Impacts of Generative AI on Creativity in Higher Education

Ziska Fields
University of Johannesburg, South Africa

A volume in the Advances in Educational Technologies and Instructional Design (AETID) Book Series

IGI Global
Publishing Tomorrow's Research Today

Vice President of Editorial Melissa Wagner
Managing Editor of Acquisitions Mikaela Felty
Managing Editor of Book Development Jocelynn Hessler
Production Manager Mike Brehm
Cover Design Phillip Shickler

Published in the United States of America by
IGI Global Scientific Publishing
701 East Chocolate Avenue
Hershey, PA, 17033, USA
Tel: 717-533-8845
Fax: 717-533-8661
Website: https://www.igi-global.com E-mail: cust@igi-global.com

Library of Congress Cataloging-in-Publication Data

Names: Fields, Ziska, 1970- editor.
Title: Impacts of generative AI on creativity in higher education / Edited by Ziska Fields.
Description: Hershey, PA : IGI Global, [2024] | Includes bibliographical references and index. | Summary: "This book offers a comprehensive overview of the current landscape of GAI in higher education"-- Provided by publisher.
Identifiers: LCCN 2024043202 (print) | LCCN 2024043203 (ebook) | ISBN 9798369324189 (hardcover) | ISBN 9798369349748 (paperback) | ISBN 9798369324196 (ebook)
Subjects: LCSH: Artificial intelligence--Educational applications. | Education, Higher--Effect of technological innovations on. | Creative ability in technology. | Generative programming (Computer science)
Classification: LCC LB1028.43 .I48 2024 (print) | LCC LB1028.43 (ebook) | DDC 370.285/63--dc23/eng/20241028
LC record available at https://lccn.loc.gov/2024043202
LC ebook record available at https://lccn.loc.gov/2024043203

British Cataloguing in Publication Data
A Cataloguing in Publication record for this book is available from the British Library.

Table of Contents

Detailed Table of Contents

full potential of AI-driven tools for the modern generation. As society increasingly integrates AI into daily life, understanding and addressing these opportunities and challenges becomes imperative for the responsible and effective deployment of AI.

The future perspectives of ChatGPT in the context of Industrial 4.0, Society 5.0, and Modern Education showcase the potential for transformative impacts on communication, decision-making, and learning processes. In Industrial 4.0, ChatGPT is anticipated to play a pivotal role in facilitating human-machine collaboration, enhancing communication in smart manufacturing, and contributing to agile decision-making processes. The integration of ChatGPT in this industrial paradigm holds promise for increased efficiency, improved troubleshooting, and streamlined interactions between workers and intelligent systems. The seamless integration of ChatGPT into the fabric of Industrial 4.0 and other terms requires a thoughtful approach, collaboration between stakeholders, and ongoing advancements in AI research and development. As ChatGPT continues to evolve, its role as a communication and decision-making tool holds significant potential to shape a future where human-machine collaboration, societal interactions, and education are enriched by the capabilities of advanced AI technologies.

Generative AI technologies such as ChatGPT have started gaining increased popularity among higher education institutions. Students, as well as teaching professionals, can utilize these tools for various academic purposes due to the immense benefits they provide by way of customization of data generated and ease of access to data. However, this chapter seeks to analyze how such tools may impact students' creative thinking

advancement, the current study concentrated on the cooperation between humans and robots in the fields of education bringing up the Research and Education Network (REN) for universities as a way to capitalize on human development. The study identified significant issues with the current REN and made an effort to resolve them through human-robot collaboration by tackling them from an organizational and pedagogical AI-robotic instructional application in light of the technological prospects highlighted in the study.

The advent of web-facing artmaking generative AI tools (A-GAI) has enabled new methods for teaching multimedia. This work explores some pedagogical approaches in harnessing combinatorial human-machine advantages in multimedia teaching and learning in higher education. This work begins with a summary of the advent of multimedia education and proposes a basic model for how A-GAI may be harnessed for teaching multimedia to early learners in higher education. This work is informed by academic research, abductive logic, and firsthand teaching,

The emergence of GenAI tools, such as OpenAI's ChatGPT, Google's Bard, and Meta's Llama, has marked the beginning of a new age in educational approaches, specifically in fostering creativity in higher education. This chapter examines the diverse effects of GenAI on promoting and assessing creativity among students and instructors. This chapter examines the capacity of these technologies to improve creative thinking, problem-solving, and personalised learning experiences. It also considers the ethical, privacy, and bias-related problems that come with using these technologies. This chapter seeks to offer valuable insights on the effective integration of GenAI into higher education curricula, with the goal of fostering the development of innovative thinkers. This was achieved by a review of current literature. The chapter proposes a strategy that harnesses the advantages of AI while reducing its potential drawbacks, therefore creating a future where technology and human ingenuity combine to promote progress and development in academics.

selective and rely less on the AI writing tools in order to help them enhance not only their English academic writing quality but also writing competences.

Preface

The emergence of generative artificial intelligence (GAI) is causing transformation in the landscape of higher education and changing how people learn, teach, are creative, and innovate. Higher education institutions are now being challenged to integrate GAI into their curricula and teaching methodologies, and questions are being asked about human and artificial creativity (Lee et al., 2024).

GAI includes a range of technologies, from natural language processing to image and music generation, and offers new capabilities for creating novel content and boosting human creativity. The ability of GAI to generate content autonomously raises fundamental questions about the nature of creativity, the role of educators, and the future of academic integrity. This rapid advancement in technology, especially GAI, is reshaping the understanding of creativity, pedagogy, teaching methodologies, research processes, the creation of artistic and intellectual outputs, and other scholarly pursuits (Bahroun et al., 2023). The symbiotic relationship between human ingenuity and machine learning is at the core of this technological advancement.

Creativity is a vital skill in the 21st century, and higher education institutions are under pressure to foster creative thinking in their students (Newton & Newton, 2014). GAI serves as a catalyst, enabling students and faculty to explore new ways of being creative, as it provides tools that enhance cognitive and creative capacities (Dawani, 2023). Whether through automated essay-writing assistance, curriculum development, or virtual learning environments, the potential of artificial intelligence (AI) to enrich the educational experience is unlimited. GAI has the potential to revolutionize how students approach creative tasks. It offers tools that can assist in brainstorming, drafting, and refining creative works. For instance, AI-powered writing assistants can help students overcome writer's block, while AI-generated art can serve as inspiration or a medium for artistic expression (Gison, 2024). The use of GAI, however, should complement rather than supplant human creativity and critical thinking.

The integration of GAI into higher education is not without its challenges. GAI raises vital questions about the nature of creativity and originality. Concerns about the authenticity of AI-generated work, algorithmic bias, the potential for academic dishonesty, and the implications for employment in creative fields necessitate a new approach (Božić, 2024). There is a fear that GAI can generate content that surpasses human creativity. The value of human-created works and how reliant students and educators will become on GAI are some of the burning issues where GAI is concerned. Moreover, there are ethical considerations surrounding the use of AI in education, particularly regarding intellectual property and the potential for misuse (Abdallah & Salah, 2023). Ethical considerations should guide the deployment of these technologies. Equitable access to GAI tools for all students, regardless of their socio-economic background, remains vital. These tools can help to enhance creativity and develop this innate ability more in students.

This book offers a comprehensive overview of the current landscape of GAI in higher education. The book aims to contribute significantly to the research community by bringing together creativity, GAI, and higher education, fostering interdisciplinary collaboration and dialogue among researchers in these domains. It offers novel pedagogical approaches that leverage GAI to encourage creativity, providing a rich ground for future research in educational technology.

The comprehensive and timely publication aims to be an essential reference source, building on the available literature and joint expertise in creativity, GAI, and higher education. Scholar-practitioners and researchers are encouraged to use the publication as reference material, and it may serve as inspiration for further research. At the same time, while having academic rigor, the book will also appeal to the general public.

Through its 16 chapters, the book explores how this technology is being utilized. Ultimately, this exploration aims to foster a deeper understanding of how GAI can enhance creativity in higher education while also addressing the challenges it presents. By examining both the positive impacts and the potential drawbacks, the authors hope to offer insights that will help educators harness the power of GAI in ways that enrich the educational experience and creative endeavors.

A breakdown of the chapters, with a brief description of each chapter, follows.

Chapter 1 is titled "Can Artificial Intelligence Promote Financial Literacy in Higher Education? A Case in the Modern World." According to the author, Bibi Zaheenah Chummun, in the higher education niche, technology goes hand in hand with understanding money-related matters. The growing knowledge of GAI and its application in the higher education sector has gained much popularity, especially for facilitating the understanding of complex financial concepts. Financial literacy is a crucial area of study in which GAI can enhance the student learning experience. However, the application of GAI is not without its challenges. The limited availability of and access to technology and a shortage of digital skills make it challenging to develop comprehensive AI-related financial literacy programs and reap their full benefits. Students are often stuck with so much information flooding their search results that they ultimately lose direction in trying to reach a conclusion. Therefore, it is important that learners are exposed to GAI and engage swiftly with financial technologies. This study is predicated on the notion that, if learners engage in using AI systems at a higher education level, they will be more inclined to make better-calculated financial decisions.

Chapter 2, titled "Exploring the Perception of Indian Educators Towards the Use of Generative AI Tools for Assessment," was contributed by Nitin Sankar Pillai and Poonam Arora. According to the authors, students have readily accepted free technological tools such as GAI, but educators differ greatly in their opinions on and willingness to embrace the same. The chapter focuses on research that was conducted among teachers of undergraduate and postgraduate management programs to ascertain their preferences regarding using AI for assessment and how they perceive it to help students and themselves. The research also revealed educators' limitations regarding the use of AI in the Indian education system.

Chapter 3, "Finding Time for Creativity in Higher Education Writing Through Generative AI," contributed by K. M. Begian-Lewis and Colleen J. Hart, discusses the relationship between time poverty, creativity, and large language models (LLMs) or GAI technologies in the writing classroom. These include ChatGPT and other GAI software in word processors such as Microsoft Word. Through examples of writing provided by ChatGPT, a student profile, and a comparative analysis of the writing supplied by two LLMs, they argue that LLMs should be integrated into the writing classroom to offer students who suffer from time poverty (limited time to devote to their classwork) the ability to practice creativity in their writing, which they may otherwise struggle to achieve. Specifically, the authors explore how ChatGPT can support students in the writing process, including researching, pre-writing, writing, revision, and reflection, to foster creativity in their writing.

In Chapter 4, "Further Research Opportunities and Challenges Towards AI-Driven Tools for the Modern Generation," Ajanthaa Lakkshmanan, S. Amudhan, Smita M. Gaikwad, and Amit Kumar Tyagi discuss the evolving landscape of AI and its applications in crafting tools tailored to the modern generation. As AI continues to advance, opportunities for further research emerge, accompanied by a set of challenges that warrant exploration. This chapter explores enhancing AI-driven tools' adaptability to dynamic user preferences, leveraging deep learning for improved context awareness, and refining natural language processing for seamless human–machine interactions. The challenges addressed encompass ethical issues, data privacy issues, and the need for transparent decision-making processes within AI systems. The chapter highlights the interdisciplinary nature of research into these topics, calling for collaboration among experts in AI and human–computer interaction to unlock the full potential of AI-driven tools for the modern generation. As society integrates AI into daily life to an ever-increasing degree, understanding and addressing these opportunities and challenges becomes imperative for it responsible and effective deployment.

Chapter 5, titled "Future Perspectives of ChatGPT Towards Industry 4.0, Society 5.0, and Modern Education," was contributed by Mansi Kukreja, Amit Kumar Tyagi, M. Sivakumar, and Senthil Kumar Arumugam. The future applications of ChatGPT in the context of Industry 4.0, Society 5.0, and modern education showcase its potential to have transformative impacts on communication, decision-making, and learning processes. In Industry 4.0, ChatGPT is anticipated to play a pivotal role in facilitating human–machine collaboration, enhancing communication in smart manufacturing, and contributing to agile decision-making processes. The integration of ChatGPT in this industrial paradigm holds promise for increased efficiency, improved troubleshooting, and streamlined interactions between workers and intelligent systems. The seamless integration of ChatGPT into the fabric of Industry 4.0 and other contexts requires a thoughtful approach, collaboration between stakeholders, and ongoing advancements in AI research and development. As ChatGPT continues to evolve, its role as a communication and decision-making tool holds significant potential to shape a future in which the capabilities of advanced AI technologies enrich human–machine collaboration, societal interactions, and education.

In Chapter 6, "Generative AI and Its Impact on Creative Thinking Abilities in Higher Education Institutions," Mareena Francis Kaitharath, K. N. Shifna, and P. S. Anuradha analyze how GAI technologies such as ChatGPT may impact students' creative-thinking ability, as well as the drawbacks that teachers face after the implementation of such tools. The methodology adopted for the study was two surveys: one administered to gather students' opinions and the other to understand teachers' perspectives. The analysis of the data collected shows that students' over-reliance on such GAI tools might hinder their ability to think creatively to some extent. The chapter also suggests some strategies that teachers may adopt to ensure that they accurately assess their students' capabilities.

Chapter 7, titled "Generative AI and its Implications for Higher Education Students' Creativity: AI and Creativity in Higher Education," by Blandina Manditereza and Mavis Chamboko-Mpotaringa, explores the impact of GAI in higher education, with the aim of understanding its transformative effects on students' creative-thinking processes and outcomes. Using the content analysis approach, the review of literature uncovers current views on how AI enables or disrupts students' creativity. GAI is a powerful tool in higher education, as it can generate original content such as text, images, music, and videos based on input data or predefined models. The adoption of GAI led to a need to understand how these advancements may shape the educational experience and develop essential skills, including creativity. Creativity is crucial in today's digital age, but the emergence of digital tools such as GAI raises questions about its potential impact on creativity. Since creativity plays a fundamental role in higher education, GAI offers students a platform for original thinking, problem-solving, and innovation.

Chapter 8, titled "Generative AI in Curriculum Development: A Framework for Adaptive, Customized, and Personalized Learning," was contributed by Mariam Tanweer and Aisha Ismail. This chapter discusses how GAI can improve educational inclusion and comprehensiveness by facilitating customized, adaptive learning experiences. The framework in this chapter provides a structured approach to integrating GAI into curriculum design to create dynamic, flexible, and personalized educational paths. GAI enables educators to create individualized and tailored learning modules by utilizing advanced machine learning and natural language processing, promoting an inclusive educational setting. The discussion in this chapter highlights the crucial significance of GAI in developing educational methods and curricula, establishing a new model for future learning environments.

Chapter 9, titled "Generative AI in Curriculum Development in Higher Education," contributed by Muhammad Usman Tariq, explores the transformative role of GAI in reshaping the development of higher education curricula. GAI, as exemplified by advanced models such as GPT-3, employs sophisticated algorithms to generate scientifically relevant content, surpassing traditional norms of teaching and learning. The overview delves into the fundamental principles of GAI, emphasizing the significance of generative models such as generative adversarial networks and the technical intricacies involved in their training. Essentially, the discourse on the importance of GAI in curriculum development underscores its disruptive potential in education. By providing personalized and adaptable pathways for growth, GAI addresses the diverse needs of students, fostering engagement and comprehension. It also underscores the role of GAI in overcoming limitations in traditional education, facilitating the creation of virtual laboratories and simulations that enhance hands-on learning.

Chapter 10, "Generative Artificial Intelligence (AI) and Sustainable Development Goal 4 on Tertiary Education: Conversational AI With User-Centric ChatGPT-4," was contributed by Ugochukwu Okwudili Matthew, David Oyewumi Oyekunle, Lateef Olawale Fatai, Edidiong Elijah Akpan, Matthew Abiola Oladipupo, Temitope Samson Adekunle, Ajibola Olaosebikan Waliu, and Victory Chibuike Onumaku. Society 5.0 seeks to create a sustainable, people-centered community. Advancements in robotics and AI research have been used in several areas of life in the modern digital society to address a wide range of problems. Despite the large body of research on the impact of human–robot cooperation on low- and high-level tasks related to robot educational advancement, the study in this chapter concentrated on the collaboration between humans and robots in education. The research and education network (REN) for universities is identified as a way to capitalize on human development. The chapter identifies significant issues with the current REN and tries to resolve them through human–robot collaboration by tackling them from an organizational and pedagogical AI-robotic instructional application in light of the technological prospects highlighted in the study.

Chapter 11, titled "Harnessing Combinatorial Human–Machine Advantages in Multimedia Teaching and Learning in Higher Education," was contributed by Shalin Hai-Jew. The advent of web-facing artmaking generative AI tools (A-GAI) has enabled new methods for teaching multimedia. This chapter explores some pedagogical approaches to harnessing combinatorial human–machine advantages in multimedia teaching and learning in higher education. This chapter begins with a summary of the advent of multimedia education and proposes a basic model for how A-GAI may be harnessed to teach multimedia to early learners in higher education. This work is informed by academic research, abductive logic, and firsthand teaching.

Chapter 12, "Revolutionizing Creative Education: The Role of Generative AI in Enhancing Innovation and Learning in Higher Education," was contributed by Khalida Akbar, Farai Donald Nyika, and Vicent Mbonye. The emergence of GAI tools, such as OpenAI's ChatGPT, Google's Bard (now Gemini), and Meta's Llama, has marked the beginning of a new age in educational approaches, specifically in fostering creativity in higher education. This chapter examines the diverse effects of GAI on promoting and assessing creativity among students and instructors. This chapter discusses the capacity of these technologies to improve creative thinking, problem-solving, and personalized learning experiences. It also considers these technologies' ethical, privacy, and bias-related problems. This chapter seeks to offer valuable insights on the effective integration of GAI into higher education curricula to foster the development of innovative thinkers. The chapter proposes a strategy that harnesses the advantages of AI while reducing its potential drawbacks, creating a future in which technology and human ingenuity combine to promote progress and development in academics.

In Chapter 13, "The Interplay Between Creativity, Thinking Styles, Higher Education, and Generative AI," Ziska Fields discusses the radical changes in education that AI, especially GAI technology, is causing. This technology can impact students' creativity, cognition, preferred thinking styles, and higher-order thinking skills. This chapter explores the link between creativity, thinking styles and skills, higher education, and GAI and indicates an interplay between them. GAI is reshaping our understanding of education and its impact on creativity and thinking styles. It forces us to reconsider and review current and traditional teaching and learning pedagogies.

In Chapter 14, titled "Transforming Assessments With Generative AI," Aisha Ismail, Mariam Tanweer, and Sadia Farooq reveal the new ways of assessment that GAI is allowing and the tools that can create engaging and innovative content. GAI is positioned to bring about a significant transformation in the educational process by promoting adaptation and customization. This chapter sheds light on the significance of GAI in assessments in higher education. It offers valuable insights into the possibilities for change and improvement in educational evaluations, indicating its capacity to revolutionize the future of education.

Chapter 15, titled "Unleashing Creative Potential: The Role of Generative AI in Business Education," was contributed by Justin Knibbe, Rosalynn Peschl, and Oleksiy Osiyevskyy. This study examines the overlooked role of creativity in business school curricula despite its recognized importance in fostering innovation and solving global challenges. It criticizes traditional educational models for failing to nurture creative thinking and argues for integrating GAI systems to enhance creativity in business education. GAI is posited as a tool to improve divergent and convergent thinking, offering practical applications across various business disciplines. However, the authors also highlight the ethical considerations surrounding data usage, intellectual property, and privacy. The study concludes that integrating GAI responsibly can revolutionize business education, preparing future leaders for an AI-augmented business world while maintaining its necessary ethical, informed, and transparent use.

Chapter 16, titled "What AI-Based Writing Assistant Actually Improve Writing Quality or Writing Skills," was contributed by Sholihatul Hamidah Daulay, Hotma Berutu, Muhammad Dalimunte, Muhammad Muslim Nasution, Eka Apriani, Muthmainnah Muthmainnah, and Shaumiwaty Shaumiwaty. Through a descriptive qualitative approach, the study reported in this chapter aimed to find out what kinds of AI-based writing assistants students used and their effect on students' English academic writing skills. The researchers employed questionnaires and semi-structured interviews with the study participants, 20 students of a master's program in English education who were purposively chosen based on their experience using AI as an assistant in English academic writing. The respondents used various AI-based writing tools. Interestingly, the study found that using AI-based writing assistants has both positive and negative impacts on students' academic writing skills. The chapter highlights that users of AI writing tools must be more selective and rely less on such tools to help them enhance their English academic writing quality and writing competencies.

The book serves as a valuable resource for educators, researchers, students, and policymakers, filling the gaps in understanding and the debates regarding the impacts of GAI on creativity in higher education. The book aims to promote the creative growth and creation of a vibrant, an innovative, and an inclusive educational future without diminishing the creative potential of future generations.

Ziska Fields
University of Johannesburg, South Africa

REFERENCES

Abdallah, M., & Salah, M. (2023). Artificial intelligence and intellectual properties: Legal and ethical considerations. *International Journal of Intelligent Systems and Applications in Engineering*, 12(1), 368–376. https://ijisae.org/index.php/IJISAE/article/view/3911

Bahroun, Z., Anane, C., Ahmed, V., & Zacca, A. (2023). Transforming education: A comprehensive review of generative artificial intelligence in educational settings through bibliometric and content analysis. *Sustainability (Basel)*, 15(17), 12983. Advance online publication. DOI:10.3390/su151712983

Božić, V. (2024). *Generative AI: Potential and peril*. ResearchGate. DOI:10.13140/RG.2.2.14861.96489

Dawani, S. (2023). *Integrating artificial intelligence into creativity education: Developing a creative problem-solving course for higher education* [Master's dissertation, SUNY Buffalo State University]. https://digitalcommons.buffalostate.edu/creativeprojects/363

Gison, C. (2024, April 2). *Overcoming writer's block with AI: Tools and techniques*. Medium. Retrieved July 2, 2024, from https://medium.com/@chasegison/overcoming-writers-block-with-ai-tools-and-techniques-4a3bcfb2d6a0

Lee, D., Arnold, M., Srivastava, A., Plastow, K., Strelan, S., Ploeckl, F., Lekkas, D., & Palmer, E. (2024). The impact of generative AI on higher education learning and teaching: A study of educators' perspectives. *Computers and Education: Artificial Intelligence*, 6, 100221. Advance online publication. DOI:10.1016/j.caeai.2024.100221

Newton, L. D., & Newton, D. P. (2014). Creativity in 21st-century education. *Prospects*, 44(4), 575–589. DOI:10.1007/s11125-014-9322-1

Chapter 1
Can Artificial Intelligence Promote Financial Literacy in Higher Education?
A Case in the Modern World

Bibi Zaheenah Chummun
University of KwaZulu-Natal, South Africa

ABSTRACT

Technology and understanding money-related matters go hand in hand together in the higher education niche. The increase in the knowledge of generative artificial intelligence and its application in the higher education sector have gained much popularity especially for complex financial terminologies. A key study area where AI can enhance the experience of student learning is financial literacy. However, the application of AI is not without its challenges; the limited availability of technology and access to digital skills leave out some from optimising the full benefits of a fledged AI-related financial literacy. Students are often stuck with so much information flooding the search engines to the extent that they ultimately lose directions for a conclusion. Therefore, it is prominent that the learners get exposed to AI and engage swiftly with financial technologies. This study is predicated on the thrust that if the learners are engaged with using AI systems at a higher education level, they will be more inclined to make more calculated financial decisions.

DOI: 10.4018/979-8-3693-2418-9.ch001

INTRODUCTION

The many industrial revolutions have been dominating the mankind evolution one after the other, and this has amended the face of the modern world . The fifth Industrial revolution also known as the society 5.0 seeks to achieve the socio-economic goals and development that is endorsed by smart digital technologies and robotics science evolution on a sustainable basis such as the Internet of Things(IoT), artificial intelligence (AI), machine learning and the big data analytics (Schoitsch, 2019). Society 5.0 is at present dawning in unexpected ways on the small village "the world" as we bank exponentially on the technologies of Industry 4.0, namely artificial intelligence (AI) (Oztemel & Gursev, 2020).

The role and importance of artificial intelligence (AI) in diverse sectors has increased a lot recently and the higher education niche is no exception. The 21st century has seen an upward surge of how higher education is rapidly evolving which is driven by advances in globalisation, technology, changing student demographics and proliferation of the internet. As per a survey conducted by CNBC in 2023, thirty five percent (35%) of businesses have adopted AI. Seventy-seven percent (77%) of devices in use feature some form of AI. Thirty seven percent (37%) of consumers having received financial assistance from AI-powered chatbots (Epperson, 2023). AI is expected to contribute to $15.7 trillion to the global economy by 2030.

One cannot deny the fact that there are more of online learning activities from a remote point and offering of more courses/programmes that can be rounded online entirely (Dieguez et al., 2021). This education trend enables young adults to gain higher education and allows better flexibility in the learner learning process and experience (Neumann et al., 2021). As the sector for higher education becomes more flexible and diverse this generates a more global citizenship cross-learning and understanding. Incorporating technology in the learning style in fostering creativity and research has been found to accelerate (Amornkitpinyo et al., 2021). As the education sector identifies new measures to improve the quality of higher education, the factoring of AI has been viewed as one of the most creative and innovative inclusion of mankind (Chedrawi & Howayeck, 2019). The future outlook of AI in higher education looks promising as technology is likely to improve the process of learning and teaching (Mishra, 2019).

This is an area where AI has a lot of potential to contribute significantly and make an impactful effect in encouraging financial literacy in the higher education institutions. Financial literacy pertains to an important skill of life which allows people in making calculated choices such as their own finances, savings, credit behaviour and investments. Financial literacy also pertains to knowledge, skills and abilities related to the financial part. It comprises of a comprehensive understanding of financial services and products with the assistance of advice, information and also the ability to understand financial allied risks and make calculated choices and decisions (Organisation for Economic Co-operation and Development, 2016). Regrettably, several young adults do not have the necessary skills and knowledge in an attempt to cope with their finances and budget as it should be, hence driving a life of financial struggles and wrong financial choices. Previously, the transfer of financial knowledge and skills has traditionally and conventionally been entrusted to educators, financial advisers and professionals. Although that not many higher education institutions fully understand the AI application in the higher education system, many educational institutions have started to action AI teaching and learning to those who have the resources in using it, potentially for an enhanced financial education systems leading to an improved financial literacy. The reliance on the use of more and more on AI nowadays is likely to be more impactful if AI is introduced at an early stage in the higher education sector.

The Fourth Industrial revolution has led to a more globalised, interconnected world that ever before (World Economic Forum 2016: 8). The digitisation and the internet of things (IOT) have been transformational in the higher education business. The education institutions are transcending borders and students are becoming increasingly global and this has led to new openings for new frontiers and opportunities through more use of AI-based tools in financial education. Since the role of AI is inevitable in future education, the learners are encouraged and motivated nowadays in the sense that the vital skill of creativity in this century in higher education institutions is a “must” in fostering creative lateral thinking . While traditional teaching methods have been effective, the integration of generative AI into higher education institutions is set to increase the measures to harness and nurture creativity in students in an attempt to improve financial literacy.

Unluckily the young adults lack the important skills, knowledge and competencies to effectively cope with their finances effectively and mainly seek or outsource advice or help for their savings, investment and preparing a budget, leading to poor financial decisions and a lifetime of financial struggles (Chummun, 2017). Teaching AI is a prominent role when engaging innovative measures to enhance financial literacy in higher education institutions. By unlocking the potential of AI, teachers can incite students to plough in the personalised learning experiences that are tailored-made to the specific learning way of every learner, related to financial literacy. An AI tool that analyses complex financial information and questions extracts the essential information and presents the scenario in a simple, understandable language and this can empower individuals to make more informed decisions (Hummingbird, 2023). Generative AI can improve financial education by providing tailored advice based on an individual's financial goals that they present. The teaching and learning processes for the two-fold; students and teachers become more interesting and enable the students to memorise the financial aspects they learn in class and it also allows the tutors to improve their teaching philosophies and styles, which is a win-win situation for both stakeholders.

This chapter seeks to analyse how AI promotes financial literacy in higher education. This is mainly related to an exploration of how AI is becoming the catalyst for reshaping the new generation financial landscape. Therefore section one addresses the role and importance and also the advantages of enhancing financial literacy in higher education sector. Section two looks at the challenges of AI in promoting financial literacy. Section three provides a snapshot of real-world examples and case studies. Section four discusses how AI can become a powerful tool in bridging the information gaps to students in higher education institutions, Section four provides recommendations on how to improve financial literacy in higher education institutions. Section five provides the future research directions for implementing AI integration in the curricula through indigenous financial education in an attempt to improve the students' learning practices and experiences. A conclusion is also found at the end of this chapter .

BACKGROUND

The Importance and Pros of AI in Higher Education Institutions in Promoting Financial Literacy

In this section of the paper, we delve into the importance of improving financial literacy and how AI has become a potent ally in improving financial literacy in higher education institutions. It is important that before factoring the importance of financial literacy and its benefits acquired by students in using AI among higher education institutions, a snapshot of how the financial services field which is headed by fintech orgnisations in brief (financial technologies) has been increasingly using machine learning (ML). For instance, AI makes use of a lot of ML capabilities in the following ways:

- **Prediction analytics**: The benefits of using large data sets are gained from using ML algorithms are used for predicting results. According to (Bolhuis & Rayner, 2020), ML capabilities usually perform better than traditional statistical models in the financial services sector and is usually undertaken in economic, credit risk scoring, risk management and to forecast economic variables.
- **Process of natural language**: AI through ML has the ability to communicate and conveying understanding by using human language. According to (Hirshberg & Manning, 2015), coupled with deep learning, natural language

processing has been used in the financial services field in applications such as chatbots, reports and contract reviews.

- **Recognition of facial/signature**: As a matter of the due diligence process, using ML in image recognition as a security measure is being made a habit by some financial companies in the fight against the combating the financing of terrorism and anti-money laundering requirements for identification and verification of customers details (Goodfellow, Bengio & Courville, 2016).
- **Detection of anomaly:** AI uses ML algorithms to identify suspicious data and insurance fraud detection (Chandola, Banerjee & Kumar, 2009).

AI is Transforming the financial services sector by automating financial processes like data entry processing of data and reports generation; investment and trading decisions which allows predictions and risk coping mechanisms and fraud detection (World Economic Forum, 2020). The recent implementation of financial technologies such as cloud computing and big data deploys AI/ML systems on an increased basis (World Economic Forum, 2020). In brief, AI has the following benefits in the financial services sector.

- **Improved efficiency and accuracy**: AI/ML have the ability to process big data sets promptly and on an accurate basis reducing errors as well as increasing efficiency. This is likely to generate a better financial analysis, risk assessment and quicker decision processes.
- **Personalised financial services:** AI through ML enables financial organisations to generate more personalized financial services customised to personal customer needs. By analyzing customer data and preferences, AI systems can offer customized references and financial advice. The budgeting applications which leverage ML algorithms allow savings, expenditure and personalized advice for mitigating expenses. The investment applications through AI/ML-based platforms assist in the identification of investment opportunities and benefits, provide customized investment recommendations and allow the individuals to manage their respective portfolios as per their individual preferences. The chatbots through AI/ ML also allow to respond to queries and help in setting debt management strategies.
- **Enhanced customer experience**: AI-based like virtual assistants and chatbots can enable quality customer support such as responding instantly and promptly the stakeholders' queries. This can only improve the customer experience on an overall basis.
- **Reduction in cost**: Through streamlined process of automation, AI/ML technologies can reduce overhead costs for financial organisations. This can lead to cost savings, resource optimization and more effective financial services.

Mitigation of Fraud in the Financial Services Industry

AI is gradually but steadily catching up and adding value in the field of insurance which forms part of the financial services area using the InsurTech and Fintech. For an insurance provider to receive the optimum value from AI/ML, understanding the systems and processes in the insurance claims detection of fraud cannot be ignored. For the process of combating fraud and detection to derive its most value, AI must be fed with lots of data. The role of big data sets in utilising new sets of information relating to the policies of insurance can assist in the process of mitigating fraud (Chummun, 2018).

Advances in AI/ML are paving the way to make it possible in leveraging unstructured data sets such as online use, credit histories and identity cards. New data types from social media and mobile phones are being used already to offer credit offering to the financially excluded customers. However, the challenges of potential risks related to fraud exist also across the insurance chain, where AI/ML could assist to enhance pricing, risk modelling, frequencies of collection and distribution as well as ultimately unlocking possibilities of fraud . The insurance providers can make use of AI/ML to unlock patterns and trends in claiming fraudulently through spotting those by self-educating sources, for instance those which can be "mined" to generate information on trends and patterns flagging those claims, need deeper investigation. As AI relies on "big data" and other sources to review a claim, it is harder that fraudulent claims applicants can suit their specifications or requirements easily. The use of AI/ML in reducing fraudulent claims will grow as more relevant data is collected through its ability to locate fraudulent activities through self-education.

The junction of AI and financial literacy has received much more attention to the extent that the education institutions have seen that AI has an unlocking potential to transform the way that financial concepts are understood, facilitated and implemented. AI technologies such as, natural language processing, machine learning and predictive analytics, are cruising the way in the organisations' operations, making the AI processes and systems more accessible. In leveraging AI related technologies, the financial education can lead to become more personalised, accessible and effective.

On a global font, financial literacy levels show different variations. The developed countries such as the United States of America, United Kingdom and Canada among others, have incorporated financial education in their system of education. However, disparities remain due to factors like age, gender, educational status and income. The emerging or developing countries are still working hard to factor this aspect of financial education to promote financial literacy especially in the underserved basics, gearing to enhance financial access and inclusion of financial sector services (Atkinson & Messy, 2013).

Financial literacy is an important skill that enables people to manage and cope effectively with their money-related decisions in the sense that they become self-sufficient on an economically point of view (Vidovićová 2013: 191). It plays a crucial part as it enhances the financial health of an individual which can contribute to economic growth and development (Huston, 2010). It comprises a consortium of skills, knowledge and competencies about savings and investments, credit management, budgeting and planning. However, one has to agree that a large portion of the population is still deprived of the basic financial literacy concepts hence leading to financial challenges. On the other hand, AI relates to the computer science field that emphasises on the creativity skills of machines which can mimic the tasks and assignments that traditionally need human intelligence in using data and algorithms to analyse, learn and make forecasts. As AI cuts across several disciplines, an increased number of financial institutions are moving their services to be digitized which result in an increased demand for AI systems in financial literacy education. Whilst several educational and financial institutions have begun to implement AI systems, there is still an immediate need for relative allied skills to be taught to young students.

The impact of AI on authentic learning on financial education is still to be researched on a deeper font. Authentic learning relates to the pedagogical approach that engages real-world problem-solving, collaboration and communication that is increasingly becoming an essential aspect of education in the modern world. AI can facilitate communication and interpersonal skills to students. This global collaboration exposes students to think critically and creatively about complex and real-world issues. By fostering a collaborative learning environment, AI can help students develop necessary skills such as individuals efforts, teamwork, problem-solving and communication which are prerequisites of a successful workforce.

Furthermore, AI can endorse project-based learning (PBL) support initiatives and development on financial topics which important for authentic learning. PBL enables students to embark on real-world projects which are complex and encourage them to use their knowledge and apply their skills. AI helps the students in the implementation of those projects by providing required resources, guidelines and feedback and students to track their own progress, feedback and performance. In undertaking PBL, AI empowers students to develop the critical thinking, creativity and problem-solving skills that are required for success nowadays

Not only AI can assist student in many spheres but also can help teachers in their development for authentic learning and teaching. In providing teachers or educators the opportunities to access data-driven insights, allows the facilitators to locate areas where they can improve, hence the ability to devise specific strategies to improve their training and teaching. This has the potential to enhance effective engaging students learning experiences through the patterns and trends of the student performance. In brief, AI can improve financial literacy through developing and accommodating intelligent teaching-based processes.

AI is at present contributing a prominent role in enhancing financial literacy in using creative and innovative measures that is geared to the individual needs of the students demographics. The following are the different ways that AI currently promotes financial education and improves better security measures and more personalized financial assistance:

- **AI based tools for financial learning**

AI based platforms such as Eduboard provide the engagement and interaction of good experiences for financial education. These powered applications use AI algorithms to generate personalised tutorials, simulations and quizzes that assist learners to grasp financial basic concepts hence enhancing understanding.

- **Gamification of financial concepts and application**

AI systems are often used to gamify financial education, making it more enjoyable . Through gamified platforms and applications, students can easily acquire understanding of financial concepts, involve in decision-making choices and obtain prompt results on their exercises.

- **Financial virtual coaches**

AI-based virtual chatbots and assistants act as financial virtual coaches, and provide guidelines in answering questions and personalised choices and help. The financial virtual coaches can also mimic real-life financial scenarios, allowing students to embark in financial decision process in a secure setting.

From the advent of algorithmic trading to the implementation of predictive analytics, the financial industry has been at the forefront of actioning AI financial technologies in higher education institutions. However, recent advancements in machine learning increased computational power, and the availability of vast datasets have propelled AI into a position of unparalleled prominence. Students at higher education institutions can derive benefits from AI in their journey of financial education. AI provides valuable insights in the present market conditions and also allows real-time data analysis which empower students to make responsible sustainable decisions. AI powered platforms like Eduboard assists students with their writing skills in their modules' assignments such as accounting, economics and finance without forgetting the research component of their respective study.

A Snapshot of Real-World Examples and Case Studies

In this modern world that we are currently living, financial security features as vital, thus the development of financial skills, knowledge, competencies and managing budget has cropped up as priority for both businesses and individuals. This section also discusses the development of budgeting and financial literacy through the lens of AI which is in turn supported by real-world examples and case studies.

AI has been transforming budgeting and financial literacy through the provision of real-time spending tracking, interactive tools tailored learning and predictive insights. Mint, Cleo, YNAB, Squirrel AI and SmartDollar are important current examples relating to the mechanism of assisting students/individuals in enhancing their respective financial skills.

- **Mint**: *A smart personal financial application driven by AI integrates data from different contexts to enable users with real-time insights into their expenses. This one-of-a-kind program employs advanced algorithms to assist users in creating realistic budgets, managing spending, and receiving notifications when their budget is about to be exceeded* (Sudharsan, 2024).
- **Cleo**: *This AI-powered chatbot captivates users on messaging platforms by delivering budgeting assistance, personalized financial advice and insight into their spending habits. Cleo uses extensive data analysis to identify potential savings opportunities and recommends strategies to improve spending habits.* (Sudharsan, 2024).
- **YNAB** (You Need A Budget): *This new budgeting application uses AI to forecast future financial circumstances by evaluating past spending patterns. YNAB's AI algorithms enable users to estimate forthcoming spending, set financial objectives, and adjust budgets accordingly, resulting in proactive financial management and smart future planning* (Sudharsan, 2024).
- **SmartDollar**: *This uses AI to provide individualized financial education and coaching. SmartDollar tailors its curriculum to each user, providing practical financial guidance. The program's effectiveness is demonstrated by its capacity to assist participants in reducing debt and increasing savings* (Sudharsan, 2024).
- **Squirrel Ai Learning**: This programme employs AI to gamify financial education by providing quizzes, challenges, and rewards to keep users engaged. Squirrel AI makes learning fun and engaging which in turn encourages the growth of financial literacy skills effectively(Sudharsan, 2024).

Case Study One: Bridging the Economic Gap: How AI is Empowering Africa's Financial Landscape – Empowering Women in Finance (Intelliverse AI, 2023)

In the African countries, addressing gender disparities relates to an important objective in today's world of financial systems and inclusion. Women under-representation in the formal financial services systems does not only prevent individual empowerment but also hinder the economic development of communities.

Artificial Intelligence emerges as a catalyst that can reshape the financial setting and also playing a crucial role in the empowerment of women in Africa. The disparities in gender in enhancing financial literacy highlights the unique challenges women face in accessing and utilizing financial services, including limited access to financial education, societal norms and cultural barriers. The AI-driven initiatives for gender equality examines successful AI initiatives that specifically target gender disparities in financial inclusion and leverages AI for financial literacy.

It discusses how AI-driven educational tools and platforms are instrumental in enhancing financial literacy among women, providing them with the knowledge needed for informed decision-making. It also breaks barriers with AI for instance showcasing how AI enables the development of personalized financial products tailored to meet the diverse needs of women and overcoming traditional one-size-fits-all approaches. Further, AI has the potential in revolutionizing microfinance, facilitating small-scale loans and empowering women entrepreneurs to drive economic growth. The role of AI in bridging societal norms can shape inclusive policies that specifically address the unique financial needs of women and can also foster entrepreneurship in driving innovation and economic participation as well as surmounting cultural barriers through change in mindset and building trust.

Case Study Two: Educational Institution Partnership (Teachflow, 2022)

A university collaborated with a financial institution to develop an AI-driven financial literacy course for students. The programme personalised financial education modules were tailored to the students' needs and goals. Further, the gamified learning platform was geared to engage students and make financial concepts more accessible. There was evidence of AI algorithms to track progress, provide feedback, and recommend additional resources The findings revealed that there was an increase in financial knowledge and skills among students. Improved financial behaviours in budgeting and managing student loans and positive impact on students' long-term financial well-being were revealed.

The above real-world examples and case studies highlight AI usefulness in enhancing financial literacy and inclusion. However, AI on promoting financial literacy is not without challenges, the next section looks at some of these challenges of AI in promoting financial literacy in higher education institutions.

Some Challenges of AI in the Enhancement Journey of Financial Literacy in Higher Education Institutions

The continent of Africa lies at the junction of its unprecedented persistent disparities and unlocked economic potential (Matchaba-Hove, Antoni & Giwe, 2019). The thriving urban sector and rural marginalised communities capture a need that requires transformation such as financial inclusion for all where financial literacy is a strong determinant (Demirgüç-Kunt & Klapper, 2013). One cannot deny that a large segment of African countries remains financially excluded (Kumar, Mishra, & Mishra, 2019) . Although that AI has emerged as a financial technology and as a token of hope in becoming a catalyst for revolutionising Africa's financial setting, it poses some challenges such as lack of access to financial technology, lack of access to physical banking, information asymmetry, cultural factors and still the perception of historical mistrust of traditional financial institutions among others. Bridging this economic gap requires innovative solutions that address the root causes of financial exclusion by students in higher education institutions. A study conducted in 2023 revealed the following challenges that lie at the forefront in promoting financial literacy (Fornero & Prete, 2023).

- **Access to financial education**: Many individuals, particularly those from marginalized communities or low-income backgrounds, lack access to quality financial education. Limited resources, lack of awareness, and systemic barriers contribute to this disparity (Fornero & Prete, 2023).
- **Misunderstanding or lack of understanding of financial concepts**: Financial concepts can be complex and intimidating, especially for those with limited exposure to financial education. Simplifying and demystifying these concepts is crucial to ensure that individuals can understand and apply them effectively (Demirgüç-Kunt & Klapper, 2013).
- **Behavioural and psychological factors**: Human behaviour and psychology play a significant role in financial decision-making. Overcoming challenges such as impulse buying, emotional spending, and the fear of financial risks require addressing these behavioural and psychological factors (Gerrans et al., 2023)

While AI enforces financial literacy education and facilitates personalised and interactive experiences' learning, it also has a myriad of challenges:

Information Privacy and the Protection of Users' Private Data

AI provides a challenge relating to the privacy rights and the users protection of data because of the algorithms' complexity that is utilised in the AI systems. AI is prone to make decisions which is based on data patterns that are not easy for individuals to differentiate, implying that end-users may not know that their private data is being compromised to make decisions that can affect them (Sher & Benchlouch, 2023). The granular, continuous, and ubiquitous data collection by AI can potentially lead to the exposure of sensitive information of the users.

Infrastructure Limitations

One of the most challenging issues encountered relates to infrastructure limitations. AI infrastructure has been using a development life cycle that does not work when building and deploying AI models (Lawton, 2021). Another problem is that modern AI applications are cobbled together across many best-of-breed tools that can cause the rise of shadow AI without integration into a coherent infrastructure. Shadow AI refers to AI that is not under the control of a company's IT department and may not have proper security or governance measures. Many regions in Africa still face limitations in terms of internet connectivity, electricity access, and technology adoption (Intelliverse AI, 2023). Bridging this infrastructure gap necessitates concerted efforts in building digital infrastructure, ensuring widespread access to reliable connectivity and fostering digital literacy. Collaboration between governments, private sector entities, and international organizations is crucial to overcoming these limitations and creating an inclusive digital ecosystem.

Other challenges relate to over dependence on AI tools that can reduce personal responsibility in financial decision making process. AI can give rise to cyber-attacks in dealing with large datasets at a go. Over-dependence on AI tools can diminish personal responsibility in financial management. AI/ML applications can also generate bias in the outcome from the training data sets which can lead to non-accurate and inappropriate recommendations.

The aspect of legal and ethical implications in the use of AI in finance raises some ethical concerns, such as algorithm bias, data security, privacy and data security (Farhud, 2019). Financial institutions must ensure that AI systems adhere to ethical standards and comply with regulations to protect customer information and avoid discriminatory practices. Another challenge relates to the Integration of AI technologies into financial systems which are currently in existence. Financial institutions need to invest in infrastructure, data management and employee training to effectively implement AI systems. Further, AI algorithms can be complex and opaque, making it difficult to understand the decision-making process. Ensuring transparency and building trust with customers and stakeholders is crucial for the widespread adoption of AI in finance.

One of the most recent generative form of AI that is impacting the field of higher education is ChatGPT (Chat Generative Pre-Trained Transformer) by using improved teaching and learning validated models in an attempt to acquire human requirements. ChatGPT is classified as an effective medium tool for educators which provide a stumbling starting block for the creation of syllabus, outlines, templates, teaching notes and the assessment deliverables. However, its integration into academic settings raises concerns regarding academic integrity, plagiarism detection and the potential impact on critical thinking skills. GenAI uses a chatbots that has been luring important details which is ultimately classified as the central box of continuous discussion with regard to the probable adverse impact for the learning and teaching processes in higher education institutions. The advances of ChatGPT as an enabler for a large language model trained to "generate human-like texts based on a given prompt or context. It can be used for a variety of natural language processing tasks, such as text completion, conversation generation, and language translation" (Baidoo-Anu & Ansah, 2023). Equipped with sophisticated generative skills and knowledge, one of the most important question in the higher education niche is that it has the ability to respond to examination questions, edit and write academic projects, assignments and generate academic reports with the probability of not being easily identified by updated anti-plagiarism software versions.

Further, academic integrity has been leading to continuous debates probably known as a major concern recently in the current academic field on whether the ChaptGPT technology should be stopped from the higher education field of academia (Lo, 2023). It is one of the policies of higher education institutions that academic misconduct for instance plagiarism, although being a serious offence, they are not classified as new misconduct components to higher education and have been researched into a lot over the years (Topsakal, 2022). However, the new comer of ChatGPT recently has augmented the misconduct for two main reasons; scarcity of transparent academic policies and also shallow detection possibilities. Subsequently, it still presents as an academic obstacle to both the facilitators and institutions in complying with maintaining and fair evaluation of academic policies' principles and standards .

Further, according to Sallam (2023), the reliability and accuracy in the use of ChatGPT in the higher education field are often a hurdle as the advances of the technology is carried out on a large quantity of data, hence the outcome can consist of inaccuracies. It is often debated that ChatGPT is equipped with limited or unavailable knowledge and these have not been updated with sets of data post 2021 (Baidoo-Anu & Owusu, 2023). Therefore, the reports generated may advance results that are not always reliable or accurate especially for subjects/modules and the other academic activities. Furthermore, ChatGPT technology can lead to biased information (Baidoo-Anu & Owusu, 2023). This challenge can affect students learning individual experiences especially those who bank on ChatGPT to inform their learning styles and provide conclusions (Pavlik, 2023). This practice can limit the effectiveness of the technology in accommodating group presentations, collaborative work, group discussions and other academic activities such as research findings that are important for a fully-fledged learning experience as well as personalized learning.

RECOMMENDATIONS: SOME MEASURES THAT ARTIFICIAL INTELLIGENCE CAN USE TO IMPROVE FINANCIAL LITERACY IN HIGHER EDUCATION INSTITUTIONS

In order to measure the effectiveness of AI in financial education requires much efforts through actioning several dimensions methods and indicators. Using a pre and post-tests questionnaire, measuring the deviations thereof and the use of interviews, surveys in assessing trends in students' financial knowledge, behaviors and attitude can assess the effectiveness of AI in financial education. The analytics, reports and dashboards can assist in monitoring students' progress, learning engagement and performance. The use of experiments, controlled surveys can be used to make a comparative study in the results non-AI and AI based financial education experiences and interventions. Quantitative and Qualitative data analysis techniques can also be employed to identify the factors that influence the effectiveness of AI for financial education.

In the realm of fostering financial literacy and inclusive financial technologies, addressing the significant gap in financial literacy stands as a critical imperative. In the light of the challenges one must accordingly adjust the way to deal with those in an innovative and creative way. One thing that is revealed found helpful is that technology can improve financial literacy of students by providing them with varied tools to learn, practice and upgrade their financial skills. By using technology, students can access, customize and enjoy financial education that suits their needs and purposes, goals, objectives and interests.

Online Courses and Modules (Online Platforms)

Online platforms are classified as reliable tools to enhance teaching and learning in generating financial education. Those learning and teaching platforms involve the use of quizzes and real-life simulations on an online interactive basis into the teaching and learning processes which equip the students with a consortium of access to educational tools from all around the world obviously, with internet connectivity. Those resources allows students to engage in different hands-on scenarios and games, for instance, budgeting, savings and investment real-life simulations. Those online interactive platforms which are flexible and accessible from anywhere has the capacity to accommodate different online interactive tools, insightful quizzes, and case-scenarios simulations into the teaching and learning process (Abuhassna et al, 2020). Factoring the online interactive tools into the financial literacy or education curricula imparts the probability of the student succeeding in both financial-related examinations and in financial-making decisions.

In utilising intensive online platforms that cater for interactive finance-related topics coupled with real-life scenarios and peer evaluation exercises can only improve both students to engage and understand the finance concepts (Abuhassna et al., 2020).

Gamification

Another way that technology can improve financial literacy for students is by using applications and games that simulate real-life scenarios and challenges. Those applications and games can help students practice and apply their financial skills in a fun and engaging way (French,McKillop & Stewart, 2023). They can also provide feedback, tips, and rewards to motivate and guide students. For example, some applications and games can help students create and track their budgets, manage their expenses, set and achieve their savings goals, or invest in virtual stocks.

First and foremost, gamification uses game design elements and principles in non-game contexts to engage and motivate individuals. It taps into a person's natural love for playing games, competition, and rewards to enhance the learning experience. Gamification can foster a positive learning environment, providing students with immediate feedback and encouraging healthy competition. Through leader boards and rewards, students can gauge their progress, compare themselves to their peers, and strive for improvement (World Economic Forum, 2023).

This sense of achievement and accomplishment serves as a powerful motivator, encouraging students to invest more time and effort into their financial education. One of the greatest benefits of gamification is that it encourages students to actively participate in their learning. They can face challenges, earn virtual rewards, and see how their decisions impact their financial situation regardless of age. Gamification is a powerful tool for motivating students and boosting engagement. The use of simulated competitions in some of finance courses has teams of students who try to run companies under different conditions. The technology is fairly flexible and lets the instructor set up a wide range of environments. The simulations are more sophisticated, allowing all sorts of fine tuning of financial inputs like interest rates, rates of return, growth rates, and others. Students can see the impact of their decisions and how changes in various constraints affect outcomes.

Chatbots and Virtual Assistants

A third way that technology can improve financial literacy for students is by using chatbots and virtual assistants that can answer questions, provide advice, and offer support (Riikkinen, Saarijärvi, & Sarlin, 2018). Those chatbots and virtual assistants can use artificial intelligence, natural language processing, and machine learning to communicate with students through text or voice. They can also use data and algorithms to personalize their responses and suggestions (Riikkinen, Saarijärvi, & Sarlin, 2018). For example, some chatbots and virtual assistants can help students find scholarships, compare loan options, or plan for retirement (Priya, & Sharma, 2023).

Podcasts and Videos

A fourth way that technology can improve financial literacy for students is by using podcasts and videos that can educate, inspire, and entertain students (Zureck, 2020). These podcasts and videos can use audio and visual elements to convey information, stories, and insights about financial topics. They can also feature experts, influencers, and peers who can share their experiences, opinions, and tips. For example, some podcasts and videos can help students learn about financial trends, strategies, and opportunities, or hear from successful entrepreneurs and investors (Zureck, 2020).

Online Communities and Platforms

Another way that technology can improve financial literacy for students is by using online communities and platforms that can connect, empower, and support students (Wanof, 2023). These online communities and platforms can use social media, forums, blogs, and websites to facilitate communication, collaboration, and learning among students. They can also provide resources, tools and opportunities for students to access, share, and create financial contents. For example, some online communities and platforms can help students find mentors, peers or experts who can offer guidance, feedback or coaching.

Technology can improve financial literacy for students by providing them with various tools to learn, practice and improve their financial skills. By using technology, students can access, customize, and enjoy financial education that suits their needs, goals, and interests. Technology can also help students overcome the barriers, challenges, and myths that prevent them from achieving financial wellness and success (Yang, Wu, & Huang, 2023).

Educators venturing into the realm of AI-enhanced financial education can adopt these leading platforms and resources. Backed by intense AI algorithms they are at the forefront of revolutionizing how financial literacy is taught and understood (WEF, 2023).

- **FinLearn:** These platforms are known for their personalized learning journeys based on individual financial goals.
- **MoneyMentor:** Uses machine learning to simulate real-world financial scenarios, helping students grasp complex financial concepts in an interactive manner.
- **EduFinance:** A repository of AI-driven financial tools, worksheets, and interactive modules for all age groups.

Regulatory and ethical framework: the ethical, supervisory and regulatory consideration should not be ignored. As AI carries more weight and integration in the financial services sector, ethical and regulatory framework considerations will act as an enabler and plays an important role. Improving financial literacy will demand fairness, transparency, accountability in AI systems and good governance which will be important prerequisites for protecting individuals' rights and building trust.

FUTURE RESEARCH DIRECTIONS

The absence of AI-based tools that generates financial literacy dissemination of information in rural communities of Africa sets the scene for future research directions. The more integration of AI at present gives rise to better opportunities of learning which thrive its way to new ways of potential learning in the financial related programmes or financial concepts at higher education institutions.

As AI integration has the potential to improve learning and learning opportunities and foster in bridging the gap between the traditional educational systems and indigenous communities. Indigenous financial education is at the crossroad of a transformative shift. Unlocking the potential to enhance the way and mechanisms indigenous students learn, AI implementation can set the scene in becoming a potent ally in fostering and preserving indigenous languages, rituals and cultures. For instance the indigenous students can learn how to prepare a budget, manage their credits, analyse how and when to save and invest as a continued learning process using AI/ML powered-based tools.

The fast pace of AI implementation in the financial education continues to be witnessed in higher education institutions as it carries a myriad of advantages and also has a lot of potential to tackle the challenges that indigenous students can face in receiving financial education. The indigenous students are mostly faced with the lack of relevant and culturally linguistic appropriate learning materials in financial education. AI can assist to surmount this hurdle in enabling the development and process of personalised learning experience that are customised to the relevant interests and needs of every student. For example the AI-based language learning systems and applications can be utilized to revitalize and preserve the indigenous languages which are mainly at risk of disappearance. By using AI-powered algorithms, the application can analyse and take cognisance of large linguistic datasets amount and enable them to foster language learning engagement and produce appropriate and accurate translations. This is most likely that indigenous students can be empowered to hold a strong bearing with their traditional cultural and ritual heritage while acquiring also important language skills that can be used and applied in various aspects of their day to day routine activities.

Furthermore, AI based tools can be used by higher education institutions to create virtual learning spaces and environments that are engaging and culturally responsive for indigenous students in their financial education. Through the immersive use of technologies such as augmented and virtual reality, AI can assist in maintaining indigenous traditions and histories that are both meaningful and interactive. This should not only lead to a more thorough understanding of indigenous cultures but also assist to break down the different stereotypes and embrace bigger cultural awareness among the non-indigenous learners . AI implementation in indigenous education has the ability to cater for personalized learning experiences for the various needs of learning to indigenous students. Through the utilisation of the ML algorithms, AI has the power to analyse, synthesize and customise to each student's learning needs, preference, style and progress through quizzes, questions and feedback which allow a more effective and targeted approach to higher education. This can be advantageous especially for indigenous learners who may face mainstream educational trauma, as AI related learning and teaching assist in fostering the creativity and supportive inclusive learning setting and environment that brings academic success and resilience. Furthermore, AI plays an important role in handling the challenges of limited internet access and connection to education in remote indigenous communities. Factoring the use of AI-based educational platforms and mechanisms, students in the indigenous communities can have access to high-quality financial learning resources and connect with peers and facilitators on a worldwide basis. This is most likely to break down the divide of digitisation and enables native students to have the opportunities to thrive into the increasingly highly technology-integrated-driven world village.

The involvement of AI in native education has a lot of potential to improve learning avenues and also tackling the specific hurdles confronted by those indigenous learners. In engaging AI/ML technologies in financial education, the learners have a lot of possible avenues to thrive into a future where indigenous cultures, traditions and languages are not only kept heartedly but also valued and celebrated as an important part of their financial educational setting. In the quest for continued research on the unlocking potential of the AI technology factoring in the future agenda of indigenous financial education, collaborative work with the indigenous people or communities are at the forefront and their perspectives are a priority of these technological advancements. Thus, the financial technologies (Fintech) organisations, higher education institutions(HEI) and education providers can factor those mentioned aspects of indigenous financial education which is likely to enhance financial literacy in higher education institutions through active innovative teaching and creative learning with the objective of driving financial literacy in developing countries and that still leave room for future stage of research.

CONCLUSION

As AI continues to advance and become more integrated into our daily lives, it is essential that we harness its full potential to improve financial literacy and education in schools. By leveraging AI's capabilities, we can create a more engaging, personalised and effective learning experiences and benefit from enhanced security measures that empower students to make informed financial decisions throughout their lives. AI is playing a transformative role in promoting financial literacy. The intelligent tutoring systems of AI also cater for the well-thought development of the teachers/educators. This will help to reduce the prevalence of financial illiteracy, its related negative consequences, such as high levels of debt and financial struggles and insecurity. The future of AI in financial literacy holds great potential for improving financial knowledge, skills, and behaviours, ultimately leading to a more financially literate society.

The main aim of this chapter is to analyse how AI can promote financial literacy in higher education institutions. This is mainly related to an exploration of how AI is becoming the catalyst for reshaping the new generation financial landscape. Therefore section one has addressed the role and importance and also the benefits of AI in enhancing financial literacy in higher education sector. Section two discussed laden challenges of AI in promoting financial literacy. Section three has provided some real-world examples of AI in driving financial literacy. Section four explained the ways that AI becomes a potent ally in bridging the information gaps to students in higher education institutions. Section four has given some insightful recommendations relating to some valuable measures in improving financial literacy . Section five caters for the future research directions by accommodating the indigenous financial education to improve financial literacy.

By embracing AI in financial literacy initiatives can empower students in their learning processes and build a more financially secure future. AI acts as an enabler, complementing traditional teaching methods. In the confluence of AI and financial literacy lies an opportunity to shape a generation that is adept, informed and empowered in their financial decisions. As we have journeyed through the transformative potential of AI in education, it is evident that the road ahead, though laden with challenges, is promising. It is an imperative call to educators, policymakers, and institutions to harness this potential and invest in AI-driven financial education, ensuring a future where financial literacy is not just a skill but a universal right. It is high time that financial education should be democratised as it transcends geographical and socio-economic barriers, making high-quality financial education accessible to all, including underserved population at large. Financial institutions and AI developers will need to collaborate closely to leverage AI technologies effectively. By combining the expertise of financial professionals with the power of AI, innovative solutions can be developed to address specific financial literacy challenges. As much as it provides educators with tools to enhance the learning and teaching experience, however it does not replace the human touch and expertise.

REFERENCES

Abuhassna, H., Al-Rahmi, W. M., Yahya, N., Zakaria, M. A. Z. M., Kosnin, A. B. M., & Darwish, M. (2020). Development of a new model on utilizing online learning platforms to improve students' academic achievements and satisfaction. *International Journal of Educational Technology in Higher Education*, 17(1), 1–23. DOI:10.1186/s41239-020-00216-z

Amornkitpinyo, T., Yoosomboon, S., Sopapradit, S., & Amornkitpinyo, P. (2021). The structural equation model of actual use of cloud learning for higher education students in the 21st century. *Journal of E-Learning and Knowledge Society*, 17(1), 72–80.

Atkinson, A., & Messy, F. A. (2013). Promoting financial inclusion through financial education: OECD/INFE evidence, policies and practice.

Baidoo-Anu, D., & Ansah, L. O. (2023). Education in the era of generative artificial intelligence (AI): Understanding the potential benefits of ChatGPT in promoting teaching and learning. *Journal of AI*, 7(1), 52–62. DOI:10.61969/jai.1337500

Baidoo-Anu, D., & Owusu Ansah, L. (2023). Education in the Era of Generative Artificial Intelligence (AI): Understanding the Potential Benefits of ChatGPT in Promoting Teaching and Learning. *SSRN*, 2023, 4337484. DOI:10.2139/ssrn.4337484

Bolhuis, M. A., & Rayner, B. (2020). *Deus ex machina? A framework for macro forecasting with machine learning*. International Monetary Fund.

Chandola, V., Banerjee, A., & Kumar, V. (2009). Anomaly detection: A survey. *ACM Computing Surveys*, 41(3), 1–58. DOI:10.1145/1541880.1541882

Chedrawi, C., & Howayeck, P. (2019). Artificial intelligence a disruptive innovation in higher education accreditation programs: Expert systems and AACSB. *Lecture Notes in Information Systems and Organisation*, 30, 115–129. DOI:10.1007/978-3-030-10737-6_8

Chummun, B. Z. (2017). An analysis of the development influences of the low-income cover market-end in South Africa. *African Journal of Science, Technology, Innovation and Development*, 9(6), 795–802. DOI:10.1080/20421338.2017.1385576

Chummun, B. Z. (2018). How can Artificial Intelligence reduce fraud in the inclusive cover niche: a case of developing African countries. *Journal of Contemporary Management, 15*(Special Edition 1), 1-17.

Demirgüç-Kunt, A., & Klapper, L. (2013). Measuring financial inclusion: Explaining variation in use of financial services across and within countries. *Brookings Papers on Economic Activity*, 2013(1), 279–340. DOI:10.1353/eca.2013.0002

Dieguez, T., Loureiro, P., & Ferreira, I. (2021). Entrepreneurship and leadership in higher education to develop the needed 21st Century skills. In *17th European Conference on Management, Leadership and Governance, ECMLG 2021*. Academic Conferences International Limited.

Epperson, S. (2023). https://www.cnbc.com/2023/09/12/3-in-10-adults-would-use-ai-for-financial-advice-cnbc-survey-finds.html

Farhud, D. (2019). Epigenetic and Ethics: How are Ethical Traits Inherited? . *International Journal of Ethics and Society*, 1(3).

Fornero, E., & Prete, A. L. (2023). Financial education: From better personal finance to improved citizenship. *Journal of Financial Literacy and Wellbeing*, 1-16.

French, D., McKillop, D., & Stewart, E. (2020). The effectiveness of smart phone apps in improving financial capability. *European Journal of Finance*, 26(4-5), 302–318. Retrieved February 27, 2023, from. DOI:10.1080/1351847X.2019.1639526

George, L. 2021. Infrastructure Limitations. https://techtarget.com/searchenterpriseai/feature/Addressing-3-infrastructure-issues-that-challenge-AI-adoption

Gerrans, P., Abisekaraj, S. B., & Liu, Z. F. (2023). The fear of missing out on cryptocurrency and stock investments: Direct and indirect effects of financial literacy and risk tolerance. *Journal of Financial Literacy and Wellbeing*, 1-35.

Goodfellow, I., Bengio, Y., & Courville, A. (2016). *Deep learning*. MIT press.

Hirshberg, J., & Manning, C. D. (2015). Advances in Natural Language Processing. *Science*, 349(6245), 261–266. DOI:10.1126/science.aaa8685 PMID:26185244

Hummingbird, J. R. (2023). https://fintechmagazine.com/articles/hummingbird-harnessing-gen-ai-for-financial-operations

Huston, S. J. (2010). Measuring financial literacy. *The Journal of Consumer Affairs*, 44(2), 296–316. DOI:10.1111/j.1745-6606.2010.01170.x

Intelliverseai. (2023). Bridging the Economic Gap: How AI is Empowering Africa's Financial Landscape. https://intelliverseai.com/

Kumar, M., Mishra, R., & Mishra, K. (2019). Correlates of financial literacy: Strategic precursor to financial inclusion. *SCMS Journal of Indian Management, 16*(4), 16-30.

Lo, C. K. (2023). What is the impact of ChatGPT on education? A rapid review of the literature. *Education Sciences*, 13(4), 410. DOI:10.3390/educsci13040410

Matchaba-Hove, T., Antoni, X., & Giwe, M. B. (2019). The use of banking products and services by low-income and under-banked consumers in the nelson mandela Bay. *Academy of Accounting and Financial Studies Journal*, 23(2), 1–13.

Mishra, R. (2019). Usage of data analytics and artificial intelligence in ensuring quality assurance at higher education institutions. In *2019 Amity International Conference on Artificial Intelligence, AICAI 2019*. Institute of Electrical and Electronics Engineers Inc. DOI:10.1109/AICAI.2019.8701392

Neumann, C., Stroud, K. M., Bailey, S., Allison, K., & Everts, S. S. (2021). 21st-century competencies in higher education: A practitioner's guide. In *Handbook of research on barriers for teaching 21st-Century competencies and the impact of digitalization* (pp. 293–315). IGI Global. DOI:10.4018/978-1-7998-6967-2.ch016

Organisation for Economic Co-operation and Development. (2016). OECD/INFE international survey of adult financial literacy competencies. *Retrieved February 27, 2023,* from http://www.oecd.org/finance/OECD-INFE-International-Survey-of -Adult Financial-Literacy-Competencies.pdf

Oztemel, E., & Gursev, S. (2020). Literature review of Industry 4.0 and related technologies. *Journal of Intelligent Manufacturing*, 31(1), 127–182. DOI:10.1007/s10845-018-1433-8

Pavlik, J. V. (2023). Collaborating with ChatGPT: Considering the Implications of Generative Artificial Intelligence for Journalism and Media Education. *J. Mass Commun. Educ.*, 2023(78), 84–93. DOI:10.1177/10776958221149577

Priya, B., & Sharma, V. (2023). Exploring users' adoption intentions of intelligent virtual assistants in financial services: An anthropomorphic perspectives and socio-psychological perspectives. *Computers in Human Behavior*, 148, 107912. DOI:10.1016/j.chb.2023.107912

Riikkinen, M., Saarijärvi, H., Sarlin, P., & Lähteenmäki, I. (2018). Using artificial intelligence to create value in insurance. *International Journal of Bank Marketing*, 36(6), 1145–1168. DOI:10.1108/IJBM-01-2017-0015

Sallam, M. (2023). The Utility of ChatGPT as an Example of Large Language Models in Healthcare Education, Research and Practice: Systematic Review on the Future Perspectives and Potential Limitations. https://www.medrxiv.org/content/10 .1101/2023.02.19.23286155v1

Schoitsch, E. (2019). Beyond smart systems-Creating a society of the future (5.0) resolving disruptive changes and social challenges. *IDIMT 2019, Proceedings*, 387-400.

Sher, G., & Benchlouch, A. (2023). The privacy paradox with AI. *Retrieved February 27, 2023,* from https://www.reuters.com/legal/legalindustry/privacy-paradox-with-ai-2023-10-31/

Sudharsan, B. (2024). The Role of AI in Enhancing Financial Literacy and Budgeting Skills. https://www.linkedin.com/pulse/role-ai-enhancing-financial-literacy-budgeting-skills-sudharsan-b

Teachflow. (2022). The role of AI in promoting financial literacy. https://teachflow.ai/the-role-of-ai-in-promoting-financial-literacy/

Topsakal, O., & Topsakal, E. (2022). Framework for a foreign language teaching software for children utilizing AR, voicebots and ChatGPT (Large Language Models). *The Journal of Cognitive Systems*, 7(2), 33–38. DOI:10.52876/jcs.1227392

Vidovićová, L. (2013). Financial literacy in retirement planning context: the case of Czech older workers. In Phellas, C. (Ed.), *Aging in European societies. Healthy aging in Europe* (pp. 191–203). Springer. DOI:10.1007/978-1-4419-8345-9_13

Wanof, M. I. (2023). Digital technology innovation in improving financial access for low-income communities. *Technology and Society Perspectives*, 1(1), 26–34. DOI:10.61100/tacit.v1i1.35

World Economic Forum. (2016). The Global Risks Report 2016. http://www3.weforum.org/docs/Media/TheGlobalRisksReport2016.pdf

World Economic Forum. (2016). The Fourth Industrial Revolution. https://www.weforum.org/agenda/2016/01/the-fourth-industrial-revolution

World Economic Forum. (2023). Gamification for financial education: building resilience through play. https://intelligence.weforum.org/topics/a1Gb0000000LPFfEAO/publications/5a6261cc30fe46b78b330a636c2318b1

Yang, J., Wu, Y., & Huang, B. (2023). Digital finance and financial literacy: Evidence from Chinese households. *Journal of Banking & Finance*, 156, 107005. DOI:10.1016/j.jbankfin.2023.107005

Zureck, A. (2020). Literature review on the use of media in financial education. *EDULEARN20 Proceedings*, 491-496.

KEY TERMS AND DEFINITIONS

Artificial Intelligence (AI): Technology that allows machines and computers to mimic problem-solving capabilities and human intelligence.

Financial Education: It teaches the knowledge, attitudes and skills that are needed to understand money-related matters.

Financial Literacy: The ability to understand financial skills, including budgeting, personal financial management, saving and investing.

Fintech: financial technology that competes with traditional financial methods in the delivery of financial services.

Insurtech: Insurance technology which is designed to process insurance policies, collects premiums, process claims and reduce costs

Machine Learning (ML): A study in artificial intelligence concerned with the development and study of statistical algorithms.

Chapter 2
Exploring the Perception of Indian Educators Towards Use of Generative AI Tools for Assessment

Nitin Sankar Pillai
https://orcid.org/0000-0002-4802-877X
Institute of Management, Nirma University, India

Poonam Arora
https://orcid.org/0000-0001-8578-3638
SKIPS School of Business, India

ABSTRACT

Educational ecosystem has always kept pace with the technological development. Stakeholders in education have had an agile reaction to the progress happening outside the classroom and have embraced these changes at the earliest for their own benefits. While students have readily accepted the free tools, there is a raging debate on the view of educators regarding the same. The present research focuses on teachers and educators who teach at undergraduate and post-graduate students of management and assimilates their opinion on the use of artificial intelligence, in one of the key aspects of the educational journey, i.e., assessment. In the research carried out engaging insights were brought forth in terms of educators preferences regarding the use of artificial intelligence for assessment and how they perceive it to help students and themselves. At the same time, the research has also shown the limitations that educators feel regarding the use of artificial intelligence from an

DOI: 10.4018/979-8-3693-2418-9.ch002

Indian perspective, due to the sheer number of human power involved in the Indian Education System.

INTRODUCTION

Artificial intelligence (AI) and the debate surrounding it is growing proportionately to its capabilities. The application of this technological progression is found in all walks of life and its presence cannot be ignored. Even in education, Artificial Intelligence is still marching at the periphery with still possible understandings being made of the impact it can have on teaching and learning (Bozkurt et al, 2021). While students have readily accepted the use of artificial intelligence for their academic work, other stakeholders such as administrative bodies, policymakers, and educators are still debating on the use and misuse of artificial intelligence in educational settings. Some of the early research in this domain has presented wonderful results in the form of better personalized learning, updating, and improvement in the learning materials at the large level while also being able to develop coding for research and drafting an email in response to queries (Chiu et al, 2023). The use of this technology has not just been limited to students and their interaction with it outside the classroom, successful integration has also been tested by researchers in the classroom (Mollick and Mollick, 2023a, 2023b). Other seminal researchers have focused on positive links between student motivation and the use of AI (Xia et al, 2022), academic performance (Khan et al, 2021), positive influence on collaboration, communication, problem-solving, creativity, and self-regulated learning skills (Porter & Grippa, 2020).

As the field grows and more researchers involve themselves in various influences of Gen AI in education, links are being established on how this technology can be harnessed for providing student benefit in the form of personalized feedback on assignments (Crompton & Burke, 2023) and academic assistance (Kim &Bennekin, 2016) while teachers can be benefitted through question and prompt generation (Ng, Leun, Chu &Qioa, 2021; Yang, Chen, Flanagan & Ogata, 2021) and may also be able to accurately predict academic performance (Chu, Tu & Yang, 2022). There has been considerable discussion and deliberation on investigating the role of artificial intelligence in the educational sector and its impact on the various stakeholders, however, more work is required as the field grows and more stakeholders get first-hand access to artificial intelligence. In India the magnitude of reach and its impact is profound, given that internet connectivity and handheld devices are cheaper, compared to the global situation, thus providing easy access to Gen AI software to students who use them for their benefits.

More research in this domain needs to be carried out as the technology is proliferating at a rapid pace and access is also easily available to the students. While students are known to use these for their academic work, there is a dearth of literature on how it is viewed from the perspective of teachers and educators. More agile universities and educational institutions have brought out AI usage policies for students and teachers by connecting it with academic requirements and concepts of academic dishonesty, however, a large number of these institutions are yet to bring out policies and a larger number of stakeholders are yet to follow these. Progressing ahead, a holistic understanding of artificial intelligence in education can only be envisaged if the perspectives of all stakeholders including teachers are collated to create a comprehensive understanding. Educators being in direct contact with the product generated through Gen AI are a primary source to understand its perception. Even if policies are in place, student's performance is finally evaluated by teachers and hence their perspectives are pivotal to creating a holistic understanding of Gen AI usage. Student performance, which has been considered as a benchmark for measuring educational program success is a result of assessment practices. Assessment practices ensure systematic collection of student performance, evaluated by teachers, suggesting whether the educational program has achieved its objectives or not. In this scenario, investigating whether AI has influenced assessment practices, especially from the viewpoint of educators needs to be conducted. All educational journeys are oriented towards one or the other form of assessment, with more emphasis being given to continuous evaluation in the form of formative assessment in the current educational milieu. Formative assessment tasks generally tend to give students more autonomy in terms of the time given for producing work and also the monitoring presented on them, thus students are expected to produce work outside the classroom over a period of time, rather than summative assessment or in-class tests. In this situation, the dependence on Gen AI cannot be fully controlled. Thus, while students depend on these technologies, it must be understood whether educators believe that student use of Gen AI in achieving their assessment goals are valid or not. The study hypothesizes that this opinion can be different for educators teaching at undergraduate and postgraduate levels and so the current research also aims to find whether there is any significant difference in the usage of AI in assessment at different levels of teaching. Hence, the present research investigates how educators view the triangulation of student performance, assessment, and influence of Generative Artificial Intelligence.

LITERATURE REVIEW

Creativity is a keystone of 21st century education. At the base level is can be understood as new and novel processes and products that come from and are present in the works of individuals, groups, and systems (Csikszentmihalyi, 1997, 2014; Creely et al, 2021). Creativity has been debated to be within humans or in the artifacts and environment (Glaveanu& Kaufman, 2019). Even if the basic understanding of creativity were to be taken it is evident that within the educational framework, this definition perfectly aligns with the expectations made of various stakeholders. The educational system has evolved to be more accepting and to present opportunities for students to present their work in new ways, more customized rather than standardized. This would require the environment to promote more novelty in expression, not only in the final product but also in the method or way the final product was arrived at. It would also require the entire system more accepting of novel and new products and processes rather than insisting on standardization.

Creativity has been established to have five elements, namely the actor, process, outcome, domain, and space (Amabile, 1996; Boden, 2004; Csikszentmihalyi, 1997, Rhodes, 1961). These elements first begin with the actor, i.e., the human capable of generative unique ideas and behavior (Glaveanu and Kaufman, 2019). However, in recent times with the involvement of artificial intelligence, the role of the primary actor has shifted from the human to that of the technology. The second element of creativity is the process which emphasizes the thoughts and actions that result in new outcomes (Lubart, 2001). Especially with problem-solving, it is expected that the main actor, i.e., humans would undergo a cognitive processing using a new process using schemata to come out with new solutions to the problems faced. Thus, creativity is broken down into the method or means by which the outcome is brought forth and the newness that these means present. However, the element of the process can be debated, as it may be possible that AI carried out the process for students effortlessly, while students do not employ any new methods for finding neoteric solutions. The result of the process, i.e., the product is the third element in creativity which has to be unique only if the other two elements are involved before the product can bring in novelty. This has not been worked on much as whether Gen AI can churn new ideas and products every time it is run is yet to be investigated. Domain, as the fourth element of creativity can range from general thematic areas, and domains to microdomains (i.e., from arts to painting) (Baer & Kaufman, 2005). Domain, with respect to AI, must be understood as the data (statistics and characteristics) that are specific to the domain of which demands are being made by the user (Anantrasirichai& Bull, 2022). The final element of space is considered as the spatial process that allows mobility between individuals and the artifacts being used which in the case of Gen AI is restricted in digital space.

CREATIVITY AND EDUCATION

Within the educational set up one must be able to see that the functional definition and understanding of creativity may be undermined with the involvement of Artificial Intelligence. The roles played by the actor and the process through which creativity is supposed to be expected are both taken on by technology rather than the individual or student. Additionally, where in classroom tasks and assessment tasks students are expected to involve themselves with the problem at hand, using higher-order thinking skills to find neoteric solutions, the use of artificial intelligence skips these two steps as the technology provides the solutions without students engaging effectively with it. The outcome that is derived sprouts from programming languages and algorithms rather than student engagement with the issue at hand. The domain knowledge, which must be built over a period of time and requires students to fall back on their schemata to effectively involve past and present knowledge for skill utilization may not happen when Gen AI is involved as domain-specific understanding is coded in terms of facts and statistics from large source pools in artificial intelligence. Consequently, we see an absence of any physical mobility between the tasks, artifacts used, students or probably the educators because the work with Gen AI happens solely between students and the technology through a device in a very restricted fashion. Hence if we are to consider whether creativity is being promoted through Artificial Intelligence in the educational setting, it may raise doubts and needs further investigation. From the accepted models, it may not seem to promote creative thinking and this may be a cause of worry, especially for the teachers as the aim of education is to do so.

CREATIVITY AND ASSESSMENT

Creativity is closely related to assessment and vice-versa. Assessment, in its basic form, must be able to assist students not only produce peak performance but also be able to use novel processes to produce new results or solutions to the problems posed by assessment tasks. Assessment requires students to encounter a challenge and employ the skills and knowledge acquired as part of their education to provide a new solution. Both the method employed to arrive at the solution and the solution itself must be customized to the situation and the learner, requiring a sense of creativity. The student becomes the actor that employs a process for a specified outcome within the confines of a domain and space in an assessment task, which is aligned with the concepts of creativity. The current challenge however is the use of Artificial Intelligence, which as stated above removes the actors, and processes and provides a generic outcome. The student is no longer required to actively engage with the problem and is not mandated to use a process that provides a natural outcome. AI could do this for the students, reducing the need for creativity for students. Thus, assessment situations pose a challenge, due to the introduction of AI with respect to creativity in current educational practices.

One of the crucial junctures where this lack comes to the forefront of discussion is that of assessment. Assessment, in its true form, must be able to elevate student learning and be able to help them find unique means for developing novel products, in the form of skill and knowledge which has future applicability. Assessment tasks, resultant of research work in this domain, are expected to help students use higher-order thinking skills, especially in college education, and promote creativity as these are the skills required by employers outside educational murals. Thus, assessment tasks need to be understood from the perspective of interventions by artificial intelligence.

ASSESSMENT AND ARTIFICIAL INTELLIGENCE

Integrating artificial intelligence in education has been a concept of research for over three decades. At its simplistic level, it was aimed at creating "computationally precise and explicit forms of educational, psychological and social knowledge which are often left implicit" (Luckin, 1999). One of the core tenets of assessment is to be able to improve the teaching-learning experience holistically. If applied with the veracity evident in its theoretical structures, assessment is a means to better the educational experience in terms of what students have learned and what is left to be learned. Additionally, it can also give insights into the washback effects that the experience created on the students, and consequently when these are combined understanding can be derived of how well the assessment has been able to fulfill the objectives that all the stakeholders agreed upon before embarking on the educational journey. Thus, assessment does play a crucial role with its impact being present not only in the lives of the students but also in the educational ecosystem including, but not limited to, teachers, policymakers and administrative bodies.

Assessment can be challenging for even experienced educators as it requires diligent crafting of items and tasks which then need to be mapped with rubrics and complex statistical models when student responses are produced (Mislevy et al, 2012). If continuous assessment is considered then the challenge is further compounded as more assessment activities would be carried out by the teacher throughout the program and many such assessment events need to be carefully crafted, adeptly administered, and responsibility-rated. The context of assessment may also pose a challenge as it may happen that in large classrooms assessment is substituted by testing. Although popularly these are used synonymously, a detailed study of the domain would delineate the two with testing being only a subset of assessment. Testing, generally presents a limited insight into student competence, probably just a snapshot of student performance at a particular time for the specific task. If we are to consider the large level of understanding of learning which is defined by a change then testing may not be able to reflect the same. Learning could be understood as a change in mental representations (Perret-Clermont, 1980), what can be done individually or with help (Vygotsky & Cole, 1978), or assimilating with new cultures (Lave & Wenger, 1991). If the educational experience is signposted by only testing then it may not be able to capture this kind of growth, which can only happen with the help of assessment. However, the difficulty with assessment being complicated has been established at the beginning due to its complexity. Assessment also deals with other challenges such as being too standardized, not providing opportunities for students to learn at their own pace, and also being inauthentic in terms of the demands made of them.

These challenges have been managed with the intervention of Artificial Intelligence in recent years. Studies have shown that the use of AI can create better assessment tasks especially multiple-choice questions and open-answer questions, given large-scale data sets are present. Question generation through LexRank has resulted in better results (Chen, Yang and Gasevic, 2019) and by using a two-step manner of input (Jia, Zhou, Sun and Wu, 2020). Use of robust data sets can assist teachers in creating automated questions that align with the need and hand and has resulted in the promotion of datasets such as RACE (Lai, Xie, Liu, Yang &Hovy, 2017) and LearningQ (Chen, Yang, Hauff & Houben, 2018). The question of carefully designed rubrics is still debated despite standard rubrics being available for the teachers. The field has given a lot to educational practice through intelligent tutoring systems (Carbonell, 1970; Mark & Greer, 1995; VanLehn, 2011), predicting learner success through log file and click stream analysis (Crossley, Paquetter, Dascalu, McNamara & Baker, 2016) using learning analytics and educational data mining.

Automated scoring has been the leading frontier in the application of AI for assessment with developers claiming its integrity and application (Moon & Pae, 2011; Pinot de Moira, 2013; Bridgeman, 2013). Automated scoring not only reduces the time taken for assessment but is also claimed to give effective feedback to the student, which is important for further improvement. However, there is still a certain hesitation in using these technologies for assessment with results showing that even in countries that have financial access to use of these technologies there is less change (Timmis et al., 2016). On both sides of the paradigm, with students and with teachers, we see that it has become evident that technological impact is high with the influence also being so. Students have taken to the use of technology for their production of academic demands while teachers and policy makers are still struggling to make sense of what AI means in the educational setting.

In this situation, it is mandated that an investigation be carried out to understand how educators feel about the involvement of AI in assessment and learning. This case becomes all the more challenging in a country like India because of the scale of education which is nearly a $180 billion industry with the Gross Enrolment Ration (GER) to reach 50% by 2035 (Financial Express, 2024). It is considered the third largest system in the world catering to nearly 40 million students through 56, 000 institutions with 15 lakh teachers (Tomar, 2023). The scale of Indian education is large and hence the challenges are also mammoth. The use of technology is proliferated with students having ready access to cheap internet connections and cost-effective hand-held devices. Thus, to understand the role of artificial intelligence in creating an ecosystem that allows creative thinking and promotes fairness in assessment research work needs to be carried out which is attempted here.

RESEARCH METHODOLOGY

The chapter aims to explore the perception of educators towards use of Generative AI tools in assessment. To understand how educators feel about the involvement of AI in assessment and learning, the authors conducted research on educators working in management institutes of Ahmedabad.

Research Method: The research aimed at capturing the state of affairs as it exits to know the perception of educators regarding usage of AI and hence follows a descriptive research method.

ResearchApproach: Quantitative approach of data collection following descriptive research method was applied to take the opinions of the respondents.

Sources of Data: The data for this research is taken from secondary as well as primary source. The scales used in this research are inspired by secondary research while the firsthand data is collected from educators following primary source.

Data Collection Tool: For data collection, a well-structured questionnaire was prepared, containing questions associated with the use of Gen AI tools. To know the perception of educators, Cochran's formula was used to calculate the sample size.

To maintain the confidentiality of the respondents, the researchers decided not to collect personal details like name, contact number, income details, name of the institute and email ids. A questionnaire was forwarded to educators through online mode. The data collection followed non-probability convenience sampling and took a total of one month to complete. After data pre-processing, 19 entries were removed, and 182 responses were selected for the analysis.

Reliability Analysis: To check the reliability of the data, Cronbach's alpha value was observed to be 0.825 which indicates a high level of internal consistency for the scale with this specific sample.

Table 1. Cronbach's alpha test

Reliability Statistics		
Cronbach's Alpha	**Cronbach's Alpha Based on Standardized Items**	**N of Items**
.811	.825	16

Normality Testing: Normality of the data was measured by calculating skewness and kurtosis where the values were found within the acceptable range of -2 and +2 and so the data was found to be normal.

Demographic Details: The data collection involved 182 respondents of Ahmedabad. The following table shows the descriptive statistics of the same gender, age, level of teaching and work experience of respondents.

Table 2. Descriptive Statistics

Sr. No.	Variable	Items	Number	Percentage
1.	Gender	Male	84	46%
		Female	98	54%
2.	Age Group	Less than 25	20	10%
		25-35	45	25%
		36-50	97	53%
		More than 50	20	12%
3.	Level of Teaching	Undergraduate	75	41%
		Postgraduate	107	59%
4.	Teaching Experience	0-5 years	32	17%
		6-10 years	45	24%
		11-15 years	72	39%
		16-20 years	23	15%
		More than 20 years	10	5%

Frequency analysis on demographic variables of educators was conducted wherein 84 respondents were males and the rest 98 females as is shown in table: 53% of the respondents were between 36 to 50 years of age, followed by 25% of the respondents belonging to the age group of 26-35 years. 10% of the respondents fall into the youngest category of less than 25 years of age and the rest 12% belong to the oldest group of respondents. Relating to the level of teaching, 107 respondents are teaching at postgraduate level while the remaining 75 at undergraduate level. On being asked about their teaching experience, majority of the respondents, i.e.,39%, have 11-15 years of experience, followed by a dominant percentage of 24% having 6-10 years, and an approximately equal percentage of respondents had 0-5 years and 16-20 years of experience. The most experienced group having more than 20 years clubs 5% of the total respondents.

The questionnaire used in this research is inspired by AIAS scale developed by Perkins, Furze, Roe, &MacVaugh in 2024. The scale is divided into 5 levels. The authors designed and asked various questions to respondents based on these five levels.

The use of Gen AI in assessment has been measured using 5 different scales and to know the opinion of the respondents, various questions on assessment were asked relating to each scale. The following table shows five scale levels and the questions asked.

Table 3. Scale Levels and Questions

Scale Level	Assessment Description	Items
1.	No AI	The assessment is completed entirely without AI assistance
2.	AI-Assisted Idea Generation and Structuring	AI can be used in the assessment for brainstorming
		AI can be used in the assessment for creating structures
		AI can be used in the assessment for generating ideas
3.	AI-Assisted Editing	AI can be used to make improvements to the clarity of student-created work
		AI can be used to make improvements to the quality of student-created work
		AI can be used to improve the final output,
4.	AI Task Completion, Human Evaluation	AI is used to complete only certain elements of the task
		AI is used to generate complete output and humans evaluating its correctness
5.	Full AI	AI should be used as a 'co-pilot' to meet the requirements of the assessment
		AI should be used for a collaborative approach
		AI should be used for complete result generation

Data Analysis

To find out the average opinion regarding the usage of AI in assessment, mean square analysis is undertaken to know the perception of respondents.

Table 4. Mean square Analysis.

Scale Description	Mean Value
AI-Assisted Editing	4.24
AI-Assisted Idea Generation and Structuring	4.20
AI Task Completion, Human Evaluation	3.01
No AI	2.89
Full AI	1.20

Based on the mean values obtained for all the five scales as shown in Table 4, the following chart is prepared.

Figure 1. Mean Values of Scales

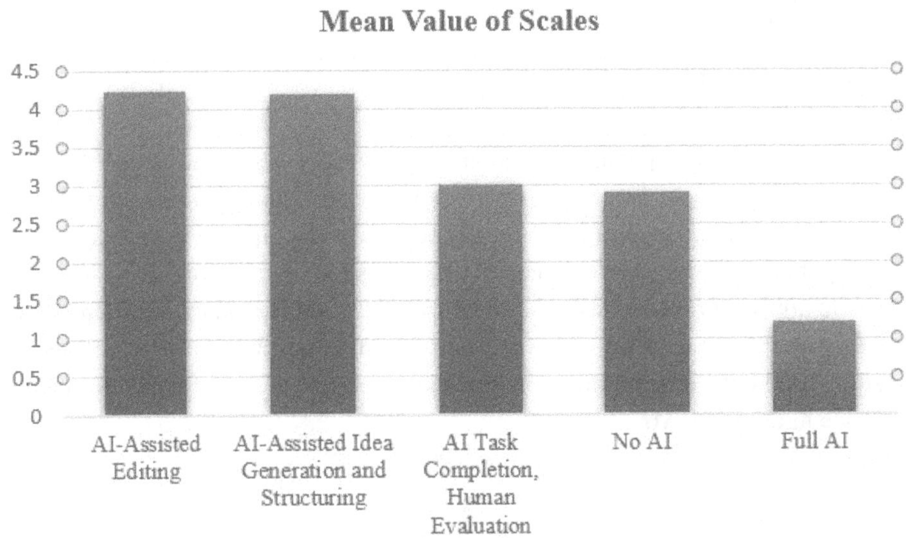

As can be seen from Fig 1, AI-assisted editing usage has the highest mean, followed by mean score of AI-Assisted Idea Generation and Structuring. For educators, AI can be helpful in assessing assignments, projects and reports of students via AI where mainly the assistance is taken in the form of plagiarism checks, copy editing checks and frame checks, and the tool is used mainly for editing purposes. Designing the multiple-choice questions and open-answer questions, for a large number of students and then later structuring and aligning with the need and context helps save time of management educators. Also, the second highest mean is when AI-generated frameworks or checklists or structures and blueprints are generated via AI to execute the work and then assessment is undertaken by educators on their own. As AI can create better assessment tasks, rubric frameworks can be designed for ongoing exams of students. The third highly rated factor by the respondents is AI task completion and human evaluation. Learner success can be calculated through AI tools such as log file and click stream analysis and then through human intervention later, the ranking and success rate of students can be predicted.

The two lowest means found by the study is no usage of AI and Full usage of AI. Living in the digital world and understanding that the future of education is tied with Gen AI, management educators agree that usage of AI is time-saving and prevents physical monotonous assessments and can be of great help to educators. Also, being in education and surrounded by ethics and integrity, full usage of AI without any human intervention is rated lowest. This says the educators of Ahmedabad do not encourage full usage of AI for task completion or merely doing an evaluation after taking or completing the whole work through AI tools as it violates the practice of academic integrity and ethical code.

Hypothesis Testing

To find out educator perceptions about various scale descriptions based on the level of teaching is also an area of interest. To signify the difference in educator perception regarding usage of AI in assessment, five hypotheses were framed. As normality check was done earlier where the data was found to be normal, researchers decided to apply parametric test of ANOVA to analyze the statistical difference in educator perception regarding usage of AI in assessment over all the levels of scales. The study used level of teaching as independent variable to find out the significant difference in usage of AI.

Table 5 shows four hypotheses framed for the study.

Table 5. Hypothesis and Statistical Tool

Sr. No.	Hypothesis	Test used
1	H_{01}: There is no significant mean difference in perception towards no AI usage in assessment and level of teaching.	ANOVA
2	H_{02}: There is no significant mean difference in perception towards AI assisted idea generation and structuring in assessment and level of teaching.	ANOVA
3	H_{03}: There is no significant mean difference in perception towards AI assisted editing in assessment and level of teaching.	ANOVA
4	H_{04}: There is no significant mean difference in perception towards no AI task completion and human evaluation in assessment and level of teaching.	ANOVA
5	H_{05}: There is no significant mean difference in perception towards Full AI usage in assessment and level of teaching.	ANOVA

The responses of educators were taken on a scale of 5 asking them to rate their perception of the usage of AI in assessment. ANOVA test is applied to check the significance difference in teacher perception over level of teaching.

ANOVA allows the comparison of the mean of two sets of data and helps in determining if there is a significant difference between the means of two datasets.

Table 6. ANOVA Table

Sr. No.	Hypothesis	P value	Hypothesis Accepted
1	H_{01}: There is no significant mean difference in perception towards no AI usage in assessment and level of teaching.	0.540	Null hypothesis
2	H_{02}: There is no significant mean difference in perception towards AI assisted idea generation and structuring in assessment and level of teaching.	0.001	Alternate hypothesis
3	H_{03}: There is no significant mean difference in perception towards AI assisted editing in assessment and level of teaching.	0.000	Alternate hypothesis
4	H_{04}: There is no significant mean difference in perception towards AI task completion and human evaluation in assessment and level of teaching.	0.320	Null hypothesis
5	H_{05}: There is no significant mean difference in perception towards Full AI usage in assessment and level of teaching.	0.231	Null hypothesis

Table 6 shows that there is no significance difference in perception of management educators teaching at undergraduate and postgraduate levels regarding usage of AI in assessment at 1st, 4th and 5th level. The educators at both levels perceive that full usage of AI is not correct for assessment. Complete assessment can't be left for machines to evaluate. Also, not using AI at all is also not acceptable, and hence the perception of educators at both levels matches. AI can be used for task completion, while assessors can then check it for corrections, agrees educators of postgraduate and undergraduate colleges, and hence no statistical difference is found here also.

Statistically significant difference is found in perception towards AI-assisted editing and AI-assisted idea generation and structuring for level 2 and 3. To analyze the variance in responses further, the data obtained for both these scales is munged again.

For, level 2, AI-assisted idea generation and structuring, the interaction (p= .001) proves that the effect of level of teaching is different across the usage of AI in assessment. A large effect (ω = 0.599) was found on AI assessment due to the level of teaching. This shows that there is significant effect size of teaching level on AI assisted idea generation and structuring in assessment. To analyze further, mean score analysis was undertaken based on the values obtained from ANOVA, to study the interaction further.

The table below depicts the extent of effect of level of teaching on assessment on AI-assisted idea generation and structuring.

Table 7. Mean Score Table for AI-Assisted Idea Generation and Structuring in Assessment

Sr. No.	Level of Teaching	Mean Score
1	Undergraduate	4.25
2	Postgraduate	2.99

According to the table 7 above, the mean value of educators working at undergraduate level is higher than the of educators at postgraduate level. Given the huge number of students being admitted at undergraduate courses, the task of assessment becomes exhaustive. With continuous evaluations and multiple deadlines for the assessment of such a huge number of students, Automated scoring can be a helpful AI tool that can be used for assessment. Rubric structuring or generating and drafting evaluations can be useful and may save monotonous tasks for educators.

For, level 3, AI-assisted editing in assessment, simple main effects variance analysis showed that level of teaching has a statistically significant effect on assessment ($p = 0.000$). ANOVA revealed that there is a statistically significant interaction and to find the significant interaction effect omega squared value is calculated. $\omega = 0.68$ shows the significant substantive large effect of level of teaching on AI-assisted editing in assessment. To understand this effect further, mean score analysis is calculated.

Table 8. Mean Score Table for AI-Assisted Editing in Assessment

Sr. No.	Level of Teaching	Mean Score
1	Undergraduate	3.15
2	Postgraduate	4.79

According to Table 8, the mean value of educators working at postgraduate level is higher than the of educators at undergraduate level. Teachers at postgraduate level agree more on using AI in assessment majorly for editing purposes. AI can be used to edit for clarity of student-created work, but they do not want any new content for assessment to be created using AI.

CONCLUSION

Artificial Intelligence has made an impact on the educational landscape along with all other industries at a rapid pace. Its ability to assist in innovative teaching and learning compounded with the benefits of assessment has provided benefits to all the stakeholders. Although the impact is felt in all areas there still exists a doubt in the utilization of this technology in its full capacity by all the stakeholders. While students have taken to it, educators and policymakers still view the technology with doubt or may still not be able to completely comprehend the use AI in the educational sector. More research in this area is required especially in the domain of assessment and subsequently creativity.

The modern educational shift has mandated a need for assessment to be more organic in providing solutions and engaging for learners. It has progressed from the rote learning and production mechanism to being an engaging activity that requires students to use all their faculties, knowledge and skills related to the specific domain of study to find solutions to challenges posed in the assessment tasks. Even the proliferation of Bloom's Taxonomy and Outcome Based Education requires educational institutes to design assessment tasks that pivot on the need for creative processes employed by students for creative outcomes. The student becomes the actor who engages effectively with the problem posed and uses cognitively high thoughts and actions for creating outcomes, assisting the educator to evaluate both the ends and the means used for arriving there. However, with the involvement of AI, these steps may have taken a step back and it is mandated that this be researched upon. With the onset of continuous assessment, which is not bound by classroom tasks students are given more time and space for them to carry out assessment tasks. In the absence of an invigilator, there are chances that students would end up using artificial intelligence only for producing the work, rather than using their own faculties to engage with the tasks. The perception of educators becomes crucial at this juncture as their consent would go a long way in creating AI-friendly assessment systems that promote creativity and critical thinking.

Based on the data analysis, the researchers found that educators working in management institutes of Ahmedabad accepted that the use of AI can be helpful in assessment. The results revealed that educators perceive AI to be helpful where the assistance is taken in the form of plagiarism checks, copy editing checks and frame checks, and the AI tools are used mainly for editing purposes. Designing assessments for students and then later structuring and aligning with the needs and context was found to be time-saving for management educators, in the present study. Educators also may like to use AI-generated frameworks or structures generated via AI to create better assessment tasks. Assessments where AI tools may complete a task and later evaluation can be undertaken is also a mode of assessments preferred by educators, however complete use of AI assessments was disagreed strongly by the educators.

The study results contribute to the debate surrounding the use of Artificial Intelligence in education by revealing the perspectives of educators teaching at undergraduate and postgraduate institutes. No significance difference was found in complete dependence on AI tools in assessments as educators at both levels believe it is against academic integrity and ethics. Statistical difference between the educators were found in usage of AI in editing and structuring assessments. While structuring or generating and drafting evaluations were preferred more by undergraduate educators, postgraduate educators prefer AI tools for editing in assessment.

REFERENCES

Ali, M., Murray, P., Momin, M., Dwivedi, Y., & Malik, T. (2024). The effects of artificial intelligence applications in educational settings: Challenges and strategies. *Technological Forecasting and Social Change*, 199, 1–18. DOI:10.1016/j.techfore.2023.123076

Amabile, T. M. (1996). *Creativity in Context: Update to the social psychology of creativity*. Westview Press.

Anantrasirichai, N., & Bull, D. (2022). Artificial Intelligence in the creative industries: A review. *Artificial Intelligence Review*, 55(1), 89–656. DOI:10.1007/s10462-021-10039-7

Arora, P., & Pillai, N. (2023). Understanding the Need for Redesigning Teachng and Learning for Indian Educators in the Digital Age. In A. A. Arinushkina, A. V. Morozov, & I. V. Robert, *Contemporary Challenges in Education: Digitalization, Methodology and Management* (pp. 289-316). IGI Global.

Baer, J., & Kaufman, J. C. (2005). Bridging generality and specificity: The amusement park theoretical (APT) model of creativity. *Roeper Review*, 27(3), 158–163. DOI:10.1080/02783190509554310

Boden, M. A. (2004). *The creative mind: myths and mechanisms*. Routledge. DOI:10.4324/9780203508527

Bozkurt, A., Karadeniz, A., Baneres, D., Guerrero-Roldan, A., & Rodriguez, M. (2021). Artificial Intellience and Reflections from Educational Landscape: A Review of AI Studies in Half a Century. *Sustainability (Basel)*, 13(2), 800. DOI:10.3390/su13020800

Bridgeman, B. (2013). Human ratings and automated essay evaluation. In Shermis, M. D., & Burnstein, J. (Eds.), *Handbook of Automated Essay Evaluation: Current applications and new directions* (pp. 221–233). Routledge.

Carbonell, J. R. (1970). An artificial-intelligence approach to computer-assisted instruction. *IEEE Transactions on Man-Machine Systems*, 11(4), 190–202. DOI:10.1109/TMMS.1970.299942

Chen, G., Yang, G., & Gasevic, D. (2019). A comparative study on question-worthy sentence selection strategies for educational question generation. *20th International Conference on Artificial Intelligence in Education* (pp. 59-70). Cham: Springer. DOI:10.1007/978-3-030-23204-7_6

Chen, G., Yang, J., Hauff, C., & Houben, G. J. (2018). LearningQ: A larg-scale dataset for educational question generation. *12th International AAAI Conference on Web and Social Media* (pp. 481-490). AAAI. DOI:10.1609/icwsm.v12i1.14987

Chu, H., Tu, Y., & Yang, R. (2022). Roles and research trends of artificial intelligence in higher education: A systematic review of the top 50 most-cited articles. *Australian Journal of Educational Technology*, 22–42.

Creely, E., Henriksen, D., & Henderson, M. (2021). Three Modes of Creativity. *The Journal of Creative Behavior*, 55(2), 306–318. DOI:10.1002/jocb.452

Crompton, H., & Burke, D. (2023). Artificial intelligence in higher education: The state of the field. *International Journal of Educational Technology in Higher Education*, 20(1), 1–22. DOI:10.1186/s41239-023-00392-8

Crossley, S., Paquette, L., Dascalu, M., McNamara, D. S., & Baker, R. S. (2016). Combining dick-stream data with Nlp tools to better understand MOOC completion. *6th international conference on learning analytics & knowledge* (pp. 6-14). New York: Association for Computing Machinery.

Csikszentmihalyi, M. (1997). *The Psychology of Discovery and Invention*. Harper Perennial.

Csikszentmihalyi, M. (2014). *The Systems Model of Creativity*. Springer. DOI:10.1007/978-94-017-9085-7

Education, F. E. (2024, February 15). *The Indian higher education sector is set to grow 3x from $55 billion in 2023 to $180 billion by 2035: Report*. Retrieved April 14, 2024, from Financial Express: https://www.financialexpress.com/jobs-career/education-the-indian-higher-education-sector-is-set-to-grow-3x-from-55-billion-in-2023-to-180-billion-by-2035-reportnbsp-3395715/

Furze, P. M., Roe, J., & MacVaugh, J. (2024). The Artificial Intelligence Assessment Scale(AIAS): A Framework for Ethical Integration of Generative AI in Educational Assessment. *Journal of University Teaching and Learning* .

Glaveanu, V. P., & Kaufman, J. C. (2019). A historical perspective. In Kaufman, J. R. (Ed.), *Sternberg, The Cambridge Handbok of Creativity* (pp. 9–26). Cambridge University Press. DOI:10.1017/9781316979839.003

Habib, A., Muhaimin, M., Danibao, B., Wibowo, Y., Wahyuni, S., & Octavia, A. (2023). ChatGPT in higher education learning: Acceptance and use. *Computers & Education. Artificial Intelligence*, 1–9.

Jia, X., Zhou, W., Sun, X., & Wu, Y. (2020). EQG-RACE: Examination-Type question generation.

Khan, I., Ahmad, A. R., Jabeur, N., & Mahdi, M. N. (2021). *An artificial intelligence approach to monitor student performance and devise preventive measure*. Smart Learning Environments. DOI:10.1186/s40561-021-00161-y

Kim, J., & Bennekin, K. N. (2016). The effectiveness of volition support (VoS) in prompting students' effort regulation and performance in a online mathematics course. *Instructional Science*, 44(4), 359–377. DOI:10.1007/s11251-015-9366-5

Lai, G., Xie, Q., Liu, H., Yang, Y., & Hovy, E. (2017). RACE: Large-scale ReAding Comprehension Dataset From Examinations. https://arxiv.org/abs/1704.04683DOI: 10.18653/v1/D17-1082

Lave, J., & Wenger, E. (1991). *Situated Learning: Legitimate peripheral participation*. Cambridge University Press. DOI:10.1017/CBO9780511815355

Lubart, T. (2001). Models of the creative process: Past, present and future. *Creativity Research Journal*, 13(3-4), 295–308. DOI:10.1207/S15326934CRJ1334_07

Mark, M. A., & Greer, J. E. (1995). The VCR tutor: Effective instruction for device operation. *Journal of the Learning Sciences*, 4(2), 209–246. DOI:10.1207/s15327809jls0402_3

Mislevy, R. J., Behrens, J. T., Dicerbo, K. E., & Levy, R. (2012). Design and discovery in educational assessment: Evidence-centered design, psychometrics and educational data mining. *Journal of educational data mining*, 11-48.

Mollick, E. R., & Mollick, L. (2023a). Assigning AI: Seven approaches for students with prompts. *SSRN*. DOI:10.2139/ssrn.4475995

Mollick, E. R., & Mollick, L. (2023b). Using AI to implement effective teaching strategies inclassroom: Five Strategies, including prompts. *SSRN*. DOI:10.2139/ssrn.4391243

Moon, Y., & Pae, J. K. (2011). Short-term effects of automated writing feedback and users' evaluation of criterion. *Applied Linguistics*, 125–150.

Ng, D., Leung, T. K., Chu, K. L., & Qia, M. S. (2021). Conceptualizing AI Literacy: an exploratory review. *Computers and Education: Artificial Inteligence*, 10-41.

Perret-Clemont, A. N. (1980). *Social interaction and cognitive development in children*. Academic Press.

Pinot de Moira, A. (2013). *Features of a level-based mark scheme and their effect on marking realiability*. Centre of Education Research and Policy.

Porter, B., & Grippa, F. (2020). A platform for AI-enabled real-time feedback to promote digital collaboration. *Sustainability (Basel)*, 12(24), 1–13. DOI:10.3390/su122410243

Rhodes, M. (1961). An analysis of creativity. *Phi Delta Kappan*, 305–310.

Timmis, S., Broadfoot, P., Sutherland, R., & Oldfield, A. (2016). Rethinking assessment in a digital age: Opportunities, challenges and risks. *British Educational Research Journal*, 42(3), 454–476. DOI:10.1002/berj.3215

Tomar, A. (2023, December 8). *How can Indian higher education prepare to leapfrog in the next two years*. Retrieved April 14, 2024, from EY.Com: https://www.ey.com/en_in/education/how-can-indian-higher-education-prepare-to-leapfrog-in-the-next-two-years

VanLehn, K. (2011). The relative effectiveness of human tutoring, intelligent tutoring systems, and other tutoring systems. *Educational Psychologist*, 46(4), 197–221. DOI:10.1080/00461520.2011.611369

Vygotsky, L. S., & Cole, M. (1978). Mind in society: Development of higher psychological processes. Harvard University Press.

Xia, Q., Chiu, T. K., Lee, M., Temiyato, I., Dai, Y., & Chai, C. S. (2022). A self-determination theory design for inclusive and diverse Artificial Intelligence (AI) K-12 education. *Computers & Education*, 189, 104582. DOI:10.1016/j.compedu.2022.104582

Yang, A. C., Chen, I. Y., Flanagan, B., & Ogata, H. (2021). Automatic generation of cloze items for repeated testing to improve reading comprehension. *Journal of Educational Technology & Society*, 147–158.

Chapter 3
Finding Time for Creativity in Higher Education Writing Through Generative AI

K. M. Begian-Lewis
Wayne State University, USA

Colleen J. Hart
Wayne State University, USA

ABSTRACT

In this chapter, the authors discuss the relationship between time poverty, creativity, and Large Language Models of AI (LLMs) or Generative AI technologies in the writing classroom, including ChatGPT and GenAI software in word processors such as Microsoft Word. Through examples of writing provided by ChatGPT, a student profile, and comparative analysis of writing provided by two LLMs, they make an argument that LLMs should be integrated into the writing classroom in order to offer students who suffer from time poverty the ability to practice creativity in their writing which they may struggle to achieve when limited to the time they can devote to their classwork. Specifically, they explore how ChatGPT can support students in the writing process, including researching, pre-writing, writing, revision, and reflection in order to foster creativity in their writing.

DOI: 10.4018/979-8-3693-2418-9.ch003

INTRODUCTION

Creativity is a privilege more common among students who are not affected by time poverty. By this, we mean that students who do not face time barriers that affect their ability to complete their coursework are those who can develop their critical thinking skills at the level of creativity. Creativity is a task that is part of the thinking process; in this process, before one can think creatively, one must first be able to understand a topic. Only once they have this grasp of an issue can they begin to think creatively about it. When students do not have the time or resources to devote to developing an understanding, they are also barred from taking their thinking to the next step and being able to think creatively. While there are compounding reasons that students may find themselves vulnerable to time poverty, in this paper, we will be focusing on this vulnerability to discuss how access to Large Language Models of AI (LLMs) can act as a counterbalance to the time poverty often experienced by students so that these students can be afforded the time it takes to be truly creative within the composition classroom (Begian-Lewis, 2023; Vickery, 1977).

Within this chapter, we will explore some of the unique ways in which modern students experience time poverty. We will also discuss both the importance of creativity in composition classrooms and how creativity can be encouraged in these spaces through the use of Generative AI (GenAI). Finally, we will suggest practical ways in which instructors can encourage students of composition to use GenAI ethically as a part of their research, pre-writing, writing, revision, and reflecting practices in ways that save time while increasing the students' ability to be creative. These practical examples will include student profiles, sample assignments, and a variety of examples of steps in the composition process that have been completed using GenAI.

TIME POVERTY

Modern students have a lot on their plates. Some factors that can cause students to experience time poverty include the need to work a job, completing coursework and studying in a second or third language, participating in sports, roles as a caretaker or other relational responsibilities, and issues that are unique to first-generation students, just to name a few (Amano et al., 2023; Begian-Lewis, 2023; Wladis, 2018; Roksa, 2018). Beyond these constraints, students with disabilities also face tremendous and hard-to-quantify time challenges that put them at greater risk of time poverty (Wood, 2017). Previously, Begian-Lewis ran the numbers on the percentage of available time that students use to work on schoolwork outside of class, comparatively, and found that, all other things being equal, a student who does not have outside time commitments devotes 4.66% less of their available time to out-of-class work when completing 24 hours of studying than a student who has an outside commitment that requires 20 hours of the student's time on top of the 24 hours that they spend studying (Begian-Lewis, 2023). This disparity in time becomes greater as the time-poor student is required to devote more of their time to commitments outside of school. Many time-poor students find themselves facing multiple time-consuming obligations beyond school at once as they go to school.

In an interview with Kim Mills of the American Psychiatric Association, Gloria Mark of the University of California, Irvine, distinguishes between rote activity—where individuals are engaged but not challenged—and focused attention—where individuals are engaged and challenged. Mark details a series of studies beginning in 2004 in which individuals were timed while doing daily activities that required focused attention and that time was stopped when they shifted into rote activities. The results of this study found that the average amount of time individuals spent using focused attention—we will call this their focused attention span—before they reverted to rote activities was approximately 2.5 minutes. The average focused attention span decreased each time researchers re-tested so that, in 2017/2018, the average focused attention span of participants was just 47 seconds, a decrease that can be attributed greatly to technological advancements. The shortening of the average focused attention span affects all students, but they particularly make online education even more difficult for many students as the students are subjected to targeted marketing and messaging and have so many other elements competing for their attention to contend with (Kavyashree et al., 2022; Mark, 2023). Students who experience time poverty due to disabilities that affect their attention spans are also disproportionately impacted by the shortening of focused attention spans (Wood, 2017).

Between compounding out-of-school time commitments and an increased number of tasks competing for a student's attention, it is no wonder that the average amount of time that students spend studying has been steadily decreasing over time (Babcock & Marks, 2011). While Babcock & Marks use Oaxaca's model for determining the effect of changing composition between data sets, they note that, between 1961 and 2003, the amount of time that students—despite their background, race, gender, and a variety of other identity characteristics—spent studying had decreased from an average of 40 hours per week to an average of about 27 hours per week. Despite the broad decrease in study time that Babcock & Marks reported, they also noted that students who did not work and had college-educated fathers averaged a greater number of hours spent studying compared to working students with college-educated fathers.[1]

Students who experience time poverty are less likely to complete their degrees than their time neutral peers (Xavier & Maneses, 2022; Xavier et al., 2022). In fact, time poverty is a common reason for students enrolling part-time or returning to school later in life. In a 2022 study by Xavier & Maneses found that the majority of non-traditional part-time students reported that they considered dropping out of their programs in their first year (Xavier & Maneses, 2022), indicating that there are multiple constraints that non-traditional students face as compared to their traditional, time-privileged peers.

WHAT IS CREATIVITY?

At its most basic level, creativity is the "...ability to make or otherwise bring into existence something new, whether a new solution to a problem, a new method or device, or a new artistic object or form" (Kerr, 2024). Creativity is invention. But, the ability to be creative requires time.

Emphasizing creativity in the composition classroom is not a new idea, though it has often been a controversial one (Bull et al., 1995; Sternberg, 2004). Sidney Dobrin references the Ancient Greek philosopher and rhetorician Cicero regarding writing and rhetoric, noting that "[l]ong before writing instructors began formally teaching "the writing process," classical rhetoricians identified the five canons of rhetoric—a means of categorizing the steps a speaker or writer needs to take in order to produce oration or writing. These canons are invention, arrangement, style, memory, and delivery" (2023, 63). Invention—as Simonson defines it, "all the ways that discourse and other materials are generated for rhetorical address" (2014, 299)—then is arguably a key element of composition education. The generation of content of which to write and speak about, of course, is creativity, and this conception occurs throughout many stages in the writing classroom. While an instructor may give an assignment requiring the student to write on a particular issue, the writing process is not linear, and the student will have to creatively build many parts of their argument, such as creating a hook in their introduction, determining topics for their body paragraphs, and possibly adding their own thoughts and experiences throughout. In his 2015 article in *College Composition and Communication,* Patrick Sullivan supports this in arguing that creativity should be valued as much as literacy in the writing classroom, as creativity can be defined as a necessary building block for developing new ideas and developing greater intellectual capabilities. In other words, creativity can be key to moving past rote activity and into the focused attention stage of composing.

From this, we argue that creativity is crucial in a student's writing; therefore, we should provide tools and instruction on ways to support this activity. Notably, creativity is not something that GenAI is currently capable of. When a student prompts an AI model, the model replies with word associations, providing the statistically most likely response (Dobrin, 2023). This lack of creativity limits GenAI to the sort of mechanical tasks that are time-consuming but do not require invention or critical thinking making a partnership between students and AI models a productive pairing.

TIME AND CREATIVITY

Some students share that they don't intend to use AI in their writing. For them, learning another technology does not feel like a contribution to their learning of how to write effectively or help them develop writing skills that they can take out of the classroom. But for many others, they are already implementing GenAI into their writing and even doing so in a way that is not noticeable by their instructors (Terry, 2023; Fyfe, 2023). Concerns about plagiarism and the ethical debates of GenAI do not find any grounding if one cannot prove a student has in fact utilized GenAI in their coursework. And ultimately, should we not support all students' capabilities in the classroom by providing an equal playing field? Many temporally unprivileged students who do not have equal time to devote to their coursework may also not have time to devote to learning how to use GenAI as a writing tool outside of the classroom. Many students are also nervous to interact with GenAI on their own for a variety of reasons including the fear of being punished or ethical concerns, concerns that are valid considering the controversy and uncertainty surrounding GenAI in writing (Fyfe, 2023). For this reason, among others, we must instruct writing with this tool.

GENERATIVE AI AND CREATIVITY

There is much debate over whether GenAI should be used in the composition classroom. This article does not engage with this conversation directly by negotiating the positives and negatives of its use and assumes that there is a place for GenAI in the composition classroom. This approach is taken so that, in this article, we can focus on practical ways of using GenAI to encourage greater creativity.

As long as the writer understands the capabilities of GenAI, Wagner et al. (2022) posit that AI has a place in the creation of literature reviews. Specifically, writers must consider which steps can and cannot be done successfully and accurately through GenAI. Though their article is specific to literature reviews, their approach can be expanded for other aspects of composition that students engage in in the college classroom, which can be supplemented through LLMs. Wagner et al. argue that GenAI is a beneficial tool in the creation of literature reviews because it allows writers to conduct more mechanical tasks more efficiently so that writers can focus on the more creative aspects of writing literature reviews. Wagner et al. were focused on research that was being conducted by professionals. If GenAI is capable of saving experts time, imagine how much time it can save new researchers who are in the early stages of learning the more mechanical tasks involved in composition.

Wagner et al. reference the use of GenAI in STEM writing, where researchers have had success in creating hypotheses with the help of AI models. While they acknowledge ethical concerns in using AI for designing research in the social sciences, Wagner et al. suggest that researchers in the social sciences can learn from the ways that GenAI is used in STEM writing and forecast a "moderate potential" for GenAI to support individuals with the early stages of idea generation. Leslie (2023) supports this, finding that content constructed by GenAI are "principal sites for human empowerment, democratic agency, and creativity" (n.p.). Within the composition classroom, GenAI can support students in jumping into conversations that could otherwise be overwhelming. We have all probably encountered students who are either so afraid of trying and failing to produce a workable idea that they simply cannot start a task or students who consider so much information when approaching composition work that they are unable to settle on an idea. While GenAI is not capable of creating new ideas, it is capable of inspiring ideas in others.

GenAI offers a unique opportunity in the writing classroom to support our students' writing processes by cutting down time and strengthening their confidence in their capabilities. In their 2023 study, Nikoloas Pellas finds that "generative AI platforms can significantly improve undergraduate students' narrative intelligence scores and writing self-efficacy," which points to how this tool can shorten the prewriting stage and prompt students to feel confident entering the writing state of their writing process. Additionally, they found no noticeable difference in AI's impact on creativity as a factor in student writing and instead argue that AI's mastery of grammar and organization offer space for students to focus on creative elements in their writing. Sidney Dobrin analogizes GenAI to the smart kid in class: "we all want collaborators who are capable of offering novel contributions to our work. Think back to those moments in high school when you had to choose a lab partner, and how students rushed to pair with the "smart kid" hoping their own grade would benefit from that student's work. In many ways, GenAI can be that smart kid for all of us" (2023, 25). Because ChatGPT and other GenAI softwares are offered online with free versions, these tools can be taken up by any student with access to the internet. While we cannot guarantee that students can access these tools at home, they could utilize them in our classrooms and through computer labs provided by their colleges or universities. And using this tool as a writing support, such as the smart kid who immediately understands what the teacher is talking about, can help students with their writing process.

There are many issues regarding the output of GenAI, as many scholars noted; in summary, Dobrin states GenAI can't "discern value, accuracy, or bias in the data they scrub.... Nor can AIs identify which data are more or less relevant in light of a provided prompt. Thus, we must be critical when assessing the accuracy and the relevance of GenAI outputs" (2023, 38). From this we can draw that the more often an idea is presented, the more likely GenAI will be to offer that information. Since it identifies patterns, stereotypes are commonly present. It is our role as a user of this tool and as a writer to be critical of this writing. Here, our role as a writer moves from the collection of information and the construction of sentences to be a critical analyzer of the content created, both for inaccuracy in information as well as in how well the writing represents our own ideas. Relieving us of a significant amount of time and labor over the search for sources and the construction of sentences, we can now focus on refining the content we want to create by adapting the prompts we request and move our time and energy to the revision of content.

EXAMPLES OF WRITING WITH GENERATIVE AI

Generative AI offers many opportunities to offload time and labor in the writing process. For example, it can assist authors in developing argument statements or theses, outline major points of an argument, and finding and summarizing texts. From there, students can critically assess the content they have been provided and spend time developing their arguments.

When I asked ChatGPT to "create an outline for an argumentative essay about how communication technologies have changed over time," ChatGPT replied with the following outline:

I. Introduction
    A. Definition of communication technologies
    B. Importance of communication technologies in society
    C. Overview of how communication technologies have evolved over time
II. Historical Perspective
    A. Early forms of communication technologies (e.g., cave paintings, smoke signals, carrier pigeons)
    B. Invention of writing systems and its impact on communication
    C. Development of postal services and its role in long-distance communication
III. Industrial Revolution and Telegraph

A. Impact of the Industrial Revolution on communication technologies
B. Invention and impact of the telegraph
C. Role of the telegraph in shaping global communication networks

IV. Rise of Telephony and Radio
A. Introduction of telephony and its impact on interpersonal communication
B. Development of radio technology and its role in mass communication
C. Influence of radio broadcasting on society and politics

V. Television and Mass Media
A. Emergence of television as a dominant communication medium
B. Impact of television on entertainment, advertising, and news dissemination
C. Role of mass media in shaping public opinion and cultural norms

VI. Digital Revolution and Internet
A. Advent of the digital revolution and its impact on communication technologies
B. Development of the internet and its transformative effect on global communication
C. Influence of social media platforms on interpersonal communication and information dissemination

VII. Mobile Communication and Wireless Technologies
A. Evolution of mobile communication devices (e.g., smartphones, tablets)
B. Impact of wireless technologies on accessibility and connectivity
C. Role of mobile communication in shaping modern society and business practices

VIII. Current Trends and Future Outlook
A. Overview of current communication technologies (e.g., 5G, IoT, AI)
B. Potential future developments in communication technologies
C. Implications of evolving communication technologies on society, culture, and economy

IX. Counterarguments and Critiques
A. Critiques of modern communication technologies (e.g., privacy concerns, digital divide)
B. Counterarguments against the notion of continuous technological progress
C. Consideration of alternative perspectives on the impact of communication technologies

X. Conclusion
A. Recap of the evolution of communication technologies over time
B. Reflection on the transformative impact of communication technologies on society
C. Call to action for responsible use and regulation of communication technologies.

From this outline, students can determine what topics they want to further explore from the many that ChatGPT has offered. Additionally, when asking for ChatGPT to outline arguments, it often includes a section prior to the conclusion that lists counterarguments---a valuable moment where students can reflect on multiple positions and strengthen their own. While all body paragraphs offer students the opportunity to find sources that are meaningful to them and write about them in thoughtful and creative ways, this prompt to address a counterargument and spend time to reinforce the importance of their own argument highlights the importance of creativity by addressing solutions to any disagreements.

In reviewing the different topics of the sample outline, a student might realize (or be guided by their instructor to recognize) that their research question that prompted this outline is quite broad. The sections of this essay range from historical technologies, the development of the telegraph and its impact, to development of the radio and telephone, to digital technologies such as social media. Each of these topics alone could be explored in depth in an argumentative essay. Whether prior to the creation of an outline or after, a student might decide to narrow their research question on a topic that resonates most with them, and many contemporary students are drawn to write about social media, so this is the next example we will explore through ChatGPT. Drawing from the language provided in the outline, I asked ChatGPT to "Write a thesis statement about the digital revolution and technologies, its development, and its impact on global communication." In response, ChatGPT wrote, "The digital revolution and advancements in technology have fundamentally transformed global communication, revolutionizing the way information is transmitted, received, and interacted with, thus shaping modern society in profound ways." This thesis statement does fulfill the request, yet it is quite general. What advancements in technology are we talking about specifically? How has it shaped modern society? To follow this up, I asked ChatGPT to be more specific about how it has shaped modern society. The new thesis statement it created is as follows:

The digital revolution and advancements in technology have not only revolutionized global communication but have also profoundly shaped modern society by fostering interconnectedness, accelerating the spread of information, redefining social interactions, transforming business models, and democratizing access to knowledge and opportunities.

This thesis statement does offer less general language, specifically regarding its narrowing to "transforming business models" and "democratizing access to knowledge and opportunities." The five major points that ChatGPT offers in this thesis all offer multiple areas for a student to research and find sources. So, I asked ChatGPT to "find sources that support this thesis." ChatGPT responded that they do not have access to external sources. But one way to receive research help is to have ChatGPT create bibliography for the specific argument statement. In response to this prompt, ChatGPT created a list of 10 sources with notes, writing:

Creating a bibliography for your argument would involve listing academic sources that support the various aspects of the digital revolution and advancements in technology as outlined in your thesis statement. Here's an example of how you could format the bibliography:

1. Castells, Manuel. "The Rise of the Network Society: The Information Age: Economy, Society, and Culture." Wiley-Blackwell, 2010.
2. Jenkins, Henry. "Convergence Culture: Where Old and New Media Collide." NYU Press, 2006.
3. Shirky, Clay. "Here Comes Everybody: The Power of Organizing Without Organizations." Penguin Books, 2008.
4. Benkler, Yochai. "The Wealth of Networks: How Social Production Transforms Markets and Freedom." Yale University Press, 2006.
5. Rheingold, Howard. "Smart Mobs: The Next Social Revolution." Basic Books, 2003.
6. Wellman, Barry, and Caroline Haythornthwaite (eds.). "The Internet in Everyday Life." Wiley-Blackwell, 2002.
7. Rifkin, Jeremy. "The Zero Marginal Cost Society: The Internet of Things, the Collaborative Commons, and the Eclipse of Capitalism." St. Martin's Griffin, 2014.
8. Turkle, Sherry. "Alone Together: Why We Expect More from Technology and Less from Each Other." Basic Books, 2011.
9. Anderson, Chris. "The Long Tail: Why the Future of Business is Selling Less of More." Hyperion, 2006.
10. Tapscott, Don, and Anthony D. Williams. "Wikinomics: How Mass Collaboration Changes Everything." Portfolio, 2006.

This bibliography includes a mix of books and authors that discuss various aspects of the digital revolution, including its impact on communication, society, business, and knowledge sharing. You can further expand this list by including specific journal articles, research papers, or other academic sources that delve deeper into each aspect of your argument.

These texts do exist, which can be an issue, as Dobrin mentions above, with using ChatGPT to write with sources. However, if a student was required to use MLA format, which is common in high school English and first-year college writing courses, this would be an incorrect format for book titles. Additionally, the texts are not organized in alphabetical order based on authors' last names. This is one example where a student must be critical of the content that ChatGPT offers. ChatGPT even recognizes the limitations of the information it has provided, reminding the searcher that they can, "further expand this list by including specific journal articles, research papers, or other academic sources that delve deeper into each aspect of your argument."

From this search, however, students can investigate these texts, and even ask ChatGPT to summarize the sources for them to understand what the sources are about and determine if they would like to use them for their project. For instance, when asked to summarize Henry Jenkin's *Convergence Culture,* ChatGPT writes a four-paragraph description, beginning with, "*Convergence Culture* by Henry Jenkins explores how digital technologies have transformed media and culture by blurring the lines between different forms of media, such as television, film, and the internet. Jenkins argues that convergence is not just a technological shift but also a cultural shift, as it changes how media is produced, consumed, and shared." This description informs the students that this text will focus on digital technologies as they relate to media studies, including television and film. This may be a specific avenue the student would want to explore further, or they may instead want to find sources in a different area of studies, such as business, building from the provision of Rifkin's text that outlines digital technologies development and the "Eclipse of Capitalism." Here, students can reflect on their own interests and incorporate them into their assignments. ChatGPT just offers them the tools to decide where they would like to explore in their research, and this summarizing function can even be used to help students confirm their reading and understanding of their sources. As each of these examples show, GenAI can be used to further the writing process, whether for pre-writing, research, writing, revision, and reflection, offering students time to save time, reflect on their goals as an author, and creatively engage with their writing work.

GenAI can be helpful in the editing stages as well. It is crucial that students develop their editing and revising skills. However, editing can take a lot of time and often doesn't genuinely teach the student how and why they are making particular changes. To illustrate both how time poverty can affect a student's experience with editing their work and minimize their creativity, we will provide a student profile and sample scenario below. This will be followed by an example of how we used ChatGPT to edit a student sample and how this approach can save time over other editing techniques.

Student Profile

Giana is a freshman who is taking Introductory Composition. She has writing anxiety that is exacerbated by her lack of confidence in her ability to write "well." She has never been a top student in English courses, where she often struggles to get her words down in a way that accurately communicates her ideas to others. Giana works while attending school both to meet her basic needs and because she is trying to keep her student loan borrowing low. She comes from a working-class background and has experienced both housing and food insecurity before. These experiences teach her that she needs to be sure to work hard at her job, but they have also taught her that higher education is the way to become socially mobile. She takes an instrumentalist stance on education, particularly when it comes to courses that she does not consider to be directly relevant to the work that she will be doing in her future career (Seitz, 2004). Giana wants to be a veterinarian, a goal that is spurred by her love for animals and her strength as a student in STEM courses.

Writing Scenario

Giana's class has been assigned an I-Search as their first major project. An I-Search is a piece that asks students to narrate their research process in three phases. Students first write about their expectations for their research and their motivation for conducting their research and think ahead to anticipate what they will do. The student then narrates their research as they are conducting it, focusing on their experiences rather than focusing on the findings. Finally, students are asked to reflect on their research and look ahead to their next steps.

Giana is efficacious and has high expectations for herself. However, her anxiety prevents her from feeling comfortable going to the university Writing Center for assistance with editing her I-Search out of fear that she will be seen as unintelligent or unworthy of studying at a college level. Giana's socioeconomic background has made her very self-conscious about being seen as unworthy and, after all, she is working hard on the paper and has been careful to edit it several times.

During peer review, Giana's peer partner struggles to follow Giana's narrative and comments that it seems like Giana is jumping back and forth between sections of the paper. Her lab partner identifies three scenes that take place at different times that Giana is discussing throughout her paper and recommends that Giana edit her paper so that the discussion of each scene is together, suggesting that this could increase clarity. Giana feels that she has a good reason for the ordering of her paper because she was not taking a chronological approach to discussing her research experience. However, Giana worries that, if she does not reorder her paper, she will receive a lower grade because her paper may be hard for her instructor to follow.

Giana knows that she could ask her instructor, but it was hard enough for her to show her writing to a peer and, again, she is nervous that her instructor will think less of her as a student. That is not the first impression that she wants to make with her English instructor. So, Giana organizes the paper chronologically and works on editing it so that this new order fits with the rest of her paper. She completes the edits in time to turn the paper in.

Analysis

In this scenario, the ideal solution would be for the instructor to find a way to make every student feel comfortable coming to them when the student has concerns. We all know, however, that this simply is not a realistic solution. No matter how much an instructor embraces a pedagogy of care or other classroom practices designed to help students feel more comfortable, we cannot always reach every student. By providing students with solutions for moments when they are not comfortable coming to you, they gain greater agency in their educational journey.

In the case of Giana's I-Search, we encounter a student who is already creative. A shortage of time is not the only issue that Giana faces in completing her work. However, a great deal of Giana's time is being spent attempting to make her work clearer without a) fully understanding the changes she is making and b) agreeing with the changes she is making. Arguably, Giana is being creative with the organization of her I-Search. She is simply struggling to learn how to express her creativity to others. Due to her time constraints, Giana had to choose between trying to learn to reorganize her paper to better illustrate her creativity and using the skills she already has to make the edits that her peer review partner suggested.

EDITING WITH GENERATIVE AI

The following is an example of a snippet of writing that could be part of a student I-Search project:

I found all of my articles through the university library system. Usually, I would have used a Google search, but now that I know more about assessing the credibility of articles, using the library system makes a lot more sense. In the future, I will make use of this system in the future because the early findings of my research have inspired me to write up a research proposal even though it is not a requirement of this class.

This sample contains areas that could benefit from editing due to repeated words being left in the draft and for clarity. Below is the same sample, which has been edited using Microsoft editor.

I found all my articles through the university library system. Usually, I would have used a Google search, but now that I know more about assessing the credibility of articles, using the library system makes a lot more sense. In the future, I will make use of this system in the future because the early findings of my research have inspired me to write up a research proposal even though it is not a requirement of this class.

The editor made two suggestions, as shown in Figure 1 and Figure 2. In the suggestion from Figure 1, the student is advised to replace the words "all of" with "all" because it would improve conciseness, stating "More concise language would be clearer for your reader." Conciseness is a word that a lot of us are familiar with, but which may be unfamiliar to some of our students, including students who speak English as a second language. Some students may need to look up the definition to understand the recommended changes. Another issue with this feedback is that the student has no way of asking further questions to clarify the editing suggestions. According to Lee, "Technology in teaching creativity should be novel, fun, and valuable" (2). However, in this scenario, if the student wants to better understand the recommendations, they must ask others or perform a search and apply what they find to their writing. Technology, in this case, only fulfills the requirement of being valuable, but is this use of technology the most valuable to the student?

The recommendation from Figure 2 states that the student should consider replacing the words "a lot" with more specific numbers or examples if they are working on a resume but the editor offers no suggestions of how the student could edit the sentence to include more specific numbers or examples. When we see this, we can identify that the student will not need to use this feedback. For one, the student is not writing a resume. For another, the suggestion does not match the content of the sentence as the editor is simply homing in on "a lot" and not "a lot" in the context of the student's sentence.

Figure 1. An editing suggestion to improve conciseness by replacing "all of" with "all"

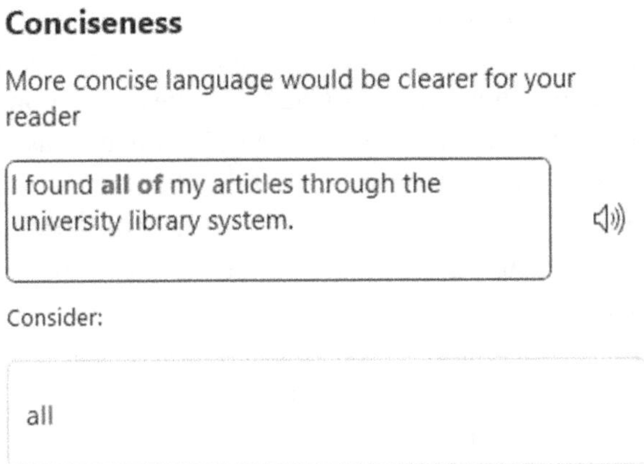

Figure 2. An editing suggestion to replace "a lot" with more specific information

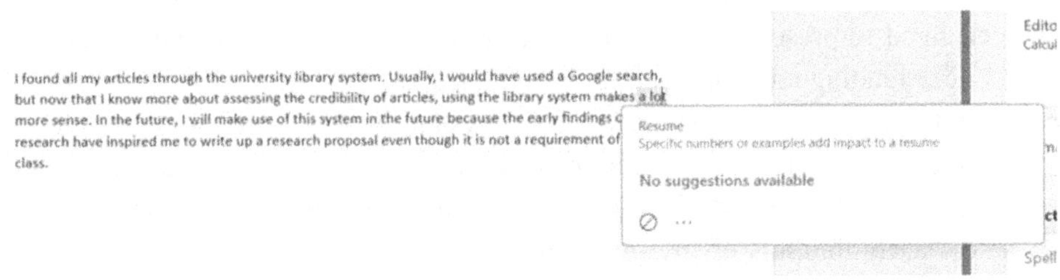

Next, we used ChatGPT to edit the same example. We did this by imputing the following prompt: "If I provide you with a piece of my writing, can you edit it?"

From which, we received the following response: "Of course! I'd be happy to help. Please go ahead and provide the piece of writing you'd like me to edit, and let me know what specific aspects you'd like me to focus on."

After we input the sample, ChatGPT returned the edited sample below:

I found all of my articles through the university library system. Previously, I would have relied on a Google search, but now that I have a better understanding of how to assess the credibility of articles, using the library system makes a lot more sense. In the future, I will continue to make use of this system because the initial findings of my research have inspired me to write up a research proposal, even though it is not a requirement for this class.

Notice that ChatGPT caught the repeated use of "in the future" where Microsoft Word's editor did. Meanwhile, ChatGPT did not prioritize conciseness, but, instead, prioritized flow. It is worth noting that ChatGPT does not automatically provide feedback on the reason that it made these changes. If a student has not been instructed to prompt ChatGPT further, this could be the end of the conversation, which is concerning because the student will not be able to make these edits themself in the future. However, if you further prompt the LLM, it can provide detailed information on why it suggested each change.

We input the following prompt: "Can you explain why you recommended these changes?" What follows is the response from ChatGPT:

Certainly! Here's an explanation of the changes I made:

- "Usually, I would have used a Google search," was changed to "Previously, I would have relied on a Google search." This change helps to clarify that the action of using Google search was in the past and now there's a different approach being taken.
- "Using the library system makes a lot more sense" was kept as is, but it was changed to present tense. This is because it's a statement about the current understanding and approach to finding articles.
- "In the future, I will make use of this system in the future" was modified to "In the future, I will continue to make use of this system." This is to avoid repetition of the word "future" and to make the sentence more concise.
- "the early findings of my research have inspired me to write up a research proposal even though it is not a requirement of this class" was changed to "the initial findings of my research have inspired me to write up a research proposal, even though it is not a requirement for this class." This change was made to improve clarity and to ensure the sentence flows smoothly. "Initial findings" sounds more formal and appropriate in an academic context, and "write up" is a common phrase meaning to compose or create a document.

Overall, the changes were made to improve clarity, consistency in tense, and to ensure the sentence structure flows well.

This response identifies each change and then lays out the reason for the recommendation in the context of the student's specific sample, which can save students the time of trying to look up the reasoning and apply it to their text.

It is important to note that the response above includes problematic ideologies that are common in GenAI due to AI replicating the most common ideas that it was trained on (Dobrin, 2023). ChatGPT's response states that "'Initial findings'" sounds more formal and appropriate in an academic context." This recommendation upholds Western ideology that associates Standard American English (SAE) with formality in harmful and racist ways. This is one example of why it is so important to talk to students about GenAI so that they can identify problematic suggestions such as this.

CONSIDERATIONS

Though this chapter has been focused on the benefits of incorporating AI into the modern writing classroom to increase student creativity and attempt to counteract time poverty among students, it is important to discuss the challenges associated with using AI in this way. Namely, as we have discussed, time poverty disproportionately affects students who are socioeconomically vulnerable. These are the same students who may have more barriers to utilizing technology. If these students do not have access (or dependable access) to technology, then the interventions discussed in this chapter cannot benefit them to the intended degree. We recommend that students be given the opportunity to use school computers in class rather than just outside of the classroom. This, too, can lead to greater concerns because the schools that will be more capable of making this accommodation are necessarily going to be the more monetarily stable institutions. K.M. has incorporated trips to the university library into their classroom to allow students to work on their paper during workshop-like sessions to help account for these issues of access.

AI use also introduces a plethora of new ethical concerns to the classroom. If time poverty is an issue, then there will be students who seek to use AI to counteract their time poverty in their own way, which can include using AI to write their assignments. However, there will be students using AI in the writing classroom whether it is allowed or not. By discussing AI and how to use it, it is more likely that students will be able to use it ethically.

The possibility that students will overuse AI makes it necessary for instructors to do extra work to attempt to counter these methods, placing a greater time burden on educators. While there are ways for educators to attempt to lessen this time burden, it will take time and trial and error to find the most effective ways. Beyond finding the AI checker that works for the educator, it is necessary to consider ways in which the student may have edited their paper so that the overuse of AI would not be detected. The authors of this chapter have had success with having students produce the majority of their writing in class so that the instructor is present for the writing process.

In order to move the writing of papers into the classroom, it is possible to partially "flip" the classroom so that students are introduced to the content between classes and then review the material together before workshopping their writing in the classroom. Again, in the early stages of adapting this approach, there is a greater time burden placed on the instructor as they may need to create video content for their students to view between classes. Videos on core content can be reused between semesters to help with instructor time poverty as the students will still be discussing this material with their instructors during the class.

Generative AI can change the writing classroom for the better, but it can also place a greater socioeconomic burden on students, a greater time burden on instructors, and lead to ethical concerns that must be considered. The process of incorporating AI into the writing classroom is not something that can be done quickly as it will require adjustments over time.

FINAL THOUGHTS

Because the conditions that result in time poverty are so broad, it is hard to determine how many students suffer from time poverty. It can be assumed, however, that there are students in most classes who are experiencing time insecurity. By actively instructing students in the use of GenAI for the research, prewriting, writing, revision, and reflection stages of composition, we allow students to take greater agency over the use of their time. When students have more time, they are able to better understand the work that they are doing, allowing for greater creativity, invention, focused attention, and critical thinking. The above recommendations are only the beginning of the possibilities for incorporating GenAI into the writing classroom, offering instructors the chance to get creative with how they utilize this exciting new tool.

REFERENCES

Amano, T., Ramirez-Castaneda, V., Berdejo-Espinola, V., Borokini, I., Chowdhury, S., Golivets, M., González-Trujillo, J. D., Montaño-Centellas, F., Paudel, K., White, R. L., & Veríssimo, D. (2023). The Manifold Costs of Being a Non-Native English Speaker in Science. *PLoS Biology*, 21(7), e3002184. DOI:10.1371/journal.pbio.3002184 PMID:37463136

Babcock, P., & Marks, M. (2011). The Falling Time Cost of College: Evidence from Half a Century of Time Use Data. *The Review of Economics and Statistics*, 93(2), 468–478. DOI:10.1162/REST_a_00093

Begian-Lewis, K. M. (2023), Time Poverty and the Socioeconomically Disadvantaged Student in Higher Education, *Socio-Economic Implications of Global Educational Inequalities*.

Bull, K. S., Montgomery, D., & Baloche, L. (1995). Teaching creativity at the college level: A synthesis of curricular components perceived as important by instructors. *Creativity Research Journal*, 8(1), 83–89. DOI:10.1207/s15326934crj0801_7

Dobrin, S. (2023). *AI and Writing*. Broadview Press.

Fyfe, P. (2023). How to cheat on your final paper: Assigning AI for student writing. *AI & Society*, 38(4), 1395–1405. DOI:10.1007/s00146-022-01397-z

Kavyashree, N., Shailaja, L. K., Anitha, J., & Sindhu, P. (2022). Real-time attention span tracking in online education. *International Journal of Innovative Technology and Exploring Engineering*, 11(9), 11–17. DOI:10.35940/ijitee.G9191.0811922

Kerr, B. (2024, February 23). *Creativity. Encyclopedia Britannica*. https://www.britannica.com/topic/creativity

Lee, K. (2023). Effectiveness of gamification and selection of appropriate teaching methods of creativity: Students' perspectives. *Heliyon*, 9(10), e20420. DOI:10.1016/j.heliyon.2023.e20420

Leslie, D. (2023). Does the sun rise ChatGPT? Scientific discovery in the age of generative AI. *AI and Ethics*. Advance online publication. DOI:10.1007/s43681-023-00315-3

Mark, G. (2023). Speaking of Psychology: Why our attention spans are shrinking, with Gloria Mark, PhD. *American Psychological Association*, https://www.apa.org/news/podcasts/speaking-of-psychology/attention-spans

Pellas, N. (2023, July). The Effects of Generative AI Platforms on Undergraduates' Narrative Intelligence and Writing Self-Efficacy. *Education Sciences*, 13(11), 1155. DOI:10.3390/educsci13111155

Roksa, J., Feldon, D. F., & Maher, M. (2018). First-generation students in pursuit of the PhD: Comparing socialization experiences and outcomes to continuing-generation peers. *The Journal of Higher Education*, 89(5), 728–752. DOI:10.1080/00221546.2018.1435134

Seitz, D. (2004). *Who Can Afford Critical Consciousness? Practicing a Pedagogy of Humility*. Hampton Press.

Simonson, P. (2014). Reinvention Invention, Again. *Rhetoric Society Quarterly*, 44(1), 299–322. DOI:10.1080/02773945.2014.938862

Sternberg, R. J. (2004). Teaching college students that creativity is a decision. *Guidance & Counselling*, 19(4), 196.

Sullivan, P. (2015). The UnEssay: Making room for creativity in the composition classroom. *College Composition and Communication*, 67(1), 6–34. DOI:10.58680/ccc201527441

Terry, O. K. (2023, May 12). I'm a Student. You Have No Idea How Much We're Using ChatGPT: No professor or software could ever pick up on it. *The Chronicle of Higher Education*.https://www.chronicle.com/article/im-a-student-you-have-no-idea-how-much-were-using-chatgpt?sra=true

Vickery, C. (1977). The Time-Poor: A New Look at Poverty. *The Journal of Human Resources*, 12(1), 27–48. DOI:10.2307/145597

Wagner, G., Lukyanenko, R., & Pare, G. (2022). Artificial Intelligence and the Conduct of Literature Reviews. *Journal of Information Technology*, 37(2), 209–226. DOI:10.1177/02683962211048201

Wladis, C., Hachey, A. C., & Conway, K. (2018). No time for college? an investigation of time poverty and parenthood. *The Journal of Higher Education*, 89(6), 807–831. DOI:10.1080/00221546.2018.1442983

Wood, T. (2017). Cripping Time in the College Composition Classroom. *College Composition and Communication*, 69(2), 260–286. DOI:10.58680/ccc201729419

Xavier, M., & Meneses, J. (2022). Persistence and time challenges in an open online university: A case study of the experiences of first-year learners. *International Journal of Educational Technology in Higher Education*, 19(1), 1–17. DOI:10.1186/s41239-022-00338-6 PMID:35013716

Xavier, M., Meneses, J., & Fiuza, P. J. (2022). Dropout, stopout, and time challenges in open online higher education: A qualitative study of the first-year student experience. *Open Learning*, 1–17. DOI:10.1080/02680513.2022.2160236

ENDNOTE

1 It is important to note that the focus on college-educated "fathers" specifically is due to the first data set being conducted in 1961 and asking only about fathers, so there were no records of the impact of college-educated mothers on their child's time spent studying.

Chapter 4
Further Research Opportunities and Challenges Towards AI-Driven Tools for Modern Generation

Ajanthaa Lakkshmanan
https://orcid.org/0000-0001-5355-2229
SRM Institute of Science and Technology, Kattankulathur, India

S. Amudhan
St Joseph's University, Bengaluru, India

Smita M. Gaikwad
CMS Business School, JAIN University, Bangalore, India

Amit Kumar Tyagi
https://orcid.org/0000-0003-2657-8700
National Institute of Fashion Technology, New Delhi, India

ABSTRACT

This chapter discusses the evolving landscape of artificial intelligence (AI) and its applications in crafting tools tailored for the modern generation. As AI continues to advance, opportunities for further research emerge, accompanied by a set of challenges that warrant exploration. This work explores key research avenues such as enhancing AI-driven tools' adaptability to dynamic user preferences, leveraging deep learning for improved context-awareness, and refining natural language processing

DOI: 10.4018/979-8-3693-2418-9.ch004

for seamless human-machine interactions. The challenges addressed ethical issues, data privacy issues, and the need for transparent decision-making processes within AI systems. This work highlights the interdisciplinary nature of this research, calling for collaboration among experts in AI, human-computer interaction, to unlock the full potential of AI-driven tools for the modern generation. As society increasingly integrates AI into daily life, understanding and addressing these opportunities and challenges becomes imperative for the responsible and effective deployment of AI.

1. INTRODUCTION TO AI-DRIVEN TOOLS AND MODERN GENERATION

Artificial intelligence (AI) has arisen as a powerful force in the ever-changing technological landscape, and it is revolutionizing our interactions and perceptions of the world (Amit Kumar Tyagi, 2024). The development of AI-powered tools tailored to the needs and tastes of the present generation is one particular way in which AI has had an impact. As technology becomes increasingly intertwined with daily life, understanding the intersection of AI and the requirements of today's tech-enabled and dynamic user base becomes imperative. AI-driven tools encompass a diverse array of applications, from virtual assistants and personalized recommendation systems to advanced automation in various industries. These tools use machine learning algorithms, neural networks, and sophisticated data processing capabilities to analyze large datasets and extract valuable information. The result is a new model of intelligent, adaptable tools that aim to enhance user experiences, streamline processes, and anticipate user needs in real-time (Richa Singh, Amit Kumar Tyagi, Senthil Kumar, 2024).

Also, this chapter discusses about the useful relationship between AI-driven tools and the modern generation. We will discuss the various form of AI integration, addressing both the opportunities and challenges that arise in the quest to create tools that resonate with the tech-savvy expectations of contemporary users (Amit Kumar Tyagi, Shrikant Tiwari, 2024). From the unified integration of AI into daily tasks to the ethical issues surrounding data usage and privacy, our exploration seeks to provide a comprehensive understanding of the impact and potential of AI-driven tools in shaping the experiences of the modern generation. As we navigate this technological frontier, it is important to note the symbiotic relationship between AI and the modern user, setting the stage for a thoughtful and informed discussion on the future of intelligent tools in our increasingly interconnected world (Meghna Manoj Nair and Amit Kumar Tyagi, 2023).

1.1 Background to AI-Driven Tools for the Modern Generation

The background to AI-driven tools for the modern generation lies in the intersection of technological advancements, changing user behaviors, and the evolving expectations of contemporary society. Over the past few decades, the field of Artificial Intelligence has witnessed rapid progress, transitioning from theoretical concepts to practical applications that impact various aspects of daily life. The advent of Big Data and connection of interconnected devices have provided an unprecedented volume of information for AI systems to analyze and derive meaningful information. Machine learning algorithms, particularly those utilizing deep neural networks, have demonstrated remarkable capabilities in tasks such as image recognition, natural language processing, and pattern recognition. These advancements have made the way for the development of intelligent tools that go beyond mere automation and instead provide personalized, context-aware experiences. Simultaneously, the modern generation, characterized by individuals born in the digital age, has cultivated a natural affinity for technology. Growing up in an era of smartphones, social media, and instant connectivity, this demographic possesses a unique set of expectations and preferences. They seek tools and applications that seamlessly integrate into their fast-paced, digitally-driven lifestyles, providing intuitive solutions to complex problems.

AI-driven tools, therefore, emerge as a response to this convergence of technological capabilities and user expectations. From smart assistants that adapt to individual preferences to recommendation systems that anticipate user needs, these tools are designed to enhance efficiency, convenience, and personalization. The background to AI-driven tools for the modern generation is marked by the recognition of the symbiotic relationship between technology and user experience, with AI acting as a catalyst for transformative advancements in how individuals interact with, benefit from, and are influenced by the digital world.

1.2 Scope and Importance of AI-Driven Tools for the Modern Generation

The scope and importance of AI-driven tools for the modern generation are large and multifaceted, encompassing a wide range of applications that significantly impact various aspects of individuals' lives. Understanding the scope and recognizing the importance of these tools provides insights into the transformative potential they hold in shaping the contemporary technological landscape.

A. Personalization and User Experience: AI-driven tools have the capability to personalize user experiences by learning from individual behaviors and preferences. From content recommendations to tailored services, these tools aim to create highly customized interactions, enhancing user satisfaction and engagement.
B. Efficiency and Automation: Systems powered by AI streamline routine operations and speed up processing times, leading to greater efficiency across many industries. Automated customer service and advanced data analysis are just two examples of the ways that technology is freeing up workers to focus on higher-level, more strategic aspects of their jobs.
C. The field of predictive analytics makes use of AI-powered technology to sift through mountains of data in search of patterns and trends. The use of machine learning techniques allows for this to be achieved. This competency is valuable in fields like marketing, healthcare, and finance, where data-driven insights may shape strategy and decision-making.
D. Enhanced Accessibility: AI-driven tools play an important role in making technology more accessible. Voice recognition, natural language processing, and other AI-powered features make it easier for individuals, including those with disabilities, to interact with digital platforms and devices.
E. Healthcare Innovations: AI-driven tools are revolutionizing healthcare by assisting in diagnostics, drug discovery, and personalized medicine. From predictive analytics for disease prevention to virtual health assistants, these tools contribute to improved patient outcomes and healthcare delivery.
F. Cybersecurity: The modern generation faces evolving cybersecurity threats, and AI-driven tools are instrumental in fortifying digital defenses. AI can detect anomalies, analyze patterns, and respond in real-time to potential security breaches, providing a proactive approach to safeguarding digital assets.

In summary, the scope and importance of AI-driven tools for the modern generation extend across diverse domains, providing opportunities for innovation, efficiency, and improved quality of life. As these tools continue to evolve, it is essential to balance technological advancements with ethical issues, ensuring that the benefits are accessible, equitable, and aligned with the values of the society they serve.

1.3 Organization of the Work

This work is summarized in nine sections.

2. CURRENT STATE OF AI-DRIVEN TOOLS

2.1 Overview of Existing AI Tools

There were several existing AI tools across various domains, each designed to address specific challenges and opportunities (Selvaraj, P., alias Muralidharan, et al., 2021) (Narayanan, L. K., & Subbiah, P, 2023). It's important to note that the field of AI is dynamic, and new tools are frequently developed. Here is an overview of some prominent existing AI tools up to that point:

A. Natural Language Processing (NLP) Tools:
   - GPT-3, like its predecessors, is a powerful language model developed by OpenAI. It can understand and generate text that is frighteningly close to human-produced writing.
   - BERT, or Bidirectional Encoder Representations from Transformers, is a Google tool. Its goal is to create a foundation for many different types of natural language processing jobs and to make it easier to read natural language.

B. Machine Learning Frameworks:
   - Google's TensorFlow is a framework for machine learning. One of the most popular ways to build and train deep learning models is with this open-source programming language.
   - The dynamic computing design and versatility of the deep learning framework PyTorch make it a favorite among developers and researchers. Many people choose it.

C. Computer Vision Tools:
   - The Open-Source Computer Vision Library, or OpenCV for short, is a popular tool for computer vision tasks. Several features and tools for working with photos and videos are included in it.
   - One such object detection system is YOLO, an acronym for "You Only Look Once," and it can detect and classify objects in the here and now.

D. Speech Recognition:
   - Google's Speech-to-Text API: This API converts spoken words into written text, enabling voice command functionality in various applications.
   - Mozilla's DeepSpeech: An open-source automatic speech recognition (ASR) engine based on deep learning.

E. Recommender Systems:
   - Collaborative Filtering Algorithms: Examples include user-based and item-based collaborative filtering algorithms, widely used in recommendation systems by companies like Netflix and Amazon.

- Content-Based Filtering: Recommender systems that suggest items based on user preferences and item characteristics.

F. AI in Healthcare:
    - With the use of medical literature, clinical trial data, and patient records, IBM Watson for Oncology can provide clinicians with information on cancer therapy.
    - Using images from the field of pathology, PathAI provides artificial intelligence to help pathologists make diagnoses.

G. Chatbots and Virtual Assistants:
    - Dialogflow: Google's natural language understanding tool for building conversational interfaces, including chatbots.
    - Microsoft's Azure Bot Service: Allows developers to create intelligent, enterprise-grade bots for various platforms.

H. AI in Cybersecurity:
    - Darktrace: Uses AI to detect and respond to cybersecurity threats, employing machine learning to understand and adapt to network behaviors.
    - Cylance: Applies AI algorithms to proactively prevent security threats by identifying and blocking malware.

Hence, this section provides a detailed explanation about the diversity of different AI tools across different domains (Meghna Manoj Nair, Amit Kumar Tyagi, 2023) (Amit Kumar Tyagi, 2023) (Tyagi, A.K., Bansal, R., Anshu, Dananjayan, S., 2023). Keep in mind that the field is rapidly evolving, and new tools may have been introduced since my last update.

2.2 Applications of AI-Driven Tools in Various Domains

AI-driven tools have found applications across a wide range of domains, revolutionizing industries and enhancing various aspects of daily life (Kung, T. H., Cheatham, M., et al., 2023) (Eysenbach, G., 2023). Here are notable applications in key domains:

A. Healthcare:
    - Health Prognosis and Forecasting: AI is used to evaluate medical images (such MRI and CT scans) to detect diseases, including cancer, at an early stage.
    - Drug development: By studying molecular interactions and predicting potential treatment options, artificial intelligence helps accelerate the drug discovery process.

- Individuals' genetic composition and medical history inform the process of personalized medicine, which involves designing treatment plans specifically for each patient.

Figure 1 illustrates the applications of AI in the field of healthcare.

Figure 1. AI application in healthcare

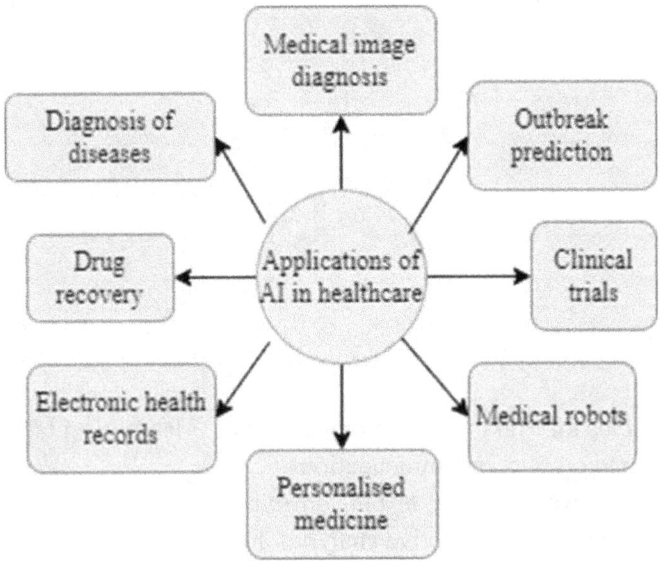

B. Finance:
- Market trends, transactions, and investment portfolio optimization are all areas that benefit from AI. Algorithmic trading describes this style of trading.
- Credit Risk Assessment: AI analyses several variables to determine credit risk, leading to more precise loan decisions.
- Automated Detection of Fraud: AI can spot suspicious trends in financial transactions and stop them in their tracks.

Figure 2 illustrates the application of AI in the field of finance.

Figure 2. AI application in finance

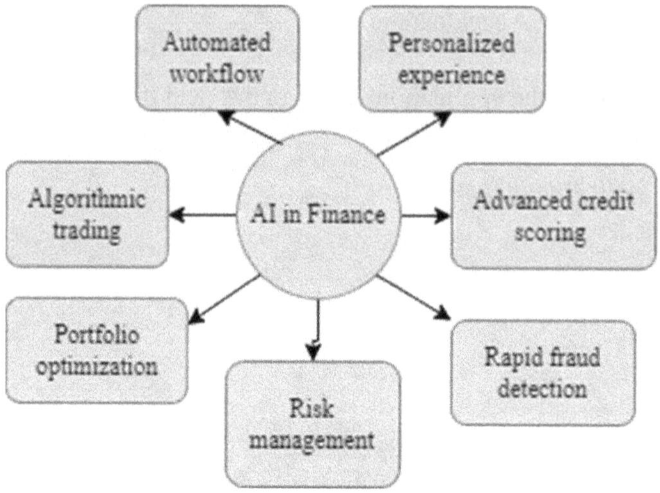

C. Retail:
    - Systems for Making Recommendations: AI learns user tastes to provide tailored product recommendations.
    - To improve inventory levels and minimize the incidence of stockouts and overstocks, predictive analytics are utilized in the field of inventory management.
    - Virtual assistants and chatbots: AI-powered chatbots enhance the shopping experience by answering client inquiries and guiding them through the purchasing process.

D. Manufacturing:
    - One such method is predictive maintenance, which makes use of AI to track machinery in motion in order to foresee when repairs would be needed and cut down on breakdowns.
    - Computer vision and machine learning technologies may be used for real-time fault identification during manufacturing, which helps with quality control.
    - Supply chain optimization is one area where artificial intelligence has shown promise. By improving logistics and doing demand forecasts, AI is helping to streamline supply chain operations.

E. Education:

- AI-powered adaptive learning platforms tailor course materials to each student's unique strengths, weaknesses, and preferred methods of acquisition.
- Automated grading: With the help of AI, it is possible to grade assignments and provide feedback quickly.
- Virtual learning assistants, or chatbots, help students with course navigation, answering queries, and studying.

Figure 3 illustrates the applications of AI in the field of education

Figure 3. Application of AI in education

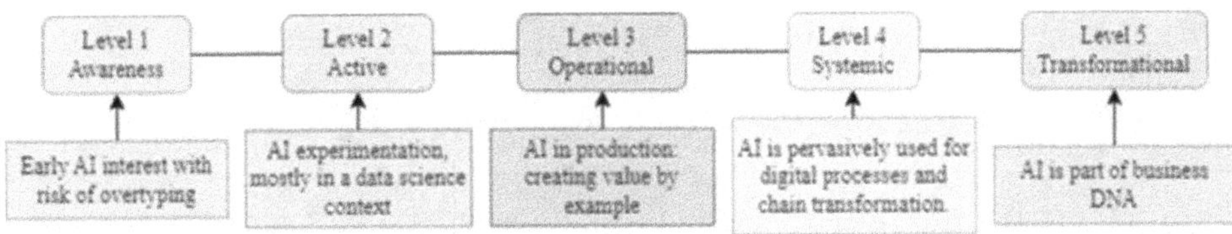

F. Automotive:
   - Self-Driving Cars: Powered by AI, these vehicles analyses data from their sensors and make decisions about their route in real time.
   - Predictive maintenance, which uses artificial intelligence to examine data from sensors, can help drivers know when their vehicles need repairs.
   - Intelligent traffic management systems, made possible by artificial intelligence, assist to enhance traffic flow and reduce congestion.

G. Human Resources:
   - Recruitment Automation: AI screens resume, conducts initial interviews, and identifies suitable candidates.
   - Employee Engagement: AI tools analyze employee feedback and behavior to enhance workplace satisfaction.
   - Performance Management: AI helps assess and manage employee performance through data-driven information.

H. Cybersecurity:
   - Anomaly Detection: AI identifies unusual patterns in network traffic to detect potential security threats.
   - Behavioral Analysis: AI analyzes user behavior to detect deviations and potential insider threats.

- Automated Incident Response: AI automates responses to security incidents, minimizing response time.

Figure 4 illustrates the applications of AI in the field of cyber security.

Figure 4. AI application in cyber security

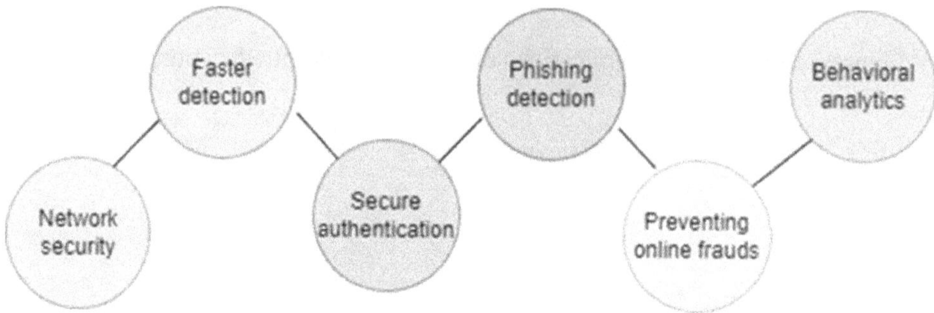

I. Energy:
    - Smart Grids: AI optimizes energy distribution and usage in smart grid systems.
    - The goal of predictive infrastructure maintenance is to improve maintenance schedules by utilizing artificial intelligence to forecast when equipment may break.
    - AI helps with the monitoring and management of industrial buildings' and operations' energy usage, which leads to greater energy efficiency.

Hence, these applications demonstrate the adaptability and transformative potential of AI-driven tools across various domains, contributing to efficiency, innovation, and improved decision-making.

2.3 Impact of AI-Driven Tools on Modern Generation

The impact of AI-driven tools on the modern generation is so useful and multifaceted (Civaner, M. M., Uncu, Y., et al., 2022) (Chen, L., Chen, P., & Lin, Z, 2020), influencing various aspects of daily life, work, and societal interactions. Here are key aspects of this impact:

A. Digital Transformation:

- AI-driven tools are instrumental in the ongoing digital transformation, shaping the way individuals interact with technology.
- The modern generation experiences a seamless integration of AI in daily activities, from personalized recommendations on streaming platforms to voice-activated virtual assistants.

B. Personalization and User Experience:

- AI enables highly personalized experiences, adapting to individual preferences and behaviors.
- Modern generation users benefit from personalized content recommendations, tailored advertising, and customized user interfaces, enhancing overall user satisfaction.

C. Automation and Efficiency:

- This generation may focus on more complex and creative aspects of their personal and professional lives since artificial intelligence can automate boring tasks.
- In industries like manufacturing, healthcare, and finance, AI-driven automation improves efficiency and contributes to faster and more accurate decision-making.

D. Education and Learning:

- AI-powered adaptive learning platforms cater to individual learning styles, providing personalized educational experiences.
- Virtual tutors, interactive learning tools, and automated grading systems enhance the learning journey for the modern generation.

E. Communication and Social Interaction:

- AI-driven chatbots and virtual assistants facilitate seamless communication and interaction.
- Social media platforms use AI for content recommendations, sentiment analysis, and personalized feeds, shaping online social experiences.

F. Career Opportunities:

- The modern workforce experiences changes in job roles and career opportunities due to AI integration.
- AI-driven tools impact industries by creating new job roles, emphasizing the importance of skills related to AI development, data analysis, and technology management.

G. Health and Wellness:

- AI applications in healthcare contribute to improved diagnostics, personalized treatment plans, and preventive care.
- Wearable devices and health apps powered by AI help the modern generation monitor and manage their well-being more proactively.

H. Entertainment and Gaming:

- AI enhances the entertainment experience through personalized content recommendations, immersive gaming experiences, and realistic simulations.
- Virtual reality (VR) and augmented reality (AR) technologies, often powered by AI, create engaging and interactive entertainment options.

I. Environmental Impact:

- AI-driven tools contribute to sustainability efforts by optimizing energy consumption, improving resource efficiency, and supporting environmental monitoring initiatives.

In summary, AI-driven technologies are having a major impact on this generation because they can change the way people live, work, learn, and interact with the environment. However, as technology progresses, it raises important questions about ethics, privacy, and societal implications, notwithstanding its many benefits. These issues must be thoroughly addressed.

2.4 Research Gaps and Limitations in Current AI-Driven Tools

As discussed above, AI field is dynamic, and ongoing research on AI may have consist few issues (Holmes, W., Porayska-Pomsta, K., Holstein, K., et al., 2021) (Williamson, B., & Eynon, R., 2020). Here are some important gaps and limitations towards AI driven tools:

- Data Uniformity and Bias: AI models can internalise biases from training data, leading to biassed predictions and unfair outcomes, especially in delicate areas like healthcare and criminal justice.
- Transparency and Explanability: The decision-making mechanisms used by many AI systems, especially deep neural networks, are sometimes described as "black boxes," which makes it difficult to access and understand. Explainability is a critical component in gaining consumers' confidence and ensuring accountability.
- As far as moral dilemmas are concerned, the creation and deployment of AI-powered systems must adhere to strict ethical guidelines. Additional research is required to address issues like as privacy, consent, and the proper use of AI.
- Generalization to Unseen Data: AI models may struggle to generalize well to data that differs from the training set. Ensuring robust performance on diverse datasets and in real-world scenarios is an ongoing challenge.
- Lack of Diversity in Training Data: Training datasets are often not representative of diverse populations, leading to biased models that may not perform well for individuals from underrepresented groups.

- Risks to Data Integrity: AI models can be attacked by malicious individuals who alter the data inputs to trick the model into making inaccurate predictions. A significant area of study is the improvement of AI system safety.
- Limited Transfer Learning: The effectiveness of transfer learning, where models trained on one task are adapted to another, is still an active research area. Improving the transferability of knowledge across tasks remains a challenge.
- Robustness to Noisy Data: AI models are often sensitive to noise and outliers in data. Developing models that are more robust to noisy inputs is important for real-world applications where data may be imperfect.
- Real-Time Processing: Some AI models, especially complex deep learning architectures, may be computationally intensive and not suitable for real-time applications. Research is needed to develop efficient models for real-time processing.
- Human-AI Collaboration: The effective collaboration between humans and AI systems, especially in decision-making processes, raised challenges in terms of user interface design, trust-building, and ensuring user comprehension of AI recommendations.
- Long-Term Dependability: Ensuring the long-term dependability and reliability of AI systems, especially in dynamic environments, remains an open research question.
- Legal and Regulatory Challenges: The legal and regulatory frameworks governing AI are still evolving, and there is a need for international standards to address issues such as liability, accountability, and data protection.

Note that these research gaps are important for the responsible development and deployment of AI-driven tools.

3. FUTURE RESEARCH OPPORTUNITIES IN AI FOR THE MODERN GENERATION

The future of AI research for the modern generation holds promising opportunities across various domains (H.R. Deekshetha, Amit Kumar Tyagi, 2023) (Tyagi AK, Dananjayan S, et al., 2023) (Akshita Tyagi, Swetta Kukreja, et al., 2022). Here are some key areas that present useful research opportunities:

- Ethical AI and Responsible Innovation: Researcher can focus on developing ethical frameworks and guidelines for AI development, ensuring responsible innovation and addressing societal issues related to bias, fairness, and transparency.

- Explainable AI (XAI): Enhancing the explainability of AI models is a critical research area. Developing methods to make AI decisions more interpretable and transparent will increase user trust and facilitate broader adoption.
- AI for Healthcare: Researcher can explain about personalized medicine, improving diagnostic accuracy, and optimizing treatment plans. Integrating AI with healthcare systems for preventive care and patient monitoring is a promising avenue.
- AI in Education: Further exploration of adaptive learning systems, intelligent tutoring, and personalized educational content delivery can enhance the effectiveness of AI in education. Research on addressing equity and access issues is also important.
- Human-AI Collaboration: Investigating effective ways for humans and AI systems to collaborate, especially in decision-making processes, can lead to the development of tools that augment human capabilities while considering user preferences and values.
- AI for Sustainability: Research opportunities exist in using AI to address environmental challenges, including optimizing energy consumption, improving resource management, and developing solutions for climate change mitigation.
- Robustness and Security: Future research can focus on developing AI models that are more robust to adversarial attacks and ensuring the security of AI systems in real-world applications, including IoT devices and critical infrastructure.
- AI and Creativity: Discussing how AI can be harnessed to enhance creativity in various domains, such as art, design, and content creation, presents exciting research opportunities.
- Human-Computer Interaction (HCI): Research can focus on improving the interaction between humans and AI systems, emphasizing natural language understanding, intuitive interfaces, and designing AI tools that align with user expectations.
- Artificial Intelligence and Edge Computing: Studying how AI and edge computing work together can make AI systems smarter and faster, which is especially important when processing data in real time is paramount.
- AI for Mental Health: Research can discuss the use of AI in mental health applications, including early detection of mental health issues, personalized interventions, and support systems for individuals.

AI Policy and Governance:

Researcher in this area can contribute to the development of robust legal and regulatory frameworks for AI, addressing issues related to privacy, accountability, and the responsible use of AI technologies. Few future works are:

- Interdisciplinary Collaboration: Encouraging collaboration between AI researchers, ethicists, psychologists, sociologists, and other disciplines can lead to a more holistic understanding of the societal impacts of AI and the development of inclusive and responsible AI systems.
- AI for Aging Population: Research opportunities exist in developing AI-driven tools to support the aging population, including assistive technologies, healthcare monitoring, and personalized services to enhance quality of life.
- Natural Language Processing Advancements: Advancements in natural language processing can contribute to more sophisticated conversational AI, sentiment analysis, and language understanding, improving communication between humans and machines.

In summary, discussing these research opportunities will contribute to the continued evolution of AI technologies, ensuring that they align with the needs and values of the modern generation while addressing ethical, social, and technical challenges. Few other uses are: Social and Emotional Intelligence in AI Tools, Ethical and Inclusive AI Development.

4. ISSUES AND CHALLENGES IN AI DEVELOPMENT FOR MODERN GENERATION

The development of AI for the modern generation is accompanied by various issues and challenges (Goyal, Deepti & Tyagi, Amit., 2020) (Varsha R., Nair S.M., Tyagi A.K., Aswathy S.U., RadhaKrishnan R., 2021) that researchers, developers, and policymakers need to address. Some of the key challenges include:

A. Ethical Issues:
    - Bias and Fairness: AI systems can inherit biases present in training data, leading to unfair outcomes and perpetuating existing societal biases.
    - Transparency: The opacity of AI decision-making processes raises issues about accountability and the ability to understand and explain AI-driven decisions.

B. Privacy and Data Security:

- Data Privacy: AI often relies on large amounts of personal data, raising issues about the privacy of individuals and the potential misuse of sensitive information.
- Security: Adversarial attacks and the vulnerability of AI systems to manipulation kept risks, especially in critical applications like healthcare and finance.

C. Explainability and Interpretability:
  - The lack of explainability in AI models, particularly in deep learning, hinders user trust and raises challenges in ensuring that AI decisions align with human values.

D. Accessibility and Inclusivity:
  - Ensuring that AI technologies are accessible to diverse populations is a challenge. Addressing issues related to the digital divide, bias in algorithms, and inclusion for individuals with disabilities is important.

E. Regulatory and Legal Frameworks:
  - The rapid evolution of AI has outpaced the development of comprehensive regulatory frameworks. Establishing clear guidelines for ethical AI development and deployment is a pressing challenge.

F. Interdisciplinary Collaboration:
  - Bridging the gap between technical experts and policymakers, ethicists, and social scientists is essential to develop comprehensive and socially responsible AI solutions.

G. Human-AI Collaboration:
  - Designing AI systems that effectively collaborate with humans, taking into account user preferences, cultural differences, and the diversity of human thought processes, raised an essential challenge.

H. Education and Skills Gap:
  - The rapid advancement of AI technology creates a gap between the skills needed for AI development and the available workforce. Developing educational programs to address this gap is essential.

I. Algorithmic Accountability:
  - Establishing mechanisms for holding AI systems and their developers accountable for their actions, especially in high-stakes applications like autonomous vehicles and healthcare, is a complex challenge.

J. Environmental Impact:
  - The computational intensity of training deep learning models contributes to an important carbon footprint. Researching and implementing environmentally sustainable AI practices is important.

K. Bias Mitigation:

- Addressing bias in AI algorithms is an ongoing challenge. Developing methods to detect and mitigate bias and ensuring fairness in AI outcomes is important for responsible AI development.

L. Public Trust and Perception:
- Building and maintaining public trust in AI technologies is challenging, especially when faced with high-profile incidents of AI system failures or misuse.

M. Robustness to Adversarial Attacks:
- Developing AI models that are resilient to adversarial attacks and can handle unforeseen situations is important for the reliability of AI applications.

So, it will need a concerted effort from the AI community, politics, and society at large to overcome these challenges. In order to succeed, one must adhere to high ethical standards, do ongoing research, and design systems that prioritise people's and communities' welfare.

5. INTERDISCIPLINARY APPROACHES IN AI RESEARCH IN THIS SMART ERA

Interdisciplinary approaches in AI research are important in the smart era, where the integration of technology into various aspects of daily life requires a holistic understanding of complex challenges. Here are some key interdisciplinary approaches in AI research:

- AI and Ethics: Collaboration between computer scientists, ethicists, and philosophers is essential to address ethical issues in AI development. This includes ensuring fairness, transparency, and accountability in AI systems.
- Human-Computer Interaction (HCI): Integrating HCI experts into AI research helps design user-friendly interfaces, ensuring that AI systems align with human expectations and preferences.
- AI and Law: Legal scholars working with AI researchers can contribute to the development of regulations and policies that govern AI use, addressing issues such as liability, privacy, and intellectual property.
- AI and Psychology/Cognitive Science: Collaboration with psychologists and cognitive scientists helps in understanding human cognition, emotion, and decision-making, improving the design of AI systems for effective human interaction.

- AI and Medicine/Healthcare: Collaboration between AI experts and medical professionals can lead to the development of AI-driven tools for diagnostics, treatment planning, and personalized medicine.
- AI and Environmental Science: Collaboration between AI researchers and environmental scientists can use AI for monitoring and managing environmental data, contributing to sustainability and climate change research.
- AI and Education: Involving educators and learning specialists in AI research leads to the development of adaptive learning systems, intelligent tutoring, and personalized educational tools.
- AI and Sociology/Anthropology: Collaboration with social scientists helps in understanding the societal impact of AI, including its effects on culture, behavior, and social structures.
- AI and Linguistics: Collaborating with linguists enhances natural language processing capabilities in AI, leading to better language understanding and generation.
- AI and Economics: Bringing together AI researchers and economists contributes to the development of AI models for economic forecasting, market analysis, and optimization of business processes.
- AI and Neuroscience: Collaboration with neuroscientists helps in developing AI models inspired by the human brain, advancing the field of neuromorphic computing and brain-computer interfaces.
- AI and Cybersecurity: Combining expertise in AI and cybersecurity helps in developing advanced threat detection systems and enhancing the security of AI applications.
- AI and Design: Collaboration with design experts contributes to the development of aesthetically pleasing and user-centric AI interfaces and products.
- AI and Agriculture: Collaborating with agronomists and agricultural scientists enables the development of AI applications for precision farming, crop monitoring, and yield prediction.
- AI and Urban Planning: Integrating AI expertise with urban planners helps in developing smart city solutions, optimizing traffic flow, energy consumption, and infrastructure planning.

Hence, an enhanced understanding of the possibilities and challenges in AI research is the end outcome of such interdisciplinary collaborations, which in turn lead to fresh approaches that account for both the technical and social aspects. The inclusion of many perspectives is growing in importance for the development of ethical and impactful AI as technology progresses.

5.1 Collaboration between AI and Psychology for the Modern Society

Collaboration between AI and psychology holds great potential for addressing challenges and enhancing various aspects of modern society. Here are several ways in which this interdisciplinary collaboration can be beneficial:

- Personalized Mental Health Support: AI tools developed in collaboration with psychologists can provide personalized mental health support. These tools can analyze behavioral patterns and provide insights to individuals, suggesting coping mechanisms or recommending professional help when needed.
- Behavioral Intervention and Therapy: AI systems working with psychologists can assist in delivering behavioral interventions and therapy. Virtual assistants equipped with natural language processing capabilities can engage in conversations, providing support and guidance in areas such as stress management and emotional well-being.
- Understanding User Emotions and Intentions: Collaboration between AI and psychology can improve AI systems' ability to understand user emotions and intentions. This can lead to more empathetic virtual assistants and customer service bots that respond appropriately to users' emotional states.
- Humanizing Human-Machine Interaction: Integrating psychological principles into AI design can contribute to more human-like interactions. AI systems can better understand non-verbal cues, emotions, and context, leading to more natural and effective communication.
- AI in Cognitive Assessment and Enhancement: Collaboration can lead to the development of AI-driven tools for cognitive assessment and enhancement. These tools can assist psychologists in evaluating cognitive abilities, identifying areas for improvement, and providing targeted interventions.
- Early Detection of Mental Health Issues: AI algorithms, developed in collaboration with psychologists, can analyze various data sources to detect early signs of mental health issues. This can enable timely interventions and support for individuals at risk.
- Improving Accessibility to Mental Health Services: AI-powered virtual therapists and chatbots, developed with psychological expertise, can enhance the accessibility of mental health services. This is particularly valuable in regions with limited access to human psychologists.
- Enhanced Diagnosis and Treatment Planning: AI can assist psychologists in the diagnosis of psychological disorders by analyzing large datasets and identifying patterns that may not be immediately apparent. It can also contribute

to more personalized treatment planning based on individual psychological profiles.

- Reducing Stigma and Increasing Awareness: AI can play a role in reducing the stigma associated with mental health issues by providing discreet and accessible avenues for seeking support. Additionally, AI can contribute to mental health awareness campaigns and educational initiatives.
- Ethical issues in AI Applications: Psychologists can contribute their expertise in ethical issues related to the application of AI in psychology. This collaboration is essential to ensure that AI tools adhere to ethical standards and prioritize the well-being and privacy of individuals.
- Research on Human-AI Interaction: Collaborative research can discuss the psychological impact of interacting with AI systems. This includes studying user perceptions, trust-building, and the potential psychological effects of long-term engagement with AI companions.
- Training and Education for Psychologists: Collaboration between AI and psychology can lead to the development of educational tools and training programs for psychologists, helping them use AI technologies in their practice more effectively.

In summary, the collaboration between AI and psychology has the potential to significantly advance mental health support, human-machine interaction, and our understanding of psychological well-being in the modern society. It is important for researchers, practitioners, and technologists to work together to ensure that these applications are ethical, effective, and aligned with psychological principles.

6. FUTURE TRENDS AND POTENTIAL IMPACT OF AI-DRIVEN TOOLS ON MODERN GENERATION

6.1 Role of Emerging Technologies in AI-Driven Tools for Modern Generation

Emerging technologies play an important role in shaping the capabilities and functionalities of AI-driven tools for the modern generation. These technologies contribute to advancements that enhance the efficiency, personalization, and overall user experience of AI-driven tools. Here are several emerging technologies influencing AI-driven tools:

- The IoT: Internet-connected gadgets generate massive amounts of data that AI systems can sift through for trends. Utilising data collected from the

Internet of Things (IoT), applications powered by artificial intelligence (AI) provide customised user experiences, predictive analytics, and context-aware decision-making.

- 5G networks' properties, such as low-latency and high-speed connectivity, allow devices and AI systems to interact more efficiently and quickly. For real-time applications like AR and autonomous vehicles, this is of the utmost importance.
- Computing at the edge: By bringing processing closer to the data source, edge computing improves the responsiveness of AI-driven tools and decreases latency. Computing at the edge is another name for it. This is a crucial factor to think about for smart device and face recognition apps that need to make choices instantly.
- Technology like Augmented Reality (AR) and Virtual Reality (VR) enhance user interactions by immersing them in interactive experiences. Tools driven by AI enable the use of these technologies in applications like interactive information dissemination, training simulations, and virtual assistants.
- Blockchain: Blockchain technology ensures secure and transparent transactions. In AI-driven tools, blockchain can be used for secure data sharing, traceability of AI decisions, and maintaining privacy in decentralized applications.
- Natural Language Processing (NLP) Advances: Ongoing advancements in NLP enable AI-driven tools to better understand and generate human-like language. This is important for the development of conversational AI, virtual assistants, and language translation services.
- When it comes to solving complex issues, quantum computing can do it at unprecedented speeds. Simulating, optimising, and training machine learning models are just a few of the AI processes that might be substantially accelerated by quantum computing.
- Biometric Technologies: Biometric authentication methods, such as facial recognition and fingerprint scanning, enhance the security and personalization of AI-driven tools. These technologies are increasingly integrated into applications like authentication and access control.
- Robotics and Automation: Robotics, coupled with AI, enables the development of intelligent autonomous systems. AI-driven tools in robotics contribute to advancements in areas such as autonomous vehicles, robotic process automation (RPA), and smart manufacturing.
- Explainable AI (XAI): Explainable AI aims to make AI decision-making processes more transparent and interpretable. This is critical for building trust and understanding in AI-driven tools, especially in applications where transparency is essential.

- Swarm Intelligence: Inspired by collective behavior in nature, swarm intelligence in AI involves coordinating the actions of multiple agents. This is applied in areas like optimization, logistics, and distributed problem-solving.
- Biotechnology Integration: AI-driven tools can benefit from advancements in biotechnology, such as bioinformatics and personalized medicine. AI analyzes biological data for information about healthcare, genetics, and drug discovery.
- Synthetic Biology: AI-driven tools in synthetic biology assist in designing and optimizing biological systems. This interdisciplinary field involves the integration of AI for genetic engineering and bioinformatics.
- Neuromorphic Computing: Inspired by the human brain, neuromorphic computing emulates neural architectures. AI-driven tools using neuromorphic computing promise energy-efficient and brain-inspired computation for tasks like pattern recognition.
- Generative Adversarial Networks (GANs): GANs enable the generation of realistic synthetic data. AI-driven tools use GANs for applications like image and content generation, enhancing the capabilities of creative and generative systems.

Hence, the integration of these emerging technologies with AI-driven tools ensures a continuous evolution of capabilities, providing innovative solutions that align with the demands and expectations of the modern generation. The synergy between AI and these technologies fosters advancements that contribute to a smarter, more connected, and efficient digital landscape.

6.2 Industry Trends and Innovations towards AI-Driven Tools for Modern Generation in near future

In near future, several industry trends and innovations will shape the development of AI-driven tools for the modern/ next generation. While the landscape is dynamic, here are some key trends and innovations expected to influence AI in the near future, as mentioned in table 1.

Table 1. Trends and Innovations (for industry) towards AI-Driven Tools for Modern Generation in near future

Types	Trend	Innovation
AI in Edge Computing	The integration of AI with edge computing is gaining momentum, allowing AI processing to occur closer to the data source. This trend enables real-time decision-making, reducing latency and bandwidth requirements.	Edge AI applications are expected to grow in various sectors, including smart devices, healthcare wearables, and industrial IoT.
Conversational AI and Natural Language Processing (NLP)	Continued advancements in NLP and conversational AI are enhancing natural language understanding and interaction. Virtual assistants and chatbots are becoming more sophisticated and capable of handling complex queries	The integration of voice interfaces and the ability to understand context in conversations will contribute to more natural and intuitive interactions with AI-driven tools.
AI for Healthcare	AI is increasingly being applied to healthcare for diagnostics, treatment planning, and personalized medicine. The use of AI in medical imaging and the analysis of health data is expected to grow.	Innovations may include AI-driven drug discovery, predictive analytics for disease prevention, and the integration of AI with wearable health devices for continuous monitoring.
Explainable AI (XAI)	The importance of transparency in AI decision-making is leading to a focus on explainable AI. This trend is important for building trust in AI systems, especially in sensitive applications.	Techniques for making AI models more interpretable and understandable are expected to evolve, facilitating their use in critical areas such as healthcare and finance.
AI in Cybersecurity	The evolving threat landscape has increased the demand for AI in cybersecurity. AI-driven tools are used for anomaly detection, threat intelligence, and real-time response to security incidents.	Advanced AI algorithms for detecting sophisticated cyber threats, as well as the use of AI in deception technologies and autonomous security systems, are expected to be key innovations.
AI-Driven Personalization	AI is playing a central role in personalizing user experiences across various industries, including retail, entertainment, and marketing. Personalized recommendations and content delivery are becoming more refined.	Innovations include AI algorithms that dynamically adapt to user preferences in real-time, creating highly customized and engaging experiences.
Responsible AI and Ethical issues	There is an increasing focus on responsible AI development, addressing ethical issues such as bias, fairness, and transparency. Organizations are incorporating ethical AI principles into their practices.	Innovations in tools and methodologies for auditing and ensuring the ethical use of AI, along with frameworks for responsible AI development, are expected to emerge.
AI in Augmented Reality (AR) and Virtual Reality (VR)	AI is enhancing AR and VR experiences by enabling more realistic simulations and immersive interactions. AI-driven tools contribute to the development of intelligent virtual environments.	Integration of AI for better object recognition, gesture tracking, and personalized content delivery within AR and VR applications will be a notable innovation.

continued on following page

Table 1. Continued

Types	Trend	Innovation
AI in Financial Services	In order to better detect fraud, manage risks, and assist customers, the banking industry is gradually embracing AI. Artificial intelligence (AI) tools are facilitating better decision-making and process simplification.	Innovations may include AI-driven robo-advisors, predictive analytics for financial markets, and enhanced fraud detection algorithms.
AI and Robotics Collaboration	Collaborative efforts between AI and robotics are creating intelligent robotic systems. AI algorithms contribute to the autonomy, adaptability, and learning capabilities of robots.	Innovations include AI-driven robots for tasks ranging from manufacturing and logistics to healthcare and service industries.
AI-Enhanced Creativity	AI is being utilized to enhance creativity in fields such as art, music, and content creation. Creative AI tools are becoming more accessible, enabling individuals to discuss new forms of expression.	Continued advancements in generative models, like GANs, are expected to lead to new tools that assist and collaborate with artists and creators.
AI and Remote Collaboration	The increasing reliance on remote work has prompted the integration of AI into collaboration tools. AI-driven features enhance virtual meetings, document collaboration, and communication.	Innovations may include AI-driven virtual assistants for business communication, automated meeting facilitation, and intelligent content curation for remote teams.

Hence, as these trends and innovations unfold, it's essential to monitor the evolving landscape of AI-driven tools, considering their impact on diverse industries and societal aspects. Ongoing research, collaboration, and responsible development practices will play an important role in shaping the future of AI for the modern generation.

7 RESPONSIBLE AI DEVELOPMENT FOR A SAFER ENVIRONMENT

7.1 Ensuring Transparency and Accountability in AI-Driven Tools

Ensuring transparency and accountability in AI-driven tools is important for building trust, addressing ethical issues, and promoting responsible AI development. Here are key practices and strategies to achieve transparency and accountability:

- Explainability and Interpretability: Implement techniques that make AI models more interpretable and explainable. This involves providing clear information about how the model makes decisions, especially in critical applications such as healthcare and finance.

- Clear Documentation: Document the development process, model architecture, and training data. This documentation should be accessible to relevant stakeholders, including developers, regulators, and end-users.
- The advancement of artificial intelligence must be guided by established and strictly enforced ethical standards. These guidelines must cover topics like fairness, anti-discrimination efforts, personal data protection, and the responsible use of AI.
- User-Friendly Interfaces: Design user interfaces that provide users information about how AI-driven tools work. This can include visualizations, explanations, and notifications about the limitations of the system.
- Algorithmic Impact Assessments: Perform assessments to understand the potential societal impact of AI algorithms. Identify and mitigate any negative consequences, and regularly review and update these assessments.
- Bias Detection and Mitigation: Regularly assess AI models for bias. Utilize techniques for bias detection and implement strategies for mitigating biases to ensure fair and equitable outcomes.
- Adherence to regulations: Get up-to-date on the current and future regulations governing AI and make sure you follow them. Data privacy, consumer protection, and ethical considerations are all areas that might be incorporated into rules.
- Accountability Frameworks: Define clear lines of accountability within development teams and organizations. Ensure that responsibility for AI systems is well-distributed and that there are mechanisms for addressing issues and issues.
- Data Governance: Practice transparent data governance. Clearly communicate how data is collected, used, and stored. Obtain explicit consent when necessary and ensure compliance with data protection regulations.
- External Audits and Third-Party Assessments: Engage external entities or third-party auditors to conduct assessments and audits of AI systems. External perspectives can provide an impartial evaluation of system transparency and accountability.
- Continuous Monitoring and Evaluation: Implement continuous monitoring of AI systems in real-world applications. Regularly evaluate the system's performance and effectiveness, addressing any issues that arise over time.
- Education and Training: Educate stakeholders, including developers, users, and decision-makers, about the capabilities and limitations of AI systems. This promotes a better understanding of AI and realistic expectations.
- Transparency Reports: Release periodic transparency reports detailing key aspects of AI systems, including performance metrics, user feedback, and any corrective actions taken.

Hence, by integrating these practices into the development lifecycle of AI-driven tools, organizations can foster transparency, accountability, and responsible AI use. As the field of AI evolves, ongoing commitment to ethical principles and open communication is essential for building and maintaining public trust in AI technologies.

7.2 Improving Public Perception, Acceptance and Regulatory Frameworks for AI-Driven Tools

Improving public perception, acceptance, and regulatory frameworks for AI-driven tools is important for using trust and responsible adoption of artificial intelligence technologies. Here are strategies to address these aspects:

- Launch public awareness campaigns to inform the public about the benefits and risks of artificial intelligence technology so that they may make an informed decision. Clear up any confusion and highlight practical uses that are making a positive impact on society.
- It is critical to be transparent with AI-driven tool interfaces and to provide easy-to-understand explanations for the decisions they make while developing these tools. This has the potential to make the technology more approachable, which may lead to more confidence and use from consumers.
- Incorporating a diverse set of perspectives and voices into the planning and execution of a project is one example of an inclusive development technique. Building AI systems that are welcoming and respectful of other cultures requires consideration of diverse perspectives and beliefs.
- The creation, deployment, and oversight of AI systems necessitates the establishment of distinct responsibilities inside companies. Mechanisms for holding people accountable should handle this. Make sure there are processes in place to assign blame and implement fixes in case problems emerge.
- Independent Audits: Have other groups examine and assess AI systems as part of the auditing process. External validation helps to increase public trust by providing an unbiased assessment.
- Take strong measures to protect customer information and let people know about them. To ensure the privacy of our users, we have taken this initial action. The public needs reassurance that their data is being treated responsibly and in line with privacy laws.
- Public Participation in Decision-Making Processes: Public participation is essential when making decisions on AI policy and deployment. To foster a sense of collective ownership and belonging, it is important to ask for public feedback in order to learn about issues and hopes.

Note that by implementing these strategies, organizations and policymakers can contribute to building a positive perception of AI technologies, enhancing public acceptance, and developing regulatory frameworks that balance innovation with ethical issues. It's essential to create an environment where AI is seen as a tool for positive impact, and where the public feels informed, engaged, and confident in the responsible use of these technologies.

8. EXISTED RESEARCH METHODOLOGIES/ TOOLS, ALGORITHMS, SIMULATORS USED IN AI DRIVEN TOOLS AND AI DEVELOPMENT

Research methodologies, tools, algorithms, and simulators in the field of AI development are diverse and continually evolving. Here is an overview of some commonly used approaches and resources, as mentioned in table 2.

Table 2. Available Research Methodologies/ Tools, Algorithms, Simulators used in AI driven tools and AI development

Area	Types	Description	Tools
Research Methodologies	Experimental Research	Conducting experiments to gather empirical data and draw conclusions. This involves designing experiments, collecting data, and analyzing results	Experimentation often involves the use of programming languages (e.g., Python, R), statistical analysis tools (e.g., R, MATLAB), and specialized frameworks.
	Case Studies	In-depth examination of a particular instance or scenario to understand its complexities and unique characteristics.	Data collection tools, interview protocols, and analytical tools depending on the nature of the case study
	Surveys and Questionnaires	Gathering information from a sample population through structured surveys or questionnaires	Survey software (e.g., Qualtrics, SurveyMonkey), statistical analysis tools for interpreting survey data.
	Literature Review	Systematic review and analysis of existing literature to understand the state of the art, identify research gaps, and inform new research.	Academic databases, citation management tools (e.g., EndNote, Zotero).

continued on following page

Table 2. Continued

Area	Types	Description	Tools
Tools for AI Development	Integrated Development Environments (IDEs)	Tools that provide a comprehensive environment for writing, testing, and debugging code.	PyCharm, Jupyter Notebooks, Visual Studio Code.
	Version Control Systems	Enables collaborative development, tracks changes in code, and facilitates versioning.	Git, SVN.
	Containerization	Allows developers to package applications and their dependencies into containers for consistent deployment.	Docker, Kubernetes.
	Collaboration Platforms	Platforms for collaborative coding, version control, and project management.	GitHub, GitLab.
	Continuous Integration/ Continuous Deployment (CI/CD) Tools	Automates building, testing, and deploying code changes.	Jenkins, Travis CI.
Algorithms	Machine Learning Algorithms	Various supervised and unsupervised learning algorithms for classification, regression, clustering, etc.	Random Forest, Support Vector Machines, Neural Networks.
	Deep Learning Architectures	Specialized neural network architectures for tasks like image recognition, natural language processing, and sequence modeling.	Convolutional Neural Networks (CNNs), Recurrent Neural Networks (RNNs), Transformer models.
	Reinforcement Learning Algorithms	Q-Learning, Deep Q Networks (DQN).	Algorithms for training agents to make sequences of decisions by interacting with an environment.
	Natural Language Processing (NLP) Algorithms	Algorithms for understanding and processing human language.	Word Embeddings (Word2Vec, GloVe), Named Entity Recognition (NER), Transformer-based models (BERT, GPT).

continued on following page

Table 2. Continued

Area	Types	Description	Tools
Simulators	Robotics Simulators	Simulate robotic systems to test algorithms and behaviors in a virtual environment.	Gazebo, V-REP (now CoppeliaSim), Webots.
	Autonomous Vehicle Simulators	Simulate driving scenarios for testing autonomous vehicle algorithms and systems.	CARLA, Apollo, AirSim.
	Game Development Engines	While primarily for game development, these engines are used to simulate environments for training AI models.	Unity, Unreal Engine.
	Traffic Simulators	Simulate traffic flow and transportation scenarios for testing AI algorithms in smart transportation systems.	SUMO, Aimsun.
	Network Simulators	Simulate computer networks to test and analyze the performance of networking algorithms.	ns-3, OMNeT++.

Hence, these tools, methodologies, algorithms, and simulators collectively contribute to the robust development and evaluation of AI-driven tools across various sectors/ domains. Researchers and developers often combine these resources to conduct experiments, build models, and ensure the effectiveness and reliability of AI applications.

9. CONCLUSION

Discovering new research opportunities and challenges in the pursuit of AI-driven tools for the modern day exemplifies the ever-changing nature of artificial intelligence, a vibrant area with the potential to shape the future. The identified research opportunities have the potential to enhance human-machine interactions, context-awareness, and adaptability. Adapting to the evolving needs of contemporary consumers is crucial for the development of artificial intelligence technology. However, there will be challenges along the way as we attempt to incorporate AI with existing technology. The necessity for transparent decision-making processes, concerns about data privacy, and ethical considerations are all significant obstacles that must be adequately addressed. We need to solve all of these problems. Research has to be more holistic as a result, bringing together experts from several domains including AI, HCI, and ethics, to tackle the problem. If we want to achieve our aim of making full use of AI-driven instruments' capabilities, we must be vigilant and tackle these difficulties directly. This highlights the need of using communication and collaboration among academics, government officials, and industry stakeholders, as well as the necessity for ongoing multi-disciplinary research projects. If we go this route, we can make sure that AI is built with ethics in mind, that user privacy is protected, and that it helps benefit the present generation. This means that the dedication of the community to doing more research, fixing problems, and supporting responsible innovation will determine the fate of AI-driven technology in the future. By working together, we can create a future where AI is a natural part of our lives, enhancing accessibility, efficiency, and the user experience without compromising on social values or ethical principles.

REFERENCES

Amit Kumar Tyagi. (2024). *Transformative Effects of ChatGPT on the Modern Era of Education and Society: From Society's and Industry's Perspectives, in book title: Machine Learning Algorithms Using Scikit and TensorFlow Environments*. IGI Global. DOI:10.4018/978-1-6684-8531-6.ch019

Amit Kumar Tyagi. (2024). *Shrikant Tiwari, The Future of Artificial Intelligence in Blockchain Applications, in book title: Machine Learning Algorithms Using Scikit and TensorFlow Environments*. IGI Global. DOI:10.4018/978-1-6684-8531-6.ch018

Chen, L., Chen, P., & Lin, Z. (2020). Artificial intelligence in education: A review. *IEEE Access : Practical Innovations, Open Solutions*, 8, 75264–75278. DOI:10.1109/ACCESS.2020.2988510

Civaner, M. M., Uncu, Y., Bulut, F., Chalil, E. G., & Tatli, A. (2022). Artificial intelligence in medical education: A cross-sectional needs assessment. *BMC Medical Education*, 22(1), 772. DOI:10.1186/s12909-022-03852-3 PMID:36352431

Deekshetha & Tyagi. (2023). Automated and intelligent systems for next-generation-based smart applications. Data Science for Genomics. Academic Press. DOI:10.1016/B978-0-323-98352-5.00019-7

Eysenbach, G. (2023). The role of ChatGPT, generative language models, and artificial intelligence in medical education: A conversation with ChatGPT and a call for papers. *JMIR Medical Education*, 9(1), e46885. DOI:10.2196/46885 PMID:36863937

Goyal & Tyagi. (2020). A Look at Top 35 Problems in the Computer Science Field for the Next Decade. .DOI:10.1201/9781003052098-40

Holmes, W., Porayska-Pomsta, K., Holstein, K., Sutherland, E., Baker, T., Shum, S. B., & Koedinger, K. R. (2021). Ethics of AI in education: Towards a community-wide framework. *International Journal of Artificial Intelligence in Education*, 1–23.

Kung, T. H., Cheatham, M., Medenilla, A., Sillos, C., De Leon, L., Elepaño, C., Madriaga, M., Aggabao, R., Diaz-Candido, G., Maningo, J., & Tseng, V. (2023). Performance of ChatGPT on USMLE: Potential for AI-assisted medical education using large language models. *PLOS Digital Health*, 2(2), e0000198. DOI:10.1371/journal.pdig.0000198 PMID:36812645

Meghna Manoj Nair & Amit Kumar Tyagi. (2023). Blockchain technology for next-generation society: current trends and future opportunities for smart era", in the book: Blockchain Technology for Secure Social Media Computing. .DOI:10.1049/PBSE019E_ch11

Nair, M. M., & Tyagi, A. K. (2023). AI, IoT, blockchain, and cloud computing: The necessity of the future. Distributed Computing to Blockchain. Academic Press. DOI:10.1016/B978-0-323-96146-2.00001-2

Richa Singh. (2024). *Imagining the Sustainable Future With Industry 6.0: A Smarter Pathway for Modern Society and Manufacturing Industries, in book title: Machine Learning Algorithms Using Scikit and TensorFlow Environments*. IGI Global. DOI:10.4018/978-1-6684-8531-6.ch016

Selvaraj, P., Muralidharan, R. R., Subbaiah, P., & Narayanan, L. K. (2021). Smart Infant and Child Monitoring System using Integrated IoT and GIS. *Design Engineering*, 15225-15235.

Tyagi, A., Kukreja, S., Nair, M. M., & Tyagi, A. K. (2022). Machine Learning: Past, Present and Future. *NeuroQuantology : An Interdisciplinary Journal of Neuroscience and Quantum Physics*, 20(8). Advance online publication. DOI:10.14704/nq.2022.20.8.NQ44468

Tyagi, A. K., & Bansal, R. (2023). A Step-To-Step Guide to Write a Quality Research Article. In Intelligent Systems Design and Applications. ISDA 2022. Lecture Notes in Networks and Systems, vol 717. Springer. DOI:10.1007/978-3-031-35510-3_36

Tyagi, A. K., Dananjayan, S., Agarwal, D., & Thariq Ahmed, H. F. (2023). Blockchain—Internet of Things Applications: Opportunities and Challenges for Industry 4.0 and Society 5.0. *Sensors (Basel)*, 23(2), 947. DOI:10.3390/s23020947 PMID:36679743

Varsha, R., Nair, S. M., Tyagi, A. K., & Aswathy, S. U. (2021) The Future with Advanced Analytics: A Sequential Analysis of the Disruptive Technology's Scope. In Hybrid Intelligent Systems. HIS 2020. Advances in Intelligent Systems and Computing, vol 1375. Springer. DOI:10.1007/978-3-030-73050-5_56

Williamson, B., & Eynon, R. (2020). Historical threads, missing links, and future directions in AI in education. *Learning, Media and Technology*, 45(3), 223–235. DOI:10.1080/17439884.2020.1798995

Chapter 5
Future Perspectives of ChatGPT Towards Industry 4.0, Society 5.0, and Modern Education

Mansi Kukreja
https://orcid.org/0000-0002-0925-1215
CMS Business School, JAIN University, Bangalore, India

Senthil Kumar Arumugam
https://orcid.org/0000-0002-5081-9183
School of Commerce, Presidency University, Bengaluru, India

Amit Kumar Tyagi
https://orcid.org/0000-0003-2657-8700
National Institute of Fashion Technology, New Delhi, India

M. Sivakumar
https://orcid.org/0000-0002-3564-4733
SRM Institute of Science and Technology, Kattankulathur, India

ABSTRACT

The future perspectives of ChatGPT in the context of Industrial 4.0, Society 5.0, and Modern Education showcase the potential for transformative impacts on communication, decision-making, and learning processes. In Industrial 4.0, ChatGPT is anticipated to play a pivotal role in facilitating human-machine collaboration, enhancing communication in smart manufacturing, and contributing to agile decision-making processes. The integration of ChatGPT in this industrial paradigm holds promise for increased efficiency, improved troubleshooting, and streamlined

DOI: 10.4018/979-8-3693-2418-9.ch005

interactions between workers and intelligent systems. The seamless integration of ChatGPT into the fabric of Industrial 4.0 and other terms requires a thoughtful approach, collaboration between stakeholders, and ongoing advancements in AI research and development. As ChatGPT continues to evolve, its role as a communication and decision-making tool holds significant potential to shape a future where human-machine collaboration, societal interactions, and education are enriched by the capabilities of advanced AI technologies.

1. INTRODUCTION TO INDUSTRIAL 4.0, SOCIETY 5.0, AND MODERN EDUCATION

In the context of Society 5.0, ChatGPT is modern tool as a catalyst for human-centric communication, providing personalized and empathetic interactions in various social contexts. The technology is expected to contribute to mental health support, counseling, and public engagement, using a harmonious balance between technology and human well-being. As Society 5.0 emphasizes the human-centric approach, ChatGPT is used to enhance societal interactions, promote inclusivity, and address challenges through intelligent conversations. In the era of Modern Education, ChatGPT is anticipated to revolutionize the learning experience by providing personalized, adaptive, and interactive educational interactions. The future holds the potential for AI-driven tutoring, mentorship, and collaborative learning environments, tailoring educational content to individual needs. ChatGPT's role in education extends to supporting teachers, providing real-time feedback, and using a dynamic and engaging learning atmosphere. The technology is expected to contribute to the evolution of education towards a more student-centric, technology-enhanced model. Note that Industrial 4.0, (Nair et al., 2021; Tyagi et al., 2020) Society 5.0, and modern education are interconnected concepts that reflect the ongoing evolution of technology and its impact on various aspects of society, industry, and education. Now we will explore each of these concepts individually:

A. Industrial 4.0

Industrial 4.0, also known as the Fourth Industrial Revolution, represents the integration of digital technologies into manufacturing and industry (Nair et al., 2021; Tyagi et al., 2020). It builds upon the previous industrial revolutions, incorporating automation, data exchange, artificial intelligence, and the Internet of Things (IoT) as shown in Figure 1. Here are the few Key Features of industry 4.0:

- Smart Manufacturing: Utilization of intelligent machines and systems.

- Interconnectivity: Devices and systems communicate and collaborate seamlessly.
- Data Analytics: Extensive use of data for decision-making and optimization.
- Automation: Increased reliance on autonomous systems and robotics.

Figure 1. Industry 4.0 Features

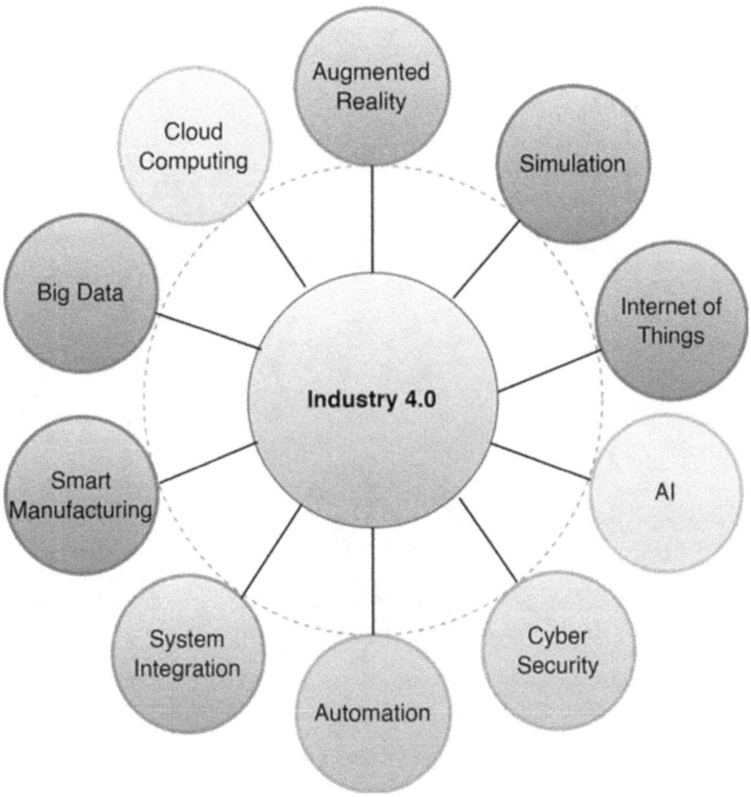

B. Society 5.0

Society 5.0 is a concept introduced by the Japanese government, envisioning the next stage of societal evolution. It focuses on the harmonious integration of technology into all aspects of human life to address social challenges and improve overall well-being as shown in Figure 2. Here are the few key components of Society 5.0:

- Technological Integration: Seamless integration of technologies like AI, IoT, and big data into daily life.
- Human-Centric Approach: Prioritizing human needs and well-being in technological advancements.
- Sustainability: Addressing environmental and social challenges through technology.
- Cross-Sector Collaboration: Collaboration across various sectors to create a comprehensive and inclusive society.

Figure 2. Society 5.0 Features

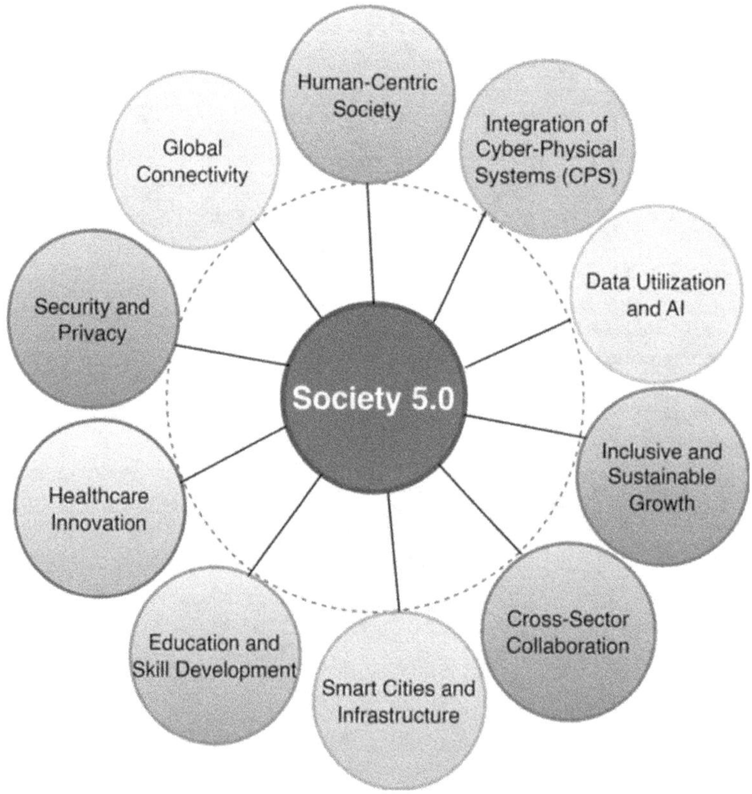

Figure 3. Key Aspects of Modern Education

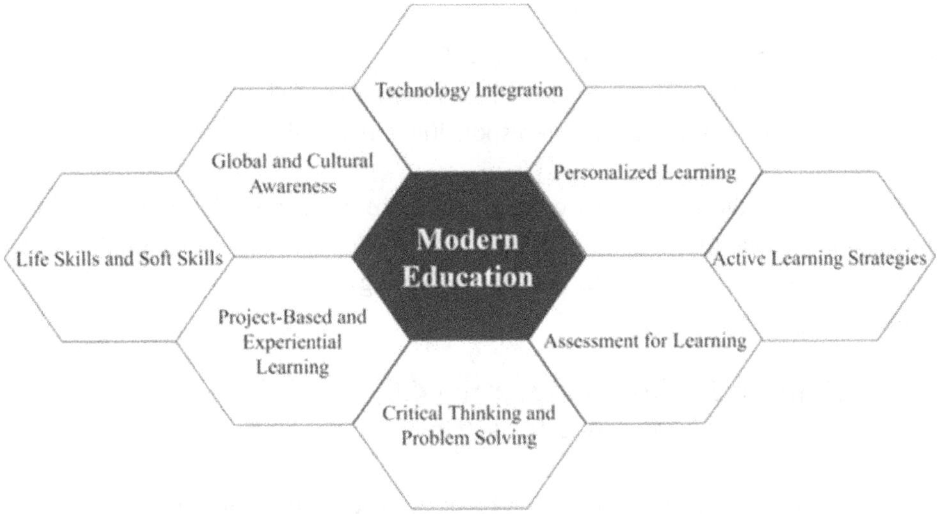

C. Modern Education

Modern education refers to the transformation of traditional educational practices through the integration of technology, updated pedagogical approaches, and a focus on preparing students for the challenges of the 21st century. Here are few key aspects of modern education as:

- Technology Integration: Use of digital tools, online resources, and interactive learning platforms.
- Personalized Learning: Tailoring education to individual needs and learning styles.
- Critical Thinking and Problem-Solving: Emphasis on developing skills for the modern workforce.
- Global Connectivity: Using technology to connect students globally and use cultural understanding.

D. Interconnections

- Skills Alignment: Industrial 4.0 and Society 5.0 necessitate a workforce with advanced technological and critical thinking skills, driving changes in education to prepare students accordingly.

- Lifelong Learning: The rapid pace of technological advancements in Industry 4.0 and Society 5.0 requires a commitment to continuous learning, influencing modern education models.
- Human-Centric Approach: Society 5.0's emphasis on human well-being aligns with the goal of modern education to prepare individuals not only for careers but also for active and responsible citizenship.

In summary, these concepts collectively represent a holistic approach to the integration of technology into various facets of society, industry, and education, with a shared goal of enhancing human well-being and addressing the challenges of the modern era.

1.1 Background Work to Industrial 4.0, Society 5.0, and Modern Education

Understanding the background and evolution of Industrial 4.0, Society 5.0, and Modern Education involves examining the historical context, technological advancements, and societal shifts that have led to the emergence of these concepts. Here's a brief overview:

A. Industrial 4.0

Historical Context:

- First Industrial Revolution (18th-19th centuries): Steam power and mechanization.
- Second Industrial Revolution (late 19th-early 20th centuries): Electricity and mass production.
- Third Industrial Revolution (mid-20th century): Automation and computerization.

Technological Advances Leading to Industrial 4.0:

- Computing Power: Increased computational capabilities and the rise of computers.
- Internet: Global connectivity and communication.
- Automation: Advancements in robotics and control systems.
- Data Analytics and IoT: Growing capacity to gather and investigate large amounts of data.

B. Society 5.0

Evolution from Previous Societal Paradigms:

- Agricultural Society (Society 1.0): Agrarian communities.
- Industrial Society (Society 2.0): Urbanization and industrialization.
- Information Society (Society 3.0): Information and communication technologies.

Technological Advances Leading to Society 5.0:

- AI and Robotics: Integration of artificial intelligence and robotics in daily life.
- Big Data and Analytics: Utilization of data for decision-making and problem-solving.
- Smart Technologies: Connected systems, IoT, and smart infrastructure.
- Human-Centric Design: Prioritizing human needs in technological development.

C. Modern Education

Historical Evolution:

- Traditional Education: Classroom-based, teacher-centered learning.
- Emergence of Technology: Introduction of computers, e-learning, and multimedia.
- Shift to Student-Centric Learning: Recognition of diverse learning styles and needs.

Technological Advances Shaping Modern Education:

- Digital Tools: Laptops, tablets, and interactive whiteboards.
- Online Learning Platforms: MOOCs, e-learning platforms, and virtual classrooms.
- Personalized Learning Software: Adaptive learning systems tailored to individual students.
- Global Connectivity: Collaboration and learning beyond geographical boundaries.

Hence, understanding the background of these concepts involves recognizing the historical progression of industrial, societal, and educational paradigms, as well as the transformative role of technology in shaping contemporary perspectives and approaches.

1.2 Organization of the Work

This work is summarized in 9 sections.

2. CHATGPT IN THE CONTEXT OF INDUSTRIAL 4.0

2.1 AI Driven Tools for Industrial 4.0 in This Smart Era

In the context of Industrial 4.0, the smart era is characterized by the integration of artificial intelligence (AI) driven tools and technologies to enhance efficiency, productivity, and decision-making in industrial processes (Tyagi, 2024; Singh et al, 2024). Here are some AI-driven tools commonly used in Industrial 4.0, as mentioned in table 1.

Table 1. AI-driven tools commonly used in Industrial 4.0

Types	Description	Benefits
Predictive Maintenance Systems	AI algorithms analyze data from sensors and equipment to predict when machinery is likely to fail.	Reduces downtime, extends the lifespan of equipment, and optimizes maintenance schedules.
Smart Manufacturing Platforms	Comprehensive platforms that integrate AI, IoT, and data analytics for end-to-end control and optimization of manufacturing processes.	Enhances production efficiency, reduces waste, and improves overall operational visibility.
AI-Enabled Robotics	Integration of AI algorithms into robotic systems for autonomous decision-making and adaptation to changing environments.	Increases efficiency, precision, and flexibility in manufacturing processes.
Quality Control and Defect Detection	AI-powered computer vision systems analyze visual data to detect defects and ensure product quality.	Improves product quality, reduces defects, and minimizes the need for manual inspection.
Supply Chain Optimization	AI algorithms examine data across the supply chain to optimize inventory management, demand forecasting, and logistics.	Reduces costs, minimizes delays, and improves overall supply chain efficiency.

continued on following page

Table 1. Continued

Types	Description	Benefits
Digital Twins	Virtual replicas of physical assets or systems that use AI to simulate and analyze real-world scenarios.	Enables better understanding, monitoring, and optimization of physical assets, leading to improved performance.
AI-Driven Energy Management	AI algorithms analyze energy consumption patterns to optimize usage and reduce costs.	Improves energy efficiency, reduces environmental impact, and lowers operational expenses.
Cognitive Automation	Integrating AI with automation to perform complex tasks that require human-like cognitive abilities.	Streamlines decision-making processes, reduces errors, and enhances operational efficiency.
AI-Based Cybersecurity Solutions	AI-driven tools that continuously monitor and analyze network data to detect and respond to cybersecurity threats.	Enhances the security of industrial systems and protects against cyberattacks.
Collaborative Robots (Cobots)	Robots are designed to work along with humans, often equipped with AI to adapt to human behavior and collaborate seamlessly.	Improves flexibility in manufacturing processes, enhances productivity, and promotes safer working environments.

Hence, the adoption of these AI-driven tools in Industrial 4.0 reflects a shift towards intelligent and interconnected systems, where data-driven insights and automation play an important role in optimizing industrial operations. These tools contribute to the overarching goals of increased efficiency, reduced costs, and improved sustainability within smart manufacturing environments.

2.2 Role of Artificial Intelligence in Smart Manufacturing

Artificial Intelligence (AI) plays an important role in smart manufacturing, also known as Industry 4.0, by introducing intelligent automation, data analytics, and decision-making capabilities (Tyagi & Tiwari, 2024) into the manufacturing processes. The incorporation of AI in smart manufacturing brings about several key benefits and transformations.

- Predictive Maintenance: AI algorithms analyze data from sensors and equipment to predict when machinery is likely to fail. It reduces downtime by allowing proactive maintenance, extends the lifespan of equipment, and optimizes maintenance costs.
- Quality Control and Defect Detection: AI-driven computer vision systems inspect and analyze visual data to identify defects and ensure product quality. It improves product quality, reduces defects, and automates the inspection process, leading to increased efficiency.
- Smart Manufacturing Platforms: Comprehensive platforms integrate AI, IoT, and data analytics for real-time monitoring, control, and optimization of

manufacturing processes. It enhances overall operational visibility, facilitates predictive analytics, and optimizes production efficiency.

- Supply Chain Optimization: AI analyzes data across the supply chain to optimize inventory management, demand forecasting, and logistics. It reduces costs, minimizes delays, and improves efficiency throughout the supply chain.
- Digital Twins: AI-driven simulations that create virtual replicas of physical assets or systems for monitoring and analysis. It enables better understanding and optimization of physical assets, leading to improved performance, maintenance, and design.
- Energy Management: AI algorithms analyze energy consumption patterns to optimize usage and reduce costs. It improves energy efficiency, reduces environmental impact, and lowers operational expenses.
- Cognitive Automation: Integrating AI with automation to perform complex tasks that require human-like cognitive abilities. It enhances decision-making processes, reduces errors, and improves operational efficiency.
- Human-Robot Collaboration: AI enables robots to work alongside humans, adapting to human behavior and collaborating seamlessly. It improves flexibility in manufacturing processes, enhances productivity, and promotes safer working environments.
- Process Optimization: AI analyzes data from various sources to discover opportunities for process optimization and efficiency improvement. It streamlines operations, minimizes waste, and enhances overall productivity.
- Data Analytics and Insights: AI processes and analyzes large amounts of data generated by sensors and systems to derive actionable insights. It enables data-driven decision-making, facilitates continuous improvement, and supports strategic planning.

Hence the collective impact of AI in smart manufacturing is the creation of more agile, efficient, and adaptive production systems. By using AI technologies, manufacturers can respond to dynamic market demands, reduce costs, and improve overall competitiveness in the rapidly evolving industrial landscape.

2.3 ChatGPT in Industrial Communication and Decision-Making

ChatGPT, or similar natural language processing models, can play a major role in industrial communication and decision-making processes in several ways (Tyagi, 2024):

- Human-Machine Interaction: ChatGPT can facilitate natural and intuitive communication between humans and machines in industrial settings. This can include voice or text-based interactions for querying information, giving commands, or receiving status updates.
- Troubleshooting and Maintenance: Employees can interact with ChatGPT to troubleshoot issues or perform routine maintenance tasks. The model can provide guidance, step-by-step instructions, and answer queries related to equipment maintenance.
- Data Analysis and Reporting: ChatGPT can assist in analyzing complex data sets and generating reports. Users can ask natural language questions about production metrics, quality control, or other key performance indicators, and the model can provide relevant insights.
- Decision Support: ChatGPT can assist in decision-making by providing information and recommendations based on historical data, current conditions, and predefined criteria. This can be particularly valuable for managers and operators in making informed choices.
- Training and Onboarding: ChatGPT can be used for training new employees or providing information on new processes and equipment. It can answer questions related to standard operating procedures, safety protocols, and other onboarding materials.
- Supply Chain Communication (Fosso Wamba et al., 2023): ChatGPT can enhance communication within the supply chain by facilitating natural language interactions between different stakeholders. This includes order status inquiries, shipment tracking, and coordination between suppliers and manufacturers.
- Real-time Monitoring and Alerts: ChatGPT can be incorporated with monitoring systems to provide real-time status updates and alerts. Users can inquire about the current state of equipment, production lines, or any anomalies detected by sensors.
- Workflow Optimization: ChatGPT can aid in optimizing workflows by providing suggestions for process improvements, identifying bottlenecks, and providing insights into efficiency enhancements.

Note that while ChatGPT can be a precious tool in industrial communication and decision-making, its implementation should be carefully designed to ensure data security, accuracy, and alignment with specific industry requirements and standards. Additionally, integrating ChatGPT with other technologies, such as IoT devices and data analytics platforms, can enhance its capabilities and effectiveness in an industrial context.

2.4 Human-Machine Collaboration in Industrial 4.0

Human-machine collaboration is a central theme in the context of Industrial 4.0, where the integration of highly developed technologies (Nair & Tyagi, 2023; Nair & Tyagi, 2023) aims to create more efficient, flexible, and responsive manufacturing processes. Here are key aspects of human-machine collaboration in the context of Industrial 4.0:

- Cobots (Collaborative Robots): These are designed to work together with humans in a shared workspace. They can assist with repetitive or physically demanding tasks, enhancing both productivity and worker safety. It benefits are: Improved efficiency, reduced physical strain on workers, and the ability to allocate tasks based on the strengths of each collaborator.
- Augmented Reality (AR) and Virtual Reality (VR): AR and VR technologies provide immersive interfaces for human-machine interaction. They can be used for training, maintenance, and real-time visualization of complex processes. Its benefits are: Enhanced training experiences, improved maintenance procedures, and better visualization of data and processes.
- Intelligent Assistance Systems: AI-driven systems assist human operators in decision-making, problem-solving, and task execution. These systems often use data analytics, machine learning, and real-time monitoring. It benefits are: Increased efficiency, better decision support, and the ability to handle complex tasks with speed and accuracy.
- Digital Twins: Digital twins are virtual replicas of physical systems or processes. They enable humans to monitor, analyze, and optimize real-world operations in a virtual environment. Its benefits are: Improved understanding of physical processes, predictive maintenance, and the ability to simulate and test changes before implementation.
- IoT Connectivity: The Internet of Things (IoT) enables seamless communication between machines and human-operated devices. Sensors and devices collect real-time data, providing valuable insights for decision-making. Its benefits are: Enhanced monitoring, proactive maintenance, and data-driven decision-making.
- Smart Devices and Wearables: Wearable devices equipped with sensors and communication capabilities provide real-time data to workers. Examples include smart glasses for augmented reality or smart gloves for gesture-based control. Its benefits are: Improved worker safety, hands-free operation, and access to relevant information on the shop floor.
- Data Analytics and Decision Support: Advanced analytics and machine learning algorithms analyze large datasets to provide insights for decision-

making. Humans interpret these insights and make informed choices. Its benefits are: Informed decision-making, identification of patterns or anomalies, and optimization of processes based on data-driven insights.

- Human-Centric Design: Industrial 4.0 systems are designed with a focus on human usability and ergonomics. User interfaces are intuitive, and technologies are implemented to augment human capabilities. Its benefits are: Improved user acceptance, reduced training times, and better collaboration between humans and machines.
- Interconnected Ecosystems: Industrial 4.0 creates interconnected ecosystems where machines, devices, and humans collaborate seamlessly. Information flows across the entire value chain. Its benefits are: Improved coordination, faster response times, and a holistic view of the entire manufacturing process.

Hence, Human-machine collaboration in Industrial 4.0 not only enhances productivity and efficiency but also contributes to a safer and more satisfying working environment. It recognizes the strengths of both humans and machines, creating synergies that lead to greater innovation and competitiveness in the manufacturing industry.

3. CHATGPT AND SOCIETY 5.0

3.1 AI Driven Tools in Society 5.0

Society 5.0 envisions the harmonious integration of technology into all aspects of human life to address social challenges and improve overall well-being. Artificial Intelligence (AI) plays an important role in realizing the goals of Society 5.0 by providing intelligent solutions (Tyagi, 2023; Tyagi et al., 2022) across various domains. Here are some AI-driven tools and applications in the context of Society 5.0, as mentioned in table 2.

Table 2. AI driven tools in Society 5.0

Area	AI tools	Benefits
Healthcare and Telemedicine	Diagnosis support systems, predictive analytics for disease outbreaks, virtual health assistants.	Enhanced healthcare provision, early identification of diseases, individualized treatment strategies, and the monitoring of patients from a distance.

continued on following page

Table 2. Continued

Area	AI tools	Benefits
Smart Cities and Urban Planning	Traffic management systems, predictive maintenance for infrastructure, intelligent energy grids	Enhanced urban efficiency, reduced traffic congestion, optimized resource usage, and improved sustainability.
Education and Learning	Personalized learning platforms, intelligent tutoring systems, adaptive educational content.	Tailored learning experiences, early identification of learning gaps, and the facilitation of lifelong learning.
Social Services and Welfare	Social welfare analytics, predictive modeling for social issues, chatbots for citizen services.	Efficient allocation of resources, early intervention in social issues, and improved citizen engagement.
Environmental Monitoring and Conservation	Remote sensing data analysis, predictive modeling for climate change, wildlife monitoring.	Improved environmental management, early detection of ecological threats, and sustainable resource management.
Agriculture and Food Security	Precision agriculture, crop disease detection, supply chain optimization.	Increased agricultural productivity, reduced environmental impact, and improved food supply chain resilience.
Finance and Economic Systems	Algorithmic trading, fraud detection, predictive analytics for economic trends.	Enhanced financial stability, improved risk management, and more accurate economic forecasting.
Public Safety and Security	Video analytics for public surveillance, predictive policing, disaster response planning.	Improved public safety, faster emergency response, and enhanced security measures.
Workplace and Human Resources	Recruitment automation, employee performance analytics, AI-driven HR chatbots.	Streamlined HR processes, improved workforce management, and enhanced employee experience.
Digital Inclusion and Accessibility	Natural language processing for accessibility, AI-driven translation services.	Increased accessibility, improved communication across language barriers, and greater inclusivity.
Personalized Services and Retail	Recommendation engines, personalized shopping experiences, AI-driven virtual shopping assistants	Enhanced customer satisfaction, personalized services, and improved retail efficiency.

Hence, the deployment of AI-driven tools in Society 5.0 contributes to creating a smarter, more connected, and human-centric society. By using AI technologies, Society 5.0 aims to address complex societal challenges and improve the overall quality of life for individuals and communities.

3.2 Human-Centric Approach to Emerging AI Based Technology

A human-centric approach to emerging AI-based technology is important to ensure that technological advancements align with human values, needs, and well-being (Nair et al., 2021; Deekshetha & Tyagi, 2023). Such an approach emphasizes ethical issues, user experience, transparency, and inclusivity. Here are key aspects of a human-centric approach to emerging AI-based technology:

A. Ethical issues:
   - Principles: Develop and adhere to ethical guidelines that prioritize fairness, transparency, accountability, and privacy.
   - Bias Mitigation: Implement measures to identify and mitigate biases in AI algorithms to ensure fair and unbiased outcomes.

B. User-Centered Design:
   - User Experience (UX): Prioritize the design of AI systems that enhance user experience and are intuitive for diverse user groups.
   - Feedback Mechanisms: Incorporate user feedback into the development process to continuously improve and adapt technology to user needs.

C. Transparency and Understandability:
   - Explainable AI: Strive for transparency in AI decision-making processes to help users understand how algorithms reach conclusions.
   - User Understanding: Provide users with clear explanations of how AI technologies work and the potential impacts on their lives.

D. Inclusivity and Accessibility:
   - Diverse Representation: Ensure diverse representation in AI development teams to address a range of perspectives and avoid biased outcomes.
   - Accessibility: Design AI technologies that are accessible to individuals with diverse abilities, ensuring inclusivity.

E. Privacy Protection:
   - Data Protection: Prioritize user privacy by implementing robust data protection measures, including anonymization and encryption.
   - Informed Consent: Obtain informed consent from users regarding data collection, processing, and storage.

F. Human-AI Collaboration:
   - Augmentation, not Replacement: Design AI systems to augment human capabilities rather than replacing human roles entirely, using collaboration.
   - User Empowerment: Empower users to have control over AI tools, allowing them to intervene and override decisions when necessary.

G. Accountability and Governance:
   - Clear Responsibility: Establish clear lines of responsibility for AI systems, including accountability for unintended consequences.
   - Ethics Committees: Form ethics committees or advisory boards to guide the development and deployment of AI technologies.

H. Continuous Monitoring and Evaluation:
   - Ongoing Assessment: Continuously monitor AI systems for potential biases, ethical issues, and unintended consequences.

- Regular Audits: Conduct regular audits and evaluations of AI systems to ensure ongoing compliance with ethical standards.

I. Education and Awareness:

- User Education: Educate users about AI technologies, their capabilities, and potential impacts to use informed decision-making.
- Public Awareness: Raise awareness about AI ethics and responsible use, engaging with the broader public.

Hence, a human-centric approach recognizes that AI technologies should be designed and implemented to enhance human well-being, promote equity, and respect fundamental human rights. It involves active collaboration between technologists, ethicists, policymakers, and the broader community to ensure that AI serves as a tool for positive societal transformation.

3.3 ChatGPT in Bridging Human-Machine Interaction

ChatGPT and similar natural language processing models play a major role in bridging human-machine interaction by providing a more natural and intuitive means of communication between humans and machines (Fui-Hoon Nah et al., 2023). Here's how ChatGPT contributes to this interaction:

- Conversational Interface: ChatGPT acts as a conversational interface, enabling users to interact with machines using natural language. This is especially valuable for individuals who may not have technical expertise.
- User Assistance and Support: ChatGPT can provide assistance and support to users by answering queries, providing guidance, and providing information on a wide range of topics.
- Accessibility: ChatGPT makes technology more accessible to a broader audience, including those who may not be familiar with complex interfaces or traditional programming languages.
- Enhanced Customer Service: In customer service applications, ChatGPT can handle routine queries, provide information, and offer assistance, freeing up human agents to focus on more complex issues.
- Language Translation: ChatGPT can facilitate language translation, enabling users who speak different languages to communicate effectively with machines.
- Learning and Education: ChatGPT can support learning and education by answering questions, providing explanations, and providing interactive learning experiences.

- Task Automation: ChatGPT can be integrated into systems to perform certain tasks based on user commands, contributing to task automation and simplifying user interactions.
- Virtual Assistants: ChatGPT can serve as the underlying technology for virtual assistants, helping users with tasks such as setting reminders, sending messages, or providing information.
- Human-Machine Collaboration: ChatGPT contributes to a more collaborative relationship between humans and machines, allowing for smoother collaboration in various domains.
- Interactive Design and Prototyping: Designers and developers can use ChatGPT to interactively prototype and refine user interfaces, discussing different conversational scenarios.
- Innovation in Human-Computer Interaction (HCI): ChatGPT and similar models drive innovation in HCI, discussing new ways for humans to interact with technology beyond traditional interfaces.
- Emotional Intelligence: As AI models improve in understanding and generating human-like responses, they contribute to the development of emotionally intelligent interactions, making interactions more nuanced and engaging.
- Entertainment and Content Creation: ChatGPT can be employed for creating interactive and entertaining content, such as conversational characters in video games or interactive storytelling applications.

While ChatGPT contributes significantly to human-machine interaction, it's important to note the ongoing challenges, including addressing biases, ensuring ethical use, and refining the technology to better understand context and user intent. The continual improvement of natural language processing models contributes to a more seamless and effective bridge between humans and machines in various applications and domains.

3.4 Ethical Issues in the Integration of AI Driven Tools/ChatGPT in Society 5.0

The integration of AI-driven tools, including models like ChatGPT, in Society 5.0 raises several ethical issues. As technology becomes increasingly pervasive, it is important to address these issues to ensure responsible development and deployment. Here are some ethical issues related to the integration of AI-driven tools in Society 5.0:

- Bias and Fairness: AI models can inherit biases from the data they are trained on, leading to biased outcomes and potential discrimination. Due to this, we face Unfair treatment, reinforcing existing social biases, and perpetuating discrimination in decision-making processes.

- Transparency and Explainability: The obscurity of AI algorithms can create difficulties in comprehending the decision-making process, resulting in a dearth of responsibility. Due to this, we face Reduced trust, difficulty in addressing errors or biases, and challenges in ensuring accountability and compliance with regulations.
- Privacy Issues: AI-driven tools often rely on large amounts of personal data, raising issues about privacy infringement. Due to this, we face Unauthorized access to sensitive information, potential misuse of personal data, and erosion of individual privacy.
- Security Risks: AI systems can be vulnerable to attacks and manipulation, leading to security breaches. So, we may Compromised system integrity, unauthorized access, and potential harm to individuals or organizations.
- Job Displacement and Economic Inequality: The widespread adoption of AI-driven tools may lead to job displacement, creating economic disparities. So, we face unemployment, economic inequality, and the need for reskilling or upskilling of the workforce.
- Dependency on Technology: Overreliance on AI-driven tools may lead to diminished human skills and decision-making abilities. We need to Reduced critical thinking skills, dependency on automated systems, and potential consequences in the absence of technology.
- Ethical Use of AI in Decision-Making: The use of AI in critical decision-making processes, such as criminal justice or healthcare, raises ethical issues. So, we may need unintended consequences, lack of empathy in decision-making, and challenges in balancing AI assistance with human judgment.
- Social Impact and Inclusion: Unequal access to AI technologies may exacerbate existing social inequalities. Hence, a digital divide, excluding certain populations from the benefits of AI-driven tools, and reinforcing societal disparities.
- Informed Consent: Users may not fully understand the implications of interacting with AI systems, leading to uninformed consent. We facelack of awareness about data usage, potential consequences, and user autonomy.
- Accountability and Liability: Assigning accountability for errors or harm resulting from AI systems might pose difficulties. So, we facelack of accountability, challenges in assigning liability, and difficulties in seeking redress for AI-related harms.

Hence, these ethical issues require collaboration among technology developers, policymakers, ethicists, and the broader society. Implementing transparent and accountable practices, promoting diversity in AI development, and ensuring ongoing monitoring and evaluation are essential steps toward responsible integration of AI-driven tools in Society 5.0.

4. MODERN EDUCATION AND CHATGPT

4.1 Evolving Trends/Role of Artificial Intelligence in Modern Education and in Personalized Learning

Artificial Intelligence (AI) is playing a transformative role in modern education (Tyagi et al., 2020; Tyagi et al., 2023), with a particular focus on personalized learning. Here are evolving trends and the roles of AI in shaping the landscape of education:

- Personalized Learning: AI enables the creation of adaptive learning systems that cater to individual student needs, adjusting the pace, content, and style of learning based on their abilities and preferences. Its benefits are: Improved student engagement, better learning outcomes, and the ability to address diverse learning styles.
- Intelligent Tutoring Systems: AI-powered tutoring systems provide personalized support to students, providing guidance, feedback, and additional resources based on individual progress and learning gaps. Its benefits are: enhanced student comprehension, increased self-directed learning, and support for educators in addressing individual student needs.
- Automated Grading and Feedback: AI automates the grading process, providing instant feedback to students. This allows educators to focus on more personalized interactions and instructional design. Its benefits are: faster assessment turnaround, more detailed feedback, and increased efficiency for both students and teachers.
- Adaptive Learning Platforms: AI-driven adaptive learning platforms analyze student performance data to dynamically adjust the difficulty and content of learning materials, ensuring an optimal learning path for each student. Its benefits are: Tailored learning experiences, addressing individual strengths and weaknesses, and using mastery of concepts.
- Predictive Analytics: AI analyzes student data to predict performance trends and identify potential challenges. This enables educators to take early action and offer specific assistance. Its benefits are: Proactive intervention, reduced dropout rates, and improved overall student success.

- Natural Language Processing (NLP) for Language Learning: NLP technologies assist in language learning by providing real-time language analysis, pronunciation feedback, and interactive language practice. It benefits are: Enhanced language acquisition, improved communication skills, and personalized language learning experiences.
- Virtual Classrooms and AI-Assisted Teaching: AI is used in virtual classrooms to facilitate teaching, monitor student engagement, and provide additional resources in real-time. Its benefits are: Improved online teaching experiences, increased student participation, and personalized learning pathways.
- Gamification and AI in Education (Zhan et al., 2022): AI-driven gamification elements are used to create interactive and engaging educational experiences, tailoring challenges to individual skill levels. Its benefits are: Increased motivation, active participation, and a more enjoyable learning process.
- Education Chatbots: AI-powered chatbots assist students in answering queries related to coursework, deadlines, and general information. Its benefits are: 24/7 support, quick access to information, and the ability to handle routine administrative tasks.
- Emotional Intelligence and Well-being: AI tools monitor student behavior and engagement to assess emotional states. This information can be used to provide support for students' well-being. Its benefits are: Early detection of emotional distress, personalized mental health resources, and a more supportive learning environment.
- Data-Driven Decision Making for Educators: AI enables educators to make informed decisions by analyzing large sets of data related to student performance, attendance, and engagement. Its benefits are: Informed teaching strategies, tailored interventions, and evidence-based decision-making.

Hence, as AI continues to advance, its role in education is likely to expand, providing more sophisticated and personalized learning experiences for students while providing valuable support to educators. Balancing the integration of AI with ethical issues, privacy issues, and maintaining a human touch in education will be key aspects of this ongoing evolution.

4.2 Challenges and Opportunities in Modern Education With AI Driven Tools

The integration of AI-driven tools in modern education presents both challenges and opportunities (Tyagi et al., 2022; Goyal & Tyagi, 2020). While these tools offer innovative solutions to enhance learning experiences, they also raise issues that need to be addressed. Here's an overview of the challenges and opportunities associated with the use of AI in education, as mentioned in Table 3.

Table 3. Issue and Challenges in Modern Education with AI Driven Tools

Types	Challenges	Issues
Bias and Fairness	AI algorithms may inherit biases present in training data, leading to unfair treatment and reinforcing existing disparities.	Unintended discrimination, exacerbation of existing inequalities, and biased decision-making
Data Privacy and Security	Collecting and analyzing large amounts of student data raise issues about privacy and the potential for data breaches.	Unauthorized access, misuse of sensitive information, and erosion of student privacy.
Teacher Training and Adoption	Teachers may lack the necessary training to effectively integrate AI tools into their teaching practices.	Ineffective use of AI tools, resistance to adoption, and potential disparities in access to training.
Ethical Use of AI in Education	Ethical issues surrounding the use of AI in decision-making, particularly in areas like student assessments and admissions.	Lack of transparency, accountability issues, and potential biases in AI-driven decisions.
Equity and Access	Unequal access to technology and AI tools may exacerbate existing disparities in education.	The digital divide, unequal opportunities for students, and disparities in educational outcomes.
Overemphasis on Standardized Testing	The use of AI in standardized testing may lead to an overemphasis on test scores as a measure of student success.	Narrow assessment criteria, neglect of other important skills, and potential stress on students.
Job Displacement and Changing Skill Requirements	The automation of certain tasks through AI may lead to issues about job displacement and the need for new skillsets.	Economic challenges, unemployment, and the need for continuous reskilling.

Opportunities: Now few opportunities in Modern Education with AI driven tools are:

- Personalized Learning: AI enables personalized learning experiences tailored to individual student needs, pace, and learning styles. Its benefits are: Improved student engagement, better learning outcomes, and increased adaptability.
- Adaptive Learning Platforms (Yakin, & Linden, 2021): AI-driven adaptive learning systems modify content and difficulty levels according to the individual performance of each student. Its benefits are: optimal learning paths, addressing learning gaps, and using mastery of concepts.
- Enhanced Teaching and Administrative Efficiency: AI tools automate administrative tasks and grading, allowing teachers to focus more on personalized instruction. Its benefits are: Time-saving, increased efficiency, and better allocation of educators' time.

- Early Intervention and Support: AI analytics can predict student performance trends, allowing for early intervention and targeted support. Its benefits are: Reduced dropout rates, improved student success, and proactive support mechanisms.
- Global Access to Education: Online education platforms and AI-driven tools enable global access to educational resources and expertise. Its benefits are: Expanded learning opportunities, cultural exchange, and increased accessibility.
- Skill Development and Lifelong Learning: AI supports continuous learning by recommending personalized professional development opportunities. Its benefits are: Lifelong learning, skill development aligned with market needs, and improved career readiness.
- Innovative Teaching Strategies: AI allows educators to implement innovative and interactive teaching strategies. Its benefits are: Improved engagement, diverse learning experiences, and the cultivation of critical thinking skills.
- Virtual Classrooms and Remote Learning: AI facilitates virtual classrooms and online learning, providing flexibility and accessibility. Its benefits are: Increased access to education, global collaboration, and adaptability to diverse learning environments.
- Gamification for Engagement: AI-driven gamification enhances student engagement and motivation. Its benefits are: active participation, enjoyable learning experiences, and increased retention of information.
- Feedback and Assessment Improvement: AI tools provide instant feedback, allowing for more detailed assessment and targeted feedback. Its benefits are: Faster assessment turnaround, improved feedback, and a deeper understanding of student progress.

While there are challenges in integrating AI into education, addressing these issues presents an opportunity to create a more equitable, efficient, and engaging educational environment. Striking a balance between using the benefits of AI and mitigating potential risks is essential for the responsible integration of technology in modern education.

5. INTEGRATION OF INDUSTRIAL 4.0, SOCIETY 5.0, AND MODERN EDUCATION

5.1 Convergence of Industrial 4.0, Society 5.0, and Modern Education

The convergence of Industry 4.0, Society 5.0, and modern education represents a holistic approach to addressing societal challenges and using sustainable development. Each of these concepts plays a unique role in shaping the future, and their convergence has the potential to create synergies that benefit individuals, industries, and society as a whole. Here's an exploration of how these concepts converge, as mentioned in table 4.

Table 4. Convergence of Industrial 4.0, Society 5.0, and Modern Education

Type	Industry 4.0	Society 5.0	Modern Education	Convergence
Technological Integration	Focuses on the integration of advanced technologies in manufacturing and industrial processes, such as IoT, AI, and automation.	Envisions a society where technology is seamlessly integrated into various aspects of life to enhance well-being.	Incorporates technology to create interactive and adaptive learning environments.	The integration of cutting-edge technologies in industry, society, and education promotes a technologically advanced and interconnected ecosystem.
Data-Driven Decision-Making	Relies on data analytics for predictive maintenance, process optimization, and improved efficiency.	Advocates for a society where data is used to address social issues, enhance quality of life, and support sustainable development.	Utilizes data analytics to personalize learning, assess student performance, and optimize educational processes.	The emphasis on data-driven decision-making across industry, society, and education uses efficiency, innovation, and informed choices.
Human-Centric Approach	Incorporates human-machine collaboration and emphasizes the well-being of workers.	Focuses on the human-centric use of technology to address societal challenges and enhance the quality of life.	Adopts a student-centered approach, using technology to cater to individual learning needs.	A shared commitment to human-centric design principles ensures that advancements in technology prioritize the well-being and needs of individuals

continued on following page

Table 4. Continued

Type	Industry 4.0	Society 5.0	Modern Education	Convergence
Lifelong Learning and Skill Development	Encourages a continuous learning mindset to adapt to evolving technologies.	Promotes lifelong learning to empower individuals to navigate a rapidly changing society.	Emphasizes the importance of continuous learning and skill development to prepare students for the future.	The integration of Industry 4.0, Society 5.0, and modern education supports a culture of lifelong learning and skill adaptation.
Global Connectivity	Facilitates global connectivity through interconnected supply chains and collaborative manufacturing processes.	Envisions a globally connected society where information and resources are shared for the collective benefit.	Utilizes technology for global collaboration, online learning, and sharing educational resources.	The convergence promotes a global perspective, using collaboration and knowledge exchange across industries, societies, and educational institutions.
Innovation Ecosystem	Drives innovation in manufacturing processes, product design, and business models.	Encourages an innovation ecosystem where technology addresses societal challenges and enhances the quality of life.	Nurtures innovation through project-based learning, STEM education, and the integration of emerging technologies.	The convergence of these concepts creates an overarching innovation ecosystem that spans industry, society, and education, using a culture of creativity and problem-solving.

Hence, the convergence of Industry 4.0, Society 5.0, and modern education represents a harmonious integration of technological advancements, societal progress, and educational innovation. This convergence aims to create a future where technology serves humanity, uses sustainable development, and prepares individuals for the challenges and opportunities of a rapidly evolving world.

5.2 Enhancing Learning and Innovation in Industry 4.0 and Society 5.0

Enhancing learning and innovation in Industry 4.0 and Society 5.0 requires a multifaceted approach that integrates education, technology, and societal collaboration (Goyal, & Tyagi, 2020; Mishra, & Tyagi, 2022). Here are key strategies to use learning and innovation in these contexts, as mentioned in table 5.

Table 5. Learning and Innovation in Industry 4.0 and Society 5.0

	Types	Learning Focus	Innovation Integration
Learning and Innovation in Industry 4.0	Continuous Training and Upskilling:	Emphasize continuous learning and upskilling for the workforce to adapt to rapidly evolving technologies.	Integrate innovation-focused training programs to cultivate a culture of creativity and problem-solving.
	Digital Learning Platforms	Implement digital learning platforms that use e-learning, virtual reality (VR), and augmented reality (AR) for interactive and immersive learning experiences.	Use digital platforms to simulate real-world scenarios, using innovation in problem-solving and decision-making.
	Collaborative Learning Environments	Facilitate collaborative learning environments that encourage knowledge-sharing and teamwork.	Use cross-disciplinary collaboration to stimulate innovation by combining diverse perspectives and expertise.
	Industry-Academia Partnerships	Establish strong partnerships between industries and academic institutions.	Promote collaborative research projects, internships, and knowledge exchange to drive innovation from academic insights to practical applications
	Experiential Learning	Provide hands-on, experiential learning opportunities to bridge theoretical knowledge with practical skills.	Encourage experimentation and prototyping to cultivate an innovation mindset among learners.
	Data Literacy Programs	Develop programs that enhance data literacy skills among the workforce.	Utilize data analytics for informed decision-making and innovation, using a data-driven culture.
	Agile Methodologies	Incorporate agile methodologies in training to instill adaptability and flexibility.	Apply agile principles to innovation processes, allowing for iterative development and quick adaptation to changing requirements.
Learning and Innovation in Society 5.0	Lifelong Learning Initiatives	Promote lifelong learning initiatives at all stages of life.	Enable individuals to acquire new skills and stay adaptable in a rapidly changing society, using a culture of continuous innovation.
	Digital Inclusion Programs	Implement programs to bridge the digital divide and ensure equal access to technology.	Use innovation by providing diverse communities with the tools and resources needed to participate in the digital economy.
	Citizen Science and Crowdsourcing	Encourage citizen science projects and crowdsourcing initiatives.	Involve the public in collecting data, solving problems, and contributing to innovative solutions for societal challenges.

continued on following page

Table 5. Continued

	Types	Learning Focus	Innovation Integration
	Cross-Sector Collaboration	Facilitate collaboration between government, industry, academia, and civil society.	Create platforms for cross-sector collaboration to address complex societal issues through innovative solutions.
	Social Innovation Programs	Develop educational programs that emphasize social innovation	Encourage individuals to address societal challenges creatively, promoting innovations that contribute to the well-being of communities.
	Human-Centric Design Thinking	Integrate human-centric design thinking into educational curricula.	Use an empathetic approach to problem-solving, ensuring that innovations are designed with the end-user in mind.
	Civic Technology Initiatives	Promote civic technology initiatives that engage citizens in using technology for societal improvement.	Enable citizens to participate in the co-creation of solutions that enhance the quality of life and address societal challenges.

6. ISSUES, CHALLENGES OF AI DRIVEN TOOLS/ CHATGPT ON INDUSTRIAL 4.0, SOCIETY 5.0, AND MODERN EDUCATION

6.1 Privacy and Security Issues Towards Role of ChatGPT in Industrial 4.0, Society 5.0, and Modern Education

The use of ChatGPT in Industrial 4.0, Society 5.0, and Modern Education raises important privacy and security issues (Nair, & Tyagi, 2021). Here are key points related to privacy and security issues in each context:

A. Industrial 4.0

Privacy Issues:

- Data Privacy: In an industrial setting, conversations involving sensitive information about manufacturing processes, trade secrets, and proprietary data may be processed by ChatGPT. Ensuring the privacy of such data is important to prevent industrial espionage or unauthorized access.
- Employee Privacy: Interactions between workers and ChatGPT in the industrial context may involve personal information. Employers must safeguard employee privacy, adhering to data protection regulations.

Security Challenges:

- Data Breaches: The storage and transmission of data during interactions with ChatGPT may be susceptible to cyber threats. Robust cybersecurity measures are essential to prevent data breaches.
- Integrity of Operations: If ChatGPT is integrated into critical industrial systems, ensuring the integrity of operations is important to prevent malicious interference that could compromise safety and productivity.

B. Society 5.0

Privacy Issues:

- Social Conversations: ChatGPT may be used in various social contexts, including counseling, mental health support, or general communication. Privacy issues arise when sensitive personal information is shared, requiring measures to protect user confidentiality.
- Public Conversations: In public forums or online spaces, the use of ChatGPT raises issues about the privacy of shared information and the potential for misuse.

Security Challenges:

- Misuse of Information: Security risks include the potential misuse of information shared during conversations. Unauthorized access to sensitive data could lead to identity theft or other malicious activities.
- Ethical issues: The ethical use of ChatGPT in sensitive contexts, such as mental health support, is important to avoid harm to individuals and maintain trust in AI systems.

C. Modern Education

Privacy Issues:

- Student Data: ChatGPT interactions in educational settings may involve student data, including performance metrics, learning preferences, and potentially sensitive information. Protecting student privacy is paramount to comply with educational regulations.

- Teacher-Student Interactions: Conversations between teachers and students using ChatGPT should be conducted with privacy in mind, ensuring that sensitive topics are handled appropriately.

Security Challenges:

- Data Security in E-Learning Platforms: If ChatGPT is integrated into e-learning platforms, securing the data exchanged during interactions is critical to prevent unauthorized access and protect the confidentiality of educational content.
- Preventing Cheating: In assessment scenarios, there may be issues about students using ChatGPT to cheat during exams. Implementing security measures to detect and prevent such behavior is essential.

Hence, balancing the benefits of ChatGPT with privacy and security issues is essential to build trust and ensure responsible deployment across Industrial 4.0, Society 5.0, and Modern Education. Stakeholders should collaborate to establish robust policies, standards, and practices that prioritize user privacy and data security.

6.2 Technical and Research Challenges Towards Role of ChatGPT in Industrial 4.0, Society 5.0, and Modern Education

The integration of ChatGPT into Industrial 4.0, Society 5.0, and Modern Education presents several technical and research challenges. Addressing these challenges is important for ensuring the effective and responsible deployment of ChatGPT in diverse contexts. Here are some key challenges, as mentioned in Table 6.

Table 6. Challenges towards role of ChatGPT in Industrial 4.0, Society 5.0, and Modern Education

Types	Challenge	Research Focus
Domain-Specific Understanding	ChatGPT may lack domain-specific knowledge required in industrial, societal, or educational settings.	Improving the model's understanding of specialized terminology, industry-specific processes, and context-dependent information.
Real-Time Responsiveness	Achieving real-time responsiveness for interactive applications in industries, society, or educational platforms.	Investigating methods to optimize model inference speed without compromising on the quality of responses.

continued on following page

Table 6. Continued

Types	Challenge	Research Focus
Customization and Adaptability	Tailoring ChatGPT for specific industry workflows, societal interactions, or educational needs.	Developing techniques for customization and adaptability to ensure the model aligns with the unique requirements of each context.
Ethical AI and Bias Mitigation	Addressing ethical issues and mitigating biases in the responses generated by ChatGPT.	Investigating methods for bias detection, mitigation, and promoting ethical behavior in the model's outputs.
Security and Privacy Preservation	Ensuring robust security measures to protect sensitive information and maintaining user privacy	Developing encryption techniques, secure communication protocols, and privacy-preserving methods for ChatGPT interactions.
Explainability and Interpretability	Enhancing the explainability and interpretability of ChatGPT's responses, especially in critical applications.	Discussing techniques to make the model's decision-making process more transparent and understandable.
Multilingual and Multimodal Capabilities	Extending ChatGPT's capabilities to handle multiple languages and modalities, including images and videos.	Investigating methods for multilingual support and integrating multimodal inputs for a more comprehensive understanding.
Collaboration with Human Experts	Facilitating effective collaboration between ChatGPT and human experts in complex industrial, societal, or educational scenarios	Developing collaborative frameworks that use the strengths of both AI and human expertise.
Dynamic Learning and Continuous Improvement	Enabling ChatGPT to adapt dynamically to changing contexts and acquire knowledge over time	Discussing techniques for continual learning and adaptive behavior, allowing the model to improve its performance with experience.
Scalability and Resource Efficiency	Enabling ChatGPT to adapt dynamically to changing contexts and acquire knowledge over time.	Discussing techniques for continual learning and adaptive behavior, allowing the model to improve its performance with experience.
Scalability and Resource Efficiency	Ensuring scalability and resource efficiency, particularly when deploying ChatGPT in resource-constrained environments.	Optimizing model architectures, discussing lightweight variants, and efficient deployment strategies.
Alignment with Educational Objectives	Aligning ChatGPT's responses with educational goals and pedagogical principles.	Integrating educational expertise into the model's training process and ensuring that responses align with instructional objectives.
Adaptation to Diverse Learning Styles:	Adapting ChatGPT to cater to diverse learning styles in educational settings.	Investigating methods to personalize educational interactions based on individual learning preferences and needs.
Long-Term Engagement and Retention	Ensuring long-term engagement and knowledge retention in educational contexts.	Developing strategies to maintain user interest, facilitate long-term learning, and enhance knowledge retention.

7.3 Societal and Educational Challenges Towards Role of ChatGPT in Industrial 4.0, Society 5.0, and Modern Education

The integration of ChatGPT in Industrial 4.0, Society 5.0, and Modern Education introduces various societal and educational challenges. Addressing these challenges is important to ensure responsible deployment and positive contributions to these domains. Here are key challenges in each context:

A. Industrial 4.0

Societal Challenges:

- Job Displacement: The implementation of ChatGPT and other AI technologies in task automation may result in job displacement, necessitating the development of measures to enhance the skills and knowledge of the workforce through reskilling and upskilling.
- Digital Divide: Socioeconomic disparities may widen as certain groups struggle to adapt to the digital nature of Industry 4.0, necessitating inclusive policies.

Educational Challenges:

- Skill Mismatch: Preparing the workforce with the necessary skills for AI-driven industrial processes faced challenge, requiring educational programs to align with industry needs.
- Continuous Learning Culture: Using a culture of continuous learning is important to adapt to evolving technologies, requiring educational systems to promote lifelong learning.

B. Society 5.0

Societal Challenges:

- Privacy Issues: The use of ChatGPT in societal interactions raises privacy issues, necessitating robust regulations and ethical guidelines.
- Digital Dependence: An over-reliance on AI for social interactions may lead to reduced face-to-face communication, impacting social skills and community engagement.

Educational Challenges:

- Ethical Literacy: Preparing individuals to navigate ethical issues in AI-driven social interactions requires incorporating ethical literacy into educational curricula.
- Cultural Competence: ChatGPT must be trained to understand and respect diverse cultural nuances in societal contexts, requiring cultural competence education.

C. Modern Education

Societal Challenges:

- Inequality in Access: The integration of ChatGPT in education may widen the digital divide, with some students lacking access to AI-driven educational tools.
- Depersonalization of Learning: Excessive reliance on AI in education may depersonalize the learning experience, impacting student-teacher relationships.

Educational Challenges:

- Assessment Integrity: Ensuring the integrity of assessments in the presence of AI tools like ChatGPT faces challenges, requiring the development of secure assessment methods.
- Teacher Training: Educators may require training to effectively integrate and collaborate with AI tools in the classroom, necessitating ongoing professional development.

Hence, these challenges require collaborative effort involving researchers, educators, policymakers, and industry stakeholders to ensure that the integration of ChatGPT in Industrial 4.0, Society 5.0, and Modern Education contributes positively to societal advancement and educational outcomes.

8. FUTURE PERSPECTIVES AND INNOVATIONS OF CHATGPT IN INDUSTRIAL 4.0, SOCIETY 5.0, AND MODERN EDUCATION

8.1 Emerging Technologies in AI and ChatGPT for Modern Society

Emerging technologies in AI and ChatGPT continue to shape and redefine modern society, providing innovative solutions, enhancing capabilities, and introducing new possibilities across various domains. Here are some key emerging technologies in AI and ChatGPT that have a major impact on modern society:

- AI-Driven Personalization: AI algorithms, including those integrated into ChatGPT, are increasingly personalized, tailoring experiences, content, and recommendations based on individual preferences and behavior. It enhances user engagement, customer satisfaction, and the overall user experience across applications such as content streaming, e-commerce, and online services.
- Generative Adversarial Networks (GANs): GANs enable the generation of realistic synthetic data by training a generator to produce data that is indistinguishable from real data, and a discriminator to differentiate between real and generated data. It is used in various applications, including image and video synthesis, creating realistic simulations, and enhancing data augmentation techniques.
- Natural Language Processing (NLP) Advancements: Ongoing advancements in NLP, a key component of ChatGPT, enable improved language understanding, sentiment analysis, and contextual interpretation. It powers more sophisticated chatbots, virtual assistants, and language translation services, making human-computer interactions more natural and effective.
- Explainable AI (XAI): XAI focuses on developing AI models that provide clear explanations for their decisions and predictions, increasing transparency and interpretability. It enhances trust in AI systems, particularly in critical applications like healthcare, finance, and autonomous vehicles, where understanding the reasoning behind AI decisions is important.
- Federated Learning: Federated Learning (Cherukuvada et al., 2023) allows AI models to be trained across decentralized devices, enabling learning without exchanging raw data. It preserves privacy by keeping data on local devices, making it applicable in healthcare, finance, and other sectors where data privacy is a primary concern.
- Reinforcement Learning Advances: Continuous advancements in reinforcement learning, a type of machine learning where agents learn by interacting with an environment, enable more sophisticated decision-making and auton-

omous control. It applied in robotics, game playing, optimization problems, and resource management, leading to more efficient and adaptable systems.

- Edge AI: Edge AI involves processing data locally on devices rather than relying on centralized cloud servers, enabling real-time decision-making and reducing latency. It powering applications such as smart devices, autonomous vehicles, and IoT devices, where low latency and real-time processing are critical.
- AI for Healthcare Diagnostics: AI is increasingly being utilized for medical imaging analysis, disease diagnosis, and treatment recommendations, improving the accuracy and efficiency of healthcare processes. It accelerates diagnostics, aids in treatment planning, and enhances medical research, ultimately improving patient outcomes.
- AI in Cybersecurity: AI technologies, including machine learning and anomaly detection algorithms, are employed in cybersecurity to identify and respond to security threats. It enhances threat detection, reduces response times, and strengthens the overall resilience of digital systems against cyberattacks.
- Quantum Computing: Quantum computing uses the principles of quantum mechanics to perform complex computations, potentially solving problems that are currently intractable for classical computers. It has the potential to revolutionize fields such as cryptography, optimization, and drug discovery, significantly impacting various industries.
- AI in Climate Science: It is employed in climate modeling, data analysis, and prediction to understand complex environmental systems and address climate-related challenges. It facilitates more accurate climate predictions, helps in the development of sustainable practices, and supports climate change mitigation and adaptation efforts.
- Robotics and Autonomous Systems: Advancements in robotics, combined with AI, enable the development of autonomous systems for tasks such as transportation, manufacturing, and exploration. It streamlines processes, enhances efficiency, and contributes to industries ranging from logistics to space exploration.
- Human Augmentation Technologies: Technologies that enhance human capabilities, including AI-powered prosthetics, brain-computer interfaces, and exoskeletons. It improves the quality of life for individuals with disabilities, enables new forms of human-machine collaboration, and holds potential for enhancing human performance.
- AI in Education Technology (EdTech): AI is integrated into educational platforms to personalize learning experiences, provide intelligent tutoring, and optimize educational content delivery. It supports adaptive learning, identifies individual learning needs, and facilitates remote and online education.

- ChatGPT-Based Virtual Assistants: Virtual assistants powered by models like ChatGPT provide conversational interfaces for users, assisting with tasks, answering queries, and facilitating natural language interactions. It enhances user engagement, productivity, and accessibility in various applications, from customer support to personal productivity tools.
- Neuromorphic Computing: Neuromorphic computing mimics the architecture and functioning of the human brain, enabling energy-efficient and parallel processing. It Holds potential for cognitive computing, pattern recognition, and AI systems that emulate human-like learning and decision-making processes.
- Blockchain and AI Integration: Integration of blockchain technology with AI for enhancing transparency, security, and traceability of AI-generated decisions and data. It Addresses issues related to data privacy, accountability, and trust in AI systems, particularly in sensitive applications.
- 5G and AI Convergence: The convergence of 5G technology and AI enables faster and more reliable communication, supporting the deployment of AI applications in real-time. It Facilitates the growth of connected devices, autonomous systems, and immersive technologies that rely on low-latency, high-bandwidth communication.
- AI in Content Creation: AI algorithms are increasingly used for content creation, including writing articles, generating art, and composing music. It Expedites creative processes, supports content creators, and introduces new possibilities in artistic expression.

Note that these emerging technologies in AI and ChatGPT collectively contribute to a transformative landscape, shaping the way we live, work, and interact in modern society. As these technologies continue to advance, it is important to address ethical, societal, and regulatory issues to ensure responsible and beneficial integration into various aspects of our lives.

8.2 Potential Innovations Towards Modern Education, Industry, and Society in Next Decade

The next decade holds exciting prospects for innovations in education, industry, and society, driven by advancements in technology, artificial intelligence, and societal needs. Here are potential innovations that could significantly impact these domains:

A. Education

- Personalized Learning Ecosystems: Integrated platforms providing personalized learning experiences tailored to individual needs, incorporating AI, adaptive learning technologies, and real-time feedback. It Uses student engagement, addresses diverse learning styles, and enhances educational outcomes.
- Augmented Reality (AR) and Virtual Reality (VR) Learning Environments: Immersive educational experiences using AR and VR technologies, enabling students to explore historical events, conduct virtual experiments, and participate in interactive simulations. It Enhances experiential learning, making complex concepts more tangible and engaging.
- Blockchain for Academic Credentials: Blockchain-based systems for securely storing and verifying academic credentials, enabling transparent and tamper-proof records of educational achievements. It Streamlines credential verification, reduces fraud, and facilitates global recognition of qualifications.
- Global Collaborative Learning Platforms: Online platforms that facilitate collaborative projects and cultural exchanges among students from diverse geographical locations, using global perspectives. It Prepares students for a globally interconnected world, promotes cross-cultural understanding, and encourages collaborative problem-solving.
- AI-Powered Tutoring and Mentoring Systems: Advanced AI systems providing personalized tutoring and mentorship to students, adapting to individual learning styles and pacing. It Supplements traditional teaching methods, supports struggling students, and encourages self-directed learning.
- Quantum Education: Integration of quantum computing concepts into educational curricula, preparing students for emerging technologies and careers in quantum computing. It Equips the workforce with skills for the quantum era, using innovation in quantum computing applications.
- Emphasis on Social-Emotional Learning (SEL):Increased focus on SEL skills such as empathy, resilience, and collaboration, integrated into educational programs to support holistic student development. It Prepares students for emotional intelligence, enhances interpersonal skills, and contributes to overall well-being.

B. Industry (Industrial 4.0)

- Autonomous Industrial Systems: Fully autonomous industrial processes using AI, robotics, and IoT, minimizing human intervention in routine tasks. It

Increases efficiency, reduces errors, and improves safety in manufacturing and logistics.

- Digital Twins for Predictive Maintenance: Enhanced digital twins of physical assets, incorporating real-time data and AI analytics for predictive maintenance and performance optimization. It Minimizes downtime, extends equipment lifespan, and optimizes resource utilization in industries.
- Blockchain in Supply Chain Management: Blockchain solutions for transparent and secure supply chain management, ensuring traceability and authenticity of products. It Mitigates fraud, improves supply chain resilience, and enhances trust among stakeholders.
- Human-Robot Collaboration in Manufacturing: Advanced collaborative robots (cobots) working alongside human workers in manufacturing settings, with improved safety features and adaptive capabilities. It Optimizes production processes, enhances worker safety, and facilitates flexible manufacturing setups.
- Energy-Optimized Smart Grids:AI-driven smart grids that dynamically optimize energy distribution, consumption, and storage in real-time, integrating renewable energy sources. It Enhances energy efficiency, reduces carbon footprint, and contributes to sustainable energy practices.
- AI-Enhanced Cybersecurity for Critical Infrastructure: AI-powered cybersecurity solutions specifically designed to protect critical infrastructure against sophisticated cyber threats. It Strengthens resilience against cyber-attacks, safeguards essential services, and ensures the integrity of industrial systems.

C. Society (Society 5.0)

- Digital Health Ecosystems: Integrated digital health platforms using AI, wearables, and telemedicine for personalized healthcare monitoring, diagnostics, and treatment. It Improves healthcare accessibility, enables early detection of health issues, and empowers individuals to manage their well-being.
- Smart Cities with AI-Driven Urban Planning: AI-powered urban planning systems optimizing city infrastructure, transportation, and public services for sustainability and efficiency. It Enhances city livability, reduces congestion, and promotes eco-friendly urban development.
- AI-Enhanced Civic Engagement: Platforms using AI to enhance citizen engagement in decision-making processes, enabling data-driven policy development and public participation. It Uses inclusive governance, strengthens democracy, and builds trust between citizens and government.
- Climate Action Technologies: Technologies using AI, IoT, and data analytics to address climate change challenges, including monitoring environmental

changes, predicting natural disasters, and promoting sustainable practices. It Supports global efforts to combat climate change, enhances environmental conservation, and builds climate resilience.

- Digital Inclusion Initiatives: Comprehensive initiatives addressing digital divides, ensuring equitable access to technology, internet connectivity, and digital literacy programs. It Reduces socioeconomic disparities, promotes equal opportunities, and facilitates broader participation in the digital economy.
- AI in Cultural Preservation: AI applications for the preservation and restoration of cultural heritage, including language preservation, art restoration, and digitization of historical artifacts. It Safeguards cultural diversity, facilitates historical conservation, and promotes cultural understanding.
- Inclusive AI Ethics Frameworks: Development and adoption of ethical frameworks for the responsible and inclusive use of AI, addressing bias, transparency, and fairness. It Guides the ethical deployment of AI technologies, ensures accountability, and builds public trust.

Hence, these potential innovations represent a glimpse into the transformative changes that could shape education, industry, and society in the coming decade. As these advancements unfold, careful consideration of ethical, regulatory, and societal implications will be essential to ensure that the benefits of innovation are widely shared and contribute positively to the well-being of individuals and communities.

9. CONCLUSION

The future perspectives of ChatGPT towards Industrial 4.0, Society 5.0, and Modern Education promise a paradigm shift in communication, decision-making, and learning. The potential applications of ChatGPT across these domains reflect a transformative landscape where human-machine collaboration, societal interactions, and education are redefined by advanced AI technologies. In Industrial 4.0, ChatGPT is poised to revolutionize smart manufacturing by enhancing communication, troubleshooting, and decision-making processes. The collaborative interplay between humans and machines, facilitated by ChatGPT, holds the key to increased efficiency, productivity, and agility in industrial workflows. Further, Society 5.0 envisions a future where technology is harnessed to enhance the well-being of individuals and society. ChatGPT emerges as a catalyst for human-centric communication, contributing to mental health support, counseling, and using meaningful interactions. As technology advances, the potential of ChatGPT to bridge the gap between humans and intelligent systems becomes increasingly evident, aligning with the principles of a harmonious and inclusive society. Hence, In the era of

Modern Education, ChatGPT is positioned to transform the learning experience. The growth of personalized, adaptive, and interactive educational interactions promises to cater to individual learning needs. ChatGPT's role as a supportive tutor, mentor, and collaborative learning tool contributes to the evolution of education towards a more dynamic, student-centric model. However, these promising prospects come with ethical responsibilities. The integration of ChatGPT must be approached with careful consideration of privacy, transparency, and the ethical implications of AI-driven interactions. Striking a balance between technological innovation and ethical considerations is essential to ensure a positive and inclusive impact on society.

As we navigate towards this future, collaboration among researchers, educators, policymakers, and industry stakeholders is paramount. Ongoing advancements in AI research, coupled with a commitment to responsible deployment, will be instrumental in harnessing the full potential of ChatGPT in shaping a future where technology enhances human experiences, uses collaboration, and contributes to the betterment of industrial processes, societal interactions, and education. The journey towards this future requires a thoughtful and collaborative effort to ensure that the transformative power of ChatGPT aligns with the values of a progressive and inclusive society.

REFERENCES

Cherukuvada, S., Krishnaraj, N., & Bellam, K. (2023, April). Federated Learning with Internet of Things for Data Privacy and Security. In *2023 International Conference on Networking and Communications (ICNWC)* (pp. 1-7). IEEE. DOI:10.1109/ICNWC57852.2023.10127281

Deekshetha, H. R., & Tyagi, A. K. (2023). Automated and intelligent systems for next-generation-based smart applications. In *Data Science for Genomics* (pp. 265–276). Academic Press., DOI:10.1016/B978-0-323-98352-5.00019-7

Fosso Wamba, S., Guthrie, C., Queiroz, M. M., & Minner, S. (2023). ChatGPT and generative artificial intelligence: An exploratory study of key benefits and challenges in operations and supply chain management. *International Journal of Production Research*, 1–21. DOI:10.1080/00207543.2023.2294116

Fui-Hoon Nah, F., Zheng, R., Cai, J., Siau, K., & Chen, L. (2023). Generative AI and ChatGPT: Applications, challenges, and AI-human collaboration. *Journal of Information Technology Case and Application Research*, 25(3), 277–304. DOI:10.1080/15228053.2023.2233814

Goyal, D., & Tyagi, A. K. (2020). A Look at Top 35 Problems in the Computer Science Field for the Next Decade. In *ICT for Competitive Strategies* (pp. 379–396). CRC Press. DOI:10.1201/9781003052098-40

Mishra, S., & Tyagi, A. K. (2022). The role of machine learning techniques in internet of things-based cloud applications. *Artificial intelligence-based internet of things systems*, 105-135. DOI:10.1007/978-3-030-87059-1_4

Nair, M. M., & Tyagi, A. K. (2023). *Blockchain technology for next-generation society: current trends and future opportunities for smart era*. Blockchain Technology for Secure Social Media Computing. DOI:10.1049/PBSE019E_ch11

Nair, M. M., & Tyagi, A. K. (2023). AI, IoT, blockchain, and cloud computing: The necessity of the future. In *Distributed Computing to Blockchain* (pp. 189–206). Academic Press. DOI:10.1016/B978-0-323-96146-2.00001-2

Nair, M. M., Tyagi, A. K., & Sreenath, N. (2021). The future with industry 4.0 at the core of society 5.0: Open issues, future opportunities and challenges. In *2021 international conference on computer communication and informatics (ICCCI)* (pp. 1-7). IEEE. DOI:10.1109/ICCCI50826.2021.9402498

Nair, M. M., & Tyagi, A. K. (2021). Privacy: History, statistics, policy, laws, preservation and threat analysis. *Journal of Information Assurance & Security, 16*(1).

Singh, R., Tyagi, A. K., & Arumugam, S. K. (2024). Imagining the Sustainable Future With Industry 6.0: A Smarter Pathway for Modern Society and Manufacturing Industries. In *Machine Learning Algorithms Using Scikit and TensorFlow Environments* (pp. 318-331). IGI Global. DOI:10.4018/978-1-6684-8531-6.ch016

Tyagi, A., Kukreja, S., Meghna, M. N., & Tyagi, A. K. (2022). Machine learning: Past, present and future. *NeuroQuantology : An Interdisciplinary Journal of Neuroscience and Quantum Physics*, 20(8), 4333. DOI:10.14704/nq.2022.20.8.NQ44468

Tyagi, A. K. (2023). Decentralized everything: Practical use of blockchain technology in future applications. In *Distributed Computing to Blockchain* (pp. 19–38). Academic Press. DOI:10.1016/B978-0-323-96146-2.00010-3

Tyagi, A. K. (2024). Transformative Effects of ChatGPT on the Modern Era of Education and Society: From Society's and Industry's Perspectives. In *Machine Learning Algorithms Using Scikit and TensorFlow Environments* (pp. 374–387). IGI Global. DOI:10.1007/978-3-030-71187-0_1

Tyagi, A. K., Bansal, R., & Dananjayan, S. (2022). A Step-To-Step Guide to Write a Quality Research Article. In *International Conference on Intelligent Systems Design and Applications* (pp. 374-383). Cham: Springer Nature Switzerland. DOI:10.1007/978-3-031-35510-3_36

Tyagi, A. K., Dananjayan, S., Agarwal, D., & Thariq Ahmed, H. F. (2023). Blockchain—Internet of Things Applications: Opportunities and Challenges for Industry 4.0 and Society 5.0. *Sensors (Basel)*, 23(2), 947. DOI:10.3390/s23020947 PMID:36679743

Tyagi, A. K., Fernandez, T. F., Mishra, S., & Kumari, S. (2020). Intelligent automation systems at the core of industry 4.0. In *International conference on intelligent systems design and applications* (pp. 1-18). Cham: Springer International Publishing. DOI:10.1007/978-3-030-71187-0_1

Tyagi, A. K., & Tiwari, S. (2024). The future of artificial intelligence in blockchain applications. In *Machine Learning Algorithms using Scikit and TensorFlow Environments* (pp. 346–373). IGI Global. DOI:10.4018/978-1-6684-8531-6.ch018

Yakin, M., & Linden, K. (2021). Adaptive e-learning platforms can improve student performance and engagement in dental education. *Journal of Dental Education*, 85(7), 1309–1315. DOI:10.1002/jdd.12609 PMID:33825184

Zhan, Z., He, L., Tong, Y., Liang, X., Guo, S., & Lan, X. (2022). The effectiveness of gamification in programming education: Evidence from a meta-analysis. *Computers and Education: Artificial Intelligence*, 100096. Advance online publication. DOI:10.1016/j.caeai.2022.100096

Chapter 6

Generative AI and Its Impact on Creative Thinking Abilities in Higher Education Institutions

Mareena Francis Kaitharath
Christ University, Bangalore, India

Shifna K. N.
Christ University, Bangalore, India

Anuradha P. S.
Christ University, Bangalore, India

ABSTRACT

Generative AI technologies such as ChatGPT have started gaining increased popularity among higher education institutions. Students, as well as teaching professionals, can utilize these tools for various academic purposes due to the immense benefits they provide by way of customization of data generated and ease of access to data. However, this chapter seeks to analyze how such tools may impact students' creative thinking ability. It also analyses the drawbacks faced by teachers after implementation of such tools. The methodology adopted for the study was two surveys: one administered to gather students' opinions and the other for understanding teachers' perspectives. The analysis of the data collected shows that the over-reliance of students on such generative AI tools might hinder students' ability to think creatively to some extent. The chapter also suggests some of the strategies that can be adopted

DOI: 10.4018/979-8-3693-2418-9.ch006

by teachers to ensure students' capabilities are assessed accurately.

INTRODUCTION

In today's world, every activity is driven by large chunks of data. There has been an increasing need to find ways to simplify and gain valuable insights from large data sets. Generative artificial intelligence technologies provide helpful information by studying the patterns of the data it is trained on and generating data with similar characteristics. Generative artificial intelligence technologies have emerged as powerful tools that can analyze and replicate patterns within the data they are trained on, offering potential opportunities to transform the educational sector significantly (Baidoo-Anu & Ansah, 2023). Unlike traditional artificial intelligence that analyzes data or interprets information, generative artificial intelligence creates new content on its own. Deep learning is one of the key techniques used in generative artificial intelligence to generate unique content in just a single click (Hwang et al., 2020). This AI system is designed to learn patterns and structures from existing data and use that knowledge to create new, similar content.

Some of the most popular generative artificial intelligence tools include ChatGPT, introduced by OpenAI in November 2022, which created a revolution in almost every field. ChatGPT is known to be great with words that seem natural and engaging compared to other chatbots. Bard, now called Gemini, the AI tool developed by Google in March 2023, simplifies the information search process by quickly summarizing relevant information from various sources on Google. LLaMa, released by Meta in February 2023, is an AI tool that proved to be more efficient and available to wide spectrum of users.

Emerging generative artificial intelligence technologies, like ChatGPT, Bard, and LLaMa, along with their growing popularity, hold the promise of significant change in the educational sphere. These AI technologies possess the capability to revolutionize education by addressing the unique learning needs of each student. They can analyze vast data sets, recognize patterns, and customize educational materials to suit the individual preferences and requirements of learners (Chan & Hu, 2023). The transformative potential of generative artificial intelligence in higher education extends beyond teaching methods, with the ability to transform content generation, research, and problem-solving. Such AI tools could also act as instruments that encourage students to explore unconventional approaches to completing assignments, thereby fostering creativity.

However, the increasing over-reliance on such technologies by students is one of the significant challenges or concerns posed by artificial intelligence in the education sector. In this era where such generative artificial intelligence technologies are transforming traditional teaching practices, it is questionable whether this transformation cultivates or hinders the development of creative thinking skills among students. Instead of utilizing generative AI-driven tools for a better understanding of concepts, some students may resort to such technologies for most of their academic work rather than using their capabilities. Over the years, it could inadvertently tarnish the core objective of the education system, which is to foster the growth and development of an individual. This would create the need for developing more reliable assessment structures to evaluate the students' true potential.

Creativity is considered as an essential skill in the 21st century, thus making it important for students to nurture their creative thinking skills in order to adapt easily (Creely et al., 2023). Creativity is essential to foster innovation and problem-solving skills which is necessary in today's rapidly changing competitive world. It encourages diverse perspectives that help students find novel solutions to problems, which helps them adapt to the evolving job markets, where creative skills are tremendously valued. Since most jobs have more automated processes, the requirement of a human touch is only necessary in areas where creativity is essential.

This chapter dwells on how generative artificial intelligence technologies will impact the creativity of the students at the higher education level, thereby evaluating the impact on their overall personal development. Overall, this study would help gain an initial understanding of the issue. Through this study, we hope to contribute to the ongoing discussions surrounding the use of artificial intelligence technologies in the educational sector and provide valuable insights that can help the development of effective policies and strategies for their use without hindering the students' creativity.

Objectives

- To analyze the extent of popularity and usage of generative AI tools for academic purposes among students at the higher education level
- To examine the impact of generative artificial intelligence technologies on the creativity of students at the higher education level
- To gather students' opinions on the benefits and concerns in utilizing generative AI tools for academic purposes
- To understand the challenges that teachers may face in accurately assessing a student's capabilities or the genuineness of assignments submitted by them during performance assessments
- To suggest methods or strategies that teachers can adopt to ensure students do not overly rely on AI tools for their academic tasks

REVIEW OF LITERATURE

Digital Transformation in the Education Sector

Human and non-human interaction is pervasive since AI is on the rise. The education field is also one among the many fields going through a digital transformation. AI studies in education in half a century is reviewed and research areas related to this are identified and presented in the article "Intelligence and Reflections from Educational Landscape: A Review of AI Studies in Half a Century". (Bozkurt et al., 2021) The study "Information and Communication Technologies in Higher Education: Comparison of Stimulated Motivation" explains the use of any kind of technology in the classroom, especially during and after the Covid-19 pandemic. How such technologies kept the students motivated is analyzed using a three-stage experimental design among engineering students. The students' perspective on employing various technologies as a teaching aid for their educational journey is analyzed and the best motivating technological tool is identified. When compared to traditional lectures, it was found that acceptance and motivation to learn were high in all of the technologies studied. (Arredondo, 2023) The paper titled "Students' voices on generative AI: perceptions, benefits, and challenges in higher education" studies the perception of students towards rising generative artificial intelligence technologies such as ChatGPT. Along with understanding its potential benefits and challenges, the study also focused on understanding students' familiarity and willingness to engage with such technologies. To enhance the teaching and learning experience in higher education, this study helps implement the responsible use of GenAI tools by overcoming the concerns. The survey involving 399 participants revealed an overall positive attitude toward the use of GenAI in education, which includes both enthusiasm and concerns. (Chan & Hu, 2023) "Exploring the Potential of Generative Artificial Intelligence in Education: Applications, Challenges, and Future Research Directions" is a paper that highlights that generative artificial intelligence (GAI) tools such as ChatGPT and Midjourney have gained a lot of popularity in recent times and it is predicted that its use will increase rapidly in the future. The paper explores the difficulties of generative AI-driven learning through the lenses of scholarly investigation and educational goals, supported by practical instances. This unique perspective distinguishes GAI from traditional AI, chatbots, and information systems. GAI-based learning applications include academic article proofreading, content analysis, question item generation, and rubric development. (Hwang & Chen, 2023)

Benefits of Generative Artificial Intelligence

The article "Vision, challenges, roles and research issues of Artificial Intelligence in Education" opens by emphasizing the growing utilization of AI in diverse fields, including voice and image recognition, decision-making, and natural language processing, employing methodologies such as machine learning and deep learning. The paper highlights aspects regarding how artificial intelligence (AI), such as intelligent tutoring systems or robots in classrooms, can improve learning, engagement, and educational policymaking. The article goes on to examine how adaptive learning systems and intelligent tutoring systems can help with this goal as well as how human teachers' knowledge and skills must be included in AI-driven educational systems. The article also investigates the impact of AI on higher-order thinking as well as the potential applications of AI outside of the traditional system. (Hwang et al., 2020) The article "The Rise of Generative Artificial Intelligence and Its Impact on Education: The Promises and Perils" examines the quick development and growing popularity of GAI-driven applications like ChatGPT, which can produce text, code, artwork, and other content in response to user input. The phrase "prompt engineering" is introduced in the article as a technique to maximize the effectiveness of GAI tools by using relevant and coherent prompts. The paper also highlights how utilizing GAI to summarize literature, identify research gaps, and enhance various components of the research process might revolutionize research. (Murugesan & Cherukuri, 2023) The impact of large language models (LLMs), including ChatGPT and GPT4, on the education industry is covered in the article "Generative Artificial Intelligence and the Education Sector". The author discusses the use of LLMs by educators to automate the grading of essays, tests, and assignments, freeing up time for other aspects of teaching. The article also addresses the potential increase in plagiarism facilitated by LLMs, and how AI tools are being developed to detect AI-generated text, known as "AIgiarism". These tools aim to distinguish between AI-generated and human-written text and are expected to provide a countermeasure to plagiarism assisted by AI tools. To evaluate student understanding and discourage cheating, institutions can impose policies, and additional requirements for assignments using AI, and oral presentations. Additionally, focusing assignments on recent news events can be a strategy to minimize the use of older training data. (Ahmad et al., 2023) The authors of 'Generative AI and the future of education: Ragnarok or Reformation? A paradoxical perspective from management educators argue that generative AI can be used for personalized learning experience for students and how it can be done by tailoring the contents as per the students' need which in turn helps to create collaborative and interactive learning. This use of generative AI can create a Ragnarok (destruction) in the educational sector. (Lim et al., 2023) In a paper titled "Generative Artificial Intelligence in Education, Part One: The Dynamic

Frontier," the potential of generative AI is examined in relation to education. The writers emphasize the need for a dynamic and flexible learning environment that can accommodate students' various demands. The application of generative AI in creating content is one of the major topics raised in the article. Teachers can develop interactive and dynamic learning materials, such as virtual simulations, interactive storytelling, and immersive virtual reality experiences, by utilizing generative AI models. These cutting-edge methods can raise student interest and encourage more thorough comprehension of the material. Generative AI models may dynamically modify the learning content and pace to suit unique learning preferences by examining student data and behavior. This personalized approach can help students grasp concepts more effectively and efficiently. (Hsu & Ching, 2023)

The paper "Artificial Intelligence in Education: Addressing Ethical Challenges in K-12 settings" discusses what artificial intelligence is and its educational applications such as personalized learning platforms, automated assessment systems, facial recognition systems and predictive analytics, social networking sites, and chatbots. It then goes on to discuss how to navigate the ethical challenges and potential risks and concerns of using AI in education. (Akgün & Greenhow, 2021) The opinion paper "So what if ChatGPT wrote it?" Multidisciplinary perspectives on opportunities, challenges and implications of generative conversational AI for research, practice and policy" provides an overview of the opportunities, challenges, and implications of generative conversational AI (GCAI). The author discusses how AI systems can assist researchers in data analysis, literature review, and hypothesis generation. The article has used a mixed methodology approach which involves both quantitative and qualitative methods to collect and analyze data. The quantitative data was collected through a survey of various industrial experts discussing their views on GCAI and the qualitative data was collected through a review of literature. (Dwivedi et al., 2023) The article "The Rise of Generative Artificial Intelligence (AI) Language Models - Challenges and Opportunities for Geographical and Environmental Education" analyzes how generative AI language models might affect geographic and environmental education. According to the author, generative AI has the ability to produce more individualized and interesting learning experiences for students, better preparing them for environmental issues in the future. The creation of accurate simulations and case studies using generative AI language models enables students to sharpen their skills in a secure setting. Students can receive immediate feedback on their performance by using AI language models, which can help them identify the areas of improvement. (Chang & Kidman, 2023) The article "Artificial Intelligence, Web 3, and the Future of Distance Education" examines the idea of Web 3 and how it might alter the nature of education. The authors discuss how Web 3 technologies can use AI to build immersive learning environments like virtual and augmented reality that replicate real-world experiences and enhance student engagement. The paper explores the possibilities of blockchain technology in providing lifelong learning records and credential verification. This enhances ongoing skill development, maintains the validity and transferability of learners' accomplishments, and fosters a more adaptable and dynamic educational ecology. (Diehl, 2023)

Concerns With the Use of Generative AI in Education

Artificial intelligence (AI) is a rapidly developing field with the potential to revolutionize many industries, including education. However, there is also a lot of hype surrounding AI, and it is important to be aware of both the potential benefits and risks of its use in education. In the paper 'The threat, hype, and promise of artificial intelligence in education', the researcher has discussed Artificial intelligence and how Artificial intelligence has a huge potential for efficiency and cost reduction. The study highlights the role of teachers in education with the use of AI, the alignment of AI with pedagogical goals, and the strengths, weaknesses, opportunities, and threats that AI can present in the educational sector. (Humble & Mozelius, 2022) The article "New Era of Artificial Intelligence in Education: Towards a Sustainable Multifaceted Revolution" explores the potential advantages and difficulties that artificial intelligence (AI) offers to modernize education. The paper analyzes the use of ChatGPT to standardize academics and the ethical issues it raises for the education system, and it makes the case that using AI in education is the only way ahead while putting safeguards in place to prevent its misuse. (Kamalov et al., 2023) The study "Ethical Principles for Artificial Intelligence in Education" investigates the requirement for ethical principles to control AI's creation, application, and utilization in educational contexts. It acknowledges that while AI has many advantages, like personalized learning, adaptive teaching, and better educational outcomes, there are ethical issues that need to be resolved to ensure its ethical and equitable usage. Transparency in AI systems used in education is one of the study's main concepts. The authors argue that transparency is essential to establish trust and comprehend how AI algorithms make judgments that affect students' learning experiences. They promote the thorough documenting of AI algorithms, data sources, and decision-making procedures to maintain accountability and prevent biases or discriminatory behaviors. (Nguyen et al., 2022)

One of the Most Prominent Generative AI Tool: ChatGPT

Natural language models like ChatGPT were trained on massive text datasets from the internet which makes it possible to respond to a large number of prompts. The use and potential implications of ChatGPT since its release in November 2022 have presented numerous advantages and disadvantages for the education sector. AI has the potential to improve the transfer of knowledge, dispel misconceptions, and promote critical thinking skills among students, while also acknowledging concerns of academic dishonesty, integrity, and malpractices. The paper "AI in Higher Education: A Literature Review of ChatGPT and Guidelines for Responsible Implementation" presents a theoretical and conceptual framework on how to utilize ChatGPT effectively, keeping in mind the possibility of its hype. (Perera & Lankathilaka, 2023) The history and the principles behind ChatGPT and other similar models are discussed in relation to its potential impact on the educational system, along with the underlying ethical issues in the article titled "ChatGPT and a New Academic Reality: Artificial Intelligence-Written Research Papers and the Ethics of the Large Language Models in Scholarly Publishing". Authorship, copyright, and plagiarism are highlighted as some of the concerns surrounding the use of ChatGPT in the academic field, and also its impact on academic job expectations, tenure and promotions is discussed. (Lund et al., 2023) The paper "Reconceptualizing ChatGPT and generative AI as a student-driven Innovation in Higher Education" focuses on the necessity to integrate AI into curricula and emphasizes the change from learning via AI to learning with AI. The article discusses the historical development and adoption of AI technologies in higher education based on the review of existing articles and the key milestones and advancements in AI applications for teaching and learning with various examples of surveys conducted in universities. (Dai et al., 2023) The paper "Education in the Era of Generative Artificial Intelligence (AI): Understanding the Potential Benefits of ChatGPT in Promoting Teaching and Learning" discusses the benefits of ChatGPT in promoting teaching and learning such as personalized tutoring, automated essay grading, language translation, interactive learning and adaptive learning. It also highlights the inherent limitations of ChatGPT such as biases in data training, privacy issues and generating wrong information, lack of human interaction, limited understanding, and lack of creativity or contextual understanding. (Baidoo-Anu & Ansah, 2023) In ground-breaking research titled "Unlocking the Power of ChatGPT: A Framework for Applying Generative AI in Education," the potential of ChatGPT, an effective generative AI model, is examined in the context of education. The author emphasizes how ChatGPT might transform the way educational content is provided and customized because it can produce human-like responses in real time. ChatGPT enables lively, engaging interactions between students, which promotes collaborative learning. Additionally, it can automate the evaluation process by reviewing student replies and providing immediate feedback. The paper brings into light different benefits and challenges that the ChatGPT possesses and also gives policies and practices that can be used to overcome such challenges. (Su & Yang, 2023) In the review paper 'The Potential Impact of ChatGPT on Education: Using History as a Rearview Mirror' an examination is made, drawing parallels between generative artificial intelligence and five educational technologies from the past.

The paper discusses that AI technology has the potential to evolve into a knowledge generator, thereby serving as an educational AI tool to enhance teaching and learning outcomes. By interacting with its historical equivalents, this cutting-edge educational technology, called generative artificial intelligence, creates a more complex landscape of educational technology. (Wang & Guo, 2023)

Future Implications of Generative AI in Education

"Chatbots in Education and Research: A Critical Examination of Ethical Implications and Solutions" is an article that examines the ethical perspective of the use of AI systems and chatbots in the academic field. The potential for its misuse and exploitation is examined and effective solutions to such dilemmas are proposed. Assessment methods will need to be more innovative and creative. The study analyzes how chatbots act as research assistants as well as how to avoid their misuse. (Kooli, 2023) The article "Generative Artificial Intelligence Empowers Educational Reform: Current Status, Issues, and Prospects" identifies problems in the present application of generative artificial intelligence in education such as opacity and unexplainability, data privacy and security, personalization and fairness, and effectiveness and reliability, through an in-depth analysis. The solutions are suggested for such problems and the prospects for future development such as personalized education, intelligent teaching, collaborative education, and virtual teaching are explored. (Yu & Guo, 2023) "The Promises and Challenges of Artificial Intelligence for Teachers: A Systematic Review of Research" is an article that gives an overview of teachers' use of artificial intelligence (AI) applications and machine learning methods. It seeks to understand what advantages and challenges teachers face when using artificial intelligence for education. Teachers can take advantage of artificial intelligence in the planning, implementation as well as assessment stages. (Celik et al., 2022) The review paper "Artificial Intelligence for Student Assessment: A Systematic Review" discusses the functionalities of AI in assessments such as automatic grading of students, particularly in other educational levels than higher education. The study involves a systematic review of 100 papers. (Calatayud et al., 2021) The article titled "On ChatGPT and Beyond: How Generative Artificial Intelligence May Affect Research, Teaching, and Practice" examines how generative AI impacts the way academic research, teaching, and business practice are conducted. By listing the opportunities and threats, the paper also highlights some interesting avenues for future research. (Peres et al., 2023) Internet of Things, swarm intelligence, deep learning, and neuroscience, as well as an assessment of AI in education, social and ethical issues due to inappropriate use of AI technologies, and the changing roles of teachers and students are the research trends suggested for further investigation in the paper "A Review of Artificial Intelligence (AI) in Education from 2010 to 2020". (Zhai et al., 2021)

METHODOLOGY

The methodology employed in this research study centers on the use of surveys in the form of questionnaires to gather diverse opinions and perspectives from students and faculty from various higher education institutions. The surveys aimed to collect valuable insights into the impact of generative artificial intelligence on the students' creativity.

The survey was conducted in two dimensions: one survey was conducted to gather students' opinions, and the second survey was to gather the teachers' perspectives. The first survey was administered to 290 respondents, who are students currently pursuing their undergraduate, postgraduate, or doctoral studies or professional courses at higher education institutions. The second survey was conducted to gather opinions and perspectives from 44 teaching professionals from the higher education sector. Participation in the survey was completely voluntary. By incorporating multiple viewpoints, the research strives to provide a comprehensive understanding of the relationship between the use of generative artificial intelligence tools and creativity in higher education students.

The surveys were administered via online questionnaire as Google form, consisting of mostly closed-ended questions and one open-ended question. The questionnaire was developed by brainstorming the aspects that would reflect the impact of the usage of generative AI tools on the creativity of students. The data collected from the survey was analyzed using SPSS software to gain better insights.

The survey among students consisted of four questions to collect their demographic details such as name, gender, age, and the course they were currently pursuing. This was followed by 11 multiple-choice questions and one open-ended question. Most of the questions have followed a 5-point Likert scale. The survey included questions to assess the popularity of various generative AI tools, the extent of their usage for academic purposes and the usefulness of such tools, how the students assess their own level of creativity, and the impact on creativity after the introduction of such tools. They were also asked for their opinion on whether the introduction of such tools has made it challenging for the teachers to assess students' capabilities and genuineness of their assignments. Finally, the benefits and challenges of using such generative AI tools are examined, and the last open-ended question seeks answers to how students could utilize such tools in a manner that does not adversely impact their creative thinking skills.

The survey among faculty consisted of three questions to collect their demographic details such as name, gender, and years of teaching experience. This is followed by 9 multiple-choice questions and one open-ended question. Most of the questions have followed a 5-point Likert scale. The survey included questions to assess the extent of familiarity of teachers with such generative AI tools, the extent of usage of such tools by students for academic purposes, and whether it has impacted the students' creative thinking ability. Then, there were questions to understand whether it has become challenging for the teachers to accurately assess students' capabilities or if they have noticed any changes in the quality, originality, or authenticity of students' work after the introduction of such tools. Finally, they were asked how well they feel equipped to differentiate the work generated using such tools and those produced independently by students, and the open-ended question sought suggestions on the methods or strategies that teachers can adopt to ensure students do not overly rely on AI tools for their academic tasks.

ANALYSIS AND INTERPRETATION

1. Findings From Survey Among Students

Table 1. Demographic Characteristics of Respondents (Total 290 Respondents)

Demographic Profile	Categories	Number of Respondents	Percentage
Gender	Male	106	36.55%
	Female	184	63.45%
Age	17 - 20	83	28.62%
	21 - 24	189	65.17%
	25 and above	18	6.21%
Education Currently Pursuing	Undergraduate	107	36.9%
	Post Graduation	172	59.31%
	Doctoral Studies	4	1.38%
	Professional Courses	7	2.41%

Figure 1. Gender-Wise Categories of Respondents (Total 290 Respondents)

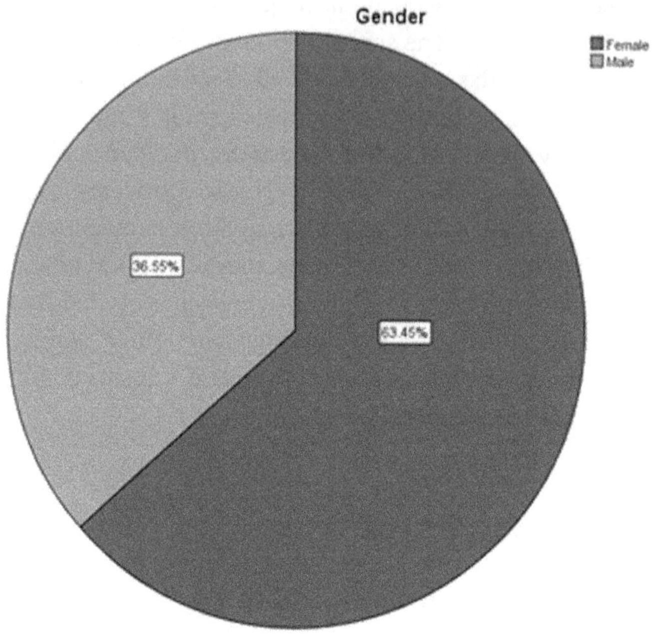

Figure 2. Age-Wise Categories of Respondents (Total 290 Respondents)

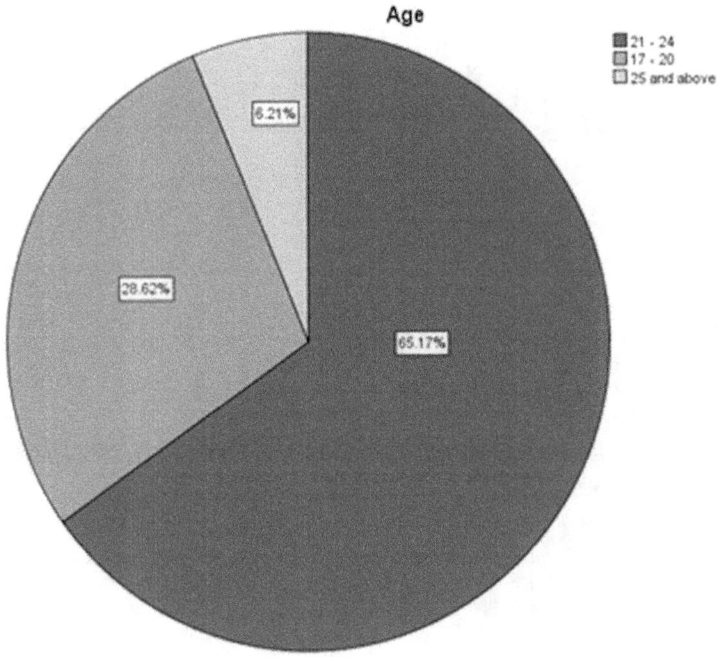

Figure 3. Categories of Respondents Based on Education Currently Pursuing (Total 290 Respondents)

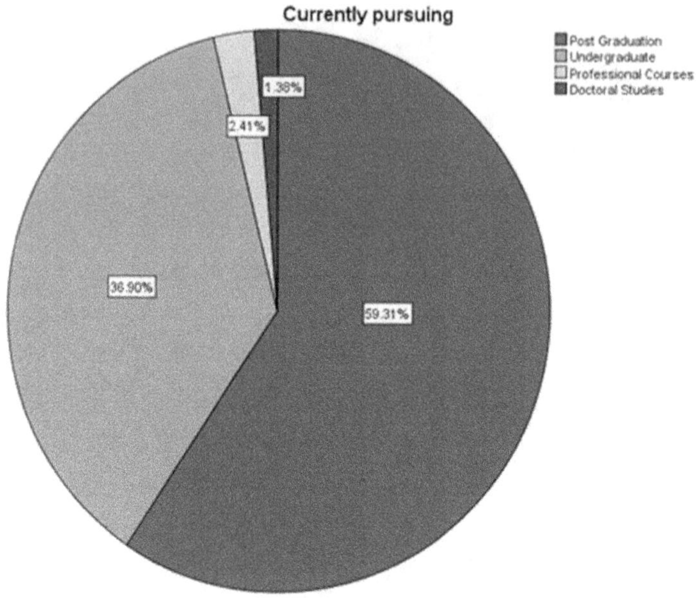

The survey circulated among the students consisted of 290 responses with the majority being female students (63.45%) and the remaining being male students (36.55%). Most of the respondents were in the range between 21-24 age group (65.17%), followed by those aged between 17-20 (28.62%). Only a small percentage of respondents were 25 years or above (6.21%). As for education, the majority of the respondents were pursuing their post-graduation studies (59.31%), followed by undergraduate studies (36.9%), a smaller number of respondents were engaged in doctoral studies (1.38%), and few respondents were also pursuing professional courses (2.41%).

2. Frequency Analysis

Table 2. Question - Have you ever referred to any generative AI tools like ChatGPT, Bard, LLaMa, etc, for your academic work?

		Frequency	Percent	Valid Percent	Cumulative Percent
Valid	Yes	273	94.1	94.1	94.1
	No	17	5.9	5.9	100.0
	Total	290	100.0	100.0	

Source: Computed

The data in Table 2 offers valuable insights into the extent of usage of generative AI tools like ChatGPT, Bard, LLaMa, etc, among respondents for academic purposes. The results show that most students, about 94.1%, have used these tools at least once. This means that many students find these tools helpful for their studies. On the other hand, a smaller group, about 5.9%, said they haven't used these tools for their academic work. This could be because they are not familiar with these generative AI tools or they prefer different ways of doing their academic work. Overall, the data shows that generative AI tools are becoming more popular among students for their academic work.

Table 3. Question - How frequently do you use generative AI tools like ChatGPT, Bard, LLaMa, etc, for your academic work?

		Frequency	Percent	Valid Percent	Cumulative Percent
Valid	1 = Not at all	16	5.5	5.5	5.5
	2.00	36	12.4	12.4	17.9
	3.00	116	40.0	40.0	57.9
	4.00	77	26.6	26.6	84.5
	5 = Always	45	15.5	15.5	100.0
	Total	290	100.0	100.0	

Source: Computed

Table 3 shows the findings from a survey done among 290 students. The goal was to see how much they use generative AI tools. The data reveals different levels of involvement with these tools. A significant 40% of respondents reported using generative AI tools regularly, rating them at 3.00 on the usage scale. This means that a considerable portion of students actively incorporate these tools into their academic work. Additionally, 26.6% of students use them even more often, rating them at 4.00, showing they really like and find them helpful. Some students, about

15.5%, said they use these tools "Always," indicating consistent usage. This highlights how often some students rely on these tools. On the other hand, 12.4% of students use these tools occasionally, rating them at 2.00. Meanwhile, a small but noticeable 5.5% of students don't use generative AI tools at all, showing that there is a notable portion of the student population who have yet to explore or utilize this technology.

Table 4. Question - On a 5-point scale, can you rate the usefulness of these generative AI tools for you?

		Frequency	Percent	Valid Percent	Cumulative Percent
Valid	1 = Not at all useful	3	1.0	1.0	1.0
	2.00	9	3.1	3.1	4.1
	3.00	74	25.5	25.5	29.7
	4.00	128	44.1	44.1	73.8
	5 = Very useful	76	26.2	26.2	100.0
	Total	290	100.0	100.0	

Source: Computed

Table 4 shows what people think about generative AI tools on a scale of 1 to 5, with 1 being "Not at all useful" and 5 being "Very useful". The data indicates a diverse range of opinions among respondents. A small minority, comprising 1.0% of the total, rated these tools at the lowest level, indicating that they find them not useful at all. Additionally, a slightly larger group, accounting for 3.1% of the total, rated the tools slightly higher, suggesting some utility but not to a significant extent. However, the most common rating among respondents was 3.00, chosen by 25.5% of the total. This indicates that a significant number of respondents consider these tools moderately helpful, showing a moderate level of acceptance and usefulness. Furthermore, a significant majority of respondents, representing 44.1% of the total, rated the usefulness of these tools at 4.00, indicating that they perceive them to be quite useful. Additionally, 26.2% of respondents rated the usefulness of these tools at the highest level, 5 = Very useful. This implies that a notable proportion of respondents strongly support and value the benefits that these generative AI tools offer in their work, demonstrating a high level of acceptance and usefulness.

Table 5. Mean Analysis (Descriptive Statistics)

	N	Minimum	Maximum	Mean
Frequency of usage of generative AI tools		1.00	5.00	3.3414
Usefulness of generative AI tools		1.00	5.00	3.9138
How generative AI impacted creative thinking ability		1.00	5.00	3.0000

continued on following page

Table 5. Continued

	N	Minimum	Maximum	Mean
Generative AI tools limits the development of creative skills		1.00	5.00	3.4276
Challenging for teachers to accurately assess students' capabilities		1.00	5.00	3.7759
Difficult for teachers to accurately assess the genuineness of the assignments		1.00	5.00	3.8069
Valid N (listwise)				

Source: Computed

The table presented above shows the mean analysis of the responses of the survey circulated among students in higher education. A total of 290 (N) participants provided responses attempting all variables, with no missing values. The Likert scale was employed for all questions, ranging from a minimum value of 1 to a maximum value of 5, with 3 representing the midpoint.

The findings revealed the frequency of using generative AI tools among participants to be moderate, as indicated by a mean score of 3.34 on a scale with a minimum value of 1, implying that they do not use these generative AI tools and a maximum value of 5, implying that they always use these generative AI tools. The result suggests that these tools are being integrated into educational practices but perhaps not extensively. In terms of usefulness, generative AI tools received relatively high ratings, with a mean score of 3.9138 on a scale with a minimum value of 1 implying that these generative AI tools are not useful and a maximum value of 5 implying that these generative AI tools are highly useful, this indicates that participants perceive these tools as effective in assisting various creative tasks, highlighting their potential to enhance productivity and creativity in their education. When assessing students' creative thinking abilities, the mean score was 3.41 on a scale of minimum value of 1 implying that they are not creative compared to their peers of the same age group, and the maximum value of 5 implying that they are highly creative; the result showed a moderate level suggesting that students possess some degree of creative thinking skills and there is room for improvement and development. Respondents reported a neutral stance on how generative AI impacted creative thinking ability, with a mean score of 3 on a scale of a minimum value of 1, implying that it has decreased their creativity and a maximum value of 5, implying that it has enhanced creativity. This suggests a lack of strong consensus among participants regarding the direct influence of generative AI on fostering creative thinking skills. The analysis also shows that concerns were raised regarding the potential limitations of generative AI tools in fostering the development of creative skills, as indicated by a mean score of 3.4276 on a scale of minimum value of 1, implying that they strongly agree and maximum value of 5 implying they strongly disagree. This suggests a perception among respondents that reliance on these tools may hinder their growth of creative abilities. Moreover, respondents highlighted challenges faced by teachers in accurately assessing students' capabilities and the genuineness of assignments, with mean scores of 3.7759 and 3.8069 on a scale of minimum value of 1, implying strongly disagree and a maximum value of 5 implying strongly agree. This highlights the complexities involved in incorporating generative AI tools into educational practices and the need for educators to navigate issues related to assessment and authenticity.

3. Independent Sample T-Test

Table 6. Group Statistics

	Gender	N	Mean	Std. Deviation	Std. Error Mean
Frequency of usage of generative AI tools	Male	106	3.2075	1.03939	.10095
	Female	184	3.4185	1.06298	.07836
Usefulness of generative AI tools	Male	106	3.9151	.85209	.08276
	Female	184	3.9130	.85765	.06323

Source: Computed

Table 6 shows group statistics based on gender as the independent variable and two dependent variables being the frequency of usage of generative AI tools and the usefulness of generative AI tools. From a total of 290 responses, it is observed that males have an average frequency of usage with a mean score of 3.2075, accompanied by a standard deviation of 1.03939 and a standard error mean of0.10095. Conversely, females exhibit a slightly higher mean score of 3.4185 for the frequency of usage, with a standard deviation of 1.06298 and a standard error mean of 0.07836. These findings suggest that, on average, females tend to utilize generative AI tools more frequently compared to males.. Regarding the usefulness of AI tools males present a mean score of 3.9151, along with a standard deviation of 0.85209 and a standard error mean of 0.08276, while for females, the mean score is 3.9130, with a standard deviation of 0.85765 and a standard error mean of 0.06323. These statistics indicate that there is a negligible difference in the perceived usefulness of AI tools between males and females.

Table 7. Independent Samples Test

		Levene's Test for Equality of Variances		t-test for Equality of Means						
									95% Confidence Interval of the Difference	
		F	Sig.	t	df	Sig. (2-tailed)	Mean Difference	Std. Error Difference	Lower	Upper
Frequency of usage of generative AI tools	Equal variances assumed	.501	.480	-1.641	288	.102	-.21093	.12858	-.46400	.04214
	Equal variances not assumed			-1.650	223.166	.100	-.21093	.12780	-.46278	.04092
Usefulness of generative AI tools	Equal variances assumed	.156	.694	.020	288	.984	.00205	.10433	-.20330	.20740
	Equal variances not assumed			.020	220.277	.984	.00205	.10415	-.20321	.20731

Source: Computed

Table 7 represents independent sample t-test results. Generally, an independent samples test holds good if there exist equal variances across the variables studied. It is tested with the help of Levene's Test for Equality of Variances. From the above table, it is clear that the computed significance value of 0.480 for the Frequency of usage of generative AI tools and 0.694 for the Usefulness of generative AI tools are both more than the acceptable significance value of 0.05. Thus, it can be concluded that mean differences between males and females are insignificant with respect to their frequency of usage of generative AI tools as well as the usefulness of generative AI tools.

4. One-Way Anova

4.1 Independent Variable - Age

Table 8. Dependent Variables - Frequency of usage of generative AI tools, Usefulness of generative AI tools

		Sum of Squares	df	Mean Square	F	Sig.
Frequency of usage of generative AI tools	Between Groups	3.650	2	1.825	1.639	
	Within Groups	319.553		1.113		
	Total	323.203				

continued on following page

Table 8. Continued

		Sum of Squares	df	Mean Square	F	Sig.
Usefulness of generative AI tools	Between Groups	5.306	2	2.653	3.704	
	Within Groups	205.539		.716		
	Total	210.845				

The table displays the results of a one-way ANOVA, examining the relationship between age (the independent variable) and two dependent variables: frequency of usage of generative AI tools and usefulness of generative AI tools. For the frequency of usage of generative AI tools, the ANOVA results indicate that there is no statistically significant difference between age groups (0.196 > 0.05). This suggests that age does not have a significant impact on the frequency of usage of these tools among respondents. However, when considering the usefulness of generative AI tools, the ANOVA results reveal a statistically significant difference between age groups (0.026 < 0.05). This indicates that there are significant differences in how different age groups perceive the usefulness of these tools.

4.2 Independent Variable - Education Currently Pursuing

Table 9. Dependent Variables - Frequency of usage of generative AI tools, Usefulness of generative AI tools

		Sum of Squares	df	Mean Square	F	Sig.
Frequency of usage of generative AI tools	Between Groups	21.323	3	7.108	6.734	
	Within Groups	301.880		1.056		
	Total	323.203				
Usefulness of generative AI tools	Between Groups	4.080	3	1.360	1.881	
	Within Groups	206.765		.723		
	Total	210.845				

The one-way ANOVA table examines the relationship between education currently pursuing (independent variable) and two dependent variables: the frequency of usage of generative AI tools and the usefulness of generative AI tools. For the frequency of usage of generative AI tools, the ANOVA results reveal a statistically significant difference between groups (0.000 < 0.05). This suggests that there are significant variations in the frequency of usage across different education levels currently being pursued by respondents. However, when considering the usefulness of generative AI tools, the ANOVA results do not show a statistically significant difference between groups (0.133 > 0.05). This indicates that the usefulness of these tools does not significantly vary across different education levels currently being pursued by the respondents. These findings suggest that factors related to education level may influence the frequency of usage of generative AI tools, but they do not seem to affect how useful these tools are perceived to be.

5. Regression

Dependent Variable - Self rating on creative thinking ability
Independent Variable - Frequency of usage of generative AI tools

Table 10. Model Summary[b]

					Change Statistics					
Model	R	R Square	Adjusted R Square	Std. Error of the Estimate	R Square Change	F Change			Sig. F Change	Durbin-Watson
1	.166[a]	.028	.024	.75836	.028	8.197	1		.005	2.063

a. Predictors: (Constant), Frequency of usage of generative AI tools
b. Dependent Variable: Creative thinking ability of the student

The above table represents the model summary. The R-value represents the correlation between observed and predicted values. Here, the R-value is 0.166, indicating a weak positive correlation between the creative thinking ability of the students and the predictor frequency of usage of generative AI tools. R square value indicates variance in the dependent variable explained by the independent variable. In this case, the R square value is 0.028, which means the 2.8% variation in the creative thinking ability of the students is explained by the frequency of usage of generative AI tools. The adjusted R square is the R square value accounted for standard error. The adjusted R square is 0.024, which considers the number of predictors in the model and is slightly lower than the R Square value. The standard error is approximately 0.75836, suggesting that the model's predictions may have a margin of error around this value. The Durbin-Watson statistic is a test for autocorrelation in the residuals of the regression model. In this case, the value of 2.063 suggests that there is no significant autocorrelation between the variables.

Table 11. ANOVA[a]

Model		Sum of Squares	df	Mean Square	F	Sig.
1	Regression	4.714	1	4.714	8.197	.005[b]
	Residual	165.630	288	.575		
	Total	170.345	289			

a. Dependent Variable: Creative thinking ability of the student
b. Predictors: (Constant), Frequency of usage of generative AI tools

The suitability of the variable to perform regression was further tested with the help of ANOVA.

ANOVA is significant at 1% level since the computed value 0.005 is less than 0.01. Thus, there is a significant difference in the creative thinking ability of the student with respect to the frequency of usage of generative AI tools.

Table 12. Coefficients[a]

Model		Unstandardized Coefficients		Standardized Coefficients			95.0% Confidence Interval for B	
		B	Std. Error	Beta	t	Sig.	Lower Bound	Upper Bound
	(Constant)	3.010	.148		20.365		2.719	3.301
	Frequency of usage of generative AI tools	.121	.042	.166	2.863		.038	.204

a. Dependent Variable: Creative thinking ability of the student

The value 0.121 represents the effect of frequency of usage of generative AI tools on the creative thinking ability of the students. It shows the degree to which the frequency of usage of generative AI tools impacts the creative thinking ability of the students.

Table 13. Residuals Statistics[a]

	Minimum	Maximum	Mean	Std. Deviation	N
Predicted Value	3.1310	3.6141	3.4138	.12772	290
Residual	-2.61411	1.86898	.00000	.75704	290
Std. Predicted Value	-2.214	1.568	.000	1.000	290
Std. Residual	-3.447	2.465	.000	.998	290

a. Dependent Variable: Creative thinking ability of the student

The residual statistics give us an idea of how well our regression model is doing. The "Predicted Value" tells us what the model expects the creative thinking ability rating to be for each student. The lowest expected rating is around 3.1310, while the highest is about 3.6141, with an average of around 3.4138. The small standard deviation of 0.12772 indicates that the predicted values are relatively close to the mean, suggesting that the model's predictions are consistent across the sample. The "Residual" shows the difference between what the model predicts and what was actually observed. A residual of 0.0000 indicates that, on average, the model's predictions are accurate with no systematic bias towards overestimation or underestimation. The largest underestimation is around 2.61411 points below the prediction, and the largest overestimation is about 1.86898 points above. On average, though, the predictions are right on target. The "Std. Predicted Value" and "Std. Residual" are standardized versions of these values, which help us compare them across different models. Overall, these numbers suggest our model does a decent job of predicting creative thinking ability based on how often students use generative AI tools.

Table 14. Correlation

	Frequency of usage of generative AI tools	Usefulness of generative AI tools	Creative thinking ability of the student	How generative AI impacted creative thinking ability	Generative AI tools limit the development of creative skills	Challenging for teachers to accurately assess students' capabilities	Difficult for teachers to accurately assess the genuineness of the assignments
Frequency of usage of generative AI tools	1	.496**	.166**	.161**	-.046	.120*	.149*
Usefulness of generative AI tools		1	.318**	.175**	-.087	.215**	.305**
Creative thinking ability of the student			1	.259**	-.080	.086	.112
How generative AI impacted creative thinking ability				1	.041	.054	.070
Generative AI tools limit the development of creative skills					1	-.344**	-.349**
Challenging for teachers to accurately assess students' capabilities						1	.558**
Difficult for teachers to accurately assess the genuineness of the assignments							1

The above table shows the Karl Pearsons' correlation between the questions from the survey that is circulated among the students.

The table shows that the correlation between the frequency of usage of generative AI tools and the usefulness of generative AI tools is 0.496, indicating a moderate positive correlation and a significant level of 1%.

The correlation between the frequency of usage of generative AI tools and the creative thinking ability of the student is 0.166, indicating a weak positive correlation and a significant level of 1%.

The correlation between the frequency of usage of generative AI tools and How generative AI impacted creative thinking ability is 0.161, indicating a weak positive correlation and a significant level at 1%.

The correlation between the frequency of usage of generative AI tools and how challenging it is for teachers to accurately assess students' capabilities is 0.120, indicating a weak positive correlation and a significant level of 5%.

The correlation between the frequency of usage of generative AI tools and the difficulty for teachers to accurately assess the genuineness of the assignments is 0.149, indicating a weak positive correlation and a significant level at 5%.

The correlation between the Usefulness of generative AI tools and the Creative thinking ability of the student is 0.318, indicating a weak positive correlation and a significant level at 1%.

The correlation between the Usefulness of generative AI tools and How generative AI impacted creative thinking ability is 0.175 indicating a weak positive correlation and significant level at 1%.

The correlation between the Usefulness of generative AI tools and how challenging it is for teachers to accurately assess students' capabilities is 0.215, indicating a weak positive correlation and a significant level at 1%.

The correlation between the Usefulness of generative AI tools and the Difficulty for teachers to accurately assess the genuineness of the assignments is 0.305, indicating a weak positive correlation and a significant level of 1%.

The correlation between the Creative thinking ability of the student and How generative AI impacted creative thinking ability is 0.259, indicating a weak positive correlation and a significant level at 1%.

The correlation between the Generative AI tools limiting the development of creative skills and How Challenging it is for teachers to accurately assess students' capabilities is -0.344, indicating a weak negative correlation and a significant level at 1%.

The correlation between how Generative AI tools limit the development of creative skills, and the Difficulty for teachers to accurately assess the genuineness of the assignments is -0.349, indicating a weak negative correlation and a significant level of 1%.

The correlation between the difficulty for teachers to accurately assess students' capabilities and the Difficulty for teachers to accurately assess the genuineness of the assignments is 0.558, indicating a moderate positive correlation and a significant level at 1%.

Figure 4. Generative AI tools that students have used or interacted with

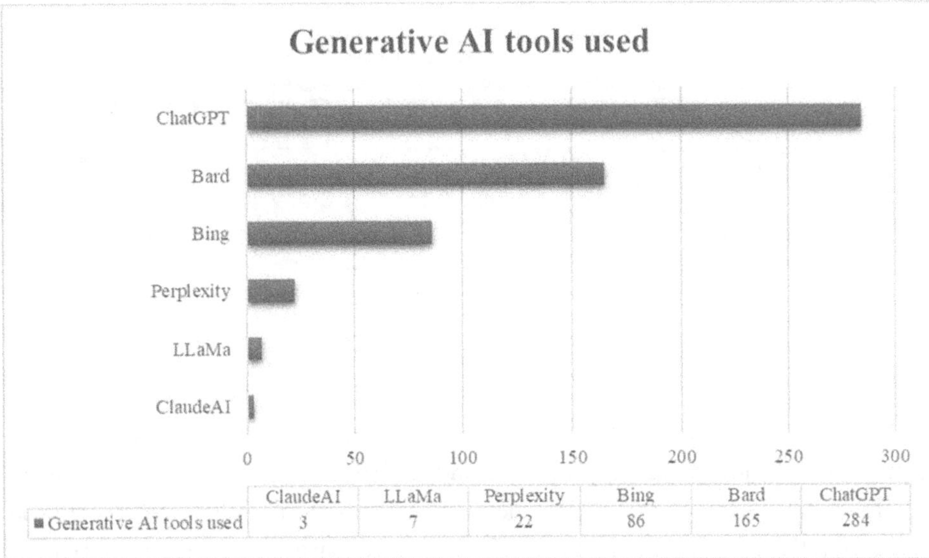

The graph depicts the various generative artificial intelligence tools students are familiar with or have utilized for academic purposes. Out of 290 responses from students pursuing higher education, 284 respondents reported familiarity with and usage of ChatGPT, making it the most commonly used tool. Following ChatGPT, Bard (now Gemini) was utilized by 165 respondents, while 86 respondents have used Bing. Perplexity garnered 22 responses, with LLaMa and ClaudeAI following with 7 and 3 responses respectively. This shows that Generative AI plays a major role in the Higher education system. Apart from the above popular tools, other generative AI tools respondents have used include Clickup, Monica, Tome, Elicit, Dall E, Eleven Labs, QuillBot, Grammarly, etc.

Figure 5. Benefits of utilizing generative AI technologies for academic purposes

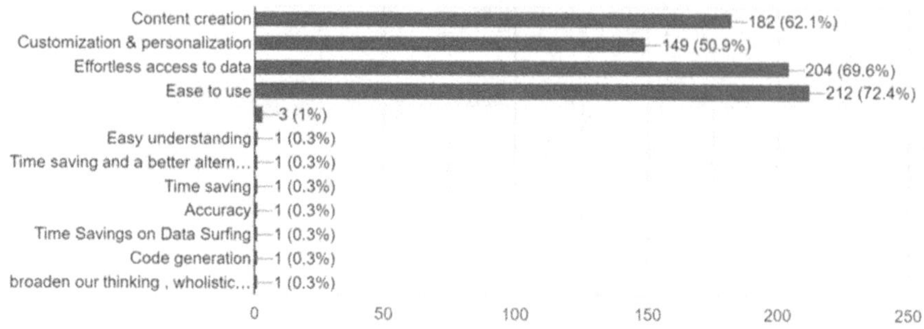

The graph shows the benefits of utilizing generative AI technologies for academic purposes. It shows that 62.1% of respondents believe these tools make content creation easier. Additionally, 50.9% mention that these tools help to customize and personalize the information. About 69.9% responded that data can be accessed easily, while 72.4% find them easy to use. A small percentage, 0.3%, also mention they improve understanding of data, save time, enhance code generation, and provide accurate data. Overall, generative AI offers various advantages for academic tasks, including content creation, customization, data access, ease of use, and improving understanding and accuracy.

Figure 6. Major concerns in the use of generative AI tools for academic purposes

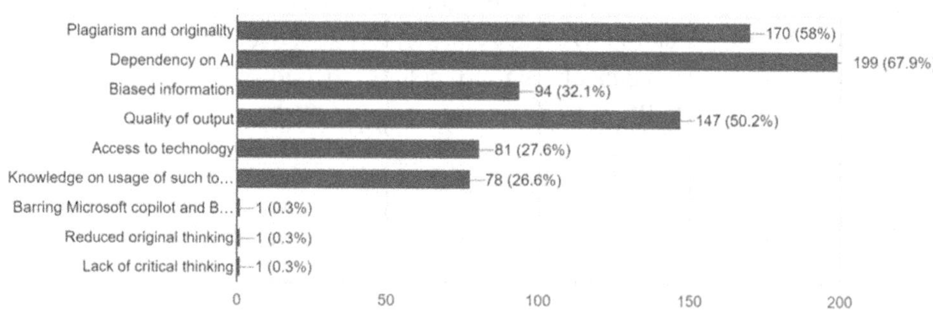

The graph depicts major concerns in the use of generative AI tools for academic purposes. Nearly 58% of the participants responded that the concern in using Generative AI is plagiarism and originality of the data. A majority of 67.9% expressed worry about becoming too reliant on AI technology. Additionally, about 50.2% of respondents expressed concerns regarding the quality of the output generated by these tools. Other notable concerns include the possibility of biased information (32.1%), limited access to technology (27.6%), and insufficient knowledge about using AI tools (26.6%). A very small percentage, 0.3%, indicated concerns about a decline in critical thinking skills and original thought.

6. How Can Students Utilize Such Tools in a Manner That Does Not Adversely Impact or Limit Their Creative Thinking Skills?

The students who responded to the survey believe that AI tools should be integrated into education carefully, with a focus on nurturing creativity and critical thinking. They recommend using AI as a backup option rather than relying on it too much, and only using it when necessary. They also highlight the importance of thinking independently. Even though technology is helpful for gathering information and generating ideas, the students warn against depending too heavily on AI, as it could hinder creative thinking. They suggest that individuals should think about and experiment with the information they get from AI, while also trying out different tools to strike a balance between using technology to boost creativity and not relying on it too much. Furthermore, the students generally agree that AI should be seen as a tool to enhance learning, rather than a replacement for creative thinking. They stress the importance of staying original and improving critical thinking skills alongside advancements in technology. To sum up, while the students acknowledge the usefulness of AI, they believe it shouldn't overshadow or replace students' natural creativity and critical thinking abilities.

2. FINDINGS FROM SURVEY AMONG TEACHING PROFESSIONALS

Table 15. Demographic Characteristics of Respondents (Total 44 respondents)

Demographic Profile	Categories	Number of Respondents	Percentage
Gender	Male Female	20 24	45.45% 54.55%
Years of Teaching Experience	Less than 6 years 6 to 10 years 11 to 15 years More than 15 years	12 9 6 17	27.27% 20.45% 13.64% 38.64%

Figure 7. Gender-wise categories of respondents (Total 44 respondents)

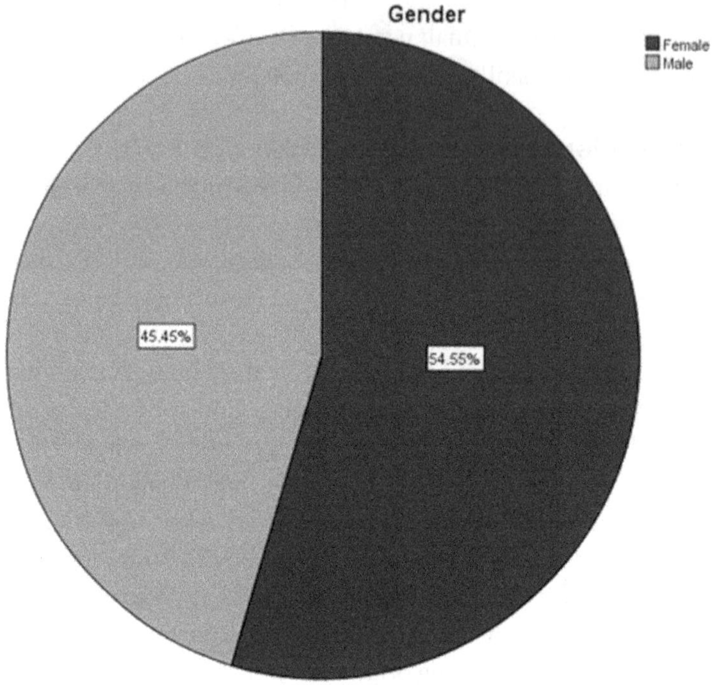

Figure 8. Categories of respondents as per number of years of teaching experience

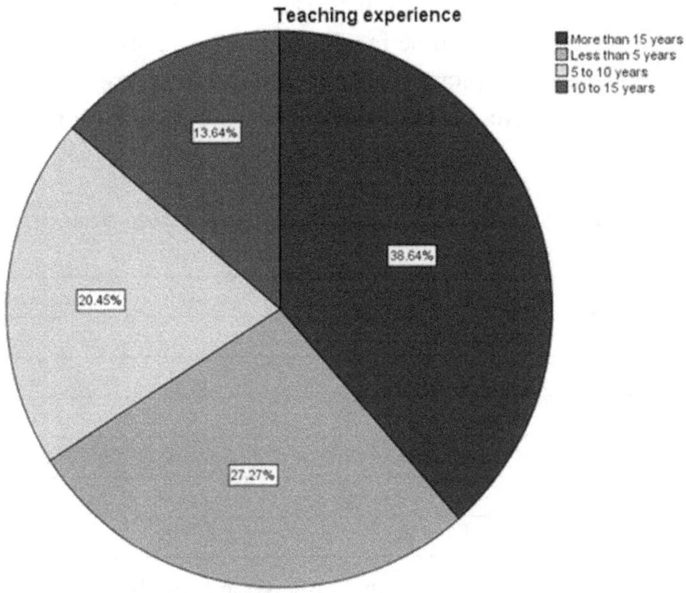

The survey among the teaching professionals had 44 respondents; the survey had a more balanced gender distribution, with 54.55% being female and 45.45% being male. The distribution of teaching experience varied, with 38.64% having experience of more than 15 years, 27.7% having less than 6 years of experience, 20.45% having 6 to 10 years of experience, and 13.64% having experience of 11 to 15 years.

1. Frequency Analysis

Table 16. Question - Have you used or interacted with generative AI technologies?

		Frequency	Percent	Valid Percent	Cumulative Percent
Valid	Yes	40	90.9	90.9	90.9
	No	4	9.1	9.1	100.0
	Total	44	100.0	100.0	

The provided table presents the results of a frequency analysis of the responses from faculties in higher education institutions, focusing on their usage or interaction with generative AI technologies. A majority of the respondents, representing 90.9% of the sample, indicated that they have used or interacted with generative AI technologies. This high percentage suggests a significant level of familiarity and engagement with these generative AI tools within the academic community. On the other hand, a smaller group, around 9.1%, haven't used these technologies yet. While this group is small, it shows that some faculty members are still not familiar with generative AI and are yet to explore or engage with these emerging technologies. The data shows that generative AI is becoming more common in higher education.

Table 17. Question - How often do you think students seek help from generative AI tools for their assignments?

		Frequency	Percent	Valid Percent	Cumulative Percent
Valid	4.00	19	43.2	43.2	43.2
	5 = ?Always	12	27.3	27.3	70.5
	3.00	8	18.2	18.2	88.6
	2.00	4	9.1	9.1	97.7
	1 = Not at all	1	2.3	2.3	100.0
	Total	44	100.0	100.0	

The above table shows a frequency analysis of responses to the question regarding the frequency of students seeking help from generative AI tools for their assignments. The scale range encompasses responses from "Not at all = 1" to "Always = 5". Among the respondents, the majority, accounting for 43.2%, indicated that students seek help, suggesting a substantial reliance on these tools. Additionally, 27.3% of respondents mentioned that students seek help "Always" on a scale of 5, indicating consistent usage. An additional 18.2% reported instances of students seeking help. Only a small fraction, 2.3%, indicated that students never seek help from generative AI tools for their assignments. Overall, the data suggests that there is a notable level of engagement with generative AI tools among students for seeking assistance with their assignments, with varying degrees of frequency reported by the respondents.

Table 18. Mean Analysis (Descriptive Statistics)

	N	Minimum	Maximum	Mean
How often students seek help from generative AI tools	44	1.00	5.00	3.8409
How generative AI impacted creative thinking ability	44	1.00	5.00	2.2273
Generative AI tools limits the development of creative skills	44	1.00	4.00	2.3182
Challenging to accurately assess students' capabilities	44	1.00	5.00	3.7500
Changes in the quality or originality of students' work	44	1.00	5.00	3.7045
Impact on the authenticity of students' work	44	2.00	5.00	3.4545
How equipped to differentiate work created with generative AI	44	1.00	5.00	3.4545
Valid N (listwise)	44			

The table displayed above illustrates the mean analysis of the responses from a survey distributed among faculties in higher education institutions. The objective was to examine the impacts of Generative AI tools on creativity in higher education. A total of 44 participants (N) contributed responses to all variables, with no missing values. A Likert scale was utilized for all scale variables, ranging from 1 to 5, where 3 represents the midpoint. It covers various dimensions related to the utilization and impact of generative AI tools in academic contexts. The mean score for "How often students seek help from generative AI tools" is 3.8409, indicating slightly higher than a moderate frequency of seeking assistance from these tools among students. Concerning the impact on creative thinking ability, the mean score is 2.2273. However, when considering the limitation of creative skill development by generative AI tools, the mean score is slightly higher at 2.3182, indicating that it may limit creativity. Moreover, the mean score for the challenging nature of accurately assessing students' capabilities is 3.7500, indicating a significant level of difficulty experienced by faculty members. Additionally, changes in the quality or originality of students' work receive a mean score of 3.7045, suggesting a noticeable impact attributed to generative AI tools. The impact on the authenticity of students' work receives a mean score of 3.4545, indicating a moderate influence. Lastly, faculty members feel moderately equipped to differentiate work created with generative AI, reflected in the mean score of 3.4545. Overall, these mean analyses provide valuable insights into faculty members' varied perceptions and experiences regarding the utilization and impact of generative AI tools in higher education.

Table 19. One-Way Anova

		Sum of Squares		Mean Square	F	Sig.
Challenging to accurately assess students' capabilities	Between Groups	7.307	3	2.436	1.991	
	Within Groups	48.943		1.224		
	Total	56.250				
Changes in the quality or originality of students' work	Between Groups	3.545	3	1.182	1.257	
	Within Groups	37.614		.940		
	Total	41.159				
Impact on the authenticity of students' work	Between Groups	1.880	3	.627	1.192	
	Within Groups	21.029		.526		
	Total	22.909				

continued on following page

Table 19. Continued

		Sum of Squares		Mean Square	F	Sig.
How equipped to differentiate work created with generative AI	Between Groups	1.791	3	.597	.486	
	Within Groups	49.118		1.228		
	Total	50.909				

Independent Variable - Years of teaching experience
Dependent Variables -
Challenging to accurately assess students' capabilities
Changes in the quality or originality of students' work
Impact on the authenticity of students' work
How equipped to differentiate work created with generative AI

The table displays the results of a one-way ANOVA, examining the relationship between Years of teaching experience (the independent variable) and four dependent variables: Challenge to accurately assess students' capabilities, Changes in the quality or originality of students' work, Impact on the authenticity of students' work, and How equipped teachers are to differentiate work created with generative AI. For the variable “Challenging to accurately assess students' capabilities,” the analysis shows no significant difference between groups based on years of teaching experience (0.131 > 0.05). Similarly, for “Changes in the quality or originality of students' work,” the ANOVA results reveal no significant differences between groups (0.302 > 0.05). Regarding the “Impact on the authenticity of students' work,” the analysis also indicates no significant variation between groups based on years of teaching experience (0.325 > 0.05). Likewise, for “How equipped to differentiate work created with generative AI,” there are no significant differences observed among groups (0.694 > 0.05). In summary, the ANOVA results suggest that years of teaching experience do not have a significant impact on the variables related to assessing students' capabilities, changes in the quality of students' work, authenticity of students' work, or the ability to differentiate work created with generative AI.

Figure 9. What are the generative AI tools or platforms that teachers are aware of?

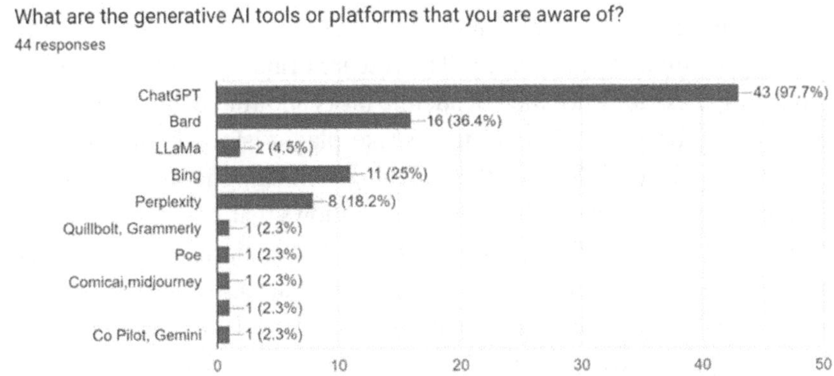

The graph depicts the generative AI tools or platforms teachers are aware of out of 44 respondents. The majority, 97.7%, indicate awareness of ChatGPT. Following this, 36.4% are familiar with Bard (now Gemini), while 25% know about Bing, and 18.2% are aware of Perplexity. A smaller proportion, 4.5%, are familiar with LLaMa. Additionally, a small percentage of 2.3% show awareness of other generative AI tools such as Quillbolt, Grammarly, Comical, Co-Pilot, Midjourney, and Poe.

2. What Could Be Some Methods or Strategies That Teachers Can Adopt to Ensure Students Do Not Overly Rely on AI Tools for Their Academic Tasks?

The tasks given to students can be more practical in nature, such as building different models and bringing in solutions to existing problems; this will ensure that such AI-based tools are not hampering students' creativity. Questions should be created in a manner that involves the application of creativity and understanding level or thought-provoking questions. Ask students for handwritten submissions. Need to prepare a policy to limit the use of AI in assignments. Use AI tools to detect if content has been copied or recycled from AI-based platforms. Increase group discussions and evaluate in-class contributions of students. Create awareness of the ethical usage of AI tools. Follow-up tests and quizzes should be designed to test whether the student understands the concept. Techniques or methods like MCQ-based assessment and Viva voce can be considered.

CONCLUSION

In conclusion, this chapter has thoroughly examined how generative AI tools are being used and how they impact higher education, considering the opinions and perspectives of students and faculty. The research findings indicate that many students are using these tools for their academic tasks and find them helpful. However, concerns have been raised about issues like plagiarism, relying too heavily on AI, and the possibility of biases in the content generated. The survey conducted between students and teachers of higher education shows that AI impacts creativity in education. Faculty members have varying levels of familiarity and involvement with generative AI tools. While many see the potential benefits, they also face challenges such as verifying the authenticity of student work and dealing with the complexities of AI-generated content. The chapter points out that excessive reliance on AI might hinder students' ability to think creatively and critically. Striking a balance between using AI effectively for learning and preserving students' creativity is crucial. Moreover, fair evaluation methods for student work must be established when AI is involved. Overall, this chapter shows that AI can be both helpful and challenging, but higher education institutions need to find ways to use AI in education that encourage creativity and critical thinking while still helping students learn effectively.

REFERENCES

Ahmad, N., Murugesan, S., & Kshetri, N. (2023). Generative artificial intelligence and the education sector. *Computer*, 56(6), 72–76. DOI:10.1109/MC.2023.3263576

Akgün, S., & Greenhow, C. (2021). Artificial intelligence in education: Addressing ethical challenges in K-12 settings. *AI and Ethics*, 2(3), 431–440. DOI:10.1007/s43681-021-00096-7 PMID:34790956

Arredondo, L. L. (2023). Information and communication technologies in higher education: Comparison of stimulated motivation. *Education and Information Technologies*. Advance online publication. DOI:10.1007/s10639-023-12160-2

Baidoo-Anu, D., & Ansah, L. O. (2023). Education in the Era of Generative Artificial Intelligence (AI): Understanding the potential benefits of ChatGPT in promoting teaching and learning. *Social Science Research Network*. https://doi.org/DOI:10.2139/ssrn.4337484

Bozkurt, A., Karadeniz, A., Baneres, D., Rodríguez, M. E., & Rodríguez, M. E. (2021). Artificial Intelligence and Reflections from Educational Landscape: A Review of AI Studies in Half a Century. *Sustainability (Basel)*, 13(2), 800. DOI:10.3390/su13020800

Calatayud, V. G., Espinosa, M. P. P., & Vila, R. R. (2021). Artificial Intelligence for Student Assessment: A Systematic review. *Applied Sciences (Basel, Switzerland)*, 11(12), 5467. DOI:10.3390/app11125467

Celik, I., Dindar, M., Muukkonen, H., & Järvelä, S. (2022). The Promises and Challenges of Artificial Intelligence for Teachers: A Systematic Review of Research. *TechTrends*, 66(4), 616–630. DOI:10.1007/s11528-022-00715-y

Chan, C. K. Y., & Hu, W. (2023). Students' voices on generative AI: Perceptions, benefits, and challenges in higher education. *International Journal of Educational Technology in Higher Education*, 20(1), 43. Advance online publication. DOI:10.1186/s41239-023-00411-8

Chang, C. H., & Kidman, G. (2023). The rise of generative artificial intelligence (AI) language models - challenges and opportunities for geographical and environmental education. *International Research in Geographical and Environmental Education*, 32(2), 85–89. DOI:10.1080/10382046.2023.2194036

Creely, E., Henriksen, D., & Henderson, M. (2023). Artificial intelligence, creativity, and education: critical questions for researchers and educators. In E. Langran, P. Christensen, & J. Sanson (Eds.), *Proceedings of Society for Information Technology & Teacher Education International Conference 2023* (pp. 1309-1317). Association for the Advancement of Computing in Education (AACE). https://www.learntechlib.org/primary/p/221998/

Dai, Y., Liu, A., & Lim, C. P. (2023). Reconceptualizing ChatGPT and generative AI as a student-driven innovation in higher education. *Procedia CIRP*, 119, 84–90. DOI:10.1016/j.procir.2023.05.002

Diehl, W. C. (2023). Artificial intelligence, Web 3, and the future of distance education. *American Journal of Distance Education*, 37(2), 83–84. DOI:10.1080/08923647.2023.2206081

Dwivedi, Y. K., Kshetri, N., Hughes, L., Slade, E., Jeyaraj, A., Kar, A. K., Baabdullah, A. M., Koohang, A., Raghavan, V., Ahuja, M., Albanna, H., Albashrawi, M. A., Al-Busaidi, A. S., Balakrishnan, J., Barlette, Y., Basu, S., Bose, I., Brooks, L., Buhalis, D., & Wright, R. T. (2023). Opinion Paper: "So what if ChatGPT wrote it?" Multidisciplinary perspectives on opportunities, challenges and implications of generative conversational AI for research, practice and policy. *International Journal of Information Management*, 71, 102642. DOI:10.1016/j.ijinfomgt.2023.102642

Hsu, Y., & Ching, Y. (2023a). Generative Artificial Intelligence in Education, Part One: The Dynamic Frontier. *TechTrends*, 67(4), 603–607. DOI:10.1007/s11528-023-00863-9

Humble, N., & Mozelius, P. (2022). The threat, hype, and promise of artificial intelligence in education. *Discover Artificial Intelligence*, 2(1), 22. Advance online publication. DOI:10.1007/s44163-022-00039-z

Hwang, G., Xie, H., Wah, B. W., & Gašević, D. (2020). Vision, challenges, roles and research issues of Artificial Intelligence in Education. *Computers & Education: Artificial Intelligence*, 1, 100001. DOI:10.1016/j.caeai.2020.100001

Hwang, G.-J., & Chen, N.-S. (2023). Editorial Position Paper: Exploring the Potential of Generative Artificial Intelligence in Education: Applications, Challenges, and Future Research Directions. *Journal of Educational Technology & Society*, 26(2). Advance online publication. DOI:10.30191/ETS.202304_26(2).0014

Kamalov, F., Calonge, D. S., & Gurrib, I. (2023). New era of Artificial intelligence in Education: Towards a sustainable Multifaceted Revolution. *Sustainability (Basel)*, 15(16), 12451. DOI:10.3390/su151612451

Kooli, C. (2023). Chatbots in Education and Research: A Critical Examination of ethical implications and solutions. *Sustainability (Basel)*, 15(7), 5614. DOI:10.3390/su15075614

Lim, W. M., Gunasekara, A., Pallant, J. L., Pallant, J., & Pechenkina, E. (2023). Generative AI and the future of education: Ragnarök or reformation? A paradoxical perspective from management educators. *International Journal of Management Education*, 21(2), 100790. DOI:10.1016/j.ijme.2023.100790

Lund, B., Wang, T., Mannuru, N. R., Nie, B., Shimray, S. R., & Wang, Z. (2023). ChatGPT and a new academic reality: Artificial Intelligence-written research papers and the ethics of the large language models in scholarly publishing. *Journal of the Association for Information Science and Technology*, 74(5), 570–581. DOI:10.1002/asi.24750

Murugesan, S., & Cherukuri, A. K. (2023). The rise of generative artificial intelligence and its impact on education: The promises and perils. *Computer*, 56(5), 116–121. DOI:10.1109/MC.2023.3253292

Nguyen, A., Ngo, H. N., Hong, Y., Dang, B., & Nguyen, B. T. (2022). Ethical principles for artificial intelligence in education. *Education and Information Technologies*, 28(4), 4221–4241. DOI:10.1007/s10639-022-11316-w PMID:36254344

Perera, P., & Lankathilaka, M. (2023). AI in Higher Education: A Literature Review of ChatGPT and Guidelines for Responsible Implementation. *International Journal of Research and Innovation in Social Science*, VII(VI), 306–314. DOI:10.47772/IJRISS.2023.7623

Peres, R., Schreier, M., Schweidel, D. A., & Sorescu, A. (2023). On ChatGPT and beyond: How generative artificial intelligence may affect research, teaching, and practice. *International Journal of Research in Marketing*, 40(2), 269–275. DOI:10.1016/j.ijresmar.2023.03.001

Su, J., & Yang, W. (2023). Unlocking the power of ChatGPT: A framework for applying generative AI in education. *ECNU Review of Education*, 6(3), 355–366. DOI:10.1177/20965311231168423

Wang, M., & Guo, W. (2023). *The potential impact of ChatGPT on Education: Using History as a rearview mirror*. ECNU Review of Education. DOI:10.1177/20965311231189826

Yu, H., & Guo, Y. (2023). Generative artificial intelligence empowers educational reform: Current status, issues, and prospects. *Frontiers in Education*, 8, 1183162. Advance online publication. DOI:10.3389/feduc.2023.1183162

Zhai, X., Chu, X., Chai, C. S., Jong, M. S., Starčič, A. I., Spector, M., Liu, J., Jing, Y., & Li, Y. (2021). A Review of Artificial Intelligence (AI) in Education from 2010 to 2020. *Complexity*, 2021, 1–18. DOI:10.1155/2021/8812542

KEY TERMS AND DEFINITIONS

Creative Thinking Skills: The ability to think and create unique ideas and original solutions to problems.

Generative Artificial Intelligence: A type of artificial intelligence tool that is used to generate textual data, images, ideas and other types of data using generative models.

Higher Education Institutions: Educational institutions that include universities, colleges and professional schools.

Students of Higher Education Institutions: Students pursuing their education in universities, colleges and higher professional schools.

Teaching Professionals: Individuals who provide teaching service in colleges, universities and professional schools.

Chapter 7
Generative AI and Its Implications for Higher Education Students' Creativity

Blandina Manditereza
https://orcid.org/0000-0003-2564-5860
University of the Free State, South Africa

Mavis Chamboko-Mpotaringa
https://orcid.org/0000-0001-8488-4330
University of Johannesburg, South Africa

ABSTRACT

This chapter explores Generative AI (artificial intelligence) in higher education regarding students' creativity. By utilising the quantitative content analysis approach, the chapter explored the impact of generative AI in higher education to understand its transformative effects on students' creative thinking processes and its outcomes. Current literature reveals the latest thinking on how AI enables or disrupts students' creativity. Generative AI is a potent tool in higher education which generates original content like text, images, music, and videos based on input data or predefined models. The adoption of generative AI led to the need to understand how these advancements may shape the educational experience to develop essential skills like creativity. Since creativity is crucial in today's digital age, generative AI raises questions about its potential impact on the imagination. The aspect of creativity, which is fundamental in higher education, offers students opportunities to enhance critical-thinking, problem-solving, and innovation; however, a balance is necessary between the utilisation of AI tools and the human element of creativity.

DOI: 10.4018/979-8-3693-2418-9.ch007

INTRODUCTION AND BACKGROUND

Konecki et al. (2023) and Vacarelu (2023) mention that AI is changing many industries and operational structures globally, thus impacting our daily lives, the workplace, and the nature of work. Its inclusion in higher education has created the possibility of revolutionising institutions of learning; but it also comes with risks and challenges. Hence, society must be conscious of the implications of AI integration to effect possible adjustments (Konecki et al., 2023; Vacarelu, 2023). Higher education has experienced significant growth since using artificial intelligence (AI), which can potentially change how institutions and students learn. However, while it offers many opportunities, it also brings several problems and risks that demand careful consideration (Saaida, 2023). One of the elements compromised through AI integration is the aspect of creativity. Importantly, creativity in higher education enhances knowledge, critical-thinking, employability, personal growth, and prepares students for the 21st century. It also connects diverse subjects and applies theoretical concepts to real-world scenarios, which promotes a richer understanding of complex issues. Moreover, employers value creativity as being critical for navigating dynamic job markets and adapting to industry demands. Encouraging creativity supports emotional and cognitive development by allowing students to express themselves accurately. It also fosters problem-solving and innovation which motivates students to overcome obstacles and push boundaries in their fields. By promoting creativity, institutions prepare students for careers that can contribute meaningfully to society. Since the utilisation of AI in the learning environment presents both challenges and prospects and given the significance of creativity in developing thinking skills, we need to be circumspect of graduate degree programmes on offer.

Previous research on artificial intelligence (AI) primarily focused on information science and technology, with limited exploration from an interdisciplinary and macro perspective (Tuo et al., 2021). More comprehensive and in-depth research is needed to investigate AI's broader implications on graduate characteristics across various disciplines and industries. The increasing reach and adoption of AI in multiple sectors have prompted the need to investigate its impact on graduate attributes (Bearman et al., 2023). As the world becomes more automated and interconnected, it is imperative to examine how AI shapes the essential skills and qualities required in the job market (Muthmainnah et al., 2022). However, to see the whole picture, there is the need to explore the negative side of generative AI pertaining to graduates' characteristics.

LITERATURE REVIEW

Artificial Intelligence in Higher Education

Artificial Intelligence (AI) in higher education refers to computer programmes that conduct human-like functions including self-correction, learning, and adaptation. It is applied to academic performance, recruiting, retention, admissions, and student support, among others. Therefore, it is essential to prepare all students in the use of AI for the future. According to Crompton and Burke (2023), AI is transforming social relationships and education by developing creative teaching and learning strategies that are being evaluated in various settings. For us to understand AI, we need to look at the examples of AI.

Examples of Innovative Uses Of Artificial Intelligence in Higher Education

Automating Administrative Tasks: AI frees administrative staff from manual tasks like paperwork and student identification (Zhihan, 2023).

Personalised learning: AI offers corrective feedback and individualised learning plans which assist students in their academic journey (Simuka, 2022; Crompton & Burke,2023).

Enhancing student support: AI assists in student support services, improves retention rates, and academic success (Simuka, 2022; Crompton & Burke,2023).

AI is utilizing generative algorithms, neural networks, and machine learning techniques to generate content that resembles human creativity from large datasets(Zhihan, 2023).

Artificial Intelligence in the Academic Space

According to Zawacki-Richter et al. (2019), AI has grown dramatically in the higher education sector over the previous five years by improving teaching, student learning, and administrative work. In this regard, predicting performance, recommending resources, automating evaluation, and customising learning experiences are critical applications. Also, AI is utilised through online platforms in higher education for assessment, resource selection, and performance prediction.

This migration towards AI requires incisive scholarly knowledge of technology which must be evaluated on its merits (Simuka, 2023). Because AI is altering the direction and processes within the teaching, learning, and administrative domains, it has drastically led to the speedy evolution of learning spaces in higher education. Although AI has gained popularity among academics and students because it enhances the calibre and accessibility of instruction, more research and discussions are necessary before users can completely embrace AI in higher education (Crompton & Burke, 2023). This means that AI has deep implications for higher education as it impacts on graduate competencies. "Graduate attributes [competencies] are emphasised in higher education as incentives to attract both learners and employers" (Rampersad, 2014, p. 2).

One of the critical graduate capabilities is the aspect of creativity which has a spin-off effect on other vital skills like problem-solving and critical thinking. Hence, creativity as a critical attribute should be nurtured in higher education as employers regard it as being invaluable. It is essential for navigating dynamic job markets and adapting to industry demands. Also, encouraging creativity supports emotional and cognitive development which allows students to express themselves naturally. It also prepares students for careers and to contribute meaningfully to uplift society. The question arises: how can this be realised and sustained through AI? Since creativity is viewed as a critical element in higher education, we need to evaluate whether or not AI is 'encroaching' on our learning spaces.

The Importance of Creativity in Higher Education

Additionally, literature indicates that creativity is critical to higher education as it enables problem-solving, innovation, adaptability, empathy, self-discovery, and having a competitive edge. In other words, it inspires graduates to think outside the box, find novel solutions, and tackle societal issues successfully. Moreover, creativity fosters empathy, connects individuals to diverse perspectives, and reveals hidden talents. As such, potential employers seek graduates with fresh ideas, innovative approaches, and cutting-edge competencies which make them valuable assets in a globally competitive job market. While students' specific attributes may vary, this study focused on creativity as a core competency. Creativity, as an element in education is valuable in various situations because it capacitates individuals to perform critical tasks. Considering the modern trends in thinking, adding machines to assist humans in problem-solving may be viewed as an opportunity or a threat. Although machines may perform tasks faster, they may dictate how humans perform their daily routine tasks – this implies that even graduates produced by the higher education system may become redundant as their thinking skills may rely too heavily on AI tools such as computers, iPads, software, and cell phones, among others.

This chapter reviewed creativity in higher education as a transactional (and transformational) tool for enhancing knowledge and stimulating original and diverse ideas (Quinn, 2018). Creativity is viewed as a fundamental graduate quality in civil engineering, science, and higher education. It enables graduates to tackle challenges in industry, while also being a requirement for professional accreditation. Consequently, assessment practices in undergraduate studies should evaluate generic capabilities (including creativity) alongside discipline-specific knowledge. Since creativity is the ability to unearth original ideas while innovation involves implementing them to create value, professors appreciate innovation in the classroom which is regarded as an integrative attribute. At engineering schools culture plays a significant role in fostering creativity and innovation which are desirable attributes that can be developed through work-integrated learning, collaborative processes, and supportive teaching practices (Quinn, 2018).

Importantly, creativity prepares and equips graduates with tools to thrive, adapt, and contribute meaningfully to their professional and personal lives. However, literature cautions that AI's impact on learning can be contextually based as it can engender threats and opportunities depending on how one adopts and uses it. Creativity as a graduate attribute may seem compromised by the introduction of AI because academics in higher education may view it as a threat, and not as an opportunity. Attributes or capabilities include sound qualities such as knowledge, skills, and dispositions that prepare students for career success, responsible citizenship, and lifelong learning. However, specific attributes may vary across institutions. These graduate attributes are often integrated into higher education institutions' (HEIs') curricula to ensure quality learning experiences for students to efficiently prepare them for future careers and roles as responsible global citizens.

Artificial Intelligence and Creativity in Higher Education

Creativity in humans is a skill that promotes the engendering of new ideas to find innovative solutions which assist us to improve different facets of the work environment; hence, AI enhances critical-thinking skills which stimulate creativity. Human creativity is a unique talent that drives innovation and progress in various industries. It allows humans to generate new ideas to solve complex problems by pushing the boundaries of what is possible. Unlike AI which operates with predefined rules, human creativity is infinite, not bound by algorithms or software restrictions. In terms of higher education and creativity research, Patston et al. (2022) contend that creativity is an essential 21st century skill that education systems should prioritise when designing their academic programmes, but this graduate attribute requires nurturing. The dilemma is whether to view AI as a threat or as an opportunity in higher education because AI is a 'revolutionary' tool because it inspires collaboration and innovation. Although critics state that AI lacks the inner understanding of human emotions which is a key aspect in driving true creativity, the future requires a balance between AI and human creativity, with humans guiding AI to enhance outputs – this implies that human creativity remains a unique driver of innovation (Quinn, 2018). Consequently, when teaching in HEIs, adopting a constructivist orientation is advisable as it enables the inclusion of creativity.

Theoretical Orientation in Teaching Creativity in Higher Education

Researchers and practitioners should adopt a constructivist orientation as a strategy for developing creativity in students in the current dynamic context of AI. A constructivist framework enables academics to motivate learners to interact with content creatively and naturally or through AI tools. Constructivism, which is a philosophical educational perspective that emphasises active problem-solving, centres on real-world problems or complex tasks that require critical thinking (Creswell & Creswell, 2018). Therefore, through applying constructivist principles, learners are encouraged to analyse, evaluate, and synthesise information to arrive at solutions. Since constructivism emphasises the learner's active role in acquiring knowledge and understanding the world, it proposes that individuals construct knowledge and make-meaning through experiences, interactions, and mental processes. In other words, constructivism in education places learners at the centre of the learning process through active engagement, social interaction, and the construction of knowledge through experience (Vygotsky, 1978). In essence, constructivism provides a fertile ground for developing critical-thinking skills that promote creativity.

Further, constructivism encourages learners to actively engage with information, consider multiple perspectives, reflect on their thinking, and apply their knowledge to solve real-world problems. This approach to AI in education recognises that learning is a vibrant and dynamic process, rather than merely passively absorbing information; thus, learning becomes a deep process. Accordingly, when using AI in learning, students should be allowed to balance AI-driven guidance and the learner's autonomy to ensure productive experiences.

Understanding Generative AI and Creativity

This research applied a qualitative analysis approach to obtain a comprehensive understanding of generative AI and its implications for higher education regarding students' creativity. In addition, it intended to evaluate the influence of generative AI on creativity among higher education students, as well as to explore its potential benefits and challenges. Also, the chapter examined strategies to enhance creativity by employing critical-thinking skills.

Qualitative content analysis is a research technique that uses secondary research for analysis and involves noting the prevalence of certain words, themes, or concepts within a given text or sets of qualitative data (Mhlanga, 2021). This is an unobstructed research technique that allows researchers to objectively analyse data (Elo et al., 2014) in congruence with the research questions which guide what should be investigated and created (Schreier, 2012). In addition, content analysis is a valuable method for studying social phenomena because it is non-invasive. Content analysis engages three approaches: conventional, directed, and summative. These help researchers to make-sense of textual data and to conform to the naturalistic paradigm. Moreover, the researcher perused peer-reviewed journal articles, conference proceedings, books, book chapters, and media articles as secondary sources, all of which were critically analysed to inform the discussions in this chapter. By adhering to the content analysis approach which involved counting and comparing keywords to interpret the underlying context of the content, this chapter discusses the findings below:

Impact of Generative AI on Students' Creative Thinking

Generative AI goes mainstream, stimulates creative thinking, promotes innovation, and enhances learning outcomes across various disciplines and educational contexts in higher education. This resonates Eaton's (2023) who suggests that determining the origins and ends of artificial intelligence and human intelligence is insufficient as the two are inextricably linked in stimulating human thinking resulting in creative related elements.

Generative AI has many creative-related applications, as shown in Figure 1 below.

The increasing reach and adoption of AI in multiple sectors prompted the need to understand its impact on graduate attributes (Bearman et al., 2023). In higher education, generative AI adoption has implications; students and practitioners can leverage generative AI for their benefit while guarding against adverse elements. Creative functions such as idea generation and brainstorming, art and design inspirations, music composition, innovative storytelling, and writing can be automated to generate various ideas and inspirations across different domains by providing students with diverse starting points for creative projects. This limits the possibility of mistakes precipitated by the lack of inspiration or creativity, while aiding the discovery of novel thoughts and solutions. (Kayser & Telukdarie, 2024).

Figure 1. Potential Real-World Creative Applications of Generative (AI)

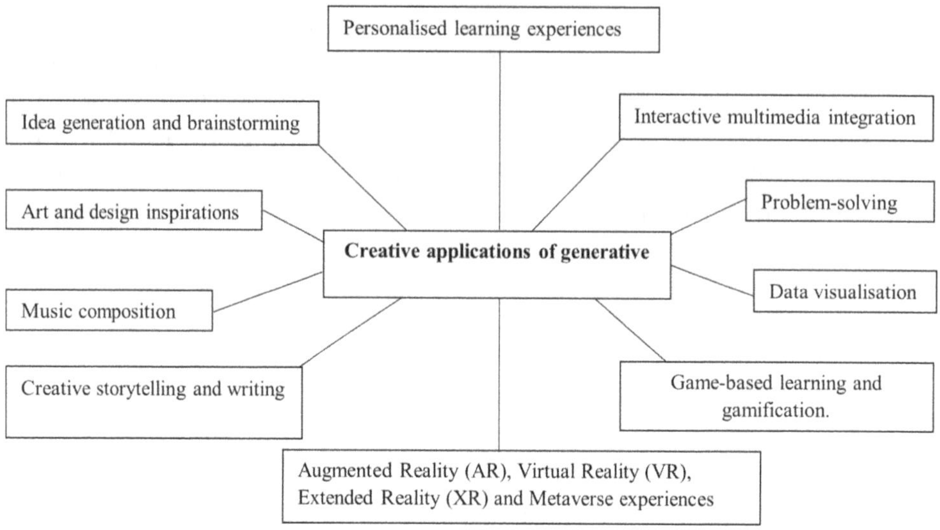

In addition, AI-powered software can automate the analysis and visualisation of complex datasets. This enables creative higher education students, researchers, and analysts to uncover insights and trends more efficiently by leveraging machine-learning algorithms. The AI systems can identify patterns, trends, correlations, and anomalies in datasets that can further reduce the likelihood of errors in presentation, interpretation, and analysis. Moreover, generative AI enhances game-based learning and gamification experiences by creating dynamic and adaptive game environments that promote creative thinking and problem-solving skills (Chamboko-Mpotaringa & Manditereza, 2023; Nguwi, 2023). Also, AI algorithms can generate randomised game elements, challenges, and puzzles that keep students engaged and encouraged to think creatively to overcome obstacles. The AI-powered adaptive learning platforms can function as virtual tutors and recommend educational resources, projects, and activities that challenge students to think creatively to pursue their intellectual passions (Simuka, 2022; Crompton & Burke, 2023). Also, by utilising students' data on learning preferences, AI can create personalised learning pathways tailored to individual needs and interests, thus positively impacting students' creative learning.

Despite its numerous advantages, the adoption of generative AI has some drawbacks regarding creativity in higher education. Students may depend excessively on productive AI tools for generating ideas, creating content, and solving problems, thus leading to a passive approach to learning with a diminished sense of personal creativity. Over-reliance on generative AI could reduce students' opportunities for hands-on learning experiences which promote creativity, experimentation, and problem-solving skills. In other words, students may miss the crucial processes of trial-and-error, exploration, and self-discovery which are essential for fostering creativity and innovation in higher education. In other words, an obsessive dependence on generative AI tools may restrict students' ability to think critically, innovatively, and independently to generate novel ideas.

We must accept that generative AI tools are machines, and despite being able to provide answers, they cannot think critically and creatively like humans. There is a high probability that generative AI models amplify existing biases in the training data they were built on (Bozkurt et al., 2023). For example, if the model developers lack the necessary literacy skills to evaluate internet texts critically, and if they fail to request generative AI models like ChatGPT or Bard to incorporate diverse examples and perspectives, there is the likelihood that biased or incorrect information will be conveyed to students.

If students do not adhere to ethical guidelines and lack guidance on academic integrity, they may unintentionally transgress plagiarism policies and compromise the credibility of their work. For educators, it may be challenging to assess the authenticity and originality of the works of students who have used generative AI tools. Distinguishing between AI-generated content and original student contributions can be difficult which raises concerns about the validity of assessment methods and academic integrity. Thus, generative AI has the potential to compromise the accuracy of assessment methods and undermine the principles of academic integrity. Hence, it becomes essential for educators to implement appropriate measures to mitigate this risk to ensure that assessments are fair and reliable.

Future Recommendations

How Should Higher Education Institutions (HEIs) Protect Creativity?

Firstly, HEIs need to know how to manage and leverage AI so as not to disrupt student creativity. Admittedly, AI can be used to support student creativity in higher education by providing tools and resources which improve learning experience and educational outcomes. Academics and researchers should acknowledge that AI can promote creativity by eliciting new ideas that might not have been thought of before, which can lead to unique and creative work. It can function as a bridge between many different kinds of information, as well as assist people to find new ways to be creative. Also, AI can play a pivotal role in deciding what ideas and information get noticed, in addition to influencing what new creative things are made of.

Although AI has proved to be popular in HEIs, the danger is that it may undermine, outperform, or supplant creative and problem-solving mental tasks that students engage in. According to Muthmainna et al. (2022), AI helps to simplify complex ideas into discrete manageable parts that can be included in different technological Apps. The general belief is that AI promotes a positive level of students' intellectual engagement. However, this study sought to determine whether AI is more of a challenge than an opportunity for learners. Since AI enables students to access masses of information at their fingertips, this can lead to students heavily relying on AI algorithms to filter and select information, potentially making them less skilled at critical evaluation and information synthesis (Crompton & Burke, 2023). Current literature asserts that AI can both positively and negatively impact creativity. Since most literature reviews emphasise mainly the potential benefits of AI in enhancing information access, this research views AI as not being a significant threat because AI operates at the physical level which humans would have created. Thus, we should understand the dynamics of AI in higher education to maintain creativity. The view that AI is not a threat to higher education and creativity is supported by Xing and Marwala (2018) who affirm that AI's current usefulness doesn't necessarily outweigh human creativity, as our internal creativity is largely responsible for its research and development.

This research suggests that in the era of AI in higher education, it is crucial to develop and maintain creativity skills. Educators should be trained to understand AI's operations, as well as recognise areas where human intelligence excels. Hence, students should acquire AI literacy skills to understand how AI can support creativity and learning, but balancing AI use with human elements is essential. In this regard, virtual assistants and chatbots are examples of AI technologies that can improve educational opportunities which can be tailored to individual needs and interests. Students should stay informed about the latest AI technologies which assist in the exploration of new perspectives. Academics and researchers must also exploit generative AI for the following reasons:

- It helps engendering new ideas and improves creative thinking in schools by providing teachers and students with many different ideas.
- It acts like a thinking friend helping with planning lessons and engaging in projects, while encouraging new and creative ways of learning.
- AI supports thinking outside the box, teamwork, and active learning by 're-inventing' school to become more engaging to enhance students' creativity.

The overhauling of higher education learning spaces resulted in the creation of personalised learning platforms that are powered by AI which can adjust to the needs of each student to improve the standard of education (Baker, 2019). Since AI has become the new pedagogical trajectory, institutions can now gain valuable insights into student performance and learning patterns from AI-powered analytics and data generation tools which help them make decisions based on available data (Siemens & Gasevic, 2017).

Previous research on AI primarily focused on information science and technology which limited exploration from an interdisciplinary and macro perspective (Tuo et al., 2021). This chapter fills this existing gap in literature. However, it is suggested that more comprehensive research should be conducted to investigate AI's broader implications on graduate attributes across various disciplines. As the world evolves to become more automated and interconnected, examining how AI will shape the skills and qualities valued in the job market is essential (Muthmainnah et al., 2022). The potential outcomes and threats of AI on the competencies of graduates should be carefully examined and evaluated. While existing research has provided insights into the multifaceted relationship between AI adoption in higher education and the development of graduate attributes among students, this study advises that although AI offers several opportunities for enhancing creativity, it also poses challenges such as over-reliance on technology, utilising technology to replace the human touch, and the potential erosion of specific cognitive skills. Academics are encouraged to employ a balanced approach to harness AI's benefits while promoting and nurturing creativity in learning.

CONCLUSION

As the world continues to evolve rapidly, educators and institutions should ensure that students acquire new literacy skills such as AI, data analysis, computational know-how, and digital competencies to effectively navigate the AI-driven future global economy. Nevertheless, further research is needed to explore the full potential of AI in education, in addition to addressing challenges related to elements that stifle graduates' creativity. A balanced approach is essential such that institutions proactively address graduate attributes and job displacement concerns while leveraging AI to enhance teaching, learning, and administrative processes. In support, Rampersad (2014, p. 2) agrees that a balanced approach is essential to take advantage of the benefits of AI while promoting graduate qualities like creativity. This implies that integrating AI in higher education raises important questions which require urgent consideration. In conclusion, the higher education sector, academics, students, and researchers must be familiar with how AI impacts the development of creativity. Researchers must distinguish between AI's advantages and disadvantages in terms of graduates' attributes. Importantly, academics should be discerning to not replace sound pedagogical strategies with technology. The answer is to adopt technology to extend human capabilities and possibilities in teaching, learning, and research without hindering human creative skills.

REFERENCES

Ahuja, R. (2019). Impact of artificial intelligence on higher education. In *Artificial Intelligence in Higher Education* (pp. 39–52). Springer.

Anderson, C. A., & Dill, K. E. (2020). Video games and aggressive thoughts, feelings, and behaviour in the laboratory and life. *Journal of Personality and Social Psychology*, 78(4), 772–790. DOI:10.1037/0022-3514.78.4.772 PMID:10794380

Anuyahong, B., Rattanapong, C., & Patcha, I. (2023). Analysing the Impact of Artificial Intelligence in Personalized Learning and Adaptive Assessment in Higher Education. *International Journal of Research and Scientific Innovation*, 10(4).

Baker, R. S. (2019). AI in Education: Promises and pitfalls. *The Future of Children*, 29(2), 181–199.

Bao, Y., Zhang, J., Liang, L., Wang, X., & Cheng, W. (2022). Enhancing creativity using generative AI techniques: An exploratory study. *IEEE Transactions on Learning Technologies*. Advance online publication. DOI:10.1109/TLT.2022.3188088

Bearman, M., Ryan, J., & Ajjawi, R. (2023). Discourses of artificial intelligence in higher education: a critical literature review. *Higher Education,* 86(2), 369–385. https://doi.orgy1007/s10734-022-00937-2

Bostrom, N., & Yudkowsky, E. (2014). The ethics of artificial intelligence. In *Cambridge Handbook of Artificial Intelligence,* 316-334. DOI:10.1017/CBO9781139046855.020

Bozkurt, A., Xiao, J., Lambert, S., Pazurek, A., Crompton, H., & Jandrić, P. (2023). Speculative futures on ChatGPT and generative artificial intelligence (AI): A collective reflection from the educational landscape. *Asian Journal of Distance Education*, 18(1), 53–130.

Buhalis, D., & Sinarta, Y. (2019). Real-time co-creation and nowness service: Lessons from tourism and hospitality. *Journal of Travel & Tourism Marketing*, 36(5), 563–582. DOI:10.1080/10548408.2019.1592059

Chamboko-Mpotaringa, M., & Manditereza, B. (2023). Innovative Language Learning Approaches: Immersive Technologies and Gamification. In Kartal, G. (Ed.), *Transforming the Language Teaching Experience in the Age of AI* (pp. 189–214). IGI-Global. DOI:10.4018/978-1-6684-9893-4.ch011

Chamboko-Mpotaringa, M., & Tichaawa, T. M. (2021a). Digital trends and tools driving change in marketing Free State tourism destinations: A stakeholder's perspective. *African Journal of Hospitality, Tourism and Leisure*, 10(6), 1973–1984. DOI:10.46222/ajhtl.19770720.204

Chamboko-Mpotaringa, M., & Tichaawa, T. M. (2021b). Tourism digital marketing tools and views on future trends: A systematic literature review. *African Journal of Hospitality, Tourism and Leisure*, 10(2), 712–726. DOI:10.46222/ajhtl.19770720-128

Creswell, J. W., & Creswell, J. D. (2018). *Research Design: Qualitative, Quantitative, And Mixed Methods Approaches* (5th ed.). SAGE.

Eaton, S. (2023). Postplagiarism: Transdisciplinary ethics and integrity in the age of artificial intelligence and neurotechnology. *International Journal for Educational Integrity*, 19(1), 23. Advance online publication. DOI:10.1007/s40979-023-00144-1

Educause. (2019). *Seven things you should know about artificial intelligence in teaching and learning*. Educause Learning Initiative.

Elo, S., Kääriäinen, M., Kanste, O., Pölkki, T., Utriainen, K., & Kyngäs, H. (2014). Qualitative Content Analysis. *SAGE Open*, 4(1). Advance online publication. DOI:10.1177/2158244014522633

Facione, P. (2015). *Critical Thinking: What It is and Why It Counts?* Insight Assessment.

Halpern, D. F. (2014). *Thought and knowledge: An introduction to critical thinking*. Psychology Press.

Kaplan, A. M., & Haenlein, M. (2019). Siri, Siri, in my hand: Who is the fairest in the land? On the interpretations, illustrations, and implications of artificial intelligence. *Business Horizons*, 62(1), 15–25. DOI:10.1016/j.bushor.2018.08.004

Karampiperis, G., & Papanikolaou, N. (2022). Integrating generative artificial intelligence in higher Education: Challenges and opportunities. *Frontiers in Education*, 7(6), 875536. DOI:10.3389/feduc.2022.875536

Konecki, M., Konecki, M., & Biškupić, I. (2023). Using Artificial Intelligence in Higher Education. *Proceedings of the 15th International Conference on Computer Supported Education*.

Martínez-Gómez, M., Jabaloyes Vivas, J. M., & Carrión García, A. (2020). Relevance of Skills in Total Quality Management in Engineering Studies as a Tool for Performing Their Jobs. *Sustainability (Basel)*, 12(5), 2065. DOI:10.3390/su12052065

Mhlanga, D. (2021). Artificial Intelligence in Industry 4.0, and Its Impact on Poverty, Innovation, Infrastructure Development, and the Sustainable Development Goals: Lessons from Emerging Economies? *Sustainability (Basel)*, 13(11), 5788. DOI:10.3390/su13115788

Murgatrotd, S. (2024). Artificial Intelligence and future of higher education. Revista Paraguaya De Educación A Distancia (REPED), 5, 4-11. DOI:10.56152/reped2024-vol5num1-art1

Muthmainnah, I., Seraj, P. M., & Oteir, I. (2022). Playing with AI to Investigate Human-Computer Interaction Technology and Improving Critical Thinking Skills to Pursue 21st Century Age. *Education Research International*, 2022, 1–17. DOI:10.1155/2022/6468995

Nguwi, Y. Y. (2023). Technologies for Education: From Gamification to AI-enabled Learning. *International Journal of Multidisciplinary Perspectives in Higher Education*, 8(1), 111–132.

Rowe, A., & Zegwaard, K. (2017). Developing graduate employability skills and attributes: Curriculum enhancement through work-integrated learning. *Asia Pacific Journal of Cooperative Education*, 18, 87–99.

Runco, M. A. (2014). Creativity. In *The Oxford Handbook of Cognitive Psychology* (pp. 371–386). OUP.

Saaida, M. (2023). AI-Driven transformations in higher Education: Opportunities and challenges. *International Journal of Educational Research and Studies*, 5, 29–36.

Schreier, M. (2012). *Qualitative content analysis in practice*. SAGE. DOI:10.4135/9781529682571

Slimi, Z., & Carballido, B. V. (2023). Navigating the Ethical Challenges of Artificial Intelligence in Higher Education: An Analysis of Seven Global AI Ethics Policies. *TEM Journal,* 12(2). https://doi.org/DOI:10.18421/TEM122-02

Tuo, Y., Ning, L., & Zhu, A. (2021). How Artificial Intelligence Will Change the Future of Tourism Industry: The Practice in China. In *Information and Communication Technologies in Tourism* (pp. 83–94). Springer International Publishing. DOI:10.1007/978-3-030-65785-7_7

Vacarelu, M. (2023). Artificial Intelligence and Higher Education Legal Limits: Bridging Human and Machine. In *Future Education with Intelligence,* 15–33. DOI:10.1007/978-981-19-8641-3_2

Vygotsky, L. S. (1978). Interaction between learning and development. *Readings on the Development of Children*, 23(3), 34–41.

Williamson, B. (2020). Governing by numbers: Algorithmic governance and the hidden algorithms that govern people's lives. *Learning, Media and Technology*, 45(3), 247–265.

Wong, B., Chiu, Y. T., Copsey-Blake, M., & Nikolopoulou, M. (2022). A mapping of graduate attributes: What can we expect from UK university students? *Higher Education Research & Development*, 41(4), 1340–1355. DOI:10.1080/07294360.2021.1882405

Xing, B., & Marwala, T. (2018). *Creativity and Artificial Intelligence: A Digital Art Perspective.* Springer. ArXiv, abs/1807.08195.

Yoder-Himes, D. R., Asif, A., Kinney, K., Brandt, T. J., Hopp, C., & Ross, E. (2022). Racial, skin tone, and sex disparities in automated proctoring software. *Frontiers in Education*, 7, 881449. Advance online publication. DOI:10.3389/feduc.2022.881449

Zhang, Y., Xiong, F., Xie, Y., Fan, X., & Gu, H. (2020). The Impact of Artificial Intelligence and Blockchain on the Accounting Profession. *IEEE Access : Practical Innovations, Open Solutions*, 10(1), 461–477. DOI:10.1109/ACCESS.2020.3000505

Zhihan, L. (2023). Generative artificial intelligence in the metaverse era. *Cognitive Robotics*, 3, 208–217. DOI:10.1016/j.cogr.2023.06.001

KEY TERMS AND DEFINITIONS

Academic Integrity: It emphasises the importance of adhering to ethical principles and honesty in academic work such as proper citation, avoiding plagiarism, and upholding academic standards.

Academic Policies: Rules, guidelines, and regulations set by educational institutions to govern academic conduct, curriculum, assessment, and other aspects of the academic environment.

ChatGPT: ChatGPT, a Chatbot by OpenAI, uses a large language model to guide conversations. With over 100 million users, it's a fast-growing consumer application available for free in premium versions. It is a key player in the AI boom.

Collaboration: Collaboration is the process of teamworking with others to achieve common objectives, exchange knowledge, and improve learning outcomes.

Creativity: It is a human trait that is being researched and debated due to the advent of AI technologies. It involves transcending traditional rules to create insightful knowledge.

Ethical Usage: The responsible and moral use of technology practices that ensure compliance with ethical standards to prevent harm.

Generative Artificial Intelligence: Artificial intelligence involves machines that can generate various types of data such as text, images, videos, or other information, often in response to specific prompts.

Higher Education: Post-secondary education is offered by universities, colleges, and other tertiary institutions.

Innovation: The promotion of original, creative, and unique ideas, methods, or technologies that foster positive change and improvement.

Pedagogical Opportunities: The focus is on providing educational spaces and openings that improve teaching methods, curriculum development, and learning experiences.

Personalised Learning: The goal is to create individualised educational experiences that cater for the unique needs, preferences, and learning styles of each student.

Chapter 8
Generative AI in Curriculum Development:
A Framework for Adaptive, Customized, and Personalized Learning

Mariam Tanweer
https://orcid.org/0000-0003-4146-6635
University of South Australia Online, Australia

Aisha Ismail
https://orcid.org/0000-0003-4458-4311
Virtual University of Pakistan, Pakistan

ABSTRACT

Generative artificial intelligence (GAI) is becoming a crucial influence in different industries, particularly transforming education through the reshaping of curriculum creation. This chapter discusses how GAI can improve educational inclusion and comprehensiveness by providing personalized, customized and adaptive learning experiences. The framework in this chapter provides a structured approach to integrating GAI into curriculum design with the goal of creating dynamic, flexible, and personalized educational paths. By utilizing advanced machine learning and natural language processing, GAI enables educators to create personalized and tailored learning modules, promoting an inclusive educational setting. The discussion in this chapter highlights the crucial significance of GAI in developing educational methods and curriculum, establishing a new model for future learning environments.

DOI: 10.4018/979-8-3693-2418-9.ch008

1. REDEFINING EDUCATION: FROM TRADITIONAL MODELS TO AI-ENHANCED PERSONALIZED LEARNING

In the rapidly changing field of education, classic approaches are increasingly considered inadequate to address the dynamic needs of modern learners and the challenges of a fast-paced environment. Historically, education has been defined by a passive learning methodology in which learners are anticipated to assimilate material provided through direct instruction (Pendy, 2023). This paradigm frequently places students in a responsive state, where they passively acquire knowledge instead of actively interacting with it.

An important limitation of this strategy is its restricted capacity to promote critical thinking, creativity, and problem-solving skills, which are crucial competencies for the 21st century (Rashid et al., 2019). It typically does not cater to a variety of learning styles and speeds, leading to a lack of interest and shallow understanding. In addition, conventional evaluations, frequently in the form of standardised exams, mainly assess the ability to memorise information and retain it temporarily, thereby neglecting to encompass a wide range of student learning.

As a result of these constraints, educational approaches have developed to incorporate strategies such as the flipped classroom. This concept disrupts conventional learning environments by providing educational content online outside of the physical classroom (Shihab et al., 2023). Flipped learning involves moving exercises, usually classified as homework, from outside the classroom to inside it. This enables students to participate in interactive sessions, where they can engage in conversations, solve problems, and work on collaborative projects with the assistance of the instructor. This fosters dynamic learning and motivates students to develop autonomy in their learning process.

Although models like the flipped classroom, blended learning, project-based learning, peer-led, and collaborative learning are considered advancements, they are only intermediate stages leading to more significant changes in educational paradigms. The incorporation of Artificial Intelligence (AI) in education offers even more favourable prospects (Pendy, 2023). AI has the capacity to customise learning experiences according to individual requirements, adapt to a student's speed, and offer immediate feedback, thereby greatly improving learning outcomes. AI-powered platforms can analyse data from student interactions to adapt content in real-time, providing tailored challenges or extra support as required.

The demand for educational models driven by artificial intelligence is especially crucial in light of the rapidly increasing speed of technology and societal transformations. Lifelong learning is essential due to the constant evolution of skills necessary in contemporary workplaces. AI, particularly generative AI, has the invaluable ability to generate customised learning pathways that are engaging, dynamic, and continuously updated in this environment.

2. OVERVIEW OF GAI IN EDUCATION

Generative Artificial Intelligence (GAI) has emerged as a powerful and impactful tool across various sectors, including education. In the realm of education, GAI possesses the potential to profoundly alter the approaches taken in instruction, knowledge acquisition, and interaction with educational materials. This technology generates, synthesises, and simulates human-like reactions by employing sophisticated machine-learning algorithms, fostering an environment conducive to personalised and adaptable learning experiences.

GAI operates through the generation of unique data that closely resembles pre-established patterns. This involves the creation of educational materials, assessments, and simulations that emulate human-like interactions. In contrast to conventional AI, generative models, such as GPT (Generative Pre-trained Transformer), operate without pre-programmed responses. Conversely, they undergo training using vast datasets, enabling them to generate coherent and contextually appropriate outputs.

The application of GAI in language-intensive disciplines yields significant advantages. These systems are equipped with sophisticated natural language processing capabilities, which enable them to understand and respond to enquiries from students, thereby facilitating interactive tutoring experiences. Generative model-driven chatbots can engage in substantial dialogues, providing prompt assistance and feedback, augmenting the educational experience beyond the traditional classroom setting.

One notable advantage of GAI in education is its capacity to facilitate personalised and customised learning experiences. Generative models can personalise and customise instructional content by the specific needs of individual learners through the analysis of their unique learning profiles, preferences, and academic achievements. This adaptability enhances engagement and comprehension, establishing a more effective educational environment. Additionally, GAI is indispensable for the development of educational content. Text, graphics, and multimedia elements are among the many types of information the system can generate to supplement conventional instructional materials. Educators can utilise generative models to generate interactive materials, simulations, and personalised educational resources tailored to each student's unique requirements.

GAI can also be significantly utilised in educational feedback and evaluation systems. The system can generate genuine assessment cases, evaluate student responses, and provide exhaustive feedback. This approach optimises particular elements of the evaluation process and ensures prompt and valuable feedback, thereby encouraging continuous improvement.

Given the continuous progression of technology, GAI is poised to emerge as an indispensable element within the realm of education. Subsequent developments may witness the creation of more sophisticated models capable of adapting to diverse learning modalities, dialects, and cultural contexts. Among the potential applications is the facilitation of educators in creating dynamic, student-centred curricula and developing immersive virtual learning environments. As we explore the manifold prospects offered by this revolutionary technology, it is imperative to conscientiously consider ethical norms and pedagogical ramifications to ensure that its complete potential for the benefit of students worldwide is realised.

This chapter unfolds GAI's potential curriculum development applications, including creating individualised content and implementing dynamic, responsive, and inclusive curricula that provide students with personalised, customised and adaptive learning paths (individualised learning from now in this chapter). However, this chapter does not focus on the ethical concerns poist by the GAI and leaves this to further research in the area. The figure 1 exhibits the framework proposed in this chapter for developing a GAI-based curriculum. The proposed framework suggests that after analysing and interpreting data using AI, GAI could assist in creating customised, personalised, and flexible educational curricula. An academic programme influenced by GAI could include several components, such as supplementary materials for customised learning experiences, adaptive learning paths for flexibility, and personalisation of content or pace, among other possibilities. The following sections of this chapter explore the different components of the proposed framework in more depth.

3. GAI AND INDIVIDUALISED LEARNING PRINCIPLES ALIGNMENT

GAI leads an education paradigm change by supporting individualised and adaptable learning. For instance, personalised learning tailors the learning process to each student. It identifies students' diverse needs to provide personalised and meaningful education. This concept works well with GAI, which uses its advanced capabilities to transform education. Another example is where GAI can analyse massive datasets with unsurpassed accuracy (Namoun & Alshanqiti, 2020). In their research, Namoun and Alshanqiti (2020) analysed a decade of research work to analyse the understanding and use of intelligent techniques such as generative AI to predict student learning outcomes. They indicated that this technology uses powerful algorithms to assess student performance data, learning preferences, and styles to create a detailed academic trajectory for each student. This analytical capacity is the foundation for creating personalised learning paths and a more flexible and responsive educational environment. It does not stop here; GAI can then use the analysis conducted through the datasets to help create customised, personalised and adaptive learning pathways for each student. Tailored instructional content can improve engagement and comprehension by considering personal preferences, academic talents, weaknesses, and other criteria. An educational experience that exceeds the usual one-size-fits-all approach allows learners to thrive at their own pace and in their preferred learning methods.

Figure 1. A Framework to Develop GAI based Curriculum

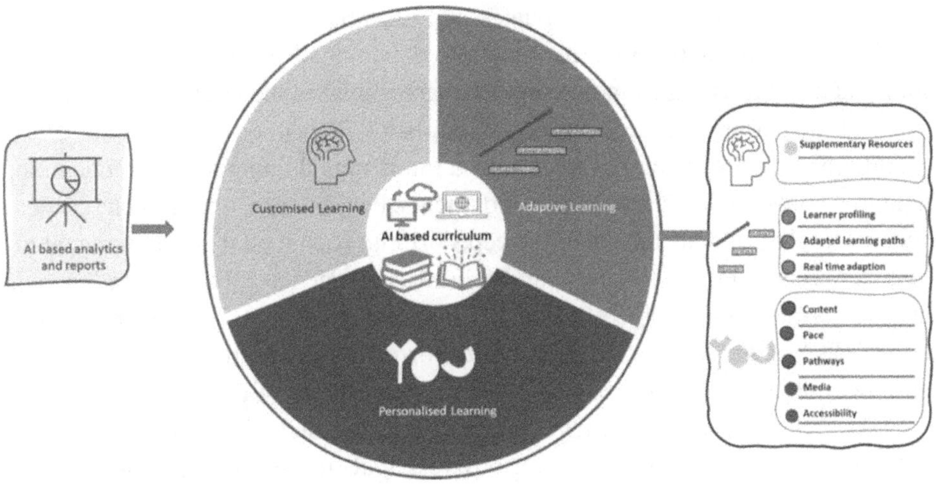

Source: Author

This section discusses GAI implementations in customised, personalised and adaptive learning through innovative curriculum design. This section also discusses the reciprocal relationship between customised, personalised and adaptive Learning and GAI and how this convergence changes education. Illustrative instances and case studies demonstrate how academic establishments are leveraging GAI to transform the way students learn and enhance the effectiveness, inclusiveness, and dynamism of education.

3.1. What is Customised, Personalised, and Adaptive Learning

Kem (2022) puts forth a persuasive point that personalised learning was defined by the Education (2010) as a process in which each learner can personalise their learning programme in accordance with their own pace (personalisation), by employing instructional methods that are distinct to their requirements (adaption), and by accessing content that is customised to their learning objectives. Adaptive learning includes continuous feedback and updating of the resources using the student data (Taylor et al., 2021). It includes the approaches to adapt to the needs of individual learners. For instance, it delivers education on a large scale by evaluating individual learners' existing skills and knowledge, offering feedback and content, and continuously tracking the progress of the individual. It uses learning algorithms to provide real-time updates and essential tools that enhance student learning outcomes. In other words, customised, personalised and adaptive learning (individualised learning from now in this chapter) places the learner's needs at the centre of the learning process (Štuikys & Burbaitė, 2024).

Individualised learning has long been a fundamental component of education, including conventional classroom environments. For instance, within such settings, students might evaluate a range of concepts prior to each lesson and, contingent on their comprehension, be assigned personalised assignments that correspond to their level of mastery of the subject matter (Campbell et al., 2007). The advent of technology has brought about a significant transformation in traditional individualised learning, much like in numerous other fields. An instance of this is the application of various learning management systems as platforms, including written and visual materials, tools for monitoring learning progress, real-time feedback, and identifying students who are at risk of requiring additional assistance and offering the same (Li & Wong, 2021).

Individualised learning can be further modernised to meet the requirements of students in the era of GAI, which has arrived. A contemporary illustration can be found in the personalised generative libraries (PGL) framework suggested by Štuikys and Burbaitė (2024), which makes use of individualised learning materials. To understand the concept of PGL, one can start from the 'digital libraries'. Digital libraries and repositories serve as resources for providing educational content. Users, whether teachers or learners, can access parts of the content they need from existing digital repositories. However, for individualised learning, the PGL framework delineates an extended process-based framework. This framework emphasises two primary processes: obtaining resources from PGLs/repositories and utilising these resources for personalised learning activities.

Both teachers and students can possess their own PGLs. The content of a teacher's PGL is highly customised. This library's generative nature stems from two key features: First the PGL structure incorporates elements that function as generators (e.g., Metadata Generator and Query Generator), utilising a generative method (Štuikys & Burbaitė, 2024). During this generative process, educators engage in the resource-gaining process by utilising PGL tools to generate individualised lesson plans that include Learning Objects (Los) inventories. They can develop a list of key resources under their personalised library for individualised lesson plans and link them to the learning objectives and outcomes. The second key feature of library's generative nature is a large body of the personalized content is characterized as a generative learning object. . Intermediate and beginner students construct individualised learning paths using the teacher's resource list, whereas advanced students have the ability to generate or alter their own lesson plans.

The main goal is to develop a lesson plan that is smoothly incorporated into the curriculum. It is essential to ensure alignment when creating a thorough lesson plan that provides several possibilities for individualisation at both beginner/intermediate and advanced levels.

3.2 Creating the Content Using (G)AI

GAI plays a crucial role in individualised learning, particularly in developing educational materials. In the past, educators faced challenges in customising curricula to suit the specific needs of each student, sometimes relying on generic materials. This was mostly attributed to the use of knowledge-based AI by educators, wherein human expert knowledge is employed to facilitate decision-making, with AI providing support in the decision-making process. GAI, on the other hand, serves as a collaborative tool, assisting in creating diverse educational content, spanning from instructional outlines to multimedia resources. This mitigates the challenges educators encounter and ensures that the curriculum remains current, relevant, and in accordance with the most recent educational benchmarks.

i. AI Algorithms

The role of GAI is evident across three educational levels: facilitating and overseeing the students at the program level, managing the entire class in a single unit, and providing individualised help to students for personalised and adaptive learning. Though we will discuss three levels below our main focus will be managing a single unit and providing individualised help for students. Taylor et al. (2021) investigated individualised learning, which entails assessing learners' knowledge and skills, employing algorithms to provide feedback, and monitoring their advancement.

According to Minn (2022), the success of an individualised learning environment depends on two key factors: providing valuable feedback and restructuring adaptive learning materials. Adapting information to suit the specific needs of each student improves the learning experience. However, a major challenge is identifying the algorithms that are successful in evaluating abilities and knowledge at both the unit and individual levels in order to individualise the learning process.

ii. Research

a) Recent research and study areas to match student aptitude

Generative AI, in this regard, can help us identify the most useful algorithms. For instance, GAI leverages cutting-edge research to harness insights regarding students' aptitudes that are applicable across different academic disciplines. This entails exploring recently studied subjects, recognising developing subfields that enhance the present state of affairs, and determining how these progressions can be advantageous to particular stakeholders.

By examining recent studies, GAI acquires knowledge about cutting-edge advancements in several disciplines, revealing the areas that are currently being explored. It comprehends the subtle complexities of specialised areas that are enhancing the current knowledge base, demonstrating the ever-evolving character of academic investigation.

Furthermore, GAI discerns the possible recipients of these scientific endeavours. It attracts attention from the academic community, industry experts, policymakers, and society as a whole, who can utilise the results for innovation, problem-solving, and societal advancement.

b) Emerging trends of pedagogical innovations and education

The research may also encompass investigations into emerging developments in pedagogical methodologies, such as open pedagogy. GAI extensively examines academic literature, including publications, conference proceedings, and scholarly articles, to discover developing patterns in instructional techniques (Guan et al., 2020). The AI utilises sophisticated semantic analysis to examine academic texts and identify crucial concepts, principles, and notable researchers driving instructional innovation's forefront. In addition to conventional research methods, the AI utilises educational platforms, blogs, and social media to gather up-to-date conversations, sentiments, and the grassroots-level acceptance of innovative techniques. One may utilise the same media to investigate current educational trends, such as the accessibility of massive online courses (MOOCs), open educational resources (OERs), and personalised libraries.

c) Aligning with the Educational Standards:

GAI can systematically incorporate data to ensure educational content is by current standards and norms. Conducting thorough research examines the existing educational standards, curriculum frameworks, and learning objectives established by academic institutions and regulatory authorities. The AI assesses that the content adheres to accreditation requirements, enhancing the quality and validity required for institutional recognition.

Aligning AI with educational standards requires training it. At first, GAI receives a thorough dataset encompassing diverse educational standards, curriculum frameworks, learning objectives, and accreditation requirements from many academic institutions and regulatory agencies. This dataset is fundamental to its learning. The training procedure commonly utilises supervised learning methods, in which the AI is trained using labelled data. For instance, educational materials that have undergone prior assessment and classification according to specific criteria are utilised. The AI scrutinises these resources to acquire knowledge of the attributes that render them compliant or non-compliant. In addition, natural language processing (NLP) techniques empower GAI to comprehend and analyse the text in these papers, recognising crucial concepts, standards, and needs. By employing methods such as pattern recognition and semantic analysis, GAI acquires the ability to compare and verify new educational material with existing standards. Over time, GAI's capacity to precisely evaluate and guarantee the adherence of instructional materials to current standards and norms is enhanced through iterative training and the integration of feedback loops. The continuous process of learning and adaptation is essential for GAI's efficacy in creating pertinent and compatible educational materials.

In addition to meeting minimum requirements, AI examines competency-based education, aligning curriculum with the crucial skills needed in the changing work market. The proactive nature of GAI goes beyond meeting current criteria; it also predicts and adjusts to changing regulations and educational trends based on past data. The AI enhances the educational experience by keeping up with the constantly evolving educational environment, ensuring alignment with present and future academic requirements.

d) Student Performance Data:

GAI surpasses established norms and recommendations by assessing many dimensions of data. The system evaluates the academic achievements, individual learning styles, and levels of involvement of students to customise the educational material. This customised method accommodates the specific requirements of individuals and groups, hence improving the overall educational experience.

For this, Montebello and Montebello (2018) propose an e-portfolio of students. They mention that a personal learning portfolio (PLP) should encompass three essential components of a student's educational experience. First and foremost, it should accurately represent the learner's academic experiences, including a wide range of courses, subjects, material, assessments, and curricular activities. The student or educational institution can preserve these elements, which may serve as end products to demonstrate successes or as procedures to illustrate the learning path. Furthermore, the PLP should meticulously record the learner's progression, encompassing individual and organisational encounters, such as work background, competencies, credentials, and other characteristics commonly seen in a curriculum vitae. The third aspect of the PLP emphasises the learner's distinct aptitudes, showcasing an enhanced collection of academic abilities, educational proficiencies, and competencies. The PLP should possess adaptability and comprehensiveness, accommodating learners of varying ages, backgrounds, cultures, and nationalities. Additionally, it should be flexible enough to operate in different contexts and learning phases, combining a vast array of distinct and blended materials.

The AI utilises PLP and other data analysis to identify trends in students' interactions with instructional materials based on various factors, enabling it to alter content delivery to accommodate multiple learning styles. Data-driven personalisation facilitates an atmosphere where students may actively and efficiently interact with the material, enhancing their understanding and ability to remember it. GAI converts unprocessed data into practical insights, enhancing a flexible and adaptable educational system that emphasises individual learners' specific needs while adhering to broader educational benchmarks.

GAI begins its procedure by utilising comprehensive datasets, including educators' research points. The datasets encompass academic publications, educational materials, institutional reports, and insights from industry professionals. Utilising Natural Language Processing (NLP), GAI analyses and understands written language, deriving subtle and detailed insights. In addition to keyword analysis, GAI utilises semantic analysis to comprehend the contextual significance. Thematic analysis is an additional computational tool revealing significant discoveries about particular topics.

In addition, GAI utilises past data to identify patterns and develops machine-learning models to forecast future events. By integrating these methodologies, GAI extracts extensive datasets and analyses and forecasts educational patterns, providing useful perspectives for educators and academics. This approach guarantees a comprehensive understanding of educational environments, allowing GAI to offer practical information and support well-informed decision-making in the education sector.

4. GAI-ASSISTED CURRICULUM DEVELOPMENT AND DELIVERY

Within the dynamic realm of education, the incorporation of GAI signifies a momentous shift in curriculum development and individualisation methodology. In light of evolving educational paradigms that prioritise personalised and dynamic learning experiences, the significance of AI in revolutionising the production and distribution of educational materials has grown substantially. As discussed in the previous section, GAI is a pioneering technology that leverages its sophisticated capabilities to analyse and process extensive datasets. It provides educators with a potent instrument to stay abreast of recent research, educational benchmarks, and pedagogical developments.

The strength of this technology resides in its capacity to thoroughly examine vast amounts of information, condensing it into current and pertinent educational resources that align with the changing requirements of students. Implementing this methodology mitigates the conventional workload that educators have borne concerning content development and guarantees that the generated materials are precisely aligned with the present educational environment. The entire content creation process is optimised by AI algorithms, including the dynamic generation of lesson plans and the development of diverse multimedia resources (e.g., informative infographics, interactive simulations, and engaging videos). By optimising the process, educational content can be presented more efficiently and effectively, considering each student's specific requirements and learning preferences.

In addition, the effectiveness and speediness facilitated by AI-powered content generation play a crucial role in seamlessly integrating educational resources with prescribed curriculum standards. AI provides educators with a valuable ally, allowing them to ensure that their instructional materials remain current and to stay informed about ongoing developments in the field of education. By delegating the laborious tasks of content generation to AI, educators can allocate additional time and effort toward facilitating learning experiences that are both captivating and influential. Instructors can assume their responsibilities with heightened assurance, bolstered by AI algorithms that aid in developing pedagogically sound, modern, and productive educational materials.

In this section, we will further explore how the GAI can assist in offering the students an adaptive, customised and personalised learning experience.

4.1. Adaptive Curriculum and Learning Pathways

Adaptive learning, a pedagogical approach tailored to meet the individual needs of learners, represents a significant shift in educational paradigms. It is a technology, as emphasised by Castañeda and Selwyn (2018), Castro (2019), and Muñoz et al. (2022), that provides an educational approach that is advantageous for teachers, students, and administrators. Adaptive learning adjusts the difficulty level and content delivery based on a learner's understanding and performance, creating a personalised learning experience. The adaptive learning theory states that when devising a strategy for incorporating adaptive learning into learning design (LD), it's crucial to consider two distinct dimensions. Firstly, implementing the adaptive approach can be internal, directly within the Unit of Learning (UOL), or external, situated outside the UOL. Secondly, the focus of adaptation varies: it could be the content within the UOL, the user interface of the UOL, or an entirely different aspect (Towle & Halm, 2005). The following section looks at the internal to UOL, which will be unit/subject-specific and external at the program level. Moreover, the adaption can be in the interface, content, difficulty level, and the type of delivery.

By leveraging advanced algorithms and data analytics, adaptive learning systems can identify specific learning gaps and adapt in real time, providing targeted instruction that optimises learning outcomes. This subsection delves into AI in adaptive learning, exploring its transformative potential to cater to diverse learning styles and abilities, fostering a more inclusive and effective educational environment.

4.1.1. How will the Adaptive Learning Modules be developed? Adaptive learning technology, harnessing the capabilities of Artificial Intelligence (AI), presents a groundbreaking method of education that accommodates the individual learning speed and comprehension level of every learner. This customised educational experience is accomplished using AI-powered algorithms that carefully analyse individual performance and learning habits. Through this approach, these systems have the ability to adapt to the level of difficulty of the content and the nature of the material provided to the student. Consequently, if a student demonstrates exceptional proficiency in a specific domain, the AI system can present more sophisticated subject matter to ensure the student remains engrossed and stimulated. On the other hand, if a student encounters difficulty with a particular topic, the system can offer supplementary materials that are easier to comprehend or present the knowledge in an alternative manner to enhance comprehension. Let's take an example which we will use throughout this chapter.

Conceptual Eclipse: Unraveling the Debits and Credits Dilemma

The problem and initial diagnostic:

Picture a tertiary education accounting curriculum wherein students are exposed to a diverse range of concepts over the course of the semester.

The AI system in this scenario gathers and evaluates data from diverse sources, including student feedback, online forum discussion boards using learning management systems (LMS), Q&A sessions on LMS or recordings, assignment grades, student progress reports and exam scores. Over the semester, the AI algorithm discerns a repetitive pattern in all the weekly modules: a notable portion of students routinely achieve lower scores on the fundamental principle of "debits and credits" and their practical implementation within the framework of the double-entry accounting system. It also identifies from the Q&A sessions and discussion boards posts that the confusion frequently arises from the counterintuitive nature of these phrases as they are employed in accounting, which may diverge from their common usage in everyday life.

After recognising this pattern, the AI system highlights the fundamental principle of "debits and credits" as a subject that needs further focus. The instructors receive this information and can subsequently investigate the situation more thoroughly. It is possible that the existing instructional approach for fundamental principle of "debits and credits" is not effectively engaging the students, requires assistance to recognise how these terms differ from the everyday use or alternatively, the allotted time for covering this topic may be inadequate.

Taking the example above, the following sections explore the components of the adaptive learning model and is further explained in the example 2: developing adaptive learning modules below.

A. Developing Adaptive Learning Modules
   i. Initial Diagnostic Assessment and Learner Profiling: The process commences with an AI-powered diagnostic assessment to evaluate the student's initial comprehension of the topic under investigation. The AI utilises the outcomes to classify the student's degree of expertise and customises the initial complexity of the modules accordingly.

The diagnostic assessment will begin with formulating diverse inquiries, encompassing multiple-choice questions, true or false statements, and brief responses. An ideal diagnostic assessment should possess adaptability, enabling it to dynamically modify the difficulty level based on the student's responses. To accomplish this, the teacher needs to construct a database of diagnostic questions spanning several difficulty levels. AI can record the number of attempts the student makes to accomplish each level, which will ascertain the student's learning requirements. After the evaluation, the AI promptly examines the results and detects patterns in the student's answers that reveal their strengths and areas where they can grow. The main objective is to evaluate the student's level of proficiency. Additionally, prompt feedback can be given on their performance, including explanations for erroneous responses, to enhance learning from the beginning.

Example 1: Conceptual Eclipse: Unraveling the Debits and Credits Dilemma

Source: Command given by Author, generated by AI

The initial evaluation marks merely the starting point. With each step forward in the adaptive learning journey, the AI persistently tracks the student's progress, continuously modifying their learning trajectory. This dynamic approach guarantees that the instructional content consistently matches the student's growing grasp of the subject matter, keeping the challenges within reach yet sufficiently stimulating and adapting to the student's developing comprehension of the concepts at hand.

ii. Adapted Learning Path: The learner begins with an interactive session to introduce the problematic concepts. Suppose the examination revealed that the student possesses a certain level of comprehension regarding the subject matter. In that case, the module may commence with a concise recapitulation before progressing towards more intricate applications. The module would begin with fundamental principles, catering to individuals without prior knowledge or experience in the subject matter.
iii. Real-Time Adaptation: The AI diligently tracks the student's replies to exercises and quizzes throughout the module. If the learner consistently answers several questions accurately, the AI may present a more challenging series of tasks or quickly progress to the next idea. In contrast, if the student encounters difficulties, the AI will adaptively modify the content to make the explanations easier or offer extra practice problems related to the same subject.

Example 2: Developing Adaptive Learning Modules

Conceptual Eclipse: Unraveling the Debits and Credits Dilemma

The learner profiling:

After the initial diagnostic of the issue with the subject of Accounting, AI can start individual learner profiling.

Data Integration: The AI system consolidates data from diverse sources including diagnostic assessments, engagement indicators (such as time spent on activities and involvement in conversations), assignment grades, and feedback from learning management systems. This extensive data gathering guarantees a full perspective of every student's educational progression.

Learning Preferences Analysis: By employing algorithms with the ability to perform natural language processing and pattern identification, the AI evaluates students' interactions with various forms of information (such as videos, text, and interactive quizzes) and determines their favored ways of learning. For example, it could identify that certain students have a stronger inclination towards visual content, while others have improved memory retention with written materials or interactive assignments. Let's assume that through individual profiling, AI discovers that Ali excels in topics presented through videos but struggles with subjects where the material is primarily text-based.

Topic mastery analysis: The AI assesses students' proficiency levels in various topics and assignments to determine their knowledge. It discerns patterns of achievement and challenge, precisely identifying particular domains in which a student demonstrates exceptional performance or has difficulties. This entails not only examining the raw scores, but also taking into account the intricacy of the activities accomplished and the advancement over time. For Ali, grasping the fundamental concepts of debit and credit appears to be a challenge.

Cognitive and affective components: Cognitive and affective components are taken into consideration by the AI through the analysis of engagement levels, time spent on tasks, and patterns in seeking assistance, such as the frequency of questions posed in discussion boards. This allows the AI to assess motivational and engagement factors. Additionally, it takes into account the input provided by students regarding their degrees of confidence and interest in different disciplines, including this qualitative information to create a more detailed and nuanced profile. Ali consistently posts on discussion boards with moderate frequency across all subjects he has been enrolled in since the beginning of his degree program. On average, he dedicates about 5 hours per week to engaging with the learning management system (LMS) for each subject. His grades in all courses range from 67% to 72%.

Dynamic Profiling: The AI system use machine learning algorithms to consistently update profiles in real-time as fresh data is received. The dynamic profiling technique enables the adjustment of learning paths in real-time, ensuring that the educational content and strategies stay in line with the changing requirements of each learner.

Example 3: AI Suggestions for Adaptive Learning

Conceptual Eclipse: Unraveling the Debits and Credits Dilemma
AI suggestions for adaptive learning

Following is the suggestion from AI for the adaptive learning paths for Ali based on the diagnosis above;

Based on Ali's individual profile as determined by AI, the suggested adaptive learning path for him would prioritise visual and interactive content, especially in areas where he faces challenges, such as the fundamental concepts of debit and credit. Here's how the adaptive learning path could be structured for Ali:

Interactive Introduction: Begin with an engaging, interactive module that introduces the concepts of debit and credit through videos and interactive activities. This approach aligns with Ali's preference for video-based learning and provides a hands-on experience to grasp the basics.

Diagnostic Assessment: Incorporate a brief, interactive assessment to gauge Ali's current understanding of debit and credit. If this reveals that Ali has some foundational knowledge, the path would then offer a succinct review segment to reinforce these basics before moving forward.

Visual and Interactive Learning Modules: Given Ali's better performance with video content, the learning path would include more video tutorials and interactive simulations that explore the principles of debit and credit in depth. These modules would use visual aids and real-life scenarios to make abstract concepts more tangible.

Discussion Board Engagement: Encourage Ali to participate more actively in discussion boards related to these topics. Since he already posts with moderate frequency, tailored prompts and questions on the boards could stimulate deeper engagement and allow him to explore the subjects more thoroughly with peers.

Customised Weekly Time Commitment: Considering Ali spends an average of 5 hours per week on the LMS for each subject, the learning path can be structured to optimise this time. Allocating specific segments of his weekly study schedule to focus on interactive and video content can ensure he remains engaged without overwhelming him.

Progressive Difficulty and Application: As Ali advances, the learning path would gradually introduce more complex applications of debit and credit, ensuring that each new concept builds upon the last. This structured progression aids in solidifying his understanding and application of these fundamental accounting principles.

Ongoing Assessments and Adjustments: Regular, formative assessments would be integrated to monitor Ali's progress, with the AI adjusting the learning path as needed. If Ali improves in his understanding of text-based materials, the path could gradually incorporate more of these resources to strengthen his reading comprehension alongside his visual learning skills.

Training Adaptive learning in GAI is a continual process of observing, analysing, and adjusting based on students' specific interactions with the learning modules. The AI undergoes intensive training utilising a varied dataset to carry out this task efficiently. This dataset is extensive, encompassing a diverse array of problems, varying in complexity levels, and containing many educational resources carefully selected by educators. By undergoing comprehensive training, the AI acquires a sophisticated comprehension of the educational environment, allowing it to distinguish the most efficient approaches for captivating students.

The AI closely observes the students' performance, preferences, and advancement as they engage with the learning environment. This encompasses their reactions to diverse forms of content, such as videos as opposed to text, and their proficiency levels in different concepts and skills. Through data analysis, the AI discerns trends and learning trajectories, enabling it to forecast and adapt to the changing educational requirements of individual students.

For instance, if a student like Ali has a predilection for video-based learning and encounters difficulties with text-laden materials, the AI adapts his educational trajectory to incorporate more visual and interactive content. This corresponds to his preferred learning method and tackles his particular difficulties, such as comprehending the fundamental principles of debit and credit in accounting.

Furthermore, the AI's capacity to flexibly adjust the learning trajectory includes altering the difficulty and format of teaching materials according to the student's present performance and feedback. If Ali exhibits growth and increasing familiarity with previously challenging subjects, the AI will gradually present more intricate ideas, providing a consistent advancement that aligns with his learning speed.

To maintain an interesting and efficient learning experience, the AI system also utilises the knowledge gained from the student's participation in discussion forums and their activity on the learning management system. Comprehensive methodology enables the AI to establish an individualised educational setting that promotes not only intellectual advancement but also drive and involvement.

Essentially, the training of GAI for adaptive learning involves a complex combination of technology and pedagogy. Its goal is to create educational experiences tailored to learners' individual needs. The AI's capacity to analyse, forecast, and adjust enables a personalised approach to education, wherein each student's experience is customised to their specific requirements, inclinations, and objectives.

4.2 Customised Learning Pathways

Customised learning adapts educational experiences to suit each student's specific requirements, increasing their involvement and efficacy. This approach utilises AI to assess the advancement and difficulties of learners, providing recommendations for supplementary resources as needed. The following way can be utilised in customised learning.

i. Supplementary Resources: Upon conducting a diagnostic assessment, the AI can identify any issues or challenges certain students may have with various sections of the unit/subject by studying the analytics. In such cases, the AI can provide supplemental resources. For example, if the AI identifies reoccurring challenges with specific components of debits and credits, it automatically proposes additional resources. Visualise GAI suggests that the student facing difficulties with fundamental accounting concepts can consider watching tailored videos from Khan Academy or AccountingCoach. This may also encompass supplementary reading resources.

Nevertheless, this necessitates a substantial dataset to be established. Additionally, this will require GAI authorisation to access scholarly reading materials, such as research papers, books, or digital libraries. The GAI can be trained by inputting information on the topic taught, the sorts of students, and the success of the teaching. Additionally, it encompasses ongoing feedback loops. This will enable GAI to acquire knowledge about patterns over time and subsequently enhance its ability to provide more accurate recommendations.

4.3 Personalised Learning Preference and Educational Material

Personalised learning personalises educational experiences to align with individual student preferences, choices and learning styles, resulting in a more captivating and efficient learning process. Personalised learning provides a wide range of options to accommodate each student's individual requirements and interests, taking into account elements like pace, content medium, evaluation methods, and cultural inclusion. Personalised learning differs from adaptive learning in that while adaptive learning involves AI diagnosing issues and suggesting various learning pathways, personalized learning allows students to choose their own paths according to their preferences.

i. Content Type

Personalised learning recognises and offers the unique preferences of individual students, guaranteeing that the educational experience is both captivating and efficient. Some students are inclined towards graphical content or learning activities within diverse preferences, as they see that visual representations and interactions augment their comprehension and memory of information. This preference utilises the cognitive process in which visual signals facilitate the rapid comprehension of concepts, enhancing the accessibility of complicated ideas.

On the other hand, other students may prefer textual content or video lectures as their preferred learning method. This group of individuals frequently discovers that engaging in self-paced reading facilitates profound reflection and a stronger bond with the content. They might value the straightforward sequence and thorough explanation that written books provide. Video lectures effectively integrate aural explanations with visual aids, appealing to individuals who excel in auditory and visual learning. Videos offer the additional benefit of allowing users to pause and replay, which is especially advantageous for intricate subjects, providing a combination of visual and textual learning opportunities.

Furthermore, the inclination towards interactive simulations or augmented/virtual reality experiences is becoming a potent instrument in personalised education. These novel approaches engage students in the learning content by providing practical experience and connecting theoretical knowledge to real-world situations. This immersive learning method is particularly attractive to kinesthetic learners who derive benefits from active participation and firsthand experiences. For example, the University of South Australia Online (will be known as Adelaide University from 2025), in partnership with Accenture, provides a virtual reality experience to students in their digital business degree program, which helps students understand real-world scenarios in exciting and innovative ways.

ii. Learning Pace

An essential feature of personalised learning is its capacity to adjust to the individualised learning pace of every student. Understanding that learners have various levels of knowledge assimilation is essential for establishing an inclusive and efficient educational setting. Some students require a fast pace in order to stay engaged and sustain momentum. These learners excel when they make rapid progress in understanding the content since it keeps them engaged and mentally stimulated. Accelerated learning paths can accommodate these individuals by offering concise lessons that efficiently address fundamental concepts, allowing them to progress rapidly to more difficult subjects without unnecessary interruptions.

On the other hand, some students gain advantages from a more deliberate and controlled learning method. These individuals may necessitate more time to grasp and assimilate the stuff offered to them comprehensively. Adopting a slower pace allows these individuals to contemplate the information thoughtfully, establish connections with prior knowledge, and fully comprehend the intricacies of the subject matter. Personalised learning environments can meet these needs by providing flexible time limits for certain subjects, additional resources for in-depth investigation, and chances for review and consolidation.

iii. Learning Pathways

Within personalised learning, learning pathways signify a significant departure from a standardised approach to education. Instructors can cater to their students' diverse interests, professional aspirations, and academic proficiencies by providing various pathways to attain identical educational objectives. Implementing various learning methodologies guarantees that each learner discovers a path that aligns with their individual and career goals.

Students who prefer the practical application of ideas might greatly benefit from educational material incorporating real-world case studies, hands-on projects, and internships. These pragmatic routes enable students to utilise theoretical information in order to resolve tangible issues, thus closing the divide between classroom education and practical implementation. For example, a student studying business management may participate in creating a marketing plan for a nearby business, providing them with a personal understanding of the complexities and difficulties involved in implementing marketing tactics.

However, students with a strong inclination towards theoretical knowledge may excel in a track that delves deeper into conceptual understanding, analytical frameworks, and examining fundamental concepts. This strategy is suitable for learners with a greater inclination towards study, academia, or acquiring a thorough comprehension of a subject. For students of this calibre, their learning trajectory could encompass advanced theoretical classes, research endeavours, and chances to interact with academic publications and texts.

iv. Media Preferences

The selection of media in instructional content plays a crucial role in meeting students' diverse learning preferences in the current digital era. In addition to conventional visual and written formats, a wide range of media formats can significantly enhance the learning process, making education more captivating and efficient.

Videos have become essential in contemporary education, allowing visual and auditory learners to observe concepts being demonstrated. Videos can streamline intricate subjects by utilising animations, demonstrations, and expert explanations, hence enhancing the accessibility of learning and sustaining student engagement.

Podcasts are a highly effective medium for auditory learners to acquire information through engaging in debates, interviews, and lectures. They enable students to acquire knowledge while travelling, converting monotonous journeys into fruitful learning opportunities. Podcasts can explore specialised subjects, providing in-depth analysis and a wide range of themes to the curriculum.

Interactive simulations are especially advantageous for kinesthetic learners who excel in hands-on activities rather than passive observation. Interactive simulations offer a tactile educational experience, enabling students to explore various situations and observe the consequences of their choices inside a regulated, digital setting. This method is indispensable in disciplines such as science, engineering, and finance, where the practical implementation is just as essential as theoretical understanding.

Augmented/Virtual Reality (AR/VR) experiences enable students to be virtually transported to historical landmarks, the interior of the human body, or even distant planets, providing immersive learning encounters that are unattainable in a conventional classroom. These technologies have the ability to transform intangible concepts into tangible ones, boost spatial comprehension, and greatly enhance retention through experience learning.

v. Accessibility Options

Personalisation in education is more than just adapting to individual learning methods and preferences; it also entails modifying learning settings to suit students with disabilities. This dedication to inclusivity guarantees that every student, irrespective of their physical or cognitive limitations, has equitable chances to excel in their educational endeavours. Through the utilisation of adaptable technologies and the application of design principles, educators can establish inclusive learning experiences that acknowledge and attend to the distinct requirements of every student.

Text-to-speech software can greatly benefit students with visual impairments or struggle with reading since it can be significantly beneficial. This technology utilises text-to-speech functionality, enabling students to access information through auditory means. Integrating text-to-speech features into digital information allows these students to access textual materials independently and effortlessly, greatly improving their learning experience.

Providing alternative text explanations for photos promotes accessibility for students who rely on screen readers, allowing them to comprehend visual content. Descriptive alternative text enables visually impaired students to comprehend the context and importance of images utilised in instructional resources, guaranteeing that they do not overlook crucial visually conveyed information.

Customisable interface designs can enhance navigability and reduce the overwhelming nature of digital learning platforms for students with visual, cognitive, or motor disabilities. Students can customise their learning environment by utilising features such as customisable font sizes, colour contrasts, and streamlined layouts.

This promotes enhanced engagement and reduces obstacles to comprehension, catering to their individual requirements.

Integrating assistive technologies such as voice recognition software, magnification tools, or specialised input devices can enhance the individualised learning experience for students with disabilities. These gadgets can assist students in overcoming physical obstacles to typing, accessing digital platforms, or perceiving small print, allowing them to fully engage in their educational pursuits.

5. AI AND GAI FOR CURRICULUM DEVELOPMENT AND IMPROVEMENT

The impact of AI on the educational industry is truly remarkable. As emphasised by Ahmad et al. (2023), AI's implementation in this field is versatile, serving a vital function at three specific levels: firstly, by providing a customised curriculum to individual students; secondly, by offering extensive support to entire classes; and thirdly, by benefiting entire student cohorts. AI's wide range of capabilities highlights its potential to significantly change and improve educational procedures and results.

Starting from the customised curriculum for individual students, AI algorithms possess the distinct capacity to systematically analyse student outcomes and feedback, facilitating a curriculum development process that relies on data-driven methods.

AI algorithms have the capability to analyse substantial amounts of student performance data, encompassing test scores, assignment marks, and progress reports. Through the analysis of these data points, AI can discern patterns and trends that serve as indicators of the efficacy of the existing curriculum. For example, if a substantial proportion of students continually encounter difficulties with a specific subject or idea, AI can identify this as an area that requires focus. This understanding enables educators to adapt or strengthen particular aspects of the curriculum to tackle these learning deficiencies. GAI can then assist in revising the parts of the content to make it customised to the needs of the students.

i. GAI Assistance

GAI can provide substantial support in personalising and adapting the curriculum to suit all students' requirements. The following describes how GAI can be utilised:

a) Tailored Learning Materials: GAI can produce individualised learning materials with a particular emphasis on the concept of credits and debits. The instructional resources may comprise individualised worksheets, practical exercises, and detailed explanations highlighting the distinctions between the accounting definitions and common utilisation of these terms.

GAI generates the following example

Example 4: GAI Generated Scenario

Consider the scenario of a small business owner, Alex, who recently started an organic coffee shop. In everyday language, Alex views a 'credit' as something positive, like receiving credit for a good idea. Conversely, a 'debit' might be thought of as something negative, like debiting money from a bank account. However, these terms take on a different meaning in the accounting world, particularly under the double-entry system.

When Alex buys coffee beans on credit for $500, the transaction involves two accounting entries. In accounting, a 'debit' increases an asset. Here, the coffee beans are an asset, so the inventory account is debited (increased) by $500. On the other hand, since Alex hasn't paid cash yet, the accounts payable—a liability account—increases. In accounting, increasing a liability account requires a 'credit'. So, accounts payable are credited by $500.

In this transaction, 'debit' doesn't signify something negative, nor does 'credit' imply something positive. Instead, they represent the dual effect of a single transaction on different accounts, ensuring the fundamental accounting equation (Assets = Liabilities + Equity) remains balanced. This example clarifies the specialised use of 'debits' and 'credits' in accounting, distinct from their common everyday usage.

Figure 2. GAI Example of Understanding Fundamentals of Accounting

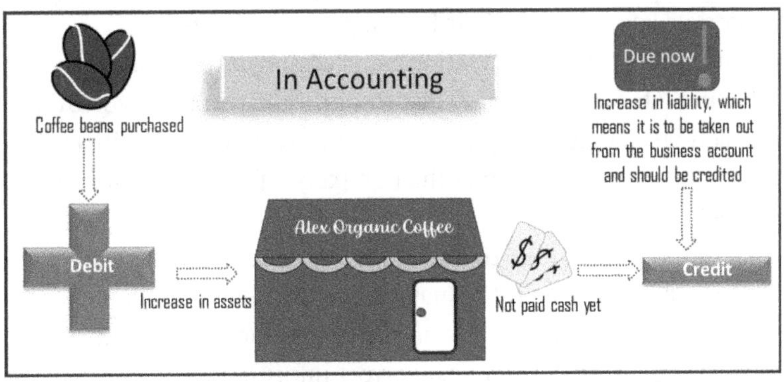

Source: Author

Figure 3. GAI Example of Understanding Fundamentals of Accounting

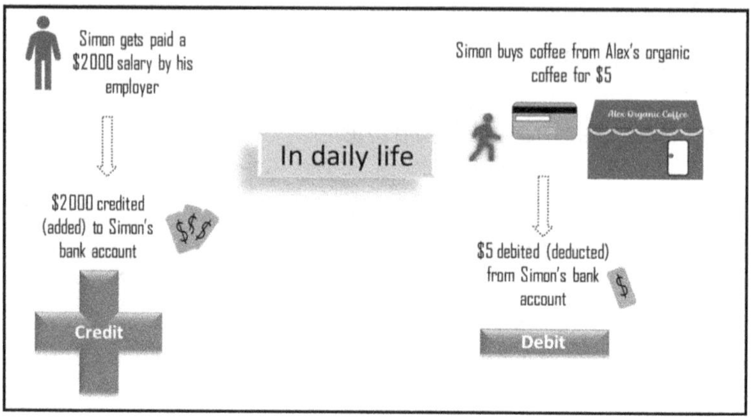

Source: Author

b) Developing engaging educational content: GAI can develop engaging and interactive educational content, including gamified learning experiences and simulations. These may facilitate a more intuitive and engaging comprehension among students regarding the pragmatic implementation of debits and credits in the double-entry accounting system.

A few examples of engaging learning material can be the following;

Create a virtual accounting laboratory for students to experiment with debits and credits. Students can analyse the effects of different entries on income and balance sheets in a controlled setting without the real possibility of financial loss. These items can be included in the virtual accounting laboratory for students to study different materials according to their learning requirements.

Create a virtual accounting simulation game where players manage the accounting activities of a simulated corporation. Their responsibility would involve documenting various transactions and deciding which accounts to credit or debit. The simulation can show how their decisions affect the company's financial statements and offer instant feedback.

Create interactive case studies that challenge students to utilise their understanding of debits and credits in real-world scenarios. Various outcomes could stem from the decisions made in the case study, offering students a practical demonstration of the consequences of inputting correct or incorrect information.

Create a game where users complete tasks or missions that include using debits and credits to solve accounting issues. Completing each quest successfully may provide higher-level entry, offering increasingly complex challenges to overcome.

Create debit and credit puzzles where participants must match the correct debit and credit entries with provided transactions. Engaging in drag-and-drop exercises or interactive crossword puzzles are two effective ways to achieve this goal.

Create a role-playing game where players take on the roles of an accountant or a business owner. They must apply their knowledge of credits and debits to make important decisions that influence the game's result as they advance.

Implement leaderboard challenges to encourage student competition by tasking them with appropriately allocating debits and credits in various scenarios. This can enhance motivation and engagement by establishing a positive competitive environment.

Figure 4. GAI Generated Engaging Learning Material Example of The Accounting Lab

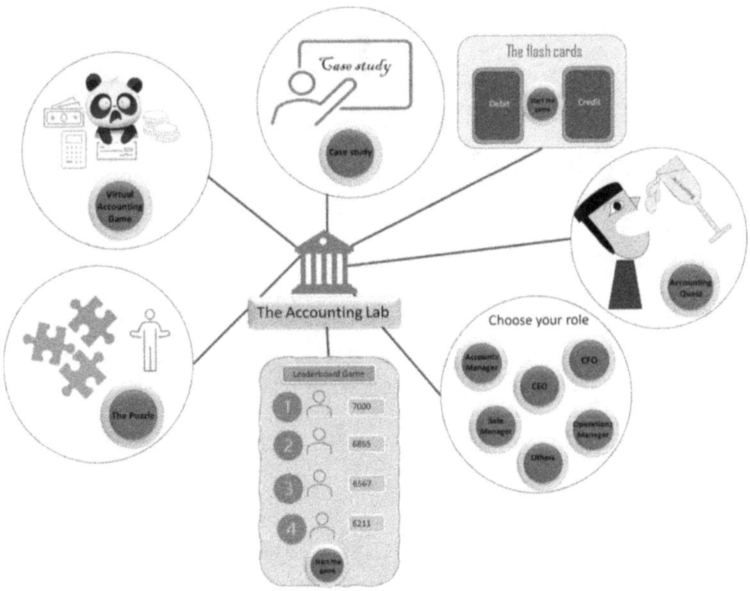

Source: Author

For example, students can select a difficulty level in the leaderboard game, as shown in Figure 5. They can further choose their team members to work in a team and exhibit their scores as a team or an individual on the live leaderboard scoreboard. Moreover, this game can be extended to use interactive boards for decision-making and assess which team has made efficient and effective decisions. The games can be extended to the entire semester.

Implement interactive exams and flashcards to assess students' comprehension of the appropriate circumstances to apply debit and credit cards. To further reinforce learning, these may consist of explanations and immediate feedback. AI-driven educational platforms enable students to obtain prompt feedback on their academic progress. GAI can analyse trainees' solutions to debit and credit-related problems and deliver immediate, individualised feedback, which may consist of suggestions or strategies to better comprehend intricate elements.

Figure 5. GAI Generated Engaging Learning Material-Detailed Example of The Accounting Lab

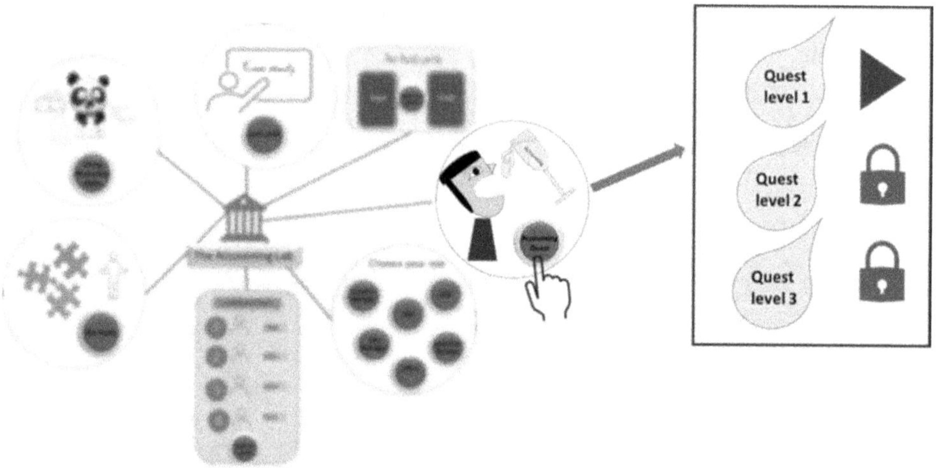

Source: Author

Figure 6. GAI Generated Engaging Learning Material-Another Detailed Example of the Accounting Lab

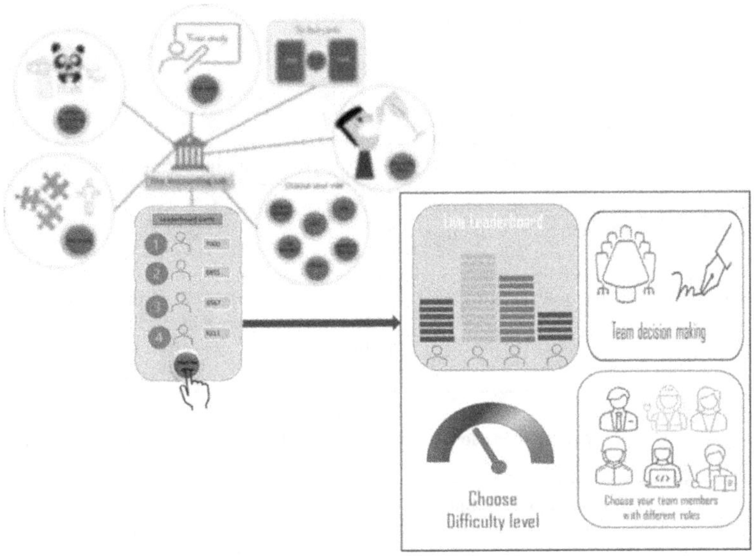

Source: Author

6. CHALLENGES IN USING AI AND GAI IN CURRICULUM DEVELOPMENT

6.1 Assessing the Reliability and Quality of Data

Generative AI technology, like natural language processing models, may create content by analysing extensive datasets from many sources. Although this technology enables quick creation of material, there is a potential issue about the accuracy and dependability of the generated content, particularly when it is unsupervised. Chaka (2023) stated that there are several methods that claim to analyse the dependability of AI-generated data, but none of them are deemed mature yet as they are all still in the early phases. In order to address this problem, it is essential to establish strong validation methods where the content produced is consistently examined and verified for accuracy. This should ideally be done using a combination of automated systems and human supervision. The assessment of the dependability of educational data necessitates the creation and training of tailored instruments that align with the specific requirements of the education sector. Moreover, it is imperative that AI models undergo training using authenticated and reliable data sources, and that they are consistently updated to enhance their precision and pertinence. This stratified method guarantees that the content remains accurate and informative.

Table 1 presents a range of tools that can be utilised to evaluate the dependability of educational data produced by GAI.

Table 1. Tools for assessing the reliability and quality of data.

Types of tools	What do they do	Example of available tools
Validation and Verification Tools	Help confirm the correctness and reliability of outputs	Astera Informatica Alteryx
Data Provenance tools	Assess the data origins	Organisation-specific/custom-build. An example can be camflow (Cambridge Information Flow) used by Cambridge University to capture data provenance
Robustness Testing	Stress test AI systems for specific scenarios	Industry-specific. Not many examples are found in education. One example is computer-assisted learning system in Åbo Akademi University
AI bias checking	Detecting and mitigating the bias in data	Google's What-If Tool IBM's AI Fairness 360 Microsoft's Fairlearn
Data quality management	Improving quality of data used to train and improve the operations of AI	Industry and organistaion specific. One example can be IBM databand

Source: Author

6.2 Impact on Student Individualised Learning

Utilising GAI in education has the capacity to dynamically customise learning materials to suit the specific requirements of each student. Through the analysis of student data, including performance indicators, learning styles, and engagement levels, AI may dynamically adjust the curriculum, providing a highly individualised learning experience. The ability to adapt can be advantageous in accommodating various learning speeds and styles, thus enhancing engagement and optimising learning outcomes. Yet, the success of this customisation relies on the AI's capacity to precisely analyse student data and provide suitable content, requiring continuous monitoring and modifications to assure consistency with educational objectives. While the training of AI should be done on an organisational level, various organisations offer services to assess and optimise student data for personalised and individualised learning. As an example, b14all collaborated with the University of Aveiro to expand the boundaries of artificial intelligence and data analytics in the field of education.

6.3 Role of Teaching Staff

The implementation of AI in education raises the question of whether it will lead to an increased workload for teaching personnel, who will be responsible for overseeing the accuracy of the work produced by AI. Instructors are crucial in providing context, facilitating debates, and delivering insights that cannot be replicated by AI. AI has the potential to decrease the amount of time instructors need to spend on producing and personalising educational materials. However, it also brings along additional responsibilities such as supervising AI operations and incorporating AI-generated information into teaching. Instead of adding to their workload, it changes their responsibilities from administrative activities to more engaging and facilitative obligations. This move has the potential to improve the educational experience by enabling teachers to allocate more attention to teaching and reduce their involvement in logistical preparation.

6.4 Training on the Use of AI Technologies

In order to successfully incorporate AI into educational environments, it is imperative that both educators and learners receive instruction on how to efficiently utilise these technologies. This training should encompass both the practical aspects of using AI tools and the analysis of AI-generated content and data. Educational institutions must to offer continuous professional development to teachers, arming them with the essential competencies to effectively utilise AI in their instructional methodologies. Incorporating modules on digital literacy and AI into the curriculum can effectively provide students with the necessary skills to proficiently engage with AI-powered systems.

Generative AI offers novel prospects for improving personalised learning, but it also brings forward obstacles that require meticulous deliberation and control. To address these problems, it is necessary to establish frameworks for verifying information, modify the roles of educators, and undertake thorough training programmes. By using and continuously improving generative AI, we can greatly enhance the teaching environment.

7. CONCLUSION: SHAPING THE FUTURE OF EDUCATION THROUGH GENERATIVE AI

The revolutionary ability of Generative Artificial Intelligence (GAI) to reshape curriculum development and delivery in the educational field signifies a substantial advancement towards a personalised and adaptable learning model. This chapter has examined the basic principles of GAI and its compatibility with personalised and adaptive learning. We have gained an understanding of how these technologies have the potential to transform educational practices.

Personalised and adaptive learning is characterised by its capacity to accommodate each individual learner's distinct requirements, inclinations, and speed. Educators and curriculum creators can produce dynamic, captivating, and highly tailored learning materials and routes through GAI. By catering to students' various learning styles and capacities, this approach not only improves the learning experience but also maximises educational results.

Current research in the sector, coupled with new teaching methods and educational trends, highlights the significance of matching curriculum development with educational standards and utilising student performance data. Generative AI is essential for this alignment since it provides the necessary capabilities to analyse extensive data, detect areas where learning is lacking, and create material that successfully fills these gaps.

The implementation and provision of GAI-supported curricula have demonstrated encouraging outcomes in establishing adaptable curricula and learning routes. The first diagnostic evaluations and learner profiling establish the foundation for customised learning experiences, while the real-time adaptation guarantees that the curriculum adjusts to the changing needs of each learner. Moreover, personalised learning and additional instructional materials enhance the academic experience, increasing accessibility and inclusivity in education.

The core focus of this strategy is the customisation of learning preferences, which includes factors such as the type of information, the pace of learning, the pathways taken, media choices, and accessibility options. GAI enables a learning environment that respects and enhances the distinctiveness of each student by accommodating their choices. This promotes the democratisation of education, enabling equal access and participation irrespective of an individual's background or talents.

Ultimately, the incorporation of GAI into curriculum development represents a fundamental change towards an educational model that prioritises the needs and preferences of the student. This approach not only questions conventional teaching methods but also establishes a new benchmark for what may be accomplished in the field of education. The consequences of this change are significant, as it can improve the standard of education, increase learner involvement, and eventually cultivate a generation of learners capable of navigating the intricacies of the contemporary world.

Looking ahead, it is certain that the integration of GAI in education will progress, propelled by technological improvements and a growing comprehension of how to cater to the requirements of varied learners effectively. The pursuit of completely harnessing the capabilities of personalized, customised and adaptive learning is a continuing endeavour, and GAI plays a crucial role in this revolutionary undertaking.

To responsibly utilise the potential of GAI in education, educators, policymakers, and technologists must work together. This collaboration will ensure everyone can access the advantages of GAI in education. By doing this, we may access unparalleled possibilities for expansion, originality, and empowerment, crafting a future where every student possesses the resources and assistance necessary to flourish.

References

Ahmad, K., Iqbal, W., El-Hassan, A., Qadir, J., Benhaddou, D., Ayyash, M., & Al-Fuqaha, A. (2023). Data-driven artificial intelligence in education: A comprehensive review. *IEEE Transactions on Learning Technologies*.

Campbell, R., Robinson, W., Neelands, J., Hewston, R., & Mazzoli, L. (2007). Personalised learning: Ambiguities in theory and practice. *British Journal of Educational Studies*, 55(2), 135–154. DOI:10.1111/j.1467-8527.2007.00370.x

Castañeda, L., & Selwyn, N. (2018). *More than tools? Making sense of the ongoing digitizations of higher education* (Vol. 15). SpringerOpen.

Castro, R. (2019). Blended learning in higher education: Trends and capabilities. *Education and Information Technologies*, 24(4), 2523–2546. DOI:10.1007/s10639-019-09886-3

Education, U. S. D. o. (2010). Transforming American education: Learning powered by technology. In: Office of Educational Technology, US Department of Education Washington, DC.

Guan, C., Mou, J., & Jiang, Z. (2020). Artificial intelligence innovation in education: A twenty-year data-driven historical analysis. *International Journal of Innovation Studies*, 4(4), 134–147. DOI:10.1016/j.ijis.2020.09.001

Kem, D. (2022). Personalised and adaptive learning: Emerging learning platforms in the era of digital and smart learning. *International Journal of Social Science and Human Research*, 5(2), 385–391. DOI:10.47191/ijsshr/v5-i2-02

Li, K. C., & Wong, B. T.-M. (2021). Features and trends of personalised learning: A review of journal publications from 2001 to 2018. *Interactive Learning Environments*, 29(2), 182–195. DOI:10.1080/10494820.2020.1811735

Minn, S. (2022). AI-assisted knowledge assessment techniques for adaptive learning environments. *Computers and Education: Artificial Intelligence*, 3, 100050.

Montebello, M., & Montebello, M. (2018). Personal learning networks, portfolios and environments. *AI Injected e-Learning: The Future of Online Education*, 39-50.

Muñoz, J. L. R., Ojeda, F. M., Jurado, D. L. A., Peña, P. F. P., Carranza, C. P. M., Berríos, H. Q., Molina, S. U., Farfan, A. R. M., Arias-Gonzáles, J. L., & Vasquez-Pauca, M. J. (2022). Systematic review of adaptive learning technology for learning in higher education. *Eurasian Journal of Educational Research*, 98(98), 221–233.

Namoun, A., & Alshanqiti, A. (2020). Predicting student performance using data mining and learning analytics techniques: A systematic literature review. *Applied Sciences (Basel, Switzerland)*, 11(1), 237. DOI:10.3390/app11010237

Pendy, B. (2023). From traditional to tech-infused: The evolution of education. *BULLET: Jurnal Multidisiplin Ilmu*, 2(3), 767–777.

Rashid, M. T., Zhang, D. Y., & Wang, D. (2019). Socialcar: A task allocation framework for social media driven vehicular network sensing systems. *Eduvest-Journal of Universal Studies, 3*(6), 1028-1039.

Štuikys, V., & Burbaitė, R. (2024). Personal Generative Libraries for Personalised Learning: A Case Study. In *Evolution of STEM-Driven Computer Science Education: The Perspective of Big Concepts* (pp. 109-134). Springer. DOI:10.1007/978-3-031-48235-9_4

Taylor, D. L., Yeung, M., & Bashet, A. (2021). Personalized and adaptive learning. *Innovative Learning Environments in STEM Higher Education: Opportunities, Challenges, and Looking Forward*, 17-34.

Towle, B., & Halm, M. (2005). Designing adaptive learning environments with learning design. *Learning Design: A Handbook on Modelling and Delivering Networked Education and Training*, 215-226.

KEY TERMS AND DEFINITIONS

Adaptive Learning: Adaptive Learning modifies teaching material and level of difficulty according to a student's performance and comprehension, guaranteeing an optimised and challenging learning journey as they advance.

Curriculum Development: Systematic development and structuring of educational courses and content.

Customised Learning: Customised Learning tailors educational experiences to individual strengths and needs.

Generative Artificial Intelligence (GAI): Artificial intelligence algorithms capable of producing novel content or data utilising large datasets to identify patterns and then using this information to create new outputs like text, graphics, and music.

Metadata Generator: Metadata Generator (MDG) is the heterogeneous metaprogram that (1) accepts values of parameters taken from the metadata concrete feature model as inputs, (2) accepts from the user (learner or teacher) the link to the content in a repository (public or individual), and (3) produces the descriptive part of this content and stores it into DB automatically (Štuikys & Burbaitė, 2024).

Personalised Learning: Customised Learning tailors educational experiences to individual preferences.

Query Generator (QG): Is the heterogeneous metaprogram that (1) forms the user interface for designing the query using parameters derived from the metadata model; (2) creates a query in SQL and sends it to the DB; (3) returns the description of the adequate content to form the LO list as a space for creating a personalised content (Štuikys & Burbaitė, 2024).

Chapter 9
Generative AI in Curriculum Development in Higher Education

Muhammad Usman Tariq
https://orcid.org/0000-0002-7605-3040
Abu Dhabi University, UAE & University of Glasgow, UK

ABSTRACT

This chapter explores the transformative role of Generative Artificial Intelligence (Generative AI) in reshaping the development of higher education curricula. Generative AI, as exemplified by advanced models like GPT-3, employs sophisticated algorithms to generate scientifically relevant content, surpassing traditional norms of teaching and learning. The overview delves into the fundamental principles of Generative AI, emphasizing the significance of generative models such as Generative Adversarial Networks (GANs) and the technical intricacies involved in their training. Essentially, the discourse on the significance of Generative AI in curriculum development underscores its disruptive potential in education. By providing personalized and adaptable pathways for growth, Generative AI addresses the diverse needs of students, fostering engagement and comprehension. It also underscores the role of Generative AI in overcoming limitations in traditional education, facilitating the creation of virtual laboratories and simulations that enhance hands-on learning.

1. INTRODUCTION

Generative Artificial Intelligence (Generative AI) stands at the forefront of technological advancements, providing innovative solutions and transformative potential across various sectors. In the realm of higher education, its application has become

DOI: 10.4018/979-8-3693-2418-9.ch009

increasingly pivotal in reshaping the landscape of curriculum development. This section aims to delve into the multifaceted role of Generative AI in higher education, examining its foundations, applications, challenges, and future prospects. Generative AI, a subset of artificial intelligence, focuses on creating new content—be it text, images, or other forms—rather than solely analyzing and interpreting existing data. The core principles of Generative AI lie in its ability to discern patterns, structures, and relationships within datasets, enabling the generation of novel, scientifically relevant content (Goodfellow et al., 2014). This unique technology has implications far beyond its immediate applications, influencing the very fabric of educational systems. The integration of Generative AI in higher education is a dynamic and evolving process, reshaping traditional paradigms of teaching and learning. As we delve into the depths of this technology, it is essential to comprehend its fundamental principles and components to grasp the full extent of its potential impact.

Overview of Generative AI

Generative AI operates on the premise of generative models, which are trained to understand and replicate patterns present in training data. One of the fundamental structures in Generative AI is the Generative Adversarial Network (GAN), introduced by Goodfellow et al. (2014). GANs consist of two neural networks—a generator and a discriminator—engaged in a continuous feedback loop. The generator aims to create content, while the discriminator evaluates its authenticity. Through this adversarial process, the generator refines its ability to produce content that becomes increasingly indistinguishable from real data. The significance of Generative AI lies not only in its capacity to mimic existing content but also in creating entirely new and scientifically meaningful material. This has significant implications for fields such as natural language processing, computer vision, and creative arts. OpenAI's GPT-3 (Generative Pre-trained Transformer 3), a powerful language model, exemplifies the capabilities of Generative AI by generating coherent and scientifically relevant text based on input prompts (Brown et al., 2020). The fundamental principles of Generative AI are grounded in mathematical concepts and computational algorithms. For instance, the training of generative models involves optimizing parameters through processes like backpropagation and stochastic gradient descent (Goodfellow et al., 2014). Understanding these technical aspects is crucial for educators and curriculum developers seeking to leverage the potential of Generative AI in higher education.

Relevance in Curriculum Development

The integration of Generative AI in curriculum development holds significant promise for fostering innovation and adaptability within educational structures. As traditional methods grapple with the challenges of accommodating diverse learning styles and evolving knowledge landscapes, Generative AI provides a dynamic solution. In the realm of curriculum development, Generative AI contributes to the creation of personalized and adaptive pathways for growth. By analyzing individual learning patterns and preferences, AI algorithms can tailor educational content to meet the specific needs of each student (Siemens and Long, 2011). This individualization of learning paths enhances student engagement and comprehension, fostering a more effective and efficient educational process. Additionally, Generative AI enables the generation of various educational materials, ranging from interactive simulations to virtual laboratories. For instance, AI-powered platforms like Labster use generative models to simulate scientific experiments, providing students with a virtual hands-on experience (Labster, n.d.). This not only enhances traditional learning methods but also transcends geographical and resource constraints, making high-quality education accessible to a broader audience. The significance of Generative AI in curriculum development extends beyond personalized pathways for growth. It plays a crucial role in addressing the ever-changing demands of the gig economy by facilitating the integration of emerging technologies and industry-relevant skills into educational curricula. As the Fourth Industrial Revolution unfolds, the ability of educational institutions to adapt their curricula becomes crucial, and Generative AI emerges as a tool for agile and responsive curriculum development. In summary, Generative AI stands as a formidable force in higher education, offering innovative solutions for curriculum development that align with the diverse needs of students in the 21st century. As we navigate through the complexities of this technology, it becomes evident that its integration has the potential to reshape not only how we teach and learn but also the very nature of educational content and delivery systems.

2. FUNDAMENTALS OF GENERATIVE ARTIFICIAL INTELLIGENCE

Generative Artificial Intelligence (Generative AI) represents a revolutionary paradigm within the realm of artificial intelligence, focusing on the generation of new content rather than mere analysis and interpretation of existing data. A comprehensive grasp of the basics of Generative AI is essential to appreciate its transformative potential across diverse domains. At its core, Generative AI operates on the principles of generative models, sophisticated algorithms designed to learn patterns and structures within datasets and thereby generate novel content. One pivotal structure within Generative AI is the Generative Adversarial Network (GAN), introduced by Goodfellow et al. (2014). GANs consist of two interconnected neural networks—a generator and a discriminator—engaged in a continuous adversarial process. The generator aims to create content, while the discriminator evaluates the authenticity of the generated content. This adversarial feedback loop refines the generator's ability to produce content that becomes increasingly indistinguishable from real data.

Understanding generative models is crucial as they have the capacity to capture and replicate complex patterns present in various datasets. Generative models are not confined to a specific type of data; they can be applied to generate images, text, and even multimedia content. For instance, OpenAI's GPT-3, a language model based on generative principles, has demonstrated unparalleled capabilities in producing coherent and scientifically relevant text based on input prompts (Brown et al., 2020). Additionally, the training process of generative models involves optimization techniques such as backpropagation and stochastic gradient descent (Goodfellow et al., 2014). Backpropagation enables the model to learn and adjust its parameters by minimizing the difference between the generated output and the real data. This iterative refinement process is crucial for the model to progress toward creating high-quality content. Understanding the basics of Generative Artificial Intelligence extends beyond the technical aspects to encompass its broader implications.

Generative AI has the potential to disrupt industries by automating content creation, enabling the generation of creative works, and contributing to scientific research through the creation of novel simulations and models. In summary, a thorough understanding of the fundamentals of Generative AI, particularly the principles of generative models and their applications, is essential for unlocking the full potential of this revolutionary technology. As we delve deeper into the intricacies of these models, it becomes evident that their applications extend far beyond the realm of artificial intelligence, influencing creativity, innovation, and problem-solving across various fields.

Understanding Generative Models

Understanding generative models is a fundamental aspect of navigating the complexities of Generative Artificial Intelligence. Generative models form the backbone of this technology, enabling the creation of new and scientifically relevant content through the learning and replication of patterns within datasets. Generative models operate in contrast to discriminative models, which focus on classifying and distinguishing different categories within data. One of the fundamental generative models is the Variational Autoencoder (VAE), introduced by Kingma and Welling

(2013). VAEs are designed to learn a probabilistic mapping between the data and a latent space, allowing the generation of new information of interest by sampling from this space. This approach facilitates the production of diverse and novel content while maintaining a coherent and sensible structure. Another crucial generative model is the Long Short-Term Memory (LSTM) network, a type of recurrent neural network (RNN) known for its ability to capture and generate sequential data (Hochreiter and Schmidhuber, 1997). LSTMs are particularly effective in generating text and have played a significant role in the advancement of language models within Generative AI. Understanding the nuances of generative models involves delving into their training mechanisms. The training of these models typically involves a large dataset, and the model learns to capture the statistical patterns present in the data. The generative process involves sampling from the learned distribution to create new instances that resemble the training data. This generative capability has been harnessed in applications like image synthesis, where models can generate realistic images based on patterns acquired from a dataset (Goodfellow et al., 2014). Furthermore, understanding generative models requires an awareness of the challenges associated with their training. Mode collapse, where the model produces limited variety in generated outputs, and training instability are common issues that researchers strive to address (Arjovsky et al., 2017). Overcoming these challenges is essential to ensure the stability and creativity of generative models.

In conclusion, understanding generative models is pivotal for unraveling the complexities of Generative Artificial Intelligence. From VAEs to LSTMs, each model contributes to the diversity and richness of generated content. As researchers continue to advance these models and address associated challenges, the potential applications of generative models in fields like creative arts, content generation, and data synthesis become increasingly apparent.

Key Concepts and Algorithms in Generative Artificial Intelligence

Generative Artificial Intelligence (Generative AI) relies on a set of fundamental concepts and algorithms that form the foundation of its functionality. A comprehensive understanding of these concepts is crucial for appreciating the inner workings of Generative AI and its applications across various domains. This discussion explores some of the crucial key concepts and algorithms that define Generative AI, shedding light on their significance and impact.

Generative Adversarial Networks (GANs): One of the foundational concepts in Generative AI is Generative Adversarial Networks (GANs), introduced by Goodfellow et al. (2014). GANs operate on the intriguing principle of adversarial training, involving two neural networks - a generator and a discriminator. The generator's role is to create content, while the discriminator evaluates the authenticity of the generated content. Through this adversarial process, GANs continuously improve the generator's ability to produce content that becomes increasingly indistinguishable from real data. The GAN framework has been instrumental in generating various types of content, from images to text, contributing significantly to advancements in Generative AI (Goodfellow et al., 2014).

Variational Autoencoders (VAEs): Variational Autoencoders, introduced by Kingma and Welling (2013), represent another fundamental concept in Generative AI. VAEs focus on learning a probabilistic mapping between input data and a latent space. This latent space allows for the generation of new pieces of information by sampling, facilitating the creation of diverse and novel content. VAEs have found applications in generating realistic images, especially in situations where capturing the underlying distribution of data is crucial (Kingma and Welling, 2013).

Long Short-Term Memory (LSTM) Networks: In the realm of sequential data generation, Long Short-Term Memory (LSTM) networks, a type of recurrent neural network (RNN), play a significant role. Introduced by Hochreiter and Schmidhuber (1997), LSTMs excel in capturing and generating sequential data, making them particularly effective in text generation tasks. The ability of LSTMs to maintain and update a 'memory' of past information enables the generation of coherent and scientifically meaningful sequences (Hochreiter and Schmidhuber, 1997).

Transformer Architecture: The Transformer architecture, introduced by Vaswani et al. (2017), has become a crucial concept in Generative AI, especially for natural language processing tasks. Transformers leverage a self-attention mechanism that allows the model to selectively weigh different parts of the input sequence. This attention mechanism has proven highly effective in capturing long-range dependencies and relationships within sequential data. Notably, OpenAI's GPT-3 (Brown et al., 2020), a language model based on the Transformer architecture, has demonstrated exceptional capabilities in generating coherent and scientifically relevant text.

Training Mechanisms: The training mechanisms used in Generative AI include optimization techniques like backpropagation and stochastic gradient descent (Goodfellow et al., 2014). Backpropagation enables the model to learn and adjust its parameters by minimizing the difference between the generated output and the real data. This iterative refinement process is crucial for the model to progress toward creating high-quality content.

Challenges in Training: Generative AI poses unique challenges during the training phase. Mode collapse, where the model produces limited variety in generated outputs, and training instability are common issues that researchers continuously address (Arjovsky et al., 2017). Striking a balance between training stability and variety in generated content is a critical consideration in developing robust Generative AI models.

Ethical Considerations: As Generative AI becomes more prevalent, ethical considerations regarding biases and misuse come to the forefront. Biases present in training data can be perpetuated in generated content, raising concerns about fairness and representation (Raji and Buolamwini, 2019). Mitigating these ethical concerns requires a concerted effort to address biases in both training data and algorithms. Thus, the key concepts and algorithms in Generative AI form a complex tapestry that underpins its functionality and applications. From the adversarial training of GANs to the probabilistic mapping of VAEs and the attention mechanisms in Transformers, these concepts shape the landscape of content generation and hold the key to unlocking the full potential of Generative AI.

3. APPLICATIONS IN HIGHER EDUCATION

Generative Artificial Intelligence (Generative AI) emerges as a transformative force in higher education, offering a spectrum of applications that extend beyond conventional teaching methodologies. As institutions strive to adapt to the evolving needs of students and the demands of the digital age, the integration of Generative AI becomes crucial in reshaping opportunities for growth and personalizing educational pathways.

Enhancing Growth Opportunities

Generative AI significantly contributes to the enhancement of growth opportunities in higher education. An exemplary application is the creation of interactive and immersive educational content. Virtual laboratories powered by Generative AI provide students with realistic simulations of scientific experiments, enabling hands-on learning experiences even in the absence of physical labs (Labster, n.d.). This not only expands the scope of learning but also addresses resource constraints in traditional educational settings.

Moreover, Generative AI plays a pivotal role in content creation and customization. OpenAI's GPT-3, a language model based on Generative AI, can generate scientifically relevant and coherent text in response to prompts. This capability can be leveraged to automate the production of learning materials, quizzes, and assessments, saving educators time and ensuring the availability of diverse and engaging content (Brown et al., 2020).

The utilization of Generative AI in the development of intelligent tutoring systems further enhances growth opportunities. These systems employ AI algorithms to adaptively guide students through their learning journey, providing real-time feedback and personalized assistance (VanLehn, 2011). This personalized guidance improves comprehension and retention, fostering a more effective and tailored educational experience. Additionally, Generative AI contributes to the creation of chatbots and virtual assistants that can assist students in their inquiries, offer support, and facilitate discussions. These intelligent systems, powered by natural language processing capabilities, create a more interactive and accessible learning environment (Wang et al., 2019). The potential to engage in meaningful conversations with AI-driven companions enhances student engagement and provides instant assistance, particularly in online learning settings. In summary, the integration of Generative AI in higher education holds promise for transforming growth opportunities. By facilitating the creation of interactive content, automating content generation, and providing personalized support through intelligent tutoring systems, Generative AI contributes to a more dynamic and responsive educational landscape.

Personalized Learning Pathways in Education

Personalization in education is a crucial focal point, aiming to address the diverse needs and learning styles of individual students. Generative AI emerges as a powerful tool in crafting personalized learning pathways, addressing the inherent variability in students' abilities, preferences, and learning paces. One prominent application of Generative AI in personalized education is adaptive learning platforms. These platforms utilize AI algorithms to analyze individual student performance, identify strengths and weaknesses, and dynamically adjust the difficulty and content of learning materials (Siemens and Long, 2011). For example, the Khan Academy employs adaptive learning technology to tailor math exercises based on students' proficiency levels, ensuring a customized learning trajectory (Khan Academy, n.d.). Furthermore, Generative AI contributes to the creation of intelligent recommendation systems within educational platforms. These systems analyze students' past interactions, preferences, and performance data to suggest relevant courses, resources, and supplementary materials (Verbert et al., 2012). By providing personalized recommendations, students can explore topics aligned with their interests and career aspirations, fostering a truly engaging and purpose-driven educational experience. Generative AI also plays a role in the development of personalized learning environments through the creation of AI-driven educational content. For instance, adaptive e-books can dynamically adjust content based on students' progress, allowing them to explore concepts at their own pace and receive additional support in areas where they may be struggling (Zapata-Rivera and Greer, 2004). This tailoring of content to individual needs enhances the effectiveness of learning materials.

Moreover, the personalization of education pathways extends to the realm of skill development and career readiness. Generative AI can analyze industry trends, job market demands, and individual skill profiles to recommend personalized learning paths aligned with students' career goals (Wang et al., 2020). This proactive approach equips students with the necessary skills and knowledge required for success in their chosen fields.

In conclusion, the integration of Generative AI in higher education facilitates the creation of personalized learning pathways, addressing the diverse needs and aspirations of students. From adaptive learning platforms to intelligent recommendation systems, Generative AI contributes to the development of an educational ecosystem that is responsive, engaging, and tailored to the unique journey of each learner.

4. INTEGRATING GENERATIVE ARTIFICIAL INTELLIGENCE IN CURRICULUM DESIGN

The incorporation of Generative Artificial Intelligence (Generative AI) into curriculum design marks a paradigm shift in educational practices, offering innovative ways to tailor growth opportunities to the evolving needs of students. This discussion explores the integration of Generative AI in curriculum design, focusing on two key aspects:

Curriculum Planning and Adaptive Learning Systems

Curriculum Planning

Curriculum planning, a fundamental aspect of effective educational preparation, involves the systematic delineation of learning objectives, content, assessments, and instructional strategies across a program or course. The integration of Generative AI in curriculum planning introduces new elements of efficiency, personalization, and adaptability.

Generative AI contributes to curriculum planning by automating the creation of learning materials and resources. OpenAI's GPT-3, a language model capable of generating realistic and coherent text, can assist educators in developing comprehensive course outlines, lecture notes, and supplementary materials. This automation not only saves time but ensures the availability of diverse and high-quality content to support various learning styles (Brown et al., 2020).

Additionally, Generative AI facilitates the dynamic adaptation of curriculum content based on real-time data and student feedback. As students engage with learning materials, AI algorithms can analyze their interactions, identify areas of difficulty, and generate additional resources or activities to address specific learning needs. This responsive approach to curriculum planning ensures that the content remains relevant and effective in facilitating student learning (Siemens and Long,

2011). The use of Generative AI in curriculum planning extends to the creation of interactive simulations and virtual laboratories. Platforms like Labster leverage generative models to simulate scientific experiments, providing students with a virtual hands-on experience (Labster, n.d.). This not only enhances the comprehension of complex concepts but also overcomes logistical challenges associated with physical labs, making quality education more accessible. However, the integration of Generative AI in curriculum planning is not without challenges. Ethical considerations, such as biases present in training data, must be carefully addressed to ensure fair and unbiased content generation (Raji and Buolamwini, 2019). Moreover, educators must actively engage in guiding the AI models to align with educational objectives and curriculum standards, striking a balance between automation and intentional curriculum design. In conclusion, the integration of Generative AI in curriculum planning holds immense potential for streamlining content creation, personalizing growth opportunities, and enhancing the overall effectiveness of educational programs.

Adaptive Learning Systems

Adaptive learning systems represent a revolutionary approach to education, tailoring growth opportunities to the individual needs and progress of each student. Generative AI plays a crucial role in the development and enhancement of adaptive learning systems, offering dynamic and personalized educational pathways.

One significant application of Generative AI in adaptive learning systems is the creation of intelligent tutoring systems. These systems leverage AI algorithms to analyze individual student performance, identify strengths and weaknesses, and adaptively guide students through their learning process (VanLehn, 2011). For example, Carnegie Learning's MATHia uses AI-driven tutoring to provide real-time feedback and personalized assistance in math education (Carnegie Learning, n.d.). Generative AI contributes to the personalization of learning content within adaptive systems. By analyzing the learning styles, preferences, and progress of each student, AI algorithms can dynamically adjust the difficulty and format of educational materials. This ensures that students are appropriately challenged, engaged, and supported in their individual learning paths (Siemens and Long, 2011).

Moreover, Generative AI enhances adaptive learning systems through the creation of customized assessments and exercises. These systems can generate tailored quizzes and assignments based on the specific needs and learning objectives of each student. The adaptive nature of these assessments ensures that students receive targeted feedback and support, fostering a deeper understanding of the material (Corbett and Anderson, 1995).

The integration of Generative AI in adaptive learning systems also extends to the development of chatbots and virtual assistants. These AI-driven interfaces provide students with instant support, answering questions, providing explanations, and facilitating discussions. The conversational nature of these systems enhances student engagement and provides additional avenues for personalized learning interactions (Wang et al., 2019). Despite the promising advancements, challenges persist in the integration of Generative AI in adaptive learning systems. Addressing issues of data security, ensuring algorithmic transparency, and mitigating biases are critical considerations to uphold ethical standards and promote a positive learning environment (Leyva and Hadwin, 2020). In conclusion, the integration of Generative AI in adaptive learning systems represents a significant leap toward personalized and effective education. By tailoring content, assessments, and support tools to individual student needs, Generative AI contributes to a dynamic and responsive educational ecosystem that empowers students on their unique educational journeys.

5. CHALLENGES AND CONSIDERATIONS IN GENERATIVE ARTIFICIAL INTELLIGENCE IN EDUCATION

Generative Artificial Intelligence (Generative AI) stands at the forefront of technological advancement, but its integration into various domains brings forth a host of challenges and considerations. This discussion delves into the intricate challenges and considerations surrounding Generative AI, with a focus on ethical implications and the crucial task of addressing bias within these systems in the educations sector.

Ethical Implications

The rapid progression of Generative AI raises significant ethical concerns that extend across various sectors, encompassing issues such as privacy, security, societal impacts, and accountability. As these systems become more integrated into daily life, understanding and addressing the ethical implications becomes crucial in the higher education as students are involved in the process.

One primary ethical concern is the potential misuse of Generative AI for malicious purposes, including the creation of deepfakes—fabricated media convincingly replacing one person's likeness with another in videos or images (Brundage et al., 2018). Deepfakes have the potential to deceive, manipulate, and cause harm by generating misleading content, thereby undermining trust in digital media.

Privacy considerations also loom large in the ethical landscape of Generative AI. The ability of these systems to generate realistic yet synthetic data poses risks to individuals' privacy, making it increasingly challenging to distinguish between authentic and generated information. Ensuring robust privacy mechanisms and regulations is crucial to protect individuals from potential infringements.

Additionally, Generative AI introduces ethical challenges related to intellectual property and copyright. Questions arise about the ownership and authorship of the generated works as these systems produce content autonomously, necessitating a reevaluation of existing legal frameworks to adapt to the dynamic nature of AI-generated content (Burrell, 2016).

Another ethical aspect revolves around the societal impacts of Generative AI, particularly exacerbating existing inequalities. Biases present in training data can be perpetuated in generated content, leading to discriminatory outcomes. Addressing this requires ongoing research and mitigation strategies to ensure fairness and equity.

Ensuring accountability in the deployment of Generative AI systems is a critical ethical consideration. The opaque nature of some AI models, coupled with their ability to generate complex outcomes, poses challenges in understanding, interpreting, and attributing responsibility for the decisions made by these systems. The lack of transparency can hinder effective oversight and accountability mechanisms.

To address these ethical concerns, a multi-faceted approach is necessary. Collaboration between technologists, ethicists, policymakers, and the public is essential to establish guidelines, frameworks, and regulations governing the responsible development and deployment of Generative AI. Ethical considerations should be embedded in the design process, and ongoing vigilance is required to adapt to emerging challenges and ethical scenarios.

Addressing Bias in AI

The pervasive issue of bias in AI systems, including Generative AI, presents significant challenges to the fair and impartial deployment of these technologies. Bias can manifest in various forms, including racial, gender, economic, and cultural preferences, and resolving these issues is essential for ensuring just and inclusive AI applications.

One primary source of bias in Generative AI lies in the training data used to develop these models. Biases present in the data, whether intentional or inadvertent, can be learned and propagated by the AI system, leading to biased outputs (Crawford and Calo, 2016). For example, language models trained on biased text corpora may produce outputs that reinforce stereotypes or exhibit discriminatory language.

Addressing bias requires a comprehensive examination of training data and proactive measures to mitigate and correct biases. Diverse and representative datasets are crucial to ensure that AI models learn from a wide range of examples, minimizing the risk of perpetuating existing biases. Continuous monitoring and auditing of training data can help identify and rectify biases in an ongoing manner.

Algorithmic transparency is a crucial aspect of addressing bias. Understanding how AI models make decisions allows for the identification of biased patterns and the development of strategies to mitigate them. Open-sourcing AI models and algorithms, where feasible, promotes transparency and enables external scrutiny by researchers and the broader community (Diakopoulos, 2016).

Moreover, incorporating diverse perspectives in the development and evaluation of AI systems is instrumental in uncovering and correcting biases. Diversity in the development team ensures that various viewpoints and experiences are considered, reducing the likelihood of biased outcomes (O'Neil, 2016). Seeking input from the communities that may be affected by AI systems enhances the nuanced understanding of potential biases. Ethical considerations play a vital role in addressing bias. Ethical AI development involves a commitment to fairness, accountability, and transparency. Implementing ethical guidelines and codes of conduct within organizations and industries can create a culture of responsibility and encourage ethical decision-making throughout the AI development lifecycle (Jobin et al., 2019). The integration of bias mitigation techniques directly into the design and deployment of AI systems is critical. Strategies such as debiasing algorithms, adversarial training, and fairness-aware AI design aim to reduce and eliminate biases within the model's decision-making processes (Zhang et al., 2018). However, it is crucial to acknowledge that addressing bias in AI is an ongoing and iterative process. As AI systems evolve and encounter new data, biases may emerge or evolve over time. Hence, continuous monitoring, evaluation, and adaptation are essential components of an effective strategy to mitigate bias in Generative AI and other AI applications.

6. CASE STUDIES IN GENERATIVE ARTIFICIAL INTELLIGENCE: EXPLORING SUCCESSFUL IMPLEMENTATIONS AND LESSONS LEARNED

Successful Implementations

Generative Artificial Intelligence (Generative AI) has witnessed remarkable success stories across various domains, showcasing its transformative potential in addressing complex challenges and enhancing diverse processes. This section examines four case studies that epitomize successful implementations of Generative AI, providing insights into the impact of these advancements.

Healthcare: Enhancing Clinical Imaging With Generative AI

In healthcare, a notable success story revolves around the use of Generative AI to expand clinical imaging datasets. Limited datasets for training diagnostic algorithms have been a persistent challenge in clinical image analysis. Researchers have successfully utilized Generative Adversarial Networks (GANs) to address this issue. By generating synthetic clinical images closely resembling real patient data, GANs contribute to the development of training datasets, leading to more robust and accurate diagnostic models (Erickson et al., 2017). This implementation has significantly improved the capabilities of clinical imaging systems, enabling more precise and reliable diagnoses. The ability to generate diverse and realistic clinical images supports training AI models to recognize patterns and abnormalities in various diseases. This case highlights the potential of Generative AI to address data scarcity challenges in healthcare, ultimately improving patient outcomes.

Art and Creativity: Mario Klingemann's AI-Generated Art

The integration of Generative AI and art has produced stunning results, as seen in the collaboration between artist Mario Klingemann and Google Arts and Culture. Klingemann utilized Generative Adversarial Networks (GANs) to create unique and mesmerizing artworks. Through the iterative process of training the GAN on a diverse range of artistic styles and themes, Klingemann generated artworks that pushed the boundaries of traditional artistic creation (Google Arts and Culture, n.d.). This case study highlights the potential of Generative AI in fostering creativity and innovation in the field of art. Klingemann's AI-generated artworks earned recognition in the art community, demonstrating how Generative AI can serve as a tool for artists to explore new realms of expression and produce exceptional visual experiences.

Natural Language Processing: GPT-3 in Content Generation and Coding Assistance

OpenAI's GPT-3, a language model based on Generative AI, has shown remarkable advancements in natural language processing tasks. GPT-3's ability to understand and generate human-like text has been harnessed for content generation and coding assistance. Developers and content creators can interact with GPT-3 to produce realistic and logically relevant text for various purposes, from writing articles to assisting with coding tasks (Brown et al., 2020). The successful implementation of GPT-3 in various applications highlights its versatility and the potential for Generative AI to revolutionize how individuals interact with language. GPT-3's few-shot learning capabilities enable it to adapt quickly to specific tasks, showcasing the flexibility and broad relevance of Generative AI in natural language understanding and generation.

AI for Anomaly Discovery in Financial Transactions

In the finance sector, Generative AI has been instrumental in the development of AI models for fraud detection. One prominent case study involves the use of Generative AI to analyze transaction patterns and identify anomalies indicative of fraudulent activities. By employing advanced AI techniques, including generative approaches, financial institutions can detect and prevent fraudulent transactions in real-time (Dal Pozzolo et al., 2015). This successful implementation showcases the potential of Generative AI in enhancing security measures in the finance industry. By analyzing large datasets and learning complex patterns, Generative AI contributes to the development of effective fraud detection systems, safeguarding financial institutions and their clients from unlawful activities. These case studies collectively demonstrate the breadth of successful implementations of Generative AI, ranging from healthcare and art to natural language processing and finance. The outcomes reflect the versatility and effectiveness of Generative AI in addressing domain-specific challenges and pushing the boundaries of possibilities in various fields.

Lessons Learned

The successful implementations of Generative AI have provided valuable lessons for researchers, developers, and organizations. Understanding the challenges faced and the insights gained from these experiences is crucial for refining future applications of Generative AI. Here are key lessons learned from the four case studies:

Data Quality is Vital for Healthcare Applications

In healthcare applications, the quality of training data is critical for the success of Generative AI models. The case study on clinical imaging expansion emphasizes the importance of ensuring diverse and representative datasets. Rigorous data preprocessing, including addressing biases and ensuring data integrity, contributes to the generation of synthetic clinical images that enhance the training of diagnostic algorithms (Erickson et al., 2017).

Interdisciplinary Collaboration Drives Creative Advancement

The collaboration between artist Mario Klingemann and Google Arts and Culture exemplifies the power of interdisciplinary collaboration. In the field of art and creativity, bringing together expertise from both the artistic and technological realms enhances the potential for innovation. This case study highlights the importance of fostering collaboration between artists, technologists, and researchers to unlock additional possibilities and push the boundaries of creative expression (Google Arts and Culture, n.d.).

Flexibility and Versatility in Natural Language Processing

The case study on GPT-3 emphasizes the flexibility and versatility of Generative AI in natural language processing. GPT-3's ability to generate realistic and logically relevant text for various tasks demonstrates its broad applicability. The lesson learned is the potential for Generative AI models, like GPT-3, to serve as powerful resources in a variety of language-related applications, transforming how individuals interact with text (Brown et al., 2020).

Improving Security Measures in Finance

The use of Generative AI in finance for fraud detection provides insights into the lessons learned in enhancing security measures. The case study emphasizes the importance of employing advanced AI techniques, including generative approaches, to analyze transaction patterns and identify anomalies. The lesson is that Generative AI contributes to the development of robust fraud detection systems, offering real-time protection against illicit activities in the finance sector (Dal Pozzolo et al., 2015).

Ethical Considerations and Transparency are Essential Across Domains

Across the case studies, the importance of ethical considerations and transparency emerges as a common theme. Whether in healthcare, art, natural language processing, or finance, it is critical to embed ethical guidelines from the inception of Generative AI projects. Transparency in how these models operate, especially in critical domains, builds trust and ensures responsible artificial intelligence development. The lessons learned emphasize the ongoing need for ethical frameworks, user education, and transparent communication about the capabilities and limitations of Generative AI systems (Crawford and Calo, 2016; Dignum et al., 2019). Thus, the case studies of successful Generative AI implementations provide valuable insights and examples for future development and deployment. These cases underscore the importance of data quality, interdisciplinary collaboration, flexibility, and ethical considerations in harnessing the full potential of Generative AI across various domains.

7. FUTURE DIRECTIONS OF GENERATIVE ARTIFICIAL INTELLIGENCE

Generative Artificial Intelligence (Generative AI) has achieved significant milestones, ushering in a new era of innovation and possibilities. Looking ahead, emerging trends and potential impacts on various sectors, including higher education, come into focus. This detailed exploration delves into the anticipated future possibilities of Generative AI, examining evolving trends and its potential influence on higher education.

Emerging Trends in Generative AI

Advancements in Generative Models

The future of Generative AI is poised for advancements in generative models, pushing the boundaries of creativity and realism. Emerging models are likely to demonstrate more sophisticated capabilities in generating high-fidelity content across domains such as images, text, and even media. Continued developments in Generative Adversarial Networks (GANs) may lead to more stable training processes, enabling the creation of synthetic data with exceptional realism (Brock et al., 2019).

Cross-Domain Applications

The future of Generative AI involves a shift toward cross-domain applications, where models trained in one domain can be adapted to perform tasks in another. This cross-domain adaptability holds promise for more efficient use of artificial intelligence models across diverse industries. For example, a model trained in natural language processing might be fine-tuned for medical image analysis, contributing to enhanced capabilities and versatility (Razavian et al., 2014).

Human-AI Collaboration

The future landscape of Generative AI envisions increased collaboration between humans and AI systems. Generative models, equipped with advanced natural language understanding, may work alongside human creators, supporting content generation, design, and problem-solving. This collaborative approach holds potential in fields like creative arts, where AI becomes a tool for artists to enhance their creative expressions rather than replacing human creativity (Bau et al., 2020).

Ethical AI and Bias Mitigation

The future trajectory of Generative AI is intertwined with an increased emphasis on ethical considerations and bias mitigation. Researchers and developers are expected to focus on the development of models that are not only technologically advanced but also ethically responsible. Efforts to address biases in training data and enhance transparency in AI decision-making processes will play a crucial role in shaping the responsible future of Generative AI (Jobin et al., 2019).

Explainability and Interpretability

As Generative AI models become increasingly complex, the need for explainability and interpretability rises. Future trends are likely to focus on developing models that provide insights into their decision-making processes. This is particularly important in applications like healthcare, where understanding why a model made a specific decision is essential for gaining trust from practitioners and ensuring patient safety (Caruana et al., 2015).

Federated Learning for Privacy

Privacy concerns in AI applications, particularly those involving sensitive data, drive the future adoption of federated learning in Generative AI. This approach allows models to be trained across decentralized devices without centralizing sensitive information. Federated learning aligns with the growing emphasis on privacy-preserving AI, making it a promising avenue for future developments in Generative AI applications involving user-generated content (McMahan et al., 2017).

Potential Impact on Higher Education

Personalized Learning Environments

Generative AI holds the potential to transform the landscape of higher education by establishing personalized learning environments. Adaptive learning systems, powered by Generative AI, can analyze individual learning patterns, preferences, and performance to tailor educational content. This level of personalization enhances the effectiveness of learning experiences, catering to various learning styles and pacing (Siemens and Long, 2011).

Curriculum Design and Content Generation

The impact of Generative AI on higher education extends to curriculum and content generation. AI models can assist instructors in designing curriculum maps that align with industry needs and societal advancements. Additionally, Generative AI can aid in generating educational content, including lecture materials, quizzes, and interactive simulations. This not only saves time for instructors but also ensures the relevance and diversity of educational resources (Dahl et al., 2013).

Enhanced Student Engagement

Generative AI has the potential to enhance student engagement through the development of interactive and immersive learning experiences. Virtual tutors and AI-driven educational games can provide personalized feedback, adapt to individual learning styles, and create engaging environments that foster active participation. These advancements contribute to a more dynamic and participatory learning environment in higher education (Murray, 2017).

Automated Assessment and Feedback

The future impact of Generative AI on higher education includes the automation of assessment and feedback processes. AI models can efficiently evaluate assignments, tests, and exams, providing instant feedback to students. This streamlines the grading process for instructors and offers timely insights to students, enabling them to identify areas for improvement and track their progress throughout a course (Dong et al., 2017).

Expanded Research Capabilities

In the realm of research, Generative AI can expand the capabilities of higher education institutions. AI models can assist researchers in generating hypotheses, analyzing vast datasets, and even suggesting novel research directions. This collaborative approach between researchers and AI systems accelerates the pace of discovery and opens new avenues for interdisciplinary research (Topol, 2019; Raimi et al. 2022).

Addressing Accessibility Challenges

Generative AI has the potential to address accessibility challenges in higher education by creating adaptable learning materials for students with diverse needs. AI-driven tools can generate alternative formats of educational content, such as audio descriptions, transcripts, and material formats, ensuring that the learning experience is inclusive and accessible to all students (Baker Sennett et al., 2019).

Thus, the future possibilities of Generative AI are marked by emerging trends that promise advancements in model capabilities, ethical considerations, and human-AI collaboration. The potential impact on higher education is vast, encompassing personalized learning environments, curriculum design, enhanced student engagement, automated assessment, expanded research capabilities, and the alleviation of accessibility challenges. As these trends continue to unfold, Generative AI is poised to play a significant role in reshaping the landscape of education and learning opportunities.

8. RECOMMENDATIONS FOR IMPLEMENTATION OF GENERATIVE ARTIFICIAL INTELLIGENCE IN EDUCATION

Generative Artificial Intelligence (Generative AI) holds significant potential for education, providing innovative ways to enhance learning opportunities, streamline administrative processes, and facilitate research endeavors within educational institutions. However, successful implementation requires careful consideration of best practices and guidelines to ensure ethical, effective, and reliable integration. This section offers recommendations for the implementation of Generative AI in education, focusing on best practices and guidelines for educational institutions (Raimi et al., 2022).

Best Practices

Ethical Considerations and Transparency

The ethical use of Generative AI is crucial in educational settings. Institutions should establish clear ethical guidelines for the development and deployment of AI technologies, emphasizing transparency in decision-making processes. Collaboration among teachers, researchers, and developers is essential to ensure that AI systems operate with fairness, accountability, and transparency, addressing biases and promoting responsible AI practices (Jobin et al., 2019).

Data Privacy and Security

Educational institutions must prioritize data privacy and security when implementing Generative AI. Sensitive student information and institutional data require robust protection measures to prevent unauthorized access or misuse. Implementing encryption, access controls, and regular security audits are essential for maintaining the integrity and confidentiality of data processed by AI systems (Beeri et al., 2016).

User-Centric Design

The successful integration of Generative AI in education relies on a user-centric design approach. Developers should collaborate with teachers, students, and administrators to understand their unique needs, challenges, and preferences. By involving end-users in the design process, AI applications can be tailored to align with the specific requirements of educational stakeholders, ensuring user acceptance and usability (Dimitrov, 2018).

Continuous Monitoring and Evaluation

To ensure the ongoing effectiveness and ethical use of Generative AI, educational institutions should establish frameworks for continuous monitoring and evaluation. Regular assessments of AI system performance, impact on learning outcomes, and adherence to ethical standards are crucial. This iterative process allows for adjustments, improvements, and the identification of potential challenges or biases that may arise over time (Hussain et al., 2020).

Interdisciplinary Collaboration

Given the multi-faceted nature of education, interdisciplinary collaboration is critical to the successful implementation of Generative AI. Bringing together experts from education, computer science, ethics, and other relevant fields facilitates a holistic approach. This collaboration ensures that AI solutions align with educational goals, pedagogical principles, and ethical considerations, contributing to the development of robust and effective applications (Yu et al., 2017).

Guidelines for Educational Institutions

Establish Ethical Review Boards

Educational institutions should establish ethical review boards or committees dedicated to addressing the ethical implications of Generative AI projects. These boards, comprising experts from various disciplines, can assess the potential impact on students, faculty, and the broader educational community. Conducting ethical reviews before and during the implementation of AI projects allows institutions to identify and address ethical concerns proactively (Tariq, 2024).

Provide Comprehensive Training

To facilitate the successful adoption of Generative AI, educational institutions should invest in comprehensive training programs for teachers, administrators, and AI developers. Training should cover both the technical aspects of AI implementation and the ethical considerations associated with AI in education. This ensures that stakeholders have the necessary knowledge and skills to make informed decisions and navigate potential challenges.

Prioritize Accessibility and Inclusivity

Guidelines for educational institutions should emphasize the importance of prioritizing accessibility and inclusivity in Generative AI implementations. AI applications should be designed to accommodate diverse learning needs, including those of students with disabilities. Ensuring that AI-driven content is accessible to all students fosters an inclusive educational environment.

Engage in Open Dialogue

Educational institutions should foster open dialogue and communication about Generative AI implementations. This includes engaging with students, faculty, parents, and the wider community to address concerns, provide information about AI initiatives, and gather feedback. Transparent communication builds trust and allows educational institutions to incorporate diverse perspectives in shaping the ethical and responsible use of Generative AI (Crawford and Calo, 2016).

Adopt Incremental Integration

Instead of rapid and widespread implementation, educational institutions should adopt a gradual and phased approach to integrating Generative AI. Pilot programs and small-scale implementations allow institutions to assess the impact, address challenges, and refine AI applications before full-scale deployment. This iterative approach ensures a thoughtful and responsible integration of AI technologies in educational settings (Wang et al., 2018; Tariq, 2024)).

Monitor and Address Bias

Guidelines should explicitly address the monitoring and mitigation of biases in Generative AI systems used in education. Educational institutions should implement measures to regularly assess AI models for biases related to gender, ethnicity, socioeconomic status, and other factors. Strategies for addressing and minimizing bias should be integrated into the development and deployment stages, promoting fair and unbiased educational experiences (Buolamwini and Gebru, 2018).

Thus, the successful implementation of Generative AI in education requires adherence to best practices and guidelines that prioritize ethical considerations, user-centric design, continuous evaluation, interdisciplinary collaboration, and responsible AI use. Educational institutions play a crucial role in shaping the future of AI in education by fostering a culture of ethical awareness, inclusivity, and transparent communication. As Generative AI continues to evolve, institutions should remain vigilant in aligning AI applications with educational values and ethical principles.

9. CONCLUSION

Generative Artificial Intelligence (Generative AI) emerges as a powerful tool with transformative potential in reshaping curriculum development in higher education. Throughout this exploration, we have delved into various facets, ranging from grasping the fundamentals of Generative AI to scrutinizing its applications, challenges, and future prospects. This conclusion summarizes key points and looks ahead to the evolving landscape of curriculum development with Generative AI (Tariq, 2022).

Recap of Key Points

Fundamentals of Generative AI

The journey commenced with an exploration of the fundamentals, unraveling the essential concepts and algorithms that underpin Generative AI. Understanding the intricacies of generative models, particularly Generative Adversarial Networks (GANs) and Variational Autoencoders (VAEs), laid the groundwork for comprehending the technology's capabilities in generating novel and realistic content.

Applications in Higher Education

The investigation extended to the diverse applications of Generative AI in higher education. From enhancing learning opportunities to personalized educational pathways, Generative AI showcased its true potential in disrupting how educators design and deliver curricula. The use of Generative AI in curriculum planning and adaptive learning systems demonstrated its adaptability to meet the evolving needs of students and institutions (Tariq, et al., 2021).

Challenges and Considerations

Recognizing the immense potential of Generative AI, we delved into the challenges and ethical considerations associated with its implementation. Addressing biases in artificial intelligence, ethical implications, and ensuring transparency emerged as crucial factors in navigating the responsible integration of Generative AI into educational settings.

Case Studies

The evaluation of case studies provided real insights into successful implementations of Generative AI. From enhancing medical imaging in healthcare to generating AI-driven art, these case studies highlighted the versatility and impact of Generative AI across different domains, showcasing its ability to address unique challenges and foster innovation.

Future Possibilities

Looking forward, the discussion extended to the future possibilities of Generative AI. Emerging trends, including advancements in generative models, cross-domain applications, and human-AI collaboration, were identified as key drivers shaping the trajectory of Generative AI. Ethical considerations, fairness, and federated learning emerged as fundamental aspects guiding future developments (Tariq and Ismail, 2024).

Guidelines for Implementation

Recognizing the need for responsible implementation, recommendations and guidelines for educational institutions were formulated. Best practices emphasizing ethical considerations, user-centric design, and continuous monitoring were presented, along with clear guidelines for institutions to ensure the ethical and effective integration of Generative AI in education.

Forward-Looking in Curriculum Development With Generative AI

As we peer into the future of curriculum development in higher education, Generative AI stands poised to play a central role in shaping the educational landscape. The journey ahead involves a dynamic interplay between technological innovation, ethical considerations, and the evolving needs of learners. Several key aspects come into focus as we project the role of Generative AI in store for curriculum development:

Dynamic and Personalized Learning Opportunities

The integration of Generative AI in curriculum development promises to usher in an era of dynamic and personalized learning opportunities. AI-driven adaptive learning systems will tailor educational content to the individual needs, preferences, and progress of each student. This shift towards personalization ensures that education becomes a tailored journey, maximizing engagement and learning outcomes.

AI as a Collaborative Partner for Educators

Educators of the future will not be replaced by AI but rather empowered by it. Generative AI will act as a collaborative partner, assisting educators in designing curriculum maps, generating interactive learning materials, and providing valuable insights into student performance. The synergy between human expertise and AI capabilities will enhance the effectiveness of teaching and learning.

Ethical Considerations at the Forefront

The future of curriculum development with Generative AI places ethical considerations at the forefront. Educational institutions must continuously assess the impact of AI-driven curricula on students, addressing biases, ensuring transparency, and upholding principles of fairness and equity. Ethical review boards and comprehensive training programs will become integral components of the implementation process.

Inclusive and Open Learning Environments

The transformative potential of Generative AI extends to establishing inclusive and accessible learning environments. AI-driven tools will generate alternative formats of educational content, ensuring that diverse learning needs are met. This inclusive approach aligns with the principles of universal design, fostering an educational ecosystem where every learner can thrive (Tariq, 2024).

Continuous Innovation and Adaptation

The future landscape of curriculum development will be characterized by continuous innovation and adaptation. As Generative AI evolves, so too will its applications in education. Institutions should embrace a culture of innovation, remaining responsive to emerging trends, and adjusting their curricula to align with the ever-changing demands of the knowledge landscape.

In conclusion, Generative AI holds the promise of redefining curriculum development in higher education. From personalized learning opportunities to ethical considerations and collaborative partnerships between humans and AI, the future presents a canvas where the integration of Generative AI will paint a dynamic and responsive educational landscape. As we navigate this transformative journey, it is crucial to approach the implementation with ethical care, technological stewardship, and a commitment to fostering an inclusive and innovative learning environment for generations to come.

REFERENCES

Baker-Sennett, J. (2019). *Accessibility in Higher Education: Promising Practices and Challenges*. Harvard Education Press.

Bau, D. (2020). Towards Demystifying the Role of Deep Learning in Creative Design. *InProceedings of the European Conference on Computer Vision (ECCV)* (pp. 510-527).

Beeri, C. (2016). Privacy-Preserving Data Synthesis. In *Proceedings of the International Conference on Extending Database Technology (EDBT)* (pp. 585-596).

Brock, A. (2019). Large Scale GAN Training for High Fidelity Natural Image Synthesis. *Proceedings of the International Conference on Learning Representations (ICLR).*

Buolamwini, J., & Gebru, T. (2018). Gender Shades: Intersectional Accuracy Disparities in Commercial Gender Classification. *InProceedings of the Conference on Fairness, Accountability, and Transparency (FAT)* (pp. 77-91).

Caruana, R. (2015). Intelligible Models for Healthcare: Predicting Pneumonia Risk and Hospital 30-day Readmission. *InProceedings of the 21th ACM SIGKDD International Conference on Knowledge Discovery and Data Mining* (pp. 1721-1730). DOI:10.1145/2783258.2788613

Crawford, K., & Calo, R. (2016). There is a blind spot in AI research. *Nature*, 538(7625), 311–313. DOI:10.1038/538311a PMID:27762391

Dahl, D. B. (2013). Large-Scale Malware Classification Using Random Projections and Neural Networks. *In Proceedings of the 22nd International Conference on World Wide Web* (WWW) (pp. 1189-1194).

Dai, Y., Liu, A., & Lim, C. P. (2023). Reconceptualizing ChatGPT and generative AI as a student-driven innovation in higher education.

Dal Pozzolo, A. (2015). Calibrating Probability with Undersampling for Unbalanced Classification. *InSymposium on Computational Intelligence and Data Mining (CIDM)* (pp. 110-117). DOI:10.1109/SSCI.2015.33

Dignum, V. (2019). Responsible Artificial Intelligence: How to Develop and Use AI in a Responsible Way. *AI & Society*, 34(3), 447–466.

Dimitrov, D. V. (2018). Medical Internet of Things and Big Data in Healthcare. *Healthcare Informatics Research*, 24(3), 195–198. PMID:27525156

Dong, C. (2017). Neural Machine Translation by Jointly Learning to Align and Translate. *Proceedings of the International Conference on Learning Representations (ICLR).*

Farrelly, T., & Baker, N. (2023). Generative artificial intelligence: Implications and considerations for higher education practice. *Education Sciences*, 13(11), 1109. DOI:10.3390/educsci13111109

Hussain, A. (2020). Ethical Considerations in Artificial Intelligence and Health Informatics: A Systematic Review. *Journal of Medical Systems*, 44(2), 37.

Jobin, A., Ienca, M., & Vayena, E. (2019). The global landscape of AI ethics guidelines. *Nature Machine Intelligence*, 1(9), 389–399. DOI:10.1038/s42256-019-0088-2

Kayabas, I. (2024). Innovative Curriculum Development and Content Creation With Generative AI. In *Transforming Education With Generative AI: Prompt Engineering and Synthetic Content Creation* (pp. 462-473). IGI Global. DOI:10.4018/979-8-3693-1351-0.ch022

Maas-Bolmer, A. (2020). Artificial Intelligence Education: An Overview of Current Initiatives and Implementation in Dutch Higher Education. *InProceedings of the European Conference on Technology Enhanced Learning (EC-TEL)* (pp. 467-471).

McDonald, N., Johri, A., Ali, A., & Hingle, A. (2024). Generative artificial intelligence in higher education: Evidence from an analysis of institutional policies and guidelines. *arXiv preprint arXiv:2402.01659.*

McMahan, B. (2017). Communication-Efficient Learning of Deep Networks from Decentralized Data. In *Proceedings of the 20th International Conference on Artificial Intelligence and Statistics (AISTATS)* (pp. 1273-1282).

Michel-Villarreal, R., Vilalta-Perdomo, E., Salinas-Navarro, D. E., Thierry-Aguilera, R., & Gerardou, F. S. (2023). Challenges and opportunities of generative AI for higher education as explained by ChatGPT. *Education Sciences*, 13(9), 856. DOI:10.3390/educsci13090856

Murray, M. (2017). *The Cybernetic Brain: Sketches of Another Future.* University of Chicago Press.

Razavian, A. S. (2014). Visualizing and Understanding Convolutional Networks. *InEuropean Conference on Computer Vision (ECCV)* (pp. 818-833).

Resnik, D. B. (2015). Data Sharing in Genomics: Ethical and Social Challenges. *Annual Review of Genomics and Human Genetics*, 16, 1–32.

Shimizu, I., Kasai, H., Shikino, K., Araki, N., Takahashi, Z., Onodera, M., Kimura, Y., Tsukamoto, T., Yamauchi, K., Asahina, M., Ito, S., & Kawakami, E. (2023). Developing medical education curriculum reform strategies to address the impact of generative AI: Qualitative study. *JMIR Medical Education*, 9(1), e53466. DOI:10.2196/53466 PMID:38032695

Siemens, G., & Long, P. (2011). Penetrating the Fog: Analytics in Learning and Education. *EDUCAUSE Review*, 46(5), 30–32.

Tariq, M. U. (2022). Maintaining sustainable production and service by mitigating impact industry 4.0 factors in the petroleum and coal sector in Pakistan. *International Journal of Services and Operations Management*, 43(2), 188. DOI:10.1504/IJSOM.2022.126815

Tariq, M. U. (2023). Role of artificial intelligence in the enabling sustainable supply chain management during COVID-19. *International Journal of Services and Operations Management*, 44(1), 115. DOI:10.1504/IJSOM.2023.128938

Tariq, M. U. (2024). Equity and Inclusion in Learning Ecosystems. In Al Husseiny, F., & Munna, A. (Eds.), *Preparing Students for the Future Educational Paradigm* (pp. 155–176). IGI Global. DOI:10.4018/979-8-3693-1536-1.ch007

Tariq, M. U. (2024). The role of AI in skilling, upskilling, and reskilling the workforce. In Doshi, R., Dadhich, M., Poddar, S., & Hiran, K. (Eds.), *Integrating generative AI in education to achieve sustainable development goals* (pp. 421–433). IGI Global. DOI:10.4018/979-8-3693-2440-0.ch023

Tariq, M. U. (2024). AI-powered language translation for multilingual classrooms. In Doshi, R., Dadhich, M., Poddar, S., & Hiran, K. (Eds.), *Integrating generative AI in education to achieve sustainable development goals* (pp. 29–46). IGI Global. DOI:10.4018/979-8-3693-2440-0.ch002

Tariq, M. U. (2024). AI and the future of talent management: Transforming recruitment and retention with machine learning. In Christiansen, B., Aziz, M., & O'Keeffe, E. (Eds.), *Global practices on effective talent acquisition and retention* (pp. 1–16). IGI Global. DOI:10.4018/979-8-3693-1938-3.ch001

Tariq, M. U. (2024). Application of blockchain and Internet of Things (IoT) in modern business. In Sinha, M., Bhandari, A., Priya, S., & Kabiraj, S. (Eds.), *Future of customer engagement through marketing intelligence* (pp. 66–94). IGI Global. DOI:10.4018/979-8-3693-2367-0.ch004

Tariq, M. U. (2024). The role of AI ethics in cost and complexity reduction. In Tennin, K., Ray, S., & Sorg, J. (Eds.), *Cases on AI ethics in business* (pp. 59–78). IGI Global. DOI:10.4018/979-8-3693-2643-5.ch004

Tariq, M. U. (2024). Challenges of a metaverse shaping the future of entrepreneurship. In Inder, S., Dawra, S., Tennin, K., & Sharma, S. (Eds.), *New business frontiers in the metaverse* (pp. 155–173). IGI Global. DOI:10.4018/979-8-3693-2422-6.ch011

Tariq, M. U. (2024). Neurodiversity inclusion and belonging strategies in the workplace. In J. Vázquez de Príncipe (Ed.), *Resilience of multicultural and multigenerational leadership and workplace experience* (pp. 182-201). IGI Global. DOI:10.4018/979-8-3693-1802-7.ch009

Tariq, M. U. (2024). AI and IoT in flood forecasting and mitigation: A comprehensive approach. In Ouaissa, M., Ouaissa, M., Boulouard, Z., Iwendi, C., & Krichen, M. (Eds.), *AI and IoT for proactive disaster management* (pp. 26–60). IGI Global. DOI:10.4018/979-8-3693-3896-4.ch003

Tariq, M. U. (2024). Empowering student entrepreneurs: From idea to execution. In Cantafio, G., & Munna, A. (Eds.), *Empowering students and elevating universities with innovation centers* (pp. 83–111). IGI Global. DOI:10.4018/979-8-3693-1467-8.ch005

Tariq, M. U. (2024). The transformation of healthcare through AI-driven diagnostics. In Sharma, A., Chanderwal, N., Tyagi, S., Upadhyay, P., & Tyagi, A. (Eds.), *Enhancing medical imaging with emerging technologies* (pp. 250–264). IGI Global. DOI:10.4018/979-8-3693-5261-8.ch015

Tariq, M. U. (2024). The role of emerging technologies in shaping the global digital government landscape. In Guo, Y. (Ed.), *Emerging developments and technologies in digital government* (pp. 160–180). IGI Global. DOI:10.4018/979-8-3693-2363-2.ch009

Tariq, M. U. (2024). Equity and inclusion in learning ecosystems. In Al Husseiny, F., & Munna, A. (Eds.), *Preparing students for the future educational paradigm* (pp. 155–176). IGI Global. DOI:10.4018/979-8-3693-1536-1.ch007

Tariq, M. U. (2024). Empowering educators in the learning ecosystem. In Al Husseiny, F., & Munna, A. (Eds.), *Preparing students for the future educational paradigm* (pp. 232–255). IGI Global. DOI:10.4018/979-8-3693-1536-1.ch010

Tariq, M. U. (2024). Revolutionizing health data management with blockchain technology: Enhancing security and efficiency in a digital era. In Garcia, M., & de Almeida, R. (Eds.), *Emerging technologies for health literacy and medical practice* (pp. 153–175). IGI Global. DOI:10.4018/979-8-3693-1214-8.ch008

Tariq, M. U. (2024). Emerging trends and innovations in blockchain-digital twin integration for green investments: A case study perspective. In Jafar, S., Rodriguez, R., Kannan, H., Akhtar, S., & Plugmann, P. (Eds.), *Harnessing blockchain-digital twin fusion for sustainable investments* (pp. 148–175). IGI Global. DOI:10.4018/979-8-3693-1878-2.ch007

Tariq, M. U. (2024). Emotional intelligence in understanding and influencing consumer behavior. In Musiolik, T., Rodriguez, R., & Kannan, H. (Eds.), *AI impacts in digital consumer behavior* (pp. 56–81). IGI Global. DOI:10.4018/979-8-3693-1918-5.ch003

Tariq, M. U. (2024). Fintech startups and cryptocurrency in business: Revolutionizing entrepreneurship. In Kankaew, K., Nakpathom, P., Chnitphattana, A., Pitchayadejanant, K., & Kunnapapdeelert, S. (Eds.), *Applying business intelligence and innovation to entrepreneurship* (pp. 106–124). IGI Global. DOI:10.4018/979-8-3693-1846-1.ch006

Tariq, M. U. (2024). Multidisciplinary service learning in higher education: Concepts, implementation, and impact. In S. Watson (Ed.), *Applications of service learning in higher education* (pp. 1-19). IGI Global. DOI:10.4018/979-8-3693-2133-1.ch001

Tariq, M. U. (2024). Enhancing cybersecurity protocols in modern healthcare systems: Strategies and best practices. In Garcia, M., & de Almeida, R. (Eds.), *Transformative approaches to patient literacy and healthcare innovation* (pp. 223–241). IGI Global. DOI:10.4018/979-8-3693-3661-8.ch011

Tariq, M. U. (2024). Advanced wearable medical devices and their role in transformative remote health monitoring. In Garcia, M., & de Almeida, R. (Eds.), *Transformative approaches to patient literacy and healthcare innovation* (pp. 308–326). IGI Global. DOI:10.4018/979-8-3693-3661-8.ch015

Tariq, M. U. (2024). Leveraging artificial intelligence for a sustainable and climate-neutral economy in Asia. In Ordóñez de Pablos, P., Almunawar, M., & Anshari, M. (Eds.), *Strengthening sustainable digitalization of Asian economy and society* (pp. 1–21). IGI Global. DOI:10.4018/979-8-3693-1942-0.ch001

Tariq, M. U. (2024). Metaverse in business and commerce. In Kumar, J., Arora, M., & Erkol Bayram, G. (Eds.), *Exploring the use of metaverse in business and education* (pp. 47–72). IGI Global., DOI:10.4018/979-8-3693-5868-9.ch004

Tariq, M. U., Babar, M., Jan, M. A., Khattak, A. S., Alshehri, M. D., & Yahya, A. (2021). Security requirement management for cloud-assisted and internet of things⇔enabled smart city. *Computers, Materials & Continua*, 67(1), 625–639. DOI:10.32604/cmc.2021.014165

Tariq, M. U., Babar, M., Poulin, M., Khattak, A. S., Alshehri, M. D., & Kaleem, S. (2021). Human behavior analysis using intelligent big data analytics. *Frontiers in Psychology*, 12, 686610. Advance online publication. DOI:10.3389/fpsyg.2021.686610 PMID:34295289

Tariq, M. U., & Ismail, M. U. S. B. (2024). AI-powered COVID-19 forecasting: A comprehensive comparison of advanced deep learning methods. *Osong Public Health and Research Perspectives*, 15(2), 2210–9099. DOI:10.24171/j.phrp.2023.0287 PMID:38621765

Tariq, M. U., & Ismail, S. B. (2024). Deep learning in public health: Comparative predictive models for COVID-19 case forecasting. *PLoS One*, 19(3), e0294289. DOI:10.1371/journal.pone.0294289 PMID:38483948

Tariq, M. U., Poulin, M., & Abonamah, A. A. (2021). Achieving operational excellence through artificial intelligence: Driving forces and barriers. *Frontiers in Psychology*, 12, 686624. Advance online publication. DOI:10.3389/fpsyg.2021.686624 PMID:34305744

Topol, E. J. (2019). High-Performance Medicine: The Convergence of Human and Artificial Intelligence. *Nature Medicine*, 25(1), 44–56. DOI:10.1038/s41591-018-0300-7 PMID:30617339

Wang, S. (2018). AI-Ed: Integrating Adaptive Learning into Intelligent Tutoring Systems. *InProceedings of the International Conference on Artificial Intelligence in Education (AIED)* (pp. 289-303).

Wang, T. (2023, August). Navigating Generative AI (ChatGPT) in Higher Education: Opportunities and Challenges. In *International Conference on Smart Learning Environments* (pp. 215-225). Singapore: Springer Nature Singapore. DOI:10.1007/978-981-99-5961-7_28

Yu, D. (2017). Bridging the Gap Between Educational Measurement and Intelligent Tutoring Systems. *Journal of Educational Measurement*, 54(2), 219–236.

Chapter 10

Generative Artificial Intelligence (AI) on Sustainable Development Goal 4 for Tertiary Education:

Conversational AI With User-Centric ChatGPT-4

Ugochukwu Okwudili Matthew
https://orcid.org/0000-0003-0828-9710
Hussaini Adamu Federal Polytechnic, Nigeria

David Oyewumi Oyekunle
https://orcid.org/0009-0007-3994-1712
University of Salford, UK

Edidiong Elijah Akpan
https://orcid.org/0009-0008-4808-860X
Arkansas Tech University, USA

Matthew Abiola Oladipupo
https://orcid.org/0000-0002-5984-6217
University of Salford, UK

Ejiofor Stanley Chukwuebuka
Arkansas Tech University, USA

Temitope Samson Adekunle
https://orcid.org/0000-0003-4828-6039
Colorado State University, USA

Ajibola Olaosebikan Waliu
https://orcid.org/0009-0002-6857-3035
Southampton Solent University, UK

Victory Chibuike Onumaku
https://orcid.org/0009-0005-7418-955X
Edge Hill University, UK

DOI: 10.4018/979-8-3693-2418-9.ch010

ABSTRACT

Emerging themes of Society 5.0 are the coexistence of humans and robots in a collaborative work environments, particularly in education. With digital transformation and newfound collaborations between people and technology, Society 5.0 seeks to create a sustainable people-centered community. Advancements in robotics and AI research have been used in several areas of life in the modern digital society to address a wide range of problems. In spite of the large body of research on human-robot cooperation on low- and high-level tasks related to robot educational advancement, the current study concentrated on the cooperation between humans and robots in the fields of education bringing up the Research and Education Network (REN) for universities as a way to capitalize on human development. The study identified significant issues with the current REN and made an effort to resolve them through human-robot collaboration by tackling them from an organizational and pedagogical AI-robotic instructional application in light of the technological prospects highlighted in the study.

1. INTRODUCTION

Society 5.0 is a civilization that prioritizes the needs of its citizens, strikes a balance between social and economic progresses, and does it through a system that is tightly integrated with both the real and technologies or digital worlds(Audrey & Paksi, 2022). The idea behind Society 5.0 is to use cutting-edge technology to enhance digital natives quality of life and build a brighter future for everybody(Matthew et al., 2024). The Sustainable Development Goals (SDGs) of the United Nations, however, serve as a roadmap for an inclusive and sustainable future for all-inclusive education. The realization of the SDGs and the provision of a blueprint for a brighter future could be greatly aided by Society 5.0. The concept of a human-centric society, where technology is created to promote people's well-being, is the foundation of Society 5.0(Yitmen, Almusaed, & Alizadehsalehi, 2023). The SDGs seek to guarantee that everyone has access to improved quality of life in a sustainable and inclusive manner, bringing Society 5.0 into its central discussion to address and resolve a number of pressing global needs. Society 5.0 may help the SDGs primarily through the use of cutting edge technologies to sustainable urban development and educational investment through enabling infrastructures(Matthew, Kazaure, & Okafor, 2021). Through the advancement of sustainable education and a reduction in the global incidence of illiteracy, Society 5.0 will enable SDG 4 to strive. By utilizing cutting-edge technologies to enhance healthcare results, Society

5.0 can also contribute to the achievement of SDG 3 which emphasized good health and general well-being.

In Society 5.0, technology and people live side by side in harmony to advance the society, with AI being a key component in resolving societal issues(Tyagi, Lakshmi Priya, Mishra, & Balamurugan, 2023). As a flexible artificial intelligence (AI) tool, ChatGPT makes a substantial contribution to this goal in a number of industries especially education. By analyzing a vast corpus of medical literature and patient data, ChatGPT helps healthcare providers diagnose conditions and suggest the best courses of action. For instance, big data and AI can assist in more precise and effective illness diagnosis, and telemedicine can be utilized to deliver healthcare services remotely(Matthew, Kazaure, Amaonwu, et al., 2021). Furthermore, by encouraging electronic learning (e-learning) and lowering the cost and increasing accessibility to education, Society 5.0 can support SDG 4 that emphasized quality education. In addition, by generating new employment prospects in industries like robotics, AI and data analytics, Society 5.0 can aid in the achievement of SDG 8 that addressed decent work and economic growth. By encouraging innovation and making investments in new infrastructure, such as smart grids and high-speed internet, Society 5.0 can also support SDG 9 with reference to industry, innovation, and infrastructure(Kasinathan et al., 2022). In order for Society 5.0 to fully contribute to the SDGs, it is crucial to make sure that its advantages are shared fairly. This entails making certain that every citizen, irrespective of socioeconomic background or geographic location, has access to the technology and services offered by Society 5.0. Society 5.0 can assist in addressing some of the most important issues facing the globe today by encouraging sustainable urban growth, enhancing healthcare outcomes, lowering the cost and increasing access to education, generating new job possibilities, and making investments in new infrastructure. To guarantee that no one is left behind, it is crucial to make sure that the advantages of Society 5.0 are dispersed fairly.

A widespread technology paradigm supporting Society 5.0 is the cyber physical system that firmly integrates cyberspace in respect to information communication and physical space relating to computational processes, which several people first thought the idea was a lofty vision with no clear indication of how it would truly play out(Oztemel & Gursev, 2020). The Fourth Industrial Revolution and the transition to Society 5.0 are considered to be analogous in that both terms relate to the current fundamental transformation of our economic system into a new paradigm(Oztemel & Gursev, 2020),(Huang et al., 2022). However, Society 5.0 is a more comprehensive idea because it envisions a radical changes in how we live, propelling industrial revolutions aimed to separate human labour from that of machines. These machines, which we may refer to as robots, will eventually assume control of the majority of the labour-intensive, monotonous, or hazardous tasks currently performed by humans(Javaid, Haleem, Singh, & Suman, 2021). There are currently accessible learning support robots that encourages active learning engagement and programming education robots for students and undergraduates(Eguchi, 2022).These robots encourages positive responses from students by fostering a calm environment where the other party is not a human and by utilizing a teaching strategy that emphasizes movement as supplementary educational pedagogy. While robots are being utilized to fill the gap left by a lack of qualified teachers in subject areas like programming and language learning, robots are actively being created for information communication technology(ICT) systems like learning apps, AI teachers, and virtual classrooms(Shahab et al., 2022).

The rate at which automation becomes ingrained in human life depends on technological advancements and public acceptance of robots. Robots may have a significant influence on civilization and the advancement of digital technology, hence it is imperative to investigate human-robot interaction and its effects on society as a whole. The conversation around Industry 5.0 had already begun among the academia and futurists, fashioning the digital collaboration between humans and robots as core objective of Industry 5.0(Taj & Zaman, 2022). However, we can be certain that digital collaboration of humans and robots will be a significant innovation for society and have a big impact on how we conduct educational businesses. The AI enabled robots are constantly being given new enriching qualities, including major gains in terms of efficiency and sharpness, as well as greater cognitive capacities, as AI is rapidly being utilized in the broad areas of robotics to engineer technology and social economic changes of the current society. Though they have a long way to go before developing relationships with people that extend beyond isolated interactions in predetermined situations, scientists are increasingly coming up with developments that are substantially obfuscating the lines between AI agents and humans(Russell, Moskowitz, & Raglin, 2017).

The game changer will be to highlight the advantages of collaboration between the fields of AI and robotics, with real-world use case demonstrations to turn any areas of mutual interest in the field of AI into a partnership geared towards guiding humanity toward a sustainable and human-centred society 5.0(Ietto, Ancillai, Sabatini, Carayannis, & Gregori, 2022). Robots have already played crucial roles in a variety of situations over the past few decades, helping to address significant global concerns. Robots are therefore being used in factories to shield employees from boring or hazardous activities(Wei & Li, 2022). Robots are being employed to disarm bombs in countries torn apart by violence(Na'inna & Anti-Dwanso, 2022), while in the healthcare sector, robots are assisting in the replacement of damaged body parts with artificial organs like prosthetic limbs(Heng, Solomon, & Gao, 2022),(Chaudhari, Loharkar, & Ingle, 2022). However, scientists are constantly working to advance robotics and give robots skills that go above and beyond what we can now imagine. Roboticists have helped a number of industries advance significantly in terms of efficiency and acuity by applying AI to their development, to enable robot welding of tiniest micro-level tolerances in the car industry(Murugamani et al., 2022). While this is going on, AI is helping healthcare robots do nano-sized medical procedures, enabling precise targeting of hereditary illnesses(Soltani et al., 2021). As a result, more industries are becoming familiar with collaborative robots, also known as Cobots, or robots designed to work alongside humans as digital colleagues, thanks to increased research being done in the subject of human-robot interaction. The Cobots can act as sales assistants in physical stores and respond in real-time to the movements of human workers in industrial applications(Storm et al., 2022). In this paper, the authors contrasted future educational methodology in Society 5.0 and Robots applications. The authors focused on the problems associated with human-robot collaborative work in educational pedagogic development and finally wrap up the study by briefly discussing potential future research areas for Nigeria's long-term educational growth.

2. RESEARCH OBJECTIVE

In an effort to support the development of an innovative societal approach to education at the 41st session of the General Conference in November 2021, United Nations Educational, Scientific, and Cultural Organization (UNESCO) produced a global report on the potential of AI in education(Mochizuki & Vickers, 2024). This includes creating an educational system in which families, schools, and society collaborate to teach and learn; establishing long-term mechanisms that support all stages of life; utilizing technology to defend the right to high-quality education for disadvantaged groups; and researching the effective integration of various knowledge gateways, approaches, and methodologies that promote social inclusion and enable knowledge transfers whenever and wherever needed(Bhandari & Bhandari, 2023). In actuality, the goal of the current study was to demonstrate the need for AI-mediated education automation in connection to the Nigerian Research and Education Network (NgREN) in order to achieve process modernity, which is a requirement for the ascent of society 5.0.

i. To create technological trends based on UNESCO's AI and education policy roadmap that promote AI-enabled learning futures with inspirations of rethinking our shared futures in order to satisfy fundamental learning demands driven by society 5.0.

ii. To Create ethical guidelines for the development, implementation, and use of AI in contemporary society's knowledge transfer and educational enterprises, as well as including the AI ethics proposals that the UNESCO Member States approved at their 41st session.
iii. To develop guiding frameworks for the AI abilities that all learners will need to live and operate with AI platform which would make it possible to reemphasize the AI curriculum paradigm in schools as a starting point for assessing NgREN efficacy.
iv. To enhance regional and global AI governance in education, which could be crucial to facilitating creative learning, innovative pedagogy, and higher-order thinking in future educational achievements.

3. LITERATURE REVIEW

Since education is a fundamental human right and the cornerstone for fostering sustainable development and peace, it is UNESCO's highest priority(Matthew & Kazaure, 2020),(Mochizuki & Vickers, 2024). The United Nations' special agency for education, UNESCO, leads the education sector both globally and regionally, fortifies national education systems, and uses education to address current global issues with a focus on gender equality and modern African civilization(Okanda, 2024). Drawing from the International Forum on AI and the Futures of Education, which took place in Beijing and concurrently online on December 7 and 8, 2020, the UNESCO Unit for Technology and AI in Education within the Future of Learning and Innovation Team has been able to provide a global roadmap for AI educational sustainability(Rof, Bikfalvi, & Marques, 2022). Since AI is spreading across national borders and becoming more and more commonplace, nations must cooperate to guarantee that AI is controlled by humans and is developed and used for the benefit of everybody. The UNESCO's acceptance of recommendations on its strategy for technological innovation in education, which emphasized new social contracts for education as discussed at the general conference's 41st session in November 2021 that focused on the ethics of AI in educational development, greatly aided in the development of the current paper(Kim, Lee, & Cho, 2022). To improve AI governance and innovation networks for the benefit of mankind and education as a whole, it is imperative that practitioners, academic institutions, international organizations, business partners, and regional government agencies collaborate.

A global forum on AI and the futures of education was organized by the People's Republic of China Ministry of Education, the National Commission of the People's Republic of China for UNESCO, and UNESCO in order to make sure that AI transformed education for a workable smart society 5.0, which will help to drive the global agenda for AI in education(Miao & Holmes, 2022). Continuing the conversation from the AI and the futures of education conferences in 2019 and 2020, the objective of the 2021 forum was to investigate the role and importance of digital humanism in AI and education. The symposium actively involved participants in discussions about how innovation and governance in AI may be enhanced for the benefit of all, as individuals and governments worldwide have a thorough understanding of the potential and constraints of AI in education. To plan out a possible future for the deployment of AI in education, representatives from academic institutions, non-governmental organizations, and international organizations joined government ministers and other senior ministry officials from Member States as forum participants. UNESCO's humanistic perspective on technology in education sees the digital world as a part of the global commons, grounded in inclusivity, equity, gender equality, and respect for human dignity(Holmes & Porayska-Pomsta, 2022). The definition of humanity must be reexamined in light of recent developments in AI, as well as the implications for learning alongside educational robots in Society 5.0. The claim that AI has the potential to improve certain aspects of education is verifiable based on pedagogical connections between education and digital media technology in the twenty-first century. However, a comprehensive solution remains problematic, especially in settings where digital flexibility and knowledge transfer are necessary for AI-robots(Flechsig, Anslinger, & Lasch, 2022). But in order for AI educational robots to fulfill their promise of accelerating the achievement of SDG4, it has been determined that they must be utilized in a way that upholds the highest moral standards and is influenced by humanistic principles(Mhlanga, 2022).

Since AI is spreading across national borders and becoming more and more commonplace, nations must cooperate to guarantee that AI is controlled by humans and is developed and used for the benefit of everybody. Specifically, it is critical that people are shielded from the negative effects of AI technologies and that the technology is employed to enhance rather than replace human abilities. Education is where this starts to enable AI-driven teaching assistants respond to each learner's unique needs and provide personalized assignments that raise knowledge levels. Through enhanced understanding of logic and algorithmic thinking, this also aids students in developing their problem-solving abilities. After identifying the essential technical and human AI competences, educational systems must make sure that every student is ready for a world where AI is pervasive. Education should only adopt AI technologies when they are demonstrably beneficial and morally just, as has already been proved. Government, business, and school leaders should all obtain extensive training in AI pedagogic innovations in order to handle the ethical dangers posed by AI. Information communication technologies (ICTs) currently in place are extremely important, as demonstrated by the COVID-19 pandemic-related school lockdown, which also showed the importance of digital technology(Ugochukwu Okwudili Matthew, Ado Saleh Kazaure, et al., 2022). Pedagogical processes in educational management were challenged to adopt new pedagogical methodologies with the emergence of remote learning facilitated by ICT-centered innovation for practical instruction and classroom teaching, in some cases(Matthew, Kazaure, Kazaure, Onyedibe, & Okafor, 2022). The development of adaptive tutoring and other tools for students is just one example of how AI is being applied in educational technology to improve online learning and teaching. Other applications include automating routine tasks for instructors, personalizing learning for students, and enabling adaptive evaluations(Seo, Tang, Roll, Fels, & Yoon, 2021).

Put differently, AI is a reflection of and an instantiation of human decision-making, which emphasizes the necessity for people to assume accountability and command. It is crucial, therefore, when AI is applied in real-world situations, such as automating low-skill professions that could harm employment opportunities or compromising students' cognitive growth in the classroom. AI has been proposed as a critical instrument to help Member States achieve SDG 4, which calls for providing high-quality education for everyone, as the China-UNESCO Conference 2021 brought to light (Miao & Holmes, 2022). To assist equitable, high-quality education for all children in preparation for lifetime learning, artificial intelligence (AI) is already being used in China, Cuba, Mexico, and Spain. Strong infrastructure development is required for this, which is a global concern, especially in countries where there are multiple schools located in remote rural areas. This method required a humanistic frame of view and an appreciation for the need for education to have a deep foundation in the human and biological sciences and to include emotive, behavioral, and cognitive aspects. In actuality, the mainstream educational programs in Portugal, Qatar, and Cuba have all included AI fundamentals into their respective ICT plans and curricula(Leogrande & Costantiello, 2023). A national AI plan that brings together the public and private sectors was recently launched in Spain, enabling students to interact and exchange knowledge while also producing new knowledge(Guenduez & Mettler, 2023). China is likewise pursuing a comprehensive approach to AI as part of its objective to transform education by 2035 (Zhu, 2022). Only eleven countries, none of which were in Africa, currently have government-approved K–12 AI curriculum, and according to UNESCO's mapping, only about 12% of the study period in these curricula was devoted to the ethical and social elements of AI (Miao & Holmes, 2022). Furthermore, few evaluations exist on the caliber of AI courses and the extent to which they were executed. Harmonized curricula are vital because countries might differ greatly from one another while sharing a great deal in common. The ultimate objective of a sustainable Society 5.0 is to guarantee that all goods and services are provided to people in the most effective manner and in accordance with their needs, helping nations overcome protracted social problems such as depopulation, social polarization, aging populations, and energy and environmental sustainability constraints. In order to address societal challenges and realize a sustainable and inclusive human-centered society, governments and their agencies should examine Society 5.0 and the SDGs and identify a set of social connectedness that support science, technology, and innovation as mainstream political agenda items(Zengin, Naktiyok, Kaygın, Kavak, & Topçuoğlu, 2021).

As today's digital society becomes increasingly automated, system-wide principles will also be involved. These principles will direct the creation of new AI innovations that will assist educators and promote future learning outcomes, in addition to knowledge sharing on best practices and the efficient use of trustworthy AI tools for education. Examining AI curriculum frameworks and AI literacy as a key policy tool for ICTs also means examining the conditions that enable their application(Matthew, Kazaure, Kazaure, Nwamouh, & Chinonso, 2022). In order to evaluate lifelong learning outcomes, identify issues with learning systems, and enhance technology for educational management, emerging methodologies in data mining across platforms and several data sources will be examined (Gumel, Abdullahi, & O, 2019). The advancement of AI is crucial to the larger digital revolution in our society, which affects public services, the workplace, education, and even day-to-day living. The digitalization of knowledge and representation, fueled by machine learning, more potent algorithms, and other AI techniques, is a part of the AI-powered instruments for earning that go beyond the distribution of conventional forms of knowledge. The swift progress of AI-human collaboration and the digital transformation of our society have a significant influence on people's conceptions of what it means to be human, their interpersonal relationships, and their technological behaviors(Bozdag, 2023). In order to steer our educational practices in the direction of sustainability, we must reinterpret conventional notions of humanism and prioritize digital humanism.

4. CONVERSATIONAL AI EDUCATIONAL ROBOTS AND NATURAL LANGUAGE PROCESSING (NLP)

As a ground-breaking tool for natural language processing (NLP) and a transformative educational business tool, generative artificial intelligence (GenAI), and more especially ChatGPT, offer a noteworthy technological achievement in terms of language models(Matthew, Bakare, Ebong, Ndukwu, & Nwanakwaugwu, 2023). The recommendations made by ChatGPT users have the power to enhance instruction and learning, which will have a significant effect on the twenty-first-century educational landscape. For several reasons, it is becoming simpler to obtain educational robots. In the days to come, human-robot collaboration which has made scientific strides in industry 5.0 excessive digital automation will most likely also become a common occurrence. This research looks at the potential applications of GenAI for both conversational agents in the classroom and NLP synthesis. By employing NLP to construct semantics, GenAI was able to understand and generate human-like language, which allowed it to replicate the most advanced human technology through detailed assumptions about patterns and structures it learns from its training data(Decardi-Nelson, Alshehri, Ajagekar, & You, 2024). The significance of GAI has increased as digital learning depends more and more on conversational agents driven by AI. It is essential to get ready for an AI-dominated future where general and educational technologies combine. This study underscored the necessity for producers to assume responsibility for reducing potential hazards by using an AI-driven instructional robotics application to demonstrate how society may impact and contribute to the development of AI pedagogic learning. As generative AI technologies have the potential to fundamentally alter teaching and learning methodologies and demand new ways of thinking, the study emphasizes that more research on organizational robotics will emerge from the technological issues raised in this study, with an emphasis on human collaboration and education.

Integrations of robots and NLP algorithms are changing the way that education is delivered by allowing for customized coaching and strategy adjustments for every learner(Younis, Ruhaiyem, Ghaban, Gazem, & Nasser, 2023). As they help students enhance their communication, collaboration, and critical-thinking abilities, they increase their participation in the classroom. Robots can now read and analyze text, respond instantly to queries in any situation, and grade assignments automatically thanks to advances in natural language processing (NLP). NLP-driven discourse and translation improves language learning because it can be used to create inclusive, adaptable, and dynamic learning environments. NLP and robotics are transforming education by enabling teachers and students to communicate, share ideas, and propose new course designs. As Dr. Janice Gobert, a professor at Rutgers University and the CEO/co-founder of Apprendis, pointed out in her essay about the creation of the Inquiry Intelligent Tutoring System(Inq-ITS), building AI for education undoubtedly involves a broad team of specialists working together (Adair, 2023). Scalable performance evaluations of science inquiry competencies were developed by Dr. Gobert and the Inq-ITS team by combining AI computational tools with a plethora of data from cognitive and learning sciences. Students work on virtual science experiments within the Inq-ITS environment, where their science practices are automatically evaluated in real-time. A pedagogical agent will assist students in finding solutions if they run across problems in the lab. At the University of Georgia, Dr. Xiaoming Zhai is an assistant professor who specializes in leveraging AI to enhance STEM teaching. She examines the effectiveness of ChatGPT, a well-known AI chatbot, in creating assessment items that are in line with nationally accepted educational standards(Adair, 2023). The ability of the chatbot to evaluate student-submitted science essays, offer personalized learning recommendations, and customize feedback for each student was another area he examined. Although Dr. Zhai believes ChatGPT has the potential to improve instruction, Dr. David Joyner, executive director of online education at the Georgia Institute of Technology, advises educators to encourage their students to use ChatGPT and related technologies. Recalling the development of calculator use in the classroom, Dr. Joyner anticipates that ChatGPT will become a valuable tool.

Figure 1. ChatGPT's General AL, NLP Enabled Architecture(Gill & Kaur, 2023)

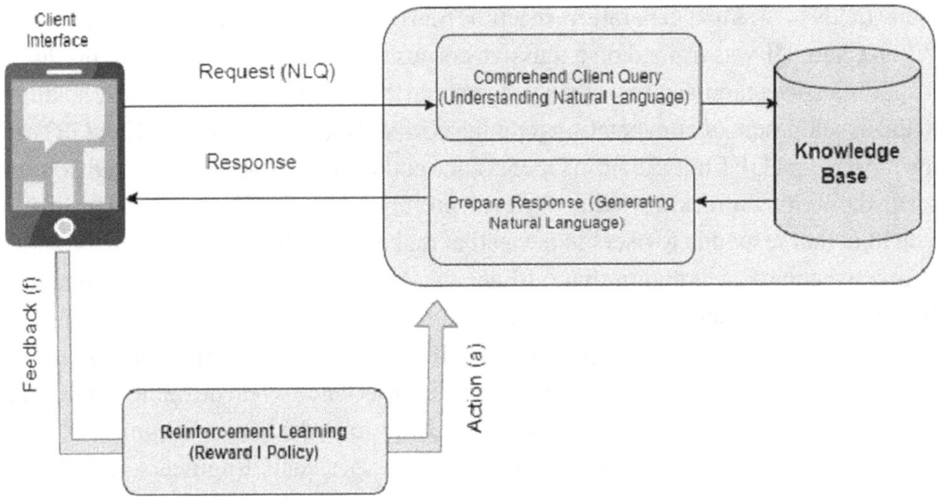

Referring to Figure 1, ChatGPT is a flexible tool with strong natural language processing (NLP) capabilities that may be used for interactive applications, text production, and language comprehension(Gill & Kaur, 2023). Comprehending ChatGPT's inception and growth is essential to its objective of propelling scientific investigation; the platform emerged from the field of NLP, a subset of artificial intelligence. With the exception of a very slight change in the setup for the data gathering architecture, OpenAI claims that ChatGPT is an enhanced version built on the well-known GPT-3.5 series that employs Reinforcement Learning from Human Feedback (RLHF) and nearly exacting methodologies to InstructGPT. It demonstrates proficiency in a wide range of difficult NLP tasks, including translating natural language into code by employing the extensive data in GPT-3.5 and fine-tuning the procedure with human input supervision. It is crucial to remember that ChatGPT is not a Generative Adversarial Network (GAN) model; rather, it is a language model built on the GPT architecture. GANs are more commonly employed for tasks like image production, whereas GPT models are intended for NLP tasks like language comprehension and text output. Building a powerful and flexible AI language model that could help with a range of activities, such as data analysis, translation, and text production, was the aim of the ChatGPT project(Rasul et al., 2023). With the purpose of addressing some limitations of previous sequence-to-sequence models for natural language processing, ChatGPT was built upon the Transformer architecture. This inventive architecture made it possible for OpenAI to produce powerful language models like the GPT series, which included the GPT-2 and GPT-3 versions that preceded ChatGPT. For ChatGPT, the GPT-3.5 architecture is the basis, built upon an improved version of OpenAI's GPT-3 model.

With fewer variables than other NLP models, GPT-3.5 produces good results in many fields such as text generation, machine translation, and language understanding. When ChatGPT was trained on a massive corpus of text data, it was able to produce responses to user inquiries that closely resembled those of a human, ultimately leading to the development of conversational replies(Gill & Kaur, 2023). Using ChatGPT-4, the most recent GPT release from OpenAI, the authors of this study explained how to set up the architecture, knowledge retrieval, prompt design, and engineering to create a chatbot that responds to users in a way that makes sense to them. Authors provide a timely technical adaptation that outlines the Application Programming Interface (API) parameters that can affect the voice, tone, and personality of the response. It was relatively simple to develop a chatbot with OpenAI's ChatGPT-4, but to get excellent results, you need to think about the user experience when utilizing ChatGPT. Although ChatGPT is a different field of study, prompt design and engineering are also included in the process of building the user experience. Engineers, designers, and product managers must take into account the chatbot's personality, tone, and user interface in addition to its understanding of and ability to respond to customer demands in order to guarantee a positive user experience. Despite the challenges of developing an effective chatbot, ChatGPT offers educational institutions incredible opportunities to improve communication with partners globally, automate customer service, and personalize student interactions. By utilizing ChatGPT's capabilities and prioritizing the user experience, educational institutions may develop chatbots that increase engagement, improve customer happiness, and accelerate business success. Since working on this prototype, OpenAI has developed plug-ins, such as the retrieval plug-in, to further boost the effectiveness and accessibility of Generative AI adoption in business solutions. Businesses should be able to construct chatbots that are even more effective and user-friendly thanks to these advancements.

5. RESEARCH MOTIVATION

In an effort to improve research and education standards, National Research and Education Networks (NRENs) were established(Pillay, Erasmus, & Pretorius, 2021). This initiative also led to the establishment of the Nigerian Research and Education Network (NgREN), a Research and Education Network (REN) similar to those established elsewhere (Bashir, 2020). All of the country's research and educational institutions must be integrated through a state-of-the-art digital hub through the use of high-speed fiber optics and other innovative technologies, such as high-capacity radios and efficient monitoring software, through an enterprise network linking these institutions(Barakabitze et al., 2019). The Nigeria Universities Commission (NUC) and the Committee of Vice Chancellors of Nigerian Universities (CVC) jointly established a foundation that allowed universities to communicate, collaborate, access, and share resources across national and international borders, mainly for research and teaching, with the additional capacity of unified communications and digital content amalgamation supplied by NgREN. With an emphasis on education to foster growth and competitiveness, African countries have continued to pursue ICT policies to encourage growth across a range of socioeconomic sectors. Almost every day, somewhere on the continent, there are announcements about new ICT projects and innovations related to ICT for education (ICT4E). However, for many years, we have noticed that funding has been focused on ensuring that new technologies function in resource-constrained educational settings a concentration that leans toward the ICT. On the other hand, well-understood ICTs are now in education, promoting ICT4E integration in African Education Systems (AES) is critical to changing the growth of African society through STEM (science, technology, engineering, and mathematics) courses in this era of knowledge (Barakabitze et al., 2019). Since Society 5.0 places a high value on human centeredness, this will be a helpful tool for reacting to creativity in research and education.

Research and education can now fully benefit from the second phase of the AfricaConnect2 Project according to a cooperative agreement negotiated by the NgREN and the West and Central African Research and Education Network (WACREN)(Bashir, 2020). This information led the present research to create an AI digital platform that allows users to customize the NgREN ecosystem through interactive educational robot engagement and the aggregation of digital resources for the end user. As part of the ICT implementation policy, integrating AI educational robots into the classroom through NgREN resource synchronization would enable the end-users (students and scholars) to participate in interactive activities with a wider range of information and knowledge during their learning. Additionally, instructors have an impact on students' views toward using ICT into their lesson plans. Just as important as students' and teachers' ICT skills and expertise are their attitudes when it comes to the successful integration of AI educational robots into the classroom. ICTs are necessary to achieve wide socioeconomic goals related to social development and educational pedagogy. Additionally, they facilitate the delivery of digital curricula in African educational institutions in both the public and commercial sectors. The design and development of the AI educational robots program should provide appropriate curricula while giving careful thought to the transformative trend that is now occurring in Africa. The curriculum for ICT implementation should include a statement on the role AI robots will play in education. It should also provide an integrated and blended designed technique for ICT teachers and students to set up an environment where students' unique skills and experiences can be reinforced(Fomunyam, 2019). Paying particular attention to Figure 1, the expansion of Internet infrastructure globally has been driven by the establishment of NRENs, or networks of research and education institutions, necessitating the adoption of proactive ICT policies in Africa(Ugochukwu Okwudili Matthew, Jazuli Sanusi Kazaure, et al., 2022).

Numerous educational and research institutions in Africa may now access essential e-resources for research and teaching, collaborate globally, and benefit from faster internet connections thanks to the establishment of successful and long-lasting NRENs across the continent. At now, there are endeavors to facilitate the establishment of an enduring NREN that prioritizes the supply of technological and services-oriented solutions, with a particular emphasis on the academic business model and financial commitment. It is crucial to support the strategies that have worked elsewhere on the continent in order to transform NRENs into vibrant, sustainable organizations. The elements that are not directly attributed to particular ICT users but are impacted by organizational culture and the ICT policy framework were covered by the institutional ICT characterizations. Every institution's ICT vision must take into account the value of ICT in teaching and learning while keeping in mind its particular financial limits in order to handle its distinct features(Ugochukwu O Matthew et al., 2022). The educational exploitation of ICT is the most important component in its integration into education. This is dependent less on the technology employed and more on the theoretical stance taken. ICT is considered to be the most effective tool for assisting the learning process. Their main contribution is their technological characteristics, which include the ways they handle, record, depict, and communicate information. These characteristics have to do with swiftly handling massive volumes of data and information, displaying data in a variety of dynamic, interactive formats, and controlling communications and the justifications they provide.

ICT indirectly contributes greatly to the educational learning process through their pedagogical interconnectedness and unique characteristics resulting from their technological properties. The main components of the contribution include activities that require active participation from teachers and students, interactive exercises involving action and counteraction, and protocols that support the formation of mental models. These align with both Vigotsky's theory that knowledge generation has a social component and Piaget's constructivist theoretical model(Kharroubi & ElMediouni, 2024), which maintains that learning is an active process of knowledge formation based on experiences gained in the real world. The study's goal, as shown in Fig. 2, was to present scenarios in which the technology actor actively engages in the resource integration and service exchange process with the user and other pertinent actors, resulting in interactive and context-aware ICT gamification. Particularly in the field of higher education, AI is making a substantial contribution to the development of ICT systems for service distribution.

Figure 2. Creation of National Research and Education Networks (NRENs) for academic and educational organizations that are networked: Authors illustration

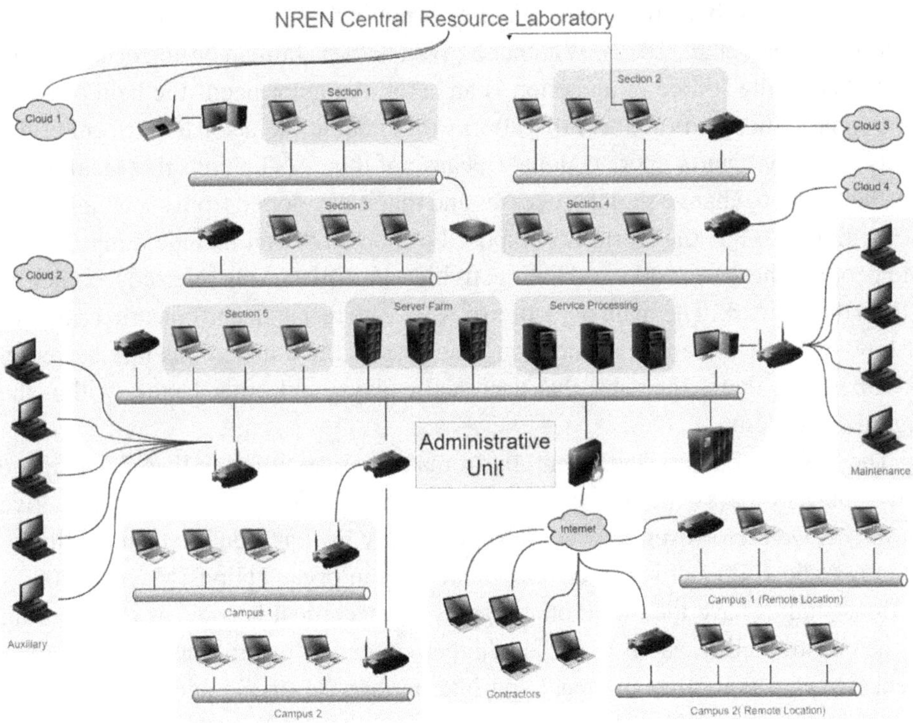

A collaborative learning environment that fosters concept development and testing, conclusion-making and deduction-making, as well as knowledge pooling and sharing, is provided by the ICT-integrated classroom. As opposed to passively processing knowledge mechanically from the teacher or textbook, students actively create their own knowledge through reflection. Content knowledge, critical thinking, and problem-solving abilities are developed in a substantial intellectual environment through the use of collaborative learning methodologies that include ICT aids(Ugochukwu Okwudili Matthew, Ado Saleh Kazaure, et al., 2022).

6. RESEARCH METHODOLOGY

The current research made use of design science methodology that requires a creation of scientific artefact. The practice of design science is intimately related to the idea of an articulated scientific model. It incorporates information technology, which provides precise criteria for evaluation and iteration inside research initiatives, and covers the methodology of numerous research disciplines. This approach enabled us create an actor network called ANT model. The actor network (ANT) is a computer-based paradigm where "actors" operate as the main computational agents and interact with both the internal and external environment to address learning issues(Kaasinen et al., 2022). Whether a given actor is human or not, according to ANT theory, the source of an action is an actor. An actor needs the help of other actors, particularly in the form of patterns that enable the actor to perform effectively; an actor cannot operate alone. Because of this, ANT thinks that technology has the power to change social processes and that it developed from social interests. According to ANT, the world is composed of networks that include things, ideas, and people. These networks and their activities are collectively referred to as actors within the network. The main objective of ANT is to research and construct a theory of how network systems can function best despite the connections that currently exist between them, the roles that each actor plays, and other factors within the digital ecosystem.

The ANT technique is efficient, but it makes the assumption that if one of the active players leaves the network, it will negatively affect all of the other active players as well. However, networks are constantly evolving due to the complexity and unpredictability of social developments within organizations(Magruk, 2022). Various studies have identified other agents and technical barriers as contributing to the constrained research in various higher education institutions. The literature identified cooperation at the local and international levels, in addition to limited access and skill to ICTs, as barriers. The suggested ANT model is presented in Figure 3, albeit it may be expanded based on the development of future technologies and scientific knowledge. The ANT model suggests that more actors should be involved in creating the NREN service portfolio and roadmap, despite the fact that the current study utilized the ANT model shown in Figure 3. These numbers and the ANT model helped to validate the study's conclusion.

Figure 3. ICT Education Development in Higher Institutions Using the ANT Model: Illustrated by the authors

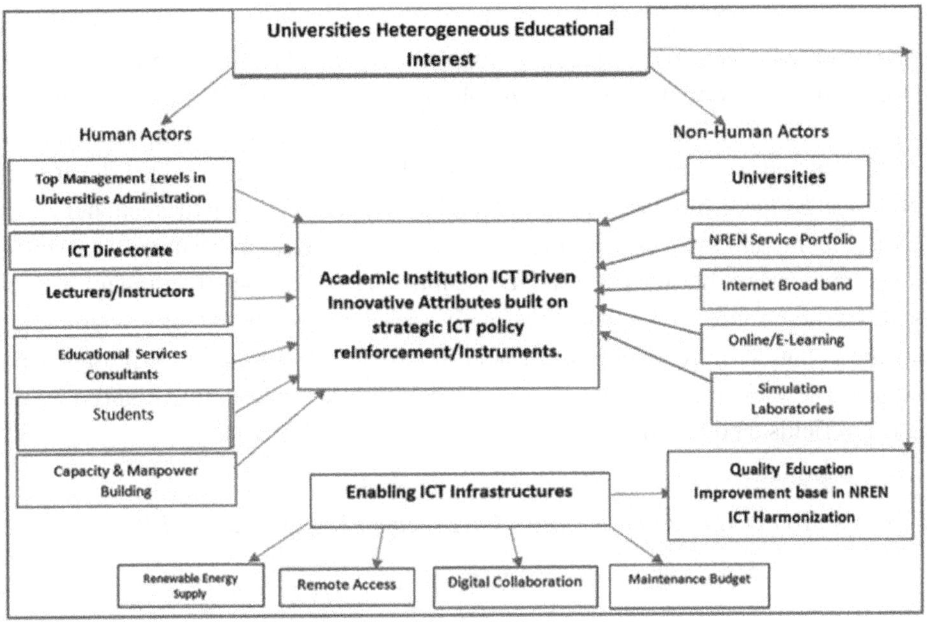

The proposed ANT model is shown in Figure 3. The truth is that more players could be included in the process of developing the roadmap and service offering. The ANT approach does not give priority to social or technological factors, in contrast to the case study, which blends problems with technology and social systems. The ANT will persistently highlight the interpretive flexibility of IT and systems in the sense that, due to specialized network-building and translation processes, ostensibly equivalent technologies yield notably different results in distinct neighborhoods. In the study, ANT demonstrated how it is possible to recognize the boundaries between technological and social structures, as well as how they are connected and how they are discussed as facts are being created, rather than taking technology for granted. NgREN must prioritize its efforts toward assisting Nigerian public higher education institutions in improving the quality of their instruction and producing more high-quality research as soon as possible in order to meet the intended goal.

7. RESEARCH IMPLEMENTATION

With reference to **Figure 1& Figure** 4, the utilization of several robots cooperating to provide more effective learning experiences is the subject of current research in educational robotics. Discovering new opportunities for educational applications and improvements in cooperative problem-solving skills and active learning encounters are the goals of research in these areas. GPT-4 and other large language models are anticipated to be essential in improving human-robot dialogue. Educational robots can be made more engaging and productive by combining these models with advancements in emotional intelligence and collaborative problem-solving skills. Educational robots has the potential to revolutionize education, give students useful skills for their future jobs, and promote a diverse student study. Educational robotics has the potential to become a useful and inclusive tool for classrooms all around the world by tackling the issues of cost and teacher preparation, investigating novel research fields, and emphasizing accessibility.

Figure 4. Higher Education Robotics Environment Using AI and NLP

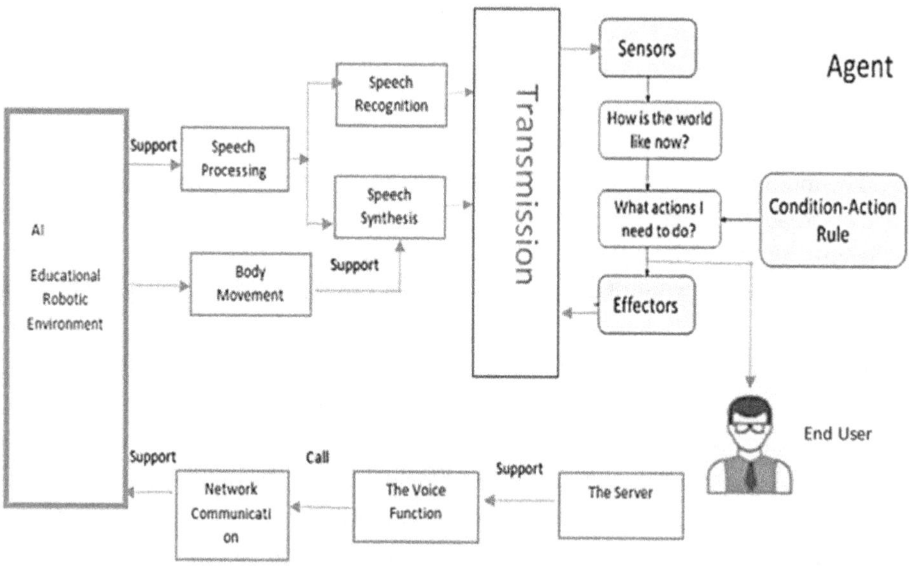

As active learning aids, educational robots can be used to improve learning experiences in a number of ways by encouraging student participation, problem-solving, and teamwork. The integration of robots into the classroom can foster student's creativity and critical thinking abilities. However, the current system will permit the following in accordance to research design, with special attention on Figure 4:

i. With an emphasis on active, interactive pedagogy, users will be able to customize their digital learning environment and study methods to suit their needs.
ii. After establishing a session and determining the chosen user's learning input, the server loads/extracts the required data and makes the appropriate platform changes.
iii. The user assigns tasks related to gathering feedback, and the server systematically specifies whether or not the student's request for information is authorized.
iv. When an operator engages in communication, the server automatically decides to share knowledge content using expressive interactive pedagogy.
v. To accomplish educational business goals with a high degree of demonstration, an AI educational robot and user will begin exchanging intelligence.
vi. AI-supported learning environments provide the kind of learning that will give struggling students the motivation and persistence to finish their education.

8. DISCUSSION OF RESEARCH FINDINGS

A priority on Africa at UNESCO was established at its 37th General Conference in 2021(Miao & Holmes, 2022). In order to fulfill the objectives of the African Union's Agenda 2063, "The Africa We Want," and the Sustainable Development Goals of the United Nations Agenda 2030, UNESCO made Africa a priority at its 37th General Conference in 2021. This was done by strengthening UNESCO's close engagement with African Member States by enhancing their capacities to harness innovation and digital transformation, including the implementation of the Recommendation on the Ethics of AI. Given AI's potential and the opportunities it presents for inclusive and sustainable development on the continent of Africa, the commission calls on the African Union, regional economic communities, governments, academic institutions, professional associations, the private sector, civil society, and international organizations to support the development of an open, accessible, and rights-based AI through a multi-stakeholder approach, with the aim of empowering Africans and transforming African societies. A unique flagship program on harnessing new and emerging technologies for sustainable development in Africa, including the implementation of the Recommendation on the Ethics of AI were added when it was modified and renewed in 2021. The primary objectives of the initiative include:

i. Enhancing the ability of African nations to accept and use AI.

ii. Strengthening the ability of all African AI actors to advance morally sound solutions and evaluate how AI affects people, the digital society, and the scientific ecosystem.
iii. Improving gender impartiality with respect to platform designs and application of AI sub-systems in the scheme of things in Africa.
iv. Mainstreaming free educational materials to help create inclusive knowledge society in Africa.
v. The enhancement of digital competences and abilities, in addition to closing the knowledge and digital inequalities.

The AI teaching robot in this study is divided into two sections: the method by which students learn and the demonstration of instinctive learning. An intelligent teaching robot designed to stimulate students' learning was presented by the authors of the present study. A speech-interacting synchronized artificial intelligence (AI) educational robot and pre-recorded educational content created with Camtasia Studio 8, a suite of software designed for creating and recording video presentations through screen casting or direct recording, may have enhanced the effectiveness of the classroom in raising student engagement in their academic work when it comes to teaching physical education. In addition to providing an instructional plan for the development of AI robotic philosophy, the study summarized Society 5.0 sustainability. The goal of the AI educational robotic application is to increase the study through the use of voice interaction in promoting education and enabling the enhancement of tailored learning to meet individual learning demands. The implementation of voice interactivity system based on AI was achieved from three aspects: speech synthesis, speech recognition, and interactive engagement. This allowed for the provision of the desired tele presence capability, improved access to the curriculum of education and coaching, and improved accuracy of speech narration through interactive experiences. When combined with the requirement of traditional education, the application of intelligent information technology (adaptive learning) will offer personalized educational experiences, successfully enabling the achievement of the 2030 global educational predictions, in accordance with UNESCO's recommendation.

9. FUTURE RESEARCH FOCUS

Education gives people the tools they need to face an uncertain and challenging future by emphasizing the development of abilities like creativity, teamwork, and entrepreneurship that are pertinent to the demands of Society 5.0. In the future, sponsoring creative education will be an investment in students' character development and their capacity to become effective leaders in this age of digital revolution, in addition to information acquisition. Education will play a significant role in promoting young people's constructive engagement in this dynamic society by embracing novel learning models, actively incorporating students, and strengthening the role of teachers as change agents. An educational strategy that is sensitive to the requirements of students and the expectations of a more interconnected society is necessary given the dynamic changes that have occurred in the digital age. Achieving learning objectives that are comprehensive and pertinent to technological advancements may be hampered by low student involvement. Thus, it is imperative to comprehend and maximize young engagement in Society 5.0 via creative teaching methods with focus on:

i. **Curriculum Update and Teaching Methodologies:** The curriculum and teaching strategies urgently need to be updated to reflect the dynamics of Society 5.0. A calculated move toward developing engaging and comprehensive learning experiences is the curriculum's inclusion of technology. Consequently, it is imperative to create educational modules that use technology as a means of augmenting students' comprehension of the subject matter. In addition to utilizing the newest gear and software, this phase also entails educating educators on how to fully utilize technology to engage and inspire their pupils. Not only is technological integration necessary, but it also needs to be thoroughly implemented in order for it to become an essential component of the learning process. Updates to the curriculum must also make the development of adaptability skills their main priority. In addition to imparting factual knowledge, the curriculum must involve students in the development of the skills required to keep up with the rapid advancement of technology. This covers abilities like teamwork, creativity, critical thinking, and problem-solving.
ii. **Creative Teaching Approaches for the Digital Natives:** Assisting students with authentic projects enables them to utilize their acquired knowledge and abilities in authentic settings. Furthermore, project-based learning offers chances for the growth of creative and problem-solving abilities when students work on assignments that call for original thought and creative solutions. By planning and carrying out their projects, students improve their comprehension of the material as well as their communication and teamwork abilities, which are vital in the rapidly changing digital world. Deep and interesting learning experiences can be made in large part by utilizing augmented and virtual reality technologies. Students can encounter abstract concepts in a more realistic context by immersing themselves in a near-real simulation thanks to this technology. Learning becomes more efficient and enjoyable when an immersive atmosphere is provided. In science education, for instance, students can use virtual reality

to see the interior of human organs or "visit" historical locations. By making use of this technology, individuals may ensure that every student has access to education in a manner that best meets their needs and preferences, even those with various learning styles. Novel learning models gain social and interactive elements via online collaboration and learning networks. Students can work together in a digital setting to accomplish coursework and projects, even with individuals from around the globe. Students and teachers develop close bonds as a result of this teamwork, which also widens the learning environment.

iii. **Empowering Teachers as Agents of Change**: Developing teacher professionalism is at the center of educational transformation in order to meet the needs of change in the era of Society 5.0. To effectively mentor students in an increasingly connected world, educators need to have a thorough understanding of how technology and learning paradigms are changing. To achieve this, a comprehensive strategy to professional development is needed, one that incorporates collaboration among instructors to exchange best practices, ongoing training, and membership in professional learning communities. Teachers need to be perpetual learners who are prepared to modify their methods in response to the most recent advancements in technology and educational research. The teacher's job description has changed dramatically from being a knowledge distributor to an active learning facilitator. In addition to being excellent sources of information, teachers also act as mentors, assisting pupils in a way that fosters critical thinking and creativity. In the setting of Society 5.0, where knowledge is readily available, educators must assist students in acquiring problem-solving, critical analysis, and teamwork abilities. In order for instructors to establish a learning environment that supports each student's full potential, teacher training must prioritize the development of these competencies. To ensure that educators can take the lead in helping students use technology effectively, it is imperative that they increase their technological proficiency. This calls for in-depth instruction in the application of technology and its integration into the curriculum, as well as knowledge of how to use digital tools to improve the learning process.

10. RECOMMENDATION

Supporting the application of AI in Africa and creating inclusive, partnership-focused, well-resourced partnerships are crucial if we are to fully grasp the potential of AI advancements. The current study aimed to improve operational partnerships for AI infrastructure development, with a focus on fostering the development of AI capabilities for important stakeholders and open-source AI tools and algorithms.

This report will also analyze earlier initiatives that were made public in the framework of UNESCO's Global Priority Africa, including the 2018 Benguerir Outcome Statement, which was unveiled at the organization's inaugural summit on artificial intelligence under the African continent. Using the knowledge given at the 2020 Forum, a synthesis report on developing competencies for the AI twenty-first century digital economy was produced. In an attempt to assist in the creation of a policy roadmap on AI as a common good towards changing education, UNESCO published a paper in April 2021 titled "AI and Education: Guidance for Policy-Makers." UNESCO had seized the opportunity presented by the 2021 International Forum to publish the book in each of the six UN languages. When UNESCO launched the AI and the future of learning program, it had three main but related goals in mind: (1) a paper offering recommendations for learning in the future with AI and expect people to use their vivid imaginations to see the many needs and problems that exist in society and the scenarios that could be used to address them, as well as their innovation in utilizing data and digital technology to make these answers a reality. (2) a set of guidelines for moral standards around the application of AI in education (3) a curriculum on AI skills for students in the classrooms, a notion that has the potential to help the United Nations accomplish its SDGs. This is connected to the completion of a survey on AI curricula for classroom instruction, the findings of which were shared at the global conference in 2021. Developing countries must provide human resources with exceptional AI skills in order to encourage regional AI developments and staff newly created jobs made possible by the usage of AI. The best approach for K–12 schools, universities, and Technical and Vocational Education and Training (TVET) institutes is to promote AI competences through national curriculum development.

11. CONCLUSION

The global world will undergo a major transformation as a result of Society 5.0 existential nomenclature, whether or not it encourages human-robot collaboration. The truth is that when robots become more commonplace in daily life, humans will likely experience a major transformation. Sustaining extreme automation raises a number of concerns, including biases in the data needed to train models, security and privacy preservation, the impact of human ingenuity, and possible employment and job displacement benefits. In order to make sure that the usage of GPT and other language models benefits society as a whole, we must constantly assess and consider their consequences. The digital revolution of our society, which impacts public services, the workplace, our everyday lives, and even education, is inextricably linked to the rise of AI in education. AI is facilitating the learning process in a number of ways, including the digital transmission of traditional information. It is also rapidly becoming about the digitization of knowledge representation and production due to machine learning and increasingly powerful algorithms. But because of the rapid advancement of human-AI integration and the digital revolution in our culture, our conception of what it means to be human and how we engage with technology has undergone a significant transformation. Our educational endeavors will be guided by the emerging field of digital humanism.

In light of the growing prevalence of AI in education, traditional ideas about humanism must be revised. Businesses will undergo a significant shift as a result of Society 5.0, whether or not it promotes human-robot collaboration. Truth be told, humans will probably undergo a significant transition as robots become more and more integrated into daily life. The authors have endeavored to construct a technological species that exhibits numerous similarities with the human species in this work. For some people, this is novel and fascinating. The current study aimed to underline the significance of using AI-mediated modernity in order to create an immersive and dynamic learning environment that gave students the increased abilities they required to become thoughtful and conscious digital natives. In this study, we introduced an AI-enabled educational robot that can provide instruction to students in both synchronous and asynchronous modes. With its network of higher education and research institutions across Nigeria, the NgREN provides an abundance of opportunities for cooperation and resource sharing. It may be possible for the university's library and other departments to operate more effectively using the AI-enabled learning system.

12. CONFLICT OF INTEREST

There is no conflict of interest regarding this publication. The paper was supported by U&J Digital Consult Limited, a Global IT and Educational Consulting Firm base in Nigeria.

REFERENCES

Adair, A. (2023). *Teaching and Learning with AI: How Artificial Intelligence is Transforming the Future of Education* (Vol. 29). ACM New York.

Audrey, A. A., & Paksi, A. K. (2022). *The Challenges of The Japanese Government to Implement Society 5.0.* Paper presented at the International Conference on Public Organization (ICONPO 2021).

Barakabitze, A. A., William-Andey Lazaro, A., Ainea, N., Mkwizu, M. H., Maziku, H., Matofali, A. X., Iddi, A., & Sanga, C. (2019). Transforming African education systems in science, technology, engineering, and mathematics (STEM) using ICTs: Challenges and opportunities. *Education Research International*, 2019, 2019. DOI:10.1155/2019/6946809

Bashir, S. (2020). Connecting Africa's Universities to Affordable High-Speed Broadband Internet.

Bhandari, S., & Bhandari, A. (2023). *Social and Economic Maxims of ICT in Education Economic and Social Implications of Information and Communication Technologies.* IGI Global.

Bozdag, A. A. (2023). AIsmosis and the pas de deux of human-AI interaction: Exploring the communicative dance between society and artificial intelligence. *Online Journal of Communication and Media Technologies*, 13(4), e202340. DOI:10.30935/ojcmt/13414

Chaudhari, R., Loharkar, P. K., & Ingle, A. (2022). *Medical Applications of Rapid Prototyping Technology Recent Advances in Industrial Production.* Springer.

Decardi-Nelson, B., Alshehri, A. S., Ajagekar, A., & You, F. (2024). Generative ai and process systems engineering: The next frontier. *Computers & Chemical Engineering*, 187, 108723. DOI:10.1016/j.compchemeng.2024.108723

Eguchi, A. (2022). *Understanding Machine Learning Through AI-powered Educational Robotics-Pilot Study with Undergraduate Students.* Paper presented at the International Conference on Robotics in Education (RiE). DOI:10.1007/978-3-031-12848-6_5

Flechsig, C., Anslinger, F., & Lasch, R. (2022). Robotic Process Automation in purchasing and supply management: A multiple case study on potentials, barriers, and implementation. *Journal of Purchasing and Supply Management*, 28(1), 100718. DOI:10.1016/j.pursup.2021.100718

Fomunyam, K. G. (2019). Education and the fourth industrial revolution: Challenges and possibilities for engineering education. *International Journal of Mechanical Engineering and Technology*, 10(8), 271–284.

Gill, S. S., & Kaur, R. (2023). ChatGPT: Vision and challenges. *Internet of Things and Cyber-Physical Systems*, 3, 262–271. DOI:10.1016/j.iotcps.2023.05.004

Guenduez, A. A., & Mettler, T. (2023). Strategically constructed narratives on artificial intelligence: What stories are told in governmental artificial intelligence policies? *Government Information Quarterly*, 40(1), 101719. DOI:10.1016/j.giq.2022.101719

Gumel, A. A., & Abdullahi, A. B., & O, U. M. (2019). The Need for a Multimodal Means of Effective Digital Learning through Data Mining and Institutional Knowledge Repository: A Proposed System for Polytechnics in Northern Nigeria. *Proceedings of the 2019 5th International Conference on Computer and Technology Applications*. DOI:10.1145/3323933.3324068

Heng, W., Solomon, S., & Gao, W. (2022). Flexible Electronics and Devices as Human–Machine Interfaces for Medical Robotics. *Advanced Materials*, 34(16), 2107902. DOI:10.1002/adma.202107902 PMID:34897836

Holmes, W., & Porayska-Pomsta, K. (2022). *The Ethics of Artificial Intelligence in Education: Practices, Challenges, and Debates*. Taylor & Francis. DOI:10.4324/9780429329067

Huang, S., Wang, B., Li, X., Zheng, P., Mourtzis, D., & Wang, L. (2022). Industry 5.0 and Society 5.0—Comparison, complementation and co-evolution. *Journal of Manufacturing Systems*, 64, 424–428. DOI:10.1016/j.jmsy.2022.07.010

Ietto, B., Ancillai, C., Sabatini, A., Carayannis, E. G., & Gregori, G. L. (2022). The Role of External Actors in SMEs' Human-Centered Industry 4.0 Adoption: An Empirical Perspective on Italian Competence Centers. *IEEE Transactions on Engineering Management*.

Javaid, M., Haleem, A., Singh, R. P., & Suman, R. (2021). Substantial capabilities of robotics in enhancing industry 4.0 implementation. *Cognitive Robotics*, 1, 58–75. DOI:10.1016/j.cogr.2021.06.001

Kaasinen, E., Anttila, A.-H., Heikkilä, P., Laarni, J., Koskinen, H., & Väätänen, A. (2022). Smooth and resilient human–machine teamwork as an Industry 5.0 design challenge. *Sustainability (Basel)*, 14(5), 2773. DOI:10.3390/su14052773

Kasinathan, P., Pugazhendhi, R., Elavarasan, R. M., Ramachandaramurthy, V. K., Ramanathan, V., Subramanian, S., & Rangasamy, S. (2022). Realization of sustainable development goals with disruptive technologies by integrating industry 5.0, society 5.0, smart cities and villages. *Sustainability (Basel)*, 14(22), 15258. DOI:10.3390/su142215258

Kharroubi, S., & ElMediouni, A. (2024). Conceptual Review: Cultivating Learner Autonomy Through Self-Directed Learning & Self-Regulated Learning: A Socio-Constructivist Exploration. *International Journal of Language and Literary Studies*, 6(2), 276–296. DOI:10.36892/ijlls.v6i2.1649

Kim, J., Lee, H., & Cho, Y. H. (2022). Learning design to support student-AI collaboration: Perspectives of leading teachers for AI in education. *Education and Information Technologies*, 27(5), 1–36. DOI:10.1007/s10639-021-10831-6

Leogrande, A., & Costantiello, A. (2023). The Impact of Government Expenditure on Education in the ESG Models at World Level. *Available atSSRN* 4438106. DOI:10.2139/ssrn.4438106

Magruk, A. (2022). The Desirable Systemic Uncertainty in Complex IoT Sensor Networks—General Anticipatory Foresight Perspective. *Sensors (Basel)*, 22(5), 1698. DOI:10.3390/s22051698 PMID:35270844

Matthew, U. O., Bakare, K. M., Ebong, G. N., Ndukwu, C. C., & Nwanakwaugwu, A. C. (2023). Generative Artificial Intelligence (AI) Educational Pedagogy Development: Conversational AI with User-Centric ChatGPT4. *Journal of Trends in Computer Science and Smart Technology*, 5(4), 401–418. DOI:10.36548/jtcsst.2023.4.003

Matthew, U. O., Kazaure, A. S., Kazaure, J. S., Hassan, I. M., Nwanakwaugwu, A. C., & Okafor, N. U. (2022). Educational Technology Adaptation & Implication for Media Technology Adoption in the Period of COVID-19. *Journal of Trends in Computer Science and Smart Technology*, 4(4), 226–245. DOI:10.36548/jtcsst.2022.4.002

Matthew, U. O., & Kazaure, J. S. (2020). Multimedia e-learning education in nigeria and developing countries of Africa for achieving SDG4. *International Journal of Information Communication Technologies and Human Development*, 12(1), 40–62. DOI:10.4018/IJICTHD.2020010103

Matthew, U. O., Kazaure, J. S., Amaonwu, O., Adamu, U. A., Hassan, I. M., Kazaure, A. A., & Ubochi, C. N. (2021). *Role of internet of health things (IoHTs) and innovative internet of 5G medical robotic things (IIo-5GMRTs) in COVID-19 global health risk management and logistics planning Intelligent Data Analysis for COVID-19 Pandemic*. Springer.

Matthew, U. O., Kazaure, J. S., Kazaure, A. S., Nwamouh, U. C., & Chinonso, A. (2022). ICT Policy Implementation as Correlate for Achieving Educational Sustainability: Approaching Development in Multi ICT Dimensions. *Journal of Information Technology*, 4(4), 250–269.

Matthew, U. O., Kazaure, J. S., Kazaure, A. S., Onyedibe, O. N., & Okafor, A. N. (2022). The Twenty First Century E-Learning Education Management & Implication for Media Technology Adoption in the Period of Pandemic. *EAI Endorsed Transactions on e-Learning, 8*(1).

Matthew, U. O., Kazaure, J. S., Ndukwu, C. C., Ebong, G. N., Nwanakwaugwu, A. C., & Nwamouh, U. C. (2024). *Artificial Intelligence Educational Pedagogy Development: ICT Pedagogy Development for Education 5.0 Educational Perspectives on Digital Technologies in Modeling and Management*. IGI Global. DOI:10.4018/979-8-3693-2314-4.ch003

Matthew, U. O., Kazaure, J. S., & Okafor, N. U. (2021). Contemporary development in E-Learning education, cloud computing technology & internet of things. *EAI Endorsed Transactions on Cloud Systems*, 7(20), e3–e3.

Mhlanga, D. (2022). The Role of Artificial Intelligence and Machine Learning Amid the COVID-19 Pandemic: What Lessons Are We Learning on 4IR and the Sustainable Development Goals. *International Journal of Environmental Research and Public Health*, 19(3), 1879. DOI:10.3390/ijerph19031879 PMID:35162901

Miao, F., & Holmes, W. (2022). International Forum on AI and Education: Ensuring AI as a Common Good to Transform Education, 7-8 December; synthesis report.

Mochizuki, Y., & Vickers, E. (2024). UNESCO, the geopolitics of AI, and China's engagement with the futures of education. *Comparative Education*, 1–20. DOI:10.1080/03050068.2024.2335125

Murugamani, C., Sahoo, S. K., Kshirsagar, P. R., Prathap, B. R., Islam, S., Noorulhasan Naveed, Q., Hussain, M. R., Hung, B. T., & Teressa, D. M. (2022). Wireless Communication for Robotic Process Automation Using Machine Learning Technique. *Wireless Communications and Mobile Computing*, 2022, 2022. DOI:10.1155/2022/4723138

Na'inna, A. M., & Anti-Dwanso, V. (2022). Arms race in the 21st century: Consequences and mitigating measures. *Global Journal of Social Sciences*, 21(1), 45–76. DOI:10.4314/gjss.v21i1.6

Okanda, E. O. (2024). Nyerere's Philosophy of Education for Self-Reliance and Its Implications for Enhancing the Socio-Economic Dimension of Current Kenyan University Education. *Futurity Philosophy*, 3(2), 4–24.

Oztemel, E., & Gursev, S. (2020). Literature review of Industry 4.0 and related technologies. *Journal of Intelligent Manufacturing*, 31(1), 127–182. DOI:10.1007/s10845-018-1433-8

Pillay, K., Erasmus, L., & Pretorius, J.-H. C. (2021). *A systems thinking approach to value-added services adoption in national research and education networks*. Paper presented at the 2021 IEEE AFRICON. DOI:10.1109/AFRICON51333.2021.9570883

Rasul, T., Nair, S., Kalendra, D., Robin, M., de Oliveira Santini, F., Ladeira, W. J., & Heathcote, L. (2023). The role of ChatGPT in higher education: Benefits, challenges, and future research directions. *Journal of Applied Learning and Teaching*, 6(1).

Rof, A., Bikfalvi, A., & Marques, P. (2022). *Digital Transformation in Higher Education: Intelligence in Systems and Business Models Intelligent Systems in Digital Transformation: Theory and Applications*. Springer.

Russell, S., Moskowitz, I. S., & Raglin, A. (2017). *Human information interaction, artificial intelligence, and errors Autonomy and Artificial Intelligence: A Threat or Savior?* Springer.

Seo, K., Tang, J., Roll, I., Fels, S., & Yoon, D. (2021). The impact of artificial intelligence on learner–instructor interaction in online learning. *International Journal of Educational Technology in Higher Education*, 18(1), 1–23. DOI:10.1186/s41239-021-00292-9 PMID:34778540

Shahab, M., Taheri, A., Mokhtari, M., Shariati, A., Heidari, R., Meghdari, A., & Alemi, M. (2022). Utilizing social virtual reality robot (V2R) for music education to children with high-functioning autism. *Education and Information Technologies*, 27(1), 819–843. DOI:10.1007/s10639-020-10392-0

Soltani, M., Moradi Kashkooli, F., Souri, M., Zare Harofte, S., Harati, T., Khadem, A., Haeri Pour, M., & Raahemifar, K. (2021). Enhancing clinical translation of cancer using nanoinformatics. *Cancers (Basel)*, 13(10), 2481. DOI:10.3390/cancers13102481 PMID:34069606

Storm, F. A., Chiappini, M., Dei, C., Piazza, C., André, E., Reißner, N., & Malosio, M. (2022). Physical and mental well-being of cobot workers: A scoping review using the Software-Hardware-Environment-Liveware-Liveware-Organization model. *Human Factors and Ergonomics in Manufacturing*, 32(5), 419–435. DOI:10.1002/hfm.20952

Taj, I., & Zaman, N. (2022). Towards Industrial Revolution 5.0 and Explainable Artificial Intelligence: Challenges and Opportunities. *International Journal of Computing and Digital Systems*, 12(1), 295–320. DOI:10.12785/ijcds/120128

Tyagi, A. K., Lakshmi Priya, R., Mishra, A. K., & Balamurugan, G. (2023). Industry 5.0: Potentials, Issues, Opportunities, and Challenges for Society 5.0. *Privacy Preservation of Genomic and Medical Data*, 409-432.

Wei, W., & Li, L. (2022). The Impact of Artificial Intelligence on the Mental Health of Manufacturing Workers: The Mediating Role of Overtime Work and the Work Environment. *Frontiers in Public Health*, 10, 10. DOI:10.3389/fpubh.2022.862407 PMID:35480579

Yitmen, I., Almusaed, A., & Alizadehsalehi, S. (2023). Investigating the Causal Relationships among Enablers of the Construction 5.0 Paradigm: Integration of Operator 5.0 and Society 5.0 with Human-Centricity, Sustainability, and Resilience. *Sustainability (Basel)*, 15(11), 9105. DOI:10.3390/su15119105

Younis, H. A., Ruhaiyem, N. I. R., Ghaban, W., Gazem, N. A., & Nasser, M. (2023). A Systematic Literature Review on the Applications of Robots and Natural Language Processing in Education. *Electronics (Basel)*, 12(13), 2864. DOI:10.3390/electronics12132864

Zengin, Y., Naktiyok, S., Kaygın, E., Kavak, O., & Topçuoğlu, E. (2021). An investigation upon industry 4.0 and society 5.0 within the context of sustainable development goals. *Sustainability (Basel)*, 13(5), 2682. DOI:10.3390/su13052682

Zhu, H. (2022). Comparative Study and Implications of Education Informatization Policies in China and the United States. *Advances in Educational Technology and Psychology*, 6(9), 25–30.

Chapter 11
Harnessing Combinatorial Human–Machine Advantages in Multimedia Teaching and Learning in Higher Education

Shalin Hai-Jew
https://orcid.org/0000-0002-8863-0175
Hutchinson Community College, USA

ABSTRACT

The advent of web-facing artmaking generative AI tools (A-GAI) has enabled new methods for teaching multimedia. This work explores some pedagogical approaches in harnessing combinatorial human-machine advantages in multimedia teaching and learning in higher education. This work begins with a summary of the advent of multimedia education and proposes a basic model for how A-GAI may be harnessed for teaching multimedia to early learners in higher education. This work is informed by academic research, abductive logic, and firsthand teaching,

INTRODUCTION

With the global rollout of a number of web-facing artmaking generative AIs (A-GAIs), higher education faculty who teach multimedia have a challenge of identifying ways to use such technologies to bolster student learning and enliven their

DOI: 10.4018/979-8-3693-2418-9.ch011

teaching. Early commentaries around generative AI have involved concerns about their safety, protections around copyright of works in the training data, and other aspects. This work suggests that it is important not to lock in opinions too early. Specifically, it is important to explore what is actually possible. For many instructors, they are learning and doing at the same time, without the luxury of a lot of testing.

Specifically, what may be done to enhance the use of human-machine collaborative advantages in visual making for multimedia learning in higher education? What do learners need to know about the models underlying the generative AI systems being used? What do they need to learn about ways to discern an AI-generated work vs. a fully human generated work (if possible)? What do learners need to know about the new creativity in the age of generative AI and how to navigate the various complexities? How can the formal learning address the informal learning (such as through video-sharing sites and social media platforms) already attained by learners through other channels? How can "born digital" and "born analog" be understood when there is so much overlap?

This chapter explores where contributions may be made in the human harnessing of artmaking generative AI tools for teaching and learning of multimedia tools in the higher education classroom. There will be consideration of creativity and innovation in this space. The digital tool used for this study is the Deep Dream Generator, which has been out in the world since 2015.

The author has spent years teaching multimedia at community college level and additional years training faculty, staff, and students, in multimedia usage at a university. With the rollout of A-GAIs and their popularization, she has experimented with a variety of tools and learned to appreciate the "mind-meld" with computers for creation. She has explored the combinatorial alchemy, that rich mixture, to produce fusion works that would not be possible otherwise. There is the mix of human culture and acquired tastes combined with the learned (trained) machine sensibility (also extracted from human works).

REVIEW OF THE LITERATURE

Multimedia, aka "interactive media" (Savage & Vogel, 1996, p. 127), refers to "the computer-controlled interactive medium that integrates in real time external visual and audio inputs with computer-generated text, graphics, animation, and audio" (Shelton, 1993, p. 694). Another definition of multimedia reads: "a computer-based system that combines at least several of text, sound, still images, full-motion video, animation, and computer graphics" (Velleman & Moore, 1996, p. 217). Multimedia involves "the combination of two or more media" with "interactivity" as a component (Galbreath, "The educational buzzword...," 1992, p. 15). Delivery of multimedia involves dependencies in hardware, software, storage, connectivity (Galbreath, "The educational buzzword...," 1992, p. 19). It is important to use proper terms to accurately represent the emergent technologies (Tolhurst, 1995). Various systems enable their hosting, searching, finding, and other means of storage and delivery. Cloud-based services enable constant access to learning materials and the related learning experience (Naidu, Bhat, & Singh, 2019, p. 81). The culmination of advanced technologies—broadband, digital authoring, multimedia—enabling "Internet-delivered online multimedia education" (Natarajan, 2006, p. 249). Said hyperbolically: multimedia "has overcome the barriers of time and space" (Malik & Agarwal, 2012, p. 468).

With multimedia, humanity needs to understand the digital and media technologies as part of new literacies in enriched informational environments (Barone & Wright, 2008, p. 292). It is important to explore "cultural forms of expression and communication" (Buckingham, "Media education goes...," 2007, p. 115). New technological affordances present "a new paradigm in information handling and delivery, with intrinsic support for profound interaction" (Gonzalez, Cranitch, & Jo, 2000, p. 90).

The changes in the information and communication technologies ecosystem have meant a rethinking of media education and competence for teachers. Said another way, instructors need to prepare learners to be digitally literate and digitally producing in a complex world (Buckingham, "Digital media literacies...," 2007). Media have an effect on culture as a whole (Masterman, 1993, p. 6), and media education involves "a quite new integration of analytical work and practical activity" among others (Masterman, 1993, p. 11). Teaching people how to participate in a democratic society is an important part of multimedia teaching and learning. Public education needs "to prepare people to participate in a democratic public sphere" (Stack & Kelly, 2006, p. 9), with a sense of personal empowerment and civics awareness. Multimedia is also seen to better align college students' skills with what is needed in industry, particularly in terms of problem-based learning and productivity (Neo & Neo, 2001) and teamwork to problem-solve (Neo & Neo, 2009). Those in education need to "attend closely to popular media and democratizing media production" to create a more prosocial and inclusive learning environment (Stack & Kelly, 2006, p. 5).

In-depth planning is required for actualizing multimedia for learning and training (Mishra & Sharma, 2005). Multimedia for education often requires the work of a team of creatives including "a producer, communication analyst, subject matter expert, script designer, interactive designer, art director, live-action director, audio engineer, and computer specialist" (Shelton, 1993, p. 694). As the digital media authoring tools have advanced, fewer staff are required to output quality multimedia. There is lower cost per "finished minute" (Galbreath, "The coming of digital..., " 1992, p. 29). Some digital desktop media may be output with professional level quality, such as for full motion video (Galbreath, "The coming of digital...," 1992, p. 27), which may have required a fully fleshed-out creative studio to achieve.

Another core feature of multimedia is its simultaneity of (requiring) perceptual channels, including sight and sound, and the use of symbolic processing via text. Animation (motion) is an aid in multimedia learning albeit with certain conditions based on human perceptual and mental processing. The predominant cognitive theory of multimedia learning, based on empirical research, suggests the following principles and practices:

> *These include the multimedia principle (present animation and narration rather than narration alone), spatial contiguity principle (present on-screen text near rather than far from corresponding animation), temporal contiguity principle (present corresponding animation and narration simultaneously rather than successively), coherence principle (present animation and narration rather than animation and on-screen text), redundancy principle (present animation and narration rather than animation, narration, and on-screen text), and personalization principle (present words in conversational rather than formal style). (Mayer & Moreno, 2002, p. 87)*

Multimedia may have three types of impacts: direct, cumulative, and subconscious (Kotiash, et al., 2022, p. 729).

Multimedia Use in Education and Learning

Educational media and multimedia are powerful for teaching and learning (Omodara & Adu, 2014). Digital-age teaching has to help learners develop "21st century skills, nonlinear thinking skills" and reflection (Lambert & Cuper, 2008, p. 264). Interactive multimedia harnesses gameplay, using both linear and nonlinear sequences (Slawson, 1993). The complexities of hypermedia, enabling different navigable paths, need to be clearly organized to aid in learner usage (Parlangeli, Marchigiani, & Bagnara, 1999).

Multimedia education supports the "informatization of society" (Kuchai, et al., 2022, p. 797). In a multimedia world, learners have their own "media spheres" (Buckingham, 2003, p. 311), and instruction benefits when it can connect with learners on their own terms. Media education bridges digital divides "between students' experiences of technology outside school and their experience in the classroom" (Buckingham, "Media education goes...," 2007, p. 111). A later work observed the widespread use of electronic devices by learners in the digital age (Putra, 2018, p. 1), so building digitally for learning stands to benefit access to this learner base. Proper instructional learning designs have to ensure that the learning is active, not passive (Stone, 1999).

Multimedia shifts the focus from the teacher to the learner, empowered by "interactive knowledge environments" (Mahajan, 2012, p. 5). Multimedia enables learner-centered teaching by aligning with learner motivations (Yap, Neo, & Neo, 2014). Interactive multimedia enables a more intuitive learning sense through adaptivity (Khoo, 1994). If designed well, media literacy learning enables learners to be critical thinkers (De Abreu, 2010). Multimedia may be used to improve learner intellectual and creativity capabilities (Adekunle, Adewale, & Boyinbode, 2019).

While digital learning objects may be stand-alone as single objects, modules, or short courses, there are also whole systems built up to enable multimedia learning. One more conceptual work proposes a "multimedia image linguistics" system to be used with multimedia:

Multimedia pictures are considered to be a language because it conforms to the definition of language; that is, it can be regarded as a symbol system and can be used to transmit knowledge information to view aesthetic hearing. (Yuejue, Xinze, Bingyue, & Xiaoyuan, 2021, p. 1)

This work conceptualizes the findings as identifying "the artistic laws of multimedia pictures" to enhance the teaching and learning materials created from multimedia (Yuejue, Xinze, Bingyue, & Xiaoyuan, 2021, p. 1). Multimedia for teaching and learning comes in various forms: tutorials, practices, simulations, experiments, and games (Putra, 2018, pp. 6-7), among others. Multimedia resources enliven traditional media like "books, tables, figures, blackboard writing" and others (Gañán, Caballé, Conesa, Barolli, Kulla, & Spaho, July 2014, p. 249), some with automation features. One study explored the use of multimedia as augmentation to documents, and it was seen as valuable to "clarify difficult concepts and better transfer information to users" in the context of "a well-structured and well-written document" (Rockley, 1994, p. 653). The architecting of multimedia environments for teaching was observed to be sophisticated (Friedland & Pauls, 2005).

Teachers need to combine "good teaching practice" with the affordances of interactive multimedia (Kennedy & McNaught, 1997). There should be clear learning goals, a reasonable workload for learners, and a sense of learner independence in the learning context. One study found that while faculty were personally active on social media that they were less willing to harness social media for teaching and learning (Seaman & Tinti-Kane, 2013). Those who would build or inherit digital works for teaching are advised to go with open-source alternatives to commercial and proprietary platforms (Fletcher, 2019). An older work puts it: "The more specialized a solution, the lower the probability of its reuse—which directly affects its sustainability" (Friedland & Pauls, 2005, p. 59).

Multimedia Authoring for Teaching and Learning

Multimedia authoring is a core part of teaching and learning (Abowd, et al., Feb. 1997). Teachers need to be aware of the variety of options for educators in terms of multimedia (Krippel, McKee, & Moody, 2010). Instructors benefit from strategies for the selection of multimedia learning aids (Kotiash, et al., 2022). Preservice teacher training is needed to strengthen their knowledge of the technologies, subject matter, and teaching in that context (Seo, Templeton, & Pellegrino, 2008). It is important to avoid traditional teaching methods that are not aligned with the necessary learning for multimedia skills training (Wang, 2010).

In terms of multimedia education, teachers need to know how to make quality multimedia aids for classroom learning (Kostolanský, Šebo, & Tomková, 2019). One research work suggests that hands-on development of multimedia applications for learning from the perspective of discipline expertise and knowledge of the learners is important (Babiker & Elmagzoub, 2015).

Audiovisual media is central in many disciplines and technology-enhanced learning (Nicolaou, Matsiola, & Kalliris, 2019). The research literature shows multimedia learning applied to various subject matters: religious education (Ziden & Rahman, 2013), statistics (Velleman & Moore, 1996), communication skills (Mukherjee, 2018), art (Motomura, 2003), foreign languages (Kramsch & Andersen, 1999, p. 31), and others. Online labs are harder to create through multimedia because of the need for "direct operation of instruments" (Junaidu, 2008, p. 98).

New forms of experiential learning ar enabled by multimedia, such as "technology-enabled active learning" (Gallou & Abrahams, 2018, p. 165). One empirical research study found positive learning effects of a multimedia intervention on student learning (Leow & Neo, 2014). Effective use of multimedia can measurably improve teaching and learning performances (Xu, 2017).

A study on multimedia "attention cueing" was found to have mixed effects based on learner visual observation characteristics (Yang, 2016, p. 249). Teachers benefit the learning when they tailor the multimedia teaching and learning to particular learning groups for learning efficacy (Abdulrahaman, et al., 2020).

Another study found students receptive to multimedia use in education (Vagg, Balta, Bolger, & Lone, 2020). Another found high motivation by learners engaging in new media (Lee, 2016).

HARNESSING COMBINATORIAL HUMAN-MACHINE ADVANTAGES IN MULTIMEDIA TEACHING AND LEARNING IN HIGHER EDUCATION

The advent of artmaking generative AI tools (A-GAI) enable users to use text and image prompts, along with other descriptors, in order to output 2d images (among other information-rich digital outputs). The output images are mashups from pixel-pieces learned in large language models (LLMs) trained on big datasets of images, with diffuse image linguistics. Resulting images come from both the human and machine imaginaries. If the world's intercommunications and global cultures and social interchanges are via social media and the Internet, the digital contents (both human- and AI-generated and human-AI generated) are the language of large swaths of society. Much of today's history is written in the digital.

For beginning learners of multimedia software tools, a typical learning sequence involves the instructor introducing the multimedia software, related terminology, principles of design (geometries, composites, underlying maths, underlying psychology), demoing the technologies, and offering short and simple assignments to enable both learning and practice. Or there may be a series of small projects that culminate in a large learner-based portfolio. Feedback is elicited from the learners, and constructive feedback is offered by the instructor. Or there may be group projects that enable learners to collaborate among themselves. Then, the instructor adds capabilities over time, especially around special effects which are glamorous and engaging. As the student becomes fluent in the various suites of tools, they work more complex design, development, and deployment work pipelines, given the ease of transcoding files and shared open or universal file types (and some open proprietary ones). The investment in acquiring the knowledge, skills, and abilities (and attitudes) [KSAs] for each of the technologies is high, so selecting the proper tools and learning sequences is important. There are tradeoffs and opportunity costs in each path. The general learning models include hands-on project-based learning and problem-based learning, among others.

The technology used for this research work is the Deep Dream Generator, released to the public in 2015, and now in Version 3. This technology is typified by an algorithm that taps into pareidolia, the portraying of shapes where there is only visual abstraction or randomness.

In Figure 1, "Teaching Multimedia Skills to Beginning Learners (with the Help of Artmaking Generative AI Tools)," the left column shows a general progressive learning sequence. Beginning learners of multimedia consume various outputs from various authoring tools and analyze them. They then learn software basics (terminology, graphical user interface, functionalities, and such) in combination with visual principles, and then they use their new skills to actualize short projects and then longer ones...with some done individually, others done as part of a team. As part of the learning, they review and revise. They also make their works available to a larger public. As to the generative AI augmentations, the A-GAI may be used for examples, ideation, design exploration, style inspirations, color palettes, reference imagery, in-painting (to correct selected sections of a visual), and others. Generative AI may be used for text-based feedback. The visuals from A-GAI may be affected by pre-production-based seeding imagery, and they may be refined further through post-production. In the figure, it is clear that the A-GAI may be harnessed for useful application at every stage. The A-GAI may be used to augment core and pedagogically solid teaching instructional designs.

Figure 1. Teaching Multimedia Skills to Beginning Learners (with the Help of Art-making Generative AI Tools)

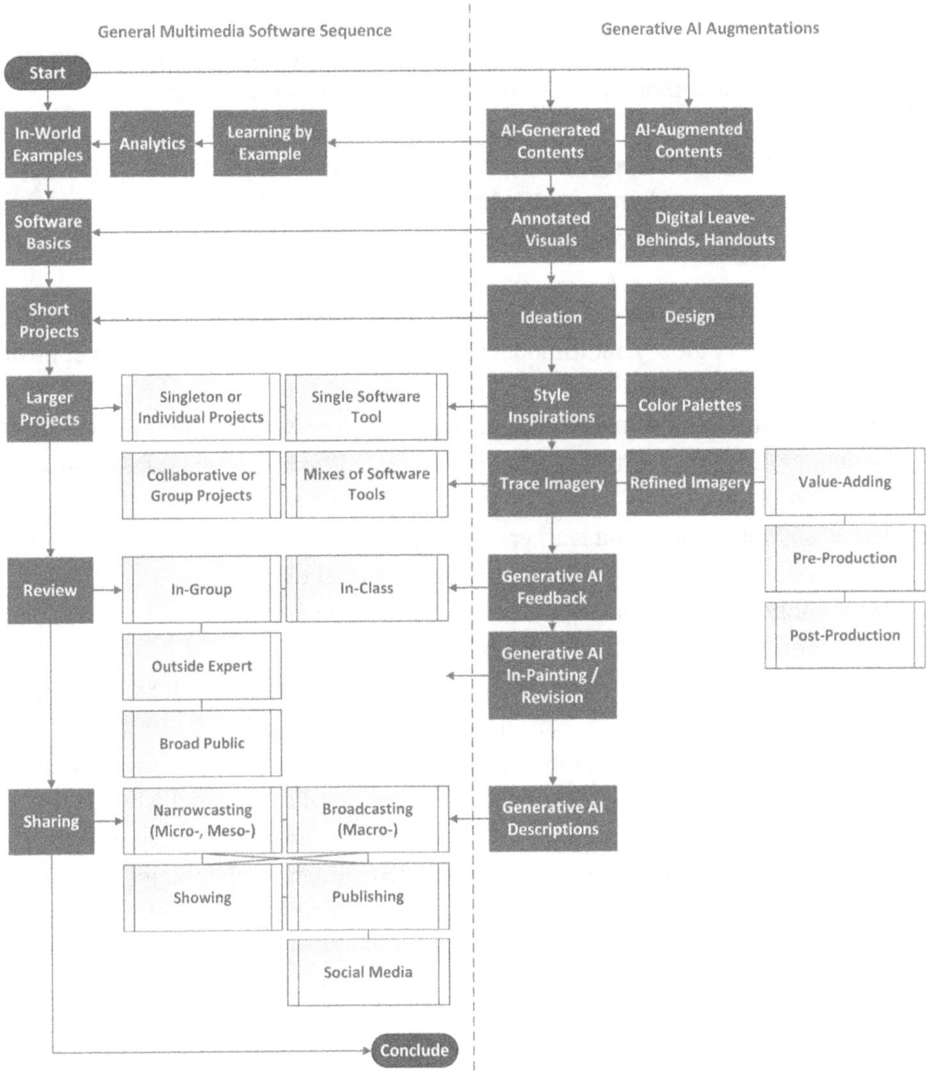

In terms of human "manual" competition, there is no efficient equivalent of outputting visuals to the same caliber of quality. If speed is important, A-GAI can help an individual fail fast. Ironically, machine-generated visuals are virtually costless except for the conceptualizing, the prompt tweaking, and the post production. The digital image editing and authoring tools, though, for all their efficiencies and power, are complex to learn (they come with a high learning curve) but enable a high level of control (down to the pixel level). As noted in the introduction, there are many questions that instructors will have to answer about their use of the A-GAI. As societies, humanity will need to define how they will incorporate A-GAI and how they will enable and support unique human voices and visions in the mix.

A generalist observation that A-GAI may be helpful in multimedia teaching and learning is asserted. Other questions have arisen in this work as well.

1. In the scenario of the beginning freshman learner, what are the various ways that instructors may harness artmaking generative AIs?
2. How can they do so in ways that are positive and constructive and conducive to learning?
3. What may be learned about effective prompting—through single modal inputs (text or imagery alone), multimodal inputs (text and imagery), and other control elements (like tagging)?
4. How can human and machine aesthetics be harnessed (in the built world—replete with so much artifice—that is co-created by humans and human-made machines)?
5. How can practitioners and learners strive for divergence, serendipity, and originality vs. convergence, predictability, and derived outputs?
6. How should pre- and post- production be brought into play for more control and more sophisticated inputs and outputs?
7. What sorts of discussions may be had around this learning context and space? How can A-GAI serve as a learning conversation starter?
8. Should the artmaking generative AI technology play a main central role or a small or peripheral one in a particular learning application, and why?
9. How can learners be encouraged to speak their own art and other truths through their work, even with so much excitement around new technologies?
10. When should the technology be "shelved" or set aside for a time? And why?

And certainly, different instructors will answer the above in different ways, perhaps collaboratively with the learners.

Discussion

A-GAI tools stand to increase productivity across a range of fields, education not least among them. This work highlights some ways these may be used in the teaching of multimedia. Indeed, many other use cases may be relevant as well. Also, given the legal requirements for accessibility in digital spaces, it would be helpful to see how the A-GAI outputs may be made accessible through both automated and human means.

FUTURE RESEARCH DIRECTIONS

The A-GAI scenario here focuses on 2d visuals, but A-GAI can produce vector graphics, 3d imagery, 4d imagery, digital writing, digital sound, and mixed and multimedia. Other enriched work processes may be explored in the multimedia space. Perhaps there may be studies of teaching and learning efficacies based on empirical research from such human-machine made contents.

Electronic (and electric) media are the *lingua franca* for the contemporaneous age. As such, computational means may be applied to their capture and study, so various multimedia training contents may be analyzed and studied for powerful in-world insights.

CONCLUSION

The SARS-CoV-2 / COVID-19 pandemic did accelerate digital transformation of higher education, and the multimodality is thought to enable more customized and adaptive learning (Rof, Bikfalvi, & Marques, 2022). This is an early moment in the hype cycle for A-GAI tools. There is so much unplumbed promise in terms of tool harnessing and usage.

REFERENCES

Abdulrahaman, M. D., Faruk, N., Oloyede, A. A., Surajudeen-Bakinde, N. T., Olawoyin, L. A., Mejabi, O. V., Imam-Fulani, Y. O., Fahm, A. O., & Azeez, A. L. (2020). Multimedia tools in the teaching and learning processes: A systematic review. *Heliyon*, 6(11), e05312. DOI:10.1016/j.heliyon.2020.e05312 PMID:33195834

Abowd, G. D., Atkeson, C. G., Feinstein, A., Hmelo, C., Kooper, R., Long, S., & Tani, M. (1997, February). Teaching and learning as multimedia authoring: the classroom 2000 project. In *Proceedings of the Fourth ACM International Conference on Multimedia* (pp. 187-198).

Adekunle, S. E., Adewale, O. S., & Boyinbode, O. K. (2019). Appraisal on perceived multimedia technologies as modern pedagogical tools for strategic improvement on teaching and learning. *International Journal of Modern Education and Computer Science*, 11(8), 15. DOI:10.5815/ijmecs.2019.08.02

Babiker, M., & Elmagzoub, A. (2015). For effective use of multimedia in education, teachers must develop their own educational multimedia applications. *Turkish Online Journal of Educational Technology-TOJET*, 14(4), 62–68.

Barone, D., & Wright, T. E. (2008). Literacy instruction with digital and media technologies. *The Reading Teacher*, 62(4), 292–302. DOI:10.1598/RT.62.4.2

Buckingham, D. (2003). Media education and the end of the critical consumer. *Harvard Educational Review*, 73(3), 309–327. DOI:10.17763/haer.73.3.c149w3g81t381p67

Buckingham, D. (2007). Digital media literacies: Rethinking media education in the age of the Internet. *Research in Comparative and International Education*, 2(1), 43–55. DOI:10.2304/rcie.2007.2.1.43

Buckingham, D. (2007). Media education goes digital: An introduction. *Learning, Media and Technology*, 32(2), 111–119. DOI:10.1080/17439880701343006

De Abreu, B. (2010). Changing technology= empowering students through media literacy Education. *New Horizons in Education*, 58(3), 26–33.

Fletcher, C. (2019). *Educational technology and the humanities: A history of control*. Debates in the Digital Humanities. DOI:10.5749/j.ctvg251hk.33

Friedland, G., & Pauls, K. (2005). Architecting multimedia environments for teaching. *Computer*, 38(6), 57–64. DOI:10.1109/MC.2005.181

Galbreath, J. (1992). The coming of digital desktop media. *Educational Technology*, 32(6), 27–32.

Galbreath, J. (1992). The educational buzzword of the 1990's: Multimedia, or is it hypermedia, or interactive multimedia, or...? *Educational Technology*, 32(4), 15–19.

Gallou, E., & Abrahams, P. (2018). Creating space for active learning:(Opportunities from) using technology in research-based education. pp. 165 - 175.

Gañán, D., Caballé, S., Conesa, J., Barolli, L., Kulla, E., & Spaho, E. (2014, July). A systematic review of multimedia resources to support teaching and learning in virtual environments. In *2014 Eighth International Conference on Complex, Intelligent and Software Intensive Systems* (pp. 249-256). IEEE. DOI:10.1109/CISIS.2014.35

Gonzalez, R., Cranitch, G., & Jo, J. (2000). Academic directions of multimedia education. *Communications of the ACM*, 43(1), 89–95. DOI:10.1145/323830.323849

Junaidu, S. (2008). Effectiveness of multimedia in learning & teaching data structures online. *Turkish Online Journal of Distance Education*, 9(4), 97–107.

Kennedy, D. M., & McNaught, C. (1997). Design elements for interactive multimedia. *Australasian Journal of Educational Technology*, 13(1). Advance online publication. DOI:10.14742/ajet.1916

Khoo, C. C. (1994). Interactive multimedia for teaching, learning and presentations. In *Proceedings of the Second International Interactive Multimedia Symposium* (pp. 230-236).

Kostolanský, L., Šebo, M., & Tomková, V. (2019). The preparation of teachers in the field of multimedia education. In *EduLearn19 Proceedings* (pp. 1477–1483). IATED. DOI:10.21125/edulearn.2019.0446

Kotiash, I., Shevchuk, I., Borysonok, M., Matviienko, I., Popov, M., Terekhov, V., & Kuchai, O. (2022). Possibilities of using multimedia technologies in education. *International Journal of Computer Science and Network Security*, 22(6), 727–732.

Kramsch, C., & Andersen, R. W. (1999). Teaching text and context through multimedia.

Krippel, G., McKee, A. J., & Moody, J. (2010). Multimedia use in higher education: Promises and pitfalls. *Journal of Instructional Pedagogies*, 2, 1–8.

Kuchai, O., Skyba, K., Demchenko, A., Savchenko, N., Necheporuk, Y., & Rezvan, O. (2022). The importance of multimedia education in the informatization of society. *IJCSNS, 797.*

Lambert, J., & Cuper, P. (2008). Multimedia technologies and familiar spaces: 21st century teaching for 21st century learners. *Contemporary Issues in Technology & Teacher Education*, 8(3), 264–276.

Lee, A. Y. (2016). *Media education in the School 2.0 era: Teaching media literacy through laptop computers and iPads*. Global Media and China.

Leow, F. T., & Neo, M. (2014). Interactive multimedia learning: Innovating classroom education in a Malaysian university. *Turkish Online Journal of Educational Technology-TOJET*, 13(2), 99–110.

Mahajan, G. (2012). Multimedia in teacher education: Perceptions & uses. *Journal of Education and Practice*, 3(1), 5–13.

Malik, S., & Agarwal, A. (2012). Use of multimedia as a new educational technology tool-A study. *International Journal of Information and Education Technology (IJIET)*, 2(5), 468–471. DOI:10.7763/IJIET.2012.V2.181

Masterman, L. (1993). The media education revolution. *Canadian Journal of Educational Communication*, 22(1), 5–14.

Mayer, R. E., & Moreno, R. (2002). Animation as an aid to multimedia learning. *Educational Psychology Review*, 14(1), 87–99. DOI:10.1023/A:1013184611077

Mishra, S., & Sharma, R. C. (2005). *Interactive multimedia in education and training*. Idea Group Pub. DOI:10.4018/978-1-59140-393-7

Motomura, K. (2003). Media literacy education in art: Motion expression and the new vision of art education. *Journal of Aesthetic Education*, 37(4), 58–64. DOI:10.1353/jae.2003.0039

Mukherjee, S. (2018). Role of multimedia in education. *Edelweiss Applied Science and Technology*, 2(1), 245–247. DOI:10.33805/2576-8484.149

Naidu, V. R., Bhat, A. Z., & Singh, B. (2019). Cloud concept for implementing multimedia based learning in higher education. In *Smart Technologies and Innovation for a Sustainable Future:Proceedings of the 1st American University in the Emirates International Research Conference—Dubai, UAE2017* (pp. 81-84). Springer International Publishing. DOI:10.1007/978-3-030-01659-3_11

Natarajan, M. (2006). Use of online technology for multimedia education. *Information Services & Use*, 26(3), 249–256. DOI:10.3233/ISU-2006-26304

Neo, M., & Neo, K. T. (2001). Innovative teaching: Using multimedia in a problem-based learning environment. *Journal of Educational Technology & Society*, 4(4), 19–31.

Neo, M., & Neo, T. K. (2009). Engaging students in multimedia-mediated Constructivist learning–Students' perceptions. *Journal of Educational Technology & Society*, 12(2), 254–266.

Nicolaou, C., Matsiola, M., & Kalliris, G. (2019). Technology-enhanced learning and teaching methodologies through audiovisual media. *Education Sciences, 9*(3), 196, 1 - 13.

Omodara, O. D., & Adu, E. I. (2014). Relevance of educational media and multimedia technology for effective service delivery in teaching and learning processes. *IOSR Journal of Research & Method in Education*, 4(2), 48–51.

Parlangeli, O., Marchigiani, E., & Bagnara, S. (1999). Multimedia systems in distance education: Effects of usability on learning. *Interacting with Computers*, 12(1), 37–49. DOI:10.1016/S0953-5438(98)00054-X

Putra, C. A. (2018). Utilization of multimedia technology for instructional media. *Journal of ICT in Education*, 5(1), 1–8. DOI:10.37134/jictie.vol5.1.2018

Rockley, A. (1994). Planning a multimedia documentation project. *Technical Communication (Washington)*, 653–661.

Rof, A., Bikfalvi, A., & Marques, P. (2022). Pandemic-accelerated digital transformation of a born digital higher education institution. *Journal of Educational Technology & Society*, 25(1), 124–141.

Savage, T. M., & Vogel, K. E. (1996). Multimedia: A revolution in higher education? *College Teaching*, 44(4), 127–131. DOI:10.1080/87567555.1996.9932339

Seaman, J., & Tinti-Kane, H. (2013). *Social media for teaching and learning*. Pearson Learning Systems.

Seo, K. K., Templeton, R., & Pellegrino, D. (2008). Creating a ripple effect: Incorporating multimedia-assisted project-based learning in teacher education. *Theory into Practice*, 47(3), 259–265. DOI:10.1080/00405840802154062

Shelton, S. M. (1993). Multimedia. *Technical Communication (Washington)*, 40(4), 694–704.

Slawson, B. (1993). Interactive multimedia: The gestalt of a gigabyte. *Art Education*, 46(6), 15–22. DOI:10.2307/3193404

Stack, M., & Kelly, D. M. (2006). Popular media, education, and resistance. *Canadian Journal of Education/Revue Canadienne de l'éducation*, 5-26.

Stone, L. L. (1999). Multimedia instruction methods. *The Journal of Economic Education*, 30(3), 265–275. DOI:10.1080/00220489909595987

Tolhurst, D. (1995). Hypertext, hypermedia, multimedia defined? *Educational Technology*, 35(2), 21–26.

Vagg, T., Balta, J. Y., Bolger, A., & Lone, M. (2020). Multimedia in education: What do the students think? *Health Profession Education*, 6(3), 325–333. DOI:10.1016/j.hpe.2020.04.011

Velleman, P. F., & Moore, D. S. (1996). Multimedia for teaching statistics: Promises and pitfalls. *The American Statistician*, 50(3), 217–225. DOI:10.1080/00031305.1996.10474383

Xu, X. (2017). Study on effective using of multimedia teaching system and enhancing teaching effect. *International Journal of Emerging Technologies in Learning*, 12(6), 187. DOI:10.3991/ijet.v12i06.7093

Yang, H. Y. (2016). The effects of attention cueing on visualizers' multimedia learning. *Journal of Educational Technology & Society*, 19(1), 249–262.

Yap, W. L., Neo, M., & Neo, T. K. (2014). Impact of learner-centred teaching environment with the use of multimedia-mediated learning modules in improving learning experience. [Sciences and Engineering]. *Jurnal Teknologi*, 68(2), 65–71.

Yuejue, Y., Xinze, S., Bingyue, L., & Xiaoyuan, W. (2021). Construct a teaching system combining image linguistics and multimedia technology. *Wireless Communications and Mobile Computing*, 2021(1), 1–11. DOI:10.1155/2021/6699010

Ziden, A. A., & Rahman, M. F. A. (2013). The effectiveness of web-based multimedia applications simulation in teaching and learning. *International Journal of Instruction*, 6(2).

ADDITIONAL READING

Hai-Jew, S. (2024). *Generative AI in Teaching and Learning*. IGI Global.

KEY TERMS AND DEFINITIONS

Artmaking Generative AI (A-GAI): A model for digital creation that is based on large language models (LLMs) trained on big data and fine-tuned for particular types of visual outputs.

Multimedia: Digital media comprised of multiple sensory channels (sight, smell, taste, touch, and hearing) simultaneously Prompt: Text, image or combination of text and imagery to elicit an output from a generative AI tool.

Prompt: Text, image or combination of text and imagery to elicit an output from a generative AI tool

Chapter 12
Revolutionizing Creative Education:
The Role of Generative AI in Enhancing Innovation and Learning in Higher Education

Khalida Akbar
Durban University of Technology, South Africa & MANCOSA, South Africa

Farai Donald Nyika
https://orcid.org/0000-0001-9759-7007
MANCOSA, South Africa

Vicent Mbonye
https://orcid.org/0000-0001-9890-614X
Partidos, South Africa

ABSTRACT

The emergence of GenAI tools, such as OpenAI's ChatGPT, Google's Bard, and Meta's Llama, has marked the beginning of a new age in educational approaches, specifically in fostering creativity in higher education. This chapter examines the diverse effects of GenAI on promoting and assessing creativity among students and instructors. This chapter examines the capacity of these technologies to improve creative thinking, problem-solving, and personalised learning experiences. It also considers the ethical, privacy, and bias-related problems that come with using these technologies. This chapter seeks to offer valuable insights on the effective integration of GenAI into higher education curricula, with the goal of fostering the development of innovative thinkers. This was achieved by a review of current literature. The chapter proposes a strategy that harnesses the advantages of AI while reducing

DOI: 10.4018/979-8-3693-2418-9.ch012

its potential drawbacks, therefore creating a future where technology and human ingenuity combine to promote progress and development in academics.

1. INTRODUCTION

The emergence of large language models, such as OpenAI's ChatGPT, signifies a monumental shift in the landscape of educational technologies, introducing a new era of generative artificial intelligence (GenAI) in higher education. These advanced AI systems, capable of generating human-like responses and engaging in complex dialogues, have sparked a significant increase in academic inquiry and interest, as evidenced by the substantial volume of research following ChatGPT's launch on November 30, 2022 (Pasquale, 2020; Kostka & Toncelli, 2023; Neumann, Rauschenberger, & Schön, 2023). The versatility of ChatGPT and similar tools, encompassing applications from assessment planning to the nuanced tasks of scientific writing, underscores the transformative potential of GenAI in academia.

While ChatGPT stands out as a prominent GenAI tool, the landscape is rich with diverse offerings, including Google's Bard and Microsoft's Bing AI, each with unique capabilities and specializations. This variety reflects a broader ecosystem of GenAI tools, each engineered with specific functionalities and based on different machine learning paradigms or large language models (LLMs) (York, 2024). This introduction seeks to delineate the scope of this chapter by focusing on the multifaceted impacts of GenAI on creative processes within higher education, exploring its potential to both enhance and challenge traditional educational paradigms. The academic discourse surrounding GenAI in higher education has been varied, ranging from optimistic speculations about its benefits to critical examinations of its ethical implications for academia (Firat, 2023; Fuchs, 2023; Rasul, et al., 2023; Baskara, 2023; Day, 2023; Huallpa, 2023; Rahimzadeh, Kostick-Quenet, Blumenthal Barby, & McGuire, 2023; Farhi, 2023). Notably, the integration of GenAI into educational practices raises important questions about authorship and originality, as Higher Education Institutions (HEIs) are traditionally centers of knowledge production. Moreover, student perceptions of GenAI have been mixed, with some highlighting its potential to support learning and creativity, while others express concerns over its reliability and the ethical ramifications of its use (Chan, & Hu, 2023; Smolansky, 2023; Ghimire, Prather, & Edwards, 2024; Dai, Liu, & Lim, 2023; Ali, Ravi, Williams, DiPaola, & Breazeal, 2024). This chapter aims to provide a comprehensive overview of GenAI technologies, examining their influence on creativity in higher education. Through a desktop analysis of the literature, this chapter will delve into how GenAI intersects with, enhances, and, at times, conflicts with creative processes in learning environments, striving for a balanced understanding that recognizes both the opportunities and challenges presented by this technological advancement.

2. IMPACTS OF GENERATIVE AI ON CREATIVITY IN HIGHER EDUCATION

GenAI is a distinct field within the realm of AI that focuses on the development of AI algorithms capable of identifying and analysing patterns and trends within training data. GenAI has the exceptional capability to independently produce novel and distinct material (Fezari, Al-Dahoud, & Al-Dahoud, 2023). It depends on multiple models, each possessing distinct strengths and limits. The models mentioned are autoencoders, variational autoencoders (VAEs), generative adversarial networks (GANs), Boltzmann Machines, and transformers (Fezari et al., 2023). These AI models are trained to understand and reproduce the fundamental framework and qualities of the data they are exposed to. This enables them to generate novel content that demonstrates analogous patterns and characteristics (Fezari et al., 2023). Nevertheless, the selection of a model is contingent upon the particular task and the nature of the data being utilised (Fezari et al., 2023).

2.1 Societal Implication of Generative Ai

The social implications refer to the effects that algorithms, data, and AI can have on many aspects of society. These effects can be positive, as they can enhance commonly held values, or negative, as they might pose a danger to those values (Whittlestone, Nyrup, Alexandrova, Dihal, & Cave, 2019). In terms of societal ramifications, the capacity of generative AI to create original material by analysing patterns and trends in training data opens up possibilities for society (Shukla, 2023). For example, ChatGPT, a type of generative AI tool, provides multiple advantages for enterprises in different business areas (Chui, Roberts, & Yee, 2022).

GenAI technologies have had a profound impact on the education sector, revolutionising both learning and teaching activities, and functioning as valuable assistants (Chiu, 2024). These technologies are essential for students as they assist in tasks like retrieving information and answering subject-specific queries (Sarker, Eiaz-Ur-Rahman, Sakib, Terano, & Rahman, 2023). Similarly, educators can take advantage of the capabilities of generative AI to build teaching plans, generate instructional resources like scripts, slides, and quizzes, evaluate and analyse student assignments, and offer constructive comments (Fui-Hoon Nah, Zheng, Cai, Siau, & Chen, 2023). GenAI has the potential to revolutionise various aspects of healthcare, including patient engagement, clinical diagnosis support, telehealth services, health education, health advising, and health promotion (Yim, et al., 2024).

3. CONQUERING THE COMPLEX TERRAIN: TECHNOLOGICAL, ETHICAL, AND REGULATORY OBSTACLES IN THE ADOPTION OF GENAI

The integration of GenAI into higher education faces numerous complex challenges (García-Peñalvo, 2023). The integration of GenAI in academic environments poses various challenges that need to be addressed in the areas of ethics, technology, and regulation, as emphasised in recent studies (Dwivedi, Pandey, Currie, & Micu, 2024; Fui-Hoon Nah et al., 2024; Ghimire, Kim, & Acharya, 2024; Michel-Villarreal, Vilalta-Perdomo, Salinas-Navarro, Thierry-Aguilera, & Gerardou, 2023).

3.1 Ethical Difficulties

In the realm of education, the use of GenAI tools raises serious ethical questions (Radwan, & Mcginty, 2024). Anxieties over AI bias, student data privacy, and AI-generated content veracity dominate ethical discussions (Cheng, Varshney, & Liu, 2021). Perera and Lankathilake (2023) emphasize the importance of transparency regarding the training of GenAI models, the use of data, and the decision-making process. Alier, García-Peñalvo, and Camba (2024) argue that GenAI's ability to generate content that is either misleading or factually incorrect poses serious risks to students' academic credibility and the quality of their training.

In the context of artificial intelligence, "ethical concerns" refers to the moral duties and obligations that come with both the system and the people who built it (Wang, Li, Ding, & Yu, 2022). For example, the incorporation of Gen AI raises ethical questions about bias. When it comes to artificial intelligence, bias occurs when the system's suggestions or replies have a propensity to favour or discriminate against certain people or groups (Patel, & Zhang, 2020). These biases can take many forms, and they frequently originate in the training data itself (Srinivasan & Uchino, 2021). Placing too much trust in the answers given by generative AI could lead to harmful or inappropriate content being generated (Iskender, 2023; Kou & Gui, 2023). Users may also get into the habit of blindly accepting answers without checking or analysing them, which could make them less good at reasoning and critical thinking (Kim, & Lee, 2021). Iskender (2023) argues that depending too much on generative AI technology can impede the growth of abilities like creativity, critical thinking, and problem-solving. With its capacity to open up new possibilities for customised learning and innovation, GenAI could have a revolutionary effect on higher education (Johnson, & Smith, 2023). Nevertheless, there are difficulties associated with this transformation, the most significant of which are concerns about AI systems' inclusivity and inherent bias. The fair and unbiased use of GenAI tools by diverse student populations is threatened by these challenges, which also raise ethical questions (Garcia, & Martinez, 2022).

Another concern pertains to the improper utilisation of AI. For example, the swift production of excellent responses by generative AI systems such as ChatGPT may lead to students who lack motivation disregarding the need to dedicate time and effort to finish their tasks and essays (Malinka, Peresíni, Firc, Hujnák, & Janus, 2023). The presence of bias in AI systems sometimes stems from training data that is imbalanced or not reflective of the real-world population (Mehrabi, et al., 2021). These biases can inadvertently perpetuate preconceptions or display discriminatory inclinations towards certain groups, hence affecting the results generated by AI models in a potentially inaccurate or unjust manner (Schwartz, et al, 2022). In higher education, the main goal is to create a learning environment that is inclusive and caters to the unique needs of students from different origins, cultures, and learning preferences. This issue is especially important in this setting (Thompson & Brewster, 2023).

Adopting strategies that mark GenAI technologies with inclusion and equity is crucial to effectively address these difficulties. One such strategy is to enhance the diversity of training datasets to ensure their representation of the entire world population (Wong & Chen, 2023). This includes a diverse array of languages and dialects, as well as a variety of cultural, socioeconomic, and demographic backgrounds. By incorporating a range of perspectives and personal backgrounds, GenAI models can be designed to understand and generate content that is characterised by reduced bias and more inclusivity (Liu & Wang, 2021). Furthermore, in terms of knowledge advancement, GenAI tools can pose challenges for educators in determining the authenticity of knowledge presented by students and peers. This entails distinguishing between original insights derived from critical analysis of information and reused content, which can range from simple replication to advanced rephrasing of AI-generated replies (Lim, Gunasekara, Pallant, Pallant, & Pechenkina, 2023). Furthermore, there are apprehensions regarding its utilisation by students for the purpose of academic dishonesty during examinations (Michel-Villarreal et al., 2023).

In addition, ethical concerns encompass potential breaches of data privacy and security (Chan & Hu, 2023; McDonald, Johri, Ali, & Hingle, 2024; Michel-Villarreal et al., 2023). Academic institutions should offer training and support to educators and students to properly utilise GenAI tools. This training should focus on developing digital literacy and critical thinking skills. By enabling users to evaluate the results of AI tools in a critical manner and acknowledge their constraints, this will encourage a more informed and perceptive use of technology in the field of creative education.

3.2 Technological Difficulties

In terms of technology, the ease of use and reliability of GenAI technologies pose significant challenges. Disparities in access to advanced technical tools worsen educational inequities, creating what is known as the digital divide (Lombardi, 2023). Furthermore, the incorporation of AI systems into educational practices is hindered by the complex nature of many of these systems, which are characterised by their "black box" features. This means that the internal mechanisms of these systems are opaque and challenging for users to understand (Liao, Gruen, & Miller, 2020). Lack of transparency can hinder instructors and students' confidence in and capacity to effectively utilise these technologies (Buckley, et al., 2022).

Generative AI, as a nascent technology, has the potential to exacerbate the current digital divide in society. This disparity may arise between individuals lacking access to gadgets or the Internet or residing in locations impeded by generative AI suppliers or websites, and those who do not (Bozkurt & Sharma, 2023).

Another challenge in GenAI is the tendency to produce hallucinations or fabricate information. Here, the AI produces output that deviates from the input source and may exhibit a lack of coherence or accuracy (Alkaissi & McFarlane, 2023). Erroneous information may consequently deceive pupils and educators.

3.3 Regulatory Difficulties

Regulatory hurdles make it much more difficult for universities to adopt GenAI (Liu, & Wongsosaputro, 2024). Unfortunately, governance institutions that can ensure the fair and ethical use of GenAI tools are lacking since regulatory frameworks lag behind the pace of technical innovation (Christoforaki & Beyan, 2022). Addressing copyright infringement is crucial, particularly as AI has the potential to produce content that mimics copyrighted materials. Additionally, there needs to be legislation that safeguards students' rights while promoting innovation (Helberger, & Diakopoulos, 2023).

Saaida (2023) argues that lawmakers, technologists, educators, and ethicists must work together to address these issues in the field of higher education. In order to make the most of GenAI's potential while limiting its risks, it is essential to implement regulations, technical standards, and ethical norms that address these issues (Christodorescu, et al. 2024). This group's goal in this AI age should be to create a sustainable academic community that values openness, fairness, and honesty (Gulumbe, Audu, & Hashim, 2024). Many governmental, ethical, and technological hurdles must be overcome before GenAI may be implemented in higher education (Lee, et al., 2023). If we want GenAI to be a force for good and equality in education, not a source of fighting and inequality, we must face these problems head-on (Zailer, & Barak-Medina, 2024).

Discordant legislation in various jurisdictions makes it even more difficult to effectively manage AI technologies (de Almeida, dos Santos, & Farias, 2021). In addition, we must immediately begin to prioritise the improvement of AI systems' explainability because this area is currently receiving insufficient attention (Mohseni, Zarei, & Ragan, 2021). The development and deployment of AI technologies have outpaced the establishment of regulatory frameworks necessary to address the intricate ethical and explainability issues they present, aggravating the pace of technological advancement (Zhang & Li, 2023).

4. CHARTING THE FUTURE WITH INNOVATING AND INTEGRATING GEN AI FOR ENHANCED CREATIVE EDUCATION

According to Chen and Wu (2022), the use of generative artificial intelligence (GenAI) in higher education has the potential to significantly change the ways in which academic institutions promote creativity. GenAI can not only improve its current capabilities but also explore new speculative and innovative uses in the future (Wang & Liu, 2023). The uncharted realms beckon researchers and professionals to delve into new areas, where the intersection of innovation and technology may reveal unprecedented opportunities for acquiring information and expressing oneself (Zhang & Wang, 2022).

A highly favourable prospect lies in the discovery and development of emerging GenAI applications specifically designed to improve innovation in higher education (Chen, & Liu, 2023). Explore technical innovations that enable students to engage in collaborative problem-solving by immersing them in virtual simulations of historical debates, where they can interact with virtual representations of historical personalities in real-time (Kim, So, & Park, 2022). These technologies could also create complex, practical problems that students can effectively solve, thus improving their creative problem-solving skills. The possible speculative applications of GenAI can serve as powerful catalysts for creativity, pushing the boundaries of what students may achieve and envision (Yusuf, Pervin, & Román-González, 2024). Examining these potential applications not only encourages intellectual curiosity but also sets a path for future research endeavours that aim to fully use the unique capacities of GenAI in educational settings (Chan, & Colloton, 2024).

The integration of GenAI into creative education requires the exploration of multidisciplinary approaches, as emphasised by Chiu (2024). A promising domain for fostering innovation is at the convergence of educational psychology, computer science, and pedagogy. Valuable knowledge from each field can be used to enhance the development and utilisation of GenAI technologies (Prather, et al., 2023). Educational psychologists can provide a deep understanding of the learning and creative processes of students, thereby revealing the cognitive and emotional mechanisms that form the basis of creativity (Lopata, Barr, Slayton, & Seli, 2022). The computer scientists' technological expertise is crucial in the advancement of sophisticated GenAI systems that can enable these groundbreaking techniques (Michel-Villarreal, et al., 2023). In the meantime, educators have the ability to ensure that the integration of GenAI into curriculum is in line with educational goals and enhances the entire learning experience from a pedagogical perspective (Sar, Nayir, & Bozkurt, 2024).

We should adopt multidisciplinary approaches to effectively integrate GenAI into creative education. These approaches ensure that technological breakthroughs are firmly grounded in an understanding of human learning and creativity (Holmes, & Miao, 2023). The integration of various areas of research has the capacity to produce GenAI applications that surpass technological progress, while also being pedagogically effective and psychologically aligned with students' needs (Bahroun, Anane, Ahmed, & Zacca, 2023). Adopting an integrated approach can greatly improve the educational environment by equipping students with resources that foster innovation, nurture creativity, and prepare them to tackle complex difficulties in the future (Adeoye, 2024).

As a result, there are numerous opportunities to cultivate innovation in the future of GenAI in higher education. The academic community can discover unexplored areas in creative education by using interdisciplinary methods and exploring new applications (Sultan, 2024). This progressive perspective encourages technologists, educators, and researchers to work together, think creatively, and explore new areas to ensure that the integration of GenAI into higher education continues to evolve in a way that improves and expands students' creative abilities (Kurtz et al., 2024).

5. PEDAGOGICAL INNOVATION LEVERAGING GEN AI: STRATEGIES AND IMPLICATIONS

The integration of GenAI into higher education presents a unique opportunity to radically revolutionise traditional teaching methods, particularly in fostering creativity and enhancing students' problem-solving abilities. When incorporating GenAI tools, it is crucial for institutions and instructors to have discussions and develop clear standards on effective tactics that improve the learning experience and prepare students for future problems.

5.1 Methods for GenAI Integration Into Pedagogy

a. The integration of GenAI technologies into problem-solving workshops has the objective of augmenting participants' creative critical thinking skills. Teachers can foster innovative thinking and encourage collaborative problem-solving by utilising GenAI to create ideas and present pupils with real-world situations (Dockterman, 2024).
b. Customised Learning Pathways: Utilise GenAI to generate personalised learning journeys that accommodate the unique interests, capabilities, and learning preferences of each individual learner. GenAI has the ability to suggest customised materials, projects, and assignments that are in line with each student's own educational journey. This fosters active engagement from students and stimulates the cultivation of novel and innovative concepts (De-Moreta-Llovet, & Gonzalez-Rodriguez, 2023).
c. Incorporate artificial intelligence (AI) into the development and execution of interactive simulations and role-playing scenarios, with the goal of actively involving learners in challenging and diverse situations. This experiential approach promotes creativity and facilitates profound learning by enabling students to apply their creative thinking and problem-solving abilities in meaningful situations (Salinas-Navarro, Vilalta-Perdomo, Michel-Villarreal, & Montesinos, 2024).
d. Use AI tools to evaluate student assignments and projects promptly and effectively within the context of feedback and revision cycles. Timely feedback facilitates iterative learning, helping students to improve their conceptualizations, boost their creative outputs, and cultivate resilience in the face of adversity (Maina, Riera, Schumacher, & Piguillem, 2021).
e. Efforts should be prioritised to encourage interdisciplinary collaboration that utilises the potential of GenAI to develop links between various academic disciplines. This method allows educators to cultivate a thorough comprehension of creativity and problem-solving that surpasses conventional academic limitations.

5.2. Addressing The Diverse Needs of Students Through Personalised and Adaptive Learning Paths

The exponential growth of available study materials, internet pages, and media for educational use, as well as the plethora of learning system information, can lead to mental and sensory fatigue and decision uncertainty (Raj & Renumol, 2022). Furthermore, there is a great deal of variation among learners in terms of their individual characteristics, learning styles, fundamental understanding, educational preferences, and engagement with the learning environment (Ciloglugil, & Inceoglu, 2018; Christudas, Kirubakaran, & Thangaiah, 2018, El-Sabagh, 2021). Adaptive learning is an instructional methodology that leverages technology to deliver individualised learning experiences that are customised to the specific requirements, inclinations, and advancement of each student (Gligorea et al., 2023). By utilising data-driven algorithms and artificial intelligence, this system adapts the instructional content, delivery, and pacing in real-time, considering the learners' engagement and performance (Gligorea et al., 2023). Personalised learning fosters a dynamic and interactive learning environment through the customisation of content to suit the unique interests, requirements, and proficiencies of individual learners (Ali, Eassa, & Hamed, 2019). This enables the instructor to incorporate a wider range of comprehensive, applicable, and diverse content into the educational environment (Alamri, Watson, & Watson, 2021).

Learning Management Systems (LMS) typically fail to cater to the specific needs of each learner based on their profile, necessitating a personalised and adaptative approach (Raj & Renumol, 2022). The move from Education 4.0 (this entailed a movement away from traditional, generalised teaching and learning) to Education 5.0 (which takes the integration of AI in education a step further by emphasizing adaptive learning) is enhanced by GenAI tools (Rane, Choudhary, & Rane, 2023). The utilisation of AI/ML algorithms empowers adaptive e-learning systems to furnish learners with immediate and constructive feedback, enabling learners to promptly recognise their errors, rectify them, and strengthen their comprehension, thereby promoting a more streamlined learning process (Bimba, Idris, Mahmud, & Al-Hunaiyyan, 2017; Gupta, Kulkarni, & Toksha, 2022).

A prevalent obstacle encountered in the field of education is the limited availability of superior annotated data, and this scarcity arises from the substantial expenses associated with annotation and the adverse effects it has on privacy (Li et al., 2024). Therefore, numerous previous models encounter challenges related to overfitting and inadequate generalisation (Li et al., 2024). However, the implementation of GenAI models can significantly mitigate these concerns (Brûhl, 2023).

5.3 Managerial Implications for Education of GenAI Integration

The potential ramifications of incorporating GenAI into instructional practices for the future of education are significant. Firstly, this necessitates a shift towards prioritising student-centred learning, where educators take on the role of facilitators rather than just providers of information, promoting inquiry and discovery. This transition emphasises the importance of fostering an educational environment that encourages innovation, rigorous assessment, and innovative exploration of unexplored areas.

In addition, the integration of GenAI poses a significant challenge to traditional assessment methods, leading to the development of new evaluation frameworks that encourage and recognise innovative ideas and processes. Educators must reassess assessment methodologies to align with the dynamic and interactive character of GenAI-facilitated learning.

In addition, ethical concerns related to GenAI, such as data privacy, bias, and the accuracy of AI-generated information, play a vital role in classroom discussions. Engaging students in critical discussions about these issues is essential for educators, as it promotes ethical awareness and responsibility in the use of AI technologies.

Integrating GenAI with teaching methods offers a promising technique to enhance creativity and address skills gaps in higher education. By utilising strategic approaches that leverage GenAI tools and addressing the associated educational implications, educators can effectively navigate this paradigm shift and foster a unique group of creative thinkers and problem solvers.

6. FUTURE RESEARCH DIRECTIONS IN GENAI AND CREATIVE EDUCATION

An area that requires additional research is the deeper integration of interdisciplinary approaches into the use of GenAI technologies (Wang & Wang, 2023). In what ways can knowledge and understandings derived from educational psychology, cognitive science, and other pertinent fields be more seamlessly integrated into GenAI applications to enhance the educational experience?

Societal and ethical implications: It is necessary to conduct additional research on the ethical consequences of GenAI in education, particularly concerning data privacy, bias, and the accuracy of AI-generated information. What ethical frameworks and governance models can we develop to address these issues? (Jiang & Zhou, 2024; Godhrawala & Kumar, 2024).

Technological Constraints and Progress: As GenAI continues to evolve, its capabilities and limitations will also progress accordingly. Future investigations should aim to keep pace with the rapid advancements in technology by closely examining the emerging tools and their possible use in educational settings (Kuhail, Alturki, Alramlawi, et al., 2023). The impact of GenAI on learning and creativity is significantly different across various educational environments due to contextual and cultural variability. Additional investigation is necessary to examine the cultural and environmental factors that influence the effectiveness of GenAI tools in the field of education. How do regional cultural norms and pedagogical practices affect the application and outcomes of GenAI in creative education? (Grassini, 2023).

These consist of longitudinal research and effect evaluation. In order to fully appreciate the impact of GenAI on higher education, it is crucial to perform longitudinal studies that monitor the adoption and outcomes of GenAI tools over time. These findings may provide a more thorough understanding of how GenAI affects not only students' academic performance and creative thinking but also their cognitive and emotional development (Lim, Lee, & Oh, 2023). The investigation into the merger of GenAI and creative education is still in its early stages.

Scholars and experts can enhance the current knowledge repository about GenAI's capabilities and establish principles for its ethical and effective integration into higher education by deliberating on suggested paths for future investigation. Although there may be challenges, the idea of a future where human creativity and technical progress work together to foster development and originality in academics is a valuable goal.

7. CONCLUSION

It is critical to address biases in GenAI algorithms, and an effective approach is to train AI models using diverse and inclusive data sets. By actively supporting and contributing to the development of these data sets, academic institutions and advocates can ensure that GenAI tools accurately reflect the global student population. Promoting the formation of interdisciplinary teams consisting of computer scientists, educators, and students to work together on GenAI projects can yield a wealth of insights, guaranteeing the development of user-friendly, pedagogically solid tools.

Curriculum integration of digital literacy and ethical AI use is an additional crucial component. By enlightening students and staff regarding the functionalities, constraints, and ethical implications of GenAI, users will be better equipped to engage with these technologies in a discerning manner. It is imperative that educational leaders and policymakers proactively collaborate with regulatory bodies to promote policies that safeguard the rights of students while promoting innovation. It is of the utmost importance to address the regulatory challenges that arise from the swift progressions of technology. The implementation of accessibility and inclusivity standards guarantees that GenAI tools are functional for students with diverse abilities.

It is imperative that this dedication to inclusivity permeates every aspect of GenAI applications, including user interfaces, content generation, and overall design. The inclusion of comprehensive feedback mechanisms enables educators and students to report concerns, propose enhancements, and participate in the iterative development of GenAI tools. The presence of this feedback loop is critical for the ongoing enhancement and continued applicability of GenAI in the field of education.

REFERENCES

Abbas, M., Jam, F. A., & Khan, T. I. (2024). Is it harmful or helpful? Examining the causes and consequences of generative AI usage among university students. *International Journal of Educational Technology in Higher Education*, 21(1), 10. DOI:10.1186/s41239-024-00444-7

Adeoye, M. A. (2024, January). Education in flux: nurturing minds for the future. *Proceeding of International Conference on Education, Society and Humanity, 2*(1), 73-82.

Alamri, H. A., Watson, S., & Watson, W. (2021). Learning technology models that support personalization within blended learning environments in higher education. *TechTrends*, 65(1), 62–78. DOI:10.1007/s11528-020-00530-3

Ali, N. A., Eassa, F., & Hamed, E. (2019). Personalized learning style for adaptive e-learning system. *International Journal of Advanced Trends in Computer Science and Engineering*, 8(1), 223–230.

Ali, S., Ravi, P., Williams, R., DiPaola, D., & Breazeal, C. (2024, March). Constructing dreams using generative AI. *Proceedings of the AAAI Conference on Artificial Intelligence*, 38(21), 23268–23275. DOI:10.1609/aaai.v38i21.30374

Alier, M., García-Peñalvo, F., & Camba, J. D. (2024). Generative Artificial Intelligence in Education: From Deceptive to Disruptive. *International Journal of Interactive Multimedia and Artificial Intelligence,* 8(5), 5-14.

Bahroun, Z., Anane, C., Ahmed, V., & Zacca, A. (2023). Transforming education: A comprehensive review of generative artificial intelligence in educational settings through bibliometric and content analysis. *Sustainability (Basel)*, 15(17), 12983. DOI:10.3390/su151712983

Baskara, F. R. (2023, May). The promises and pitfalls of using ChatGPT for self-determined learning in higher education: An argumentative review. In Prosiding Seminar Nasional Fakultas Tarbiyah dan Ilmu Keguruan IAIM Sinjai, 2, 95-101.

Bimba, A. T., Idris, N., Mahmud, R. B., & Al-Hunaiyyan, A. (2017). A cognitive knowledge-based framework for adaptive feedback. In Computational Intelligence in Information Systems: Proceedings of the Computational Intelligence in Information Systems Conference (CIIS 2016) (pp. 245-255). Springer International Publishing. DOI:10.1007/978-3-319-48517-1_22

Bozkurt, A. (2023). Generative artificial intelligence (AI) powered conversational educational agents: The inevitable paradigm shift. *Asian Journal of Distance Education*, 18(1), 198–204. DOI:10.5281/zenodo.7716416

Buckley, J., Adams, L., Aribilola, I., Arshad, I., Azeem, M., Bracken, L., Breheny, C., Buckley, C., Chimello, I., Fagan, A., Fitzpatrick, D. P., Garza Herrera, D., Gomes, G. D., Grassick, S., Halligan, E., Hirway, A., Hyland, T., Imtiaz, M. B., Khan, M. B., & Zhang, L. (2022). An assessment of the transparency of contemporary technology education research employing interview-based methodologies. *International Journal of Technology and Design Education*, 32(4), 1963–1982. DOI:10.1007/s10798-021-09695-1

Chan, C. K. Y., & Colloton, T. (2024). *Generative AI in Higher Education: The ChatGPT Effect*. Taylor & Francis. DOI:10.4324/9781003459026

Chan, C. K. Y., & Hu, W. (2023). Student's voices on generative AI: Perceptions, benefits, and challenges in higher education. *International Journal of Educational Technology in Higher Education*, 20(1), 43. DOI:10.1186/s41239-023-00411-8

Chen, H., & Liu, Q. (2023). Advancing Innovation in Higher Education: Nascent Applications of Generative Artificial Intelligence. *Journal of Educational Innovation and Technology*, 10(3), 150–165. DOI:10.1080/12345678.2023.9012345

Chen, L., & Wu, H. (2022). Transforming Creativity in Higher Education: The Role of Generative Artificial Intelligence. *Journal of Educational Technology and Creativity*, 9(1), 55–68. DOI:10.1080/12345678.2022.8765432

Cheng, L., Varshney, K. R., & Liu, H. (2021). Socially responsible ai algorithms: Issues, purposes, and challenges. *Journal of Artificial Intelligence Research*, 71, 1137–1181. DOI:10.1613/jair.1.12814

Chiu, T. K. (2024). Future research recommendations for transforming higher education with generative AI. *Computers and Education: Artificial Intelligence*, 6, 100197. DOI:10.1016/j.caeai.2023.100197

Christodorescu, M., Craven, R., Feizi, S., Gong, N., Hoffmann, M., Jha, S., ... Turek, M. (2024). Securing the Future of GenAI: Policy and Technology. *Cryptology ePrint Archive*.

Christoforaki, M., & Beyan, O. (2022). Applying the ethics of AI: A systematic review of tools for developing and accessing AI-based systems. *Artificial Intelligence Review*. Advance online publication. DOI:10.1007/s10462-022-10060-7

Christudas, B. C. L., Kirubakaran, E., & Thangaiah, P. R. J. (2018). An evolutionary approach for personalization of content delivery in e-learning systems based on learner behavior forcing compatibility of learning materials. *Telematics and Informatics*, 35(3), 520–533. DOI:10.1016/j.tele.2017.02.004

Chui, M., Roberts, R., & Yee, L. (2022, December 20). *Generative AI is Here: How Tools Like ChatGpt Could Change Your Business*. Quantum Black AI by McKinsey. https://www.mckinsey.com/capabilities/quantumblack/our-insights/generative-ai-is-here-how-tools-like-chatgpt-could-change-your-business#/

Ciloglugil, B., & Inceoglu, M. M. (2018). A learner ontology based on learning style models for adaptive e-learning. *Computational Science and Its Applications–ICCSA 2018: 18th International Conference, Melbourne, VIC, Australia, July 2-5, 2018Proceedings*, 18(Part II), 199–212.

Dai, Y., Liu, A., & Lim, C. P. (2023). Reconceptualizing ChatGPT and generative AI as a student-driven innovation in higher education. *Procedia CIRP*, 119, 84–90. DOI:10.1016/j.procir.2023.05.002

Day, M. J. (2023). Towards Ethical Artificial Intelligence in Universities: ChatGPT, Culture, and Mental Health Stigmas in Asian Higher Education Post COVID-19. *Journal of Technology in Counsellor Education and Supervision*, 4(1), 7. DOI:10.61888/2692-4129.1097

de Almeida, P. G. R., dos Santos, C. D., & Farias, J. S. (2021). Artificial intelligence regulation: A framework for governance. *Ethics and Information Technology*, 23(3), 505–525. DOI:10.1007/s10676-021-09593-z

De-Moreta-Llovet, J., & Gonzalez-Rodriguez, M. (2023). Empowering education with generative artificial intelligence tools: Approach with an instructional design matrix. *Sustainability (Basel)*, 15(15), 11524. DOI:10.3390/su151511524

Dockterman, D. (2024, February 7). Harnessing GenAI as a collaborative tool in educational problem-solving. *Generative AI @ Harvard*. Retrieved from https://www.harvard.edu/ai/2024/02/07/david-dockterman-harnessing-genai-as-a-collaborative-tool-in-educational-problem-solving/

Dwivedi, Y. K., Pandey, N., Currie, W., & Micu, A. (2024). Leveraging ChatGPT and other generative artificial intelligence (AI)GenAI-based applications in the hospitality and tourism industry: Practices, challenges, and research agenda. *International Journal of Contemporary Hospitality Management*, 36(1), 1–12. DOI:10.1108/IJCHM-05-2023-0686

El-Sabagh, H. A. (2021). Adaptive e-learning environment based on learning styles and its impact on development students' engagement. *International Journal of Educational Technology in Higher Education*, 18(1), 53. DOI:10.1186/s41239-021-00289-4

Farhi, F., Jeljeli, R., Aburezeq, I., Dweikat, F. F., Al-shami, S. A., & Slamene, R. (2023). Analyzing the students' views, concerns, and perceived ethics about ChatGPT usage. Computers and Education: Artificial Intelligence. https://www.researchgate.net/profile/Mohamed-Fezari-2/publication/370107237_From_GPT_to_AutoGPT_a_Brief_Attention_in_NLP_Processing_using_DL/links/643fd87a2eca706c8b6d151b/From-GPT-to-AutoGPT-a-Brief-Attention-in-NLP-Processing-using-DL.pdf

Firat, M. (2023). What ChatGPT means for universities: Perceptions of scholars and students. *Journal of Applied Learning and Teaching*, 6(1), 57–63.

Fui-Hoon Nah, F., Zheng, R., Cai, J., Siau, K., & Chen, L. (2023). Generative AI and ChatGPT: Applications, challenges, and AI-human collaboration. *Journal of Information Technology Case and Application Research*, 25(3), 277–304. DOI:10.1080/15228053.2023.2233814

Garcia, A., & Martinez, L. (2022). Overcoming Bias and Inclusiveness Concerns in Generative Artificial Intelligence Tools for Education. *Technology in Education Quarterly*, 37(4), 215–230. DOI:10.1177/1234567890123456

García-Peñalvo, F. J. (2023). Generative Artificial Intelligence. Open Challenges, Opportunities, and Risks in Higher Education. Proceedings for the 14th International Conference on e-Learning 2023, September 28-19, 2023, Belgrade, Serbia. https://ceur-ws.org/Vol-3696/article_1.pdf

Ghimire, A., Prather, J., & Edwards, J. (2024). Generative AI in Education: A Study of Educators' Awareness, Sentiments, and Influencing Factors. *arXiv preprint arXiv:2403.15586*.

Ghimire, P., Kim, K., & Acharya, M. (2024). Opportunities and Challenges of Generative AI in Construction Industry: Focusing on Adoption of Text-Based Models. *Buildings*, 14(1), 220. DOI:10.3390/buildings14010220

Godhrawala, A., & Kumar, A. (2024). How GenAI governance framework can help build trust in tomorrow's tech. *EY*. Retrieved from https://www.ey.com

Grassini, S. (2023). Shaping the future of education: Exploring the potential and consequences of AI and ChatGPT in educational settings. *Education Sciences*, 13(7), 692. DOI:10.3390/educsci13070692

Gulumbe, B. H., Audu, S. M., & Hashim, A. M. (2024). Balancing AI and academic integrity: What are the positions of academic publishers and universities? *AI & Society*, 1–10. DOI:10.1007/s00146-024-01946-8

Helberger, N., & Diakopoulos, N. (2023). ChatGPT: A case study on copyright challenges for generative artificial intelligence systems. *European Journal of Risk Regulation*. Cambridge Core. DOI:10.1017/err.2023.42

Holmes, W., & Miao, F. (2023). *Guidance for generative AI in education and research*. UNESCO Publishing.

Huallpa, J. J. (2023). Exploring the ethical considerations of using Chat GPT in university education. *Periodicals of Engineering and Natural Sciences*, 11(4), 105–115. DOI:10.21533/pen.v11i4.3770

Iskender, A. (2023). Holy or unholy? Interview with open AI's ChatGPT. *European Journal of Tourism Research*, 34, 1–11. DOI:10.54055/ejtr.v34i.3169

Jiang, Z., & Zhou, J. (2024). Ethical considerations and challenges of AI in higher education: Analysis from the perspective of international organizations. In Peters, M. A., & Heraud, R. (Eds.), *Encyclopedia of Educational Innovation*. Springer., DOI:10.1007/978-981-13-2262-4_293-1

Johnson, M., & Smith, T. (2023). Leveraging Generative Artificial Intelligence for Personalized Learning and Innovation in Higher Education. *Journal of Educational Technology*, 45(2), 78–92. DOI:10.1080/12345678.2023.4567890

Kim, H., So, H. J., & Park, J. Y. (2022). Examining the effect of socially engaged art education with virtual reality on creative problem solving. *Journal of Educational Technology & Society*, 25(2), 117–129.

Kim, S., & Lee, J. (2021). The Influence of Answer Acceptance on Critical Thinking in Online Learning Environments. *Journal of Educational Technology & Society*, 24(3), 112–125. DOI:10.2307/jetems.24.3.112

Kostka, I., & Toncelli, R. (2023). Exploring applications of ChatGPT to English language teaching: Opportunities, challenges, and recommendations. *TESL-EJ*, 27(3), n3. DOI:10.55593/ej.27107int

Kou, Y., & Gui, X. (2023, July). Harmful design in the metaverse and how to mitigate it: A case study of user-generated virtual worlds on roblox. In *Proceedings of the 2023 ACM Designing Interactive Systems Conference* (pp. 175-188). DOI:10.1145/3563657.3595960

Kuhail, M. A., Alturki, N., & Alramlawi, S. (2023). Generative AI in Education, Part One: The Dynamic Frontier. *TechTrends*. Retrieved from https://link.springer.com/article/10.1007/s11528-023-00735-7

Kurtz, G., Amzalag, M., Shaked, N., Zaguri, Y., Kohen-Vacs, D., Gal, E., Zailer, G., & Barak-Medina, E. (2024). Strategies for Integrating Generative AI into Higher Education: Navigating Challenges and Leveraging Opportunities. *Education Sciences*, 14(5), 503. DOI:10.3390/educsci14050503

Lee, G. G., Shi, L., Latif, E., Gao, Y., Bewersdorf, A., Nyaaba, M., . . . Zhai, X. (2023). Multimodality of ai for education: Towards artificial general intelligence. *arXiv preprint arXiv:2312.06037*.

Liao, Q. V., Gruen, D., & Miller, S. (2020, April). Questioning the AI: informing design practices for explainable AI user experiences. In *Proceedings of the 2020 CHI conference on human factors in computing systems* (pp. 1-15). DOI:10.1145/3313831.3376590

Lim, J., Lee, S., & Oh, S. (2023). Generative AI and the future of higher education: A threat to academic integrity or reformation? Evidence from multicultural perspectives. *International Journal of Educational Technology in Higher Education*, 20(1), 25. DOI:10.1186/s41239-023-00363-2 PMID:37131502

Lim, W. M., Gunasekara, A., Pallant, J. L., Pallant, J. I., & Pechenkina, E. (2023). Generative AI and the future of education: Ragnarök or reformation? A paradoxical perspective from management educators. *International Journal of Management Education*, 21(2), 100790. DOI:10.1016/j.ijme.2023.100790

Liu, I., & Wongsosaputro, M. (2024). Compliance redefined: Using GenAI to navigate a complex regulatory landscape with reduced risks and costs. *Journal of Digital Banking*, 8(4), 313–322. DOI:10.69554/LGTJ4498

Liu, Y., & Wang, Q. (2021). Enhancing Inclusivity and Addressing Originality Concerns in Generative Artificial Intelligence Models. *Journal of Computational Intelligence and Education*, 8(2), 45–60. DOI:10.1080/12345678.2021.9876543

Lombardi, M. (2023). Digital Economy and Digital Divide. In *Global Handbook of Inequality* (pp. 1–27). Springer International Publishing. DOI:10.1007/978-3-030-97417-6_48-1

Lopata, J. A., Barr, N., Slayton, M., & Seli, P. (2022). Dual modes of creative thought in the classroom: Implications of network neuroscience for creativity education. *Translational Issues in Psychological Science*, 8(1), 79–89. DOI:10.1037/tps0000317

Maina, M. F., Riera, D., Schumacher, M., & Piguillem, J. (2021). Artificial Intelligence and Learning Analytics in Educational Contexts: A Bibliometric Review. *Sustainability*, 13(4), 2541. Advance online publication. DOI:10.3390/su13042541

Malinka, K., Peresíni, M., Firc, A., Hujnák, O., & Janus, F. (2023, June). On the educational impact of chatgpt: Is artificial intelligence ready to obtain a university degree? In *Proceedings of the 2023 Conference on Innovation and Technology in Computer Science Education* (pp. 47-53). DOI:10.1145/3587102.3588827

McDonald, N., Johri, A., Ali, A., & Hingle, A. (2024). Generative artificial intelligence in higher education: Evidence from an analysis of institutional policies and guidelines. *arXiv preprint arXiv:2402.01659.*

Mehrabi, N., Morstatter, F., Saxena, N., Lerman, K., & Galstyan, A. (2021). A survey on bias and fairness in machine learning. *ACM Computing Surveys*, 54(6), 1–35. DOI:10.1145/3457607

Michel-Villarreal, R., Vilalta-Perdomo, E., Salinas-Navarro, D. E., Thierry-Aguilera, R., & Gerardou, F. S. (2023). Challenges and opportunities of generative AI for higher education as explained by ChatGPT. *Education Sciences*, 13(9), 856. DOI:10.3390/educsci13090856

Mohseni, S., Zarei, N., & Ragan, E. D. (2021). A multidisciplinary survey and framework for design and evaluation of explainable AI systems. *ACM Transactions on Interactive Intelligent Systems*, 11(3-4), 1–45. DOI:10.1145/3387166

Neumann, M., Rauschenberger, M., & Schön, E. M. (2023, May). "We Need To Talk About ChatGPT": The Future of AI and Higher Education. In 2023 IEEE/ACM 5th International Workshop on Software Engineering Education for the Next Generation (SEENG) (pp. 29-32). IEEE.

Pasquale, F. (2020). *New laws of robotics*. Harvard University Press.

Patel, R., & Zhang, L. (2020). Understanding and mitigating bias in machine learning systems. *Journal of Artificial Intelligence Research*, 68, 895–940. DOI:10.1613/jair.1.12112

Perera, P., & Lankathilake, M. (2023). Preparing to revolutionize education with the multi-model GenAI tool Google Gemini? A journey towards effective policy making. *J. Adv. Educ. Philos*, 7(8), 246–253. DOI:10.36348/jaep.2023.v07i08.001

Prather, J., Denny, P., Leinonen, J., Becker, B. A., Albluwi, I., Craig, M., & Savelka, J. (2023). The robots are here: Navigating the generative ai revolution in computing education. In *Proceedings of the 2023 Working Group Reports on Innovation and Technology in Computer Science Education* (pp. 108-159). DOI:10.1145/3623762.3633499

Radwan, A., & Mcginty, J. (2024). Toward a Conceptual Generative AI Ethical Framework in Teacher Education. *Exploring New Horizons: Generative Artificial Intelligence and Teacher Education, 88.*

Rahimzadeh, V., Kostick-Quenet, K., Blumenthal Barby, J., & McGuire, A. L. (2023). Ethics education for healthcare professionals in the era of ChatGPT and other large language models: Do we still need it? *The American Journal of Bioethics*, 23(10), 17–27. DOI:10.1080/15265161.2023.2233358 PMID:37487184

Saaida, M. B. (2023). AI-Driven transformations in higher education: Opportunities and challenges. *International Journal of Educational Research and Studies*, 5, 29–36.

Salinas-Navarro, D. E., Vilalta-Perdomo, E., Michel-Villarreal, R., & Montesinos, L. (2024). Using generative artificial intelligence tools to explain and enhance experiential learning for authentic assessment. *Education Sciences*, 14(1), 83. DOI:10.3390/educsci14010083

Sarı, T., Nayir, F., & Bozkurt, A. (2024). Reimagining education: Bridging artificial intelligence, transhumanism, and critical pedagogy. *Journal of Educational Technology and Online Learning*, 7(1), 102–115. DOI:10.31681/jetol.1308022

Sarker, D., Eiaz-Ur-Rahman, A. F. M., Sakib, A. R., Terano, H. J. R., & Rahman, M. M. (2023). ChatGPT's Applications in Higher Education: Unmasking Opportunities and Challenges. *Journal of Education. Management and Development Studies*, 3(4), 37–47.

Schwartz, R., Schwartz, R., Vassilev, A., Greene, K., Perine, L., Burt, A., & Hall, P. (2022). *Towards a standard for identifying and managing bias in artificial intelligence* (Vol. 3, p. 00). US Department of Commerce, National Institute of Standards and Technology.

Shukla, S. (2023). Creative Computing and Harnessing the Power of Generative Artificial Intelligence. *Journal of Environmental Science and Technology*, 2(1), 556–579.

Smolansky, A., Cram, A., Raduescu, C., Zeivots, S., Huber, E., & Kizilcec, R. F. (2023, July). Educator and student perspectives on the impact of generative AI on assessments in higher education. In *Proceedings of the tenth ACM conference on Learning@ Scale* (pp. 378-382). DOI:10.1145/3573051.3596191

Srinivasan, R., & Uchino, K. (2021, March). Biases in generative art: A causal look from the lens of art history. In *Proceedings of the 2021 ACM Conference on Fairness, Accountability, and Transparency* (pp. 41-51). DOI:10.1145/3442188.3445869

Sultan, F. (2024). The Future of Multidisciplinary Research: Trends and Opportunities in the 21st Century. *Kashf Journal of Multidisciplinary Research*, 1(05), 35–46.

Thompson, D., & Brewster, S. (2023). Inclusive placement learning for diverse higher education students: Anxiety, uncertainty and opportunity. *Educational Review*, 75(7), 1406–1424. DOI:10.1080/00131911.2021.2023470

Wang, M. Y., & Wang, P. (2023). Decoding business applications of generative AI: A bibliometric analysis and text mining approach. *ICEB 2023 Proceedings (Chiayi, Taiwan)*. 15. https://aisel.aisnet.org/iceb2023/15

Wang, X., & Liu, Q. (2023). Exploring Speculative and Imaginative Applications of Generative Artificial Intelligence. *Journal of Artificial Intelligence Futures*, 16(4), 210–225. DOI:10.1080/12345678.2023.9876543

Whittlestone, J., Nyrup, R., Alexandrova, A., Dihal, K., & Cave, S. (2019). *Ethical and societal implications of algorithms, data, and artificial intelligence: a roadmap for research*. Nuffield Foundation.

Wong, K., & Chen, H. (2023). Promoting Inclusivity and Equity in Generative Artificial Intelligence Tools: Diversifying Training Datasets. *Journal of Artificial Intelligence in Education*, 12(3), 150–165. DOI:10.1080/12345678.2023.9012345

Yim, D., Khuntia, J., Parameswaran, V., & Meyers, A. (2024). Preliminary Evidence of the Use of Generative AI in Health Care Clinical Services: Systematic Narrative Review. *JMIR Medical Informatics*, 12(1), e52073. DOI:10.2196/52073 PMID:38506918

York, A. (March 18, 2024). 15 Best ChatGPT Alternatives & Competitors in 2024. https://clickup.com/blog/chatgpt-alternatives/#:~:text=Jasper%20Chat,-via%20Jasper&text=Jasper%20Chat%20is%20part%20of,questions%20and%20respond%20to%20requests

Yusuf, A., Pervin, N., & Román-González, M. (2024). Generative AI and the future of higher education: A threat to academic integrity or reformation? Evidence from multicultural perspectives. *International Journal of Educational Technology in Higher Education*, 21(1), 21. DOI:10.1186/s41239-024-00453-6

Zailer, G., & Barak-Medina, E. (2024). Strategies for integrating generative AI into higher education: Navigating challenges and leveraging opportunities. *Education Sciences*, 14(5), 503. DOI:10.3390/educsci14050503

Zhang, Q., & Li, W. (2023). The Ethical Dilemma of Rapid Technological Advancement: Addressing AI Regulatory Gaps. *Ethics in Technology Quarterly*, 15(1), 30–45. DOI:10.1177/1234567890123456

Zhang, Y., & Wang, S. (2022). Unveiling Unparalleled Prospects: Exploring Unexplored Domains in Innovation and Technology Convergence. *Journal of Innovation and Technology Exploration*, 7(2), 88–102. DOI:10.1080/12345678.2022.8765432

Chapter 13
The Interplay Between Creativity, Thinking Styles, Higher Education, and Generative AI

Ziska Fields
https://orcid.org/0000-0001-5353-1807
University of Johannesburg, South Africa

ABSTRACT

The use of artificial intelligence and especially Generative AI technology is creating radical change in education. This technology can impact studentss creativity, their cognition, preferred thinking styles, and higher order thinking skills. This chapter's main objective is to explore the link betweem creativity, thinking styles and skills, higher education, and GAI. The research question was explored using literature that was screened non-systematically using Google Scholar, EBSCO, and omni-linked databases for articles published between 2019 and 2024 due to the fact that it is a rapidly emerging field of study. It was found that there is an interplay between creativity, thinking styles, education, and GAI. GAI is reshaping our understanding of education and its impact on creativity and thinking styles. It is forcing humans to reconsider and review current and traditional teaching and learning pedagogies.

INTRODUCTION AND BACKGROUND

In the 17th century, John Locke claimed that the mind is a blank state (*tabula rasa*) at birth in his 'An Essay concerning Humane Understanding in four books' (1690). As one grows up, the blank slate is 'filled up' as the result of one's experi-

DOI: 10.4018/979-8-3693-2418-9.ch013

ences of and interaction with the world (Maden, 2021). The brain lacks developed thinking preferences and acquired thinking skills at birth. One's thinking style preferences start to develop due to genetic inclination (one's DNA), social pressure, job requirements, life experiences, and education, each of which comes with benefits and consequences (Bueno, 2019).

Thinking style preferences influence human interactions daily (Baez, García,& Ibáñez, 2018; Zhaoyang, Sliwinski, Martire, & Smyth, 2019) and have an impact on virtually everything humans do, including their creativity, decision-making, and problem-solving (Lin, Duan, Wang & Duan, 2024), which are collectively referred to as higher-order thinking (HOT) skills. Each individual's approach to a specific thinking style preference will differ from another's, which can cause conflict in relationships (Lin et al, 2024). The challenge is to identify the thinking style preferences of individuals and group members to improve understanding and communication.

Education develops thinking style preferences in individuals (Lin et al., 2024) and impacts the development of creativity. The higher education institutions (HEIs) in the context of this chapter refer to universities. When students enter universities, they have established thinking style preferences based on schooling and life experiences (De Boer & Bothma, 2003, Zhang, 2004). These preferred thinking styles influence the cognitive activities of students, the ways they communicate, absorb information during the learning process, make decisions, and create new ideas (De Boer & Bothma, 2003, Shi, 2011). It is essential that educators understand this and know their own thinking style preferences as educators. Educators need to know the advantages and challenges linked to their preferred thinking styles to be able to teach students with diverse thinking style preferences. This is easier said than done because groups are mainly formed ad hoc without consideration of students' thinking style preferences, and educators are seldom conscious of their preferred thinking style unless they are made aware of it. What makes teaching challenging is that educators need to ensure that they train students to use their HOT skills and develop thinking styles to ensure that they can fit into the new world of work as graduates. Students should also be able to work with robots, machines, and artificial intelligence (AI). Therefore, students' preferred thinking styles must be identified, developed, and enhanced through education and the use of generative AI (GAI).

The use of AI, especially GAI technology, is creating radical change in education and the very understanding of its applications. GAI technology in higher education (HE) has become a contentious issue over the past few years. The issue in education is that the adoption of AI in real-world educational settings is not moving as quickly as technologies are developed and introduced (Luckin, Cukurova, Kent, & du Boulay, 2022). The rapid development of GAI caught educators and HEIs off guard due to the lack of understanding, planning, and ways to implement it in the classroom (Baidoo-Anu & Ansah, 2023). Questions continue to be raised about its impact and ethical use (Stahl & Eke (2024). What is certain is that AI will modify the cognition of present and future generations (Hughes, 2023).

According to Creely and Blannin (2023), GAI has an impact on the creative output of educators and students. This can affect their cognition, preferred thinking styles, and HOT skills. The ideal is for education to focus on preparing students to collaborate with AI to survive an interconnected and fast-changing future while developing their cognitive skills and using their preferred thinking styles. This requires evolving pedagogies and using GAI in various learning settings (Carvahlo, 2022).

Not only has GAI created a dilemma for HEIs, but it has also shaped the concept of human creativity as a cognitive skill linked to preferred thinking preferences. Creativity is seen as an inherently human capacity (Prasch, 2021); however, according to Gašević, Siemens, & Sadiq (2023), acts of creation can now be performed by GAI. Interest in artificial creativity has therefore grown due to questions being asked about the uniqueness of human creativity.

Block (2022) states that in the philosophy of technology, the role of human creativity in human-technology relations is a pressing matter. HEIs (universities) are changing rapidly due to the development of AI technology (Rodway & Schepman, 2023). The integration of GAI seems to foster a more engaging and effective learning environment that enhances creativity and learning experiences. Educators strive to cultivate an environment that encourages creative thinking and the proper use of GAI. The aim is to enable students to develop their different thinking styles to solve a variety of problems. It is unclear whether HEIs and GAI impact directly on human creativity and the development of thinking skills to enhance the creative thinking process. This chapter tries to address these uncertainties to discover if there is a link between creativity, thinking styles, HE and GAI.

The main research objective of this chapter is to explore the interplay between creativity, thinking styles, HE, and GAI. To achieve this objective, four secondary objectives have been set out. These are (1) to determine the link between creativity and GAI; (2) to explore the link between thinking styles and GAI; (3) to identify the influence between higher HE and GAI; and (4) to establish whether creativity, thinking styles, HE, and GAI can be linked. This chapter does not explore the ethical issues of GAI.

CREATIVITY

Creativity refers not to some rare gift but to a natural set of behaviors that can be taught and learned (Glăveanu & Beghetto, 2020). Everyone has the potential to create something new, different, and unexpected (Rank, as cited in De Sousa et al., 2012). Creativity inspires people to behave in creative ways, generate novel ideas, and solve problems. Naiman (2023) explains that "creativity is characterized by the ability to perceive the world in new ways, to find hidden patterns, to make connections between seemingly unrelated phenomena, and to generate solutions" (para. 1). Creative individuals can shift between abstract, analytical, and dreaming modes of thinking and make associations between unrelated elements (Fink et al., 2009, Zedelius, Protzko, Broadway & Schooler, 2020). Cropley (2016) summarized creativity as the ability to solve problems and satisfying needs. This is done by developing news and solutions with value and as being "all about the aptitudes, processes, and environmental factors that help us to generate new and useful products" (p. 63). According to Lubert (1994), creative performance relies on five aspects. These aspects are a person's intelligence, knowledge, personality attributes, thinking styles, and these are impacted by the environment. For this chapter, creativity is understood as the use and application of divergent and convergent (whole-brain) thinking to create something that is novel and original. Creativity is helpful in solving complex problems and allows people to think in different ways.

The focus on creativity in this chapter is essential and therefore different schools of thought about creativity need to be explored to understand this multifaceted phenomenon.

Models and Theories of Creativity

There are a variety of models and theories of creativity that have been developed by different schools of thought. Table 1 summarizes some useful models and theories.

Table 1. Creativity models and theories

Type	Model/theory	Description	Source(s)
Psychometric theories	Guilford's structure of intellect (SOI) model	The model proposes that creativity consists of different cognitive abilities, including divergent thinking, convergent thinking, and memory.	Baer (2016); Singh and Pathak (2019)
Cognitive theories	Wallas's four-stage model	Graham Wallas proposed a linear model of creativity consisting of four stages: preparation, incubation, illumination, and verification.	Sadler-Smith (2015); Savic (2016)
	Systems model by Csikszentmihalyi	Suggests that creativity occurs when individuals find a balance between their skills and their challenges, leading to a state of "flow."	Davis (2010); McIntyre (2008); Piccardo (2017)

continued on following page

Table 1. Continued

Type	Model/theory	Description	Source(s)
Psychodynamic theories	Freud's psychoanalytic theory	Explores the role of the unconscious mind and the influence of childhood experiences on creative expression.	Odokuma (2010); Sibi (2020)
Sociocultural theories	Vygotsky's sociocultural theory	Emphasizes the importance of cultural and social factors in shaping creativity, including the role of social interactions and language.	Hamalataha (2016); Shabani (2016)
	Five A's framework matrix	Focuses on actor, action, artifact, audience, and affordances – expanded on the 4Ps (person, process, product, and press) model of Rhodes (1961).	Glăveanu (2013)
Creative problem-solving models	Osborn–Parnes creative problem solving (CPS)	Outlines a systematic approach to generating creative ideas and solving problems.	Evans (1997); Sousa et al. (2013)
	IDEO design thinking	A human-centered problem-solving approach that promotes creativity through empathy, ideation, and prototyping.	Schwab (2019); Turnali (2015)
	Amabile's componential theory of creativity	Creativity is influenced by three components: domain-relevant skills, creativity-relevant processes, and intrinsic motivation.	Adil and Habid (2019); Amabile and Pratt (2016)
	Torrance's creativity framework	Torrance Tests of Creative Thinking focuses on assessing various aspects of creativity, such as fluency, flexibility, and originality.	Alabbasi et al. (2022); Kim (2017)
Complex systems theories	Csikszentmihalyi's systems model	Considers creativity as an emergent property of complex systems, including individuals, their social environment, and cultural context. It goes beyond individual creativity.	Davis (2010); McIntyre (2008)
Conceptual framework or set of principles	Four Cs framework	Represents key elements that are believed to contribute to a creative mindset and process – the four Cs: curiosity, connections, constraints, and courage.	Helfand et al (2017); Kaufman and Beghetto (2009)

Source: Author's compilation (2023)

These theories and models offer different perspectives on how creativity works and can be fostered. Researchers often draw on multiple theories to gain a comprehensive understanding of this complex and multifaceted phenomenon. The dawn of AI and GAI led to questions about creativity, specifically human creativity and artificial creativity. The following section explores these two types of creativity and highlights some of the research that has been conducted on creativity and AI in education.

Creativity and GAI

Human creativity is something inherently unique to humans; it is limitless (Habib et al. 2024). The rise of AI has led to questioning whether AI can increase human creativity (Habib et al., 2024), especially after it was adopted widely by creative industries, as it has proved to be a collaborative assistant for human creativity.

Habib et al. (2024) conducted research to learn about the impact of GAI on students' creative-thinking skills. The aim was to guide educators in the use of AI in the classroom and, by doing so, increasing creative output. The study highlighted the interaction between AI and students' creative-thinking processes and showed that the use of AI increased fluency. Fluency can be explained as the ability to generate a lot of ideas easily at a given time. Some students felt, however, that AI is taking over the thinking process and thereby stifles human creativity. The study suggests that AI resources should be integrated with traditional teaching methodologies. This will enhance the development of thinking skills and boost creative confidence. The danger of AI is that it has the potential the reduce the students' self-efficacy and lead to cognitive fixation. The key in human–AI collaboration is the role of the human partner, which is to provide prompts for the AI to answer. It became evident in Habib et al.'s study that classroom instruction can either support or undermine skills to solve problems and think creatively.

Marrone et al. (2022) explored how students perceive AI and creativity and the importance of developing AI and creativity in educational contexts. The study results showed that students understood the relationship between creativity and AI in technology, social, and learning factors. Students were of the opinion that AI could negatively impact their social skills because AI can weaken social intelligence, which plays a role in the development of social skills. A comment from one of the study participants was: "It is taking away from people's lives, and they are more concerned about having a digital platform to present themselves on, rather than focusing on presenting themselves in the physical world" (Marrone et al., 2022, p. 5).

An important finding was that students indicated that AI will never work in fields in which human skills are required for problem-solving. As one of the aims of creativity is to solve problems, specifically complex ones, the students felt that AI could not be useful. This made the students reluctant to adopt AI technologies in the classroom. The concept of social good was also highlighted. The students' perceptions of AI's potential for creating social good was the most powerful indicator of their willingness to learn with AI. Students who understood AI were more comfortable using AI in creative endeavors and in the classroom than those who did not. Chiu (2017) and Teao and Tan (2012), both cited in Marrone et al. (2022), explained that the confident use of AI can create a positive attitude toward technology.

In Marrone's et al. (2022) study, students were asked whether AI can match human creativity. The students strongly believed that AI cannot, although AI is technically superior to humans. One student explained that AI is made by humans, and unless humans create a robot that can be a human, human creativity cannot be matched. Some students, however, believed AI might match human creativity in the future. They also noted that AI could spark creativity rather than be creative per se, and this can support human creativity. With regard to learning factors, the students were positive about using AI to support them in gaining access to information, to provide global connections, to support their ideas, and to help in the learning process. However, they viewed their school environment as having a negative impact on their ability to exhibit creativity. This confirms the views of Sir Ken Robinson in his 2006 and 2007 TED Talks that schools can kill student creativity. Students state that they do not have enough time to be creative and that assignments are structured in such a way as to discourage creativity. Creativity can, however, be encouraged through assignments using AI that can encourage independent thinking and creative opportunities (Maronne et al., 2022). This chapter aims to elebarate on the findings of Maronne et al. (2022) to determine if a link exists between creativity, learning with GAI, and thinking styles to enhance creative outputs and to use GAI more effectively in creative pursuits.

In the next section, a link between thinking styles and skills, education, and GAI is explored.

THINKING STYLES AND SKILLS

According to Belousova and Pishchik (2015), Harrison and Bramson developed the theory of thinking styles, which states that a thinking style is a system of intellectual strategies determined by one's own individual characteristics. Belousova and Pishchik (2015) state that a thinking style is a "characteristic set of functions actualized by a person in different situations of problem-solving" (p. 1). The authors concurred with Sternberg (1990) that a thinking style refers to the way a person processes information and solves problems using mental structures. These mental structures include the right and left brain hemispheres and a person's preference to rely mostly on one hemisphere (right or left) in most situations.

Each person has preferred thinking styles to make sense of the world. Their thinking style affects their daily mental processes, how they see things and understand the world, and how they behave with others to make logical choices and to solve problems, through their own values and beliefs and cognitive processes (Baez et al., 2018, Drew, 2023; Sternberg 1994). Thinking styles are fluid and not fixed (Cilliers & Sternberg, 2001). Cognitive processes can be linked to four thinking skills: convergent thinking, divergent thinking, critical thinking, and creative thinking (Drew, 2023).

The *convergent thinking skill* is also referred to as analytical thinking. It is used to find the best answers to questions. This skill is not helpful to solving complex problems, thinking creatively or out of the box, but is best suited to relatively straightforward thought processes such as logic and memory recall (Drew, 2023). A skilled convergent thinker thinks quickly, accurately, and logically.

The *divergent thinking* skill is helpful in solving complex problems, being creative, and generating multiple solutions because it recognizes that there is not just one answer to the problem. A skilled divergent thinker can identify multiple possible solutions to a problem using their creativity (Drew, 2023).

The *critical thinking skill* uses intellectual knowledge to critique assumptions and avoid taking anything at face value. It is used in developing critical insights, deduction, induction, and abduction thinking. Deductive thinking is used to draw conclusions based on the facts. Inductive thinking draws conclusions based on a generalization. Abduction thinking (educated guess) is used to make conclusions based on the limited amount of knowledge that one has.

The *creative thinking skill* may appear to be illogical, unusual, and unconventional in generating new ideas. A creative thinker uses a new perspective and way of approaching issues (Drew, 2023).

Neethling (2005) identified four metaphorical thinking styles graphically representing the area linked to the right-brain and left-brain thinking (see Figure 1). Quadrant 1 (L1) represents a logical, quantitatively orientated, critical, objective, analytical, and fact-based thinking style. Quadrant 2 (L2) represents a planning-based orientation and encompasses thinking processes that are sequential, controlled, structured, detailed, and procedural. Quadrant 3 (R1) is associated with long-term, strategic, explorative, and conceptual thinking preferences. The R1 person is less risk-averse and likely to challenge the status quo. Quadrant 4 (R2) is associated with a strong relational focus and encompasses a preference for interpersonal cooperation and empathy (De Boer & Bothma, 2003).

Figure 1. Thinking style quadrants

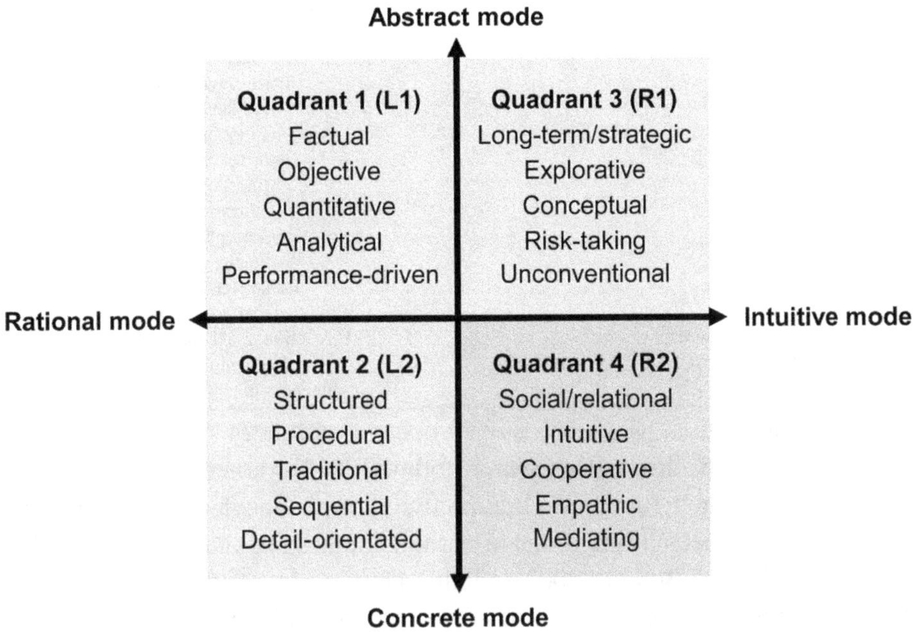

Source: Adapted from Neethling (2005)

The right and left brain hemispheres are responsible for specialized functions. The two hemispheres control different aspects of thought and action and have their own specialization and limitations. The left hemisphere is logical, analytical, rational, and verbal. The right hemisphere is intuitive, imaginative, and non-verbal (De Boer & Bothma, 2003). Table 2 contains a list of each hemisphere's areas of specialization.

Table 2. Specialized functions associated with each brain hemisphere

Left hemisphere	Right hemisphere
Speech/verbal	Spatial/musical
Logical, mathematical	Holistic
Linear, detailed	Artistic, symbolic
Sequential	Simultaneous
Controlled	Emotional
Intellectual	Intuitive, creative
Dominant	Minor (quiet)
Worldly	Spiritual
Active	Receptive
Analytic	Synthetic, gestalt
Reading, writing, naming	Facial recognition
Sequential ordering	Simultaneous comprehension
Perception of significant order	Perception of abstract patterns
Complex motor sequences	Recognition of sequences of complex figures

Source: Adapted from Trotter (1976, p. 219), as cited in De Boer and Bothma (2013)

Herrmann (1996, cited in De Boer & Bothma, 2003) warned, however, that the brain works as a whole (integrated brain activity), even though each hemisphere is different. This is especially important in learning. Lumsdaine and Lumsdaine (1995, as cited in De Boer & Bothma, 2003) identified four modes of students' learning, as shown in Figure 2. Each classroom consists of students with different thinking styles and expectations. Figure 2, therefore, also highlights the expectations of students who are dominant in the thinking styles of the respective quadrant; for example, students who have an L1 thinking style will expect precise and to-the-point information.

Figure 2. Modes of learning and students' associated expectations

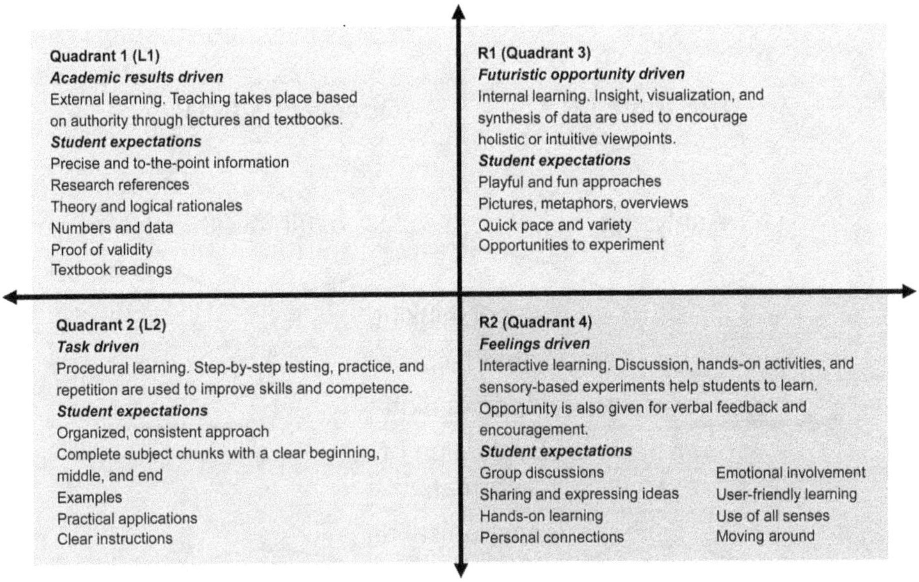

Source: Adapted from Trotter (1976, as cited in De Boer & Bothma, 2003).

These differences in thinking styles can make teaching and learning challenging to manage. If a student wants to gain new skills, developing whole-brain thinking is critical for them. The processes to achieve outcomes and gain skills are linked to quadrants in the Herrmann model and the Neethling brain instruments. Some cut across all of the quadrants, while others are specific to a particular thinking style (quadrant). The processes are displayed in Figure 3. Educators should be aware of this in their teaching and learning efforts.

Figure 3. Processes to achieve learning outcomes associated with a whole-brain approach

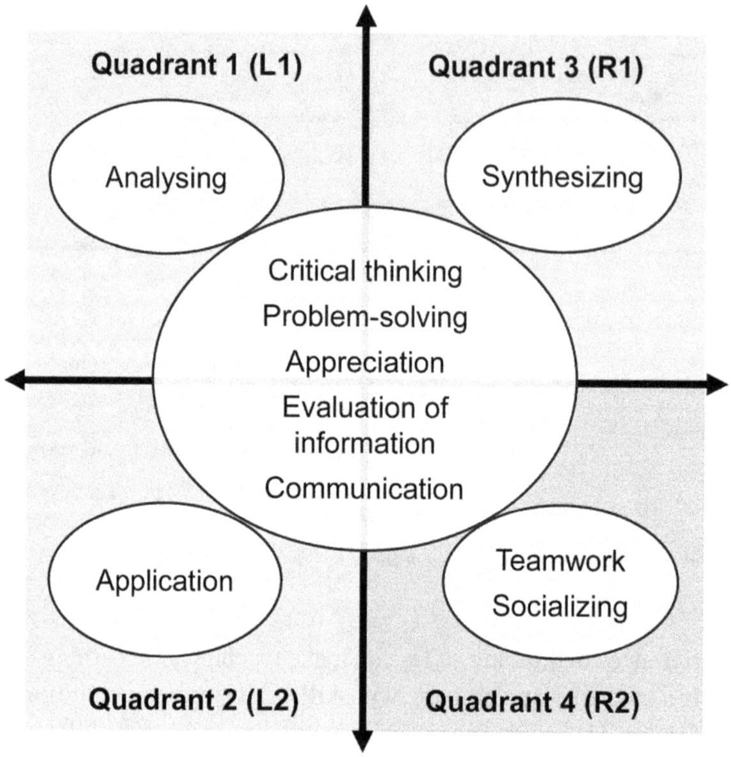

Source: Author's compilation, based on De Boer and Bothma (2003); Neethling (2005)

Various thinking styles are needed to be creative, and this requires HOT skills. HOT refers to the top levels of cognitive thinking (Staake, 2023). HOT skills are a series of essential competencies that improve learning progress and critical thinking. These competencies include analyzing and evaluating complex information, connecting facts, making connections, problem-solving, big-picture thinking, and ideating. These are skills that GAI lacks and which therefore make thinking styles in humans unique.

Carucci (2023) states that in the age of AI, critical thinking, as a HOT skill, has never been more important. It is required to enable people to use and train AI properly and to make GAI a more reliable tool. Carucci believes that people who apply their critical-thinking skills are better positioned to work with GAI to improve their own capabilities and GAI outputs, objectively evaluate the content for accuracy, and make improvements. The need for critical thinking will remain, even as AI continues to improve. The benefit of GAI is that it can adapt the instructions to accommodate each student's unique learning style, which can have an impact on the thinking skills of students (Grassini, 2023). AI tools can also provide questions and prompts based on course materials that may impact the problem-solving skills and critical-thinking abilities of students.

According to Luckin et al. (2022), metacognition is something that is not available to any AI. Meta-cognition impacts thinking styles, thinking skills, and creativity. It includes meta-intelligence (social intelligence and meta-emotion, such as the sensitive awareness of how people feel as well as others around them) and meta-contextual awareness (the ability to be self-aware).

The various models and theories that exist on thinking styles are discussed next.

Models and Theories of Thinking Styles

Various theories and models have been developed to identify and describe different thinking styles. Some examples are listed in Table 3.

Table 3. Models and theories of thinking styles

Theories and models	Description	Thinking styles focus	Sources
Myers-Briggs Type Indicator® (MBTI®)	Focus on personality and thinking styles to provide insights into cognitive preferences and how individuals process information and make decisions.	This tool classifies individuals into 16 personality types based on extraversion/introversion, sensing/intuition, thinking/feeling, and judging/perceiving.	Simkus (2024), Fetvadjiev and van de Vijver (2015)
Herrmann Brain Dominance Instrument (HBDI) and Whole Brain® Model	Helps individuals understand their dominant thinking styles and provides a framework for leveraging different modes of thinking to enhance problem-solving and creativity	Categorizes thinking styles into four quadrants, representing analytical, practical, relational, and experimental thinking preferences.	Herrmann International Asia (2024)

continued on following page

Table 3. Continued

Theories and models	Description	Thinking styles focus	Sources
Sternberg's triarchic theory of intelligence	Provides a broader and more flexible framework for understanding human intelligence. It acknowledges that intelligence goes beyond traditional measures of IQ and encompasses a range of cognitive abilities that are relevant in different life situations.	Identifies three aspects of intelligence: analytical (problem-solving), creative (novelty-seeking), and practical (adaptation to real-world situations), which can be seen as different thinking styles.	Looti (2022); Vinney (2020)
Gardner's multiple intelligences	Helps to broaden our understanding of human intelligence by recognizing and valuing diverse forms of intelligence beyond the traditional concept of IQ.	Proposes multiple intelligences, including logical–mathematical, linguistic, interpersonal, intrapersonal, spatial, musical, bodily–kinesthetic, and naturalistic intelligence, each reflecting a different thinking style.	Cherry (2023); Marenus (2024)
Kirton's adaption–innovation (KAI) theory	Helps to identify an individual's preferred approach to tackling challenges and generating new ideas.	Classifies individuals as adaptors (preferring incremental change) or innovators (seeking radical change) in their problem-solving and thinking approaches.	Mudd (1995); Stum (2009)
Cognitive styles model	Provides a framework for recognizing and leveraging individual and group cognitive preferences. It contributes to improved self-awareness, better interpersonal relationships, and enhanced problem-solving and decision-making in various personal and professional contexts.	Suggests that people have different cognitive styles, such as field dependence/independence, which relates to how individuals perceive and process information. The focus is on self-awareness, effective communication, team building, conflict resolution, learning and teaching strategies, problem solving and decision making, organizational development, and cross-cultural understanding.	Miller et al. (2012)
Rational–experiential inventory (REI)	Measures an individual's thinking style by assessing the relative dominance of two cognitive processes: rational thinking and experiential thinking.	Identifies two thinking styles: rational thinking (analytical and logical) and experiential thinking (intuitive and creative).	Phillips (2020); Shirzadifard et al. (2018)

continued on following page

Table 3. Continued

Theories and models	Description	Thinking styles focus	Sources
Neethling Brain Instruments - NBI™ Thinking Preference Assessments	Measures an individual's thinking preferences based on the concept that people have different ways of thinking and problem-solving. These instruments are neuroscience-based.	Categorizes thinking styles into four quadrants: Analytical thinking (A Quadrant, associated with logical, linear, and structured thinking), practical thinking (B Quadrant, characterized by realistic and pragmatic thinking), relational thinking (C Quadrant, emphasizing interpersonal and emotional intelligence) and experimental thinking (D Quadrant, associated with creative and holistic thinking).	Coetzee (2023); Raath (2023)
FourSight	Helps individuals understand their natural strengths in the creative process and provide strategies for enhancing each stage.	Identifies an individual's preferred thinking style across four stages of the creative problem-solving process: clarifying, ideating, developing, and implementing.	Bratsberg (2012)

Source: Author's compilation, from sources cited.

These theories and models provide frameworks for understanding how individuals approach problem-solving, decision-making, and learning, based on their thinking preferences and cognitive styles. Different contexts may require different thinking styles, and individuals often combine these styles to varying degrees based on their personality traits and experiences. But how can thinking styles and GAI be linked, if at all?

Thinking Styles and GAI

Humans' ability to analyze, evaluate, and synthesize information makes human cognition complex (Carucci, 2023). The ability of humans to think critically remains important as AI continues to develop. Even though AI is developing fast, according to Carucci (2023), it:

- does not have the ability to grasp the intricacies of human language and context;
- struggles to generate truly novel ideas to be creative and innovative;
- lacks human values and moral intuition to make ethical decisions;
- does not have emotional intelligence or the ability to understand human emotions and motivations; and
- lacks the adaptability and flexibility of human thinking.

Education equips people with these skills and develops thinking styles. AI, like GAI, cannot use different thinking styles to solve complex problems or analyze it because GAI generates "high-quality text, images, and other content based on the data they were trained on" (IBM, 2023). AI cannot be trained to think differently and critically. What AI can do is collect data about students and their interaction with a teaching interface. For this to be effective, students need to be able to work with AI, know how it will affect their studies, and determine whether it is trustworthy (Khosravi et al., 2022). AI can improve the efficiency of educators, as it takes over the mundane work of teaching, but it cannot replace the social role of teaching (Khosravi et al., 2022). What is important is that the use of AI in the classroom should protect students and their social wellbeing and assist educators to facilitate co-creation of knowledge and develop HOT in students and themselves (Carvalho et al., 2022). Carvalho et al. state that pedagogical practices that develop human HOT—for example creativity, critical thinking, and problem-solving—are also needed to support the understanding of, use of, and co-creation with AI tools. Co-creation is especially important in using GAI. The role of universities in developing higher-order skills such as creativity and preferred thinking styles with AI is crucial for the ever-changing environment in which we live.

A link between thinking styles and skills, education, and GAI is evident. The next section explores the link between creativity, thinking styles and skills, education, and GAI.

HIGHER EDUCATION

The Impact of GAI in the Classroom: Challenges and Benefits

GAI is changing the way that students study and how educators teach and assess in the classroom. Yet, according to UNESCO, "fewer than 10% of schools and universities have formal guidance on AI" (North, 2023, p. 4). This needs to change because GAI-based tools are increasing and are becoming more focused on the classroom than ever before. This development creates a set of challenges and benefits that need to be addressed.

Some educators are using GAI to support teaching and learning activities. One challenge is that GAI displays the dominant worldview (information from northern-hemisphere teachings), and can therefore have a negative impact on minority opinions, ideas, and educational priorities (North, 2023). Another challenge is that the outputs of GAI are not completely reliable and trustworthy, and there are copyright issues (Chiu, 2023). In addition, many HEIs do not have AI policies that deal with academic dishonesty. Another challenge is that the use of GAI by educators can become problematic if all the educators are not at the same level of professional development. This influences the educator's ability to teach using adaptive teaching strategies, analyze real-time data in the classrooms, and design learning strategies and self-regulated tasks or activities (Chiu, 2023). Winkler et al. (2023) add that GAI tools can diminish students' cognitive abilities, such as creative, critical thinking, and writing skills. Another major challenge, according to Luckin (2022), is that people who understand the educational problems that need to be solved mostly have limited understanding of AI, and people who understand, design, and build AI systems are unlikely to understand educational contexts and know what AI needs to do to help humans achieve success.

Winkler et al. (2023) identified the following benefits for education:

- GAI can improve students' ability to meet learning objectives.
- The efficiency of the educational process may be increased.
- GAI supports a student-centered approach.
- Using tools such as GAI can improve students' critical-thinking skills, self-reflection, and use of knowledge.
- GAI can help educators to design assignments and suggest experiential activities.
- GAI can save educators time in developing teaching materials.

The classroom became a place for both educators and students to be exposed to GAI. For educators, AI literacy is critical to curriculum leadership, facilitation skills, interdisciplinary teaching, and assessment approaches. For students, AI literacy is key to evaluating the information provided by GAI in a critical manner. They need to be able to use digital, media, and information literacies together when using GAI (Chiu, 2023) and be able to make immediate judgment on the information generated by GAI. There are areas that should be focused on when dealing with AI from an educator and student perspective. Educators and students should have basic AI technical knowledge, and understand AI applications and the impact that these have on humans and society.

GAI and Its Influence on Cognitive Skills

A human-centered approach should be the main priority in education, according to UNESCO (North, 2023). Future educators should teach students critical-reasoning and thinking skills at a foundational level. Student cognitive skills and emotional intelligence should be nurtured through education. This is what makes us human and what will distinguish us from AI technologies such as GAI.

North (2023), based on UNESCO's view, speculates that the development of intellectual skills might be compromised because students might become too dependent on GAI to help them with assignments and research. The danger exists that GAI can negatively affect the development of students' cognitive abilities. It can also make low-achieving or low self-esteem students struggling with GAI feel embarrassed.

In contrast, however, Chiu (2023) notes that GAI could have a positive influence on students in that it may "allow students to learn faster and in different ways" (p. 2) and enable them to judge whether a GAI output is trustworthy and suitable for the task it is used for. AI-enabled feedback learning systems can improve problem-solving skills and creativity (Mokmin, 2020, as cited in Chiu, 2023).

Role of HE in Developing Creativity, Thinking Styles, and HOT Skills

According to the Organisation for Economic Co-operation and Development (OECD), technology will transform nearly a third of the world's jobs—over a billion people's careers—in the short span of only a decade (Towers, 2023). Some jobs today will no longer exist in the future.

Employers, especially in today's constantly changing environment, expect graduates to have HOT skills. They will need to be resilient and use their HOT skills to collaborate, innovate, and adapt more quickly than ever to a constantly changing environment (Elfond, 2020). A degree is currently not an indicator of these skills, which is the reason Chamorro-Premuzic and Frankiewicz (2019), in their article "Does higher education still prepare people for jobs?", state that the link between the education level and the job performance of individuals remains weak. A candidate with higher intelligence scores and the ability to think and learn constantly is usually preferred over a person with a degree.

There is a growing awareness that the traditional education system does not serve all students and that a new way of teaching and learning must be developed and used globally (Cilliers & Sternberg, 2001, Lubin, 2024). An overhaul of the education system is essential to enable students to reach their full potential, be employable, and be resilient in ever-changing circumstances. Students should therefore be lifelong learners and be able to use AI technologies such as GAI. However, change is easier said than done. To change an education system requires much discussion, planning, and effort before and during its implementation.

One of the persisting challenges in the education system is the fact that educators and students have different thinking styles, which can cause some students to be left behind. Educators need to be aware of their own thinking styles and those of the students and understand how they impact teaching and learning activities (Betoret, 2007; Lin et al., 2024; Staake, 2023). Common thinking styles are analytical, creative, practical, reflective, global, systems, and collaborative thinking. These thinking styles are not mutually exclusive, and individuals may exhibit a blend of these characteristics. Understanding students' thinking styles can help educators to tailor instructional strategies, provide diverse learning opportunities, and foster an inclusive learning environment that caters to different thinking preferences. Academic grades, it seems, are more of an indicator of simply how much graduates studied, rather than their actual ability to learn, reason, and think logically (Chamorro-Premuzic & Frankiewicz, 2019). It is for this reason that developing HOT skills is so crucial at HE levels. HOT refers to skills beyond memorizing information, referring to critical and analytical skills. It is thought that HOT skills more challenging to teach and learn than lower-order skills. However, this is essential at an HE level. Teaching and learning activities that are developed to enhance critical, analytical, and creative thinking can increase collaboration, understanding, communication, and innovation in the classroom and beyond.

Teaching and learning activities at HE level can use various instruments to identify preferred thinking styles in students with the view to enhance these skills. This is important because a graduate with these skills will be able to better understand people and how they think, and be able to tap into the collective intelligence in a team. It will also have profound implications for personal effectiveness. Several tools can be used to help determine the preferred thinking styles and HOT skills of students and graduates to enhance their creativity. This chapter identified several of these tools, for example Table 3. It is important to note that these tools can provide insights into thinking styles and skills to enhance creativity. Nevertheless, they should be used with other assessment forms and qualitative observations to comprehensively understand each student's unique cognitive preferences and creative potential.

According to the World Economic Forum (WEF), by 2025, graduates will need skills in the areas of problem-solving, self-management, working with people, and technology use and development. These require creativity and HOT skills (Whiting, 2020). Of the Top 10 skills identified as necessary for the workplace of 2025 and beyond, six are linked to preferred thinking styles, thinking skills, and creativity, namely:

- analytical thinking and innovation (innovation cannot happen without creativity);
- active learning and learning strategies (creativity can play a role in learning and as quickly as demanded in the workplace);
- complex problem-solving (creativity plays a role in the ideation of ideas to solve the problems);

- critical thinking and analysis (to evaluate creative ideas and select the best ideas that can lead to innovation);
- creativity, originality, and initiative (seeing things differently and understanding the links between things that are generally not seen); and
- reasoning, problem-solving, and ideation (which have already been indicated as necessary in the top five skills).

It is important that the abovementioned skills are specifically developed in HE to ensure that graduates are exposed to different thinking styles. Graduates can then use and identify these styles when working in teams and developing themselves. Applying their HOT skills will prepare graduates for an ever-changing business environment (Jackson et al., 2022). Critical-thinking skills learned in the classroom help graduates to think deeply and critically about workplace issues and their roles and help to build corporate cultures (Murawski, 2014).

The question is whether AI, especially GAI, can develop HOT skills and various thinking styles in students. The challenge for GAI is that different disciplines require different thinking skills and thinking styles. Moreover, the intersections between students and AI require greater collaboration and coordination (Gašević et al., 2023).

Variations in Thinking Styles in Education

Thinking styles vary based on various factors. Some key variations are discussed in the sections that follow.

Academic Discipline

According to Stokel-Walker (2023, cited in Farrelly & Baker, 2023), disciplinary knowledge is under attack due to the development of GAI in education. The issue is that students are mostly developed to use a certain thinking style, depending on their discipline. For example:

- **Science, technology, engineering, and mathematics (STEM) versus the humanities:** Students in STEM fields often employ analytical and logical thinking styles, focusing on problem-solving and quantitative analysis. In contrast, humanities students may lean more toward critical thinking, creativity, and qualitative analysis (Borg Preca et al. 2023)
- **Business and social sciences:** In research, business students may adopt a practical and results-oriented thinking style, emphasizing decision-making and resource allocation. Social science students often exhibit critical think-

ing, empathy and enjoy exploring complex societal issues (Sellars et al., 2018).

- **Fine arts and creative disciplines:** Students in fine arts and creative disciplines may have a highly creative thinking style, emphasizing imagination, intuition, and innovation (Kasirer & Shnitzer-Meirovich, 2021; Samaniego et al., 2024).

However, in order to meet the challenges of an ever more rapidly changing world, it is no longer sufficient for students to train only one dominant thinking style. Students should be developed in multidisciplinary and interdisciplinary thinking. A multidisciplinary thinking style develops when two or more disciplines collaborate for a specific purpose.

Teaching and Learning

Hughes (2023) is of the opinion that "human pedagogies are being replaced by artificial tutors and automated feedback loops that could change the development of our neurocircuitry" (p. 3). Educators play a crucial role in shaping students' thinking styles and the development of HOT skills through their teaching methods, types of assessment, and expectations (Darling-Hammonda et al., 2019). The availability of resources, such as libraries, laboratories, and digital technologies (Haleema et al. 2022), can also impact how students develop their thinking styles and HOT skills. The types of assessment used in educational settings, such as exams, essays, or projects, can shape students' thinking styles and HOT skills as they adapt to meet evaluation criteria. Students' preferred thinking styles may align with their career aspirations. For example, those aiming for research careers may develop analytical and critical-thinking skills, while those pursuing creative fields may cultivate innovative thinking.

It is important to recognize that individuals are not limited to one thinking style but can adapt their thinking styles to different situations and contexts (Murawski, 2014; Sternberg, 1990; Zhang & Sternberg, 2010). Moreover, these factors are interconnected, and the development of thinking styles is a complex interplay of various influences throughout an individual's life. Cultural values and norms can strongly influence thinking styles (De Oliveira & Nisbett, 2017). For example, collectivist cultures may prioritize consensus and group harmony, leading to a thinking style that emphasizes cooperation and interdependence. In contrast, individualistic cultures may encourage independent and competitive thinking. The communication patterns prevalent in a culture, such as high- or low-context communication, can influence how individuals process information and convey their thoughts (Nam, 2015).

Carvalho (2022) states that pedagogical practices should emphasize human skills, which include creativity, solving complex problems, collaboration, and critical thinking, to support the abilities of students to communicate effectively with AI tools. A high-level pedagogy needs to have a humanistic approach (Qin, 2022) and create value by supporting value-based learning and discussions about the future. The aim is to ensure that educators and students focus on co-creation with AI to build knowledge and deal with potential challenges in the future (Damochowier, 2020, as cited in Carvalho, 2023).

One of the challenges with pedagogical tools is that educators need to prepare students for a future that is unknown but will do doubt feature AI and wicked problems. The term wicked problems refers to problems that are extremely difficult or near impossible to solve, and using only one way of thinking, even with multiple viewpoints, cannot yield possible solutions. One pedagogical strategy could be to build collective capabilities and empower students to co-create possibilities of the future world (Carvalho, 2022). It is important to break connections from the traditional way of thinking and create knowledge that can enhance shared imagination and learning. Futures intelligence in education is critical.

Goodyear et al. (2021) and Carvalho et al. (2022) devised the Activity-Centered Analysis and Design (ACAD) framework, designed for learning in an AI world. Three levels were identified: the macro, meso, and micro levels.

Table 4. ACAD framework

Philosophy	SET DESIGN Learning is physically situated. AI impacts the planet's ecosystem.	EPISTEMIC DESIGN Learning is epistemically situated. Value-creation framework.	SOCIAL DESIGN Learning is socially situated. Capability approach.
Macro The global Level 1 patterns	**Buildings and technology** Digital and physical infrastructure to support AI discussions and technological advances.	**Stakeholder value** Involving AI to support the development of future education focusing on policies. Value-creation cycles and indicators.	**Organizational structures** Supporting the development of principles that connect human agency, inclusion, wellbeing, and co-creation
Meso The local Level 2 patterns	**Allocation/ use of space and technology** Technology provision and access. Role of algorithms in education. Rooms to gather and discuss.	**Curriculum** Institutional rules for different future AI scenarios. Speculative and forward-thinking methodologies.	**Community** Schools, universities, community settings. Learning networks.

continued on following page

Table 4. Continued

Philosophy	**SET DESIGN** **Learning is physically situated.** **AI impacts the planet's ecosystem.**	**EPISTEMIC DESIGN** **Learning is epistemically situated.** **Value-creation framework.**	**SOCIAL DESIGN** **Learning is socially situated.** **Capability approach.**
Micro The detail Level 3 patterns	**Artifacts, tools, and resources** Technologies, sticky notes, paper, materials to facilitate design conversations.	**Selection, sequence, and pace** Use of AI future scenarios. Techniques to facilitate collaborative work.	**Roles and divisions of labor** Educators and students working together. Humans and bots.

Source: Based on Goodyear et al. (2021)

The ACAD framework can be a helpful guide to map where the multiple designable elements should be laid out at the macro, meso, and micro levels. This framework can help educators and students to stimulate and engage in co-design activities. The epistemic design may help in creating AI scenarios. This includes learning about and with AI, and considering how AI can support learning processes. The set-design approach includes humanistic characteristics to help guide the human agency and co-creation by looking at AI in relation to its impact on the broader global ecosystems. The social-design approach is a capability approach. Here, the educators and learners co-design conversations about different elements such as learning networks and the link between humans and bots.

Personality Traits

Personalities can affect thinking styles. Introverted individuals may exhibit more reflective, introspective, and solitary thinking styles, while extroverts might have more interactive and social thinking styles (Chazin, 2023). Those with high openness to experience tend to have a more exploratory, creative, and unconventional thinking style, whereas individuals with lower openness to experience may lean towards conventional thinking. Highly conscientious individuals may exhibit structured and organized thinking styles, emphasizing planning and attention to detail.

Personal habits and preferences, such as reading habits, problem-solving techniques, and time management, can shape an individual's thinking style (Lubart, 1994). It is important to note that these variations are not absolute, and individuals may exhibit a combination of thinking styles influenced by multiple factors. Additionally, individuals are able to adapt their thinking styles to different situations and contexts. Researchers in psychology, education, and cross-cultural studies often explore these variations to gain a deeper understanding of how other factors shape thinking styles and cognitive processes.

RESEARCH METHODOLOGY

This chapter aims to explore the interconnections between creativity, thinking styles, higher education, and generative AI. The methodology adopted is qualitative, focusing on a comprehensive literature review and theoretical analysis to construct a robust conceptual framework.

The literature review encompassed:

- Peer-reviewed journals, articles, and conference papers on creativity and thinking styles.
- Scholarly works on the role of higher education in fostering creativity.
- Recent publications and studies on generative AI and its implications for education and creativity.
- Books and authoritative sources in the fields of psychology, education, and artificial intelligence.

Academic databases were accessed such as Google Scholar, JSTOR, PubMed, and IEEE Xplore. Using keywords and phrases like "creativity in education," "thinking styles," "higher education," "generative AI," "AI and creativity," and "AI in education." Inclusion criteria was literature that is relevant and recent.

The Conceptual Framework was developed identifying key concepts. Creativity, examining various definitions and dimensions of creativity, including divergent thinking, innovation, and problem-solving. Thinking styles, reviewing theories on thinking styles, such as Sternberg's Thinking Styles. Higher education, exploring the role of higher education institutions in nurturing creativity and diverse thinking styles among students. GAI, analyzing the capabilities of generative AI and their applications in creative processes. A visual representation was used to illustrate the interplay between creativity, thinking styles, higher education, and GAI.

In the thematic analysis, the themes that were identified were: Creativity enhancement, how GAI can enhance creativity in higher education. Thinking styles and AI, the interaction between different thinking styles and the use of GAI in creative tasks. Educational strategies, effective educational strategies and curricula that leverage AI to foster creativity.

Data was extracted using relevant data and insights from the reviewed literature and synthesized to identify patterns, trends, and gaps in the current research.

This methodology provides a structured approach to exploring the theoretical underpinnings of the topic and aims to offer valuable insights into the synergistic relationship between these dynamic elements.

FINDINGS

The link between thinking styles and creativity among university students is a subject of interest for researchers in psychology, education, and creativity studies. Understanding how thinking styles relate to creativity can provide valuable insights into how educators and HE may foster creativity in higher education (Moss, 2021; Setiamurti & Kurnaiwati, 2024). The aim of this chapter is to do just that by explaining the link between creativity, thinking styles, higher education and GAI. Some of the findings are discussed below.

Four important thinking styles impact creativity among university students. *Divergent thinking* involves generating multiple possible solutions or ideas from a single starting point. Students who exhibit this thinking style are open-minded, curious, and willing to explore various perspectives (Cherry, 2023b). Effective problem-solving often requires creative thinking. University students who excel in problem-solving through innovative approaches and exploring unconventional solutions often have thinking styles conducive to creativity (Gardiner, 2020). The Foundation of Critical Thinking states that *critical thinking* is characterized by the ability to analyze, evaluate, and synthesize information and can enhance creativity (Paul & Elder, 2010). Students with strong critical-thinking skills are often better equipped to identify problems, challenge assumptions, and develop innovative solutions. Creative individuals display *flexible thinking styles*, which are essential for learning in technology-enhanced environments (Barak & Levenberg, 2016). This ability means they can adapt their thinking to different situations, consider alternative viewpoints, and embrace ambiguity. University students with flexible thinking styles are more likely to approach challenges with creativity and adaptability. *Interdisciplinary thinking* enhances creativity at the intersection of different disciplines and can help solve complex problems (Gardiner, 2020). Students with a thinking style that encourages interdisciplinary exploration and integrating ideas from various fields are more likely to produce creative solutions.

The relationship between thinking styles and creativity is a multifaceted and dynamic topic. Universities and educators may leverage these insights to create learning experiences that encourage and support creative thinking styles among their students. This can foster innovation and problem-solving abilities that are valuable in various academic and professional contexts.

Cultural backgrounds and societal norms can shape thinking styles and influence creativity in education (Chua, et al., 2015). Some cultures may value conformity and tradition, while others may encourage individualism and innovation. Students from culturally diverse backgrounds may bring unique perspectives that enhance creativity.

The educational environment plays a significant role in fostering or inhibiting creativity. This is especially important during puberty, during which factors such as personality development, peer pressure, and ridicule for coming up with unconventional ideas play a major part in an individual's development. University students are mostly at the end of puberty, and at this point the learning atmosphere and test culture may encourage creativity.

Students who are motivated and passionate about a subject or project are likelier to exhibit creative thinking styles. Motivation and interest can drive students to explore, experiment, collaborate, and take risks in their thinking (The Education Hub, 2020). Creative thinking often involves a willingness to take risks and explore unconventional ideas.

There is an interplay between creativity, thinking styles, education, and GAI. GAI is reshaping our understanding of education and its impact on creativity and thinking styles. It is forcing humans to reconsider and review current and traditional teaching and learning pedagogies (Bahroun et al., 2023). This review is necessary due to GAI's current and potential impact on student creativity and the development of their thinking styles. Thinking styles affect students' approach to solving problems, their thinking skills, reasoning, motivation, and critical-thinking and communication skills. GAI promotes collaboration by encouraging group activities, personalized guidance, and real-time feedback. The main issue is how creative output using GAI will be defined in HE and how students will leverage GAI in new idea generation, the creative process, and final creative output. Banks and De Graaf (2020) believe that a hybrid and collaborative relationship should be developed between GAI, HE, and creative output.

Zaglas (2019) warns that the overreliance on GAI could hamper creativity and hinder thinking style development and thinking skills specifically. Liu et al. (2023) concur, stating that it can also hinder students' opportunities to develop problem-solving skills, impede creativity and stunt long-term cognitive development. Creely and Blannin (2023) further explain that GAI should be used as a learning tool and should be used to support creativity and education, otherwise it might impact students' academic, career, and social performance negatively. GAI can also cause educators to overlook students' critical-thinking-skill development and ignore emotional communication.

From a positive perspective, Liu et al. (2023) suggest that GAI can encourage students to question and apply knowledge generation and this will positively impact their reasoning skills. For educators, GAI can propose suggestions to help them to come up with new ideas and approaches, and to think more creatively and innovatively in their teaching approaches.

Luckin (2022) asserts that "an engaged, competent and human educator (with all their emotional and social sensing skills) who excels in his or her field is irreplaceable" (p. 3). Educators may cultivate students' emotional development, analytical thinking, independent thoughts, creativity, and innovation, as well as enable students to engage in meaningful discussions (Liu et al., 2023). Human-centered approaches and focusing on students' HOT skills remain extremely important in education, with or without the support of GAI.

This section summarized the key findings of the conceptual chapter, emphasizing the importance of the interconnections between creativity, thinking styles, higher education, and GAI.

RECOMMENDATIONS

The interplay between creativity, thinking styles, education, and GAI becomes evident in the recommendations (technological and pedagogical aspects) proposed in Table 5.

Table 5. Ideas to enhance the interplay between creativity, thinking styles, HOT skills, education, and GAI

Recommendations	Proposals for implementing recommendations
Integration into curriculum	1. Incorporate GAI tools and techniques into the curricula of various disciplines. 2. Require students to participate in interdisciplinary projects that encourage them to explore the creative potential of GAI in solving complex problems from multiple perspectives, fostering innovation, and combining their ideas. 3. Encourage students, through the development of curricula, to use GAI to enhance their HOT skills such as creativity, problem-solving, critical thinking, innovation, and communication.
Training and support	4. Train and support educators to integrate GAI technologies into their teaching practices effectively. 5. Establish communities of practice in which educators can share best practices, resources, and experiences related to the use of GAI. 6. Train educators to create an educational environment in which students will feel safe to be creative and evaluate information. 7. Foster a culture of experimentation and continuous improvement among educators. 8. Encourage students to publish their research findings on GAI and its impact on creativity, thinking styles, and education.

continued on following page

Table 5. Continued

Recommendations	Proposals for implementing recommendations
Access to tools and resources	9. Obtain institutional licenses and/or establish relationships with industry partners to enable educators and students to have access to GAI tools and resources. 10. Provide access to high-quality datasets and pre-trained models to facilitate experimentation and exploration. 11. Balance the use of GAI tools with other resources to cultivate HOT skills in higher education.
Project-based learning	12. Allow students to apply GAI techniques to real-world problems using project-based learning and case studies. 13. Encourage students to collaborate on projects that leverage GAI to create innovative solutions or artifacts.
Critical thinking and ethical considerations	14. Include discussions on the ethical use of GAI technologies in teaching content. 15. Encourage students to critically evaluate the outputs generated by GAI and the trustworthiness thereof.
Feedback	16. Provide opportunities for students to receive feedback on their use of GAI techniques and their creative outputs.
Customization and personalization	17. Allow students to customize and personalize their learning experiences with GAI technologies. 18. Provide opportunities for students to explore different GAI techniques to find those that impact their learning and thinking styles the most.
Interdisciplinary collaboration	19. Facilitate interdisciplinary collaboration between different disciplines. 20. Encourage students to work in multidisciplinary teams to tackle complex problems that require diverse perspectives and expertise. 21. Encourage students to publish their research.

Other recommendations that experts have made include the following:

- Universities should promote experiential learning, interdisciplinary collaboration, and a culture of exploration to nurture creative thinking styles among students (Ayob et al., 2011).
- Adaptive teaching strategies in blended and diverse learning environments (Bahroun et al., 2023) are important to benefit the development and use of creativity and thinking styles in educators and students.
- There should be a shift from "goal-orientated" to "meaningful learning." Adding practical and personalized courses, using a variety of learning methods and fostering diverse and HOT thinking skills can be beneficial (Zhang, 2023, as cited in Liu et al., 2023).

To enhance the interplay between creativity, thinking styles, HE, and GAI, the actions shown in Figure 5 should be taken by the educator and student, respectively.

Figure 4. Educator and student actions to enhance teaching and learning

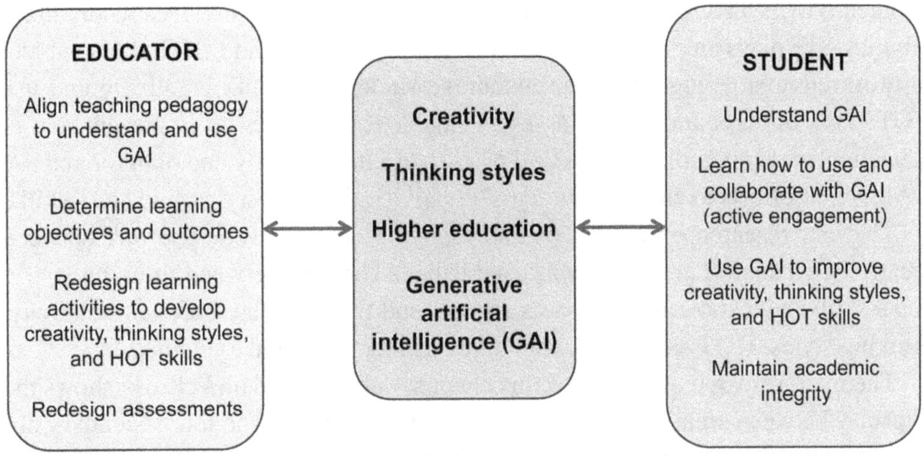

Source: Author's compilation

GAI should be used as a supportive tool in the cognitive growth and development of students' thinking processes and HOT skills. Students should develop critical thinking, ethical reasoning, and humanistic sensibilities to ensure that AI does not control or manipulate them (Carvalho et al., 2022).

CONCLUSION

The convergence of creativity, thinking styles, GAI, and HE presents a unique opportunity. The first section of the chapter focused on creativity, models, theories on creativity, and their link to GAI. It became evident in this section that graduates need to be creative. The section stressed that HE and the use of GAI to develop and enhance creativity have become important in the workplace, especially in the future.

The second section explored the various thinking preferences and identified six essential HOT skills. Four preferred thinking styles are linked to right-brain (R1 and R2) and left-brain thinking (L1 and L2). Each person uses a preferred style or styles in different situations. The aim should be to develop whole-brain thinking, by which all four styles are used effectively and interdependently in various situations. Models and theories on thinking styles and the impact of education and GAI's role on thinking style preferences were discussed.

The third section focused on education, specifically higher education and GAI. HE challenges and the impact of GAI in the classroom were discussed. GAI and its effect on cognitive skills, as well as the role of HE in developing creativity, thinking styles, and HOT skills, were examined. Finally, variations in thinking styles in education were highlighted.

Creativity is a HOT skill and requires a thinking style that involves whole-brain thinking. HE plays an essential role in developing creativity and HOT skills, which, in turn, requires pedagogies that encourage students to think creatively and use HOT skills in class and during assessments. GAI also plays an important role in education, and educators need to find ways to use it efficiently and plan for and use GAI in their efforts to enhance students' creativity, thinking styles, and HOT skills.

The four research objectives of this chapter were achieved. The link between creativity, education, and GAI was established. The link between thinking styles, HOT skills, education and GAI was shown, and the interplay between creativity, thinking styles, HOT skills, HE, and GAI was identified and explained.

The main research objective of this chapter was achieved and clearly shows the interplay between creativity, thinking styles, HE, and GAI. The four secondary objectives were also achieved. Links between creativity and GAI, and thinking styles and GAI were established. In addition, these links showed that they influenced and were influenced by HE and GAI. Therefore, creativity, thinking styles, HE, and GAI can be linked.

THE WAY FORWARD

As this is a relatively new research focus area, more research is needed in the form of longitudinal studies tracking the long-term impact of GAI on creativity and thinking styles in education. Longitudinal studies may also be used to evaluate the effectiveness of incorporating GAI into HE curricula in fostering creativity, critical thinking, and HOT skills, and its impact on preferred thinking styles. In addition, future empirical research can be based on the conceptual framework developed in this chapter. Possible methodologies for investigating the framework's practical applications can also enhance the understanding of the importance of GAI as a supportive tool in the cognitive growth and development of students' thinking processes, creativity and HOT skills.

REFERENCES

Adil, S., & Hamid, K. B. A. (2019). The relationships between leader creativity expectations, intrinsic motivation, and creative performance. *SEISENSE Journal of Management*, 2(2), 58–68. DOI:10.33215/sjom.v2i2.123

Afolabi, M. O., Dionne, S., & Lewis, H. (2009, November 18). *Are we there yet? A review of creativity methodologies* [Paper presentation]. American Society for Engineering Education St. Lawrence Section Conference, Cornell University, New York, NY, United States. Retrieved December 2, 2023, from https://www.cs.cornell.edu/Conferences/ASEE2006/ASEE%20Papers/Session%204/ASEE%20Final%20vs%203_Afolabi.pdf

Alabbasi, A. M. A., Paek, S. H., Kim, D., & Cramond, B. (2022). What do educators need to know about the Torrance Tests of Creative Thinking: A comprehensive review. *Frontiers in Psychology*, 13, 1000385. Advance online publication. DOI:10.3389/fpsyg.2022.1000385 PMID:36389550

Amabile, T., & Khaire, M. (2008). *Creativity and the role of the leader*. Harvard Business Review. Retrieved December 2, 2023, from https://hbr.org/2008/10/creativity-and-the-role-of-the-leader

Amabile, T. M., & Pratt, M. G. (2016). The dynamic componential model of creativity and innovation in organizations: Making progress, making meaning. *Research in Organizational Behavior*, 36(5), 157–183. DOI:10.1016/j.riob.2016.10.001

Anderson, L. W., & Krathwohl, D. R. (Eds.). (2001). *A taxonomy for learning, teaching, and assessing: A revision of Bloom's Taxonomy of Educational Objectives*. Longman.

Ayob, A., Hussain, A., Mustafa, M., & Shaarani, M. (2011). Nurturing Creativity and Innovative Thinking through Experiential Learning. *Procedia: Social and Behavioral Sciences*, 18, 247–254. DOI:10.1016/j.sbspro.2011.05.035

Baer, J. (2016). *Implications of domain specificity for creativity theory*. In J. Baer, Domain Specificity of Creativity (pp. 55–83). Academic Press. DOI:10.1016/B978-0-12-799962-3.00003-3

Baez, S., García, A. M., & Ibáñez, A. (2018). How does social context influence our brain and behavior? *Frontiers for Young Minds*, 6(3), 3. DOI:10.3389/frym.2018.00003

Bahroun, Z., Anane, C., Ahmed, V., & Zacca, A. (2023). Transforming education: A comprehensive review of generative artificial intelligence in educational settings through bibliometric and content analysis. *Sustainability (Basel)*, 15(17), 12983. Advance online publication. DOI:10.3390/su151712983

Baidoo-Anu, D., & Ansah, L. O. (2023). Education in the era of generative artificial intelligence (AI): Understanding the potential benefits of ChatGPT in promoting teaching and learning. *Journal of AI*, 7(1), 52–62. DOI:10.61969/jai.1337500

Barak, M., & Levenberg, A. (2016). Flexible Thinking in Learning: An Individual Differences Measure for Learning in Technology-Enhanced Environments. *Computers & Education*, 99, 39–52. DOI:10.1016/j.compedu.2016.04.003

Bawaneh, A. K. A., Zain, A. N. M., & Saleh, S. (2011). The Effect of Herrmann Whole Brain Teaching Method on Students' Understanding of Simple Electric Circuits. *European Journal of Physics Education*, 2, 1–23.

Belousova, A., & Pishchik, V. (2015). Technique of thinking evaluating. *International Journal of Cognitive Research in Science Engineering and Education*, 3(2), 1–8. DOI:10.23947/2334-8496-2015-3-2-1-8

Betoret, F. D. (2007). The Influence of Students' and Teachers' Thinking Styles on Student Course Satisfaction and on Their Learning Process. *Educational Psychology*, 27(2), 219–234. DOI:10.1080/01443410601066701

Blok, V. (2022, September). The Role of Human Creativity in Human-Technology Relations. *Philosophy & Technology*, 35(59), 1–19. DOI:10.1007/s13347-022-00559-7

Blose, A. (2023, April 12). *As ChatGPT enters the classroom, teachers weigh pros and cons*. NEA Today. Retrieved May 10, 2024, from https://www.nea.org/nea-today/all-news-articles/chatgpt-enters-classroom-teachers-weigh-pros-and-cons

Borg Preca, C., Baldacchino, L., Briguglio, M., & Mangion, M. (2023). Are STEM students creative thinkers? *Journal of Intelligence*, 11(6), 106. Advance online publication. DOI:10.3390/jintelligence11060106 PMID:37367508

Bratsberg, H. M. (2012). *Empathy maps of the FourSight Preferences* [Master's research project]. Creativity and Change Leadership Graduate Student Master's Projects. https://digitalcommons.buffalostate.edu/creativeprojects/176/

Bueno, D. (2019). Genetics and Learning: How the Genes Influence Educational Attainment. *Frontiers in Psychology*, 10, 1622. DOI:10.3389/fpsyg.2019.01622 PMID:31354597

Carucci, R. (2023, May 21). *How to harmonize human creativity with machine learning*. Forbes. Retrieved May 10, 2024, from https://www.forbes.com/sites/roncarucci/2023/05/21/how-to-harmonize-human-creativity-with-machine-learning/?sh=50f2424e2687

Carvalho, L., Martinez-Maldonado, R., Tsai, Y.-S., Markauskaite, I., & De Laat, M. (2022). How can we design for learning in an AI world? Computers and Education. *Artificial Intelligence*, 3, 100053. Advance online publication. DOI:10.1016/j.caeai.2022.100053

Chamorro-Premuzic, T., & Frankiewicz, B. (2019, January 14). *Does higher education still prepare people for jobs*? Harvard Business Review. Retrieved December 2, 2023, from https://hbr.org/2019/01/does-higher-education-still-prepare-people-for-jobs

Chazin, S. (2023, August 24). *Introverted vs. extroverted leadership styles: Finding your authentic approach*. Medium. Retrieved May 2, 2024, from https://medium.com/@stacey_76464/introverted-vs-extroverted-leadership-styles-finding-your-authentic-approach-9bb78aaa6a27

Cherry, K. (2023a, March 11). *Gardner's theory of multiple intelligences*. Verywell Mind. Retrieved May 2, 2024, from https://www.verywellmind.com/gardners-theory-of-multiple-intelligences-2795161

Cherry, K. (2023b, March 22). *How to be open-minded and why it matters*. Verywell Mind. Retrieved May 2, 2024, from https://www.verywellmind.com/be-more-open-minded-4690673

Chiu, T. K. F. (2023). The impact of Generative AI (GenAI) on practices, policies and research direction in education: A case of ChatGPT and Midjourney. *Interactive Learning Environments*, •••, 1–17. DOI:10.1080/10494820.2023.2253861

Chua, R. Y. J., Toth, Y., & Lemoine, J. (2015). The impact of culture on creativity: How cultural tightness and cultural distance affect global innovation crowdsourcing work. *Administrative Science Quarterly*, 60(2), 189–227. DOI:10.1177/0001839214563595

Cilliers, C. D., & Sternberg, R. J. (2001). Thinking styles: Implications for optimising learning and teaching in university education. *South African Journal of Higher Education*, 15(1), 13–24. DOI:10.4314/sajhe.v15i1.25375

Coetzee, F. (2023, December 4). *Unlocking the creative mind: Insights from Kobus Neethling and the Neethling Brain Instruments*. Medium. Retrieved May 2, 2024, from https://nlpwithpurpose.medium.com/unlocking-the-creative-mind-insights-from-kobus-neethling-and-the-neethling-brain-instruments-418706cc42b7

Creely, E., & Blannin, J. (2023). The implications of generative AI for creativity composition. In Cochrane, T., Narayan, V., Brown, C., MacCallum, K., Bone, E., Deneen, C., Vanderburg, R., & Hurren, B. (Eds.), *People, Partnerships and Pedagogies:Proceedings ASCILITE 2023* (pp. 357–361). https://doi.org/DOI:10.14742/apubs.2023.618

Cropley, D. H. (2016). Creative products: Defining and measuring novel solutions. In Plucker, J. (Ed.), *Creativity and innovation: Theory, research, and practice* (pp. 61–74). Prufrock. DOI:10.4324/9781003233930

Cropley, D. H., Madeiros, K., & Demadzic, A. (2022). The Intersection of Human and Artificial Creativity, D. Henriksen. P. Mishra (Eds.), *Creative Provocations: Speculations on the Future of Creativity, Technology & Learning* (pp. 19-34). Cham, Switzerland: Springer.

Darling-Hammond, L., Flook, L., Cook-Harvey, C., Barron, B., & Osher, D. (2019). Implications for educational practice of the science of learning and development. *Applied Developmental Science, 24*(2), 97–140. https://psycnet.apa.org/doi/10.1080/10888691.2018.1537791

David Baidoo-Anu, D., & Ansah, L. O. (2023). Education in the Era of Generative Artificial Intelligence (AI): Understanding the Potential Benefits of ChatGPT in Promoting Teaching and Learning. *Journal of AI*, 7(1), 52–62. DOI:10.61969/jai.1337500

Davis, S. (2010). Creativity in drama: Explanations and explorations. *Drama Australia Journal*, 33, 31–44.

De Boer, A., & Bothma, T. J. D. (2003). *Thinking styles and their role in teaching and learning*. Retrieved December 2, 2023, from https://www.researchgate.net/publication/252400208_Thinking_styles_and_their_role_in_teaching_and_learning

De Oliveira, S., & Nisbett, R. E. (2017). Culture changes how we think about thinking: From "human inference" to "geography of thought". *Perspectives on Psychological Science*, 12(5), 782–790. DOI:10.1177/1745691617702718 PMID:28972847

De Sousa, F. C., Pellissier, R., & Monteiro, I. P. (2012). Creativity, innovation and collaborative organizations. *The International Journal of Organizational Innovation*, 5(1), 26–64.

Drew, C. (2023, September 10). *The 4 types of critical thinking skills – explained!* HelpfulProfessor.com. Retrieved May 2, 2024, from https://helpfulprofessor.com/thinking-skills/

Evans, J. R. (1997). Creativity in OR/MS: The creative problem-solving process, Part 1. *Interfaces*, 27(5), 78–83. DOI:10.1287/inte.27.5.78

Extance, A. (2023, November 15). ChatGPT has entered the classroom: How LLMs could transform education. *Nature*, 623(7987), 474–477. DOI:10.1038/d41586-023-03507-3 PMID:37968523

Farrelly, T., & Baker, N. (2023). Generative Artificial Intelligence: Implications and considerations for Higher Education Practice. *Education Sciences*, 13(11), 1109. Advance online publication. DOI:10.3390/educsci13111109

Fetvadjiev, V., & Van de Vijver, F. J. R. (2015). Measures of personality across cultures. In Boyle, G. J., Saklofske, D. H., & Matthews, G. (Eds.), *Measures of personality and social psychological constructs* (pp. 752–776). Elsevier. DOI:10.1016/B978-0-12-386915-9.00026-7

Fink, A., Grabner, R. H., Benedek, M., Reishofer, G., Hauswirth, V., Fally, M., Neuper, C., Ebner, F., & Neubauer, A. C. (2009). The creative brain: Investigation of brain activity during creative problem solving by means of EEG and fMRI. *Human Brain Mapping*, 30(3), 734–748. DOI:10.1002/hbm.20538 PMID:18266217

Gardiner, P. (2020). Learning to think together: Creativity, interdisciplinary collaboration and epistemic control. *Thinking Skills and Creativity*, 38, 100749. Advance online publication. DOI:10.1016/j.tsc.2020.100749 PMID:35996661

Gašević, D., Siemens, G., & Sadiq, S. (2023). Empowering learners for the age of artificial intelligence. Computers and Education. *Artificial Intelligence*, 4, 100130. Advance online publication. DOI:10.1016/j.caeai.2023.100130

Gazzaniga, M. S. (1998). The split brain revisited. *Scientific American*, 279(1), 35–39. DOI:10.1038/scientificamerican0798-50 PMID:9648298

Glăveanu, V., & Beghetto, R. (2020). Creative experience: A non-standard definition of creativity. *Creativity Research Journal*, 33(2), 75–80. DOI:10.1080/10400419.2020.1827606

Glăveanu, V. P. (2013). Rewriting the language of creativity: The five A's framework. *Review of General Psychology*, 17(1), 69–81. DOI:10.1037/a0029528

Goodyear, P., Carvalho, L., & Yeoman, P. (2021). Activity-Centred Analysis And Design (ACAD): Core purposes, distinctive qualities and current developments. *Educational Technology Research and Development*, 69(2), 445–464. DOI:10.1007/s11423-020-09926-7 PMID:33456288

Grassini, S. (2023). Shaping the future of education: Exploring the potential and consequences of AI and ChatGPT in educational settings. *Education Sciences*, 13(7), 692. Advance online publication. DOI:10.3390/educsci13070692

Groenewald, D. (Ed.). (2013). *Contemporary management aspects*. Juta.

Gunning, D. (2017). *Explainable artificial intelligence (XAI)* (Program update DARPA/I20). Defense Advanced Research Projects Agency (DARPA). Retrieved December 2, 2023, from https://nsarchive.gwu.edu/sites/default/files/documents/5794867/National-Security-Archive-David-Gunning-DARPA.pdf

Habib, S., Vogel, T., Anli, X., & Thorne, E. (2024). How does generative artificial intelligence impact student creativity? *Journal of Creativity*, 34(1), 100072. Advance online publication. DOI:10.1016/j.yjoc.2023.100072

Harvard Business Review – Analytic Services. (2023). *Weighing the open-source, hybrid option for adopting generative AI*. Retrieved May 2, 2024, from https://hbr.org/sponsored/2023/11/weighing-the-open-source-hybrid-option-for-adopting-generative-ai

Helfand, M., Kaufman, J. C., & Beghetto, R. A. (2017). The Four C Model of Creativity: Culture and context. In Glăveanu, V. P. (Ed.), *Palgrave handbook of creativity and culture research* (pp. 15–360). Palgrave.

Hemalataha, S. S. (2016). Vygotsky's socio cultural theory: A study. *International Journal of English, Language. Literature and Humanities*, 4(12), 391–398.

Henriksen, D., & Mishra, P. (2015). We teach who we are: Creativity in the lives and practices of accomplished teachers. *Teachers College Record*, 117(7), 1–46. DOI:10.1177/016146811511700708

Herrmann, N. (1996). *The Whole Brain business book*. McCraw-Hill.

Herrmann International Asia. (2024). *The Herrmann Brain Dominance Instrument® (HBDI®)*. Retrieved May 26, 2024, from https://herrmann.com.au/what-we-do/

Hughes, C. (2023). *Generative AI won't kill education – unless we allow it to*. World Economic Forum. Retrieved May 2, 2024, from https://www.weforum.org/agenda/2023/09/navigating-the-rise-of-generative-artificial-intelligence-and-its-implications-for-education/

IBM. (2023). *What is generative AI?* Retrieved May 2, 2024, from https://research.ibm.com/blog/what-is-generative-AI

Jackson, D., Shan, H., & Meek, S. (2022). Enhancing graduates' enterprise capabilities through work-integrated learning in co-working spaces. *Higher Education*, 84(1), 101–120. DOI:10.1007/s10734-021-00756-x PMID:34511633

Kasirer, A., & Shnitzer-Meirovich, S. (2021). The perception of creativity and creative abilities among general education and special education teachers. *Thinking Skills and Creativity*, 40(4), 100820. Advance online publication. DOI:10.1016/j.tsc.2021.100820

Kaufman, J., & Beghetto, R. (2009). Beyond big and little: The Four C model of creativity. *Review of General Psychology*, 13(1), 1–12. DOI:10.1037/a0013688

Kelly, R. (2023). *The four thinking quadrants explained, and how to communicate with them*. Herrmann. Retrieved May 2, 2024, from https://herrmann.co.nz/2023/12/the-four-thinking-quadrants-explained-and-how-to-communicate-with-them/

Khosravi, H., Shum, S. B., Chen, G., Conati, C., Tsai, Y., Kay, J., Knight, S., Martinez-Maldonado, R., Sadiq, S., & Gašević, D. (2022). Explainable artificial intelligence in education. *Computers and Education: Artificial Intelligence*, 3, 100074. Advance online publication. DOI:10.1016/j.caeai.2022.100074

Kim, K. H. (2017). The Torrance Tests of Creative Thinking - Figural or Verbal: Which one should we use? *Creativity. Theories – Research – Applications, 4*(2), 302–321. https://doi.org/DOI:10.1515/ctra-2017-0015

Lim, W. M., Gunasekara, A., Pallant, J. I., & Pechenkina, E. (2023). Generative AI and the future of education: Ragnarök or reformation? A paradoxical perspective from management educators. *International Journal of Management Education*, 21(2), 100790. Advance online publication. DOI:10.1016/j.ijme.2023.100790

Lin, S., Duan, W., Wang, Y., & Duan, H. (2024). Thinking style moderates the impact of the classroom environment on language creativity. *Journal of Intelligence*, 12(1), 5. Advance online publication. DOI:10.3390/jintelligence12010005 PMID:38248903

Liu, M., Ren, Y., Nyagoga, L. M., Stonier, F., Wu, Z., & Yu, L. (2023). Future of education in the era of generative artificial intelligence: Consensus among Chinese scholars on application of ChatGPT in schools. *Future Education Research*, 1(1), 72–101. DOI:10.1002/fer3.10

Looti, M. (2022). *Sternberg's theory of intelligence*. Psychological Scales. Retrieved December 2, 2023, from https://scales.arabpsychology.com/2022/11/19/sternbergs-theory-of-intelligence/

Lubart, T. I. (1994). Creativity. In R. J. Sternberg (Ed.), *Handbook of Perception and Cognition: Vol. 2. Thinking and Problem Solving* (2nd ed., pp. 289–332). Academic Press.

Lubin, K. (2024). Our outdated educational system is failing students. Retrieved June, 25, 2024, from https://kemlaurin.medium.com/our-outdated-educational-system-is-failing-todays-students-b062ef668257

Luckin, R., Cukurova, M., Kent, C., & du Boulay, B. (2022). Empowering educators to be AI-ready. *Computers and Education: Artificial Intelligence*, 3, 100076. Advance online publication. DOI:10.1016/j.caeai.2022.100076

Luckin, R., Holmes, W., Griffiths, M., & Forcier, L. B. (2016). *Intelligence unleashed: An argument for AI in education*. Pearson Education.

Lum, J. (2022). *How to embody creativity in leadership*. Forbes. Retrieved December 2, 2023, from https://www.forbes.com/sites/forbescoachescouncil/2022/07/14/how-to-embody-creativity-in-leadership/?sh=1f09f7d64a99

Lv, Z. (2023). Generative artificial intelligence in the metaverse era. *Cognitive Robotics*, 3, 208–217. DOI:10.1016/j.cogr.2023.06.001

Maden, J. (2021, March). *John Locke's empiricism: Why we are all tabula rasas (blank slates)*. Philosophy Break. Retrieved December 2, 2023, from https://philosophybreak.com/articles/john-lockes-empiricism-why-we-are-all-tabula-rasas-blank-slates/

Marenus, M. (2024, February 2). *Howard Gardner's theory of multiple intelligences*. Simply Psychology. Retrieved May 2, 2024, from https://www.simplypsychology.org/multiple-intelligences.html

Marrone, R., Taddeo, V., & Hill, G. (2022). Creativity and artificial intelligence—A student perspective. *Journal of Intelligence*, 10(3), 65. Advance online publication. DOI:10.3390/jintelligence10030065 PMID:36135606

McIntyre, P. (2008). The systems model of creativity: Analyzing the distribution of power in the studio. *Journal of Art and Record Production*. Retrieved December 2, 2023, from https://www.arpjournal.com/asarpwp/the-systems-model-of-creativity-analyzing-the-distribution-of-power-in-the-studio/

Miller, M. B., Donovan, C.-L., Bennett, C. M., Aminoff, E. M., & Mayer, R. E. (2012). Individual differences in cognitive style and strategy predict similarities in the patterns of brain activity between individuals. *NeuroImage*, 59(1), 83–93. DOI:10.1016/j.neuroimage.2011.05.060 PMID:21651986

Moss, P. G. (2021, August 5). *Creativity in higher education.* Learning Design by Paul G Moss. Retrieved December 2, 2023, from https://paulgmoss.com/2021/08/05/creativity-in-higher-education/

Mudd, S. (1995). Kirton adaption-innovation theory: Organizational implications. *Technovation*, 15(3), 165–175. DOI:10.1016/0166-4972(95)96617-3

Murawski, L. M. (2014). Critical thinking in the classroom…and beyond. *The Journal of Learning in Higher Education*, 10(1), 25–30. https://eric.ed.gov/?id=EJ1143316

Naiman, L. (2023). *What is creativity? And why is it crucial for success?* Retrieved May 2, 2024, from https://www.creativityatwork.com/what-is-creativity/

Nam, K. A. (2015). High-context and low-context communication. In Bennett, J. M. (Ed.), *The SAGE encyclopedia of intercultural competence* (pp. 377–381). Sage Publication, Inc.

Neethling, K. (2005). *Practitioner training manual* [Unpublished manual].

North, M. (2023). *Generative AI has disrupted education. Here's how it can be used for good – UNESCO*. World Economic Forum. Retrieved May 2, 2023, from https://www.weforum.org/agenda/2023/09/generative-ai-education-unesco/

Odokuma, E. (2010). Explanations of Freud's psychoanalysis theories on the lives and works of some western artist: An African perspective. *African Research Review*, 4(3, 3a), 227–233. DOI:10.4314/afrrev.v4i3.60179

Paul, R., & Elder, L. (2010). *The miniature guide to critical thinking concepts and tools*. Foundation for Critical Thinking Press.

Phillips, W. J. (2020). Rational-experiential inventory. In Zeigler-Hill, V., & Shackelford, T. K. (Eds.), *Encyclopedia of personality and individual differences*. Springer., DOI:10.1007/978-3-319-24612-3_68

Piccardo, E. (2017). Plurilingualism as a catalyst for creativity in superdiverse societies: A systemic analysis. *Frontiers in Psychology*, 8, 2069. Advance online publication. DOI:10.3389/fpsyg.2017.02169 PMID:29312046

Prasch, L.K. (2021). Creativity: a human factors challenge. Retrieved June 1, 2024, from file:///C:/Users/ziskaf/Downloads/prasch_2022_creativity.pdf

Qin, H. (2022). A humanistic approach to Education 2030: Perspective and practice in China. *Beijing International Review of Education*, 4(2), 274–300. DOI:10.1163/25902539-04020006

Raath, E. (2023). *Whole brain empowerment for leaders and teams*. Highwire Leadership. Retrieved May 2, 2024, from https://www.highwireleadership.com/whole-brain-empowerment/

Robinson, K. (2007). *Do schools kill creativity*. Retrieved May 2, 2024, from https://www.youtube.com/watch?v=iG9CE55wbtY

Rodway, P., & Schepman, A. (2023). The impact of adopting AI educational technologies on projected course satisfaction in university students. *Computers and Education: Artificial Intelligence*, 5, 100150. DOI:10.1016/j.caeai.2023.100150

Sadler-Smith, E. (2015). Wallas' four-stage model of the creative process: More than meets the eye? *Creativity Research Journal*, 27(4), 342–352. DOI:10.1080/10400419.2015.1087277

Sahl, B. C., & Eke, D. (2024). The ethics of ChatGPT – Exploring the ethical issues of an emerging technology. Opinion paper. *International Journal of Information Management*, 74, 102700. DOI:10.1016/j.ijinfomgt.2023.102700

Samaniego, M., Usca, N., Salguero, J., & Quevedo, W. (2024). Creative thinking in art and design education: A systematic review. *Education Sciences*, 14(2), 192. Advance online publication. DOI:10.3390/educsci14020192

Savic, M. (2016). Mathematical problem-solving via Wallas' four stages of creativity: Implications for the undergraduate classroom. *The Montana Math Enthusiast*, 13(3), 255–278. DOI:10.54870/1551-3440.1377

Schwab, K. (2018, October 29). *IDEO breaks its silence on design thinking critics*. Fast Company. Retrieved December 2, 2023, from https://www.fastcompany.com/90257718/ideo-breaks-its-silence-on-design-thinkings-critics

Sellars, M., Fakirmohammad, R., Bui, L., Fishetti, J., Niyozov, S., Reynolds, R., Thapliyal, N., Liu-Smith, Y. L., & Ali, N. (2018). Conversations on critical thinking: Can critical thinking find its way forward as the skill set and mindset of the century? *Education Sciences*, 8(4), 205. Advance online publication. DOI:10.3390/educsci8040205

Setiamurti, A., & Kurniawati, F. (2024). Fostering Creativity in Higher Education Institution: A Systematic Review (2018–2022). *Open Education Studies*, 6(1), 20220221. Advance online publication. DOI:10.1515/edu-2022-0221

Shabani, K. (2016). Applications of Vygotsky's sociocultural approach for teachers' professional development. *Cogent Education*, 3(1), 1252177. Advance online publication. DOI:10.1080/2331186X.2016.1252177

Shi, C. (2011). A Study of the Relationship between Cognitive Styles and Learning Strategies. *Higher Education Studies*, 1(1), 20–26. DOI:10.5539/hes.v1n1p20

Shirzadifard, M., Shahghasemi, E., Hejazi, E., Naghsh, Z., & Ranjbar, G. (2018). Psychometric properties of Rational-Experiential Inventory for adolescents. *SAGE Open*, 8(1). Advance online publication. DOI:10.1177/2158244018767219

Simkus, J. (2024, January 29). *Myers-Briggs Type Indicator (MBTI): 16 personality types*. Simply Psychology. Retrieved May 20, 2024, from https://www.simplypsychology.org/the-myers-briggs-type-indicator.html

Singh, R. N., & Pathak, N. (2019). Guilford's structure of intellect (SOI) model of intelligence: A critical review. *Recent Advances in Psychology*, 6(1&2), 29–37.

Sousa, F., Monteiro, I., Walton, A., & Pissarra, J. (2013). Learning from failure: A case study on creative problem solving. *Procedia: Social and Behavioral Sciences*, 75, 570–580. DOI:10.1016/j.sbspro.2013.04.062

Staake, J. (2023, May 22). *What is higher-order thinking and how do i teach it?* We Are Teachers. Retrieved May 2, 2023, from https://www.weareteachers.com/higher-order-thinking/

Sternberg, R. J. (1990). Thinking styles: Keys to understanding student performance. *Phi Delta Kappan*, 71(5), 366–371.

Sternberg, R. J. (1994). Thinking styles: Theory and assessment at the interface between intelligence and personality. In Sternberg, R. J., & Ruzgis, P. (Eds.), *Personality and intelligence* (pp. 105–127). Cambridge University Press.

Stum, J. (2009). Kirton's adaption-innovation theory: Managing cognitive styles in times of diversity and change. *Emerging Leadership Journeys,* 2(1), 66–78. https://www.regent.edu/journal/emerging-leadership-journeys/kirton-adaption-innovation/

The Education Hub. (2020, January 20). *The role of motivation in learning*. Retrieved December 2, 2023, from https://theeducationhub.org.nz/motivation/

Towers, G. (2023). *10 essential skills for every future proof organization according to the World Economic Forum*. Lepaya. Retrieved May 2, 2024, from https://www.lepaya.com/blog/top-10-skills-of-the-future

Turnali, K. (2015, May 10). *What is design thinking?* Forbes. Retrieved December 2, 2023, from https://www.forbes.com/sites/sap/2015/05/10/what-is-design-thinking/

Vinchon, F., Lubart, T., Bartolotta, S., Gironnay, V., Botella, M., Bourgeois-Bougrine, S., Burkhardt, J., Bonnardel, N., Corazza, G. E., Glăveanu, V., Hanchett Hanson, M., Ivcevic, Z., Karwowski, M., Kaufman, J. C., Okada, T., Reiter-Palmon, R., & Gaggioli, A. (2023). Artificial intelligence & creativity: A manifesto for collaboration. *The Journal of Creative Behavior*, 57(4), 472–484. DOI:10.1002/jocb.597

Vinney, C. (2020). *Understanding the triarchic theory of intelligence*. ThoughtCo. Retrieved December 2, 2023, from https://www.thoughtco.com/triarchic-theory-of-intelligence-4172497

Vygotsky, L.S. (1967, 2004). Imagination and creativity in childhood. *Journal of Russian & East European Psychology, 42*(1), 7–97. (Original work published 1967)

Whiting, K. (2020). *These are the top 10 job skills of tomorrow – and how long it takes to learn them*. World Economic Forum. Retrieved December 2, 2023, from https://www.weforum.org/agenda/2020/10/top-10-work-skills-of-tomorrow-how-long-it-takes-to-learn-them/

Wieland, B., De Wit, J., & De Rooij, A. (2022). Electronic brainstorming with a chatbot partner: A good idea due to increased productivity and idea diversity. *Frontiers in Artificial Intelligence*, 5, 880673. Advance online publication. DOI:10.3389/frai.2022.880673 PMID:36213166

Winkler, C., Hammoda, B., Noyes, E., & Van Gelderen, M. (2023). Entrepreneurship education at the dawn of generative artificial intelligence. *Entrepreneurship Education and Pedagogy*, 6(4), 579–589. DOI:10.1177/25151274231198799

Yazdanian, R., Davis, R. L., Guo, X., Lim, F., Dillenbourg, P., & Kan, M. Y. (2022). On the radar: Predicting near-future surges in skills' hiring demand to provide early warning to educators. *Computers and Education: Artificial Intelligence*, 3, 100043. Advance online publication. DOI:10.1016/j.caeai.2021.100043

Zaglas, W. (2019, September 23). *Uni experts consider whether robots can really take over the classroom*. Campus Review. Retrieved December 2, 2023, from https://www.campusreview.com.au/2019/09/uni-experts-consider-whether-robots-can-really-take-over-in-the-classroom/

Zawacki-Richter, O., Marín, V. I., Bond, M., & Gouverneur, F. (2019). Systematic review of research on artificial intelligence applications in higher education – where are the educators? *International Journal of Educational Technology in Higher Education*, 16(1), 39. Advance online publication. DOI:10.1186/s41239-019-0171-0

Zhang, L., & Sternberg, R. J. (2010). Thinking styles and teachers' characteristics. *International Journal of Psychology*, 37(1), 3–12. DOI:10.1080/00207590143000171

Zhang, L. F. (2004). Thinking styles: University students' preferred teaching styles and their conceptions of effective teachers. *The Journal of Psychology*, 138(3), 233–252. DOI:10.3200/JRLP.138.3.233-252 PMID:15264441

Zhaoyang, R., Sliwinski, M. J., Martire, L. M., & Smyth, J. M. (2019). Social interactions and physical symptoms in daily life: Quality matters for older adults, quantity matters for younger adults. *Psychology & Health*, 34(7), 867–885. DOI:10.1080/08870446.2019.1579908 PMID:30821176

Chapter 14
Transforming Assessments With Generative AI

Aisha Ismail
https://orcid.org/0000-0003-4458-4311
Virtual University of Pakistan, Pakistan

Mariam Tanweer
https://orcid.org/0000-0003-4146-6635
University of South Australia Online, Australia

Sadia Farooq
University of the Punjab, Lahore, Pakistan

ABSTRACT

The potential of generative AI is evident in every field of life and education is also experiencing a paradigm shift. Generative AI is opening new ways of assessment and the tools that can create engaging and innovative contents. Through the promotion of adaptation and customization, generative AI is positioned to bring about a significant transformation in the educational process. This chapter sheds light on the significance of generative AI in assessment of higher education. It offers valuable insights into the possibilities for change and improvement in the field of educational evaluations, indicating its capacity to revolutionize the future of education.

DOI: 10.4018/979-8-3693-2418-9.ch014

1. INTRODUCTION

Assessment takes a critical position in a learning process, providing a signal to both the learners and teachers about the success of a learning process, therefore it should be properly integrated with pedagogy. Assessments if designed and implemented as per needs of the learners and the curriculum, result into effective outcomes in the form of creative and efficient learners. This effectiveness is highly related to the extent to which teachers analyze what the learner is going to be after taking an assessment. Figure 1 highlights the need of assessment for various stakeholders; in higher education the need of assessment is not limited to teachers and learners, but it is also equally important for other stakeholders including policy makers, administrators, and overall education system.

Figure 1. Need of Assessment

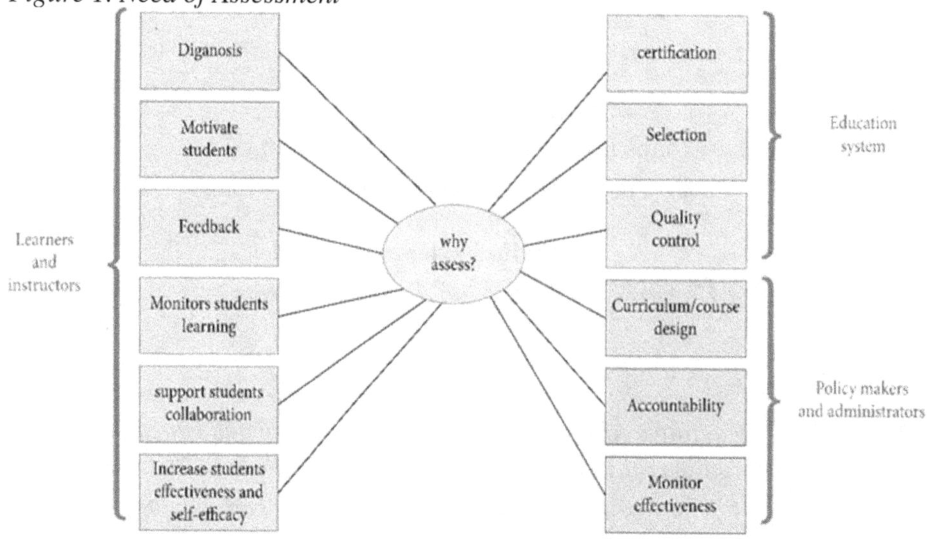

Source: (Hooda, Rana, Dahiya, Rizwan, & Hossain, 2022)

The changing dynamics of current era with the inclusion of artificial intelligence in every field of life has revolutionized the education sector and the process of learning as well. Education is experiencing a transformative change with the addition of artificial intelligence (AI) where the most significant area which offers opportunities of improvement for the educators and learners is "assessment"(Cope, Kalantzis, & Searsmith, 2021; Swiecki et al., 2022). The integration of artificial intelligence (AI), specifically Generative AI (GenAI), into assessment practices is causing a significant transformation in the field of education. As we grapple with the intricacies of the contemporary educational landscape in the 21st century, the influence of AI in re-configuring evaluations assumes a progressively noteworthy position. A paradigm shift has been observed in learning landscape, from one size fits all approach to customized, adaptive, and personalized assessments.

The learning avenues are changing enormously for both students and teachers with the availability of diverse, adaptive, and real-time learning contents. Now assessment designs are changing depending upon learner profiles which helps in identification of individual preferences. Consideration of varied nature of individual student skill level, their academic achievements, and aptitudes in development of assessments is supported by GenAI. It specifically allows educators to design and implement the right assessment tools in this paradigm which requires onerous efforts. GenAI allows teachers to develop creative assessments by offering new ideas and tools which can transform the assessment canvas. GenAI promises to address the issues of in-adaptability, uniformity, creativity, and delayed feedback attached with traditional assessments.

This introduction seeks to offer insight into the significant impact of GenAI on transforming the methods by which student learning is assessed and measured. GenAI, driven by advanced algorithms and deep learning models, exhibits the capacity to autonomously produce a wide range of intricate assessment queries and providing timely feedback. This technical innovation eradicates the limitations associated with conventional assessment approaches, granting instructors the ability to utilize a vast and ever-evolving repository of questions (Swiecki et al., 2022). When seen from the perspective of GenAI, assessments transcend their traditional role as simply evaluations and instead transform into adaptive instruments that possess the ability to cater to the individualized learning requirements of every student.

The application of GenAI in evaluations encompasses more than just the production of questions. This innovation provides access to a range of tailored exams that are specifically designed to cater to the unique learning trajectory of every student leading towards an interest driven creative learning experiences. The capacity of technology to comprehend and adjust to various learning styles and speeds guarantees that assessments serve not only as evaluation tools but also as formative instruments, offering useful insights for both educators and learners. Coping with the changing need for evaluation tools it is important to understand the two critical factors. First is the scale of using the assessment tool i.e. whether it is being used individually or collaboratively and second is whether the cognition is offloaded or extended by the assessment tool Elizabeth Koh & Shayan Doroudi (2023). This second factor is related to creativity, it is important to know how GenAI can help educators and learners in developing creative assessments by applying innovative ways. GenAI has a potential to potential to enhance creative pursuit among students by introducing new ways of assessments.

This chapter explores the complexities of utilizing GenAI for automating the process of question production, providing instructors with an extensive collection of assessment questions which are customized and personalized as per learner's needs. The chapter also highlights the role of GenAI in developing creative assessment methods for the students which can improve the critical thinking among students. Furthermore, this chapter delves into the possibilities of personalized evaluations, providing insights into the transformational influence of artificial intelligence in adapting evaluation techniques to suit the distinct capabilities and difficulties of individual learners. In the subsequent sections of this discourse, we shall explore the pragmatic implementations, advantages, and factors to be considered when integrating GenAI into the framework of educational evaluations.

2. ASSESSMENT AND GENAI: AN OVERVIEW OF CHANGING LANDSCAPE

Artificial intelligence (AI) has revolutionized the education journey with the involvement of advanced learning systems which has made learning more engaging, customized, creative, and adaptive. The integration of technology in education process demands a pedagogic shift, learning content, assessments, and evaluation system. Therefore, a complete revamping of learning system is inevitable. AI in education is useful at different levels, educator-facing AIED (AI in education for teachers), learner-facing AIED (AI in education for learners), Institutions-facing AIED (AI for institutional and infrastructural support). Key areas for academic support by AIED include profiling and prediction, curriculum design, assessment and evaluation, adaptive and personalized learning pathways, intelligent tutoring system, and collaborating learning (Luckin, Cukurova, Kent, du Boulay, & Intelligence, 2022). The traction of new learning systems lies in its ability to provide high quality learning material, engaging content, adaptive assessment, quick and constructive feedback and a continuous monitoring of learner's need to update the learning material (Cope et al., 2021). Owing to the central place in a learning system, assessment design, tools and methods are critical in determining the success of a learning system.

Traditionally, teachers used one-to-many teaching approach for students which ignores specific needs of each student (Naseer et al., 2024). The limited assessment tools, availability of resources, and delayed feedback are few issues attached with traditional assessment.

Figure 2. Traditional Assessment

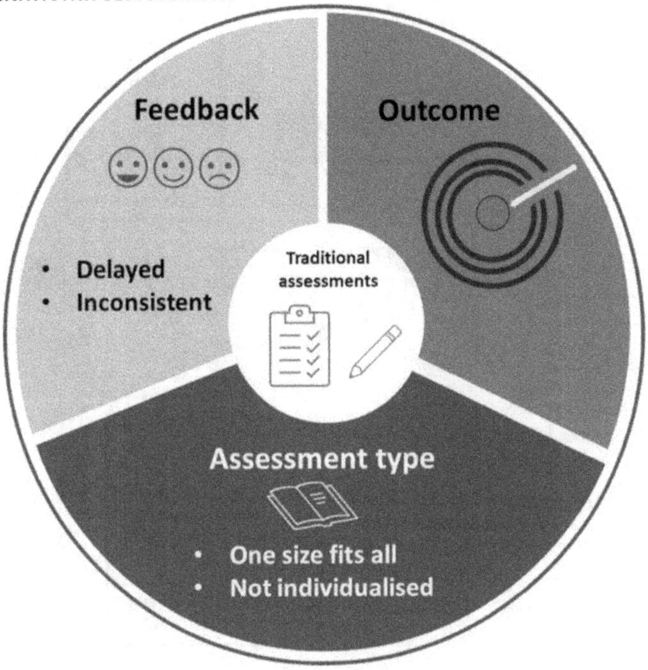

(Source: Author)

Figure 2 depicts how assessment is carried out in a traditional learning system. The role of assessment in a learning system is not restricted to assess the learners' ability to understand a concept, it is now becoming an effective tool to gauge the individual needs of learners, restructure the assessment methods and determine learner's capability. The integration GenAI in assessment has opened new opportunities for both the students and teachers. Figure 3 highlights the role of GenAI in assessment in this era of AI.

Figure 3. GenAI based Assessment

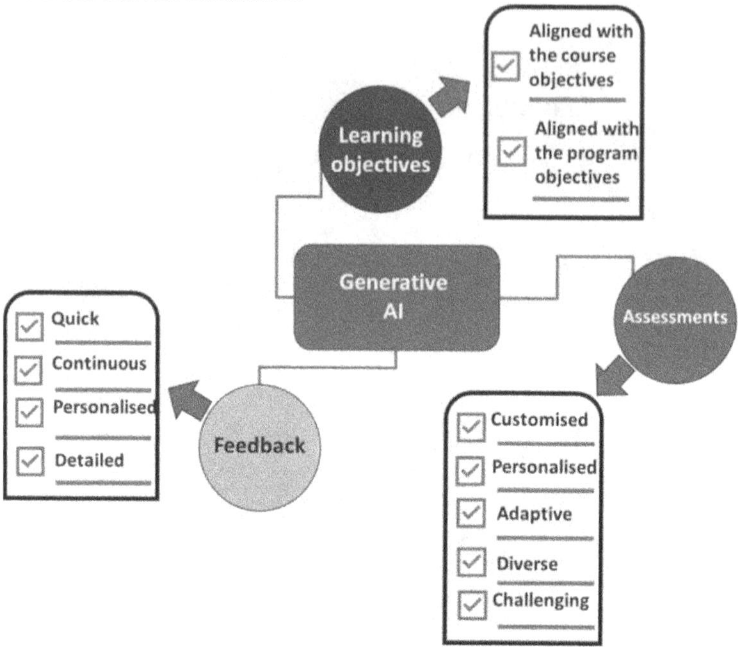

(Source: Author)

GenAI based assessments are customized, diverse, challenging, adaptive, personalized, and creative. Feedback is continuous, quick, detailed and personalized which guides learners to determine the next level of learning and the areas for improvement (Salinas-Navarro, Vilalta-Perdomo, Michel-Villarreal, & Montesinos, 2024). With the use of GenAI, technology has not only shaped the expectations of the students but also improved their ability to access, acquire, manipulate, and create information in the digital environment. Students are now thriving in the learning system with more meaningful experiences and involvement. GenAI in assessment enabled the teachers to provide personalized platforms for the students and develop the assessment activities which are adaptive to the strategies of students, the difficulty level and sequence of a task, preferences of the students and the availability of feedback. Now students are able to determine the level and sequence of a task depending upon their performance in a prior task, their ability and capability to understand a concept that is possible with a continuous monitoring of their performance. GenAI based platforms used for assessment encourage students to monitor their learning journeys through automated feedback cycles embedded in the systems and allow them to progress independently. AI tools has enabled teachers to come out of traditional assessment methods, focusing on creativity of students through independent thinking and encouraging them to use new ways to approach different situations.

These benefits can be achieved if assessment is designed in accordance with needs of curriculum and adaptive to the learners' profiles. Therefore, an important area to be focused on is development of assessment using GenAI tools. The next section discusses how GenAI tools can be used effectively in development of assessment.

3. GENAI AND DEVELOPMENT OF ASSESSMENTS

This section highlights the role of GenAI in development of assessment addressing both student and teacher sides. GenAI has a significant role in both formative and summative assessment. Teachers can use GenAI in formative assessments to create personalized assessments along with immediate feedback that will help students to improve their learning and creativity. Furthermore, based on pre-trained transformer GenAI will also help in automating the process of question development both for the formative and summative assessments (Naseer et al., 2024). Training AI tools on student's data will also assist teachers in improving assessment tools and to focus more on personalized assessments. GenAI tools monitor students' performance and progress, makes predictions, and recommend instructional suggestions to teachers which can be used in assessment re-design (Gil et al.,2021).

For students the use of personalized and adaptive assessment tools will empower them to conduct a rigorous self-assessment. Students will be more creative in dealing with different situations independently. For example, Jauhiainen and Guerra (2023) examined the application of GenAI tools in school education and highlighted that GenAI tools has potential to personalize learning material to address students with different levels of knowledge and skills. The findings revealed that most of the students enjoyed learning through GenAI modified learning material.

GenAI based assessment tools are effective in identifying learning patterns which are data-driven and creating interactive assessments for the students. Moreover, teachers can make the assessments challenging, engaging, creative and rewarding with the use of gamification. Ogunleye et al. (2024) highlighted that student engagement can be enhanced by using interactive tool during teaching to stimulate student learning, for example, a comparative activity in the form of group work exercise during lectures is helpful to discuss, compare and critique their findings of the AI-generated solutions for a given case.

3.1 GenAI and Creativity in Assessments

Being a driving force, assessments have a critical role in teaching and learning process. In the era of changing educational landscape, it is need of the hour to shift from traditional knowledge-based assessments towards problem-solving, case-study-based, and creative assessments. GenAI helps to design assessment in ways that center the process of learning, higher order thinking, and authentic tasks leading towards more innovative and creative assessment methods. In the era of AI, assessments should focus more on higher order thinking and problem-solving skills of students along with creativity. Teachers can add the element of creativity in assessments by using real-life experiences, implementing authentic assessments, and focusing on alternative modes of developing assessments(Chan, 2023; Moorhouse, Yeo, & Wan, 2023). Developing assessments using GenAI tools help in reducing reliance on a routine repetitive memorization. It also assists teachers to get new teaching ideas, revise their teaching strategies, and create personalized assessments that fits the needs of students (Xia et al., 2024). At student side, GenAI encourages independent thinking, and providing opportunities to be creative by using new ways to approach different situations smartly. For example, chatbots can act brainstorming partners for both the teachers and students in developing and attempting assessments respectively. The use of chatbots in assessment development assists teachers in generating number of assessments with different tones on a similar topic, and adding difficulty and creativity level as per students' needs (Wieland et al.,2022).

The important consideration to incorporate creativity in assessments using GenAI is the digital literacy for both the teachers and students. Digital literacy skills are critical for teachers to revise their instructional strategies, to develop different assessment methods, and to address diverse learning needs of students. Therefore, training on use of GenAI tools in assessments is essential for its effective use.

3.2 Diagnostic Assessment

Developing assessment using GenAI is a critical task for the teachers. They need to consider the re-designed curriculum and the needs of learners. Traditionally, it was difficult for the teachers to analyze historical data and to explore the patterns of student performance. It is now easy for the teachers to use GenAI tools that predict trends, develop more creative and challenging assessment tasks (use of gamification, role playing etc.) for the students. An important step in development of assessment is the use of diagnostic assessment to know the initial understanding of student about a concept, this is done by using diagnostic questions database including multiple choice questions, true false statements, and brief questions. Diagnostic assessments are pre-assessments which are designed to explore the interests of the learners, skills set they have, strength and weakness of the learners and the learning preferences.

Figure 4. Diagnostic Assessment

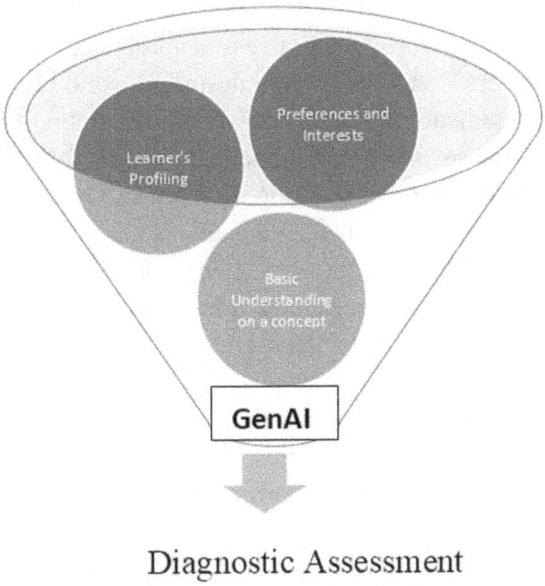

Figure 4 explains the outcomes of diagnostic assessment, here the role of GenAI is very important. GenAI records the student responses in terms of number of attempts, and correctness of tasks, detects the patterns to reveal the strength and weakness of the students. This mainly helps the teachers to identify the level of skill students have, their interests and proficiency. Moreover, prompt feedback is also attached with these tasks to make it more effective in the journey of learning for the students. Continuous monitoring and feedback allow learners to take adaptive learning pathways and help teachers to match the student competencies with learning material. Teachers can help students to modify their learning trajectories with the help of feedback. This first level of assessment is a starting point for formative and summative assessment design.

3.2 Formative Assessment

Second important area of assessment which needs attention of teachers is formative assessment. Formative assessment, also known as assessment-for-learning is on-going and performed throughout the learning process (Hooda et al., 2022). After diagnostic assessment, teachers are aware of individual learner profiles, their skills and learning preferences which is further helpful for the design of formative assessment. Formative assessment is used to assess the performance of the students during learning journey. One of the limitations of traditional assessment methods is lack of creativity, teachers develop similar assessments for all the students irrespective of their learning needs. This limitation can be addressed with the help of GenAI which allows to develop creative assessments depending upon the capability of learners. For teachers GenAI helps in brainstorming and bringing new ideas to develop creative assessments which was a difficult task in traditional settings.

GenAI enabled assessment offers experiential learning for the students, providing them customized content by analyzing their needs. On the other hand, it also enables teachers to develop more challenging, diverse, multiple, feedback oriented, flexible, and experiential assessment tasks. GenAI provides teachers assistance in development of assessment activities, now it is easier for the teachers to develop multiple assessment, with more interactive contents and quick feedback which was not possible in traditional settings.

Here are few examples which can clarify how teachers can use GenAI tools to generate real-time problem-based scenarios, case studies, games-based assessment, and role-playing scenarios to enhance learning experience of the students.

Example 1: GenAI Based Case Study Generated for Students

Case Study: "Capital Rationing Dilemma at Tech Innovations Inc."

"Tech Innovations Inc. is a technology startup that has recently secured a new round of funding to expand its operations. However, the company is facing a capital rationing situation where the available funds are not sufficient to undertake all the profitable investment opportunities identified. The company has three potential projects on hand:

- Project A: Developing a new software product with an initial investment of $150,000 and expected annual cash flows of $40,000 for the next 4 years.
- Project B: Upgrading existing infrastructure with an initial investment of $100,000 and expected annual cash flows of $30,000 for the next 3 years.
- Project C: Launching a marketing campaign with an initial investment of $80,000 and expected annual cash flows of $25,000 for the next 2 years.

Due to capital constraints, Tech Innovations Inc. can only select one project to pursue. Questions:

- Analyze the capital rationing dilemma faced by Tech Innovations Inc. and explain the implications of limited funds on project selection.
- Suggest potential solutions or strategies that the company could consider to address the capital rationing problem and maximize its profitability.

- Recommend which project (A, B, or C) Tech Innovations Inc. should prioritize based on your analysis and justification.

This case study challenges students to understand the concept of capital rationing and its impact on investment decision-making in businesses. By exploring potential solutions to overcome capital constraints and recommending the most suitable project for Tech Innovations Inc., students can develop critical thinking skills in addressing financial challenges related to limited resources

The above GenAI generated case study can be further modified by the teacher based on skills and ability of the students, embedded feedback and prompts to help them if they are unable to solve the problem. For example, if a student is unable to solve the above case study, prompt feedback with suggestions to review concept of time value of money and capital budgeting techniques can be referred. It is possible because GenAI continuously monitors the performance of students in terms of attempt, right and wrong criteria and the search of material for the case study solution by different students. So, GenAI tool makes the learning journey smooth and progressive instead of making it slower if any learner stuck on a certain level.

The use of supplementary material with assessment, feedback prompts and monitoring make the learning more effective. This practice saves time in developing multiple assessment and that time can be utilized in improving quality of assessment by incorporating more challenging tasks. Furthermore, continuous monitoring of student attempts and performance can also help in identifying patterns of learners, determining the difficulty level for an individual or group of students and re-designing the assessment. Yang, Flanagan, and Ogata (2022) highlighted deep learning models and natural language algorithms as useful tools which not only accurately estimates learners' ability but also recommend items with appropriate difficulty based on performance data of learners. Hence, based on training from existing data GenAI algorithms produce newly synthesized content, like text or images that can be used by teachers to redesign assessment and learning contents.

Example 2: Managerial Challenge

Game Title: "Managerial Mindset Challenge: Theory X vs. Theory Y"

"Scenario: You are a manager in a company facing a common workplace problem. Your team is experiencing low motivation and productivity due to a lack of communication and guidance. As a manager, you have the opportunity to apply either Theory X or Theory Y management styles to address this issue".

Instructions:

- Choose your preferred management style - Theory X or Theory Y.
- Based on your chosen style, provide a solution to improve motivation and productivity within your team.
- Justify your decision by explaining how your chosen approach aligns with the problem at hand.
- Compare the potential outcomes of applying both theories in this scenario.

Example 2 depicts how teachers can generate a game for management students to take one of management style considering the scenario generated by GenAI. This will help students to understand the concept and teachers on the other side can identify the learning level of the students. Here it is evident that GenAI enhances the capacity of generating diverse ideas for a single concept testing among students, it not only adds creativity to the assessments but also help teachers in developing multiple assessments for a concept.

Another assessment method that can be used in formative assessment is "Role Playing". Students in groups can be assigned a situation and asked to play a role. Example 3 presents GenAI generated assessment by teacher. Teachers can save time by giving detailed prompts i.e. for specific needs of students, for a specific skill set. It can be further enriched with timeline instructions and other instructions for the solution.

Example 3: Role-Play Scenario

Title: A Strategic Investment Role-Play Scenario for Student Portfolio

Managers Background: This role-playing scenario is designed to provide students with hands-on experience in creating and managing an optimized investment portfolio while developing essential skills such as risk assessment, diversification strategies, and market analysis. The following fictional framework will guide the exercise.

Scenario Overview: Students are tasked with forming an investment club that manages a $5 million endowment fund on behalf of their university's alumni association. They must build a well-diversified portfolio within six months using real financial instruments (stocks, bonds, ETFs) from various sectors and regions.

Objectives:

- To develop critical thinking and decision-making abilities related to investment strategy formulation.
- To enhance understanding of asset allocation principles and portfolio optimization techniques.

- To improve teamwork and communication among members.

Roles: Each student group should consist of five members, each taking on specific roles:

- Chief Executive Officer (CEO): Leads meetings, communicates with stakeholders, and ensures compliance with rules and regulations.
- Chief Financial Officer (CFO): Oversees budgeting, accounting, and reporting activities.
- Head of Research & Analysis: Conducts fundamental and technical research on potential investments, monitors market trends, and provides recommendations based on findings.
- Risk Management Specialist: Assesses risks associated with individual assets and overall portfolio exposure, recommends hedging or diversification strategies.
- Marketing & Communications Manager: Promotes the investment club's performance and achievements through presentations, reports, and social media channels.

Timeline:

Week 1: Introduction to the scenario, formation of teams, and assignment of roles.

Weeks 2–6: Team members conduct research, analyze data, and collaborate to select appropriate securities for inclusion in the portfolio.

Weekly meetings to discuss progress, share insights, and make decisions about asset allocations.

Week 7: Finalize the portfolio composition and submit it to the instructor for review.

Week 8: Present the final portfolio to the class and receive feedback from peers and instructors.

Summing up, GenAI has made assessment development more creative and engaging. Now teachers are more equipped with GenAI tools to develop diverse content, multiple tasks addressing more complex and cognitive assessment. Figure 5 summarizes the learning pathway for personalized and adaptive assessment. Adaptive learning pathway designed for a finance student starts from applying a suitable capital budgeting technique for students followed by a continuous monitoring by the system. Based on student performance data of students, AI algorithms identify the patterns and classify students as slow learners, and fast learners. After this identification system gives feedback, for slow learners to go back and revise the concept and for fast learners to move on to the next level. Furthermore, these feedback prompts are used to restructure assessment and learning contents.

Figure 5. Learning pathway for Personalized and Adaptive assessment

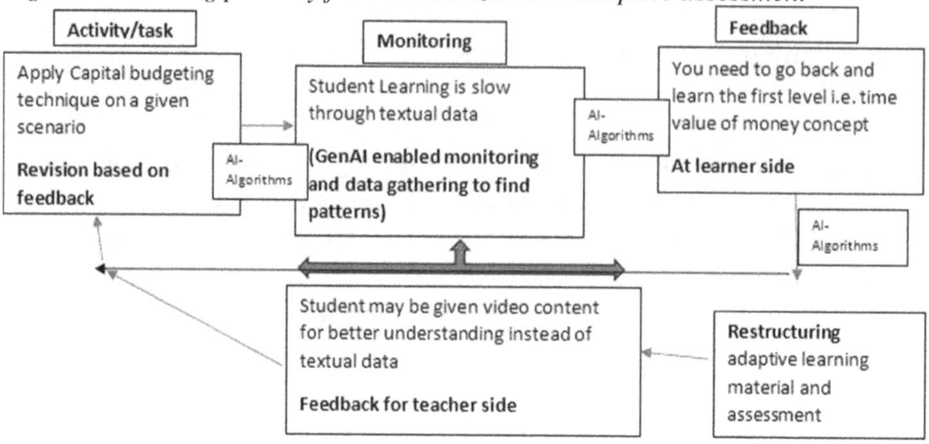

Source (Author)

3.3 Summative Assessment

GenAI also has potential to generate unique summative assessments. Summative assessment is done at the end of an instructional period and also known as assessment-of-learning (Hooda et al., 2022). GenAI tools can make summative assessment more effective and adaptive. Teachers can develop a greater number of questions with ease and creativity. More scenario-based questions with inclusion of customized and contextual data makes the assessment an effective tool of evaluation. Teachers can get patterners of responses to determine the level of understanding and to find the areas of improvement. The use of GenAI tools is very critical in this phase of assessment because this is the point where learners are judged about their performance for a whole period, and this also highlights the performance gaps in formative assessment and teaching methodology. The success and effectiveness of an assessment dependents on how it is designed, the selection of assessment tool and techniques, the way outcomes are analyzed and identified patterns are incorporated in the learning process.

4. GENAI AND EVALUATION OF ASSESSMENT

Assessment evaluation takes a crucial position in the learning environment of higher education. A quality assessment evaluation is a must ingredient for an effective learning. Therefore, teachers can use GenAI to make their assessment evaluation more meaningful, quick, automated, and personalized. Traditionally, it is a tedious task to evaluate the assessment, especially text based or case study-based questions which requires resources and time. This effort further increases as the number of students increases, specifically in behavioral studies evaluating formative and summative assessment is resource intensive task (Tobler, 2024). The capability of GenAI to automate the tasks possibly provides a support for evaluation of assessment. The predictive powers of GenAI tools and processing of large data also make it attractive to be used in evaluation process. For example, Ogunleye et al. (2024), used ChatGPT-4 and Google Bard as GenAI tools to evaluate three case studies from three disciplines including data science, data analytics, and construction management disciplines. The findings revealed that these tools depict subject-knowledge, problem solving, analytical, presentation, and critical-thinking skills and are helpful for the teachers in evaluation process.

a. Enhancing Grading and Evaluation

The use of GenAI changes question-generation, evaluation, and assessment systems. The use of GenAI in grading helps educators evaluate exams more efficiently. GenAI automates grading to save time on manual assessment evaluation. This technology saves educators time by reducing their workload. The speedy and unbiased analysis capabilities of technology optimize the grading process, ensuring students receive prompt feedback. GenAI tools also help in generating evaluation criteria which acts as assistance for teachers and make grading easier. This effect magnifies where number of students are more i.e. online learning systems. Moreover, automated grading systems not only generate grading for the students but also help students in developing their conceptual skills by providing personalized feedback (Bates et al., 2020).

AI-based software allows teachers to input sample solutions and evaluation instructions along with student answers to grade the textual data. This model can be further enhanced by using GenAI tool at output level to analyze patterns and student performance which can be further utilized to restructure the assessment and learning content. Automated grading model presented by Tobler (2024) is presented in Figure 6.

Figure 6. Automated Grading Model

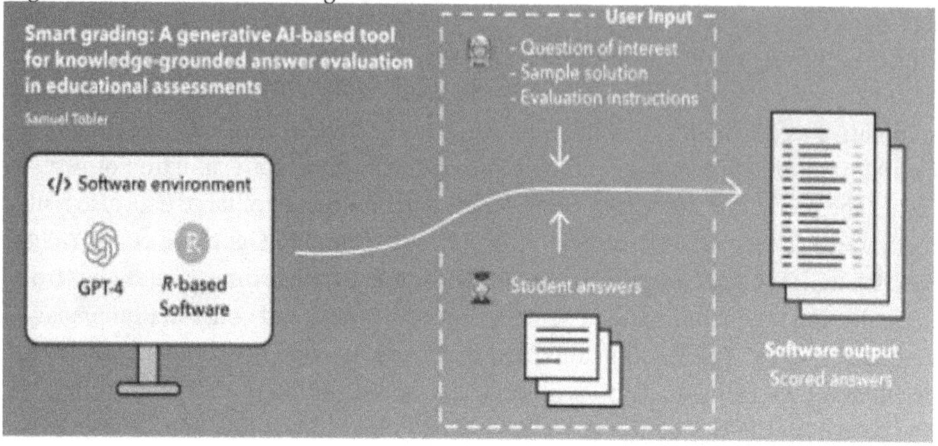

Source: (Tobler, 2024)

Automated assessment algorithms have potential to reduce teachers' workload, extend their capacity and productivity by providing course support, management, and evaluation tools. For example, reporting the results of a quantitative study, Watermeyer et al. (2024) highlighted that GenAI tools are relief for relief for teachers from bureaucratic burdens, support them in research activities, provide more time for planning for more interactive and engaging teaching contents, and help in supporting students.

Some big online learning platforms are successfully using automated grading system and proved that these grading/scoring systems have potential to deal with complexities of teaching design, adaptive learning pathways, and to support students' learning process through immediate feedback (Akgun & Greenhow, 2022).

b. Feedback

Grading of assessment is incomplete without detailed feedback; feedback timing is critical in formative assessment while in summative assessment it is not time bound. GenAI allows the development of advanced algorithms that can assess answer accuracy, understanding, critical thinking, and knowledge application. Availability of big data and learning analytics, GenAI in assessment help to provide just-in-time feedback rather than a stop-and-test approach (Luckin et al., 2022). It also allows to re-structure the assessment task based on on-going analysis of student performance. For teachers it is now easy to provide one-to-one feedback to students depending upon their achievements during learning process. Furthermore, the feature of quick and in-time feedback of GenAI based assessment also makes the teachers pro-active in providing guidance and support to the learners.

Students learn more about their strengths and weaknesses with this detailed feedback in formative assessment tasks. Feedback is important for improving the quality of assessment and learning process. It helps the students identify their areas for improvement, the difficulty level, their thinking skills, and competencies for an assigned task and to know how well they have understood a concept. GenAI enables teachers to provide feedback with attached rewards in the form of badges, moving upward on difficulty level and many more.

Another important factor in feedback is timing. GenAI allows teachers to provide detailed and quick feedback with formative assessment to make the learning journey more adaptive and personalized. Instant feedback also helps students to progressively solve problems and learn from their mistakes during learning pathways. Furthermore, to meet learners' proximal learning patterns, feedback is an important approach. Immediate feedback according to students' input guide to gradually understand the abstract concepts and perform practical exercises in a sequence leading towards improved abilities to reason in specific manner (Zhai et al., 2021). Furthermore, timely feedback is effective if it is valid and reliable, GenAI tools make it possible through algorithms. Algorithms allow systematic monitoring of student's performance which further helps in identifying good and struggling students. This identification is critical for valid and reliable feedback from teachers.

The role of assessment and feedback is not only limited to students' learning but also important for right curriculum design, instructions of teachers, and administrators' settings (Hooda et al., 2022). Feedback can take various forms including real time feedback, post hoc feedback, aggregated feedback, and feedback on feedback depending upon assessment activity and the requirements of the learners. As we examine the effects of GenAI on grading, we see a future where assessments are efficiently reviewed and provide valuable and tailored feedback, creating a more immersive and rewarding learning environment.

Comprehensively, feedback in an assessment process is essential element in a learning process; feedback if embedded in right manner, using right GenAI tools at right time can have positive impact on students in terms of increasing self-reflection, effective engagement, satisfaction, motivation, level of achievement, self-regulated learning, creativity, improved higher order skills, and scaling up personalized and adaptive learning. Whereas the use of GenAI tools in providing feedback also help teachers in various ways including effective curriculum design, supports collaborative and adaptive learning, promotes learner-centered pedagogy, improves learning design strategies, refines instructional-strategies and course contents, promotes instructors' skills in instruction delivery, and supports quality education(Hooda et al., 2022).

c. Ensuring Fairness and Bias Mitigation

Addressing evaluative bias is crucial to fair education. This section discusses biases and how GenAI promotes fair and impartial evaluation procedures. Assessments may be biased by cultural, gender, or socioeconomic factors, which might obscure a student's abilities. GenAI based tools used for assessment and feedback may result in inaccurate or discriminatory predictions at different phases including data pre-processing, model selection, and post-data processing.

GenAI can examine large datasets and find patterns, which could help reduce evaluation biases. GenAI uses unbiased algorithms to reduce bias in student performance assessment (Naseer et al., 2024). Technology's ability to assess and generate material without perpetuating prior prejudices allows for more inclusive and diverse evaluation systems. GenAI tools used in grading and evaluation are trained on large data sets, grading instruction and evaluation criteria which reduces the possible bias attached with grading. GenAI grading tools provide fair and unbiased grades based on instructions, hence, removes the chances of various bias. Although the instructions for grading are human made but the ability of algorithms to learn from data and creation of self-benchmarks for grading based on instructions are quite fair. Still there are lot of questions on fairness of GenAI based grading tools but the increasing advancement in this field is never ending which are in efforts to address these limitations.

5. CREATING ADAPTIVE LEARNING ENVIRONMENTS

GenAI plays a major role in adaptive learning systems, changing education landscape. This section examines how GenAI improves adaptive learning environments. Using complex algorithms, GenAI adapts knowledge dissemination to individual learning styles and speeds. Technology's ability to create adaptive learning materials ensures that students receive knowledge tailored to their needs, making education more engaging and effective. The enquiry also considers real-time evaluation changes based on student performance. GenAI lets adaptive learning systems adapt to each person's growth. The system may quickly modify assessment difficulty, structure, and nature-based on student performance. This responsive technique guarantees that each student is challenged at the right level and provides immediate support for those who need it. As GenAI is integrated into adaptive learning, education becomes personalized, ever-changing, creative, and flexible, maximizing student outcomes.

Figure 7 presents a comprehensive picture of an adaptive learning pathway, the key elements include learning outcomes, learners' profiling, effective assessment tools, and suitable methods with an integration of GenAI in all these elements.

Figure 7. Adaptive and Personalized Learning Pathway

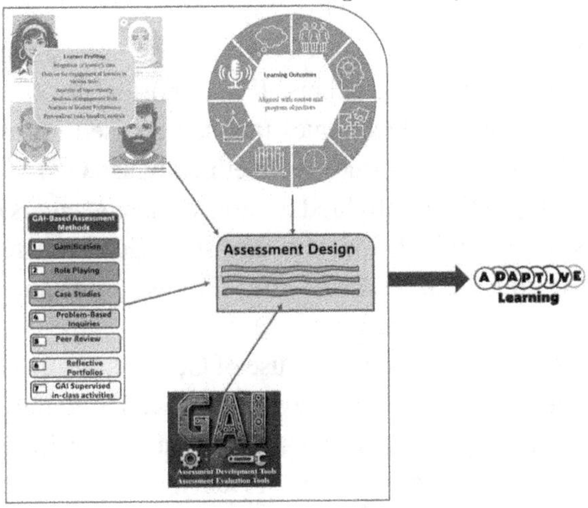

Source: (Author)

Using advanced algorithms, GenAI tools generate personalized learning content, analyze student data, create customized and creative materials, enhance student motivation for learning and active participation in assessment. As a result, an adaptive and personalized learning environment was created for the students where they can have experiential learning, creative and authentic assessment, and constructive feedback. Adaptive learning environments place students at the center of the learning process, provide tailored learning material, and assess for constructive feedback. Students are active participants in adaptive and personalized learning environments where learning is progress focused, creative, and empowers the learners.

6. CHALLENGES AND ETHICAL CONSIDERATIONS

GenAI in assessments could be promising. However, this approach's drawbacks must be acknowledged and addressed. The complicated design of GenAI models makes it difficult to explain and validate decision-making processes. Since GenAI learns from datasets with historical biases, there were concerns about biases. Integrating this technology makes assessment fairness and objectivity difficult. Furthermore, privacy and data security ethics are also major concerns for the learners. GenAI requires large datasets, raising concerns about data security and use. Finding a balance between using GenAI for educational advancement and protecting student privacy is vital.

One of the big challenges of using GenAI tools in assessment is digital literacy both for the learners and the teachers. It is important for the teachers to first understand and learn tools and techniques that can be used for assessment. Their understanding is a key to help the students to ethically use GenAI in their learning process. Swiecki et al. (2022) highlighted the areas where teachers can focus to deal with ethical issues rise at student side with the use of GenAI. A few areas of focus for the teachers are testing the assessment with AI tools, re-designing of assessment, and developing authentic assessment.

Another challenge is about responsible use of GenAI tools in assessment. There exist concerns about the use of technology beyond academic integrity, plagiarism and intellectual property rights. Furthermore, the issues regarding reliability, accessibility, privacy, security, and transparency of GenAI tools should also be addressed using new ways (Salinas-Navarro et al., 2024). Some other challenges pointed out by Molenaar (2022) with respect to working with GenAI tools are: developing a synergy between GenAI tools and human, learning and adaptability of Gen AI tools with environment, ethical and responsible behavior of learners, sharing of strategies among GenAI and human. These ethical concerns and challenges must be addressed in the learning process using GenAI tools. The responsible use of GenAI for all stakeholders of a learning system is key to its success. It is crucial to emphasis that use of GenAI is not just about technology, it is the pedagogical, ethical, social, cultural and economic dimensions of AI in education which should be of top concern for all stakeholders of a learning system (Zawacki-Richter, Marín, Bond, & Gouverneur, 2019). The training of existing and future members of GenAI community, and other relevant stakeholders is crucial to unleash its benefits while mitigating its potential harm. It is therefore important to create awareness among stakeholders to embrace their responsibilities while using GenAI tools in education. It can be ensured if ethics has a central place in a framework of use of GenAI in education (Borenstein & Howard, 2021).

7. FUTURE TRENDS AND IMPLICATIONS

It becomes evident that there is a notable transition towards a state of ongoing adjustment and customization in the field of education with the use of GenAI. The capacity of technology to generate customized information in a dynamic manner is in accordance with the increasing need for adaptive and personalized learning. Referring to the tremendous growth of GenAI tools in education, it is assumed that GenAI has a crucial function in facilitating more comprehensive, tailored, and efficient learning encounters. With a continuous evolution of the intersection between GenAI tools and education, avenues for the researchers are open to take leverage from its strengths, unleash potential opportunities, and learn from challenges and limitations. Currently, in the field of education, big data, educational data mining, and learning analytic are the areas of focus for the stakeholders (Paek & Kim, 2021).

REFERENCES

Baidoo-Anu, D., & Ansah, L. O. (2023). Education in the era of generative artificial intelligence (AI): Understanding the potential benefits of ChatGPT in promoting teaching and learning. *Journal of AI*, 7(1), 52–62. DOI: 10.61969/jai.1337500

Bates, T., Cobo, C., Mariño, O., & Wheeler, S. (2020). Can artificial intelligence transform higher education? *International Journal of Educational Technology in Higher Education*, 17(1), 1–12. DOI: 10.1186/s41239-020-00218-x

Borenstein, J., & Howard, A. (2021). Emerging challenges in AI and the need for AI ethics education. *AI and Ethics*, 1(1), 61–65. DOI: 10.1007/s43681-020-00002-7 PMID: 38624388

Chan, C. K. Y. (2023). A comprehensive AI policy education framework for university teaching and learning. *International Journal of Educational Technology in Higher Education*, 20(1), 38. DOI: 10.1186/s41239-023-00408-3

Cope, B., Kalantzis, M., & Searsmith, D. (2021). Artificial intelligence for education: Knowledge and its assessment in AI-enabled learning ecologies. *Educational Philosophy and Theory*, 53(12), 1229–1245. DOI: 10.1080/00131857.2020.1728732

Gil, P. D., da Cruz Martins, S., Moro, S., & Costa, J. M. (2021). A data-driven approach to predict first-year students' academic success in higher education institutions. *Education and Information Technologies*, 26(2), 2165–2190. DOI: 10.1007/s10639-020-10346-6 PMID: 34400873

Hooda, M., Rana, C., Dahiya, O., Rizwan, A., & Hossain, M. S. (2022). Artificial intelligence for assessment and feedback to enhance student success in higher education. *Mathematical Problems in Engineering*, 2022(1), 5215722. DOI: 10.1155/2022/5215722

Jauhiainen, J. S., & Guerra, A. G. (2023). Generative AI and ChatGPT in school children's education: Evidence from a school lesson. *Sustainability (Basel)*, 15(18), 14025. DOI: 10.3390/su151814025

Koh, E., & Doroudi, S. (2023). Learning, teaching, and assessment with generative artificial intelligence: Towards a plateau of productivity. *Learning: Research and Practice*, 9(2), 109–116. DOI: 10.1080/23735082.2023.2264086

Luckin, R., Cukurova, M., Kent, C., & Du Boulay, B. (2022). Empowering educators to be AI-ready. *Computers and Education: Artificial Intelligence*, 3, 100076.

Mao, J., Chen, B., & Liu, J. C. (2024). Generative artificial intelligence in education and its implications for assessment. *TechTrends*, 68(1), 58–66. DOI: 10.1007/s11528-023-00911-4

Molenaar, I. (2022). The concept of hybrid human-AI regulation: Exemplifying how to support young learners' self-regulated learning. *Computers and Education: Artificial Intelligence*, 3, 100070. DOI: 10.1016/j.caeai.2022.100070

Moorhouse, B. L., Yeo, M. A., & Wan, Y. (2023). Generative AI tools and assessment: Guidelines of the world's top-ranking universities. *Computers and Education Open*, 5, 100151. DOI: 10.1016/j.caeo.2023.100151

Naseer, F., Khalid, M. U., Ayub, N., Rasool, A., Abbas, T., & Afzal, M. W. (2024). Automated Assessment and Feedback in Higher Education Using Generative AI. In *Transforming Education With Generative AI: Prompt Engineering and Synthetic Content Creation* (pp. 433-461). IGI Global. DOI: 10.4018/979-8-3693-1351-0.ch021

Ogunleye, B., Zakariyyah, K. I., Ajao, O., Olayinka, O., & Sharma, H. (2024). Higher education assessment practice in the era of generative AI tools. *arXiv preprint arXiv*:2404.01036.

Paek, S., & Kim, N. (2021). Analysis of worldwide research trends on the impact of artificial intelligence in education. *Sustainability (Basel)*, 13(14), 7941. DOI: 10.3390/su13147941

Salinas-Navarro, D. E., Vilalta-Perdomo, E., Michel-Villarreal, R., & Montesinos, L. (2024). Using generative artificial intelligence tools to explain and enhance experiential learning for authentic assessment. *Education Sciences*, 14(1), 83. DOI: 10.3390/educsci14010083

Swiecki, Z., Khosravi, H., Chen, G., Martinez-Maldonado, R., Lodge, J. M., Milligan, S., Selwyn, N., & Gašević, D. (2022). Assessment in the age of artificial intelligence. *Computers and Education: Artificial Intelligence*, 3, 100075. DOI: 10.1016/j.caeai.2022.100075

Tobler, S. (2024). Smart grading: A generative AI-based tool for knowledge-grounded answer evaluation in educational assessments. *MethodsX*, 12, 102531. DOI: 10.1016/j.mex.2023.102531 PMID: 38204981

Watermeyer, R., Phipps, L., Lanclos, D., & Knight, C. (2024). Generative AI and the Automating of Academia. *Postdigital Science and Education*, 6(2), 446–466. DOI: 10.1007/s42438-023-00440-6

Wieland, B., de Wit, J., & de Rooij, A. (2022). Electronic brainstorming with a chatbot partner: A good idea due to increased productivity and idea diversity. *Frontiers in Artificial Intelligence*, 5, 880673. DOI: 10.3389/frai.2022.880673 PMID: 36213166

Xia, Q., Weng, X., Ouyang, F., Lin, T. J., & Chiu, T. K. (2024). A scoping review on how generative artificial intelligence transforms assessment in higher education. *International Journal of Educational Technology in Higher Education*, 21(1), 40. DOI: 10.1186/s41239-024-00468-z

Yang, A. C., Flanagan, B., & Ogata, H. (2022). Adaptive formative assessment system based on computerized adaptive testing and the learning memory cycle for personalized learning. *Computers and Education: Artificial Intelligence*, 3, 1. DOI: 10.1016/j.caeai.2022.100104

Zawacki-Richter, O., Marín, V. I., Bond, M., & Gouverneur, F. (2019). Systematic review of research on artificial intelligence applications in higher education–where are the educators? *International Journal of Educational Technology in Higher Education*, 16(1), 1–27. DOI: 10.1186/s41239-019-0171-0

KEY TERMS AND DEFINITIONS

Adaptive Learning: Adaptive learning is a teaching method that uses technology to facilitate the learning process based on the unique needs of each individual learner, it accommodates individual differences of the learners, and provides customized learning contents. For this learning, data and analytics are used first track student performance and to design learning path where a tailored learning material is recommended on strengths and weakness of the learners.

Formative Assessment: Formative assessment refers to assessment, which is done during the learning process, it is an ongoing assessment to supporting learning process. Continuous and prompt feedback can be given in this type of assessment. Teachers can provide customized feedback to students based on their performance and need of learning journey.

Generative Artificial Intelligence (GenAI): Generative AI is defined as a type of AI technology that can produce human-like content in response to prompts. It not only responds to prompts but also generates new and original content, including text, images, audio, and synthetic data going beyond its explicit programming. It works on deep learning models and generative adversarial networks (GANs) to response and generate content. Various GenAI tools include GPT-4, ChatGPT, AlphaCode, GitHub Copilot, Claude, Bard etc.

Personalized Learning: In personalized learning, students actively shape their learning journey based on their interests, goals and unique needs. In a personalized learning environment, students have a control over activities, learning material, and the pace which make their learning more experiential. It empowers students to customize their learning experience through their active participations and feedback.

Summative Assessment: The assessment which is done at the end of a learning process is known as summative assessment, for this type of assessment limited feedback is provided to the learners.

Chapter 15
Unleashing Creative Potential:
The Role of Generative AI in Business Education

Justin Knibbe
University of Calgary, Canada

Rosalynn Peschl
University of Calgary, Canada

Oleksiy Osiyevskyy
https://orcid.org/0000-0002-5765-6161
University of Calgary, Canada

ABSTRACT

This study examines the overlooked role of creativity in business school curricula, despite its recognized importance in fostering innovation and solving global challenges. It critiques traditional educational models for failing to nurture creative thinking and argues for the integration of Generative AI (GAI) systems to enhance creativity in business education. Using an exploratory case study approach, the authors examined the existing literature that supports the business imperative for creativity; then, GAI was posited as a tool to improve divergent and convergent thinking, offering practical applications across various business disciplines. Additionally, ethical considerations surrounding data usage, intellectual property, and privacy were highlighted. The study concludes that responsibly integrating GAI can revolutionize business education, preparing future leaders for an AI-augmented business world while maintaining the necessity for ethical, informed, and transparent use.

DOI: 10.4018/979-8-3693-2418-9.ch015

INTRODUCTION

In the dynamic global business arena, entrepreneurial thinking and innovation represent pivotal elements underpinning organizational competitive advantage, growth, and prosperity (Osiyevskyy et al., 2020). Creativity, defined as the ability to generate novel and useful ideas, is a crucial component of the innovation process (Sarooghi et al., 2015; Anderson et al., 2014). This critical aspect, however, faces a significant shortfall within business education as there is a marked lack of emphasis on creativity in business schools' curricula. This gap is more than an academic concern; it poses a substantial risk to the development of versatile, innovative leaders capable of tackling the complexities of contemporary business challenges. The relevance and urgency of addressing this educational deficiency are evident, given the proven success of creatively driven companies such as Apple and Amazon in achieving market dominance and resolving intricate global issues (Kelly & Kelly, 2013).

To bridge this educational void, the current study aims to offer an intervention involving the incorporation of Generative AI (GAI) systems – such as ChatGPT, Perplexity AI or Gemini – into business school programs. This approach seeks to cultivate creativity in students by leveraging GAI's capability to augment both divergent and convergent thinking processes (Girotra et al., 2023). The ability of GAI to process extensive data and generate innovative ideas presents a novel avenue for stimulating creative thought, prompting students to venture into unexplored territories of business models, strategies, and solutions. The integration of Generative AI across various fundamental business disciplines – from strategy and marketing to entrepreneurship and finance – is posited to transform the educational experience, equipping future business leaders with essential creative competencies for thriving in an AI-influenced business world.

Nevertheless, the adoption of Generative AI in business education brings forth significant ethical considerations. The study highlights the imperative to address concerns surrounding data ethics, intellectual property rights, and data privacy in the use of GAI (Gutiérrez, 2023). Ensuring responsible usage of GAI involves a comprehensive understanding of its functions and limitations, aimed at enhancing rather than substituting human creativity (Mahama et al., 2023). Moreover, it necessitates transparency in the application of GAI tools and the establishment of guidelines to ensure the ethical and legal integrity of AI-generated outputs. Through an exploratory case study approach, this paper will first examine the creativity deficiency in business schools. Following that, numerous suggestions for ways in which GAI can support divergent and convergent thinking will be provided across a spectrum of business disciplines. Finally, the study underscores that while GAI holds the potential to significantly elevate the process of creative thinking in business education, its integration must be carefully navigated, considering these ethical dimensions to ensure that the technology serves as a complement to human ingenuity.

THE CREATIVITY DEFICIENCY IN BUSINESS SCHOOLS' CURRICULA

Creativity is the ability to "envision, assess, formulate, express, and achieve buy-in for ideas that are novel" (Eisner, 2017, p. 5); it is at the core of what many successful companies do, including Apple, Amazon, Facebook, and 3M. Oft-repeated warnings abound of companies that failed to innovate, including Blockbuster, Blackberry, and Nokia. The management guru Peter Drucker once declared, "innovate or die" (as cited in Ignatius, 2014, para. 1), stressing the need for businesses to be vigilant, agile, and creative in their quest to remain relevant. Creativity helps people and companies to "see problems in a new way" (Baker & Baker, 2012) and allows them to imagine "novel solutions" (Eisner, 2017). David Kelly, the founder of IDEO, describes various innovations that have resulted from creativity, including more effective surgical tools, appropriate housing for service men and women returning from war, and low-cost hearing aids for elderly villagers in developing countries (Kelly & Kelly, 2013, p. 2). Creativity is also needed to tackle massive global issues such as poverty, inequality, climate change, clean energy, and protection of land and water resources. According to Dr. Seelig of the Stanford Institute of Design, companies that can innovate are succeeding "in every field" (as cited in Eisner, 2017).

In 2010, an IBM study of 1,500 leaders discovered that creativity was the top competency required for future business leaders (IBM, 2010), while in 2017, a PWC survey of 1,379 CEOs found that innovation (of which creativity is a necessary part (Baker & Baker, 2012)), was the top skill that companies wanted to hone (PWC, 2017).

As stated above, most businesses do recognize the importance of creativity. According to Aylesworth and Cleary (2020), the need for creativity in business has been "well documented" (p. 248), and Titus and Koppitsch (2018) show that businesses see creativity as an "essential business skill" (p. 242). Boulocher-Passet et al. (2016) support these sentiments, calling creativity an "essential twenty-first-century competence" and the most sought-after trait in leadership (p. 574). Eisner (2017) agrees, describing creativity as a "core competency" (p. 5). In addition to the IBM and PWC studies cited above, an Adobe Systems poll of 5,000 people revealed that 80% of respondents see "unlocking creative potential" as critical for economic growth (as cited in Kelly & Kelly, 2013, p. 4). Finally, in 2020, LinkedIn rated creativity as the top soft skill needed by companies (Van Nuys, 2019).

Creativity is clearly crucial - and sought after - for business success. It is only logical, then, that business schools should be energetically promoting and enhancing this skill in their students. Unfortunately, this does not seem to be the case. A good illustration of this point comes from the two most recent reputable Graduate Business Education Curriculum Surveys by the MBA Roundtable[1]: when summarizing the core elements of graduate business curricula of hundreds of business schools, none of them mention "creativity".

Boulocher-Passet et al. (2016) argue that business schools are not interested in providing an understanding of creativity, nor do they have the resources to do so. Creativity training is often overlooked or shuffled into certain electives. Baker and Baker (2012) also accuse business schools of doing "little to advance the abilities of students to think critically or creatively" (p. 704), while Sosa and Kayrouz (2020) show that some business schools are consciously rejecting aspects of teaching creativity. Author Daniel Pink gave an even more scathing critique of business schools when he declared that the Master of Fine Arts (MFA) "is the new MBA" (Baker & Baker, 2012, p. 705), arguing that the more creative arts students are better equipped than business students to solve complex problems. This was echoed by Adrien Wooldridge, management editor for The Economist when, in 2011, he suggested that businesses should seek out artists for their creative ideas (as cited in Baker & Baker, 2012). If this is true – that fine arts programs are better preparing students for business than business schools are – then what purpose do business schools serve? This might be why Glenn (2011) pondered whether there is still a need for a business major at all.

One reason for this may be that business schools are slow and onerous systems, unwieldy, and maybe even unable to change. A prominent thinker on this topic, Henry Mintzberg, seems to validate this hypothesis by saying that business school curriculums have remained relatively unchanged since the 1950s (as cited in Baker & Baker, 2012). An article in the Economist (2014) also declared that the current model of "lecturing, cramming and examination has barely changed for centuries" (para. 1). The ramifications of the status quo on creativity cannot be understated, and Sir Ken Robinson (2006), in the most watched TED talk of all time, chastised schools for killing creativity by giving students narrow parameters within which to work (Robinson, 2006). In his book, The Educational Psychology of Creativity, Houtz stated that business schools "punish" students who deviate from the rigid expectations given to them (as cited in Baker & Baker, 2012, p. 718). The current teaching practices do not create a culture conducive to enhancing creativity.

GENERATIVE AI AND CREATIVITY

Creativity is the ability to produce ideas (for products, services, processes, solutions) that are both novel and useful (Sarooghi et al., 2015; Anderson et al., 2014), fitting within a specific context (Amabile, 2018). It can be represented as a combination of two consecutive cognitive processes: *divergent thinking*, which refers to the capacity to generate a variety of ideas, and *convergent thinking*, which focuses on critically assessing and refining these ideas (Cropley, 2006; de Vries & Lubart, 2019; Kenworthy et al., 2021). The effectiveness of the creativity process is governed by four factors (Girotra et al., 2010; Terwiesch, & Loch, 2004; Dahan & Mendelson, 2001): (1) the quality of generated ideas on average; (2) the total number of generated ideas; (3) the variance (dispersion) of the quality of generated ideas; and (4) the effectiveness of the selection mechanism. The first three factors describe the effectiveness of the divergent thinking process, while the last factor reflects the quality of the convergent thinking. Generative AI technologies can complement human decision-makers by substantively enhancing the effectiveness of both the divergent and convergent phases of creativity. Within the business education context, early evidence suggests that a Large Language Model (LLM), like Chat-GPT-4 can generate a larger number of ideas in a shorter time frame than student participants; moreover, the AI-generated ideas are of higher quality on average and demonstrate higher dispersion/variability (Girotra et al., 2023). In other words, Generative AI systems can substantively increase all three effectiveness factors of divergent thinking, or idea generation. Interestingly, the initial critique of Generative AI or Large Language Models concerning their inability to generate truly novel ideas (as opposed to recombination of what is already known from their training datasets) turns out to be false: a recent study in Nature demonstrates the ability of LLMs to bring true discoveries of new knowledge, along with the ability to describe the emerging solutions (Romera-Paredes et al., 2023). The same study demonstrates the effectiveness of AI systems for evaluating emerging solutions, hence augmenting the convergent thinking process in addition to divergent thinking.

Not surprisingly, the prominent global 2023 AI Index Report[2] indicates that more than half of companies are actively adopting AI; moreover, "*organizations that have adopted AI report realizing meaningful cost decreases and revenue increases*" (p.4). AI technologies are substantively shaping all aspects of management practices (Shtepa et al., 2023). Hence, the demand for AI-related professional skills is increasing across nearly every industry. Gregersen & Bianzino (2023) argue that the true potential of AI extends beyond mere efficiency and cost-saving benefits; it lies in fostering inspiration, imagination, and innovation. The true value occurs when the technology is used in such a way that people can ask smarter questions, which in turn makes them better problem solvers and breakthrough innovators. Given the rapid expansion of AI adoption in business, business schools need to be at the forefront of preparing future leaders to manage organizations in a digital, AI-enabled world. According to Doan Winkel, Sr. Endowed Chair of Entrepreneurship at John Carrol University and Eric Liguori, Associate Dean at Florida State University (2024), AI can be used to reimagine how we teach to keep our curriculum aligned with what employers want. They believe that the longer we wait to incorporate AI, "the more risk we create for our students and institutions" (AI and the Future Section, para. 5). Already, organizations such as KPMG are expecting their employees to make use of GAI in their work. Chief Operating Officer, Laura Newinski, was "appalled" to learn in early 2024 that the majority of their 800 interns are not comfortable using GAI as they have been discouraged or even forbidden from using GAI in their studies (Boehm & Heath, 2024).

As such, Generative AI technologies can substantively improve the effectiveness of creative processes in business. Based on this, the primary premise of our study is that the integration of Generative AI into business school curricula can effectively dismantle the barriers to creative thinking and foster a new era of innovative business education. Generative AI is believed to be the "most important general-purpose technology of our era" for businesses (Brynjolfsson & McAfee, 2017, para. 2), and with its capacity to analyze vast datasets and produce original patterns, designs, and ideas, generative AI can serve as a powerful tool in business education, enhancing learning and encouraging creative thought. Research corroborates these insights, showing that AI can catalyze human creativity by: (a) helping to identify the patterns; (b) revealing a bigger picture; and (c) helping to guide exploration and experimentation (Bieser, 2023). Its application across various core business courses—e.g., Strategy, Marketing, Entrepreneurship, Accounting, Finance, and Leadership—can revolutionize the learning experience. By providing a hands-on, data-driven, and simulation-based learning experience, Generative AI has the potential to inspire a new generation of business leaders who are as creative as they are analytical. According to the most popular GAI system today, ChatGPT itself, it is a tool that can be used to enhance human creativity by generating ideas and inspiring users (as cited in Mahama et al., 2023). Magni et al., (2023) believe that as AI increasingly performs generative duties, humans will become the gatekeepers tasked with understanding, evaluating, and applying generated ideas. The challenge for business schools is to embrace this technology, not just as a tool for efficiency but as a catalyst for creativity. Darshak Patal, director and senior lecturer in economics at Gatton College, states that generative AI is a tool to help students brainstorm (as cited in Butterman et al., 2023). With the thoughtful integration of Generative AI across business disciplines, students can develop the creativity that will be a hallmark of successful leadership in the business world of tomorrow. In the remaining sections, the authors discuss practical approaches to achieving this goal across the key domains of the business school curriculum.

USING GENERATIVE AI ACROSS BUSINESS DISCIPLINES TO SPARK CREATIVITY

Accounting

Within the accounting field itself, Generative AI promises to streamline operations, boost efficiency, and open new avenues for strategic and value-added activities (Khalifeh, 2023; Lundaas, 2023) within a broad range of applications:

1. ***Data Analysis and Reporting:*** Generative AI systems excel in analyzing historical data, identifying financial trends, and generating comprehensive financial reports. This capability enhances financial decision-making and forecasting.
2. ***Compliance and Regulatory Assistance:*** AI tools can ensure adherence to various financial regulations and compliance requirements, offering valuable support in navigating complex legal landscapes.
3. ***Process Automation and Efficiency:*** Generative AI takes on repetitive tasks such as bookkeeping, data entry, and invoice processing. This automation not only saves time but also reduces human errors.
4. ***Client Communication and Service Improvement:*** AI aids in customer interactions, providing timely and relevant information, thereby improving customer relationships and service quality.
5. ***Tax Preparation and Advisory:*** GAI tools can assist in tax preparation by offering guidance on new tax laws, identifying deductions, and calculating preliminary tax liabilities.
6. ***Fraud Detection and Risk Analysis:*** Generative AI can be utilized in detecting fraudulent activities and conducting risk analysis in financial markets, thus enhancing the security of financial operations.

Not surprisingly, the evidence emerges about the effectiveness of using GAI in accounting classes within business schools to improve the student learning (Calderon et al., 2023). Moreover, it is reasonable to expect that GAI in accounting education can significantly enhance creativity and innovation in teaching and learning. In the context of business education, integrating GAI into accounting courses offers several transformative opportunities:

1. ***Creative Problem-Solving:*** GAI can be used to present complex, real-world accounting problems, challenging students to devise innovative solutions. This hands-on approach fosters critical thinking and creativity in problem-solving.
2. ***Scenario Simulation and Analysis:*** Students can use GAI to simulate various accounting scenarios, such as market fluctuations or regulatory changes. This helps them understand the dynamic nature of accounting in a practical, engaging manner.
3. ***Interactive Learning***: By interacting with AI tools, students can explore various accounting concepts and their applications in a more interactive and engaging way than traditional methods allow.
4. ***Data-Driven Creativity:*** GAI can assist students in analyzing vast datasets, helping them to identify patterns and insights that can lead to creative accounting strategies and solutions.
5. ***Collaborative Learning***: GAI can facilitate collaborative projects where students work together to solve accounting problems, encouraging teamwork and the exchange of creative ideas.

To achieve these goals, a potential ChatGPT prompt might be, "Act like an experienced curriculum designer with over 20 years of experience specializing in experiential learning. Create a scenario for accounting students where they will need to be creative problem solvers." From there, professors can adjust as necessary to create an activity that promotes creative problem solving.

In conclusion, by incorporating GAI into accounting education, business schools can cultivate a new generation of accountants who are not only technically proficient but also creative thinkers, capable of adapting to and shaping the rapidly evolving business landscape.

International Business

Prior research stresses the potential of GAI in enhancing International Business (IB) education, including improving engagement, collaboration, and maintaining academic integrity (Benmamoun, 2023). Within the topic of this study, incorporating GAI into the International Business courses in business schools arguably offers a transformative approach to education, particularly in fostering creativity among students.

1. ***Enhancing Creative Problem-Solving:*** GAI tools enable students to engage with complex, real-world business scenarios from an international perspective. By simulating diverse global business environments and challenges, these tools encourage students to think creatively and develop innovative solutions. For

instance, students can use GAI to model international market entry strategies, navigating different cultural, legal, and economic landscapes. This experiential learning approach nurtures creative problem-solving skills, essential for future business leaders.

2. ***Facilitating Cross-Cultural Understanding and Innovation:*** International business requires a deep understanding of various cultures and markets. GAI can assist in analyzing and understanding different cultural nuances and business practices. By leveraging GAI's vast database and analytical capabilities, students can explore and compare business strategies across different regions, fostering a global mindset and creative thinking in developing culturally sensitive business models.
3. ***Interactive Learning and Engagement***: GAI's conversational interfaces, like chatbots and virtual assistants, provide interactive and personalized learning experiences. These tools can engage students in dialogues, debates, and discussions on international business topics, enhancing their understanding and encouraging them to think creatively. Interactive learning through GAI can also include role-playing scenarios, where students navigate complex negotiations or business decisions, simulating real-world international business environments.
4. ***Data-Driven Insights and Creativity:*** In IB education, understanding and interpreting global market data is crucial. GAI tools can process and analyze large sets of international business data, providing students with insights into global market trends, consumer behaviors, and economic forecasts. This data-driven approach helps students in identifying creative opportunities and strategies for international business growth and expansion.
5. ***Collaboration and Diverse Perspectives:*** GAI facilitates collaboration among students from different backgrounds and locations, simulating a global business environment. By working on projects using GAI tools, students can share and combine their diverse perspectives, leading to more creative and inclusive business solutions. This collaborative approach not only enhances creativity but also prepares students for the collaborative nature of modern international business.
6. ***Simulating International Business Scenarios:*** GAI can create realistic simulations of international business environments, allowing students to experiment with various strategies and decisions. These simulations provide a safe space for creative experimentation, where students can learn from their successes and failures without real-world consequences. This hands-on approach is invaluable in developing creative and strategic thinking skills.
7. ***Ethical Considerations and Creative Leadership:*** The integration of GAI in IB education also involves discussing the ethical implications of AI in business. By critically examining issues such as data privacy, cultural sensitivity, and AI

bias, students develop a deeper understanding of the ethical dimensions of international business. This fosters a sense of responsible and creative leadership, essential for navigating the complex ethical landscape of global business.

As such, the integration of Generative AI into international business education represents a significant step forward in fostering creativity and innovation among business students. By providing interactive, data-driven, and collaborative learning experiences, GAI equips future business leaders with the creative competencies necessary to thrive in an increasingly globalized and technologically advanced business world. As business schools embrace these technologies, they will not only enhance the efficiency of education but also spark a new wave of creative and innovative thinking in international business.

An example ChatGPT prompt to enhance creativity in an international business class might be, "Act like an experienced curriculum designer with over 20 years of experience specializing in experiential learning. Create an activity for a university-level international business course that promotes creativity and cross-cultural understanding between two distinct countries…"

Strategic Management

In strategic management, creativity is essential for developing unique value propositions and competitive advantages. GAI can help students identify unseen opportunities and risks by analyzing market trends and generating strategic scenarios. GAI can also be used to author case studies that can be used in the classroom. Because case studies often do not have one right answer, they can promote innovation and creativity. Dominic Slauson shows how they use case studies in their OpenRN Project to allow students to "grapple with an endless number of critical thinking situations" (as cited in Nerantzi, Abegglen, Karatsiori, & Arboleda, 2023, p. 39). In a strategy context, this means that there is an endless number of cases that can be created with AI and given to students – cases with no one right answer. This will promote their strategic skills as well as their creativity as they grapple with numerous scenarios.

More broadly, integrating GAI into strategy education in business schools offers a promising pathway to enhance creativity and innovation. It provides a dynamic, data-driven, and interactive learning environment that goes beyond traditional teaching methods. This integration not only equips students with advanced strategic thinking skills but also prepares them for the complexities of an AI-augmented business landscape. Responsible and ethical use of GAI can revolutionize strategy education, nurturing a new generation of creative, innovative leaders equipped to navigate and shape the future of business:

1. ***Interactive Scenario Analysis and Planning:*** The ability to conceive of and strategize in the multi-scenario future of the business environment is crucial for strategic thinking (Mortlock & Osiyevskyy, 2023) and strategic flexibility (Biloshapka & Osiyevskyy, 2021). GAI tools can simulate the development of diverse business scenarios (arguably, better than human decision-makers), enabling students to experiment with various strategic models and approaches. This interactive learning experience fosters creativity by allowing students to explore and test their ideas in simulated real-world conditions. GAI can also create realistic, immersive simulations of business environments, allowing students to apply strategic concepts in simulated real-world scenarios. This experiential approach enhances students' ability to think creatively and adapt to rapidly changing business landscapes.
2. ***Data-Enhanced Strategic Innovation:*** GAI's ability to analyze vast datasets offers students unique insights into market trends and competitive dynamics, encouraging the development of forward-thinking, data-informed strategies. This exposure to data-driven decision-making processes fosters a culture of innovation in strategic planning.
3. ***Fostering Ethical and Sustainable Strategic Thinking:*** The integration of GAI in strategy education provides an opportunity to embed ethical and sustainable thinking into strategic decision-making. Students can explore the ethical implications of various strategic choices, preparing them to make responsible decisions in their future careers.
4. ***Collaborative Strategy Development:*** Utilizing GAI for collaborative projects enables students to integrate diverse perspectives into strategic development. This collaborative approach not only enhances creativity but also reflects the real-world complexity of strategic planning in a globalized business environment.
5. ***Bridging Theory with Real-Time Strategic Analysis:*** GAI bridges the gap between academic theory in strategic management and practical application by providing real-time analysis of current market conditions and business scenarios. This connection enriches students' understanding of strategic concepts and their application in a dynamic business world.

The prompts that can be used to create strategic problem-solving situations are endless. An example ChatGPT prompt includes, "Act like an experienced curriculum designer with over 20 years of experience specializing in experiential learning. You are teaching a strategy class to university students. Create a current case study for students to think creatively and strategically."

In summary, the integration of Generative AI into international business classes represents a significant advancement in education, offering students the tools and opportunities to cultivate their creativity, critical thinking, and innovation skills.

Entrepreneurship

In entrepreneurship education, creativity serves as the cornerstone of venture creation and innovation. It propels students to envision novel business models, identify untapped market opportunities, and devise unique solutions to often complex problems. The ability to think creatively is not only about generating new ideas but also about the capacity to critically evaluate opportunities, adapt to change, and persevere through the uncertainties inherent in launching new ventures. Entrepreneurial thinkers are the embodiment of creativity in business, requiring a blend of innovation, risk-taking, and problem-solving.

Generative AI can serve as a co-creator in this space, providing entrepreneurs with a multitude of business models, product designs, and market entry strategies. By leveraging GAI's ability to simulate business outcomes, students of entrepreneurship can learn to navigate the entrepreneurial landscape more creatively and with greater calculated risks (Darnell & Gopalkrishnan, 2023; Chalmers et al., 2021).

1. ***Brainstorming:*** GAI tools can revolutionize the brainstorming process by generating a plethora of ideas, concepts, and perspectives at an unprecedented scale (Meincke et al., 2024). In entrepreneurship classes, students can use GAI to simulate market scenarios, generate business ideas, or explore the potential impacts of emerging technologies on new ventures. It can be as easy as using ChatGPT prompts such as, "List 20 new business ideas", "What problems need solving?" or "How can we solve world hunger?" or "What solutions exist to solve hunger?" These ideas often lead to others in the classic brainstorming sense, sending students on wonderful chases for problems and solutions that they might want to tackle.
2. ***Communicating Ideas:*** being able to describe a problem statement or value proposition, quickly and concisely is foundational to the development of a viable business model. GAI can assist students in generating diverse problem statements by analyzing data from various sources, identifying trends, and highlighting unmet needs within specific markets or demographics. It can also offer feedback on the clarity and impact of their statements, guiding students toward more precise and compelling formulations.
3. ***Rapid Prototypes:*** It is hard to overstate the importance of prototyping in entrepreneurship education. Prototyping itself is considered a means of increasing creativity, innovation, and synthesis skills (Berglund & Grimheden, 2011). Design and innovation gurus at IDEO refer to "Boyle's Law:" never attend a meeting without a prototype (Rodirguez, 2017). GAI can facilitate rapid prototyping, allowing students to visualize their business models or products and iterate on them in real time. DALL-E and other AI visualization tools can help

by providing rapid prototypes. Instead of describing an idea, students create a visual representation to show their peers or even potential end-users. Rapid visualization can help both with explaining the problem to the early adopters, or customers, and identifying if these people fit the criteria, but it can also be used to show mock-ups or visuals of the potential solution. Based on the early adopter feedback, many iterations could be provided until the students have something their early adopters are happy with. AI can greatly expedite the information-gathering and interview processes in this way.

4. ***AI for Feedback:*** Beyond content creation, GAI can support the development of students' communication skills by providing platforms for practicing pitches, receiving feedback on clarity and persuasiveness, and refining their messaging to better articulate their problem statements, value propositions, and customer descriptions. Students can provide like ChatGPT or Gemini GAI systems with criteria on which to grade and ask it to provide feedback. Custom versions of ChatGPT, such as VenturusAI or ValidatorAI can be used to analyze entrepreneurial ideas and give an indication of feasibility. Canva and Grammarly are tools that can support compelling presentations and ensure impact in communication. GAIs can also ask students questions based on functionality, practicality, target market, distribution, etc., so that they can practice the Q&A portion of a pitch.

In sum, the integration of GAI into entrepreneurship education can significantly enhance the learning experience by providing tools and insights that support the critical elements of problem statement formulation, value proposition development, and customer description. By leveraging GAI, educators can equip students with the skills necessary to navigate the complexities of starting a new venture, ensuring they are prepared to meet the demands of the modern business world with creativity, clarity, and precision.

Marketing

In marketing, creativity is indispensable for developing compelling narratives, designing innovative campaigns, and crafting strategies that resonate with diverse audiences. Marketing asks students to explore the psychological and social dimensions of consumer behavior, leverage emerging trends, and use storytelling to connect with customers on a deeper level. GAI can process and analyze vast amounts of data, offering insights that might not be immediately apparent through traditional research methods. This capability is invaluable for identifying market trends and predicting consumer preferences. This predictive capability allows students to experiment with creating personalized marketing strategies that could be more effective and engaging.

1. ***Content Creation & Curation:*** GAI can assist in creating diverse advertising concepts and content ideas (Zhang & Prebensen, 2024; Bhattarai, 2023), and simulate consumer reactions to certain campaigns, providing a richer, data-driven foundation for creative thinking. Tools like OpenAI's GPT (for text generation) and DALLE (for image creation) can revolutionize how marketing content is created and curated. These tools serve as conduits for imaginative content creation, enabling students to craft compelling narratives, design innovative visuals, and conceive holistic advertising campaigns. Assignments leveraging these GAI tools can stimulate creative thinking and problem-solving, as students learn to blend AI-generated content with human creativity to produce marketing materials that resonate on a profound level.
2. ***Creating Customer Personas:*** Understanding and describing the target customer is crucial for tailoring products or services to meet specific needs. Marketing education that prioritizes this aspect prepares students to adopt a customer-first approach, which is vital for creating meaningful and sustainable marketing campaigns. GAI tools can aggregate and analyze consumer data, social media trends, and market reports to offer a nuanced understanding of target customers. This can help students in developing and then refining detailed customer personas and tailoring their marketing efforts to better meet these customers' needs.
3. ***Gleaning Insights from Customer Data:*** AI-driven analytics platforms, exemplified by IBM Watson, offer profound insights into consumer behaviors, preferences, and trends. By harnessing these tools, students can delve into the complexities of audience segmentation and consumer insights, applying theoretical knowledge to real-world data. This application not only enhances their understanding of target markets but also fosters a data-driven approach to marketing strategy development.
4. ***Simulating Market Dynamics:*** The utilization of virtual marketplaces and simulations, such as those provided by Hubro Marketing Simulation, allows students to experience the consequences of their marketing decisions in simulated environments. This experiential learning approach deepens their understanding of market analysis, campaign management, and strategic execution, offering a safe space to experiment with and refine their marketing strategies.
5. ***Optimizing Social Media Engagement:*** With the integration of AI-enhanced tools like Buffer or Hootsuite, students can engage in practical exercises in social media management, learning to optimize content delivery and engagement strategies based on AI-generated insights. These exercises not only enhance their skills in social media marketing but also underscore the importance of data-driven decision-making in engaging diverse audiences.

For an example ChatGPT prompt for customer personas that can be discussed in class, used as a creative activity, or to help students brainstorm, an instructor might begin with something like, "Act as a marketing expert with 20 years of experience. Create two distinct and appropriate customer personas for a [add type of business here]."

ETHICAL CONSIDERATIONS

In the evolving landscape of business education, the integration of Generative AI and Large Language Models (LLMs) presents a compelling opportunity to reshape how future corporate leaders are trained. The potential of these technologies to revolutionize the development of creativity and strategic thinking in business students is immense. However, as we chart this exciting territory, it is crucial to navigate the ethical complexities and potential pitfalls that accompany the use of such advanced AI tools in academic settings.

As discussed in this study, the primary allure of incorporating GAI into business courses is its ability to foster creativity and innovation. By leveraging AI's capacity to process vast amounts of information and generate novel outcomes, educators can offer students a unique sandbox to experiment with new business models, strategies, and solutions. This approach not only encourages students to think beyond traditional frameworks but also prepares them for a future where AI is an integral part of the business environment.

However, there's a fine line between using AI as a tool for sparking creativity and becoming overly reliant on it. Mahama et al., (2023) emphasize that while AI can assist humans, it cannot fully replace the nuances of human creativity. The challenge for educators is to achieve the right balance between teaching effective AI usage and ensuring that the essence of creativity – human thought and emotion – remains at the core of the learning process. Students should view Generative AI as a means to enhance their creative capabilities, not as a substitute for their own innovative thinking. Ongoing and enhanced creativity through Generative AI use can be encouraged in a number of ways, (1) encouraging collaboration among students allows them to work together, share ideas, and give each other feedback to build on ideas developed by Generative AI; (2) continue providing new and innovative tools, resources and activities to continue creative development; (3) encouraging iteration and experimentation with Generative AI outputs; (4) encourage reflective practice on the Generative AI output, students should not simply stop and what is provided but reflect and assess the merits and opportunities that are generated.

Another significant concern is the ethicality of data used by GAI. These models often learn from existing data, which can inadvertently perpetuate historical biases. Business schools must ensure that the datasets employed in teaching are not only unbiased but also representative of diverse perspectives. Furthermore, the question of intellectual property in AI-generated content is complex. Who owns the output – the AI, the user, the institution? Clarity in legal and ethical guidelines is essential in addressing these concerns within an educational framework.

The use of AI in creative processes also brings to the forefront issues of data privacy. Students and educators must be aware of how their data is utilized and protected. The potential for data misuse, such as the creation of deep fakes or misleading content, is a real concern. To mitigate these risks, business schools must establish robust policies and educate their community on digital ethics.

To navigate these ethical waters, several key principles should guide the use of GAI in business education (Gutiérrez, 2023):

(1) Informed Use: Before employing any AI tool, it is imperative to understand its origins, development process, capabilities, limitations, and associated risks. This knowledge ensures that users are fully aware of the tool's context and implications.
(2) Transparent Use: Transparency in the use of AI tools is critical. Students and educators must clearly indicate which tools were used and how they were applied in their work. This practice not only fosters academic honesty but also enhances the learning process by demystifying the role of AI in research.
(3) Ethical Use: It's crucial to distinguish between content directly produced by the user and that generated by AI. This distinction upholds the integrity of the work and respects intellectual property norms.

Responsible Use: AI tools should primarily be used in the early stages of research to inspire or suggest directions. The responsibility lies with the user to ensure that the final deliverables are the result of their own intellectual efforts and critical analysis.

CONCLUSION

In conclusion, the integration of Generative AI into business school curricula offers an unprecedented opportunity to cultivate a new breed of creative, tech-savvy corporate leaders. By embracing the transformative potential of these technologies, while conscientiously addressing the associated ethical challenges, business education can evolve to meet the demands of an AI-augmented future. The key lies in balancing the innovative capabilities of AI with a steadfast commitment to ethical, transparent, and responsible use, ensuring that the human element remains at the forefront of business creativity and decision-making.

Keeping pace with the rapid evolution of GAI technologies poses a major challenge for any business school. New features, capabilities, and best practices emerge regularly, requiring continuous learning and adaptation by business educators and IT staff. Consequently, curriculum development must be an ongoing effort, evolving to leverage new GAI capabilities and address emerging ethical considerations. This necessitates not only a commitment to continuous technological upgrades but also to the professional development of faculty. They must stay abreast of the latest trends and techniques in GAI, encompassing both the technical skills and pedagogical approaches necessary for effective integration into teaching.

To navigate these challenges, business school might consider forming partnerships and collaborations with technology companies and other industry players through business school associations. Such alliances can help distribute the costs and open access to a wider range of expertise. Designing educational programs and IT infrastructures that are modular and flexible can also ease the integration of new technologies, reducing the need for extensive overhauls when updating GAI tools. Moreover, incorporating industry-wide training on ethics and bias in AI as part of professional development for educators can aid in better understanding and mitigating these issues.

Overall, while the integration of GAI into business education heralds exciting opportunities for enhancing creativity and learning, it also brings with it a constellation of technological, financial, and educational challenges. A proactive, informed approach that includes continuous investment in technology, training, and ethical considerations is crucial. This ensures that the benefits of GAI are fully realized while minimizing its potential drawbacks, thereby maintaining the human element at the forefront of business creativity and decision-making.

REFERENCES

Amabile, T. M. (2018). *Creativity in context: Update to the social psychology of creativity*. Routledge. DOI:10.4324/9780429501234

Anderson, N., Potočnik, K., & Zhou, J. (2014). Innovation and creativity in organizations: A state-of-the-science review, prospective commentary, and guiding framework. *Journal of Management*, 40(5), 1297–1333. DOI:10.1177/0149206314527128

Aylesworth, A., & Cleary, R. (2020). Reawakening creativity for business leaders: Removing obstacles. *Journal of Education for Business*, 95(4), 248–254. DOI:10.1080/08832323.2019.1632780

Baker, D., & Baker, S. (2012). To "catch the sparkling glow": A canvas for creativity in the management classroom. *Academy of Management Learning & Education*, 11(4), 704–721. DOI:10.5465/amle.2010.0003

Benmamoun, M. (2023). Reinventing internationals business education: Integrating the power of generative AI. *AIB Insights*. Advance online publication. DOI:10.46697/001c.90397

Berglund, A., & Grimheden, M. (2011). The importance of prototyping for education in product innovation engineering. *ICORD 11: Proceedings of the 3rd International Conference on Research into Design Engineering*.

Bhattarai, A. (2023). Exploring Customer Engagement through Generative AI Innovative Strategies in Digital Marketing Campaigns. *Quarterly Journal of Emerging Technologies and Innovations*, 8(12), 1–9.

Bieser, J. (2023). How can AI support human creativity? World Economic Forum._https://www.weforum.org/agenda/2023/02/ai-can-catalyze-and-inhibit-your-creativity-here-is-how/

Biloshapka, V., & Osiyevskyy, O. (2021). Strategic optionality: Managing assets portfolio for achieving growth and longevity in turbulent environments. *Rutgers Business Review*, 6(1), 24–36.

Boehm, J., & Heath, R. (2024, January 18). OpenAI launches university partnership with Arizona State, allowing use of CHATGPT. *Axios Phoenix*. https://www.axios.com/local/phoenix/2024/01/18/openai-asu-university-partnership-school-arizona-chatgpt

Boulocher-Passet, V., Daly, P., & Sequeira, I. (2016). Fostering creativity understanding: Case study of an exercise designed for a large undergraduate business cohort at EDHEC Business School. *Journal of Management Development*, 35(5), 574–591. DOI:10.1108/JMD-08-2014-0087

Brynjolfsson, McAfee, A. (2017). The business of artificial intelligence: What it can – and cannot – do for your organization. *Harvard Business Review*.https://hbr.org/2017/07/the-business-of-artificial-intelligence

Butterman, E., Patel, D., Garvey, A., Commerford, B., & Stone, D. (2023). How is AI changing education – and business? *AACSB*. https://www.aacsb.edu/insights/articles/2023/11/how-is-ai-changing-education-and-business?

Calderon, T. G., Gao, L., & Cardoso, R. L. (2023). Generative artificial intelligence in the classroom: a financial accounting experience. In *Advances in Accounting Education: Teaching and Curriculum Innovations* (pp. 125-144). Emerald Publishing Limited. DOI:10.1108/S1085-462220230000027006

Chalmers, D., MacKenzie, N. G., & Carter, S. (2021). Artificial intelligence and entrepreneurship: Implications for venture creation in the fourth industrial revolution. *Entrepreneurship Theory and Practice*, 45(5), 1028–1053. DOI:10.1177/1042258720934581

Cropley, A. (2006). In praise of convergent thinking. *Creativity Research Journal*, 18(3), 391–404. DOI:10.1207/s15326934crj1803_13

Dahan, E., & Mendelson, H. (2001). An extreme-value model of concept testing. *Management Science*, 47(1), 102–116. DOI:10.1287/mnsc.47.1.102.10666

Darnell, J., & Gopalkrishnan, S. (2023). Entrepreneurship Teaching Exercises: integrating generative AI. https://papers.ssrn.com/sol3/papers.cfm?abstract_id=4587097

de Vries, H. B., & Lubart, T. I. (2019). Scientific creativity: Divergent and convergent thinking and the impact of culture. *The Journal of Creative Behavior*, 53(2), 145–155. DOI:10.1002/jocb.184

Dewett, T., & Gruys, M. L. (2007). Advancing the case for creativity through graduate business education. *Thinking Skills and Creativity*, 2(2), 85–95. DOI:10.1016/j.tsc.2007.04.001

Eisner, S. (2017). What if? Teaching creativity to business undergraduates. *S.A.M. Advanced Management Journal*, 82(3), 4–76.

Girotra, K., Meincke, L., Terwiesch, C., & Ulrich, K. T. (2023). Ideas are dimes a dozen: Large language models for idea generation in innovation. *Available atSSRN* 4526071. DOI:10.2139/ssrn.4526071

Girotra, K., Terwiesch, C., & Ulrich, K. T. (2010). Idea generation and the quality of the best idea. *Management Science*, 56(4), 591–605. DOI:10.1287/mnsc.1090.1144

Glenn, D. (2011, April 14). The default major: Skating through B-school. *The New York Times*. https://www.nytimes.com/2011/04/17/education/edlife/edl-17business-t.html

Gregersen, H., & Bianzino, N. M. (2023). AI can help you ask better questions – and solve bigger problems. *Harvard Business Review*. https://hbr.org/2023/05/ai-can-help-you-ask-better-questions-and-solve-bigger-problems?ab=hero-subleft-2

Gutiérrez, J. (2023) *Guidelines for the Use of Artificial Intelligence in University Courses*. Version 4.3, Universidad del Rosario. https://forogpp.files.wordpress.com/2023/02/guidelines-for-the-use-of-artificial-intelligence-in-university-courses-v4.3.pdf

IBM. (2010, May 18). *IBM 2010 Global CEO study: Creativity selected as most crucial factor for future success*. https://www.ibm.com/news/ca/en/2010/05/20/v384864m81427w34.html

Ignatius, A. (2014, December). Innovation on the fly. *Harvard Business Review*. https://hbr.org/2014/12/innovation-on-the-fly

Kelley, T., & Kelley, D. (2013). *Creative confidence: Unleashing the creative potential within us all*. Currency.

Kelly, T., & Kelly, D. (2013). *Creative confidence: Unleashing the creative potential within us all*. Penguin Random House LLC.

Kenworthy, J. B., Paulus, P. B., Minai, A. A., & Doboli, S. (2021). Divergent and convergent creativity. *Creativity and Innovation: Cognitive, Social, and Computational Approaches*, 69-98.

Khalifeh, T. (2023). Accounting in the age of Generative AI. *Strategic Finance*, October 2023, 55-64.

Levy, F., & Cannon, C. (2016, February 9). The Bloomberg job skills report 2016: What recruiters want. *Bloomberg*. https://www.bloomberg.com/graphics/2016-job-skills-report/

Livingston, L. (2010). Teaching creativity in higher education. *Arts Education Policy Review*, 111(2), 59–62. DOI:10.1080/10632910903455884

Lundaas, L. (2023). Top 7 use cases of generative AI in accounting. VIC.AI blog, May 15, https://www.vic.ai/resources/top-7-use-cases-of-generative-ai-in-accounting

Magni, F., Park, J., & Chao, M. M. (2023). Humans as creativity gatekeepers: Are we biased against AI creativity? *Journal of Business and Psychology*. Advance online publication. DOI:10.1007/s10869-023-09910-x

Mahama, I., Baidoo-Anu, D., Eshun, P., Ayimbire, B., & Eggley, V. E. (2023). ChatGPT in academic writing: A threat to human creativity and academic integrity? An exploratory study. *Indonesian Journal of Innovation and Applied Sciences*, 3(3), 228–239. DOI:10.47540/ijias.v3i3.1005

Meincke, L., Mollick, E. R., & Terwiesch, C. (2024). Prompting Diverse Ideas: Increasing AI Idea Variance. arXiv preprint, https://arxiv.org/abs/2402.01727

Mortlock, L., & Osiyevskyy, O. (2023). Strategic scenario planning in practice: Eight critical applications and associated benefits. *Strategy and Leadership*, 51(6), 22–29. DOI:10.1108/SL-08-2023-0090

Nerantzi, C., Abegglen, S., Karatsiori, M., & Martinez-Arboleda, A. (Eds.). (2023). 101 creative ideas to use AI in education. *A collection curated by #creativeHE*. Graphic design by Bushra Hashim. CC-BY-NC-SA 4.0

Osiyevskyy, O., Radnejad, A. B., & MahdaviMazdeh, H. (2020). An Entrepreneurial Management System for established companies. *Strategy and Leadership*, 48(2), 24–31. DOI:10.1108/SL-12-2019-0190

Powers, A. (2018, April 30). Creativity is the skill of the future. *Forbes*. https://www.forbes.com/sites/annapowers/2018/04/30/creativity-is-the-skill-of-the-future/?sh=63211de64fd4

PWC. (2017). *20th CEO Survey*. https://www.pwc.com/gx/en/ceo-survey/2017/pwc-ceo-20th-survey-report-2017.pdf

Reynolds, C., Stevens, D. D., & West, E. (2013). "I'm in a professional school! Why are you making me do this?" A cross-disciplinary study of the use of creative classroom projects on student learning. *College Teaching*, 61(2), 51–59. DOI:10.1080/87567555.2012.731660

Robinson, K. (2006, February). *Do schools kill creativity?* [video]. TED. https://www.ted.com/talks/sir_ken_robinson_do_schools_kill_creativity?

Rodriguez, D. (2017, February 2). Unleashing the Power of Boyle's Law. *LinkedIn Blog*.https://www.linkedin.com/pulse/boyles-law-diego-rodriguez/

Romera-Paredes, B., Barekatain, M., Novikov, A., Balog, M., Kumar, M. P., Dupont, E., & Fawzi, A. (2023). Mathematical discoveries from program search with large language models. *Nature*, 1-3. Advance online publication. DOI:10.1038/s41586-023-06924-6 PMID:38096900

Sarooghi, H., Libaers, D., & Burkemper, A. (2015). Examining the relationship between creativity and innovation: A meta-analysis of organizational, cultural, and environmental factors. *Journal of Business Venturing*, 30(5), 714–731. DOI:10.1016/j.jbusvent.2014.12.003

Shtepa, S., Bao, Y., & Osiyevskyy, O. (2023). The impact of artificial intelligence on management practice. In Cennamo, C., Dagnino, G. B., & Zhu, F. (Eds.), *Research Handbook on Digital Strategy* (pp. 324–341). Edward Elgar. DOI:10.4337/9781800378902.00027

Sosa, R., & Kayrouz, D. (2020). Creativity in graduate business education: Constitutive dimensions and connections. *Innovations in Education and Teaching International*, 57(4), 484–495. DOI:10.1080/14703297.2019.1628799

Stone, B. (2017). *The upstarts: Uber, Airbnb, and the battle for Silicon Valley*. Hachette Book Group.

Terwiesch, C., & Loch, C. H. (2004). Collaborative prototyping and the pricing of custom-designed products. *Management Science*, 50(2), 145–158. DOI:10.1287/mnsc.1030.0178

The Economist. (2014, June 28). *The digital degree*. https://www.economist.com/briefing/2014/06/27/the-digital-degree

Titus, P. A., & Koppitsch, S. (2018). Exploring business students' creative problem-solving preferences. *Journal of Education for Business*, 93(5), 242–251. DOI:10.1080/08832323.2018.1465021

Van Nuys, A. (2019, December 28). New LinkedIn research: Upskill your employees with the skill companies need most in 2020. *LinkedIn Learning Blog*. https://www.linkedin.com/business/learning/blog/learning-and-development/most-in-demand-skills-2020

Winkel, D., & Liguori, E. (2024, June 24). *From AI integration to AI co-creation*. AACSB. https://www.aacsb.edu/insights/articles/2024/06/from-ai-integration-to-ai-co-creation?

Zhang, Y., & Prebensen, N. K. (2024). Co-creating with ChatGPT for tourism marketing materials. *Annals of Tourism Research Empirical Insights*, 5(1), 100124. DOI:10.1016/j.annale.2024.100124

KEY TERMS AND DEFINITIONS

Artificial Intelligence (AI): The IT system (hardware, algorithms and software, and data) aimed at simulation of human intelligence, including rationalizing, making decisions, and learning from experience. AI systems also enable perception and processing of visual and audio information, and language translation.

Convergent Thinking: An individual or team-based cognitive process aimed at evaluating a set of ideas to find a single best solution to a problem that has a clear answer. It involves critical thinking, decision-making, and the evaluation of multiple alternatives to arrive at a solution that best fits the problem criteria.

Creativity: The cognitive process of developing original ideas (for solutions, products, processes) that are both novel and useful. It involves thinking that breaks away from established patterns or norms to generate innovative and original ideas. Creativity usually comprises two consecutive stages: divergent and convergent thinking.

Divergent Thinking: An individual or team-based cognitive process aimed at generating a large number of novel ideas. Can be done individually or in teams.

Generative Artificial Intelligence (GAI): A subset of AI aimed at creating new content, ideas, or data that were not explicitly programmed into the system. It involves AI algorithms capable of generating outputs such as text, images, sound and video by learning from a set of data inputs. GAI can produce novel and original content, making it particularly useful for tasks that require creativity and innovation.

Innovation: The application of new ideas, concepts, products, or processes that bring about significant improvements or create new value for the stakeholders. It goes beyond creativity by not only generating novel ideas but also successfully implementing them in a way that impacts markets, technologies, or society.

Large Language Model (LLM): A type of AI that processes, understands, and generates human language. These models are 'large' due to their extensive training on vast datasets of text, enabling them to perform a variety of language-related tasks like translation, summarization, and question-answering. LLMs are known for their ability to understand context and generate coherent and contextually relevant text.

ENDNOTES

1 2023: https://gbcroundtable.org/files/GBCRoundtable_2023CurriculumSurveyReport%20-%20May%201%202023.pdf 2021: https://www.mbaroundtable.org/files/SummaryReport_MBARoundtable_CurriculumSurvey2021.pdf

2 https://aiindex.stanford.edu/wp-content/uploads/2023/04/HAI_AI-Index-Report_2023.pdf

Chapter 16

What AI-Based Writing Assistant Actually Improved: Writing Quality or Writing Skills?

Sholihatul Hamidah Daulay
https://orcid.org/0000-0002-7660-8763
Universitas Islam Negeri Sumatera Utara, Indonesia

Hotma Berutu
Universitas Islam Negeri Sumatera Utara, Indonesia

Muhammad Dalimunte
https://orcid.org/0000-0003-2089-514X
Universitas Islam Negeri Sumatera Utara, Indonesia

Muhammad Muslim Nasution
Universitas Medan Area, Indonesia

Eka Apriani
Institut Agama Islam Negeri Curup, Indonesia

Muthmainnah Muthmainnah
https://orcid.org/0000-0003-3170-2374
Universitas Al-Asyariah Mandar, Indonesia

Shaumiwaty Shaumiwaty
Institut Agama Islam Negeri Takengon, Indonesia

ABSTRACT

Technological advancement has affected various aspects of human life. The existence of technology has made it easier for people, especially for the educational realm. This study aimed to find out what kinds of AI-based writing assistant used by students and the effect of utilizing the tools on students' English academic writing skills. Descriptive qualitative used as the research approach in this study. The participants of the study were 20 students of master's program in English Education who were

DOI: 10.4018/979-8-3693-2418-9.ch016

chosen purposively based on their experience in using AI as an assistant in English academic writing. The instruments employed for this study were questionnaire and semi-structured interview. This study came up with the findings that there are various AI-based writing tools used by the respondents. Interestingly, it is found that using AI-based writing assistant gives not only positive but also the negative impact on the students' academic writing skills. The users of AI writing tools need to be more selective and rely less on the AI writing tools in order to help them enhance not only their English academic writing quality but also writing competences.

INTRODUCTION

The presence of technology has given a huge change in human life, including education. It is now crucial to integrate technology in education to make it easier for the academic circles in carrying out their activities, both for learners and instructors as well as people who are involved in education. The integration of technology advancement in educational realm, particularly in English language teaching is considered as a basic needs to facilitate the teaching learning process to be better (Huang et al., 2022). According to Audrain et.al. (2022) in (Reimers, 2021), teacher and students can make a better class atmosphere by involving technology in the learning process. Through technology, students will be more enjoyable and can contribute more in teaching learning process. It is believed by putting technology in education can give more convenience in learning, both for teachers and learners (Hidayat et al., 2022). Moreover, the utilization of technology in education can assist teachers and students in delivering and perceiving the materials (Arif & Handayani, 2021). Therefore, it can be stated that the integration of technology in English language teaching can help and support the students, particularly in academic writing.

Writing is one of the compulsory proficiencies in English that need to be mastered besides reading, listening and speaking skill. According to UNESCO in (Steven, 2021), writing is one of the basic competences in lifelong study. Writing is a mode of communication that allows for the interpretation of information, the recording of experiences, self-expression, and the facilitation of important learning processes (Graham et al., 2013; Singaravelu et al., 2020). According to (Rahimi & Zhang, 2019), writing is considered as a complex, difficult, and emotive process. The English academic writing is such a problematic thing not only for non-native English learners but also for native and international learners (Campbell, 2019). The difficulties in academic writing are also supported by insufficient time of instructors in checking their students' writing. (Lim & Phua, 2019) stated that it needs a long in checking and giving valuable feedback on the learners' writing. As a result, there are still many students in higher education, particularly in Indonesia, who have not good competence in academic writing.

Due to the lack of competence in English academic writing, most of learner endeavour to find solution in order to make a better writing that worthy to be published. They try both in terms of human assistance (teachers/instructors) and also technology like Artificial Intelligence (AI). AI is a broad term that refers to automated technologies that can perform human-like intelligence processes such as learning, reasoning, and self-correction. (Popenici & Kerr, 2017). The main goal of AI is to create automated devices that can analyse, check and make correction just like humans do (Utami et al., 2023). The utilization of AI-based tools become more popular nowadays. The existence of AI is believed can be an alternative for students in English academic writing. AI-based writing assistant used as an automated writing evaluation (AWE), automated written corrective feedback (AWCF), and automated essay scoring (AES) (Utami et al., 2023).

There are various AI tools that can be utilized to support English academic writing. Interestingly, these tools can also be used not only in computer devices but also in mobile devices. This makes using the application become easier and more practical. Moreover, the AI tools can help and support students in doing their academic writing and it is easier to learn from it than from the traditional one. Based on the explanation stated previously, the researcher in this study is interested to conduct research in order to find out kinds of AI-based writing tools used by post graduate students in supporting their English academic writing. This present study also aims to investigate the impact of using AI-based writing assistant on the students' English academic writing skills.

There has been a spike study interest related to AI-based writing tools in some region, including Indonesia. However, the participants are still limited on certain level. (Gayed et al., 2022) in their research found that the utilization of AI-based writing tools can positively improve the learners' English academic writing skill for undergraduate students. Meanwhile, research by (Utami et al., 2023) only focused on 3 senior high school students as the participant. It is stated that AI-based writing assistant can definitely help students in improving their English academic writing skills. Another research comes from Zulfa et al. (2023) who also revealed that the AI-based writing tools can assist students in doing English academic writing skill. However, again, the participants only focused on higher education in undergraduate students.

Previous studies were just focused on senior high school students and higher education in undergraduate as the research participants. The findings also indicated that the utilization of AI-based writing assistant is moderately help learners in improving their English academic writing quality. Meanwhile, this present study chose master students in English education as the participants in order to give deeper research related to AI-based writing assistant for English academic writing. Furthermore, the participants are students who are now actively composing English academic work that will be published to a journal. Besides, this study is also aimed to investigate the impact of using AI-based writing assistance on the students' English academic writing, not only for the writing performance but the students' skill in English academic writing as well. The significance of this study is hopefully can be a reference to what extent the AI-based writing tools used in supporting the students' English academic writing. Furthermore, the findings of this study can be a consideration for them who are massively used AI as tools in helping on English academic writing to not rely too much on the AI-based writing tools in order to be more competence in writing professionally.

LITERATURE REVIEW

A written work's structure and content both play major roles in influencing the reader's comprehension and involvement (I. Lee & Yuan, 2021). Any written piece's content is its central idea. It contains the messages, ideas, and thoughts that the author want to get across. It is the writing's "what" or substance. Content that meets the audience's needs—whether they be to entertain, convince, educate, or stimulate thought—is considered high-quality when it is original, significant, relevant, and instructive (Molina et al., 2021). Organization, on the other hand, refers to the writing's structure or "how." It is the arrangement of the information, tying concepts together logically and coherently to lead the reader through the work.

How an argument is presented effectively, how well the reader understands the content, or how captivating a narrative is can all be greatly impacted by the organization. A seamless flow of ideas is ensured by good organization, which increases the writing's impact and readability (Awada et al., 2020). Thus, the importance of content and order in writing is overlooked when grammar and syntax are the only things being focused on. Effective communication depends not just on using the appropriate words but also on what those words communicate and how they are put together. Therefore, from the standpoint of EFL educators, it is imperative to investigate what kinds of AI writing tools are available and how they handle these other important writing components.

AI Writing Tools (AIWTs) are being utilized more often to support conventional writing techniques. Or, more specifically, ChatGPT can perform many activities in a single application, such creating an entire text, finishing a paragraph, editing a paragraph, paraphrasing, and altering formatting. Students can enhance their writing abilities in ways that might be challenging to do through conventional training methods with the use of these AI-powered writing tools, which are now accessible on mobile devices and the web. The way second language (L2) writing is approached is also changing as a result of this encouraging progress in the field of education (Nazari et al., 2021). (Barrot, 2021).

Garlinska et al. (2023) talk on how the field of writing instruction is changing, and how cloud-based writing tools, online workshops, and virtual classrooms are a few examples. Features like collaborative editing, plagiarism checks, and real-time feedback are available on these platforms. According to Nykyporets's (2023) study, these elements not only improve students' writing skills but also encourage critical thinking and autonomous reasoning in them. In this day of rapid technological growth, it is impossible to separate the evolution of writing instruction from the quick advancement of digital tools. The research by Haleem et al. (2022) eloquently discusses how this change is caused by the growing integration of digital tools in the educational space, which effectively turns paper and pen methods into significantly innovative and not static learning.

Writing abilities are so important to learning English, especially when learning the language as a second language (Brown, 2000; Celce-Murcia & Olshtain, 2000). Writers must engage in cognitive processes that involve thinking, just as speakers do (Hirvela & Belcher, 2016) and lexical density (Malvern et al., 2004; Yu, 2010). This is also true for writers (Brown, 2001: 336). Given that it calls for a methodical approach to problem solving and thought processes, it is a crucial procedure that supports the development of analytical skills (Jasper, 2005).Along with requiring the writer to confront their thoughts and give them more careful, cogent thought, writing also requires cognitive processes related to the production and manipulation of mental images.

Writing analysis and commentary on various aspects of the text, including syntax, vocabulary, grammar, content, and structure, are the general goals of AI writing tools (Hosseini et al., 2023; Strobl et al., 2019; Thorp, 2023). Machine-learning algorithms that compare the produced text to a large library of correctly and incorrectly written examples produce this kind of feedback. Stated differently, EFL students have the ability to receive immediate, customized feedback on their writing, which can help them recognize and fix errors more quickly. In addition to helping students understand the core ideas of successful writing, this real-time feedback can also provide them with guidance on how to improve their writing skills (Akgun & Greenhow, 2022; Nazari et al., 2021; Rudolph et al., 2023).

While some researchers (Kurniati & Fithriani, 2022; Wang, 2022; Zhao, 2022) have expressed concerns about the potential negative effects of these tools, others (Y. Liu et al., 2022; Lund & Wang, 2023; Qadir, 2022) have shown promise in improving students' writing skills through the use of AI-powered writing tools. However, all of the material that is offered concentrates on how AI writing tools can help with grammar and syntax. This is unquestionably an important component, but it only touches on a small portion of what makes writing effective. Additionally, the current study restricted the analysis to a single writing quality indicator. Contrarily, factors other than writing expertise are included in literature as indicators of writing quality. These factors include L2 proficiency (Cumming, 1989; Yanyan, 2010), motivation, interests, requirements, constraints, and opportunities (Scarcella and Oxford, 1992). Thus, several characteristics can be examined by researchers in the future as possible indicators of writing quality.

METHOD

This study used qualitative as the research methodology. Ary et.al (2002) stated that instead of dealing with numbers and statistics, qualitative research deals with data that is expressed in words. The data gathered are the experiences and perspectives of the subjects; qualitative research seeks to produce a more accurate depiction of the individuals, things, events, places, conversations, and so forth. Likewise, as highlighted by Creswell (2007), qualitative research involves the collection of a textual database, with data analysis revolving around the segmentation of information into sets of sentences. To elucidate, the researcher conveys the data by articulating descriptions in sentence form. Since the researcher analysed the questionnaire results and interview produced by the participants, the type of methodology in this study used was content analysis. According to Ary et.al (2002), content analysis is the approach of acquiring and examining the text's document. The content includes any message that can be conveyed by words, meaning, images, symbols, concepts, or themes. The researchers chose for a qualitative research methodology employing a content analysis approach to aid in providing a more comprehensive description of the limitations associated with the types of AI-based writing assistants utilized by students. Furthermore, the study aimed to examine the impact of using such tools on the English academic writing skills of students.

As many as twenty master students in English education from two universities in North Sumatera made as the research participant. The participants were chosen purposively based on their experience in using AI-based writing tools and they are now actively composing English academic writing for publication. Questionnaire and semi-structured interview were employed as the research instruments. As outlined by Creswell (2007: 382), a questionnaire is a survey design wherein participants complete and submit responses to the researcher. Consequently, participants opt to address queries and furnish fundamental personal or demographic details. The rationale behind choosing a questionnaire as the data collection method in this study lies in its capacity to extrapolate data from a sample to the broader population (Creswell, 2003). The researcher created the questionnaire by adapting ideas from previous studies' instruments (Utami et al., 2023) and modifying them to meet the objectives of this study. The questionnaires were prepared well to ensure the standard and quality of the questions before shared via online. The questionnaires focused on the participants' response related to what kind of AI-based writing tools used to support their English academic writing and the function of the tools as well.

The other instrument used was semi-structured interview. According to Dicicco-Bloom & Crabtree (2006), semi-structured interview furnishes interviewers with explicit instructions, ensuring the generation of dependable and comparable qualitative data. Similarly, Opdennaker (2006) elucidated that when there is a synchronous arrangement in time and place between the interviewer and interviewee, additional information beyond the verbal responses to posed questions can be provided by the interviewee.

The semi-structured interview was developed based on the respondents' response in the questionnaire. Bilingual semi-structured interviews were administered to willing participants in both Indonesian and English. Each interview session was allotted approximately 5 minutes. Owing to the availability and cost considerations of the participants, interviews were conducted at various times and locations. Because the main focus of this study was the content of the participants' responses rather than the way in which they provided the information, there was no transcription of any prosodic elements that occurred throughout the interviews. The interviews were meticulously transcribed and translated into English. Following that, all transcriptions were reviewed, re-read, and thoroughly examined, line by line, through description. Following the completion of the data collection procedures, the data was analysed in order to answer the research question. The researcher used several data analysis techniques to analyse the data, including: (1) reading and analysing all responses, (2) sorting the data, (3) organising, coding, and analysing the data, and (4) elaborating the data analysis to obtain the findings (Cresswell, 2007).

FINDINGS AND DISCUSSION

The data in this research was obtained from students' responses to both an online questionnaire and a semi-structured interview. The questionnaire items are focused on what kinds of AI-based writing tools used by master students in English education and the usefulness of the AI tools in enhancing students' English academic writing skills.

Open-ended questionnaire used as one of the research instruments in collecting the data. This questionnaire item focused on the participants' response related to what kind of AI-based writing tools are utilized to support their English academic writing. The result of open-ended questionnaire is presented in the following chart.

Figure 1. AI-Based Writing Assistant Used in English Academic Writing

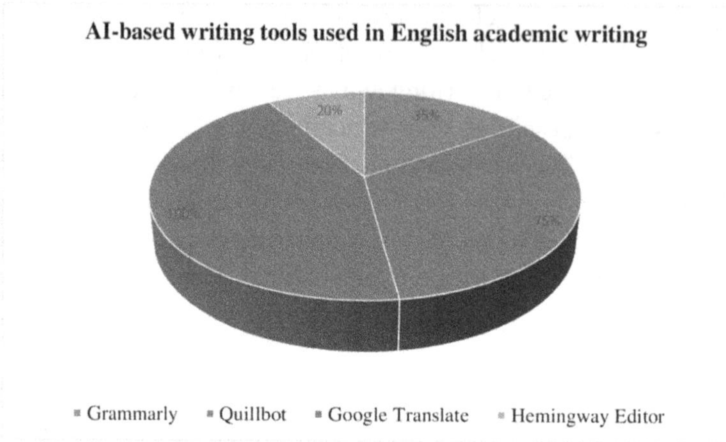

Based on the chart, there are four AI-based writing tools used by respondents in supporting their English academic writing. The most popular AI tools used is Google Translate (100%), followed by Quillbot (75%), Grammarly (35%), and the last is Hemingway Editor (20%). This data indicates that one participant can use more than one AI-based writing tools to power their English academic writing. In other words, one student can use more than one AI tools in helping them improve their English academic writing quality. The data revealed that all the participants (20 students) use Google Translate (GT) as an assistant in writing, particularly used to find out difficult words. Means, all respondents utilized GT to translate English words into Indonesia and vice versa.

To look for tricky words in both English and Indonesia, I frequently use Google Translate. Google Translate, in my opinion, is quite straightforward and offers a wide range of language options. (Excerpt 1)

I've been utilizing GT for an extended period, and I find it highly beneficial. It allows me to swiftly and effortlessly identify unfamiliar words. Additionally, I appreciate the convenience of not having to carry printed dictionaries since GT is accessible on my mobile phone, enabling me to use it anytime and anywhere. It's worth noting, though, that having an internet connection is essential for utilizing GT. (Excerpt 4)

I used Google Translate because it is free and simple to use. As long as the device is connected to the internet, the users just need to type unfamiliar words and AI will display me the meaning right away. (Excerpt 2)

I greatly appreciate Google Translate as a translation tool. It enables me to translate individual words, sentences, paragraphs, or entire texts, and the best part is that it's free. I can utilize Google Translate for translation purposes anytime I have an internet connection, without the need to download or install the application on my mobile phone. (Excerpt 8).

Users can simply search the meaning of unfamiliar words through Google Translate because it is commonly used as an online dictionary. This finding is in line with (Berutu et al., 2023), stating that students tend to use Google Translate to translate simple word level such as word, collocation and phrase rather than longer sentences or paragraph. Another AI-based writing tool used is Quilbot. As many as 15 students utilized it in their English academic writing. Quillbot serves as an artificial intelligence paraphraser. Users enter sentences that need to be paraphrased based on their requirements, and the results will be available soon.

Quillbot is one of my AI-based writing tools that I frequently use to help me rephrase lines and paragraphs in English. Quillbot gives its users a plethora of paraphrase options. Users simply need to click 'paraphrase' several times to select the best paraphrase that the Quillbot provided. (Excerpt 3)

Having incorporated Quillbot into my process of composing articles for college assignments, I have experienced an increase in confidence and a reduction in over-thinking, particularly concerning grammar and content. Prior to using Quillbot, my writing often left me uncertain. Presently, I find myself inclined to read and appreciate the neatness in both language and structure of the compositions I produce, fostering a sense of achieving a native-like quality in my writing (Excerpt 2).

Quillbot is an excellent English writing assistant for me. The web-based application offers a variety of free and premium services. For me, the free features are more than adequate because the free mode has provided a variety of elements that have assisted me in improving my English writing performance. (Excerpt 4)

At the start of the semester, I faced uncertainty about how to initiate academic writing. The necessity for a bodynote in academic writing posed a challenge since my approach was predominantly copy-pasting, leading to a significant plagiarism level in my work. This circumstance led to frustration and a lack of motivation when attempting to compose academic papers. The application brought joy to my writing process, making it an enjoyable experience by aiding in paraphrasing through synonym replacement, adjusting writing structures, and employing various methods (Excerpt 5).

Based on the participants' response, it can be inferred that Quillbot is significantly influence the English writing performance through some paraphrase features provide by the application. Kurniati & Fithriani (2022) revealed that Quillbot has an important role in enhancing students' English academic writing quality. Grammarly has the third highest percentage (7 students). Grammarly is another prominent AI-powered writing tool. Grammarly is said to be able to boost students' English academic writing proficiency due to the application's suggestions. Users must simply choose whether or not to accept Grammarly's suggestion/correction.

Grammarly assists me in improving my English academic writing performance because I may select the best correction supplied by the application directly. I also find Grammarly particularly advantageous when I upload my files, as it provides direct suggestions that can be implemented with a simple click on the revision option within Grammarly. It also automatically makes changes in our writing, enhancing the overall quality. (Excerpt 5)

Grammarly aids me in automatically correcting my spelling, eliminating the need for me to search for the correct spelling of words in the dictionary. It highlights the mistake words/sentences in distinct colours, so I can see them right away. (Excerpt 3)

Grammarly can directly identify errors in my thesis writing, particularly pinpointing my grammar mistakes. It aids me in rectifying these errors by providing constructive feedback. Additionally, Grammarly assists me in reviewing my punctuation usage, as there are instances when I overlook incorporating punctuation marks in my writing. (Excerpt 6)

This research reveals that participants have a favourable opinion of Grammarly as an AI-based writing help in English academic writing. This evidence backs up (Fitria, 2021; Maulidina & Wibowo, 2022) claiming that Grammarly can increase students' English writing quality moderately. Hemingway Editor is the latest AI-based writing assistant utilized by respondents. Four students reported that they utilize Hemingway Editor as an AI-based writing help in English academic writing. This web-based app works similarly to Grammarly in that users are provided suggestions and corrections for incorrect words/sentences. The difference is that Hemingway Editor includes a grading system for sentences that must be analysed and repaired by the application.

In my experience, Hemingway Editor proves to be a valuable writing tool for refining my writing style. The free online platform is particularly effective for editing shorter pieces. Furthermore, when I find myself writing longer and more intricate sentences, Hemingway motivates me to enhance clarity and conciseness in my writing. Additionally, it serves as a useful tool for evaluating the readability and complexity of my work. (Excerpt 11).

Even though I am not an active user of Hemingway Editor, I believe this web-based tool is extremely beneficial in boosting the quality of my English academic writing. However, I was occasionally perplexed by the app's suggestions/corrections. I mean, sometimes the correction is less precise, resulting in uncertainty in the sentences. (Excerpt 7)

Based on the response, it can be stated that using Hemingway Editor besides give positive effect, it also gives the negative one. The users need to be more selective in choosing the best correction offered by the application. However, it cannot be denied that the Hemingway editor can significantly help students in enhancing their English writing skill. It is line with (Chairil Imran, 2022) stating that applying Hemingway application can significantly influence the quality of students' English academic writing.

Another research instrument employed in this study is close-ended questionnaire. The followings presented the data obtained from questionnaire related to the usefulness of the AI-based writing tools for the students following by the interviews. The questionnaire used Likert scale (SA: Strongly agree; A: Agree; D: Disagree; & SD: Strongly disagree).

Table 1. Respondents' responses on the questionnaires

No	Statement	SA	A	DA	SDA
1	My performance in writing is better using AI-based writing tools	80%	20%	-	-
2	My writing skills are improved using AI-based writing tools	30%	20%	30%	20%
3	The quality of my writing is moderately improved using AI-based writing tools	70%	30%	-	-
4	It is flexible and accessible to use AI-based writing tools	60%	40%	-	-
5	There are various features on AI-based writing tools	30%	50%	20%	-
6	I love using AI-based writing tools in helping my English academic writing.	80%	20%	-	-
7	Using AI-based writing tools makes me more motivated in writing..	20%	40%	30%	10%

Based on the questionnaire results, it is found that most of the respondents tend to share positive responses related to the utilization of AI-based writing tools on their English academic writing. However, it cannot be denied that some participants also revealed the negative impact on using AI-based writing tools. Therefore, the researcher in this study classified the questionnaire results into positive and negative impact. In the positive side, more than half of respondents said that utilizing AI-based writing tools increased their writing quality. Questionnaire items 1 and 3 suggest that over a hundred percent (80% and 70%, respectively) strongly agree that

AI-based writing tools can improve their English writing performance. Nobody on the 'disagree and strongly disagree' side agreed with these claims. subsequently is, all of the respondents had a favourable attitude toward using AI-based writing tools to assist them with their English academic writing.

My ability to develop my ideas further has been positively impacted by AI writing tools. More often than not, these technologies provide users with several methods to more effectively articulate their ideas by providing phrases or sentences that build upon an initial notion. Furthermore, these resources can show how a concept can be expanded upon and supported by arguments or facts; this is very helpful when writing professionally. (Excerpt 7)

My writing performance has improved after adopting AI-based writing tools. My writing language is great, and I never expected to be able to write that well. (Excerpt 8).

By providing ideas and expanding on them, AI writing tools have been crucial in helping me become more creative. These resources can offer different viewpoints or angles when I'm stuck or experiencing writer's block, which helps me get past obstacles in my creative process. (Excerpt 9).

Based on the data, it can be inferred that the result offered by AI-based writing assistant is out the users' expectation. In other words, the quality of students' English academic writing is moderately improved. Chen & Wei (2021), stated that students' writing quality is overall improved powered by AI-based writing assistant.

AI writing tools are extremely helpful for arranging arguments, identifying logical errors, and fostering effective communication. I can correct mistakes and acquire insights in real time thanks to their prompt comments, which helps me better understand the fundamentals of excellent writing. (Excerpt 6)

Questionnaire items 4 and 6 also received positive responses on the use of AI-based writing tools. According to questionnaire 4, no one of the participants is on the 'disagree and strongly disagree' side. As much as 60% and 40% of respondents, respectively, are on the 'strongly agree and agree' side, claiming that the use of AI-based writing tools is flexible and accessible.

I can immediately access the AI-based writing tools because they can be used on both computer and mobile devices. I may instantly access the web-based program via my mobile phone and surf what I need to know and work on my writing. (Excerpt 9).

According to the response, AI tools can be accessed everywhere and at any time as long as the device has an internet connection. Because of the flexibility of computer and mobile devices, the use of AI tools has grown increasingly effective. In addition, questionnaire item 6 discovered that the 'strongly agree' and 'agree' sides are as high as 80% and 20%, respectively. It implies that respondents are interested in using AI-based writing tools to help them with their English academic writing. Questionnaire item 2 has the lowest percentage of favourable responses to the use of AI-based writing tools. Only half of the participants believe AI-based writing tools can help them enhance their English writing skills. This means that 50% of respondents stated that AI tools had no substantial effect on their English academic writing skills. In other words, while the existence of an AI-based writing aid is believed to boost writing performance, it does not always have a favourable impact on users' English academic writing skills.

I've found that using AI writing tools has had varying results on my ability to come up with ideas. On the one hand, they can serve as a springboard for me when I'm having trouble coming up with ideas. But sometimes the tool's ideas come off as overly general or impersonal. As such, they might not always inspire me to think carefully or critically about a subject, even though they can be useful in some situations. (Excerpt 14)

I've become more casual with my writing. I mean, when I utilize AI tools on my writing, I sometimes completely accept the application's suggestion/correction. As a result, my ability to write English academically has not improved. In doing my English academic writing, I've gotten overly reliant on AI tools. I am aware that my writing performance may be better, but not for my English academic writing skills. (Excerpt 10).

I've found that sometimes using AI writing tools can make it harder for me to come up with creative ideas. This might be explained by my reliance on the tool's recommendations, which made me stop challenging myself to think creatively. In certain cases, I think it would be better for me to work on coming up with ideas and solving problems because I know these are useful abilities that can be improved with regular practice. (Excerpt 13)

According to the responses of the participants, the existence of AI-based writing tools does not aid all students in terms of skills. In contrast, other respondents stated that their writing skills have deteriorated as a result of their reliance on web-based applications. It is undeniably a critical issue, as the existence of AI technologies causes students to stagnate or stop progressing in English academic writing. Kornfeld & Roy (2021) stated that the users of AI-based writing tools fail to develop their own writing skills due to the high dependency on the AI tools. In relation to questionnaire item 5, it was discovered that up to 80% of respondents claimed that AI-based writing tools such as Grammarly and Quillbot give diverse features. However, 20% of participants stated that the AI tool lacked functionality such as Google Translate.

The AI-based writing I used is diverse. It means that each tool has its own set of features. I believe that we should not compare the characteristics of each tool. Quillbot and Grammarly both offer a variety of functionality dependent on the needs of the user, with free and paid versions available. For Google Translate, for example, there are no features other than language selection. (Excerpt 11).

Although these tools can offer me a broader range of sophisticated vocabulary, there is a risk of employing these words without a complete grasp of their context or connotations. This may result in sentences that sound awkward or excessively formal. (Excerpt 8)

Item 7 is the final questionnaire in this investigation. According to the study, as many as 60% of respondents stated that utilizing AI-based writing tools has greatly motivated them to write.

AI writing tools have played a pivotal role in enhancing my writing skills, particularly in crafting pieces that are logically cohesive and well-flowing. Through grammar suggestions, improved vocabulary use, and the assurance of logical consistency in arguments, these tools have served effectively as individualized writing mentors. (Excerpt 12)

I enjoy employing an AI-based writing help. Sometimes the sentences or paragraphs I write are redundant. Long sentences can be reduced without compromising the sense when using AI-based writing tools. Furthermore, the terminology is more scientific. (Excerpt 12)

The use of AI writing tools has clearly improved my vocabulary selection, in my opinion. Synonyms and more sophisticated words that I might not have thought of on my own are regularly suggested by these techniques. As a result, I am able to express myself more complexly and captivatingly by using a wider variety of vocabulary. Gradually, my writing becomes increasingly refined and complex. (Excerpt 10)

However, it is also found that as much as 40% of the respondents stated that they are not motivated in writing using AI-based writing assistant. It indicates that their willingness in writing is not improved after using the AI-based writing tools.

Certainly, there's a discernible enhancement in how I incorporate transition words and phrases since integrating AI writing tools. My sentences exhibit improved flow, showcasing clearer connections between ideas and implying a heightened comprehension of cohesion in writing. However, it's important to acknowledge that, conversely, there is a potential downside of excessive reliance on these tools, which could impede my personal creativity and unique writing styles. Like any technology, the crucial aspect lies in maintaining a balanced usage and receiving ongoing guidance. (Excerpt 16)

I'm not very driven to write now that I've used AI-powered writing tools. Personally, I only create and utilize the AI tool because it is required for a routine project. So I don't believe there has been a substantial change in my willingness to write. (Excerpt 13).

AI writing tools serve as beneficial learning resources for acquiring and applying new vocabulary. Nevertheless, there is a potential drawback wherein users may excessively depend on these tools and neglect the effort to memorize and autonomously incorporate the newly learned words into their usage. (Excerpt 1)

Based on this data, it can be concluded that not all respondents' writing motivation improved after utilizing the AI-based writing assistance. The respondents' positive and negative effects are based on their motivation to undertake English academic writing (Krajcik and Kim (2020).

CONCLUSION

The use of AI-based writing assistants has gained popularity in the academic community, particularly in higher education. The presence of AI-based writing tools benefits many sectors of academic circles, especially those who actively compose English academic writing for publication. Grammarly, Quillbot, Google Translate (GT), and Hemingway Editor are some of the AI-based writing tools that students in higher education utilize to improve their English academic writing quality. AI writing assistants can significantly contribute to writing improvement also, they are not a substitute for a deep understanding of language, style, and context. Users are encouraged to critically evaluate the suggestions provided and actively engage with the learning opportunities offered by these tools. Additionally, human feedback and continuous practice remain essential for developing strong writing skills.

AI-based writing tools are thought to be extremely beneficial in increasing the quality of students' English academic writing. After utilizing AI-based tools, writing performance has greatly improved. Furthermore, the web-based application is adaptable and simple to use, allowing users to include it into their English academic writing. Despite the beneficial effects of employing AI-based writing tools, it has been discovered that the AI tools do not considerably improve students' English academic writing skills. It is true that the performance of the writing is getting better but not for the students' skill in English academic writing. The students are not motivated to write eve after using the AI tools. Surprisingly, students who rely too heavily on AI tools tend to stagnate or stop improving in English academic writing. As a result, individuals frequently follow what the AI tools recommend for their writing without rethinking the optimal language context for their academic writing. Therefore, it is important to be noted so that the users of AI tools become more selective and rely less on the AI tools in supporting their English academic writing.

REFERENCES

Adelita, D., Kurniati, E. Y., & Daulay, S. H. (2023). Difficulties and Strategies in Producing English Writing Text: What do EFL Students' Perceive? What do EFL Students' Perceive? *Education and Human Development Journal*, 8(1), 93–108. DOI:10.33086/ehdj.v8i1.3698

Akgun, S., & Greenhow, C. (2022). Artificial intelligence in education: Addressing ethical challenges in K-12 settings. *AI and Ethics*, 2(3), 431–17. DOI:10.1007/s43681-021-00096-7 PMID:34790956

Al Arif, T. Z. Z., & Handayani, R. (2021). Factors Influencing the Use of ICT for English Language Learning of Indonesian EFL University Students. *Elsya : Journal of English Language Studies*, 4(1), 24–33. DOI:10.31849/elsya.v4i1.6882

Ary, D., & Jacobs, L. (2002). *Introduction to Research in Education* (6th ed.). SAGE Publication.

Audrain, R. L., Weinberg, A. E., Bennett, A., O'Reilly, J., & Basile, C. G. (2022). Ambitious and Sustainable Post-Pandemic Workplace Design for Teachers: A Portrait of the Arizona Teacher Workforce. In Reimers, F. M. (Ed.), *Primary and Secondary Education During Covid-19 Disruptions to Educational Opportunity During a Pandemic* (pp. 353–382). Springer. DOI:10.1007/978-3-030-81500-4_14

Barrot, J. S. (2021). Using automated written corrective feedback in the writing classrooms: Effects on L2 writing accuracy. *Computer Assisted Language Learning*, 1–24. DOI:10.1080/09588221.2021.1936071

Berutu, H., Dewi, U., & Daulay, S. H. (2023). Post-Graduate Students ' Perceptions on the Utilization of Google Translate. *International Conference on English Language Teaching, 4*(1), 80–86. https://conference.unisma.ac.id/index.php/ICON/ICON-ELT

Bockting, C. L. (2023). ChatGPT: Five priorities for research. *Nature*, 614(7947), 224–226. DOI:10.1038/d41586-023-00288-7 PMID:36737653

Campbell, M. (2019). Teaching Academic Writing in Higher Education. *Education Quarterly Eeview*, 2(3), 608–614. DOI:10.31014/aior.1993.02.03.92

Chairil Imran, M. (2022). *Applying Hemingway App to Enhance Students' Writing Skill.* https://jurnal-eureka.com/index.php/edulecj

Cresswell, J. W. (2007). *Qualitative Inquiry & Research Design: Choosing Among Five Approaches.* Sage.

Creswell, J. W. (2003). *Research design: Qualitative, quantitative and mixed approaches* (2nd ed.). Sage.

Dicicco-Bloom, B., & Crabtree, B. F. (2006). The qualitative research interview. *Medical Education*, 40(4), 314–321. DOI:10.1111/j.1365-2929.2006.02418.x PMID:16573666

Fitria, T. N. (2021). Grammarly as AI-powered English Writing Assistant: Students' Alternative for Writing English. *Metathesis: Journal of English Language, Literature, and Teaching*, 5(1), 65. DOI:10.31002/metathesis.v5i1.3519

Garlinska, M., Osial, M., Proniewska, K., & Pregowska, A. (2023). The influence of emerging technologies on distance education. *Electronics (Basel)*, 12(7), 1550. DOI:10.3390/electronics12071550

Gayed, J. M., Carlon, M. K. J., Oriola, A. M., & Cross, J. S. (2022). Exploring an AI-based writing Assistant's impact on English language learners. *Computers and Education: Artificial Intelligence, 3*(October), 100055. DOI:10.1016/j.caeai.2022.100055

Graham, S., Gillespie, A., & McKeown, D. (2013). Writing: Importance, development, and instruction. *Reading and Writing*, 26(1), 1–15. DOI:10.1007/s11145-012-9395-2

Haleem, A., Javaid, M., & Singh, R. P. (2022). An era of ChatGPT as a significant futuristic support tool: A study on features, abilities, and challenges. *BenchCouncil Transactions on Benchmarks. Standards and Evaluations*, 2(4), 100089. DOI:10.1016/j.tbench.2023.100089

Hidayat, D. N., Lee, J. Y., Mason, J., & Khaerudin, T. (2022). Digital technology supporting English learning among Indonesian university students. *Research and Practice in Technology Enhanced Learning*, 17(1), 23. Advance online publication. DOI:10.1186/s41039-022-00198-8 PMID:35693547

Huang, F., Qi, J., & Xie, A. (2022). Sustaining Teaching with Technology after the Quarantine: Evidence from Chinese EFL Teachers' Technological, Pedagogical and Content Knowledge. *Sustainability (Basel)*, 14(14), 8774. Advance online publication. DOI:10.3390/su14148774

Hz, L., & Sarumaha, S. (2023). Navigating English Writing Proficiency Tests in the Era of Artificial Intelligence. *Journal of English Education and Teaching*, 7(3), 480–498. DOI:10.33369/jeet.7.3.480-498

Kurniati, E. Y., & Fithriani, R. (2022). Post-Graduate Students' Perceptions of Quillbot Utilization in English Academic Writing Class. *Journal of English Language Teaching and Linguistics*, 7(3), 437. DOI:10.21462/jeltl.v7i3.852

Lim, F. V., & Phua, J. (2019). Teaching Writing with Language Feedback Technology. *Computers and Composition, 54*(June). DOI:10.1016/j.compcom.2019.102518

Maulidina, P., & Wibowo, H. (2022). the Use of Grammarly Tools To Enrich Student'S Writing Ability. *Lingua*, 18(2), 179–189. DOI:10.34005/lingua.v18i2.2246

Nasution, A. H., Daulay, S. H., & Dewi, U. (2023). Using Rosetta Stone Application as a Mobile Assited Language Learning (MALL) in EFL: Documentary Study. *Scope: Journal of English Language Teaching, 8*(1), 8-13.

Nazari, N., Shabbir, M. S., & Setiawan, R. (2021). Application of Artificial Intelligence powered digital writing assistant in higher education: Randomized controlled trial. *Heliyon*, 7(5), e07014. DOI:10.1016/j.heliyon.2021.e07014 PMID:34027198

Nykyporets, S. S. (2023). Harnessing cloud technologies for foreign language acquisition among masters in energy engineering. *Moderní aspekty vědy: Svazek XXXI mezinárodní*, 21–56. http://ir.lib.vntu.edu.ua/handle/123456789/37121

Popenici, S. A. D., & Kerr, S. (2017). Exploring the impact of artificial intelligence on teaching and learning in higher education. *Research and Practice in Technology Enhanced Learning*, 12(1), 22. Advance online publication. DOI:10.1186/s41039-017-0062-8 PMID:30595727

Qadir, J. (2022). Engineering education in the era of ChatGPT: Promise and pitfalls of generative AI for education. *TechRxiv*. Preprint. DOI:10.36227/techrxiv.21789434.v1

Rahimi, M., & Zhang, L. J. (2019). Writing task complexity, students' motivational beliefs, anxiety and their writing production in English as a second language. *Reading and Writing*, 32(3), 761–786. DOI:10.1007/s11145-018-9887-9

Reimers, F. M. (2021). Primary and Secondary Education During Covid-19: Disruptions to Educational Opportunity During a Pandemic. *Primary and Secondary Education During Covid-19: Disruptions to Educational Opportunity During a Pandemic*, 1–475. DOI:10.1007/978-3-030-81500-4

Samosir, S. A., & Daulay, S. H. (2023). EFL Students' Perception of the use "Grammarly Application" as Automated Writing Evaluation (AWE). *Conference on English Language Teaching*, 928–940. Retrieved from https://proceedings.uinsaizu.ac.id/index.php/celti/article/view/562

Sari, W., & Daulay, S. H. (2023). Analysis of Teacher's Feedback on Students in Writing Recount Text at Senior High School. *ENGLISH FRANCA: Academic Journal of English Language and Education*, 7(1), 93–104. DOI:10.29240/ef.v7i1.6442

Singaravelu, G., Peter, J., & Singaravelu, G. (2020). Problems in Writing in English among High School Learners. *Aegaeum Journal, 8*(9), 1502–1515. https://www.researchgate.net/publication/351048985

Steven, D. (2021). AI In Education Change at the speed of Learning. *Unesco, 12*(1), 70. https://dialnet.unirioja.es/servlet/tesis?codigo=286366%0Ahttp://www.tdx.cat/bitstream/handle/10803/85876/GONZALES_Tesis Doctoral_FV.pdf?sequence=1%0Ahttps://unesdoc.unesco.org/ark:/48223/pf0000368303%0Ahttps://ec.europa.eu/jrc/en/publication/eur-scientific-and

Suryani, I., & Daulay, S. H. (2022). Students' Perceptions on Writing Activities by Using Padlet Application. *The Proceedings of English Language Teaching, Literature, and Translation*, 11, 175–188.

Utami, S. P. T., Andayani, A., Winarni, R., & Sumarwati, S. (2023). Utilization of artificial intelligence technology in an academic writing class: How do Indonesian students perceive? *Contemporary Educational Technology*, 15(4), ep450. DOI:10.30935/cedtech/13419

Wagner, G., Lukyanenko, R., & Paré, G. (2022). Artificial intelligence and the conduct of literature reviews. *Journal of Information Technology*, 37(2), 209–226. DOI:10.1177/02683962211048201

Zhao, X. (2022). Leveraging artificial intelligence (AI) technology for English writing: Introducing wordtune as a digital writing assistant for EFL writers. *RELC Journal*, 0(0), 1–5. DOI:10.1177/00336882221094089

Zulfa, S., Sari Dewi, R., Nuruddin Hidayat, D., Hamid, F., & Defianty, M. (2023). The Use of AI and Technology Tools in Developing Students' English Academic Writing Skills. *The Annual International Conference on Education*, 47–63.

Compilation of References

Abbas, M., Jam, F. A., & Khan, T. I. (2024). Is it harmful or helpful? Examining the causes and consequences of generative AI usage among university students. *International Journal of Educational Technology in Higher Education*, 21(1), 10. DOI:10.1186/s41239-024-00444-7

Abdulrahaman, M. D., Faruk, N., Oloyede, A. A., Surajudeen-Bakinde, N. T., Olawoyin, L. A., Mejabi, O. V., Imam-Fulani, Y. O., Fahm, A. O., & Azeez, A. L. (2020). Multimedia tools in the teaching and learning processes: A systematic review. *Heliyon*, 6(11), e05312. DOI:10.1016/j.heliyon.2020.e05312 PMID:33195834

Abowd, G. D., Atkeson, C. G., Feinstein, A., Hmelo, C., Kooper, R., Long, S., & Tani, M. (1997, February). Teaching and learning as multimedia authoring: the classroom 2000 project. In *Proceedings of the Fourth ACM International Conference on Multimedia* (pp. 187-198).

Abuhassna, H., Al-Rahmi, W. M., Yahya, N., Zakaria, M. A. Z. M., Kosnin, A. B. M., & Darwish, M. (2020). Development of a new model on utilizing online learning platforms to improve students' academic achievements and satisfaction. *International Journal of Educational Technology in Higher Education*, 17(1), 1–23. DOI:10.1186/s41239-020-00216-z

Adair, A. (2023). *Teaching and Learning with AI: How Artificial Intelligence is Transforming the Future of Education* (Vol. 29). ACM New York.

Adekunle, S. E., Adewale, O. S., & Boyinbode, O. K. (2019). Appraisal on perceived multimedia technologies as modern pedagogical tools for strategic improvement on teaching and learning. *International Journal of Modern Education and Computer Science*, 11(8), 15. DOI:10.5815/ijmecs.2019.08.02

Adelita, D., Kurniati, E. Y., & Daulay, S. H. (2023). Difficulties and Strategies in Producing English Writing Text: What do EFL Students' Perceive? What do EFL Students' Perceive? *Education and Human Development Journal*, 8(1), 93–108. DOI:10.33086/ehdj.v8i1.3698

Adeoye, M. A. (2024, January). Education in flux: nurturing minds for the future. *Proceeding of International Conference on Education, Society and Humanity, 2*(1), 73-82.

Adil, S., & Hamid, K. B. A. (2019). The relationships between leader creativity expectations, intrinsic motivation, and creative performance. *SEISENSE Journal of Management*, 2(2), 58–68. DOI:10.33215/sjom.v2i2.123

Afolabi, M. O., Dionne, S., & Lewis, H. (2009, November 18). *Are we there yet? A review of creativity methodologies* [Paper presentation]. American Society for Engineering Education St. Lawrence Section Conference, Cornell University, New York, NY, United States. Retrieved December 2, 2023, from https://www.cs.cornell.edu/Conferences/ASEE2006/ASEE%20Papers/Session%204/ASEE%20Final%20vs%203_Afolabi.pdf

Ahmad, K., Iqbal, W., El-Hassan, A., Qadir, J., Benhaddou, D., Ayyash, M., & Al-Fuqaha, A. (2023). Data-driven artificial intelligence in education: A comprehensive review. *IEEE Transactions on Learning Technologies*.

Ahmad, N., Murugesan, S., & Kshetri, N. (2023). Generative artificial intelligence and the education sector. *Computer*, 56(6), 72–76. DOI:10.1109/MC.2023.3263576

Ahuja, R. (2019). Impact of artificial intelligence on higher education. In *Artificial Intelligence in Higher Education* (pp. 39–52). Springer.

Akgün, S., & Greenhow, C. (2021). Artificial intelligence in education: Addressing ethical challenges in K-12 settings. *AI and Ethics*, 2(3), 431–440. DOI:10.1007/s43681-021-00096-7 PMID:34790956

Al Arif, T. Z. Z., & Handayani, R. (2021). Factors Influencing the Use of ICT for English Language Learning of Indonesian EFL University Students. *Elsya : Journal of English Language Studies*, 4(1), 24–33. DOI:10.31849/elsya.v4i1.6882

Alabbasi, A. M. A., Paek, S. H., Kim, D., & Cramond, B. (2022). What do educators need to know about the Torrance Tests of Creative Thinking: A comprehensive review. *Frontiers in Psychology*, 13, 1000385. Advance online publication. DOI:10.3389/fpsyg.2022.1000385 PMID:36389550

Alamri, H. A., Watson, S., & Watson, W. (2021). Learning technology models that support personalization within blended learning environments in higher education. *TechTrends*, 65(1), 62–78. DOI:10.1007/s11528-020-00530-3

Alier, M., García-Peñalvo, F., & Camba, J. D. (2024). Generative Artificial Intelligence in Education: From Deceptive to Disruptive. *International Journal of Interactive Multimedia and Artificial Intelligence,* 8(5), 5-14.

Ali, M., Murray, P., Momin, M., Dwivedi, Y., & Malik, T. (2024). The effects of artificial intelligence applications in educational settings: Challenges and strategies. *Technological Forecasting and Social Change*, 199, 1–18. DOI:10.1016/j.techfore.2023.123076

Ali, N. A., Eassa, F., & Hamed, E. (2019). Personalized learning style for adaptive e-learning system. *International Journal of Advanced Trends in Computer Science and Engineering*, 8(1), 223–230.

Ali, S., Ravi, P., Williams, R., DiPaola, D., & Breazeal, C. (2024, March). Constructing dreams using generative AI. *Proceedings of the AAAI Conference on Artificial Intelligence*, 38(21), 23268–23275. DOI:10.1609/aaai.v38i21.30374

Amabile, T., & Khaire, M. (2008). *Creativity and the role of the leader*. Harvard Business Review. Retrieved December 2, 2023, from https://hbr.org/2008/10/creativity-and-the-role-of-the-leader

Amabile, T. M. (1996). *Creativity in Context: Update to the social psychology of creativity*. Westview Press.

Amabile, T. M. (2018). *Creativity in context: Update to the social psychology of creativity*. Routledge. DOI:10.4324/9780429501234

Amabile, T. M., & Pratt, M. G. (2016). The dynamic componential model of creativity and innovation in organizations: Making progress, making meaning. *Research in Organizational Behavior*, 36(5), 157–183. DOI:10.1016/j.riob.2016.10.001

Amano, T., Ramirez-Castaneda, V., Berdejo-Espinola, V., Borokini, I., Chowdhury, S., Golivets, M., González-Trujillo, J. D., Montaño-Centellas, F., Paudel, K., White, R. L., & Veríssimo, D. (2023). The Manifold Costs of Being a Non-Native English Speaker in Science. *PLoS Biology*, 21(7), e3002184. DOI:10.1371/journal.pbio.3002184 PMID:37463136

Amit Kumar Tyagi. (2024). *Shrikant Tiwari, The Future of Artificial Intelligence in Blockchain Applications, in book title: Machine Learning Algorithms Using Scikit and TensorFlow Environments*. IGI Global. DOI:10.4018/978-1-6684-8531-6.ch018

Amit Kumar Tyagi. (2024). *Transformative Effects of ChatGPT on the Modern Era of Education and Society: From Society's and Industry's Perspectives, in book title: Machine Learning Algorithms Using Scikit and TensorFlow Environments.* IGI Global. DOI:10.4018/978-1-6684-8531-6.ch019

Amornkitpinyo, T., Yoosomboon, S., Sopapradit, S., & Amornkitpinyo, P. (2021). The structural equation model of actual use of cloud learning for higher education students in the 21st century. *Journal of E-Learning and Knowledge Society*, 17(1), 72–80.

Anantrasirichai, N., & Bull, D. (2022). Artificial Intelligence in the creative industries: A review. *Artificial Intelligence Review*, 55(1), 89–656. DOI:10.1007/s10462-021-10039-7

Anderson, C. A., & Dill, K. E. (2020). Video games and aggressive thoughts, feelings, and behaviour in the laboratory and life. *Journal of Personality and Social Psychology*, 78(4), 772–790. DOI:10.1037/0022-3514.78.4.772 PMID:10794380

Anderson, L. W., & Krathwohl, D. R. (Eds.). (2001). *A taxonomy for learning, teaching, and assessing: A revision of Bloom's Taxonomy of Educational Objectives*. Longman.

Anderson, N., Potočnik, K., & Zhou, J. (2014). Innovation and creativity in organizations: A state-of-the-science review, prospective commentary, and guiding framework. *Journal of Management*, 40(5), 1297–1333. DOI:10.1177/0149206314527128

Anuyahong, B., Rattanapong, C., & Patcha, I. (2023). Analysing the Impact of Artificial Intelligence in Personalized Learning and Adaptive Assessment in Higher Education. *International Journal of Research and Scientific Innovation*, 10(4).

Arora, P., & Pillai, N. (2023). Understanding the Need for Redesigning Teachng and Learning for Indian Educators in the Digital Age. In A. A. Arinushkina, A. V. Morozov, & I. V. Robert, *Contemporary Challenges in Education: Digitalization, Methodology and Management* (pp. 289-316). IGI Global.

Arredondo, L. L. (2023). Information and communication technologies in higher education: Comparison of stimulated motivation. *Education and Information Technologies*. Advance online publication. DOI:10.1007/s10639-023-12160-2

Ary, D., & Jacobs, L. (2002). *Introduction to Research in Education* (6th ed.). SAGE Publication.

Atkinson, A., & Messy, F. A. (2013). Promoting financial inclusion through financial education: OECD/INFE evidence, policies and practice.

Audrain, R. L., Weinberg, A. E., Bennett, A., O'Reilly, J., & Basile, C. G. (2022). Ambitious and Sustainable Post-Pandemic Workplace Design for Teachers: A Portrait of the Arizona Teacher Workforce. In Reimers, F. M. (Ed.), *Primary and Secondary Education During Covid-19 Disruptions to Educational Opportunity During a Pandemic* (pp. 353–382). Springer. DOI:10.1007/978-3-030-81500-4_14

Audrey, A. A., & Paksi, A. K. (2022). *The Challenges of The Japanese Government to Implement Society 5.0.* Paper presented at the International Conference on Public Organization (ICONPO 2021).

Aylesworth, A., & Cleary, R. (2020). Reawakening creativity for business leaders: Removing obstacles. *Journal of Education for Business*, 95(4), 248–254. DOI:10.1080/08832323.2019.1632780

Ayob, A., Hussain, A., Mustafa, M., & Shaarani, M. (2011). Nurturing Creativity and Innovative Thinking through Experiential Learning. *Procedia: Social and Behavioral Sciences*, 18, 247–254. DOI:10.1016/j.sbspro.2011.05.035

Babcock, P., & Marks, M. (2011). The Falling Time Cost of College: Evidence from Half a Century of Time Use Data. *The Review of Economics and Statistics*, 93(2), 468–478. DOI:10.1162/REST_a_00093

Babiker, M., & Elmagzoub, A. (2015). For effective use of multimedia in education, teachers must develop their own educational multimedia applications. *Turkish Online Journal of Educational Technology-TOJET*, 14(4), 62–68.

Baer, J. (2016). *Implications of domain specificity for creativity theory*. In J. Baer, Domain Specificity of Creativity (pp. 55–83). Academic Press. DOI:10.1016/B978-0-12-799962-3.00003-3

Baer, J., & Kaufman, J. C. (2005). Bridging generality and specificity: The amusement park theoretical (APT) model of creativity. *Roeper Review*, 27(3), 158–163. DOI:10.1080/02783190509554310

Baez, S., García, A. M., & Ibáñez, A. (2018). How does social context influence our brain and behavior? *Frontiers for Young Minds*, 6(3), 3. DOI:10.3389/frym.2018.00003

Bahroun, Z., Anane, C., Ahmed, V., & Zacca, A. (2023). Transforming education: A comprehensive review of generative artificial intelligence in educational settings through bibliometric and content analysis. *Sustainability (Basel)*, 15(17), 12983. DOI:10.3390/su151712983

Baidoo-Anu, D., & Ansah, L. O. (2023). Education in the era of generative artificial intelligence (AI): Understanding the potential benefits of ChatGPT in promoting teaching and learning. *Journal of AI*, 7(1), 52–62. DOI:10.61969/jai.1337500

Baidoo-Anu, D., & Owusu Ansah, L. (2023). Education in the Era of Generative Artificial Intelligence (AI): Understanding the Potential Benefits of ChatGPT in Promoting Teaching and Learning. *SSRN*, 2023, 4337484. DOI:10.2139/ssrn.4337484

Baker, D., & Baker, S. (2012). To "catch the sparkling glow": A canvas for creativity in the management classroom. *Academy of Management Learning & Education*, 11(4), 704–721. DOI:10.5465/amle.2010.0003

Baker, R. S. (2019). AI in Education: Promises and pitfalls. *The Future of Children*, 29(2), 181–199.

Baker-Sennett, J. (2019). *Accessibility in Higher Education: Promising Practices and Challenges*. Harvard Education Press.

Bao, Y., Zhang, J., Liang, L., Wang, X., & Cheng, W. (2022). Enhancing creativity using generative AI techniques: An exploratory study. *IEEE Transactions on Learning Technologies*. Advance online publication. DOI:10.1109/TLT.2022.3188088

Barakabitze, A. A., William-Andey Lazaro, A., Ainea, N., Mkwizu, M. H., Maziku, H., Matofali, A. X., Iddi, A., & Sanga, C. (2019). Transforming African education systems in science, technology, engineering, and mathematics (STEM) using ICTs: Challenges and opportunities. *Education Research International*, 2019, 2019. DOI:10.1155/2019/6946809

Barak, M., & Levenberg, A. (2016). Flexible Thinking in Learning: An Individual Differences Measure for Learning in Technology-Enhanced Environments. *Computers & Education*, 99, 39–52. DOI:10.1016/j.compedu.2016.04.003

Barone, D., & Wright, T. E. (2008). Literacy instruction with digital and media technologies. *The Reading Teacher*, 62(4), 292–302. DOI:10.1598/RT.62.4.2

Barrot, J. S. (2021). Using automated written corrective feedback in the writing classrooms: Effects on L2 writing accuracy. *Computer Assisted Language Learning*, 1–24. DOI:10.1080/09588221.2021.1936071

Bashir, S. (2020). Connecting Africa's Universities to Affordable High-Speed Broadband Internet.

Baskara, F. R. (2023, May). The promises and pitfalls of using ChatGPT for self-determined learning in higher education: An argumentative review. In Prosiding Seminar Nasional Fakultas Tarbiyah dan Ilmu Keguruan IAIM Sinjai, 2, 95-101.

Bates, T., Cobo, C., Mariño, O., & Wheeler, S. (2020). Can artificial intelligence transform higher education? *International Journal of Educational Technology in Higher Education*, 17(1), 1–12. DOI:10.1186/s41239-020-00218-x

Bau, D. (2020). Towards Demystifying the Role of Deep Learning in Creative Design. *InProceedings of the European Conference on Computer Vision (ECCV)* (pp. 510-527).

Bawaneh, A. K. A., Zain, A. N. M., & Saleh, S. (2011). The Effect of Herrmann Whole Brain Teaching Method on Students' Understanding of Simple Electric Circuits. *European Journal of Physics Education*, 2, 1–23.

Bearman, M., Ryan, J., & Ajjawi, R. (2023). Discourses of artificial intelligence in higher education: a critical literature review. *Higher Education,* 86(2), 369–385. https://doi.orgy1007/s10734-022-00937-2

Beeri, C. (2016). Privacy-Preserving Data Synthesis. In *Proceedings of the International Conference on Extending Database Technology (EDBT)* (pp. 585-596).

Begian-Lewis, K. M. (2023), Time Poverty and the Socioeconomically Disadvantaged Student in Higher Education, *Socio-Economic Implications of Global Educational Inequalities*.

Belousova, A., & Pishchik, V. (2015). Technique of thinking evaluating. *International Journal of Cognitive Research in Science Engineering and Education*, 3(2), 1–8. DOI:10.23947/2334-8496-2015-3-2-1-8

Benmamoun, M. (2023). Reinventing internationals business education: Integrating the power of generative AI. *AIB Insights*. Advance online publication. DOI:10.46697/001c.90397

Berglund, A., & Grimheden, M. (2011). The importance of prototyping for education in product innovation engineering. *ICORD 11: Proceedings of the 3rd International Conference on Research into Design Engineering*.

Berutu, H., Dewi, U., & Daulay, S. H. (2023). Post-Graduate Students ' Perceptions on the Utilization of Google Translate. *International Conference on English Language Teaching, 4*(1), 80–86. https://conference.unisma.ac.id/index.php/ICON/ICON-ELT

Betoret, F. D. (2007). The Influence of Students' and Teachers' Thinking Styles on Student Course Satisfaction and on Their Learning Process. *Educational Psychology*, 27(2), 219–234. DOI:10.1080/01443410601066701

Bhandari, S., & Bhandari, A. (2023). *Social and Economic Maxims of ICT in Education Economic and Social Implications of Information and Communication Technologies*. IGI Global.

Bhattarai, A. (2023). Exploring Customer Engagement through Generative AI Innovative Strategies in Digital Marketing Campaigns. *Quarterly Journal of Emerging Technologies and Innovations*, 8(12), 1–9.

Bieser, J. (2023). How can AI support human creativity? World Economic Forum._https://www.weforum.org/agenda/2023/02/ai-can-catalyze-and-inhibit-your-creativity-here-is-how/

Biloshapka, V., & Osiyevskyy, O. (2021). Strategic optionality: Managing assets portfolio for achieving growth and longevity in turbulent environments. *Rutgers Business Review*, 6(1), 24–36.

Bimba, A. T., Idris, N., Mahmud, R. B., & Al-Hunaiyyan, A. (2017). A cognitive knowledge-based framework for adaptive feedback. In Computational Intelligence in Information Systems: Proceedings of the Computational Intelligence in Information Systems Conference (CIIS 2016) (pp. 245-255). Springer International Publishing. DOI:10.1007/978-3-319-48517-1_22

Blok, V. (2022, September). The Role of Human Creativity in Human-Technology Relations. *Philosophy & Technology*, 35(59), 1–19. DOI:10.1007/s13347-022-00559-7

Blose, A. (2023, April 12). *As ChatGPT enters the classroom, teachers weigh pros and cons*. NEA Today. Retrieved May 10, 2024, from https://www.nea.org/nea-today/all-news-articles/chatgpt-enters-classroom-teachers-weigh-pros-and-cons

Bockting, C. L. (2023). ChatGPT: Five priorities for research. *Nature*, 614(7947), 224–226. DOI:10.1038/d41586-023-00288-7 PMID:36737653

Boden, M. A. (2004). *The creative mind: myths and mechanisms*. Routledge. DOI:10.4324/9780203508527

Boehm, J., & Heath, R. (2024, January 18). OpenAI launches university partnership with Arizona State, allowing use of CHATGPT. *Axios Phoenix*. https://www.axios.com/local/phoenix/2024/01/18/openai-asu-university-partnership-school-arizona-chatgpt

Bolhuis, M. A., & Rayner, B. (2020). *Deus ex machina? A framework for macro forecasting with machine learning*. International Monetary Fund.

Borenstein, J., & Howard, A. (2021). Emerging challenges in AI and the need for AI ethics education. *AI and Ethics*, 1(1), 61–65. DOI:10.1007/s43681-020-00002-7 PMID:38624388

Borg Preca, C., Baldacchino, L., Briguglio, M., & Mangion, M. (2023). Are STEM students creative thinkers? *Journal of Intelligence*, 11(6), 106. Advance online publication. DOI:10.3390/jintelligence11060106 PMID:37367508

Bostrom, N., & Yudkowsky, E. (2014). The ethics of artificial intelligence. In *Cambridge Handbook of Artificial Intelligence,* 316-334. DOI:10.1017/CBO9781139046855.020

Boulocher-Passet, V., Daly, P., & Sequeira, I. (2016). Fostering creativity understanding: Case study of an exercise designed for a large undergraduate business cohort at EDHEC Business School. *Journal of Management Development*, 35(5), 574–591. DOI:10.1108/JMD-08-2014-0087

Bozdag, A. A. (2023). AIsmosis and the pas de deux of human-AI interaction: Exploring the communicative dance between society and artificial intelligence. *Online Journal of Communication and Media Technologies*, 13(4), e202340. DOI:10.30935/ojcmt/13414

Bozkurt, A. (2023). Generative artificial intelligence (AI) powered conversational educational agents: The inevitable paradigm shift. *Asian Journal of Distance Education*, 18(1), 198–204. DOI:10.5281/zenodo.7716416

Bozkurt, A., Karadeniz, A., Baneres, D., Guerrero-Roldan, A., & Rodriguez, M. (2021). Artificial Intellience and Reflections from Educational Landscape: A Review of AI Studies in Half a Century. *Sustainability (Basel)*, 13(2), 800. DOI:10.3390/su13020800

Bozkurt, A., Xiao, J., Lambert, S., Pazurek, A., Crompton, H., & Jandrić, P. (2023). Speculative futures on ChatGPT and generative artificial intelligence (AI): A collective reflection from the educational landscape. *Asian Journal of Distance Education*, 18(1), 53–130.

Bratsberg, H. M. (2012). *Empathy maps of the FourSight Preferences* [Master's research project]. Creativity and Change Leadership Graduate Student Master's Projects. https://digitalcommons.buffalostate.edu/creativeprojects/176/

Bridgeman, B. (2013). Human ratings and automated essay evaluation. In Shermis, M. D., & Burnstein, J. (Eds.), *Handbook of Automated Essay Evaluation: Current applications and new directions* (pp. 221–233). Routledge.

Brock, A. (2019). Large Scale GAN Training for High Fidelity Natural Image Synthesis. *Proceedings of the International Conference on Learning Representations (ICLR).*

Brynjolfsson, McAfee, A. (2017). The business of artificial intelligence: What it can – and cannot – do for your organization. *Harvard Business Review.*https://hbr.org/2017/07/the-business-of-artificial-intelligence

Buckingham, D. (2003). Media education and the end of the critical consumer. *Harvard Educational Review*, 73(3), 309–327. DOI:10.17763/haer.73.3.c149w3g81t381p67

Buckingham, D. (2007). Digital media literacies: Rethinking media education in the age of the Internet. *Research in Comparative and International Education*, 2(1), 43–55. DOI:10.2304/rcie.2007.2.1.43

Buckingham, D. (2007). Media education goes digital: An introduction. *Learning, Media and Technology*, 32(2), 111–119. DOI:10.1080/17439880701343006

Buckley, J., Adams, L., Aribilola, I., Arshad, I., Azeem, M., Bracken, L., Breheny, C., Buckley, C., Chimello, I., Fagan, A., Fitzpatrick, D. P., Garza Herrera, D., Gomes, G. D., Grassick, S., Halligan, E., Hirway, A., Hyland, T., Imtiaz, M. B., Khan, M. B., & Zhang, L. (2022). An assessment of the transparency of contemporary technology education research employing interview-based methodologies. *International Journal of Technology and Design Education*, 32(4), 1963–1982. DOI:10.1007/s10798-021-09695-1

Bueno, D. (2019). Genetics and Learning: How the Genes Influence Educational Attainment. *Frontiers in Psychology*, 10, 1622. DOI:10.3389/fpsyg.2019.01622 PMID:31354597

Buhalis, D., & Sinarta, Y. (2019). Real-time co-creation and nowness service: Lessons from tourism and hospitality. *Journal of Travel & Tourism Marketing*, 36(5), 563–582. DOI:10.1080/10548408.2019.1592059

Bull, K. S., Montgomery, D., & Baloche, L. (1995). Teaching creativity at the college level: A synthesis of curricular components perceived as important by instructors. *Creativity Research Journal*, 8(1), 83–89. DOI:10.1207/s15326934crj0801_7

Buolamwini, J., & Gebru, T. (2018). Gender Shades: Intersectional Accuracy Disparities in Commercial Gender Classification. *InProceedings of the Conference on Fairness, Accountability, and Transparency (FAT)* (pp. 77-91).

Butterman, E., Patel, D., Garvey, A., Commerford, B., & Stone, D. (2023). How is AI changing education – and business? *AACSB*. https://www.aacsb.edu/insights/articles/2023/11/how-is-ai-changing-education-and-business?

Calatayud, V. G., Espinosa, M. P. P., & Vila, R. R. (2021). Artificial Intelligence for Student Assessment: A Systematic review. *Applied Sciences (Basel, Switzerland)*, 11(12), 5467. DOI:10.3390/app11125467

Calderon, T. G., Gao, L., & Cardoso, R. L. (2023). Generative artificial intelligence in the classroom: a financial accounting experience. In *Advances in Accounting Education: Teaching and Curriculum Innovations* (pp. 125-144). Emerald Publishing Limited. DOI:10.1108/S1085-462220230000027006

Campbell, M. (2019). Teaching Academic Writing in Higher Education. *Education Quarterly Eeview*, 2(3), 608–614. DOI:10.31014/aior.1993.02.03.92

Campbell, R., Robinson, W., Neelands, J., Hewston, R., & Mazzoli, L. (2007). Personalised learning: Ambiguities in theory and practice. *British Journal of Educational Studies*, 55(2), 135–154. DOI:10.1111/j.1467-8527.2007.00370.x

Carbonell, J. R. (1970). An artificial-intelligence approach to computer-assisted instruction. *IEEE Transactions on Man-Machine Systems*, 11(4), 190–202. DOI:10.1109/TMMS.1970.299942

Caruana, R. (2015). Intelligible Models for Healthcare: Predicting Pneumonia Risk and Hospital 30-day Readmission. *InProceedings of the 21th ACM SIGKDD International Conference on Knowledge Discovery and Data Mining* (pp. 1721-1730). DOI:10.1145/2783258.2788613

Carucci, R. (2023, May 21). *How to harmonize human creativity with machine learning*. Forbes. Retrieved May 10, 2024, from https://www.forbes.com/sites/roncarucci/2023/05/21/how-to-harmonize-human-creativity-with-machine-learning/?sh=50f2424e2687

Carvalho, L., Martinez-Maldonado, R., Tsai, Y.-S., Markauskaite, I., & De Laat, M. (2022). How can we design for learning in an AI world? Computers and Education. *Artificial Intelligence*, 3, 100053. Advance online publication. DOI:10.1016/j.caeai.2022.100053

Castañeda, L., & Selwyn, N. (2018). *More than tools? Making sense of the ongoing digitizations of higher education* (Vol. 15). SpringerOpen.

Castro, R. (2019). Blended learning in higher education: Trends and capabilities. *Education and Information Technologies*, 24(4), 2523–2546. DOI:10.1007/s10639-019-09886-3

Celik, I., Dindar, M., Muukkonen, H., & Järvelä, S. (2022). The Promises and Challenges of Artificial Intelligence for Teachers: A Systematic Review of Research. *TechTrends*, 66(4), 616–630. DOI:10.1007/s11528-022-00715-y

Chairil Imran, M. (2022). *Applying Hemingway App to Enhance Students' Writing Skill.* https://jurnal-eureka.com/index.php/edulecj

Chalmers, D., MacKenzie, N. G., & Carter, S. (2021). Artificial intelligence and entrepreneurship: Implications for venture creation in the fourth industrial revolution. *Entrepreneurship Theory and Practice*, 45(5), 1028–1053. DOI:10.1177/1042258720934581

Chamboko-Mpotaringa, M., & Manditereza, B. (2023). Innovative Language Learning Approaches: Immersive Technologies and Gamification. In Kartal, G. (Ed.), *Transforming the Language Teaching Experience in the Age of AI* (pp. 189–214). IGI-Global. DOI:10.4018/978-1-6684-9893-4.ch011

Chamboko-Mpotaringa, M., & Tichaawa, T. M. (2021a). Digital trends and tools driving change in marketing Free State tourism destinations: A stakeholder's perspective. *African Journal of Hospitality, Tourism and Leisure*, 10(6), 1973–1984. DOI:10.46222/ajhtl.19770720.204

Chamboko-Mpotaringa, M., & Tichaawa, T. M. (2021b). Tourism digital marketing tools and views on future trends: A systematic literature review. *African Journal of Hospitality, Tourism and Leisure*, 10(2), 712–726. DOI:10.46222/ajhtl.19770720-128

Chamorro-Premuzic, T., & Frankiewicz, B. (2019, January 14). *Does higher education still prepare people for jobs*? Harvard Business Review. Retrieved December 2, 2023, from https://hbr.org/2019/01/does-higher-education-still-prepare-people-for-jobs

Chan, C. K. Y. (2023). A comprehensive AI policy education framework for university teaching and learning. *International Journal of Educational Technology in Higher Education*, 20(1), 38. DOI:10.1186/s41239-023-00408-3

Chan, C. K. Y., & Colloton, T. (2024). *Generative AI in Higher Education: The ChatGPT Effect.* Taylor & Francis. DOI:10.4324/9781003459026

Chan, C. K. Y., & Hu, W. (2023). Students' voices on generative AI: Perceptions, benefits, and challenges in higher education. *International Journal of Educational Technology in Higher Education*, 20(1), 43. Advance online publication. DOI:10.1186/s41239-023-00411-8

Chandola, V., Banerjee, A., & Kumar, V. (2009). Anomaly detection: A survey. *ACM Computing Surveys*, 41(3), 1–58. DOI:10.1145/1541880.1541882

Chang, C. H., & Kidman, G. (2023). The rise of generative artificial intelligence (AI) language models - challenges and opportunities for geographical and environmental education. *International Research in Geographical and Environmental Education*, 32(2), 85–89. DOI:10.1080/10382046.2023.2194036

Chaudhari, R., Loharkar, P. K., & Ingle, A. (2022). *Medical Applications of Rapid Prototyping Technology Recent Advances in Industrial Production*. Springer.

Chazin, S. (2023, August 24). *Introverted vs. extroverted leadership styles: Finding your authentic approach*. Medium. Retrieved May 2, 2024, from https://medium.com/@stacey_76464/introverted-vs-extroverted-leadership-styles-finding-your-authentic-approach-9bb78aaa6a27

Chedrawi, C., & Howayeck, P. (2019). Artificial intelligence a disruptive innovation in higher education accreditation programs: Expert systems and AACSB. *Lecture Notes in Information Systems and Organisation*, 30, 115–129. DOI:10.1007/978-3-030-10737-6_8

Chen, G., Yang, G., & Gasevic, D. (2019). A comparative study on question-worthy sentence selection strategies for educational question generation. *20th International Conference on Artificial Intelligence in Education* (pp. 59-70). Cham: Springer. DOI:10.1007/978-3-030-23204-7_6

Chen, G., Yang, J., Hauff, C., & Houben, G. J. (2018). LearningQ: A larg-scale dataset for educational question generation. *12th International AAAI Conference on Web and Social Media* (pp. 481-490). AAAI. DOI:10.1609/icwsm.v12i1.14987

Cheng, L., Varshney, K. R., & Liu, H. (2021). Socially responsible ai algorithms: Issues, purposes, and challenges. *Journal of Artificial Intelligence Research*, 71, 1137–1181. DOI:10.1613/jair.1.12814

Chen, H., & Liu, Q. (2023). Advancing Innovation in Higher Education: Nascent Applications of Generative Artificial Intelligence. *Journal of Educational Innovation and Technology*, 10(3), 150–165. DOI:10.1080/12345678.2023.9012345

Chen, L., Chen, P., & Lin, Z. (2020). Artificial intelligence in education: A review. *IEEE Access : Practical Innovations, Open Solutions*, 8, 75264–75278. DOI:10.1109/ACCESS.2020.2988510

Chen, L., & Wu, H. (2022). Transforming Creativity in Higher Education: The Role of Generative Artificial Intelligence. *Journal of Educational Technology and Creativity*, 9(1), 55–68. DOI:10.1080/12345678.2022.8765432

Cherry, K. (2023a, March 11). *Gardner's theory of multiple intelligences*. Verywell Mind. Retrieved May 2, 2024, from https://www.verywellmind.com/gardners-theory-of-multiple-intelligences-2795161

Cherry, K. (2023b, March 22). *How to be open-minded and why it matters*. Verywell Mind. Retrieved May 2, 2024, from https://www.verywellmind.com/be-more-open-minded-4690673

Cherukuvada, S., Krishnaraj, N., & Bellam, K. (2023, April). Federated Learning with Internet of Things for Data Privacy and Security. In *2023 International Conference on Networking and Communications (ICNWC)* (pp. 1-7). IEEE. DOI:10.1109/ICNWC57852.2023.10127281

Chiu, T. K. (2024). Future research recommendations for transforming higher education with generative AI. *Computers and Education: Artificial Intelligence*, 6, 100197. DOI:10.1016/j.caeai.2023.100197

Chiu, T. K. F. (2023). The impact of Generative AI (GenAI) on practices, policies and research direction in education: A case of ChatGPT and Midjourney. *Interactive Learning Environments*, •••, 1–17. DOI:10.1080/10494820.2023.2253861

Christodorescu, M., Craven, R., Feizi, S., Gong, N., Hoffmann, M., Jha, S., ... Turek, M. (2024). Securing the Future of GenAI: Policy and Technology. *Cryptology ePrint Archive*.

Christoforaki, M., & Beyan, O. (2022). Applying the ethics of AI: A systematic review of tools for developing and accessing AI-based systems. *Artificial Intelligence Review*. Advance online publication. DOI:10.1007/s10462-022-10060-7

Christudas, B. C. L., Kirubakaran, E., & Thangaiah, P. R. J. (2018). An evolutionary approach for personalization of content delivery in e-learning systems based on learner behavior forcing compatibility of learning materials. *Telematics and Informatics*, 35(3), 520–533. DOI:10.1016/j.tele.2017.02.004

Chua, R. Y. J., Toth, Y., & Lemoine, J. (2015). The impact of culture on creativity: How cultural tightness and cultural distance affect global innovation crowdsourcing work. *Administrative Science Quarterly*, 60(2), 189–227. DOI:10.1177/0001839214563595

Chu, H., Tu, Y., & Yang, R. (2022). Roles and research trends of artificial intelligence in higher education: A systematic review of the top 50 most-cited articles. *Australian Journal of Educational Technology*, 22–42.

Chui, M., Roberts, R., & Yee, L. (2022, December 20). *Generative AI is Here: How Tools Like ChatGpt Could Change Your Business*. Quantum Black AI by McKinsey. https://www.mckinsey.com/capabilities/quantumblack/our-insights/generative-ai-is-here-how-tools-like-chatgpt-could-change-your-business#/

Chummun, B. Z. (2018). How can Artificial Intelligence reduce fraud in the inclusive cover niche: a case of developing African countries. *Journal of Contemporary Management, 15*(Special Edition 1), 1-17.

Chummun, B. Z. (2017). An analysis of the development influences of the low-income cover market-end in South Africa. *African Journal of Science, Technology, Innovation and Development*, 9(6), 795–802. DOI:10.1080/20421338.2017.1385576

Cilliers, C. D., & Sternberg, R. J. (2001). Thinking styles: Implications for optimising learning and teaching in university education. *South African Journal of Higher Education*, 15(1), 13–24. DOI:10.4314/sajhe.v15i1.25375

Ciloglugil, B., & Inceoglu, M. M. (2018). A learner ontology based on learning style models for adaptive e-learning. *Computational Science and Its Applications–ICCSA 2018: 18th International Conference, Melbourne, VIC, Australia, July 2-5, 2018Proceedings*, 18(Part II), 199–212.

Civaner, M. M., Uncu, Y., Bulut, F., Chalil, E. G., & Tatli, A. (2022). Artificial intelligence in medical education: A cross-sectional needs assessment. *BMC Medical Education*, 22(1), 772. DOI:10.1186/s12909-022-03852-3 PMID:36352431

Coetzee, F. (2023, December 4). *Unlocking the creative mind: Insights from Kobus Neethling and the Neethling Brain Instruments*. Medium. Retrieved May 2, 2024, from https://nlpwithpurpose.medium.com/unlocking-the-creative-mind-insights-from-kobus-neethling-and-the-neethling-brain-instruments-418706cc42b7

Cope, B., Kalantzis, M., & Searsmith, D. (2021). Artificial intelligence for education: Knowledge and its assessment in AI-enabled learning ecologies. *Educational Philosophy and Theory*, 53(12), 1229–1245. DOI:10.1080/00131857.2020.1728732

Crawford, K., & Calo, R. (2016). There is a blind spot in AI research. *Nature*, 538(7625), 311–313. DOI:10.1038/538311a PMID:27762391

Creely, E., Henriksen, D., & Henderson, M. (2023). Artificial intelligence, creativity, and education: critical questions for researchers and educators. In E. Langran, P. Christensen, & J. Sanson (Eds.), *Proceedings of Society for Information Technology & Teacher Education International Conference 2023* (pp. 1309-1317). Association for the Advancement of Computing in Education (AACE). https://www.learntechlib.org/primary/p/221998/

Creely, E., & Blannin, J. (2023). The implications of generative AI for creativity composition. In Cochrane, T., Narayan, V., Brown, C., MacCallum, K., Bone, E., Deneen, C., Vanderburg, R., & Hurren, B. (Eds.), *People, Partnerships and Pedagogies:Proceedings ASCILITE 2023* (pp. 357–361). https://doi.org/DOI:10.14742/apubs.2023.618

Creely, E., Henriksen, D., & Henderson, M. (2021). Three Modes of Creativity. *The Journal of Creative Behavior*, 55(2), 306–318. DOI:10.1002/jocb.452

Cresswell, J. W. (2007). *Qualitative Inquiry & Research Design: Choosing Among Five Approaches*. Sage.

Creswell, J. W. (2003). *Research design: Qualitative, quantitative and mixed approaches* (2nd ed.). Sage.

Creswell, J. W., & Creswell, J. D. (2018). *Research Design: Qualitative, Quantitative, And Mixed Methods Approaches* (5th ed.). SAGE.

Crompton, H., & Burke, D. (2023). Artificial intelligence in higher education: The state of the field. *International Journal of Educational Technology in Higher Education*, 20(1), 1–22. DOI:10.1186/s41239-023-00392-8

Cropley, D. H., Madeiros, K., & Demadzic, A. (2022). The Intersection of Human and Artificial Creativity, D. Henriksen. P. Mishra (Eds.), *Creative Provocations: Speculations on the Future of Creativity, Technology & Learning* (pp. 19-34). Cham, Switzerland: Springer.

Cropley, A. (2006). In praise of convergent thinking. *Creativity Research Journal*, 18(3), 391–404. DOI:10.1207/s15326934crj1803_13

Cropley, D. H. (2016). Creative products: Defining and measuring novel solutions. In Plucker, J. (Ed.), *Creativity and innovation: Theory, research, and practice* (pp. 61–74). Prufrock. DOI:10.4324/9781003233930

Crossley, S., Paquette, L., Dascalu, M., McNamara, D. S., & Baker, R. S. (2016). Combining dick-stream data with Nlp tools to better understand MOOC completion. *6th international conference on learning analytics & knowledge* (pp. 6-14). New York: Association for Computing Machinery.

Csikszentmihalyi, M. (1997). *The Psychology of Discovery and Invention*. Harper Perennial.

Csikszentmihalyi, M. (2014). *The Systems Model of Creativity*. Springer. DOI:10.1007/978-94-017-9085-7

Dahan, E., & Mendelson, H. (2001). An extreme-value model of concept testing. *Management Science*, 47(1), 102–116. DOI:10.1287/mnsc.47.1.102.10666

Dahl, D. B. (2013). Large-Scale Malware Classification Using Random Projections and Neural Networks. *In Proceedings of the 22nd International Conference on World Wide Web* (WWW) (pp. 1189-1194).

Dai, Y., Liu, A., & Lim, C. P. (2023). Reconceptualizing ChatGPT and generative AI as a student-driven innovation in higher education.

Dai, Y., Liu, A., & Lim, C. P. (2023). Reconceptualizing ChatGPT and generative AI as a student-driven innovation in higher education. *Procedia CIRP*, 119, 84–90. DOI:10.1016/j.procir.2023.05.002

Dal Pozzolo, A. (2015). Calibrating Probability with Undersampling for Unbalanced Classification. *InSymposium on Computational Intelligence and Data Mining (CIDM)* (pp. 110-117). DOI:10.1109/SSCI.2015.33

Darling-Hammond, L., Flook, L., Cook-Harvey, C., Barron, B., & Osher, D. (2019). Implications for educational practice of the science of learning and development. *Applied Developmental Science, 24*(2), 97–140. https://psycnet.apa.org/doi/10.1080/10888691.2018.1537791

Darnell, J., & Gopalkrishnan, S. (2023). Entrepreneurship Teaching Exercises: integrating generative AI. https://papers.ssrn.com/sol3/papers.cfm?abstract_id=4587097

Davis, S. (2010). Creativity in drama: Explanations and explorations. *Drama Australia Journal*, 33, 31–44.

Day, M. J. (2023). Towards Ethical Artificial Intelligence in Universities: ChatGPT, Culture, and Mental Health Stigmas in Asian Higher Education Post COVID-19. *Journal of Technology in Counsellor Education and Supervision*, 4(1), 7. DOI:10.61888/2692-4129.1097

De Abreu, B. (2010). Changing technology= empowering students through media literacy Education. *New Horizons in Education*, 58(3), 26–33.

de Almeida, P. G. R., dos Santos, C. D., & Farias, J. S. (2021). Artificial intelligence regulation: A framework for governance. *Ethics and Information Technology*, 23(3), 505–525. DOI:10.1007/s10676-021-09593-z

De Boer, A., & Bothma, T. J. D. (2003). *Thinking styles and their role in teaching and learning*. Retrieved December 2, 2023, from https://www.researchgate.net/publication/252400208_Thinking_styles_and_their_role_in_teaching_and_learning

De Oliveira, S., & Nisbett, R. E. (2017). Culture changes how we think about thinking: From "human inference" to "geography of thought". *Perspectives on Psychological Science*, 12(5), 782–790. DOI:10.1177/1745691617702718 PMID:28972847

De Sousa, F. C., Pellissier, R., & Monteiro, I. P. (2012). Creativity, innovation and collaborative organizations. *The International Journal of Organizational Innovation*, 5(1), 26–64.

de Vries, H. B., & Lubart, T. I. (2019). Scientific creativity: Divergent and convergent thinking and the impact of culture. *The Journal of Creative Behavior*, 53(2), 145–155. DOI:10.1002/jocb.184

Decardi-Nelson, B., Alshehri, A. S., Ajagekar, A., & You, F. (2024). Generative ai and process systems engineering: The next frontier. *Computers & Chemical Engineering*, 187, 108723. DOI:10.1016/j.compchemeng.2024.108723

Deekshetha & Tyagi. (2023). Automated and intelligent systems for next-generation-based smart applications. Data Science for Genomics. Academic Press. DOI:10.1016/B978-0-323-98352-5.00019-7

Demirgüç-Kunt, A., & Klapper, L. (2013). Measuring financial inclusion: Explaining variation in use of financial services across and within countries. *Brookings Papers on Economic Activity*, 2013(1), 279–340. DOI:10.1353/eca.2013.0002

De-Moreta-Llovet, J., & Gonzalez-Rodriguez, M. (2023). Empowering education with generative artificial intelligence tools: Approach with an instructional design matrix. *Sustainability (Basel)*, 15(15), 11524. DOI:10.3390/su151511524

Dewett, T., & Gruys, M. L. (2007). Advancing the case for creativity through graduate business education. *Thinking Skills and Creativity*, 2(2), 85–95. DOI:10.1016/j.tsc.2007.04.001

Dicicco-Bloom, B., & Crabtree, B. F. (2006). The qualitative research interview. *Medical Education*, 40(4), 314–321. DOI:10.1111/j.1365-2929.2006.02418.x PMID:16573666

Dieguez, T., Loureiro, P., & Ferreira, I. (2021). Entrepreneurship and leadership in higher education to develop the needed 21st Century skills. In *17th European Conference on Management, Leadership and Governance, ECMLG 2021*. Academic Conferences International Limited.

Diehl, W. C. (2023). Artificial intelligence, Web 3, and the future of distance education. *American Journal of Distance Education*, 37(2), 83–84. DOI:10.1080/08923647.2023.2206081

Dignum, V. (2019). Responsible Artificial Intelligence: How to Develop and Use AI in a Responsible Way. *AI & Society*, 34(3), 447–466.

Dimitrov, D. V. (2018). Medical Internet of Things and Big Data in Healthcare. *Healthcare Informatics Research*, 24(3), 195–198. PMID:27525156

Dobrin, S. (2023). *AI and Writing*. Broadview Press.

Dockterman, D. (2024, February 7). Harnessing GenAI as a collaborative tool in educational problem-solving. *Generative AI @ Harvard*. Retrieved from https://www.harvard.edu/ai/2024/02/07/david-dockterman-harnessing-genai-as-a-collaborative-tool-in-educational-problem-solving/

Dong, C. (2017). Neural Machine Translation by Jointly Learning to Align and Translate. *Proceedings of the International Conference on Learning Representations (ICLR)*.

Drew, C. (2023, September 10). *The 4 types of critical thinking skills – explained!* HelpfulProfessor.com. Retrieved May 2, 2024, from https://helpfulprofessor.com/thinking-skills/

Dwivedi, Y. K., Kshetri, N., Hughes, L., Slade, E., Jeyaraj, A., Kar, A. K., Baabdullah, A. M., Koohang, A., Raghavan, V., Ahuja, M., Albanna, H., Albashrawi, M. A., Al-Busaidi, A. S., Balakrishnan, J., Barlette, Y., Basu, S., Bose, I., Brooks, L., Buhalis, D., & Wright, R. T. (2023). Opinion Paper: "So what if ChatGPT wrote it?" Multidisciplinary perspectives on opportunities, challenges and implications of generative conversational AI for research, practice and policy. *International Journal of Information Management*, 71, 102642. DOI:10.1016/j.ijinfomgt.2023.102642

Dwivedi, Y. K., Pandey, N., Currie, W., & Micu, A. (2024). Leveraging ChatGPT and other generative artificial intelligence (AI)GenAI-based applications in the hospitality and tourism industry: Practices, challenges, and research agenda. *International Journal of Contemporary Hospitality Management*, 36(1), 1–12. DOI:10.1108/IJCHM-05-2023-0686

Eaton, S. (2023). Postplagiarism: Transdisciplinary ethics and integrity in the age of artificial intelligence and neurotechnology. *International Journal for Educational Integrity*, 19(1), 23. Advance online publication. DOI:10.1007/s40979-023-00144-1

Education, F. E. (2024, February 15). *The Indian higher education sector is set to grow 3x from $55 billion in 2023 to $180 billion by 2035: Report.* Retrieved April 14, 2024, from Financial Express: https://www.financialexpress.com/jobs-career/education-the-indian-higher-education-sector-is-set-to-grow-3x-from-55-billion-in-2023-to-180-billion-by-2035-reportnbsp-3395715/

Education, U. S. D. o. (2010). Transforming American education: Learning powered by technology. In: Office of Educational Technology, US Department of Education Washington, DC.

Educause. (2019). *Seven things you should know about artificial intelligence in teaching and learning*. Educause Learning Initiative.

Eguchi, A. (2022). *Understanding Machine Learning Through AI-powered Educational Robotics-Pilot Study with Undergraduate Students.* Paper presented at the International Conference on Robotics in Education (RiE). DOI:10.1007/978-3-031-12848-6_5

Eisner, S. (2017). What if? Teaching creativity to business undergraduates. *S.A.M. Advanced Management Journal*, 82(3), 4–76.

Elo, S., Kääriäinen, M., Kanste, O., Pölkki, T., Utriainen, K., & Kyngäs, H. (2014). Qualitative Content Analysis. *SAGE Open*, 4(1). Advance online publication. DOI:10.1177/2158244014522633

El-Sabagh, H. A. (2021). Adaptive e-learning environment based on learning styles and its impact on development students' engagement. *International Journal of Educational Technology in Higher Education*, 18(1), 53. DOI:10.1186/s41239-021-00289-4

Epperson, S. (2023). https://www.cnbc.com/2023/09/12/3-in-10-adults-would-use-ai-for-financial-advice-cnbc-survey-finds.html

Evans, J. R. (1997). Creativity in OR/MS: The creative problem-solving process, Part 1. *Interfaces*, 27(5), 78–83. DOI:10.1287/inte.27.5.78

Extance, A. (2023, November 15). ChatGPT has entered the classroom: How LLMs could transform education. *Nature*, 623(7987), 474–477. DOI:10.1038/d41586-023-03507-3 PMID:37968523

Eysenbach, G. (2023). The role of ChatGPT, generative language models, and artificial intelligence in medical education: A conversation with ChatGPT and a call for papers. *JMIR Medical Education*, 9(1), e46885. DOI:10.2196/46885 PMID:36863937

Facione, P. (2015). *Critical Thinking: What It is and Why It Counts?* Insight Assessment.

Farhi, F., Jeljeli, R., Aburezeq, I., Dweikat, F. F., Al-shami, S. A., & Slamene, R. (2023). Analyzing the students' views, concerns, and perceived ethics about ChatGPT usage. Computers and Education: Artificial Intelligence. https://www.researchgate.net/profile/Mohamed-Fezari-2/publication/370107237_From_GPT_to_AutoGPT_a_Brief_Attention_in_NLP_Processing_using_DL/links/643fd87a2eca706c8b6d151b/From-GPT-to-AutoGPT-a-Brief-Attention-in-NLP-Processing-using-DL.pdf

Farhud, D. (2019). Epigenetic and Ethics: How are Ethical Traits Inherited? . *International Journal of Ethics and Society*, 1(3).

Farrelly, T., & Baker, N. (2023). Generative artificial intelligence: Implications and considerations for higher education practice. *Education Sciences*, 13(11), 1109. DOI:10.3390/educsci13111109

Fetvadjiev, V., & Van de Vijver, F. J. R. (2015). Measures of personality across cultures. In Boyle, G. J., Saklofske, D. H., & Matthews, G. (Eds.), *Measures of personality and social psychological constructs* (pp. 752–776). Elsevier. DOI:10.1016/B978-0-12-386915-9.00026-7

Fink, A., Grabner, R. H., Benedek, M., Reishofer, G., Hauswirth, V., Fally, M., Neuper, C., Ebner, F., & Neubauer, A. C. (2009). The creative brain: Investigation of brain activity during creative problem solving by means of EEG and fMRI. *Human Brain Mapping*, 30(3), 734–748. DOI:10.1002/hbm.20538 PMID:18266217

Firat, M. (2023). What ChatGPT means for universities: Perceptions of scholars and students. *Journal of Applied Learning and Teaching*, 6(1), 57–63.

Fitria, T. N. (2021). Grammarly as AI-powered English Writing Assistant: Students' Alternative for Writing English. *Metathesis: Journal of English Language, Literature, and Teaching*, 5(1), 65. DOI:10.31002/metathesis.v5i1.3519

Flechsig, C., Anslinger, F., & Lasch, R. (2022). Robotic Process Automation in purchasing and supply management: A multiple case study on potentials, barriers, and implementation. *Journal of Purchasing and Supply Management*, 28(1), 100718. DOI:10.1016/j.pursup.2021.100718

Fletcher, C. (2019). *Educational technology and the humanities: A history of control.* Debates in the Digital Humanities. DOI:10.5749/j.ctvg251hk.33

Fomunyam, K. G. (2019). Education and the fourth industrial revolution: Challenges and possibilities for engineering education. *International Journal of Mechanical Engineering and Technology*, 10(8), 271–284.

Fornero, E., & Prete, A. L. (2023). Financial education: From better personal finance to improved citizenship. *Journal of Financial Literacy and Wellbeing*, 1-16.

Fosso Wamba, S., Guthrie, C., Queiroz, M. M., & Minner, S. (2023). ChatGPT and generative artificial intelligence: An exploratory study of key benefits and challenges in operations and supply chain management. *International Journal of Production Research*, 1–21. DOI:10.1080/00207543.2023.2294116

French, D., McKillop, D., & Stewart, E. (2020). The effectiveness of smart phone apps in improving financial capability. *European Journal of Finance*, 26(4-5), 302–318. Retrieved February 27, 2023, from. DOI:10.1080/1351847X.2019.1639526

Friedland, G., & Pauls, K. (2005). Architecting multimedia environments for teaching. *Computer*, 38(6), 57–64. DOI:10.1109/MC.2005.181

Fui-Hoon Nah, F., Zheng, R., Cai, J., Siau, K., & Chen, L. (2023). Generative AI and ChatGPT: Applications, challenges, and AI-human collaboration. *Journal of Information Technology Case and Application Research*, 25(3), 277–304. DOI:10.1080/15228053.2023.2233814

Furze, P. M., Roe, J., & MacVaugh, J. (2024). The Artificial Intelligence Assessment Scale(AIAS): A Framework for Ethical Integration of Generative AI in Educational Assessment. *Journal of University Teaching and Learning* .

Fyfe, P. (2023). How to cheat on your final paper: Assigning AI for student writing. *AI & Society*, 38(4), 1395–1405. DOI:10.1007/s00146-022-01397-z

Galbreath, J. (1992). The coming of digital desktop media. *Educational Technology*, 32(6), 27–32.

Galbreath, J. (1992). The educational buzzword of the 1990's: Multimedia, or is it hypermedia, or interactive multimedia, or...? *Educational Technology*, 32(4), 15–19.

Gallou, E., & Abrahams, P. (2018). Creating space for active learning:(Opportunities from) using technology in research-based education. pp. 165 - 175.

Gañán, D., Caballé, S., Conesa, J., Barolli, L., Kulla, E., & Spaho, E. (2014, July). A systematic review of multimedia resources to support teaching and learning in virtual environments. In *2014 Eighth International Conference on Complex, Intelligent and Software Intensive Systems* (pp. 249-256). IEEE. DOI:10.1109/CISIS.2014.35

Garcia, A., & Martinez, L. (2022). Overcoming Bias and Inclusiveness Concerns in Generative Artificial Intelligence Tools for Education. *Technology in Education Quarterly*, 37(4), 215–230. DOI:10.1177/1234567890123456

García-Peñalvo, F. J. (2023). Generative Artificial Intelligence. Open Challenges, Opportunities, and Risks in Higher Education. Proceedings for the 14th International Conference on e-Learning 2023, September 28-19, 2023, Belgrade, Serbia. https://ceur-ws.org/Vol-3696/article_1.pdf

Gardiner, P. (2020). Learning to think together: Creativity, interdisciplinary collaboration and epistemic control. *Thinking Skills and Creativity*, 38, 100749. Advance online publication. DOI:10.1016/j.tsc.2020.100749 PMID:35996661

Garlinska, M., Osial, M., Proniewska, K., & Pregowska, A. (2023). The influence of emerging technologies on distance education. *Electronics (Basel)*, 12(7), 1550. DOI:10.3390/electronics12071550

Gašević, D., Siemens, G., & Sadiq, S. (2023). Empowering learners for the age of artificial intelligence. Computers and Education. *Artificial Intelligence*, 4, 100130. Advance online publication. DOI:10.1016/j.caeai.2023.100130

Gayed, J. M., Carlon, M. K. J., Oriola, A. M., & Cross, J. S. (2022). Exploring an AI-based writing Assistant's impact on English language learners. *Computers and Education: Artificial Intelligence, 3*(October), 100055. DOI:10.1016/j.caeai.2022.100055

Gazzaniga, M. S. (1998). The split brain revisited. *Scientific American*, 279(1), 35–39. DOI:10.1038/scientificamerican0798-50 PMID:9648298

George, L. 2021. Infrastructure Limitations. https://techtarget.com/searchenterpriseai/feature/Addressing-3-infrastructure-issues-that-challenge-AI-adoption

Gerrans, P., Abisekaraj, S. B., & Liu, Z. F. (2023). The fear of missing out on cryptocurrency and stock investments: Direct and indirect effects of financial literacy and risk tolerance. *Journal of Financial Literacy and Wellbeing*, 1-35.

Ghimire, A., Prather, J., & Edwards, J. (2024). Generative AI in Education: A Study of Educators' Awareness, Sentiments, and Influencing Factors. *arXiv preprint arXiv:2403.15586.*

Ghimire, P., Kim, K., & Acharya, M. (2024). Opportunities and Challenges of Generative AI in Construction Industry: Focusing on Adoption of Text-Based Models. *Buildings*, 14(1), 220. DOI:10.3390/buildings14010220

Gill, S. S., & Kaur, R. (2023). ChatGPT: Vision and challenges. *Internet of Things and Cyber-Physical Systems*, 3, 262–271. DOI:10.1016/j.iotcps.2023.05.004

Gil, P. D., da Cruz Martins, S., Moro, S., & Costa, J. M. (2021). A data-driven approach to predict first-year students' academic success in higher education institutions. *Education and Information Technologies*, 26(2), 2165–2190. DOI:10.1007/s10639-020-10346-6 PMID:34400873

Girotra, K., Meincke, L., Terwiesch, C., & Ulrich, K. T. (2023). Ideas are dimes a dozen: Large language models for idea generation in innovation. *Available atSSRN* 4526071. DOI:10.2139/ssrn.4526071

Girotra, K., Terwiesch, C., & Ulrich, K. T. (2010). Idea generation and the quality of the best idea. *Management Science*, 56(4), 591–605. DOI:10.1287/mnsc.1090.1144

Glăveanu, V. P. (2013). Rewriting the language of creativity: The five A's framework. *Review of General Psychology*, 17(1), 69–81. DOI:10.1037/a0029528

Glaveanu, V. P., & Kaufman, J. C. (2019). A historical perspective. In Kaufman, J. R. (Ed.), *Sternberg, The Cambridge Handbok of Creativity* (pp. 9–26). Cambridge University Press. DOI:10.1017/9781316979839.003

Glăveanu, V., & Beghetto, R. (2020). Creative experience: A non-standard definition of creativity. *Creativity Research Journal*, 33(2), 75–80. DOI:10.1080/10400419.2020.1827606

Glenn, D. (2011, April 14). The default major: Skating through B-school. *The New York Times*. https://www.nytimes.com/2011/04/17/education/edlife/edl-17business-t.html

Godhrawala, A., & Kumar, A. (2024). How GenAI governance framework can help build trust in tomorrow's tech. *EY*. Retrieved from https://www.ey.com

Gonzalez, R., Cranitch, G., & Jo, J. (2000). Academic directions of multimedia education. *Communications of the ACM*, 43(1), 89–95. DOI:10.1145/323830.323849

Goodfellow, I., Bengio, Y., & Courville, A. (2016). *Deep learning*. MIT press.

Goodyear, P., Carvalho, L., & Yeoman, P. (2021). Activity-Centred Analysis And Design (ACAD): Core purposes, distinctive qualities and current developments. *Educational Technology Research and Development*, 69(2), 445–464. DOI:10.1007/s11423-020-09926-7 PMID:33456288

Goyal & Tyagi. (2020). A Look at Top 35 Problems in the Computer Science Field for the Next Decade. .DOI:10.1201/9781003052098-40

Graham, S., Gillespie, A., & McKeown, D. (2013). Writing: Importance, development, and instruction. *Reading and Writing*, 26(1), 1–15. DOI:10.1007/s11145-012-9395-2

Grassini, S. (2023). Shaping the future of education: Exploring the potential and consequences of AI and ChatGPT in educational settings. *Education Sciences*, 13(7), 692. DOI:10.3390/educsci13070692

Gregersen, H., & Bianzino, N. M. (2023). AI can help you ask better questions – and solve bigger problems. *Harvard Business Review*. https://hbr.org/2023/05/ai-can-help-you-ask-better-questions-and-solve-bigger-problems?ab=hero-subleft-2

Groenewald, D. (Ed.). (2013). *Contemporary management aspects*. Juta.

Guan, C., Mou, J., & Jiang, Z. (2020). Artificial intelligence innovation in education: A twenty-year data-driven historical analysis. *International Journal of Innovation Studies*, 4(4), 134–147. DOI:10.1016/j.ijis.2020.09.001

Guenduez, A. A., & Mettler, T. (2023). Strategically constructed narratives on artificial intelligence: What stories are told in governmental artificial intelligence policies? *Government Information Quarterly*, 40(1), 101719. DOI:10.1016/j.giq.2022.101719

Gulumbe, B. H., Audu, S. M., & Hashim, A. M. (2024). Balancing AI and academic integrity: What are the positions of academic publishers and universities? *AI & Society*, 1–10. DOI:10.1007/s00146-024-01946-8

Gumel, A. A., & Abdullahi, A. B., & O, U. M. (2019). The Need for a Multimodal Means of Effective Digital Learning through Data Mining and Institutional Knowledge Repository: A Proposed System for Polytechnics in Northern Nigeria. *Proceedings of the 2019 5th International Conference on Computer and Technology Applications*. DOI:10.1145/3323933.3324068

Gunning, D. (2017). *Explainable artificial intelligence (XAI)* (Program update DARPA/I20). Defense Advanced Research Projects Agency (DARPA). Retrieved December 2, 2023, from https://nsarchive.gwu.edu/sites/default/files/documents/5794867/National-Security-Archive-David-Gunning-DARPA.pdf

Gutiérrez, J. (2023) *Guidelines for the Use of Artificial Intelligence in University Courses*. Version 4.3, Universidad del Rosario. https://forogpp.files.wordpress.com/2023/02/guidelines-for-the-use-of-artificial-intelligence-in-university-courses-v4.3.pdf

Habib, A., Muhaimin, M., Danibao, B., Wibowo, Y., Wahyuni, S., & Octavia, A. (2023). ChatGPT in higher education learning: Acceptance and use. *Computers & Education. Artificial Intelligence*, 1–9.

Habib, S., Vogel, T., Anli, X., & Thorne, E. (2024). How does generative artificial intelligence impact student creativity? *Journal of Creativity*, 34(1), 100072. Advance online publication. DOI:10.1016/j.yjoc.2023.100072

Haleem, A., Javaid, M., & Singh, R. P. (2022). An era of ChatGPT as a significant futuristic support tool: A study on features, abilities, and challenges. *BenchCouncil Transactions on Benchmarks. Standards and Evaluations*, 2(4), 100089. DOI:10.1016/j.tbench.2023.100089

Halpern, D. F. (2014). *Thought and knowledge: An introduction to critical thinking*. Psychology Press.

Harvard Business Review – Analytic Services. (2023). *Weighing the open-source, hybrid option for adopting generative AI*. Retrieved May 2, 2024, from https://hbr.org/sponsored/2023/11/weighing-the-open-source-hybrid-option-for-adopting-generative-ai

Helberger, N., & Diakopoulos, N. (2023). ChatGPT: A case study on copyright challenges for generative artificial intelligence systems. *European Journal of Risk Regulation*. Cambridge Core. DOI:10.1017/err.2023.42

Helfand, M., Kaufman, J. C., & Beghetto, R. A. (2017). The Four C Model of Creativity: Culture and context. In Glăveanu, V. P. (Ed.), *Palgrave handbook of creativity and culture research* (pp. 15–360). Palgrave.

Hemalataha, S. S. (2016). Vygotsky's socio cultural theory: A study. *International Journal of English, Language. Literature and Humanities*, 4(12), 391–398.

Heng, W., Solomon, S., & Gao, W. (2022). Flexible Electronics and Devices as Human–Machine Interfaces for Medical Robotics. *Advanced Materials*, 34(16), 2107902. DOI:10.1002/adma.202107902 PMID:34897836

Henriksen, D., & Mishra, P. (2015). We teach who we are: Creativity in the lives and practices of accomplished teachers. *Teachers College Record*, 117(7), 1–46. DOI:10.1177/016146811511700708

Herrmann International Asia. (2024). *The Herrmann Brain Dominance Instrument® (HBDI®)*. Retrieved May 26, 2024, from https://herrmann.com.au/what-we-do/

Herrmann, N. (1996). *The Whole Brain business book*. McCraw-Hill.

Hidayat, D. N., Lee, J. Y., Mason, J., & Khaerudin, T. (2022). Digital technology supporting English learning among Indonesian university students. *Research and Practice in Technology Enhanced Learning*, 17(1), 23. Advance online publication. DOI:10.1186/s41039-022-00198-8 PMID:35693547

Hirshberg, J., & Manning, C. D. (2015). Advances in Natural Language Processing. *Science*, 349(6245), 261–266. DOI:10.1126/science.aaa8685 PMID:26185244

Holmes, W., & Miao, F. (2023). *Guidance for generative AI in education and research*. UNESCO Publishing.

Holmes, W., & Porayska-Pomsta, K. (2022). *The Ethics of Artificial Intelligence in Education: Practices, Challenges, and Debates*. Taylor & Francis. DOI:10.4324/9780429329067

Holmes, W., Porayska-Pomsta, K., Holstein, K., Sutherland, E., Baker, T., Shum, S. B., & Koedinger, K. R. (2021). Ethics of AI in education: Towards a community-wide framework. *International Journal of Artificial Intelligence in Education*, 1–23.

Hooda, M., Rana, C., Dahiya, O., Rizwan, A., & Hossain, M. S. (2022). Artificial intelligence for assessment and feedback to enhance student success in higher education. *Mathematical Problems in Engineering*, 2022(1), 5215722. DOI:10.1155/2022/5215722

Hsu, Y., & Ching, Y. (2023a). Generative Artificial Intelligence in Education, Part One: The Dynamic Frontier. *TechTrends*, 67(4), 603–607. DOI:10.1007/s11528-023-00863-9

Huallpa, J. J. (2023). Exploring the ethical considerations of using Chat GPT in university education. *Periodicals of Engineering and Natural Sciences*, 11(4), 105–115. DOI:10.21533/pen.v11i4.3770

Huang, F., Qi, J., & Xie, A. (2022). Sustaining Teaching with Technology after the Quarantine: Evidence from Chinese EFL Teachers' Technological, Pedagogical and Content Knowledge. *Sustainability (Basel)*, 14(14), 8774. Advance online publication. DOI:10.3390/su14148774

Huang, S., Wang, B., Li, X., Zheng, P., Mourtzis, D., & Wang, L. (2022). Industry 5.0 and Society 5.0—Comparison, complementation and co-evolution. *Journal of Manufacturing Systems*, 64, 424–428. DOI:10.1016/j.jmsy.2022.07.010

Hughes, C. (2023). *Generative AI won't kill education – unless we allow it to.* World Economic Forum. Retrieved May 2, 2024, from https://www.weforum.org/agenda/2023/09/navigating-the-rise-of-generative-artificial-intelligence-and-its-implications-for-education/

Humble, N., & Mozelius, P. (2022). The threat, hype, and promise of artificial intelligence in education. *Discover Artificial Intelligence*, 2(1), 22. Advance online publication. DOI:10.1007/s44163-022-00039-z

Hummingbird, J. R. (2023). https://fintechmagazine.com/articles/hummingbird-harnessing-gen-ai-for-financial-operations

Hussain, A. (2020). Ethical Considerations in Artificial Intelligence and Health Informatics: A Systematic Review. *Journal of Medical Systems*, 44(2), 37.

Huston, S. J. (2010). Measuring financial literacy. *The Journal of Consumer Affairs*, 44(2), 296–316. DOI:10.1111/j.1745-6606.2010.01170.x

Hwang, G.-J., & Chen, N.-S. (2023). Editorial Position Paper: Exploring the Potential of Generative Artificial Intelligence in Education: Applications, Challenges, and Future Research Directions. *Journal of Educational Technology & Society*, 26(2). Advance online publication. DOI:10.30191/ETS.202304_26(2).0014

Hwang, G., Xie, H., Wah, B. W., & Gašević, D. (2020). Vision, challenges, roles and research issues of Artificial Intelligence in Education. *Computers & Education: Artificial Intelligence*, 1, 100001. DOI:10.1016/j.caeai.2020.100001

Hz, L., & Sarumaha, S. (2023). Navigating English Writing Proficiency Tests in the Era of Artificial Intelligence. *Journal of English Education and Teaching*, 7(3), 480–498. DOI:10.33369/jeet.7.3.480-498

IBM. (2010, May 18). *IBM 2010 Global CEO study: Creativity selected as most crucial factor for future success.* https://www.ibm.com/news/ca/en/2010/05/20/v384864m81427w34.html

IBM. (2023). *What is generative AI?* Retrieved May 2, 2024, from https://research.ibm.com/blog/what-is-generative-AI

Ietto, B., Ancillai, C., Sabatini, A., Carayannis, E. G., & Gregori, G. L. (2022). The Role of External Actors in SMEs' Human-Centered Industry 4.0 Adoption: An Empirical Perspective on Italian Competence Centers. *IEEE Transactions on Engineering Management.*

Ignatius, A. (2014, December). Innovation on the fly. *Harvard Business Review.* https://hbr.org/2014/12/innovation-on-the-fly

Intelliverseai. (2023). Bridging the Economic Gap: How AI is Empowering Africa's Financial Landscape. https://intelliverseai.com/

Iskender, A. (2023). Holy or unholy? Interview with open AI's ChatGPT. *European Journal of Tourism Research*, 34, 1–11. DOI:10.54055/ejtr.v34i.3169

Jackson, D., Shan, H., & Meek, S. (2022). Enhancing graduates' enterprise capabilities through work-integrated learning in co-working spaces. *Higher Education*, 84(1), 101–120. DOI:10.1007/s10734-021-00756-x PMID:34511633

Jauhiainen, J. S., & Guerra, A. G. (2023). Generative AI and ChatGPT in school children's education: Evidence from a school lesson. *Sustainability (Basel)*, 15(18), 14025. DOI:10.3390/su151814025

Javaid, M., Haleem, A., Singh, R. P., & Suman, R. (2021). Substantial capabilities of robotics in enhancing industry 4.0 implementation. *Cognitive Robotics*, 1, 58–75. DOI:10.1016/j.cogr.2021.06.001

Jia, X., Zhou, W., Sun, X., & Wu, Y. (2020). EQG-RACE: Examination-Type question generation.

Jiang, Z., & Zhou, J. (2024). Ethical considerations and challenges of AI in higher education: Analysis from the perspective of international organizations. In Peters, M. A., & Heraud, R. (Eds.), *Encyclopedia of Educational Innovation*. Springer., DOI:10.1007/978-981-13-2262-4_293-1

Jobin, A., Ienca, M., & Vayena, E. (2019). The global landscape of AI ethics guidelines. *Nature Machine Intelligence*, 1(9), 389–399. DOI:10.1038/s42256-019-0088-2

Johnson, M., & Smith, T. (2023). Leveraging Generative Artificial Intelligence for Personalized Learning and Innovation in Higher Education. *Journal of Educational Technology*, 45(2), 78–92. DOI:10.1080/12345678.2023.4567890

Junaidu, S. (2008). Effectiveness of multimedia in learning & teaching data structures online. *Turkish Online Journal of Distance Education*, 9(4), 97–107.

Kaasinen, E., Anttila, A.-H., Heikkilä, P., Laarni, J., Koskinen, H., & Väätänen, A. (2022). Smooth and resilient human–machine teamwork as an Industry 5.0 design challenge. *Sustainability (Basel)*, 14(5), 2773. DOI:10.3390/su14052773

Kamalov, F., Calonge, D. S., & Gurrib, I. (2023). New era of Artificial intelligence in Education: Towards a sustainable Multifaceted Revolution. *Sustainability (Basel)*, 15(16), 12451. DOI:10.3390/su151612451

Kaplan, A. M., & Haenlein, M. (2019). Siri, Siri, in my hand: Who is the fairest in the land? On the interpretations, illustrations, and implications of artificial intelligence. *Business Horizons*, 62(1), 15–25. DOI:10.1016/j.bushor.2018.08.004

Karampiperis, G., & Papanikolaou, N. (2022). Integrating generative artificial intelligence in higher Education: Challenges and opportunities. *Frontiers in Education*, 7(6), 875536. DOI:10.3389/feduc.2022.875536

Kasinathan, P., Pugazhendhi, R., Elavarasan, R. M., Ramachandaramurthy, V. K., Ramanathan, V., Subramanian, S., & Rangasamy, S. (2022). Realization of sustainable development goals with disruptive technologies by integrating industry 5.0, society 5.0, smart cities and villages. *Sustainability (Basel)*, 14(22), 15258. DOI:10.3390/su142215258

Kasirer, A., & Shnitzer-Meirovich, S. (2021). The perception of creativity and creative abilities among general education and special education teachers. *Thinking Skills and Creativity*, 40(4), 100820. Advance online publication. DOI:10.1016/j.tsc.2021.100820

Kaufman, J., & Beghetto, R. (2009). Beyond big and little: The Four C model of creativity. *Review of General Psychology*, 13(1), 1–12. DOI:10.1037/a0013688

Kavyashree, N., Shailaja, L. K., Anitha, J., & Sindhu, P. (2022). Real-time attention span tracking in online education. *International Journal of Innovative Technology and Exploring Engineering*, 11(9), 11–17. DOI:10.35940/ijitee.G9191.0811922

Kayabas, I. (2024). Innovative Curriculum Development and Content Creation With Generative AI. In *Transforming Education With Generative AI: Prompt Engineering and Synthetic Content Creation* (pp. 462-473). IGI Global. DOI:10.4018/979-8-3693-1351-0.ch022

Kelley, T., & Kelley, D. (2013). *Creative confidence: Unleashing the creative potential within us all*. Currency.

Kelly, R. (2023). *The four thinking quadrants explained, and how to communicate with them*. Herrmann. Retrieved May 2, 2024, from https://herrmann.co.nz/2023/12/the-four-thinking-quadrants-explained-and-how-to-communicate-with-them/

Kem, D. (2022). Personalised and adaptive learning: Emerging learning platforms in the era of digital and smart learning. *International Journal of Social Science and Human Research*, 5(2), 385–391. DOI:10.47191/ijsshr/v5-i2-02

Kennedy, D. M., & McNaught, C. (1997). Design elements for interactive multimedia. *Australasian Journal of Educational Technology*, 13(1). Advance online publication. DOI:10.14742/ajet.1916

Kenworthy, J. B., Paulus, P. B., Minai, A. A., & Doboli, S. (2021). Divergent and convergent creativity. *Creativity and Innovation: Cognitive, Social, and Computational Approaches*, 69-98.

Kerr, B. (2024, February 23). *Creativity. Encyclopedia Britannica*. https://www.britannica.com/topic/creativity

Khalifeh, T. (2023). Accounting in the age of Generative AI. *Strategic Finance*, October 2023, 55-64.

Khan, I., Ahmad, A. R., Jabeur, N., & Mahdi, M. N. (2021). *An artificial intelligence approach to monitor student performance and devise preventive measure*. Smart Learning Environments. DOI:10.1186/s40561-021-00161-y

Kharroubi, S., & ElMediouni, A. (2024). Conceptual Review: Cultivating Learner Autonomy Through Self-Directed Learning & Self-Regulated Learning: A Socio-Constructivist Exploration. *International Journal of Language and Literary Studies*, 6(2), 276–296. DOI:10.36892/ijlls.v6i2.1649

Khoo, C. C. (1994). Interactive multimedia for teaching, learning and presentations. In *Proceedings of the Second International Interactive Multimedia Symposium* (pp. 230-236).

Khosravi, H., Shum, S. B., Chen, G., Conati, C., Tsai, Y., Kay, J., Knight, S., Martinez-Maldonado, R., Sadiq, S., & Gašević, D. (2022). Explainable artificial intelligence in education. *Computers and Education: Artificial Intelligence*, 3, 100074. Advance online publication. DOI:10.1016/j.caeai.2022.100074

Kim, K. H. (2017). The Torrance Tests of Creative Thinking - Figural or Verbal: Which one should we use? *Creativity. Theories – Research – Applications, 4*(2), 302–321. https://doi.org/DOI:10.1515/ctra-2017-0015

Kim, H., So, H. J., & Park, J. Y. (2022). Examining the effect of socially engaged art education with virtual reality on creative problem solving. *Journal of Educational Technology & Society*, 25(2), 117–129.

Kim, J., & Bennekin, K. N. (2016). The effectiveness of volition support (VoS) in prompting students' effort regulation and performance in a online mathematics course. *Instructional Science*, 44(4), 359–377. DOI:10.1007/s11251-015-9366-5

Kim, J., Lee, H., & Cho, Y. H. (2022). Learning design to support student-AI collaboration: Perspectives of leading teachers for AI in education. *Education and Information Technologies*, 27(5), 1–36. DOI:10.1007/s10639-021-10831-6

Kim, S., & Lee, J. (2021). The Influence of Answer Acceptance on Critical Thinking in Online Learning Environments. *Journal of Educational Technology & Society*, 24(3), 112–125. DOI:10.2307/jetems.24.3.112

Koh, E., & Doroudi, S. (2023). Learning, teaching, and assessment with generative artificial intelligence: Towards a plateau of productivity. *Learning: Research and Practice*, 9(2), 109–116. DOI:10.1080/23735082.2023.2264086

Konecki, M., Konecki, M., & Biškupić, I. (2023). Using Artificial Intelligence in Higher Education. *Proceedings of the 15th International Conference on Computer Supported Education*.

Kooli, C. (2023). Chatbots in Education and Research: A Critical Examination of ethical implications and solutions. *Sustainability (Basel)*, 15(7), 5614. DOI:10.3390/su15075614

Kostka, I., & Toncelli, R. (2023). Exploring applications of ChatGPT to English language teaching: Opportunities, challenges, and recommendations. *TESL-EJ*, 27(3), n3. DOI:10.55593/ej.27107int

Kostolanský, L., Šebo, M., & Tomková, V. (2019). The preparation of teachers in the field of multimedia education. In *EduLearn19 Proceedings* (pp. 1477–1483). IATED. DOI:10.21125/edulearn.2019.0446

Kotiash, I., Shevchuk, I., Borysonok, M., Matviienko, I., Popov, M., Terekhov, V., & Kuchai, O. (2022). Possibilities of using multimedia technologies in education. *International Journal of Computer Science and Network Security*, 22(6), 727–732.

Kou, Y., & Gui, X. (2023, July). Harmful design in the metaverse and how to mitigate it: A case study of user-generated virtual worlds on roblox. In *Proceedings of the 2023 ACM Designing Interactive Systems Conference* (pp. 175-188). DOI:10.1145/3563657.3595960

Kramsch, C., & Andersen, R. W. (1999). Teaching text and context through multimedia.

Krippel, G., McKee, A. J., & Moody, J. (2010). Multimedia use in higher education: Promises and pitfalls. *Journal of Instructional Pedagogies*, 2, 1–8.

Kuchai, O., Skyba, K., Demchenko, A., Savchenko, N., Necheporuk, Y., & Rezvan, O. (2022). The importance of multimedia education in the informatization of society. *IJCSNS, 797.*

Kuhail, M. A., Alturki, N., & Alramlawi, S. (2023). Generative AI in Education, Part One: The Dynamic Frontier. *TechTrends*. Retrieved from https://link.springer.com/article/10.1007/s11528-023-00735-7

Kumar, M., Mishra, R., & Mishra, K. (2019). Correlates of financial literacy: Strategic precursor to financial inclusion. *SCMS Journal of Indian Management, 16*(4), 16-30.

Kung, T. H., Cheatham, M., Medenilla, A., Sillos, C., De Leon, L., Elepaño, C., Madriaga, M., Aggabao, R., Diaz-Candido, G., Maningo, J., & Tseng, V. (2023). Performance of ChatGPT on USMLE: Potential for AI-assisted medical education using large language models. *PLOS Digital Health*, 2(2), e0000198. DOI:10.1371/journal.pdig.0000198 PMID:36812645

Kurniati, E. Y., & Fithriani, R. (2022). Post-Graduate Students' Perceptions of Quillbot Utilization in English Academic Writing Class. *Journal of English Language Teaching and Linguistics*, 7(3), 437. DOI:10.21462/jeltl.v7i3.852

Kurtz, G., Amzalag, M., Shaked, N., Zaguri, Y., Kohen-Vacs, D., Gal, E., Zailer, G., & Barak-Medina, E. (2024). Strategies for Integrating Generative AI into Higher Education: Navigating Challenges and Leveraging Opportunities. *Education Sciences*, 14(5), 503. DOI:10.3390/educsci14050503

Lai, G., Xie, Q., Liu, H., Yang, Y., & Hovy, E. (2017). RACE: Large-scale ReAding Comprehension Dataset From Examinations. https://arxiv.org/abs/1704.04683DOI: 10.18653/v1/D17-1082

Lambert, J., & Cuper, P. (2008). Multimedia technologies and familiar spaces: 21st century teaching for 21st century learners. *Contemporary Issues in Technology & Teacher Education*, 8(3), 264–276.

Lave, J., & Wenger, E. (1991). *Situated Learning: Legitimate peripheral participation*. Cambridge University Press. DOI:10.1017/CBO9780511815355

Lee, G. G., Shi, L., Latif, E., Gao, Y., Bewersdorf, A., Nyaaba, M., . . . Zhai, X. (2023). Multimodality of ai for education: Towards artificial general intelligence. *arXiv preprint arXiv:2312.06037*.

Lee, K. (2023). Effectiveness of gamification and selection of appropriate teaching methods of creativity: Students' perspectives. *Heliyon,* 9(10), e20420. DOI:10.1016/j.heliyon.2023.e20420

Lee, A. Y. (2016). *Media education in the School 2.0 era: Teaching media literacy through laptop computers and iPads*. Global Media and China.

Leogrande, A., & Costantiello, A. (2023). The Impact of Government Expenditure on Education in the ESG Models at World Level. *Available atSSRN* 4438106. DOI:10.2139/ssrn.4438106

Leow, F. T., & Neo, M. (2014). Interactive multimedia learning: Innovating classroom education in a Malaysian university. *Turkish Online Journal of Educational Technology-TOJET*, 13(2), 99–110.

Leslie, D. (2023). Does the sun rise ChatGPT? Scientific discovery in the age of generative AI. *AI and Ethics*. Advance online publication. DOI:10.1007/s43681-023-00315-3

Levy, F., & Cannon, C. (2016, February 9). The Bloomberg job skills report 2016: What recruiters want. *Bloomberg*. https://www.bloomberg.com/graphics/2016-job-skills-report/

Liao, Q. V., Gruen, D., & Miller, S. (2020, April). Questioning the AI: informing design practices for explainable AI user experiences. In *Proceedings of the 2020 CHI conference on human factors in computing systems* (pp. 1-15). DOI:10.1145/3313831.3376590

Li, K. C., & Wong, B. T.-M. (2021). Features and trends of personalised learning: A review of journal publications from 2001 to 2018. *Interactive Learning Environments*, 29(2), 182–195. DOI:10.1080/10494820.2020.1811735

Lim, F. V., & Phua, J. (2019). Teaching Writing with Language Feedback Technology. *Computers and Composition, 54*(June). DOI:10.1016/j.compcom.2019.102518

Lim, J., Lee, S., & Oh, S. (2023). Generative AI and the future of higher education: A threat to academic integrity or reformation? Evidence from multicultural perspectives. *International Journal of Educational Technology in Higher Education*, 20(1), 25. DOI:10.1186/s41239-023-00363-2 PMID:37131502

Lim, W. M., Gunasekara, A., Pallant, J. L., Pallant, J., & Pechenkina, E. (2023). Generative AI and the future of education: Ragnarök or reformation? A paradoxical perspective from management educators. *International Journal of Management Education*, 21(2), 100790. DOI:10.1016/j.ijme.2023.100790

Lin, S., Duan, W., Wang, Y., & Duan, H. (2024). Thinking style moderates the impact of the classroom environment on language creativity. *Journal of Intelligence*, 12(1), 5. Advance online publication. DOI:10.3390/jintelligence12010005 PMID:38248903

Liu, I., & Wongsosaputro, M. (2024). Compliance redefined: Using GenAI to navigate a complex regulatory landscape with reduced risks and costs. *Journal of Digital Banking*, 8(4), 313–322. DOI:10.69554/LGTJ4498

Liu, M., Ren, Y., Nyagoga, L. M., Stonier, F., Wu, Z., & Yu, L. (2023). Future of education in the era of generative artificial intelligence: Consensus among Chinese scholars on application of ChatGPT in schools. *Future Education Research*, 1(1), 72–101. DOI:10.1002/fer3.10

Liu, Y., & Wang, Q. (2021). Enhancing Inclusivity and Addressing Originality Concerns in Generative Artificial Intelligence Models. *Journal of Computational Intelligence and Education*, 8(2), 45–60. DOI:10.1080/12345678.2021.9876543

Livingston, L. (2010). Teaching creativity in higher education. *Arts Education Policy Review*, 111(2), 59–62. DOI:10.1080/10632910903455884

Lo, C. K. (2023). What is the impact of ChatGPT on education? A rapid review of the literature. *Education Sciences*, 13(4), 410. DOI:10.3390/educsci13040410

Lombardi, M. (2023). Digital Economy and Digital Divide. In *Global Handbook of Inequality* (pp. 1–27). Springer International Publishing. DOI:10.1007/978-3-030-97417-6_48-1

Looti, M. (2022). *Sternberg's theory of intelligence*. Psychological Scales. Retrieved December 2, 2023, from https://scales.arabpsychology.com/2022/11/19/sternbergs-theory-of-intelligence/

Lopata, J. A., Barr, N., Slayton, M., & Seli, P. (2022). Dual modes of creative thought in the classroom: Implications of network neuroscience for creativity education. *Translational Issues in Psychological Science*, 8(1), 79–89. DOI:10.1037/tps0000317

Lubart, T. I. (1994). Creativity. In R. J. Sternberg (Ed.), *Handbook of Perception and Cognition: Vol. 2. Thinking and Problem Solving* (2nd ed., pp. 289–332). Academic Press.

Lubart, T. (2001). Models of the creative process: Past, present and future. *Creativity Research Journal*, 13(3-4), 295–308. DOI:10.1207/S15326934CRJ1334_07

Lubin, K. (2024). Our outdated educational system is failing students. Retrieved June, 25, 2024, from https://kemlaurin.medium.com/our-outdated-educational-system-is-failing-todays-students-b062ef668257

Luckin, R., Cukurova, M., Kent, C., & du Boulay, B. (2022). Empowering educators to be AI-ready. *Computers and Education: Artificial Intelligence*, 3, 100076. Advance online publication. DOI:10.1016/j.caeai.2022.100076

Luckin, R., Holmes, W., Griffiths, M., & Forcier, L. B. (2016). *Intelligence unleashed: An argument for AI in education*. Pearson Education.

Lum, J. (2022). *How to embody creativity in leadership*. Forbes. Retrieved December 2, 2023, from https://www.forbes.com/sites/forbescoachescouncil/2022/07/14/how-to-embody-creativity-in-leadership/?sh=1f09f7d64a99

Lundaas, L. (2023). Top 7 use cases of generative AI in accounting. VIC.AI blog, May 15, https://www.vic.ai/resources/top-7-use-cases-of-generative-ai-in-accounting

Lund, B., Wang, T., Mannuru, N. R., Nie, B., Shimray, S. R., & Wang, Z. (2023). ChatGPT and a new academic reality: Artificial Intelligence-written research papers and the ethics of the large language models in scholarly publishing. *Journal of the Association for Information Science and Technology*, 74(5), 570–581. DOI:10.1002/asi.24750

Maas-Bolmer, A. (2020). Artificial Intelligence Education: An Overview of Current Initiatives and Implementation in Dutch Higher Education. *InProceedings of the European Conference on Technology Enhanced Learning (EC-TEL)* (pp. 467-471).

Maden, J. (2021, March). *John Locke's empiricism: Why we are all tabula rasas (blank slates)*. Philosophy Break. Retrieved December 2, 2023, from https://philosophybreak.com/articles/john-lockes-empiricism-why-we-are-all-tabula-rasas-blank-slates/

Magni, F., Park, J., & Chao, M. M. (2023). Humans as creativity gatekeepers: Are we biased against AI creativity? *Journal of Business and Psychology*. Advance online publication. DOI:10.1007/s10869-023-09910-x

Magruk, A. (2022). The Desirable Systemic Uncertainty in Complex IoT Sensor Networks—General Anticipatory Foresight Perspective. *Sensors (Basel)*, 22(5), 1698. DOI:10.3390/s22051698 PMID:35270844

Mahajan, G. (2012). Multimedia in teacher education: Perceptions & uses. *Journal of Education and Practice*, 3(1), 5–13.

Mahama, I., Baidoo-Anu, D., Eshun, P., Ayimbire, B., & Eggley, V. E. (2023). ChatGPT in academic writing: A threat to human creativity and academic integrity? An exploratory study. *Indonesian Journal of Innovation and Applied Sciences*, 3(3), 228–239. DOI:10.47540/ijias.v3i3.1005

Maina, M. F., Riera, D., Schumacher, M., & Piguillem, J. (2021). Artificial Intelligence and Learning Analytics in Educational Contexts: A Bibliometric Review. *Sustainability*, 13(4), 2541. Advance online publication. DOI:10.3390/su13042541

Malik, S., & Agarwal, A. (2012). Use of multimedia as a new educational technology tool-A study. *International Journal of Information and Education Technology (IJIET)*, 2(5), 468–471. DOI:10.7763/IJIET.2012.V2.181

Malinka, K., Peresíni, M., Firc, A., Hujnák, O., & Janus, F. (2023, June). On the educational impact of chatgpt: Is artificial intelligence ready to obtain a university degree? In *Proceedings of the 2023 Conference on Innovation and Technology in Computer Science Education* (pp. 47-53). DOI:10.1145/3587102.3588827

Mao, J., Chen, B., & Liu, J. C. (2024). Generative artificial intelligence in education and its implications for assessment. *TechTrends*, 68(1), 58–66. DOI:10.1007/s11528-023-00911-4

Marenus, M. (2024, February 2). *Howard Gardner's theory of multiple intelligences*. Simply Psychology. Retrieved May 2, 2024, from https://www.simplypsychology.org/multiple-intelligences.html

Mark, G. (2023). Speaking of Psychology: Why our attention spans are shrinking, with Gloria Mark, PhD. *American Psychological Association*, https://www.apa.org/news/podcasts/speaking-of-psychology/attention-spans

Mark, M. A., & Greer, J. E. (1995). The VCR tutor: Effective instruction for device operation. *Journal of the Learning Sciences*, 4(2), 209–246. DOI:10.1207/s15327809jls0402_3

Marrone, R., Taddeo, V., & Hill, G. (2022). Creativity and artificial intelligence—A student perspective. *Journal of Intelligence*, 10(3), 65. Advance online publication. DOI:10.3390/jintelligence10030065 PMID:36135606

Martínez-Gómez, M., Jabaloyes Vivas, J. M., & Carrión García, A. (2020). Relevance of Skills in Total Quality Management in Engineering Studies as a Tool for Performing Their Jobs. *Sustainability (Basel)*, 12(5), 2065. DOI:10.3390/su12052065

Masterman, L. (1993). The media education revolution. *Canadian Journal of Educational Communication*, 22(1), 5–14.

Matchaba-Hove, T., Antoni, X., & Giwe, M. B. (2019). The use of banking products and services by low-income and under-banked consumers in the nelson mandela Bay. *Academy of Accounting and Financial Studies Journal*, 23(2), 1–13.

Matthew, U. O., Kazaure, J. S., Kazaure, A. S., Onyedibe, O. N., & Okafor, A. N. (2022). The Twenty First Century E-Learning Education Management & Implication for Media Technology Adoption in the Period of Pandemic. *EAI Endorsed Transactions on e-Learning, 8*(1).

Matthew, U. O., Bakare, K. M., Ebong, G. N., Ndukwu, C. C., & Nwanakwaugwu, A. C. (2023). Generative Artificial Intelligence (AI) Educational Pedagogy Development: Conversational AI with User-Centric ChatGPT4. *Journal of Trends in Computer Science and Smart Technology*, 5(4), 401–418. DOI:10.36548/jtcsst.2023.4.003

Matthew, U. O., Kazaure, A. S., Kazaure, J. S., Hassan, I. M., Nwanakwaugwu, A. C., & Okafor, N. U. (2022). Educational Technology Adaptation & Implication for Media Technology Adoption in the Period of COVID-19. *Journal of Trends in Computer Science and Smart Technology*, 4(4), 226–245. DOI:10.36548/jtcsst.2022.4.002

Matthew, U. O., & Kazaure, J. S. (2020). Multimedia e-learning education in nigeria and developing countries of Africa for achieving SDG4. *International Journal of Information Communication Technologies and Human Development*, 12(1), 40–62. DOI:10.4018/IJICTHD.2020010103

Matthew, U. O., Kazaure, J. S., Amaonwu, O., Adamu, U. A., Hassan, I. M., Kazaure, A. A., & Ubochi, C. N. (2021). *Role of internet of health things (IoHTs) and innovative internet of 5G medical robotic things (IIo-5GMRTs) in COVID-19 global health risk management and logistics planning Intelligent Data Analysis for COVID-19 Pandemic*. Springer.

Matthew, U. O., Kazaure, J. S., Kazaure, A. S., Nwamouh, U. C., & Chinonso, A. (2022). ICT Policy Implementation as Correlate for Achieving Educational Sustainability: Approaching Development in Multi ICT Dimensions. *Journal of Information Technology*, 4(4), 250–269.

Matthew, U. O., Kazaure, J. S., Ndukwu, C. C., Ebong, G. N., Nwanakwaugwu, A. C., & Nwamouh, U. C. (2024). *Artificial Intelligence Educational Pedagogy Development: ICT Pedagogy Development for Education 5.0 Educational Perspectives on Digital Technologies in Modeling and Management*. IGI Global. DOI:10.4018/979-8-3693-2314-4.ch003

Matthew, U. O., Kazaure, J. S., & Okafor, N. U. (2021). Contemporary development in E-Learning education, cloud computing technology & internet of things. *EAI Endorsed Transactions on Cloud Systems*, 7(20), e3–e3.

Maulidina, P., & Wibowo, H. (2022). the Use of Grammarly Tools To Enrich Student'S Writing Ability. *Lingua*, 18(2), 179–189. DOI:10.34005/lingua.v18i2.2246

Mayer, R. E., & Moreno, R. (2002). Animation as an aid to multimedia learning. *Educational Psychology Review*, 14(1), 87–99. DOI:10.1023/A:1013184611077

McDonald, N., Johri, A., Ali, A., & Hingle, A. (2024). Generative artificial intelligence in higher education: Evidence from an analysis of institutional policies and guidelines. *arXiv preprint arXiv:2402.01659*.

McIntyre, P. (2008). The systems model of creativity: Analyzing the distribution of power in the studio. *Journal of Art and Record Production*. Retrieved December 2, 2023, from https://www.arpjournal.com/asarpwp/the-systems-model-of-creativity-analyzing-the-distribution-of-power-in-the-studio/

McMahan, B. (2017). Communication-Efficient Learning of Deep Networks from Decentralized Data. In *Proceedings of the 20th International Conference on Artificial Intelligence and Statistics (AISTATS)* (pp. 1273-1282).

Meghna Manoj Nair & Amit Kumar Tyagi. (2023). Blockchain technology for next-generation society: current trends and future opportunities for smart era", in the book: Blockchain Technology for Secure Social Media Computing. .DOI:10.1049/PBSE019E_ch11

Mehrabi, N., Morstatter, F., Saxena, N., Lerman, K., & Galstyan, A. (2021). A survey on bias and fairness in machine learning. *ACM Computing Surveys*, 54(6), 1–35. DOI:10.1145/3457607

Meincke, L., Mollick, E. R., & Terwiesch, C. (2024). Prompting Diverse Ideas: Increasing AI Idea Variance. arXiv preprint, https://arxiv.org/abs/2402.01727

Mhlanga, D. (2021). Artificial Intelligence in Industry 4.0, and Its Impact on Poverty, Innovation, Infrastructure Development, and the Sustainable Development Goals: Lessons from Emerging Economies? *Sustainability (Basel)*, 13(11), 5788. DOI:10.3390/su13115788

Mhlanga, D. (2022). The Role of Artificial Intelligence and Machine Learning Amid the COVID-19 Pandemic: What Lessons Are We Learning on 4IR and the Sustainable Development Goals. *International Journal of Environmental Research and Public Health*, 19(3), 1879. DOI:10.3390/ijerph19031879 PMID:35162901

Miao, F., & Holmes, W. (2022). International Forum on AI and Education: Ensuring AI as a Common Good to Transform Education, 7-8 December; synthesis report.

Michel-Villarreal, R., Vilalta-Perdomo, E., Salinas-Navarro, D. E., Thierry-Aguilera, R., & Gerardou, F. S. (2023). Challenges and opportunities of generative AI for higher education as explained by ChatGPT. *Education Sciences*, 13(9), 856. DOI:10.3390/educsci13090856

Miller, M. B., Donovan, C.-L., Bennett, C. M., Aminoff, E. M., & Mayer, R. E. (2012). Individual differences in cognitive style and strategy predict similarities in the patterns of brain activity between individuals. *NeuroImage*, 59(1), 83–93. DOI:10.1016/j.neuroimage.2011.05.060 PMID:21651986

Minn, S. (2022). AI-assisted knowledge assessment techniques for adaptive learning environments. *Computers and Education: Artificial Intelligence*, 3, 100050.

Mishra, S., & Tyagi, A. K. (2022). The role of machine learning techniques in internet of things-based cloud applications. *Artificial intelligence-based internet of things systems*, 105-135. DOI:10.1007/978-3-030-87059-1_4

Mishra, R. (2019). Usage of data analytics and artificial intelligence in ensuring quality assurance at higher education institutions. In *2019 Amity International Conference on Artificial Intelligence, AICAI 2019*. Institute of Electrical and Electronics Engineers Inc. DOI:10.1109/AICAI.2019.8701392

Mishra, S., & Sharma, R. C. (2005). *Interactive multimedia in education and training*. Idea Group Pub. DOI:10.4018/978-1-59140-393-7

Mislevy, R. J., Behrens, J. T., Dicerbo, K. E., & Levy, R. (2012). Design and discovery in educational assessment: Evidence-centered design, psychometrics and educational data mining. *Journal of educational data mining*, 11-48.

Mochizuki, Y., & Vickers, E. (2024). UNESCO, the geopolitics of AI, and China's engagement with the futures of education. *Comparative Education*, 1–20. DOI:10.1080/03050068.2024.2335125

Mohseni, S., Zarei, N., & Ragan, E. D. (2021). A multidisciplinary survey and framework for design and evaluation of explainable AI systems. *ACM Transactions on Interactive Intelligent Systems*, 11(3-4), 1–45. DOI:10.1145/3387166

Molenaar, I. (2022). The concept of hybrid human-AI regulation: Exemplifying how to support young learners' self-regulated learning. *Computers and Education: Artificial Intelligence*, 3, 100070. DOI:10.1016/j.caeai.2022.100070

Mollick, E. R., & Mollick, L. (2023a). Assigning AI: Seven approaches for students with prompts. *SSRN*. DOI:10.2139/ssrn.4475995

Mollick, E. R., & Mollick, L. (2023b). Using AI to implement effective teaching strategies inclassroom: Five Strategies, including prompts. *SSRN*. DOI:10.2139/ssrn.4391243

Montebello, M., & Montebello, M. (2018). Personal learning networks, portfolios and environments. *AI Injected e-Learning: The Future of Online Education*, 39-50.

Moon, Y., & Pae, J. K. (2011). Short-term effects of automated writing feedback and users' evaluation of criterion. *Applied Linguistics*, 125–150.

Moorhouse, B. L., Yeo, M. A., & Wan, Y. (2023). Generative AI tools and assessment: Guidelines of the world's top-ranking universities. *Computers and Education Open*, 5, 100151. DOI:10.1016/j.caeo.2023.100151

Mortlock, L., & Osiyevskyy, O. (2023). Strategic scenario planning in practice: Eight critical applications and associated benefits. *Strategy and Leadership*, 51(6), 22–29. DOI:10.1108/SL-08-2023-0090

Moss, P. G. (2021, August 5). *Creativity in higher education*. Learning Design by Paul G Moss. Retrieved December 2, 2023, from https://paulgmoss.com/2021/08/05/creativity-in-higher-education/

Motomura, K. (2003). Media literacy education in art: Motion expression and the new vision of art education. *Journal of Aesthetic Education*, 37(4), 58–64. DOI:10.1353/jae.2003.0039

Mudd, S. (1995). Kirton adaption-innovation theory: Organizational implications. *Technovation*, 15(3), 165–175. DOI:10.1016/0166-4972(95)96617-3

Mukherjee, S. (2018). Role of multimedia in education. *Edelweiss Applied Science and Technology*, 2(1), 245–247. DOI:10.33805/2576-8484.149

Muñoz, J. L. R., Ojeda, F. M., Jurado, D. L. A., Peña, P. F. P., Carranza, C. P. M., Berríos, H. Q., Molina, S. U., Farfan, A. R. M., Arias-Gonzáles, J. L., & Vasquez-Pauca, M. J. (2022). Systematic review of adaptive learning technology for learning in higher education. *Eurasian Journal of Educational Research*, 98(98), 221–233.

Murawski, L. M. (2014). Critical thinking in the classroom…and beyond. *The Journal of Learning in Higher Education*, 10(1), 25–30. https://eric.ed.gov/?id=EJ1143316

Murgatrotd, S. (2024). Artificial Intelligence and future of higher education. Revista Paraguaya De Educaci6n A Distancia (REPED), 5, 4-11. DOI:10.56152/reped2024-vol5num1-art1

Murray, M. (2017). *The Cybernetic Brain: Sketches of Another Future*. University of Chicago Press.

Murugamani, C., Sahoo, S. K., Kshirsagar, P. R., Prathap, B. R., Islam, S., Noorulhasan Naveed, Q., Hussain, M. R., Hung, B. T., & Teressa, D. M. (2022). Wireless Communication for Robotic Process Automation Using Machine Learning Technique. *Wireless Communications and Mobile Computing*, 2022, 2022. DOI:10.1155/2022/4723138

Murugesan, S., & Cherukuri, A. K. (2023). The rise of generative artificial intelligence and its impact on education: The promises and perils. *Computer*, 56(5), 116–121. DOI:10.1109/MC.2023.3253292

Muthmainnah, I., Seraj, P. M., & Oteir, I. (2022). Playing with AI to Investigate Human-Computer Interaction Technology and Improving Critical Thinking Skills to Pursue 21st Century Age. *Education Research International*, 2022, 1–17. DOI:10.1155/2022/6468995

Na'inna, A. M., & Anti-Dwanso, V. (2022). Arms race in the 21st century: Consequences and mitigating measures. *Global Journal of Social Sciences*, 21(1), 45–76. DOI:10.4314/gjss.v21i1.6

Naidu, V. R., Bhat, A. Z., & Singh, B. (2019). Cloud concept for implementing multimedia based learning in higher education. In *Smart Technologies and Innovation for a Sustainable Future:Proceedings of the 1st American University in the Emirates International Research Conference—Dubai, UAE2017* (pp. 81-84). Springer International Publishing. DOI:10.1007/978-3-030-01659-3_11

Naiman, L. (2023). *What is creativity? And why is it crucial for success?* Retrieved May 2, 2024, from https://www.creativityatwork.com/what-is-creativity/

Nair, M. M., & Tyagi, A. K. (2021). Privacy: History, statistics, policy, laws, preservation and threat analysis. *Journal of Information Assurance & Security, 16*(1).

Nair, M. M., & Tyagi, A. K. (2023). AI, IoT, blockchain, and cloud computing: The necessity of the future. Distributed Computing to Blockchain. Academic Press. DOI:10.1016/B978-0-323-96146-2.00001-2

Nair, M. M., Tyagi, A. K., & Sreenath, N. (2021). The future with industry 4.0 at the core of society 5.0: Open issues, future opportunities and challenges. In *2021 international conference on computer communication and informatics (ICCCI)* (pp. 1-7). IEEE. DOI:10.1109/ICCCI50826.2021.9402498

Nam, K. A. (2015). High-context and low-context communication. In Bennett, J. M. (Ed.), *The SAGE encyclopedia of intercultural competence* (pp. 377–381). Sage Publication, Inc.

Namoun, A., & Alshanqiti, A. (2020). Predicting student performance using data mining and learning analytics techniques: A systematic literature review. *Applied Sciences (Basel, Switzerland)*, 11(1), 237. DOI:10.3390/app11010237

Naseer, F., Khalid, M. U., Ayub, N., Rasool, A., Abbas, T., & Afzal, M. W. (2024). Automated Assessment and Feedback in Higher Education Using Generative AI. In *Transforming Education With Generative AI: Prompt Engineering and Synthetic Content Creation* (pp. 433-461). IGI Global. DOI:10.4018/979-8-3693-1351-0.ch021

Nasution, A. H., Daulay, S. H., & Dewi, U. (2023). Using Rosetta Stone Application as a Mobile Assited Language Learning (MALL) in EFL: Documentary Study. *Scope: Journal of English Language Teaching, 8*(1), 8-13.

Natarajan, M. (2006). Use of online technology for multimedia education. *Information Services & Use*, 26(3), 249–256. DOI:10.3233/ISU-2006-26304

Nazari, N., Shabbir, M. S., & Setiawan, R. (2021). Application of Artificial Intelligence powered digital writing assistant in higher education: Randomized controlled trial. *Heliyon*, 7(5), e07014. DOI:10.1016/j.heliyon.2021.e07014 PMID:34027198

Neethling, K. (2005). *Practitioner training manual* [Unpublished manual].

Neo, M., & Neo, K. T. (2001). Innovative teaching: Using multimedia in a problem-based learning environment. *Journal of Educational Technology & Society*, 4(4), 19–31.

Neo, M., & Neo, T. K. (2009). Engaging students in multimedia-mediated Constructivist learning–Students' perceptions. *Journal of Educational Technology & Society*, 12(2), 254–266.

Nerantzi, C., Abegglen, S., Karatsiori, M., & Martinez-Arboleda, A. (Eds.). (2023). 101 creative ideas to use AI in education. *A collection curated by #creativeHE.* Graphic design by Bushra Hashim. CC-BY-NC-SA 4.0

Neumann, M., Rauschenberger, M., & Schön, E. M. (2023, May). "We Need To Talk About ChatGPT": The Future of AI and Higher Education. In 2023 IEEE/ ACM 5th International Workshop on Software Engineering Education for the Next Generation (SEENG) (pp. 29-32). IEEE.

Neumann, C., Stroud, K. M., Bailey, S., Allison, K., & Everts, S. S. (2021). 21st-century competencies in higher education: A practitioner's guide. In *Handbook of research on barriers for teaching 21st-Century competencies and the impact of digitalization* (pp. 293–315). IGI Global. DOI:10.4018/978-1-7998-6967-2.ch016

Ng, D., Leung, T. K., Chu, K. L., & Qia, M. S. (2021). Conceptualizing AI Literacy: an exploratory review. *Computers and Education: Artificial Inteligence*, 10-41.

Nguwi, Y. Y. (2023). Technologies for Education: From Gamification to AI-enabled Learning. *International Journal of Multidisciplinary Perspectives in Higher Education*, 8(1), 111–132.

Nguyen, A., Ngo, H. N., Hong, Y., Dang, B., & Nguyen, B. T. (2022). Ethical principles for artificial intelligence in education. *Education and Information Technologies*, 28(4), 4221–4241. DOI:10.1007/s10639-022-11316-w PMID:36254344

Nicolaou, C., Matsiola, M., & Kalliris, G. (2019). Technology-enhanced learning and teaching methodologies through audiovisual media. *Education Sciences, 9*(3), 196, 1 - 13.

North, M. (2023). *Generative AI has disrupted education. Here's how it can be used for good – UNESCO*. World Economic Forum. Retrieved May 2, 2023, from https://www.weforum.org/agenda/2023/09/generative-ai-education-unesco/

Nykyporets, S. S. (2023). Harnessing cloud technologies for foreign language acquisition among masters in energy engineering. *Moderní aspekty vědy: Svazek XXXI mezinárodní*, 21–56. http://ir.lib.vntu.edu.ua/handle/123456789/37121

Odokuma, E. (2010). Explanations of Freud's psychoanalysis theories on the lives and works of some western artist: An African perspective. *African Research Review*, 4(3, 3a), 227–233. DOI:10.4314/afrrev.v4i3.60179

Ogunleye, B., Zakariyyah, K. I., Ajao, O., Olayinka, O., & Sharma, H. (2024). Higher education assessment practice in the era of generative AI tools. *arXiv preprint arXiv*:2404.01036.

Okanda, E. O. (2024). Nyerere's Philosophy of Education for Self-Reliance and Its Implications for Enhancing the Socio-Economic Dimension of Current Kenyan University Education. *Futurity Philosophy*, 3(2), 4–24.

Omodara, O. D., & Adu, E. I. (2014). Relevance of educational media and multimedia technology for effective service delivery in teaching and learning processes. *IOSR Journal of Research & Method in Education*, 4(2), 48–51.

Organisation for Economic Co-operation and Development. (2016). OECD/INFE international survey of adult financial literacy competencies. *Retrieved February 27, 2023,* from http://www.oecd.org/finance/OECD-INFE-International-Survey-of -Adult Financial-Literacy-Competencies.pdf

Osiyevskyy, O., Radnejad, A. B., & MahdaviMazdeh, H. (2020). An Entrepreneurial Management System for established companies. *Strategy and Leadership*, 48(2), 24–31. DOI:10.1108/SL-12-2019-0190

Oztemel, E., & Gursev, S. (2020). Literature review of Industry 4.0 and related technologies. *Journal of Intelligent Manufacturing*, 31(1), 127–182. DOI:10.1007/s10845-018-1433-8

Paek, S., & Kim, N. (2021). Analysis of worldwide research trends on the impact of artificial intelligence in education. *Sustainability (Basel)*, 13(14), 7941. DOI:10.3390/su13147941

Parlangeli, O., Marchigiani, E., & Bagnara, S. (1999). Multimedia systems in distance education: Effects of usability on learning. *Interacting with Computers*, 12(1), 37–49. DOI:10.1016/S0953-5438(98)00054-X

Pasquale, F. (2020). *New laws of robotics*. Harvard University Press.

Patel, R., & Zhang, L. (2020). Understanding and mitigating bias in machine learning systems. *Journal of Artificial Intelligence Research*, 68, 895–940. DOI:10.1613/jair.1.12112

Paul, R., & Elder, L. (2010). *The miniature guide to critical thinking concepts and tools*. Foundation for Critical Thinking Press.

Pavlik, J. V. (2023). Collaborating with ChatGPT: Considering the Implications of Generative Artificial Intelligence for Journalism and Media Education. *J. Mass Commun. Educ.*, 2023(78), 84–93. DOI:10.1177/10776958221149577

Pellas, N. (2023, July). The Effects of Generative AI Platforms on Undergraduates' Narrative Intelligence and Writing Self-Efficacy. *Education Sciences*, 13(11), 1155. DOI:10.3390/educsci13111155

Pendy, B. (2023). From traditional to tech-infused: The evolution of education. *BULLET: Jurnal Multidisiplin Ilmu*, 2(3), 767–777.

Perera, P., & Lankathilaka, M. (2023). AI in Higher Education: A Literature Review of ChatGPT and Guidelines for Responsible Implementation. *International Journal of Research and Innovation in Social Science*, VII(VI), 306–314. DOI:10.47772/IJRISS.2023.7623

Perera, P., & Lankathilake, M. (2023). Preparing to revolutionize education with the multi-model GenAI tool Google Gemini? A journey towards effective policy making. *J. Adv. Educ. Philos*, 7(8), 246–253. DOI:10.36348/jaep.2023.v07i08.001

Peres, R., Schreier, M., Schweidel, D. A., & Sorescu, A. (2023). On ChatGPT and beyond: How generative artificial intelligence may affect research, teaching, and practice. *International Journal of Research in Marketing*, 40(2), 269–275. DOI:10.1016/j.ijresmar.2023.03.001

Perret-Clemont, A. N. (1980). *Social interaction and cognitive development in children*. Academic Press.

Phillips, W. J. (2020). Rational-experiential inventory. In Zeigler-Hill, V., & Shackelford, T. K. (Eds.), *Encyclopedia of personality and individual differences*. Springer., DOI:10.1007/978-3-319-24612-3_68

Piccardo, E. (2017). Plurilingualism as a catalyst for creativity in superdiverse societies: A systemic analysis. *Frontiers in Psychology*, 8, 2069. Advance online publication. DOI:10.3389/fpsyg.2017.02169 PMID:29312046

Pillay, K., Erasmus, L., & Pretorius, J.-H. C. (2021). *A systems thinking approach to value-added services adoption in national research and education networks*. Paper presented at the 2021 IEEE AFRICON. DOI:10.1109/AFRICON51333.2021.9570883

Pinot de Moira, A. (2013). *Features of a level-based mark scheme and their effect on marking realiability*. Centre of Education Research and Policy.

Popenici, S. A. D., & Kerr, S. (2017). Exploring the impact of artificial intelligence on teaching and learning in higher education. *Research and Practice in Technology Enhanced Learning*, 12(1), 22. Advance online publication. DOI:10.1186/s41039-017-0062-8 PMID:30595727

Porter, B., & Grippa, F. (2020). A platform for AI-enabled real-time feedback to promote digital collaboration. *Sustainability (Basel)*, 12(24), 1–13. DOI:10.3390/su122410243

Powers, A. (2018, April 30). Creativity is the skill of the future. *Forbes*. https://www.forbes.com/sites/annapowers/2018/04/30/creativity-is-the-skill-of-the-future/?sh=63211de64fd4

Prasch, L.K. (2021). Creativity: a human factors challenge. Retrieved June 1, 2024, from file:///C:/Users/ziskaf/Downloads/prasch_2022_creativity.pdf

Prather, J., Denny, P., Leinonen, J., Becker, B. A., Albluwi, I., Craig, M., & Savelka, J. (2023). The robots are here: Navigating the generative ai revolution in computing education. In *Proceedings of the 2023 Working Group Reports on Innovation and Technology in Computer Science Education* (pp. 108-159). DOI:10.1145/3623762.3633499

Priya, B., & Sharma, V. (2023). Exploring users' adoption intentions of intelligent virtual assistants in financial services: An anthropomorphic perspectives and socio-psychological perspectives. *Computers in Human Behavior*, 148, 107912. DOI:10.1016/j.chb.2023.107912

Putra, C. A. (2018). Utilization of multimedia technology for instructional media. *Journal of ICT in Education*, 5(1), 1–8. DOI:10.37134/jictie.vol5.1.2018

PWC. (2017). *20th CEO Survey*. https://www.pwc.com/gx/en/ceo-survey/2017/pwc-ceo-20th-survey-report-2017.pdf

Qadir, J. (2022). Engineering education in the era of ChatGPT: Promise and pitfalls of generative AI for education. *TechRxiv*. Preprint. DOI:10.36227/techrxiv.21789434.v1

Qin, H. (2022). A humanistic approach to Education 2030: Perspective and practice in China. *Beijing International Review of Education*, 4(2), 274–300. DOI:10.1163/25902539-04020006

Raath, E. (2023). *Whole brain empowerment for leaders and teams*. Highwire Leadership. Retrieved May 2, 2024, from https://www.highwireleadership.com/whole-brain-empowerment/

Radwan, A., & Mcginty, J. (2024). Toward a Conceptual Generative AI Ethical Framework in Teacher Education. *Exploring New Horizons: Generative Artificial Intelligence and Teacher Education, 88.*

Rahimi, M., & Zhang, L. J. (2019). Writing task complexity, students' motivational beliefs, anxiety and their writing production in English as a second language. *Reading and Writing*, 32(3), 761–786. DOI:10.1007/s11145-018-9887-9

Rahimzadeh, V., Kostick-Quenet, K., Blumenthal Barby, J., & McGuire, A. L. (2023). Ethics education for healthcare professionals in the era of ChatGPT and other large language models: Do we still need it? *The American Journal of Bioethics*, 23(10), 17–27. DOI:10.1080/15265161.2023.2233358 PMID:37487184

Rashid, M. T., Zhang, D. Y., & Wang, D. (2019). Socialcar: A task allocation framework for social media driven vehicular network sensing systems. *Eduvest-Journal of Universal Studies, 3*(6), 1028-1039.

Rasul, T., Nair, S., Kalendra, D., Robin, M., de Oliveira Santini, F., Ladeira, W. J., & Heathcote, L. (2023). The role of ChatGPT in higher education: Benefits, challenges, and future research directions. *Journal of Applied Learning and Teaching*, 6(1).

Razavian, A. S. (2014). Visualizing and Understanding Convolutional Networks. *InEuropean Conference on Computer Vision (ECCV)* (pp. 818-833).

Reimers, F. M. (2021). Primary and Secondary Education During Covid-19: Disruptions to Educational Opportunity During a Pandemic. *Primary and Secondary Education During Covid-19: Disruptions to Educational Opportunity During a Pandemic*, 1–475. DOI:10.1007/978-3-030-81500-4

Resnik, D. B. (2015). Data Sharing in Genomics: Ethical and Social Challenges. *Annual Review of Genomics and Human Genetics*, 16, 1–32.

Reynolds, C., Stevens, D. D., & West, E. (2013). "I'm in a professional school! Why are you making me do this?" A cross-disciplinary study of the use of creative classroom projects on student learning. *College Teaching*, 61(2), 51–59. DOI:10.1080/87567555.2012.731660

Rhodes, M. (1961). An analysis of creativity. *Phi Delta Kappan*, 305–310.

Richa Singh. (2024). *Imagining the Sustainable Future With Industry 6.0: A Smarter Pathway for Modern Society and Manufacturing Industries, in book title: Machine Learning Algorithms Using Scikit and TensorFlow Environments*. IGI Global. DOI:10.4018/978-1-6684-8531-6.ch016

Riikkinen, M., Saarijärvi, H., Sarlin, P., & Lähteenmäki, I. (2018). Using artificial intelligence to create value in insurance. *International Journal of Bank Marketing*, 36(6), 1145–1168. DOI:10.1108/IJBM-01-2017-0015

Robinson, K. (2006, February). *Do schools kill creativity?* [video]. TED. https://www.ted.com/talks/sir_ken_robinson_do_schools_kill_creativity?

Robinson, K. (2007). *Do schools kill creativity*. Retrieved May 2, 2024, from https://www.youtube.com/watch?v=iG9CE55wbtY

Rockley, A. (1994). Planning a multimedia documentation project. *Technical Communication (Washington)*, 653–661.

Rodriguez, D. (2017, February 2). Unleashing the Power of Boyle's Law. *LinkedIn Blog*.https://www.linkedin.com/pulse/boyles-law-diego-rodriguez/

Rodway, P., & Schepman, A. (2023). The impact of adopting AI educational technologies on projected course satisfaction in university students. *Computers and Education: Artificial Intelligence*, 5, 100150. DOI:10.1016/j.caeai.2023.100150

Rof, A., Bikfalvi, A., & Marques, P. (2022). *Digital Transformation in Higher Education: Intelligence in Systems and Business Models Intelligent Systems in Digital Transformation: Theory and Applications*. Springer.

Rof, A., Bikfalvi, A., & Marques, P. (2022). Pandemic-accelerated digital transformation of a born digital higher education institution. *Journal of Educational Technology & Society*, 25(1), 124–141.

Roksa, J., Feldon, D. F., & Maher, M. (2018). First-generation students in pursuit of the PhD: Comparing socialization experiences and outcomes to continuing-generation peers. *The Journal of Higher Education*, 89(5), 728–752. DOI:10.1080/00221546.2018.1435134

Romera-Paredes, B., Barekatain, M., Novikov, A., Balog, M., Kumar, M. P., Dupont, E., & Fawzi, A. (2023). Mathematical discoveries from program search with large language models. *Nature*, 1-3. Advance online publication. DOI:10.1038/s41586-023-06924-6 PMID:38096900

Rowe, A., & Zegwaard, K. (2017). Developing graduate employability skills and attributes: Curriculum enhancement through work-integrated learning. *Asia Pacific Journal of Cooperative Education*, 18, 87–99.

Runco, M. A. (2014). Creativity. In *The Oxford Handbook of Cognitive Psychology* (pp. 371–386). OUP.

Russell, S., Moskowitz, I. S., & Raglin, A. (2017). *Human information interaction, artificial intelligence, and errors Autonomy and Artificial Intelligence: A Threat or Savior?* Springer.

Saaida, M. (2023). AI-Driven transformations in higher Education: Opportunities and challenges. *International Journal of Educational Research and Studies*, 5, 29–36.

Saaida, M. B. (2023). AI-Driven transformations in higher education: Opportunities and challenges. *International Journal of Educational Research and Studies*, 5, 29–36.

Sadler-Smith, E. (2015). Wallas' four-stage model of the creative process: More than meets the eye? *Creativity Research Journal*, 27(4), 342–352. DOI:10.1080/10400419.2015.1087277

Sahl, B. C., & Eke, D. (2024). The ethics of ChatGPT – Exploring the ethical issues of an emerging technology. Opinion paper. *International Journal of Information Management*, 74, 102700. DOI:10.1016/j.ijinfomgt.2023.102700

Salinas-Navarro, D. E., Vilalta-Perdomo, E., Michel-Villarreal, R., & Montesinos, L. (2024). Using generative artificial intelligence tools to explain and enhance experiential learning for authentic assessment. *Education Sciences*, 14(1), 83. DOI:10.3390/educsci14010083

Sallam, M. (2023). The Utility of ChatGPT as an Example of Large Language Models in Healthcare Education, Research and Practice: Systematic Review on the Future Perspectives and Potential Limitations. https://www.medrxiv.org/content/10.1101/2023.02.19.23286155v1

Samaniego, M., Usca, N., Salguero, J., & Quevedo, W. (2024). Creative thinking in art and design education: A systematic review. *Education Sciences*, 14(2), 192. Advance online publication. DOI:10.3390/educsci14020192

Samosir, S. A., & Daulay, S. H. (2023). EFL Students' Perception of the use "Grammarly Application" as Automated Writing Evaluation (AWE). *Conference on English Language Teaching*, 928–940. Retrieved from https://proceedings.uinsaizu.ac.id/index.php/celti/article/view/562

Sarı, T., Nayir, F., & Bozkurt, A. (2024). Reimagining education: Bridging artificial intelligence, transhumanism, and critical pedagogy. *Journal of Educational Technology and Online Learning*, 7(1), 102–115. DOI:10.31681/jetol.1308022

Sari, W., & Daulay, S. H. (2023). Analysis of Teacher's Feedback on Students in Writing Recount Text at Senior High School. *ENGLISH FRANCA: Academic Journal of English Language and Education*, 7(1), 93–104. DOI:10.29240/ef.v7i1.6442

Sarker, D., Eiaz-Ur-Rahman, A. F. M., Sakib, A. R., Terano, H. J. R., & Rahman, M. M. (2023). ChatGPT's Applications in Higher Education: Unmasking Opportunities and Challenges. *Journal of Education. Management and Development Studies*, 3(4), 37–47.

Sarooghi, H., Libaers, D., & Burkemper, A. (2015). Examining the relationship between creativity and innovation: A meta-analysis of organizational, cultural, and environmental factors. *Journal of Business Venturing*, 30(5), 714–731. DOI:10.1016/j.jbusvent.2014.12.003

Savage, T. M., & Vogel, K. E. (1996). Multimedia: A revolution in higher education? *College Teaching*, 44(4), 127–131. DOI:10.1080/87567555.1996.9932339

Savic, M. (2016). Mathematical problem-solving via Wallas' four stages of creativity: Implications for the undergraduate classroom. *The Montana Math Enthusiast*, 13(3), 255–278. DOI:10.54870/1551-3440.1377

Schoitsch, E. (2019). Beyond smart systems-Creating a society of the future (5.0) resolving disruptive changes and social challenges. *IDIMT 2019, Proceedings*, 387-400.

Schreier, M. (2012). *Qualitative content analysis in practice*. SAGE. DOI:10.4135/9781529682571

Schwab, K. (2018, October 29). *IDEO breaks its silence on design thinking critics*. Fast Company. Retrieved December 2, 2023, from https://www.fastcompany.com/90257718/ideo-breaks-its-silence-on-design-thinkings-critics

Schwartz, R., Schwartz, R., Vassilev, A., Greene, K., Perine, L., Burt, A., & Hall, P. (2022). *Towards a standard for identifying and managing bias in artificial intelligence* (Vol. 3, p. 00). US Department of Commerce, National Institute of Standards and Technology.

Seaman, J., & Tinti-Kane, H. (2013). *Social media for teaching and learning*. Pearson Learning Systems.

Seitz, D. (2004). *Who Can Afford Critical Consciousness? Practicing a Pedagogy of Humility*. Hampton Press.

Sellars, M., Fakirmohammad, R., Bui, L., Fishetti, J., Niyozov, S., Reynolds, R., Thapliyal, N., Liu-Smith, Y. L., & Ali, N. (2018). Conversations on critical thinking: Can critical thinking find its way forward as the skill set and mindset of the century? *Education Sciences*, 8(4), 205. Advance online publication. DOI:10.3390/educsci8040205

Selvaraj, P., Muralidharan, R. R., Subbaiah, P., & Narayanan, L. K. (2021). Smart Infant and Child Monitoring System using Integrated IoT and GIS. *Design Engineering*, 15225-15235.

Seo, K. K., Templeton, R., & Pellegrino, D. (2008). Creating a ripple effect: Incorporating multimedia-assisted project-based learning in teacher education. *Theory into Practice*, 47(3), 259–265. DOI:10.1080/00405840802154062

Seo, K., Tang, J., Roll, I., Fels, S., & Yoon, D. (2021). The impact of artificial intelligence on learner–instructor interaction in online learning. *International Journal of Educational Technology in Higher Education*, 18(1), 1–23. DOI:10.1186/s41239-021-00292-9 PMID:34778540

Setiamurti, A., & Kurniawati, F. (2024). Fostering Creativity in Higher Education Institution: A Systematic Review (2018–2022). *Open Education Studies*, 6(1), 20220221. Advance online publication. DOI:10.1515/edu-2022-0221

Shabani, K. (2016). Applications of Vygotsky's sociocultural approach for teachers' professional development. *Cogent Education*, 3(1), 1252177. Advance online publication. DOI:10.1080/2331186X.2016.1252177

Shahab, M., Taheri, A., Mokhtari, M., Shariati, A., Heidari, R., Meghdari, A., & Alemi, M. (2022). Utilizing social virtual reality robot (V2R) for music education to children with high-functioning autism. *Education and Information Technologies*, 27(1), 819–843. DOI:10.1007/s10639-020-10392-0

Shelton, S. M. (1993). Multimedia. *Technical Communication (Washington)*, 40(4), 694–704.

Sher, G., & Benchlouch, A. (2023). The privacy paradox with AI. *Retrieved February 27, 2023,* from https://www.reuters.com/legal/legalindustry/privacy-paradox-with-ai-2023-10-31/

Shi, C. (2011). A Study of the Relationship between Cognitive Styles and Learning Strategies. *Higher Education Studies*, 1(1), 20–26. DOI:10.5539/hes.v1n1p20

Shimizu, I., Kasai, H., Shikino, K., Araki, N., Takahashi, Z., Onodera, M., Kimura, Y., Tsukamoto, T., Yamauchi, K., Asahina, M., Ito, S., & Kawakami, E. (2023). Developing medical education curriculum reform strategies to address the impact of generative AI: Qualitative study. *JMIR Medical Education*, 9(1), e53466. DOI:10.2196/53466 PMID:38032695

Shirzadifard, M., Shahghasemi, E., Hejazi, E., Naghsh, Z., & Ranjbar, G. (2018). Psychometric properties of Rational-Experiential Inventory for adolescents. *SAGE Open*, 8(1). Advance online publication. DOI:10.1177/2158244018767219

Shtepa, S., Bao, Y., & Osiyevskyy, O. (2023). The impact of artificial intelligence on management practice. In Cennamo, C., Dagnino, G. B., & Zhu, F. (Eds.), *Research Handbook on Digital Strategy* (pp. 324–341). Edward Elgar. DOI:10.4337/9781800378902.00027

Shukla, S. (2023). Creative Computing and Harnessing the Power of Generative Artificial Intelligence. *Journal of Environmental Science and Technology*, 2(1), 556–579.

Siemens, G., & Long, P. (2011). Penetrating the Fog: Analytics in Learning and Education. *EDUCAUSE Review*, 46(5), 30–32.

Simkus, J. (2024, January 29). *Myers-Briggs Type Indicator (MBTI): 16 personality types*. Simply Psychology. Retrieved May 20, 2024, from https://www.simplypsychology.org/the-myers-briggs-type-indicator.html

Simonson, P. (2014). Reinvention Invention, Again. *Rhetoric Society Quarterly*, 44(1), 299–322. DOI:10.1080/02773945.2014.938862

Singaravelu, G., Peter, J., & Singaravelu, G. (2020). Problems in Writing in English among High School Learners. *Aegaeum Journal, 8*(9), 1502–1515. https://www.researchgate.net/publication/351048985

Singh, R. N., & Pathak, N. (2019). Guilford's structure of intellect (SOI) model of intelligence: A critical review. *Recent Advances in Psychology*, 6(1&2), 29–37.

Slawson, B. (1993). Interactive multimedia: The gestalt of a gigabyte. *Art Education*, 46(6), 15–22. DOI:10.2307/3193404

Slimi, Z., & Carballido, B. V. (2023). Navigating the Ethical Challenges of Artificial Intelligence in Higher Education: An Analysis of Seven Global AI Ethics Policies. *TEM Journal,* 12(2). https://doi.org/DOI:10.18421/TEM122-02

Smolansky, A., Cram, A., Raduescu, C., Zeivots, S., Huber, E., & Kizilcec, R. F. (2023, July). Educator and student perspectives on the impact of generative AI on assessments in higher education. In *Proceedings of the tenth ACM conference on Learning@ Scale* (pp. 378-382). DOI:10.1145/3573051.3596191

Soltani, M., Moradi Kashkooli, F., Souri, M., Zare Harofte, S., Harati, T., Khadem, A., Haeri Pour, M., & Raahemifar, K. (2021). Enhancing clinical translation of cancer using nanoinformatics. *Cancers (Basel),* 13(10), 2481. DOI:10.3390/cancers13102481 PMID:34069606

Sosa, R., & Kayrouz, D. (2020). Creativity in graduate business education: Constitutive dimensions and connections. *Innovations in Education and Teaching International*, 57(4), 484–495. DOI:10.1080/14703297.2019.1628799

Sousa, F., Monteiro, I., Walton, A., & Pissarra, J. (2013). Learning from failure: A case study on creative problem solving. *Procedia: Social and Behavioral Sciences*, 75, 570–580. DOI:10.1016/j.sbspro.2013.04.062

Srinivasan, R., & Uchino, K. (2021, March). Biases in generative art: A causal look from the lens of art history. In *Proceedings of the 2021 ACM Conference on Fairness, Accountability, and Transparency* (pp. 41-51). DOI:10.1145/3442188.3445869

Staake, J. (2023, May 22). *What is higher-order thinking and how do i teach it?* We Are Teachers. Retrieved May 2, 2023, from https://www.weareteachers.com/higher-order-thinking/

Stack, M., & Kelly, D. M. (2006). Popular media, education, and resistance. *Canadian Journal of Education/Revue Canadienne de l'éducation*, 5-26.

Sternberg, R. J. (1990). Thinking styles: Keys to understanding student performance. *Phi Delta Kappan*, 71(5), 366–371.

Sternberg, R. J. (1994). Thinking styles: Theory and assessment at the interface between intelligence and personality. In Sternberg, R. J., & Ruzgis, P. (Eds.), *Personality and intelligence* (pp. 105–127). Cambridge University Press.

Sternberg, R. J. (2004). Teaching college students that creativity is a decision. *Guidance & Counselling*, 19(4), 196.

Steven, D. (2021). AI In Education Change at the speed of Learning. *Unesco, 12*(1), 70. https://dialnet.unirioja.es/servlet/tesis?codigo=286366%0Ahttp://www.tdx.cat/bitstream/handle/10803/85876/GONZALES_Tesis Doctoral_FV.pdf?sequence=1%0Ahttps://unesdoc.unesco.org/ark:/48223/pf0000368303%0Ahttps://ec.europa.eu/jrc/en/publication/eur-scientific-and

Stone, B. (2017). *The upstarts: Uber, Airbnb, and the battle for Silicon Valley.* Hachette Book Group.

Stone, L. L. (1999). Multimedia instruction methods. *The Journal of Economic Education*, 30(3), 265–275. DOI:10.1080/00220489909595987

Storm, F. A., Chiappini, M., Dei, C., Piazza, C., André, E., Reißner, N., & Malosio, M. (2022). Physical and mental well-being of cobot workers: A scoping review using the Software-Hardware-Environment-Liveware-Liveware-Organization model. *Human Factors and Ergonomics in Manufacturing*, 32(5), 419–435. DOI:10.1002/hfm.20952

Štuikys, V., & Burbaitė, R. (2024). Personal Generative Libraries for Personalised Learning: A Case Study. In *Evolution of STEM-Driven Computer Science Education: The Perspective of Big Concepts* (pp. 109-134). Springer. DOI:10.1007/978-3-031-48235-9_4

Stum, J. (2009). Kirton's adaption-innovation theory: Managing cognitive styles in times of diversity and change. *Emerging Leadership Journeys,* 2(1), 66–78. https://www.regent.edu/journal/emerging-leadership-journeys/kirton-adaption-innovation/

Sudharsan, B. (2024). The Role of AI in Enhancing Financial Literacy and Budgeting Skills. https://www.linkedin.com/pulse/role-ai-enhancing-financial-literacy-budgeting-skills-sudharsan-b

Su, J., & Yang, W. (2023). Unlocking the power of ChatGPT: A framework for applying generative AI in education. *ECNU Review of Education*, 6(3), 355–366. DOI:10.1177/20965311231168423

Sullivan, P. (2015). The UnEssay: Making room for creativity in the composition classroom. *College Composition and Communication*, 67(1), 6–34. DOI:10.58680/ccc201527441

Sultan, F. (2024). The Future of Multidisciplinary Research: Trends and Opportunities in the 21st Century. *Kashf Journal of Multidisciplinary Research*, 1(05), 35–46.

Suryani, I., & Daulay, S. H. (2022). Students' Perceptions on Writing Activities by Using Padlet Application. *The Proceedings of English Language Teaching, Literature, and Translation*, 11, 175–188.

Swiecki, Z., Khosravi, H., Chen, G., Martinez-Maldonado, R., Lodge, J. M., Milligan, S., Selwyn, N., & Gašević, D. (2022). Assessment in the age of artificial intelligence. *Computers and Education: Artificial Intelligence*, 3, 100075. DOI:10.1016/j.caeai.2022.100075

Taj, I., & Zaman, N. (2022). Towards Industrial Revolution 5.0 and Explainable Artificial Intelligence: Challenges and Opportunities. *International Journal of Computing and Digital Systems*, 12(1), 295–320. DOI:10.12785/ijcds/120128

Tariq, M. U. (2024). Multidisciplinary service learning in higher education: Concepts, implementation, and impact. In S. Watson (Ed.), *Applications of service learning in higher education* (pp. 1-19). IGI Global. DOI:10.4018/979-8-3693-2133-1.ch001

Tariq, M. U. (2024). Neurodiversity inclusion and belonging strategies in the workplace. In J. Vázquez de Príncipe (Ed.), *Resilience of multicultural and multigenerational leadership and workplace experience* (pp. 182-201). IGI Global. DOI:10.4018/979-8-3693-1802-7.ch009

Tariq, M. U. (2022). Maintaining sustainable production and service by mitigating impact industry 4.0 factors in the petroleum and coal sector in Pakistan. *International Journal of Services and Operations Management*, 43(2), 188. DOI:10.1504/IJSOM.2022.126815

Tariq, M. U. (2023). Role of artificial intelligence in the enabling sustainable supply chain management during COVID-19. *International Journal of Services and Operations Management*, 44(1), 115. DOI:10.1504/IJSOM.2023.128938

Tariq, M. U. (2024). AI and IoT in flood forecasting and mitigation: A comprehensive approach. In Ouaissa, M., Ouaissa, M., Boulouard, Z., Iwendi, C., & Krichen, M. (Eds.), *AI and IoT for proactive disaster management* (pp. 26–60). IGI Global. DOI:10.4018/979-8-3693-3896-4.ch003

Tariq, M. U. (2024). AI and the future of talent management: Transforming recruitment and retention with machine learning. In Christiansen, B., Aziz, M., & O'Keeffe, E. (Eds.), *Global practices on effective talent acquisition and retention* (pp. 1–16). IGI Global. DOI:10.4018/979-8-3693-1938-3.ch001

Tariq, M. U. (2024). Application of blockchain and Internet of Things (IoT) in modern business. In Sinha, M., Bhandari, A., Priya, S., & Kabiraj, S. (Eds.), *Future of customer engagement through marketing intelligence* (pp. 66–94). IGI Global. DOI:10.4018/979-8-3693-2367-0.ch004

Tariq, M. U. (2024). Challenges of a metaverse shaping the future of entrepreneurship. In Inder, S., Dawra, S., Tennin, K., & Sharma, S. (Eds.), *New business frontiers in the metaverse* (pp. 155–173). IGI Global. DOI:10.4018/979-8-3693-2422-6.ch011

Tariq, M. U. (2024). Emerging trends and innovations in blockchain-digital twin integration for green investments: A case study perspective. In Jafar, S., Rodriguez, R., Kannan, H., Akhtar, S., & Plugmann, P. (Eds.), *Harnessing blockchain-digital twin fusion for sustainable investments* (pp. 148–175). IGI Global. DOI:10.4018/979-8-3693-1878-2.ch007

Tariq, M. U. (2024). Emotional intelligence in understanding and influencing consumer behavior. In Musiolik, T., Rodriguez, R., & Kannan, H. (Eds.), *AI impacts in digital consumer behavior* (pp. 56–81). IGI Global. DOI:10.4018/979-8-3693-1918-5.ch003

Tariq, M. U. (2024). Empowering educators in the learning ecosystem. In Al Husseiny, F., & Munna, A. (Eds.), *Preparing students for the future educational paradigm* (pp. 232–255). IGI Global. DOI:10.4018/979-8-3693-1536-1.ch010

Tariq, M. U. (2024). Empowering student entrepreneurs: From idea to execution. In Cantafio, G., & Munna, A. (Eds.), *Empowering students and elevating universities with innovation centers* (pp. 83–111). IGI Global. DOI:10.4018/979-8-3693-1467-8.ch005

Tariq, M. U. (2024). Enhancing cybersecurity protocols in modern healthcare systems: Strategies and best practices. In Garcia, M., & de Almeida, R. (Eds.), *Transformative approaches to patient literacy and healthcare innovation* (pp. 223–241). IGI Global. DOI:10.4018/979-8-3693-3661-8.ch011

Tariq, M. U. (2024). Equity and Inclusion in Learning Ecosystems. In Al Husseiny, F., & Munna, A. (Eds.), *Preparing Students for the Future Educational Paradigm* (pp. 155–176). IGI Global. DOI:10.4018/979-8-3693-1536-1.ch007

Tariq, M. U. (2024). Fintech startups and cryptocurrency in business: Revolutionizing entrepreneurship. In Kankaew, K., Nakpathom, P., Chnitphattana, A., Pitchayadejanant, K., & Kunnapapdeelert, S. (Eds.), *Applying business intelligence and innovation to entrepreneurship* (pp. 106–124). IGI Global. DOI:10.4018/979-8-3693-1846-1.ch006

Tariq, M. U. (2024). Leveraging artificial intelligence for a sustainable and climate-neutral economy in Asia. In Ordóñez de Pablos, P., Almunawar, M., & Anshari, M. (Eds.), *Strengthening sustainable digitalization of Asian economy and society* (pp. 1–21). IGI Global. DOI:10.4018/979-8-3693-1942-0.ch001

Tariq, M. U. (2024). Metaverse in business and commerce. In Kumar, J., Arora, M., & Erkol Bayram, G. (Eds.), *Exploring the use of metaverse in business and education* (pp. 47–72). IGI Global., DOI:10.4018/979-8-3693-5868-9.ch004

Tariq, M. U. (2024). Revolutionizing health data management with blockchain technology: Enhancing security and efficiency in a digital era. In Garcia, M., & de Almeida, R. (Eds.), *Emerging technologies for health literacy and medical practice* (pp. 153–175). IGI Global. DOI:10.4018/979-8-3693-1214-8.ch008

Tariq, M. U. (2024). The role of AI ethics in cost and complexity reduction. In Tennin, K., Ray, S., & Sorg, J. (Eds.), *Cases on AI ethics in business* (pp. 59–78). IGI Global. DOI:10.4018/979-8-3693-2643-5.ch004

Tariq, M. U. (2024). The role of AI in skilling, upskilling, and reskilling the workforce. In Doshi, R., Dadhich, M., Poddar, S., & Hiran, K. (Eds.), *Integrating generative AI in education to achieve sustainable development goals* (pp. 421–433). IGI Global. DOI:10.4018/979-8-3693-2440-0.ch023

Tariq, M. U. (2024). The role of emerging technologies in shaping the global digital government landscape. In Guo, Y. (Ed.), *Emerging developments and technologies in digital government* (pp. 160–180). IGI Global. DOI:10.4018/979-8-3693-2363-2.ch009

Tariq, M. U. (2024). The transformation of healthcare through AI-driven diagnostics. In Sharma, A., Chanderwal, N., Tyagi, S., Upadhyay, P., & Tyagi, A. (Eds.), *Enhancing medical imaging with emerging technologies* (pp. 250–264). IGI Global. DOI:10.4018/979-8-3693-5261-8.ch015

Tariq, M. U., Babar, M., Jan, M. A., Khattak, A. S., Alshehri, M. D., & Yahya, A. (2021). Security requirement management for cloud-assisted and internet of things⇔enabled smart city. *Computers, Materials & Continua*, 67(1), 625–639. DOI:10.32604/cmc.2021.014165

Tariq, M. U., Babar, M., Poulin, M., Khattak, A. S., Alshehri, M. D., & Kaleem, S. (2021). Human behavior analysis using intelligent big data analytics. *Frontiers in Psychology*, 12, 686610. Advance online publication. DOI:10.3389/fpsyg.2021.686610 PMID:34295289

Tariq, M. U., & Ismail, M. U. S. B. (2024). AI-powered COVID-19 forecasting: A comprehensive comparison of advanced deep learning methods. *Osong Public Health and Research Perspectives*, 15(2), 2210–9099. DOI:10.24171/j.phrp.2023.0287 PMID:38621765

Tariq, M. U., & Ismail, S. B. (2024). Deep learning in public health: Comparative predictive models for COVID-19 case forecasting. *PLoS One*, 19(3), e0294289. DOI:10.1371/journal.pone.0294289 PMID:38483948

Tariq, M. U., Poulin, M., & Abonamah, A. A. (2021). Achieving operational excellence through artificial intelligence: Driving forces and barriers. *Frontiers in Psychology*, 12, 686624. Advance online publication. DOI:10.3389/fpsyg.2021.686624 PMID:34305744

Taylor, D. L., Yeung, M., & Bashet, A. (2021). Personalized and adaptive learning. *Innovative Learning Environments in STEM Higher Education: Opportunities, Challenges, and Looking Forward*, 17-34.

Teachflow. (2022). The role of AI in promoting financial literacy. https://teachflow.ai/the-role-of-ai-in-promoting-financial-literacy/

Terry, O. K. (2023, May 12). I'm a Student. You Have No Idea How Much We're Using ChatGPT: No professor or software could ever pick up on it. *The Chronicle of Higher Education*.https://www.chronicle.com/article/im-a-student-you-have-no-idea-how-much-were-using-chatgpt?sra=true

Terwiesch, C., & Loch, C. H. (2004). Collaborative prototyping and the pricing of custom-designed products. *Management Science*, 50(2), 145–158. DOI:10.1287/mnsc.1030.0178

The Economist. (2014, June 28). *The digital degree.*https://www.economist.com/briefing/2014/06/27/the-digital-degree

The Education Hub. (2020, January 20). *The role of motivation in learning*. Retrieved December 2, 2023, from https://theeducationhub.org.nz/motivation/

Thompson, D., & Brewster, S. (2023). Inclusive placement learning for diverse higher education students: Anxiety, uncertainty and opportunity. *Educational Review*, 75(7), 1406–1424. DOI:10.1080/00131911.2021.2023470

Timmis, S., Broadfoot, P., Sutherland, R., & Oldfield, A. (2016). Rethinking assessment in a digital age: Opportunities, challenges and risks. *British Educational Research Journal*, 42(3), 454–476. DOI:10.1002/berj.3215

Titus, P. A., & Koppitsch, S. (2018). Exploring business students' creative problem-solving preferences. *Journal of Education for Business*, 93(5), 242–251. DOI:10.1080/08832323.2018.1465021

Tobler, S. (2024). Smart grading: A generative AI-based tool for knowledge-grounded answer evaluation in educational assessments. *MethodsX*, 12, 102531. DOI:10.1016/j.mex.2023.102531 PMID:38204981

Tolhurst, D. (1995). Hypertext, hypermedia, multimedia defined? *Educational Technology*, 35(2), 21–26.

Tomar, A. (2023, December 8). *How can Indian higher education prepare to leapfrog in the next two years.* Retrieved April 14, 2024, from EY.Com: https://www.ey.com/en_in/education/how-can-indian-higher-education-prepare-to-leapfrog-in-the-next-two-years

Topol, E. J. (2019). High-Performance Medicine: The Convergence of Human and Artificial Intelligence. *Nature Medicine*, 25(1), 44–56. DOI:10.1038/s41591-018-0300-7 PMID:30617339

Topsakal, O., & Topsakal, E. (2022). Framework for a foreign language teaching software for children utilizing AR, voicebots and ChatGPT (Large Language Models). *The Journal of Cognitive Systems*, 7(2), 33–38. DOI:10.52876/jcs.1227392

Towers, G. (2023). *10 essential skills for every future proof organization according to the World Economic Forum*. Lepaya. Retrieved May 2, 2024, from https://www.lepaya.com/blog/top-10-skills-of-the-future

Towle, B., & Halm, M. (2005). Designing adaptive learning environments with learning design. *Learning Design: A Handbook on Modelling and Delivering Networked Education and Training*, 215-226.

Tuo, Y., Ning, L., & Zhu, A. (2021). How Artificial Intelligence Will Change the Future of Tourism Industry: The Practice in China. In *Information and Communication Technologies in Tourism* (pp. 83–94). Springer International Publishing. DOI:10.1007/978-3-030-65785-7_7

Turnali, K. (2015, May 10). *What is design thinking?* Forbes. Retrieved December 2, 2023, from https://www.forbes.com/sites/sap/2015/05/10/what-is-design-thinking/

Tyagi, A. K., & Bansal, R. (2023). A Step-To-Step Guide to Write a Quality Research Article. In Intelligent Systems Design and Applications. ISDA 2022. Lecture Notes in Networks and Systems, vol 717. Springer. DOI:10.1007/978-3-031-35510-3_36

Tyagi, A. K., Lakshmi Priya, R., Mishra, A. K., & Balamurugan, G. (2023). Industry 5.0: Potentials, Issues, Opportunities, and Challenges for Society 5.0. *Privacy Preservation of Genomic and Medical Data*, 409-432.

Tyagi, A. K. (2023). Decentralized everything: Practical use of blockchain technology in future applications. In *Distributed Computing to Blockchain* (pp. 19–38). Academic Press. DOI:10.1016/B978-0-323-96146-2.00010-3

Tyagi, A. K. (2024). Transformative Effects of ChatGPT on the Modern Era of Education and Society: From Society's and Industry's Perspectives. In *Machine Learning Algorithms Using Scikit and TensorFlow Environments* (pp. 374–387). IGI Global. DOI:10.1007/978-3-030-71187-0_1

Tyagi, A. K., Dananjayan, S., Agarwal, D., & Thariq Ahmed, H. F. (2023). Blockchain—Internet of Things Applications: Opportunities and Challenges for Industry 4.0 and Society 5.0. *Sensors (Basel)*, 23(2), 947. DOI:10.3390/s23020947 PMID:36679743

Tyagi, A., Kukreja, S., Nair, M. M., & Tyagi, A. K. (2022). Machine Learning: Past, Present and Future. *NeuroQuantology : An Interdisciplinary Journal of Neuroscience and Quantum Physics*, 20(8). Advance online publication. DOI:10.14704/nq.2022.20.8.NQ44468

Utami, S. P. T., Andayani, A., Winarni, R., & Sumarwati, S. (2023). Utilization of artificial intelligence technology in an academic writing class: How do Indonesian students perceive? *Contemporary Educational Technology*, 15(4), ep450. DOI:10.30935/cedtech/13419

Vacarelu, M. (2023). Artificial Intelligence and Higher Education Legal Limits: Bridging Human and Machine. In *Future Education with Intelligence*, 15–33. DOI:10.1007/978-981-19-8641-3_2

Vagg, T., Balta, J. Y., Bolger, A., & Lone, M. (2020). Multimedia in education: What do the students think? *Health Profession Education*, 6(3), 325–333. DOI:10.1016/j.hpe.2020.04.011

Van Nuys, A. (2019, December 28). New LinkedIn research: Upskill your employees with the skill companies need most in 2020. *LinkedIn Learning Blog*.https://www.linkedin.com/business/learning/blog/learning-and-development/most-in-demand-skills-2020

VanLehn, K. (2011). The relative effectiveness of human tutoring, intelligent tutoring systems, and other tutoring systems. *Educational Psychologist*, 46(4), 197–221. DOI:10.1080/00461520.2011.611369

Varsha, R., Nair, S. M., Tyagi, A. K., & Aswathy, S. U. (2021) The Future with Advanced Analytics: A Sequential Analysis of the Disruptive Technology's Scope. In Hybrid Intelligent Systems. HIS 2020. Advances in Intelligent Systems and Computing, vol 1375. Springer. DOI:10.1007/978-3-030-73050-5_56

Velleman, P. F., & Moore, D. S. (1996). Multimedia for teaching statistics: Promises and pitfalls. *The American Statistician*, 50(3), 217–225. DOI:10.1080/00031305.1996.10474383

Vickery, C. (1977). The Time-Poor: A New Look at Poverty. *The Journal of Human Resources*, 12(1), 27–48. DOI:10.2307/145597

Vidovićová, L. (2013). Financial literacy in retirement planning context: the case of Czech older workers. In Phellas, C. (Ed.), *Aging in European societies. Healthy aging in Europe* (pp. 191–203). Springer. DOI:10.1007/978-1-4419-8345-9_13

Vinchon, F., Lubart, T., Bartolotta, S., Gironnay, V., Botella, M., Bourgeois-Bougrine, S., Burkhardt, J., Bonnardel, N., Corazza, G. E., Glăveanu, V., Hanchett Hanson, M., Ivcevic, Z., Karwowski, M., Kaufman, J. C., Okada, T., Reiter-Palmon, R., & Gaggioli, A. (2023). Artificial intelligence & creativity: A manifesto for collaboration. *The Journal of Creative Behavior*, 57(4), 472–484. DOI:10.1002/jocb.597

Vinney, C. (2020). *Understanding the triarchic theory of intelligence*. ThoughtCo. Retrieved December 2, 2023, from https://www.thoughtco.com/triarchic-theory-of-intelligence-4172497

Vygotsky, L. S., & Cole, M. (1978). Mind in society: Development of higher psychological processes. Harvard University Press.

Vygotsky, L.S. (1967, 2004). Imagination and creativity in childhood. *Journal of Russian & East European Psychology, 42*(1), 7–97. (Original work published 1967)

Vygotsky, L. S. (1978). Interaction between learning and development. *Readings on the Development of Children*, 23(3), 34–41.

Wagner, G., Lukyanenko, R., & Pare, G. (2022). Artificial Intelligence and the Conduct of Literature Reviews. *Journal of Information Technology*, 37(2), 209–226. DOI:10.1177/02683962211048201

Wang, M. Y., & Wang, P. (2023). Decoding business applications of generative AI: A bibliometric analysis and text mining approach. *ICEB 2023 Proceedings (Chiayi, Taiwan)*. 15. https://aisel.aisnet.org/iceb2023/15

Wang, T. (2023, August). Navigating Generative AI (ChatGPT) in Higher Education: Opportunities and Challenges. In *International Conference on Smart Learning Environments* (pp. 215-225). Singapore: Springer Nature Singapore. DOI:10.1007/978-981-99-5961-7_28

Wang, M., & Guo, W. (2023). *The potential impact of ChatGPT on Education: Using History as a rearview mirror*. ECNU Review of Education. DOI:10.1177/20965311231189826

Wang, S. (2018). AI-Ed: Integrating Adaptive Learning into Intelligent Tutoring Systems. *InProceedings of the International Conference on Artificial Intelligence in Education (AIED)* (pp. 289-303).

Wang, X., & Liu, Q. (2023). Exploring Speculative and Imaginative Applications of Generative Artificial Intelligence. *Journal of Artificial Intelligence Futures*, 16(4), 210–225. DOI:10.1080/12345678.2023.9876543

Wanof, M. I. (2023). Digital technology innovation in improving financial access for low-income communities. *Technology and Society Perspectives*, 1(1), 26–34. DOI:10.61100/tacit.v1i1.35

Watermeyer, R., Phipps, L., Lanclos, D., & Knight, C. (2024). Generative AI and the Automating of Academia. *Postdigital Science and Education*, 6(2), 446–466. DOI:10.1007/s42438-023-00440-6

Wei, W., & Li, L. (2022). The Impact of Artificial Intelligence on the Mental Health of Manufacturing Workers: The Mediating Role of Overtime Work and the Work Environment. *Frontiers in Public Health*, 10, 10. DOI:10.3389/fpubh.2022.862407 PMID:35480579

Whiting, K. (2020). *These are the top 10 job skills of tomorrow – and how long it takes to learn them*. World Economic Forum. Retrieved December 2, 2023, from https://www.weforum.org/agenda/2020/10/top-10-work-skills-of-tomorrow-how-long-it-takes-to-learn-them/

Whittlestone, J., Nyrup, R., Alexandrova, A., Dihal, K., & Cave, S. (2019). *Ethical and societal implications of algorithms, data, and artificial intelligence: a roadmap for research*. Nuffield Foundation.

Wieland, B., De Wit, J., & De Rooij, A. (2022). Electronic brainstorming with a chatbot partner: A good idea due to increased productivity and idea diversity. *Frontiers in Artificial Intelligence*, 5, 880673. Advance online publication. DOI:10.3389/frai.2022.880673 PMID:36213166

Williamson, B. (2020). Governing by numbers: Algorithmic governance and the hidden algorithms that govern people's lives. *Learning, Media and Technology*, 45(3), 247–265.

Williamson, B., & Eynon, R. (2020). Historical threads, missing links, and future directions in AI in education. *Learning, Media and Technology*, 45(3), 223–235. DOI:10.1080/17439884.2020.1798995

Winkel, D., & Liguori, E. (2024, June 24). *From AI integration to AI co-creation*. AACSB. https://www.aacsb.edu/insights/articles/2024/06/from-ai-integration-to-ai-co-creation?

Winkler, C., Hammoda, B., Noyes, E., & Van Gelderen, M. (2023). Entrepreneurship education at the dawn of generative artificial intelligence. *Entrepreneurship Education and Pedagogy*, 6(4), 579–589. DOI:10.1177/25151274231198799

Wladis, C., Hachey, A. C., & Conway, K. (2018). No time for college? an investigation of time poverty and parenthood. *The Journal of Higher Education*, 89(6), 807–831. DOI:10.1080/00221546.2018.1442983

Wong, B., Chiu, Y. T., Copsey-Blake, M., & Nikolopoulou, M. (2022). A mapping of graduate attributes: What can we expect from UK university students? *Higher Education Research & Development*, 41(4), 1340–1355. DOI:10.1080/07294360.2021.1882405

Wood, T. (2017). Cripping Time in the College Composition Classroom. *College Composition and Communication*, 69(2), 260–286. DOI:10.58680/ccc201729419

World Economic Forum. (2016). The Fourth Industrial Revolution. https://www.weforum.org/agenda/2016/01/the-fourth-industrial-revolution

World Economic Forum. (2016). The Global Risks Report 2016. http://www3.weforum.org/docs/Media/TheGlobalRisksReport2016.pdf

World Economic Forum. (2023). Gamification for financial education: building resilience through play. https://intelligence.weforum.org/topics/a1Gb0000000LPFfEAO/publications/5a6261cc30fe46b78b330a636c2318b1

Xavier, M., & Meneses, J. (2022). Persistence and time challenges in an open online university: A case study of the experiences of first-year learners. *International Journal of Educational Technology in Higher Education*, 19(1), 1–17. DOI:10.1186/s41239-022-00338-6 PMID:35013716

Xavier, M., Meneses, J., & Fiuza, P. J. (2022). Dropout, stopout, and time challenges in open online higher education: A qualitative study of the first-year student experience. *Open Learning*, 1–17. DOI:10.1080/02680513.2022.2160236

Xia, Q., Chiu, T. K., Lee, M., Temiyato, I., Dai, Y., & Chai, C. S. (2022). A self-determination theory design for inclusive and diverse Artificial Intelligence (AI) K-12 education. *Computers & Education*, 189, 104582. DOI:10.1016/j.compedu.2022.104582

Xia, Q., Weng, X., Ouyang, F., Lin, T. J., & Chiu, T. K. (2024). A scoping review on how generative artificial intelligence transforms assessment in higher education. *International Journal of Educational Technology in Higher Education*, 21(1), 40. DOI:10.1186/s41239-024-00468-z

Xing, B., & Marwala, T. (2018). *Creativity and Artificial Intelligence: A Digital Art Perspective.* Springer. ArXiv, abs/1807.08195.

Xu, X. (2017). Study on effective using of multimedia teaching system and enhancing teaching effect. *International Journal of Emerging Technologies in Learning*, 12(6), 187. DOI:10.3991/ijet.v12i06.7093

Yakin, M., & Linden, K. (2021). Adaptive e-learning platforms can improve student performance and engagement in dental education. *Journal of Dental Education*, 85(7), 1309–1315. DOI:10.1002/jdd.12609 PMID:33825184

Yang, A. C., Chen, I. Y., Flanagan, B., & Ogata, H. (2021). Automatic generation of cloze items for repeated testing to improve reading comprehension. *Journal of Educational Technology & Society*, 147–158.

Yang, A. C., Flanagan, B., & Ogata, H. (2022). Adaptive formative assessment system based on computerized adaptive testing and the learning memory cycle for personalized learning. *Computers and Education: Artificial Intelligence*, 3, 1. DOI:10.1016/j.caeai.2022.100104

Yang, H. Y. (2016). The effects of attention cueing on visualizers' multimedia learning. *Journal of Educational Technology & Society*, 19(1), 249–262.

Yang, J., Wu, Y., & Huang, B. (2023). Digital finance and financial literacy: Evidence from Chinese households. *Journal of Banking & Finance*, 156, 107005. DOI:10.1016/j.jbankfin.2023.107005

Yap, W. L., Neo, M., & Neo, T. K. (2014). Impact of learner-centred teaching environment with the use of multimedia-mediated learning modules in improving learning experience. [Sciences and Engineering]. *Jurnal Teknologi*, 68(2), 65–71.

Yazdanian, R., Davis, R. L., Guo, X., Lim, F., Dillenbourg, P., & Kan, M. Y. (2022). On the radar: Predicting near-future surges in skills' hiring demand to provide early warning to educators. *Computers and Education: Artificial Intelligence*, 3, 100043. Advance online publication. DOI:10.1016/j.caeai.2021.100043

Yim, D., Khuntia, J., Parameswaran, V., & Meyers, A. (2024). Preliminary Evidence of the Use of Generative AI in Health Care Clinical Services: Systematic Narrative Review. *JMIR Medical Informatics*, 12(1), e52073. DOI:10.2196/52073 PMID:38506918

Yitmen, I., Almusaed, A., & Alizadehsalehi, S. (2023). Investigating the Causal Relationships among Enablers of the Construction 5.0 Paradigm: Integration of Operator 5.0 and Society 5.0 with Human-Centricity, Sustainability, and Resilience. *Sustainability (Basel)*, 15(11), 9105. DOI:10.3390/su15119105

Yoder-Himes, D. R., Asif, A., Kinney, K., Brandt, T. J., Hopp, C., & Ross, E. (2022). Racial, skin tone, and sex disparities in automated proctoring software. *Frontiers in Education*, 7, 881449. Advance online publication. DOI:10.3389/feduc.2022.881449

York, A. (March 18, 2024). 15 Best ChatGPT Alternatives & Competitors in 2024. https://clickup.com/blog/chatgpt-alternatives/#:~:text=Jasper%20Chat,-via%20Jasper&text=Jasper%20Chat%20is%20part%20of,questions%20and%20respond%20to%20requests

Younis, H. A., Ruhaiyem, N. I. R., Ghaban, W., Gazem, N. A., & Nasser, M. (2023). A Systematic Literature Review on the Applications of Robots and Natural Language Processing in Education. *Electronics (Basel)*, 12(13), 2864. DOI:10.3390/electronics12132864

Yu, D. (2017). Bridging the Gap Between Educational Measurement and Intelligent Tutoring Systems. *Journal of Educational Measurement*, 54(2), 219–236.

Yuejue, Y., Xinze, S., Bingyue, L., & Xiaoyuan, W. (2021). Construct a teaching system combining image linguistics and multimedia technology. *Wireless Communications and Mobile Computing*, 2021(1), 1–11. DOI:10.1155/2021/6699010

Yu, H., & Guo, Y. (2023). Generative artificial intelligence empowers educational reform: Current status, issues, and prospects. *Frontiers in Education*, 8, 1183162. Advance online publication. DOI:10.3389/feduc.2023.1183162

Zaglas, W. (2019, September 23). *Uni experts consider whether robots can really take over the classroom.* Campus Review. Retrieved December 2, 2023, from https://www.campusreview.com.au/2019/09/uni-experts-consider-whether-robots-can-really-take-over-in-the-classroom/

Zawacki-Richter, O., Marín, V. I., Bond, M., & Gouverneur, F. (2019). Systematic review of research on artificial intelligence applications in higher education – where are the educators? *International Journal of Educational Technology in Higher Education*, 16(1), 39. Advance online publication. DOI:10.1186/s41239-019-0171-0

Zengin, Y., Naktiyok, S., Kaygın, E., Kavak, O., & Topçuoğlu, E. (2021). An investigation upon industry 4.0 and society 5.0 within the context of sustainable development goals. *Sustainability (Basel)*, 13(5), 2682. DOI:10.3390/su13052682

Zhai, X., Chu, X., Chai, C. S., Jong, M. S., Starčič, A. I., Spector, M., Liu, J., Jing, Y., & Li, Y. (2021). A Review of Artificial Intelligence (AI) in Education from 2010 to 2020. *Complexity*, 2021, 1–18. DOI:10.1155/2021/8812542

Zhang, L. F. (2004). Thinking styles: University students' preferred teaching styles and their conceptions of effective teachers. *The Journal of Psychology*, 138(3), 233–252. DOI:10.3200/JRLP.138.3.233-252 PMID:15264441

Zhang, L., & Sternberg, R. J. (2010). Thinking styles and teachers' characteristics. *International Journal of Psychology*, 37(1), 3–12. DOI:10.1080/00207590143000171

Zhang, Y., & Prebensen, N. K. (2024). Co-creating with ChatGPT for tourism marketing materials. *Annals of Tourism Research Empirical Insights*, 5(1), 100124. DOI:10.1016/j.annale.2024.100124

Zhang, Y., Xiong, F., Xie, Y., Fan, X., & Gu, H. (2020). The Impact of Artificial Intelligence and Blockchain on the Accounting Profession. *IEEE Access : Practical Innovations, Open Solutions*, 10(1), 461–477. DOI:10.1109/ACCESS.2020.3000505

Zhan, Z., He, L., Tong, Y., Liang, X., Guo, S., & Lan, X. (2022). The effectiveness of gamification in programming education: Evidence from a meta-analysis. *Computers and Education: Artificial Intelligence*, 100096. Advance online publication. DOI:10.1016/j.caeai.2022.100096

Zhao, X. (2022). Leveraging artificial intelligence (AI) technology for English writing: Introducing wordtune as a digital writing assistant for EFL writers. *RELC Journal*, 0(0), 1–5. DOI:10.1177/00336882221094089

Zhaoyang, R., Sliwinski, M. J., Martire, L. M., & Smyth, J. M. (2019). Social interactions and physical symptoms in daily life: Quality matters for older adults, quantity matters for younger adults. *Psychology & Health*, 34(7), 867–885. DOI:10.1080/08870446.2019.1579908 PMID:30821176

Zhihan, L. (2023). Generative artificial intelligence in the metaverse era. *Cognitive Robotics*, 3, 208–217. DOI:10.1016/j.cogr.2023.06.001

Zhu, H. (2022). Comparative Study and Implications of Education Informatization Policies in China and the United States. *Advances in Educational Technology and Psychology*, 6(9), 25–30.

Ziden, A. A., & Rahman, M. F. A. (2013). The effectiveness of web-based multimedia applications simulation in teaching and learning. *International Journal of Instruction*, 6(2).

Zulfa, S., Sari Dewi, R., Nuruddin Hidayat, D., Hamid, F., & Defianty, M. (2023). The Use of AI and Technology Tools in Developing Students' English Academic Writing Skills. *The Annual International Conference on Education*, 47–63.

Zureck, A. (2020). Literature review on the use of media in financial education. *EDULEARN20 Proceedings*, 491-496.

About the Contributors

Ziska Fields is an Associate Professor in the College of Business and Economics, Department of Business Management at the University of Johannesburg (UJ). Prof Fields is an Alumna at the University of KwaZulu-Natal (UKZN) in Durban and an external researcher and habilitator at the Chair of Innovation Research and Technology Management, Chemnitz University of Technology. She has recently qualified as a Neethling Brain Instruments (NBI) Practitioner focusing on identifying and developing peoples preferred thinking styles and to help them think more creatively at school, university and in the workplace. She has been appointed as the Ambassador for the World Creativity and Innovation Week (WCIW) and World Creativity and Innovation Day (WCID) in South Africa, as well as some southern African countries like Namibia and Botswana for 2021. The purpose of this role is to connect cities, regions and countries to the WCIW creative community and to foster creativity by promoting, empowering and supporting the WCIW's creativity mission. Professor Fields has 13 years' experience in the Financial Industry and 12 years' experience in Higher Education experience. Her qualifications include a BA degree (Communication Sciences), Diploma in Management Studies, MBA (Cum Laude) and PhD (Business Administration). She teaches and supervises various Management and Entrepreneurship focus area at undergraduate and postgraduate levels. Her research and supervisory focus areas include Entrepreneurship, Higher Education, Responsible Management and Human Resources with a focus on the Fourth Industrial Revolution. Her main research focus area and passion is theoretical and applied creativity across various disciplines and contexts. She developed two theoretical models to measure creativity in South Africa, focusing on youth and tertiary education. She edited five books published by IGI Global titled "Incorporating Business Models and Strategies into Social Entrepreneurship", "Collective creativity for responsible and sustainable business practice", "Handbook of Research on Information and Cyber Security in the Fourth Industrial Revolution", "Responsible, Sustainable, and Globally Aware Management in the Fourth Industrial Revolution" and "Imagination, Creativity and Responsible Management in the Fourth Industrial Revolution". She is currently busy with a book titled "Using Global Collective Intelligence and Creativity to Solve Wicked Problems: Emerging Research and Opportunities" which should be published by the end of 2020. She also has various other research areas, which include Entrepreneurship, Management, Innovation, Higher Education, Responsible Management Education, Human Resources, Future Studies and Information Technology. She edited four books titled "Incorporating Business Models and Strategies into Social Entrepreneurship", "Collective creativity for responsible and sustainable business practice", "Handbook of Research on Information and Cyber Security in the Fourth Industrial Revolution", "Responsible, Sustainable, and Globally Aware Management in the Fourth Industrial Revolution" and "Imagination, Creativity, and Responsible Management in the Fourth Industrial

Revolution". She has published various book chapters and papers and presented various conference papers. Professor Fields developed two theoretical models to measure creativity in South Africa, focusing on youth and tertiary education. Professor Fields is a driven, dedicated and passionate person who loves animals, learning new things and is constantly inspired by the positive and life-changing impact that education can have on people. Her objective is to make a difference by empowering people and helping them to reach their full potential. She strongly believes that creativity and entrepreneurial action can help people to create a better and sustainable future for themselves and society.

* * *

Temitope Samson Adekunle received the B. Tech. (Hon's) degree in Pure Mathematics from the Federal University of Technology, Minna, Nigeria, the M.Tech. degree in Mathematics (Fluid Dynamics) from the Federal University of Technology, Minna, Nigeria and also MSc degree in Data Science from the University of Salford, Manchester, United Kingdom. He is a PhD student at the Department of Computer Science, Colorado State University, Fort Collins, United State. His major research focus is on the aspect of Artificial Intelligent and Machine Learning, Fluid Dynamics, Mathematics Modelling, Data Engineering, Simulation and Modeling, Big Data Mining. Temitope had reviewed several Journals. A member of Association for the Advancement of Artificial Intelligence, Association for Computing Machinery, International Society for Data Science and Analytics, British Computer Society (BCS) The Chartered Institute for IT and Nigerian Mathematical Society.

Khalida Akbar is an accomplished academic and researcher with a distinguished career spanning the realms of higher education, cognitive rehabilitation, and human resource management. Currently serving as a Senior Research Associate at MANCOSA, she brings a wealth of expertise and experience to her role. Professional Experience: Senior Research Associate at MANCOSA: Dr.Akbar presently holds the position of Senior Research Associate at MANCOSA, where she is actively engaged in cutting-edge research and scholarship. She dedicated to academic excellence and commitment to advancing knowledge. Notably, she previously served as the DBA Coordinator at MANCOSA, demonstrating her leadership skills and contributions to academic program development. Research and Ethics Committees: Dr.Akbar has also been a pivotal member of research and ethics committees at MANCOSA, exemplifying her dedication to upholding the highest standards of academic research and ethical conduct. Post-Doctoral Fellow at DUT: From 2018 to 2023, Dr.Akbar served as a Post-Doctoral Fellow at the Durban University of Technology (DUT) within the Faculty of Research Innovation and Engagement. During this time, she specialized in the intersection of acquired brain injury and human resource management . Dr.Akbar achieved the remarkable distinction of graduating with a Ph.D. from the University of KwaZulu-Natal at the age of 26. Teaching and Supervision: Dr.Akbar 's passion for education is reflected in her ten-year tenure as a part-time lecturer at the University of KwaZulu-Natal. She has delivered lectures across various disciplines, including Human Resource Management, Entrepreneurship, Public Governance, and Industrial Organizational and Labour Studies. Dr.Akbar has also provided guidance to numerous honours, master's, and Ph.D. students, further contributing to the development of the next generation of scholars. International Engagement: Dr.Akbar has showcased her research prowess on a global stage, attending and presenting at international conferences in countries such as South Africa, France, Germany, and Mauritius. Her participation in collaborative research projects with Germany underscores her commitment to cross-border knowledge exchange and collaboration. Research Interests: Dr.Akbar 's research interests encompass a wide spectrum, including Higher Education and Development, Cognitive Function/Brain Injury, Human Resource Management, Entrepreneurship, and Management, with a particular focus on sustainability. Her multidisciplinary approach to research showcases her versatility and dedication to addressing critical issues in academia and society. Inspirational Quote:"In a world where you can be anything, be kind." Dr.Akbar embodies this ethos through her contributions to academia, research, and her unwavering commitment to making a positive impact in the lives of others. Her exemplary career trajectory and dedication to knowledge dissemination make her a respected figure in her field. Dr.Akbar continues to inspire and lead by example, leaving an indelible mark on the academic landscape.

Edidiong Elijah Akpan is a versatile professional with a wide range of specialized and academic experiences. He obtained a bachelor's degree in Biochemistry, an MBA in Business Administration and a master's degree in Information Technology. These established a strong basis for scientific investigation and analysis. Edidiong had a prosperous career for himself in the banking industry, gaining ten years of experience there. His work in banking helped him hone his managerial, strategic planning, and operational efficiency skills, which highlights his ability to work with complicated data sets, draw conclusions, and use technology to address challenging issues. Edidiong is about to start a PhD program with an emphasis on artificial intelligence and machine learning. His goal of expanding his knowledge of cutting-edge technology and making a positive impact on the quickly developing field of artificial intelligence is consistent with this endeavor. Edidiong is in a unique position to bridge the gap between scientific research, commercial strategy, technology innovation, and medicine because of his multidisciplinary skills and experience. He is a member of Chattered Institute of Bankers of Nigeria (CIBN), National Society of Black Engineers (NSBE), Nigeria Society of Biochemistry and Molecular Biology (NSBMB).

Eka Apriani, M.Pd., is an English Lecturer at English Tadris Study Program of the Faculty of Tarbiyah in Islamic State Institute of Curup. She is a Editor in Chief in Journal of English Franca and International Journal of Education Research and Development. She is also the secretary of Corolla Education Centre Foundation, Indonesia. She Received her Master Degree (Master of Language Education) from Sriwijaya University in 2013 and Doctor of Education in Bengkulu University 2022. She has published some researchs in international journal and national journal. She has Scopus Id and WOS Id. She is a member of profession organisation: ADRI, TEFLIN, PDPI and ELITE. She is treasurer of ADRI in Bengkulu Province. Her research interest is in Writing skill and ICT in learning English. She write some books: The beauty of Rejang Lebong, Semantics Crossword, Metode Pengajaran BIPA, Drama Manuscript: The Marriage of Siti Zubaidah. She has also some Intelektual Property Right: Semantics Crossword, The beauty of Rejang Lebong, The Marriage of Siti Zubaidah, Metode Pengajaran BIPA.

Poonam Arora has rich and vivid experience of almost two decades in imparting knowledge in the field of Data Sciences, Quantitative Techniques, Research, Analytical Skill Building, and HR. Dr. Poonam is a certified actuarial scientist who is a research enthusiast and an active researcher and an active researcher who has more than 50 publications to her credit. She has been the recipient of numerous academic achievement awards for her contribution to research in management. She is a passionate number cruncher and is inclined towards innovating ways to analyze data and apply the knowledge in research surveys. She is an active member of data analytics communities and is associated with editorial advisory boards in numerous national and international peer-reviewed journals and publications. She has delivered numerous guest sessions, FDPs and workshops on data analysis at various reputed institutions across Gujarat. She has keen interest in disseminating her knowledge in Statistics. She is known for guiding research scholars in the application areas of Statistics, Mathematics, Operations and Research. She is currently associated as Professor with SKIPS School of Business, SKIPS University, Ahmedabad.

Senthil Kumar Arumugam is a Professor in the School of Commerce at Presidency University, Bengaluru, India. His areas of specialization include Finance, Accounting, Marketing, Computer Applications in Business, and Research Methodology. He earned a PhD in Commerce from Bharathiar University, India, in 2014, and holds an M.Phil in Commerce, an M.Phil in Computer Science, a Master of Computer Applications, and a Master of Commerce. He has 23 years of experience in teaching, research, and administration in the fields of Commerce and Computer Applications. He is the author of 65 research articles, 11 edited books, and 18 book chapters. He has presented 60 research papers at international and national conferences and has served as a resource person, chair, and co-chair at various conferences and workshops. Additionally, he has guided two PhD students.

K. M. Begian-Lewis (they/them) is a Ph.D. candidate and Graduate Teaching Assistant concentrating in Rhetoric and Composition. Their areas of research include socioeconomic barriers to higher education, prison education, the rhetoric of health and medicine, and generative AI for writing. For their dissertation, K.M. is researching the rhetoric of female pain as it relates to the prescribing of birth control for menstrual bleeding conditions.

Hotma Berutu is a Magister student in the English Education Department at the State Islamic University, North Sumatra. She is also an English teacher.

Mavis Chamboko-Mpotaringa is a Postdoctoral Research Fellow at the School of Tourism and Hospitality, University of Johannesburg, South Africa. She holds a PhD, Masters and B.Com (Hons) in Tourism and Hospitality, a Postgraduate Certificate in Education (PGCE), Teaching English as a Foreign Language (TEFL) certification and has more than ten years of combined experience in education and tourism, a reflection of her expertise. Dr. Chamboko-Mpotaringa is a multidiscipline researcher, whose interest lies in digital technologies focusing on education, consumer behaviour and tourism marketing. Currently, Dr. Mavis is exploring the potential of the metaverse to transform education, consumer behaviour and tourism marketing.

Stanley Ejiofor Chukwuebuka is an accomplished academic and emerging researcher with a robust foundation in insurance and actuarial science. He earned his Bachelor of Science degree in Insurance and Actuarial Science from Imo State University, Owerri, Nigeria, where he gained comprehensive knowledge in risk management, financial analysis, and actuarial principles. Currently, Stanley is advancing his expertise by pursuing a Master's degree in Information Technology at Arkansas Tech University in Russellville, Arkansas, USA. His decision to specialize in IT underscores his forward-thinking approach and his recognition of the pivotal role technology plays in the modern financial and insurance sectors. Stanley is actively engaged in cutting-edge research, with a recent focus on "Generative Artificial Intelligence (AI) and Sustainable Development Goal 4 on Tertiary Education: Conversational AI with User-Centric ChatGPT-4." This research explores the transformative potential of AI in enhancing educational outcomes, particularly in higher education, and demonstrates his commitment to leveraging technological advancements for social good. Stanley's interdisciplinary academic journey equips him with a unique blend of skills, combining analytical acumen from his actuarial science background with advanced technological knowledge. This combination positions him to effectively address contemporary challenges in the insurance and education sectors, leveraging AI and IT to innovate and improve industry practices. Beyond his academic pursuits, Stanley is passionate about continuous learning and professional development. His commitment to integrating IT with insurance and actuarial science, coupled with his research on AI and education, highlights his drive to stay at the forefront of industry advancements and contribute meaningfully to the field. Stanley Ejiofor's dedication to excellence, his international educational experiences, and his innovative research make him a promising figure in the evolving landscapes of insurance, information technology, and education. His goal is to harness his diverse skill set to impact these industries positively, fostering innovation, efficiency, and sustainable development.

Bibi Zaheenah Chummun is a Senior Lecturer at the University of KwaZulu-Natal (UKZN) Graduate School of Business and Leadership (GSB&L) based on Westville Campus in Durban - South Africa. Dr. Chummun has published several papers in the field of management, microenterprises, microfinance, microinsurance and financial inclusion. She is supervising Masters and PhD students in the field of management She is a Chartered Insurer from the Chartered Insurance Institute in UK. She obtained her MBA from Nelson Mandela Metropolitan University (NMMU-South Africa) in 2010 and her PhD is from North West University (NWU-South Africa). Dr. Chummun is originally from the island of Mauritius.

Muhammad Dalimunte is a Magister lecturer in the English Education Department at the State Islamic University, North Sumatra.

Sholihatul Hamidah Daulay was born in Surabaya on June 22, 1975. She completed her bachelor's degree in English Language Education Department of the North Sumatra State Islamic Institute (IAIN SU) in 1999, then continued her Master's degree in the Linguistics Study Program at the University of North Sumatra (USU) in 2002, and then completed a Ph.D. in the Linguistics Study Program at the University of North Sumatra (USU) in 2014. The author is a permanent lecturer at the Tadris English Study Program at the State Islamic University of North Sumatra (UINSU) from 2003 till now. The author actively conducts research and writes books including Let's Study English (Cita Pustaka, 2007), Introduction to General Linguistics (La-Tansa, 2011), Language and Society (LPPP Medan, 2019), Reading Comprehension (Kencana, 2020), Basic Morphology (UMSU Press, 2021), Developing Vocabulary by Educational Game (Cakrawala Satria Mandiri, 2021), Introduction to Linguistics (UMSU Press, 2022), Student Difficulties in Learning Speaking (Muslim Intellectual Education Foundation, 2022), Fun Writing for Children: Games and Activities (Muslim Scholars Education Foundation, 2023), Designing an ICT-Based Practical Interactive Guide Interactive Quiz for Educators (Akademia Pustaka, 2023), Quick on the Draw for Writing Recount Text (Muslim Scholars Education Foundation, 2023).

Smita M. Gaikwad is a renowned professor in marketing . She has 22 year rich academic experience and research flair. Her area of research is Gren Marketing, Branding and Consumer behavior . She has presented papers in national and International Conferences. She has won several awards in research and out standing education .

Shalin Hai-Jew works as the grant writer for Hutchinson Community College in Hutchinson, Kansas. Prior, she worked as an instructional designer at Kansas State University (K-State) for 17.5 years. She has taught at the university and college levels for many years (including four years in the People's Republic of China) and was tenured at Shoreline Community College. She has Bachelor's degrees in English and psychology, a Master's degree in Creative Writing from the University of Washington (Hugh Paradise Scholar), and an Ed.D in Educational Leadership with a focus on public administration from Seattle University (where she was a Morford Scholar). She tested into the University of Washington at 14 and started her university studies at 15. She reviews for several publishers and publications. She has authored and edited a number of books. Hai-Jew was born in Huntsville, Alabama, in the U.S.

Colleen Hart (she/her) is a doctoral candidate studying rhetoric and writing studies at Wayne State University. Her dissertation research couples feminist rhetoric with empathy studies, but she also studies the impact of AI on student writing; diversity, equity, and inclusion in higher education; and visual rhetoric.

Aisha Ismail is serving Virtual University of Pakistan as a Faculty Accounting & Finance. She has completed PhD. Commerce from Hailey College of Commerce. She has more than 12 years of academic experience. Her areas of interest are corporate finance, Investment analysis and portfolio management, Risk management, microfinance and ODL practices. Currently, she is actively working on microfinance and under-served communities.

Justin Knibbe is an assistant professor (teaching) at the Haskayne School of Business. He is an experienced entrepreneur who has been teaching since 2020. He teaches undergraduate and graduate students entrepreneurial thinking, creativity, innovation, and new venture creation. He loves supporting his students and seeing their ideas come to life, and he has won multiple awards for his teaching effectiveness.

Mansi Kukreja is presently Professor, Faculty of Management Studies, CMS Business School JAIN (Deemed to be University).She got into academic in the year 2008. Her primary area of interest is financial decisions making skills. She has completed her B.Com, M.Com, and Ph.D.She is a dedicated, resourceful, and goal-driven professional educator with a solid commitment to the academic growth and development of every student with successful experience of more than 16 years also efficiently guided UG and PG students through their project work and has published several research papers, attended conferences and FDP's at national and International level. Dr. Mansi primary objective is to leverage her extensive knowledge and experience to mentor the young generation with finance domain.

Blandina Manditereza is a lecturer in Childhood Education at the University of the Free State, Bloemfontein, South Africa. She holds a PhD in curriculum Studies from the same University. Her research areas of interest include Early Childhood Language and Pedagogy, Early Childhood Teacher Education and Digital Education.

Ugochukwu O. Matthew presently is an Academic scholar with Hussaini Adamu Federal Polytechnic, Nigeria, in the Department of Computer Science with specialty in AI, Big Data Science, Cloud Computing, Internet of Things, Data Mining, Multimedia and E-Learning Education. A Member of Nigeria Computer Society (NCS), Nigeria Institute of Management (NIM), International Association of Computer Science & Information Technology (IACSIT), European Alliance for Innovation(EAI) and also a member of Teaching & Education Research Association (TERA). Ugochukwu O. Matthew hold Masters in Computer Applications from Bayero University Kano, Nigeria. Ugochukwu O. Matthew had reviewed several Journals and a member of Review Board Committee of Journals Indexed by Scopus and Web of Science including IEEE Access, SN Computer Science (Springer), International Journal of Information Communication Technologies & Human Development(IJICTHD), International Journal of Business Data Communications and Networking (IJBDCN), International Journal of Cloud Applications and Computing (IJCAC). Ugochukwu O. Matthew is a cofounder of U&J Digital Consult Limited, an IT and Educational Consulting Firm in Nigeria.

Vincent Mbonye is a dedicated information technology specialist with a keen interest in the transformative power of technology on both societal and organizational levels. Currently pursuing a PhD in Information Systems and Technology at the University of KwaZulu-Natal (UKZN), Vincent holds a Master's degree and Bachelor of Commerce Honours degree in Information Systems and Technology from UKZN, along with a Bachelor's degree in Information Technology, with honors, from Kampala International University in Uganda. With a strong foundation in academia and a proven track record of professional success, Vincent has been recognized for his analytical skills, teamwork, and ability to excel under pressure. As an Emerging Researcher Award recipient and a member of the Golden Key International Honour Society, Vincent is committed to driving innovation and making meaningful contributions to the field of information systems and technology.

Muhammad Nasution is an English lecturer in the English Education Department at the Medan Area University, North Sumatra.

Farai Nyika is an economics and public administration academic at MANCOSA. His research interest lie in local government, development economics and higher education.

Matthew Abiola Oladipupo is the Lead Data Analyst at Perch Group Ltd in Manchester, United Kingdom. He earned his Master of Science in Data Science from The University of Salford and holds a Bachelor of Technology in Electronics and Electrical Engineering, as well as a Postgraduate Diploma, from Ladoke Akintola University of Technology. As a passionate scholar in Artificial Intelligence, he brings years of experience in researching machine learning and boasts a distinguished academic profile. His expertise spans across applied statistics and data mining techniques, enabling him to develop decision-making systems for business organizations. This involves collecting extensive datasets and transforming them into actionable insights and reports, aiding organizations in strategic decision-making, business improvement, and future trend prediction.

Ajibola Olaosebikan has a background in Industrial Engineering— where he honed his business, engineering and management skills. Understanding that challenges are local, and that solving them requires sustainable tailored solutions, Ajibola has three goals: to research local problems, develop globally acknowledged solution and make societal impactful by mainstreaming technical skills through teaching. Through his job exposure at Nestle and his master's degree in Applied AI and Data Science at Southampton Solent University—where he was also a Junior Data Scientist and worked collaboratively to deliver an AI-powered decision support system, he has developed capabilities in data analytics and engineering, applied artificial intelligence in business, software engineering and research in other to actualize these goals. Currently, he is pursuing the Food Market Vision (FMV) project. This project, that span areas such as route optimization, data acquisition and storage, process automation, cloud computing etc. is aimed at enhancing the core retailing processes in the Sub-Saharan Africa (Nigeria) informal food markets. Among others, this project's major objective is to ensure verified and real-time primary data and information needed to shape food policies are obtainable the source—the informal food markets. Ajibola's research interests spans across application of AI in Business, big data, data strategy, cloud computing. Ajibola's hobby is teaching and to further showcase this, he is building LearniT—a Learning Management System to educate interested users on developing end-to-end data and software projects.

Victory Chibuike Onumaku is an accomplished data Scientist with a robust background in programming and data science, earning his B.Sc in Computer Science from Imo State University and currently doing his M.Sc at Edgehill University, UK. He is the Pioneer and Chairman of the British Computer Society (Student Chapter) at Edgehill University, also a member of Nigeria Association of Computer Science Student. Victory's expertise spans Cloud Computing, Big Data, AI, Machine Learning, NLP, Business Intelligence, and Database Management, utilizing tools like Big Query, Python, R-Studio, and SAS, Power BI, SQL. His research interest is Data, AI and NLP and using Machine learning algorithms to make predictions focusing on health. He has co authored in the comparative and predictive analysis of prostrate cancer diagnosis and using Machine learning and SAS in predicting online customer behaviour. Beyond his academic pursuits, Victory actively writes Data Science blogs, share Machine learning personal projects online and share data resources on LinkedIn, Dev community and medium, showcasing his commitment to advancing knowledge and addressing real-world challenges. His multifaceted involvement establishes him as a dynamic force in data and Machine learning and artificial intelligence world.

Oleksiy Osiyevskyy is an Associate Professor of Entrepreneurship & Innovation at the Haskayne School of Business, University of Calgary. In his scholarship, supported by the Future Fund Fellowship, he concentrates on the problem of achieving and sustaining firm growth and prosperous longevity through successful engagement in entrepreneurial strategies. Oleksiy founded his first Internet startup back in 2003, during his undergraduate studies. Since that time, he has been actively engaged in real-world business practice across the globe as an entrepreneur, manager within large companies, consultant and educator. Oleksiy has mentored, co-founded, invested in, and served on the boards of numerous startups within a broad range of industries (education, food, medical devices, transportation, e-commerce, among others), and engaged in strategic innovation projects within large organizations.

David Oyekunle is a highly esteemed expert with extensive education and experience in the fields of information technology research, project management, business analysis, and artificial intelligence. He earned his Bachelor of Science degree in statistics from the University of Ilorin in Nigeria. He obtained a Postgraduate Diploma in International Business Administration and Management from the National Open University in Nigeria and a (summer online) Master of Business Administration in Leadership and Team Building from the University of New Haven in the United States of America. He excelled as a postgraduate research scholar at the University of Salford, graduating with a Master of Science degree in project management with distinctions. David's significant organizational experience includes leading cross-functional teams, developing strategic project policies, implementing logistics, ensuring adherence to risk standards and compliance, and analyzing vast datasets to uncover trends and patterns. Among his achievements are the successful implementation of intelligent lean management and Six Sigma with data analysis, the delivery of comprehensive business reports, and the use of technological innovation to improve customer service in the banking and media sectors. I am currently serving as an educational consultant at U&J Digital Consult Limited in Nigeria. David is a personal and business coach, and he continues to contribute significantly to the fields of information technology and educational consulting. Global journals have published his research on various subjects such as strategic management, project management, international business, business informatics, and ethics in project management. Demonstrating his commitment to academic collaboration and human capital development, David actively participates in volunteer positions and committee memberships at conferences both locally and internationally. David aims to continue leveraging his expertise to drive innovation and excellence in research, education, project management, and information technology.

Anuradha P. S., Professor at CHRIST (Deemed to be University) Bangalore, India, has rich experience in the field of Finance and Commerce. Has published more than 15 papers in various international journals, authored a book titled ‘Women in the Service sector: Career Opportunities and Challenges’, has received Certificate of Excellence for the Article titled ‘Impact of Rupee volatility on the financials of the Indian IT Companies’, is awarded first prize for the paper ‘Demographics, Investment and Economic growth’ by Jain University and has served as a member of B.O.S. for various Universities.

Muthmainnah, Ph.D., an accomplished Assistant Professor at Universitas Al Asyariah Mandar in West Sulawesi, Indonesia, stands as a distinguished academician with a diverse and impactful professional portfolio. Her multifaceted career spans roles such as Chairman of the Indonesian Language Department, Public Relations Officer, Director of Women's Centre Studies, Deputy Director of Quality Assurance Unit, and her current position as Deputy Director of the Language and Character Development Institute. In addition to her administrative roles, Muthmainnah is a prolific author, contributing to the scholarly landscape with 58 national and international books. Her publications, hosted by prestigious publishers such as Springer, Emerald, IGI Global, Wiley, Routledge, and Taylor and Francis, underscore her commitment to advancing knowledge in various domains. Her profile of authored books is accessible via the Science and Technology Index (SINTA) portal: https://sinta.kemdikbud.go.id/profile/books. Muthmainnah's global influence extends beyond her academic achievements. As an international board member for several scientific innovation research groups and a member of the United Nations Volunteers roster, she actively contributes to international research collaborations and initiatives. Her exceptional contributions have earned her over 100 international awards, including recognitions as Outstanding Professor, Outstanding Leadership, Best International Influencer, Best Emerging Professor of the Year, and the International Award for Working Women and SDGs Warrior. Notably, she holds an honorary doctorate degree from Layahe University and has been honored with the Doctor of Excellence award from the Philippines. Muthmainnah's dedication to education is further evidenced by her membership in the United Nations Volunteers' roster and her advisory role in the Indonesian Education Share to Care Volunteers. Her research interests encompass a broad spectrum, including the development of literary works, instructional teaching materials, Assurance of Learning (Assure), Teaching English to Speakers of Other Languages (TESOL), ICT in education, digital education, and cybergogy. Muthmainnah's scholarly impact is quantified by her Sinta score of 2052, h-index of 18, and her role as an External Examiner for Ph.D. students at three A+ accredited campuses in India and Australia. Her commitment to international collaboration and teamwork positions her as an ideal candidate for various academic and leadership roles. For further details and engagement, Muthmainnah can be reached through her Scopus id: 57200720707, Google Scholar link: https://scholar.google.co.id/citations?user=6oeh6qmaaaaj, ResearchGate id: https://www.researchgate.net/profile/muthmainnah, Orcid id: https://orcid.org/0000-0003-3170-2374, and Wos id: 1950-2017.

Rosalynn Peschl is an Assistant Professor (Teaching) at the Haskayne School of Business at the University of Calgary. In the Entrepreneurship & Innovation area, she teaches a mandatory class on entrepreneurial thinking and optional, senior level courses on social enterprise & systems change.

Nitin Sankar Pillai has over 12 years of teaching experience in the domain of pedagogy and communication. In addition to his Masters in English he also earned a Post Graduate Diploma in Teaching English (PGDTE) from EFL University, Hyderabad and followed it with a Master of Philosophy in English Language Teaching and Higher Order Thinking Skills. He was awarded a PhD for this work in Alternative Language Assessment Strategies that investigated the need for better assessment practices in order to develop communicative abilities. He holds a Post Graduate Certificate in General Management from Indian Institute of Management, Nagpur (IIM N). He is trained in Language Assessment and Critical Thinking Strategies in EFL Context by University of Maryland (Baltimore, USA) & SIT Graduate Institute (USA) through RELO (Regional English Language Office). He has worked on various pedagogy tools through Faculty Development Programs (Gurudakshata) organized by UGC-HRDC.

Amudhan S., a distinguished academician specializing in Finance and Management, holds an illustrious 13-year career in teaching and industry practice. Presently an Assistant Professor at St. Joseph's University in Bengaluru since June 2019, Dr. Amudhan has been instrumental in shaping the academic discourse. His prior roles, including an Associate Professorship at Brindavan College, Yelahanka, and extensive service as an Assistant Professor at AVS Engineering and AVS Arts & Science Colleges in Salem, Tamil Nadu, reflect a wealth of experience across various educational settings. Alongside their academic journey, Dr. Amudhan gained significant industry insights, serving as a Senior Marketing Executive at IFFCO TOKIO General Insurance Company Ltd., Chennai, and as a Sales Executive at HCL Info systems Ltd., Chennai, accumulating two years of industry expertise. With an unwavering dedication to education, profound subject knowledge, and a rich blend of academic and industry experience, Dr. Amudhan has left an indelible mark on higher education and industry practices throughout their remarkable career.

Shaumiwaty is a Magister lecturer in the English Education Department at the IAIN Takengon, Aceh.

Mariam Tanweer is an online educator, researcher, and practitioner with expertise in talent management, the future of work, and human resource management 4.0. Since 2006, she has applied her profound knowledge to advance online education, integrating technology with traditional pedagogy. Holding a Ph.D. in Management and Commerce, Mariam's academic endeavours focus on making complex theories accessible to students. She contributes significantly to the University of South Australia-online, developing digital business courses in collaboration with industry leaders like Accenture. Mariam is also delving into the applications of Generative Artificial Intelligence in education to enhance personalized learning experiences.

Muhammad Usman Tariq has more than 16+ year's experience in industry and academia. He has authored more than 200+ research articles, 100+ case studies, 60+ book chapters and several books other than 4 patents. He has been working as a consultant and trainer for industries representing six sigma, quality, health and safety, environmental systems, project management, and information security standards. His work has encompassed sectors in aviation, manufacturing, food, hospitality, education, finance, research, software and transportation. He has diverse and significant experience working with accreditation agencies of ABET, ACBSP, AACSB, WASC, CAA, EFQM and NCEAC. Additionally, Dr. Tariq has operational experience in incubators, research labs, government research projects, private sector startups, program creation and management at various industrial and academic levels. He is Certified Higher Education Teacher from Harvard University, USA, Certified Online Educator from HMBSU, Certified Six Sigma Master Black Belt, Lead Auditor ISO 9001 Certified, ISO 14001, IOSH MS, OSHA 30, and OSHA 48. He has been awarded Principal Fellowship from Advance HE UK & Chartered Fellowship of CIPD.

Amit Kumar Tyagi is working as Assistant Professor, at National Institute of Fashion Technology, 110016, New Delhi, India. Previously he has worked as Assistant Professor (Senior Grade 2), and Senior Researcher at Vellore Institute of Technology (VIT), Chennai Campus, 600127, Chennai, Tamilandu, India for the period of 2019-2022. He received his Ph.D. Degree (Full-Time) in 2018 from Pondicherry Central University, 605014, Puducherry, India. About his academic experience, he joined the Lord Krishna College of Engineering, Ghaziabad (LKCE) for the periods of 2009-2010, and 2012-2013. He was an Assistant Professor and Head- Research, Lingaya's Vidyapeeth (formerly known as Lingaya's University), Faridabad, Haryana, India for the period of 2018-2019. His supervision experience includes more than 10 Masters' dissertations and one PhD thesis. He has contributed to several projects such as "AARIN" and "P3- Block" to address some of the open issues related to the privacy breaches in Vehicular Applications (such as Parking) and Medical Cyber Physical Systems (MCPS). He has published over 240 papers in refereed high impact journals, conferences and books.

Index

A

B

C

D

E

F

G

H

I

L

M

N

P

S

T

U

W

www.ingramcontent.com/pod-product-compliance
Lightning Source LLC
LaVergne TN
LVHW080614300926
849162LV00005B/1153

* 9 7 9 8 3 6 9 3 2 4 1 8 9 *